The Individual Investor's Guide to

The Top

Mutual
Funds®

The American Association
of Individual Investors

25th
Edition
2006

The American Association of Individual Investors is an independent, nonprofit corporation formed in 1978 for the purpose of assisting individuals in becoming effective managers of their own assets through programs of education, information, and research.

American Association of Individual Investors
625 North Michigan Avenue
Chicago, Illinois 60611
(312) 280-0170; (800) 428-2244
E-mail: members@aaii.com
Web site: www.aaii.com

ISBN 1-883328-21-7
ISSN: 1538-7070

Data in this guide was provided by Standard & Poor's Micropal and directly from the funds. While the material in this Guide cannot be guaranteed to be error free, it has been obtained from sources believed to be reliable.

Preface

The purpose of this *Guide* is to highlight the funds that would be of most interest to investors: funds open to new investors with historically superior returns in their classes, low expenses, no or low loads and that are directly available from the fund, no intermediary required. The funds are classified into useful categories of similar funds, the way investors approach fund selection, which makes comparison of fund alternatives more efficient and effective. This will allow you to dedicate more time to evaluating the better fund opportunities.

Inside the *Guide* are the information and performance statistics you will need to make well-informed decisions on your mutual fund investments. Our goal is to provide pertinent information, organized to minimize your time spent collecting and comparing data on the increasingly large universe of mutual funds.

AAII members who would like performance figures for no-load and low-load mutual funds that do not appear in this *Guide* can access this information on our Web site at www.aaii.com in the AAII Guides area.

Information for this *Guide* was gathered from direct contact with funds and from Standard & Poor's Micropal. As always, our objective is full, accurate, and timely disclosure of investment information.

John Bajkowski oversaw the development of the fund analysis format and supervised the data collection and verification. Cara Scatizzi provided research assistance, Jean Henrich provided copy editing and Marika Bonaguidi designed the cover. Alyna Johnson served as project editor for the *Guide*.

Chicago
March 2006

John Markese, Ph.D.
President

Table of Contents

How to Use This Guide

Selecting a mutual fund, while less time-consuming than investing in individual securities, does require some homework. No one should put money into an investment that is not understood. This does not require a detailed investigation of the fund's investments, but it does require an understanding of the investment objectives and strategies and the possible risks and returns of a fund.

This *Guide* is designed to provide you with that understanding. We have kept the chapters brief and to the point, so that individuals new to mutual fund investing will not be overwhelmed with unnecessary details.

Chapters 2 through 10 deal with the basics of investing in mutual funds—diversification; loads; various categories of mutual funds and what they mean; how to read a mutual fund's prospectus and annual report, as well as any other material they send you; how to evaluate the risk of a mutual fund; how to invest and redeem; common sense rules for mutual fund investors; practical answers to common questions; tie-breakers when choosing a mutual fund; and when to sell.

Chapter 11 describes how the mutual funds were chosen for inclusion in the *Guide*. Chapter 12 is a key to the terms used in the performance tables and the mutual fund data pages, and includes an explanation of how the returns were calculated and what the different risk measures mean.

Chapter 13 presents performance tables, which include the historical performance of funds along with corresponding benchmarks. While past performance is no indication of future performance, it may indicate the quality and consistency of fund management. From this section, you should pick out mutual funds that meet your investment objectives and risk tolerance. These funds can then be examined more closely in the individual mutual fund data pages that follow each performance category listing (Chapter 14).

The funds are grouped by category and listed alphabetically within each category; their ticker symbol and investment category are indicated at the top of the page after the fund's name. These pages provide 10 years of per share data, performance statistics and risk measures, portfolio information, and shareholder services provided by the fund. Use the telephone numbers and Web addresses provided to contact the funds to request a copy of the prospectus and annual report. Make sure you read the prospectus carefully before investing in any mutual fund.

At the back of the *Guide* is a list of a special category of funds, index funds. And finally, there is an index of all funds that appear in the *Guide*.

2

Investing in Mutual Funds

A mutual fund is an investment company that pools investors' money to invest in securities. An open-end mutual fund continuously issues new shares when investors want to invest in the fund, and it redeems shares when investors want to sell. A mutual fund trades directly with its shareholders, and the share price of the fund represents the market value of the securities that the fund holds.

There are several advantages that mutual funds offer individual investors. They provide:

- Professional investment management usually at a low cost, even for small accounts;
- A diversified group of securities that only a large portfolio can provide;
- Information through prospectuses and annual reports that facilitates comparisons among funds;
- Special services such as check writing, dividend reinvestment plans, telephone switching, and periodic withdrawal and investment plans;
- Account statements that make it easy to track the value of your investment and that ease the paperwork at tax time.

Successful investing takes time and effort, and it requires special knowledge and relevant, up-to-date information. Investors must spend a considerable amount of energy searching for opportunities and monitoring each investment. Professional investment management is relatively cheap with mutual funds. The typical adviser charges about 0.5% annually for managing a fund's assets. For an individual making a $10,000 investment, that comes to only $50 a year.

Of course, mutual fund investing does not preclude investing in securities on your own. One useful strategy would be to invest in mutual funds and individual securities. The mutual funds would ensure your participation in overall market moves and lend diversification to your portfolio, while the individual securities would provide you with the opportunity to apply your specific investment analysis skills.

DIVERSIFICATION

If there is one ingredient to successful investing that is universally agreed upon, it is the benefit of diversification. This is a concept that is backed by a great deal of research, market experience, and common sense. Diversification reduces risk. Risk to investors is frequently defined as volatility of return—in other words, how much an investment's return might vary over a year. Investors prefer returns that are relatively predictable, and thus less volatile. On the other hand, they want returns that are high, but higher returns are accompanied by higher risks. Diversification eliminates some of the risk without reducing potential returns.

Mutual funds, because of their size and the laws governing their operation, provide investors with diversification that might be difficult for an individual to duplicate. This is true not only for common stock funds, but also for bond funds, municipal bond funds, international bond and stock funds—in fact, for almost all mutual funds. Even the sector funds that invest only within one industry offer diversification within that industry. The degree of diversification will vary among funds, but most will provide investors with some amount of diversification.

AVOIDING EXCESSIVE CHARGES

This book focuses on no-load and low-load mutual funds. Investors should realize that:

- A load is a sales commission that goes to the seller of the fund shares;
- A load does not go to anyone responsible for managing the fund's assets and does not serve as an incentive for the fund manager to perform better;
- Funds with loads, on average, consistently underperform no-load funds when the load is taken into consideration in performance calculations;
- For every high-performing load fund, there exists a similar no-load or low-load fund that can be purchased more cheaply;
- Loads understate the real commission charged because they reduce the total amount being invested: $10,000 invested in a 6% front-end load fund results in a $600 sales charge and only a $9,400 investment in the fund;
- If the money paid for the load had been working for you, as in

a no-load fund, it would have been compounding over your holding period.

The bottom line in any investment is how it performs for you, the investor, and that performance includes consideration of all loads, fees, and expenses. There may be some load funds that will do better even if you factor in the load, but you have no way of finding that fund in advance. The only guide you have is historical performance, which is not necessarily an indication of future performance. With a heavily loaded fund, you are starting your investment with a significant loss—the load. Avoid unnecessary charges whenever possible.

SORTING OUT CHARGES

It is best to stick with no-load or low-load funds, but they are becoming more difficult to distinguish from heavily loaded funds. The use of high front-end loads has declined, and funds are now turning to other kinds of charges. Some mutual funds sold by brokerage firms, for example, have lowered their front-end loads, and others have introduced back-end loads (deferred sales charges), which are sales commissions paid when exiting the fund. In both instances, the load is often accompanied by annual charges.

On the other hand, some no-load funds have found that to compete, they must market themselves much more aggressively. To do so, they have introduced charges of their own.

The result has been the introduction of low loads, redemption fees, and annual charges. Low loads—up to 3%—are sometimes added instead of the annual charges. In addition, some funds have instituted a charge for investing or withdrawing money.

Redemption fees work like back-end loads: You pay a percentage of the value of your fund when you get out. Loads are on the amount you have invested, while redemption fees are calculated against the value of your fund assets. Some funds have sliding scale redemption fees, so that the longer you remain invested, the lower the charge when you leave. Some funds use redemption fees to discourage short-term trading, a policy that is designed to protect longer-term investors. These funds usually have redemption fees that disappear after six months.

Some funds, usually index funds, may charge a fee, 1% for example, on all new money invested in the fund. This charge defrays the cost of investing the new money. In effect, the new investment pays its way rather than having the transaction costs charged to investments already in the fund.

Probably the most confusing charge is the annual charge, the 12b-1 plan. The adoption of a 12b-1 plan by a fund permits the adviser to use fund assets to pay for distribution costs, including advertising, distribution of fund literature such as prospectuses and annual reports, and sales commissions paid to brokers. Some funds use 12b-1 plans as masked load charges: They levy very high rates on the fund and use the money to pay brokers to sell the fund. Since the charge is annual and based on the value of the investment, this can result in a total cost to a long-term investor that exceeds a high up-front sales load. A fee table (see Chapter 4: Understanding Mutual Fund Statements) is required in all prospectuses to clarify the impact of a 12b-1 plan and other charges.

The fee table makes the comparison of total expenses among funds easier. Selecting a fund based solely on expenses, including loads and charges, will not give you optimal results, but avoiding funds with high expenses and unnecessary charges is important for long-term performance.

3

Mutual Fund Categories

Mutual funds come in all shapes and sizes; there are thousands of mutual funds, each with its own characteristics. Many mutual funds, however, have shared investments that generally lead to other characteristics that are similar.

These shared characteristics allow us to divide mutual funds into categories. This chapter defines the mutual fund categories we used for this book. In this guide, the individual fund data pages appear alphabetically within each category; the fund's category is indicated beneath the fund's name.

The tables on pages 25 and 69 provide average returns and risk (see Chapter 12 for definitions of these terms) of funds by category, which illustrate some of the differences between these categories.

STOCK FUNDS

Portfolio managers of mutual funds that invest in common stocks can choose from the stocks of different industries, stocks at different stages of development, and even stocks of different countries and regions. Over the stock market cycles, large stocks behave differently from small stocks, domestic stocks do not move in unison with foreign or emerging market stocks, and stocks in different sectors or industries react differently to the same economic and business conditions.

For investors to make initial investment decisions on stock mutual funds and to compare and evaluate the ongoing performance of investments in stock mutual funds, grouping similar funds together into cohesive categories is a logical first step. The stock fund categories provided in this guide to facilitate your selection and monitoring of fund investments encompass domestic funds, sector funds, and international funds.

DOMESTIC STOCK FUNDS

In funds categorized by stock size, the "cap" stands for capitalization (market share price times number of shares of common stock

Fund Categories

Domestic Stock Funds
- Large-Cap Stock
- Mid-Cap Stock
- Small-Cap Stock

Sector Stock Funds
- Energy/Resources Sector Stock
- Financial/Banking Sector Stock
- Gold Sector Stock
- Health Sector Stock
- Real Estate Sector Stock
- Technology Sector Stock
- Telecommunications Sector Stock
- Utilities Sector Stock

International Stock Funds
- Global Stock
- Foreign Stock
- Regional/Country Stock
- Emerging Stock

Balanced Stock/Bond Funds
- Balanced Stock/Bond

Taxable Bond Funds
- Corporate Bond
- Corporate High-Yield Bond
- Mortgage-Backed Bond
- Government: Short-Term Bond
- Government: Intermediate-Term Bond
- Government: Long-Term Bond
- General Bond

outstanding).

Large-cap stocks are usually stocks of national or multinational firms with well-known products or services provided to consumers, other businesses, or governments. Most of the stocks in the Dow Jones industrial average, the S&P 500 and the NASDAQ 100 are, for example, large-cap stocks. While some large-cap stocks are more volatile than

Municipal Bond Funds
National Muni: Short-Term Bond
National Muni: Intermediate-Term Bond
National Muni: Long-Term Bond
National Muni: High-Yield Bond

State-Specific Bond Funds
Muni: Arizona Bond
Muni: California Bond
Muni: Colorado Bond
Muni: Connecticut Bond
Muni: Florida Bond
Muni: Georgia Bond
Muni: Hawaii Bond
Muni: Kentucky Bond
Muni: Maryland Bond
Muni: Massachusetts Bond
Muni: Michigan Bond
Muni: Minnesota Bond
Muni: New Jersey Bond
Muni: New York Bond
Muni: Ohio Bond
Muni: Pennsylvania Bond
Muni: Tennessee Bond
Muni: Virginia Bond
Muni: West Virginia Bond
Muni: Wisconsin Bond

International Bond Funds
International Bond

others, a well-diversified mutual fund portfolio of large-cap stocks would perform similarly to most investors' conception of the stock market. Large-cap stocks, as a category, also tend to pay the highest cash dividends, although many large-cap stocks pay no dividends. Large-cap stock funds, in summary, tend to have the lowest volatility and highest dividend yield in the domestic common stock group.

Mid-cap stocks are, as their name implies, smaller than the largest domestic stocks. They are usually established firms in established industries with regional, national and sometimes international markets for their products and services. The S&P MidCap 400 index is a common benchmark for mid-cap stocks. These funds would tend to have lower dividend yields than large-cap funds and to have somewhat higher volatility.

Small-cap stocks are often emerging firms in sometimes emerging industries. But also, these small companies can be established firms with local, regional and sometimes even national and international markets. The benchmark for this group is the S&P SmallCap 600. These stocks must have liquid enough trading for mutual funds to invest and, although small, are still listed on the New York Stock Exchange, the American Stock Exchange or NASDAQ. These small-cap funds tend to be more volatile than large-cap and mid-cap funds, have very low dividend yields, and often do not move in tandem with large-cap and mid-cap funds.

The large-, mid- and small-cap categories capture a fund's predominant focus and are important because these size categories do not all behave alike in a market sense. The stocks do tend to move in somewhat different cycles and have pronounced differences in risk and return over time.

One other element can be superimposed over these stock size distinctions to better understand performance and risk in different market environments: the growth or value investment management style of the fund portfolio manager.

A small-cap growth fund will act differently than a small-cap value fund and a mid-cap growth fund is more likely to correlate with a small-cap growth fund than a mid-cap value fund. Portfolio managers of growth-managed funds seek out stocks that have either experienced rapid growth in sales or earnings or are expected to have rapid growth. Often these stocks have high price-earnings ratios (price per share divided by earnings per share) and are volatile when expectations for earnings or sales growth change even slightly. Few growth stocks pay any significant dividend, and they are often concentrated in industries such as technology, health, telecommunications and software.

The value style of investment management emphasizes low price to earnings, low price to sales (price per share divided by sales per share), and higher dividend yields. The trade-off relative to growth stocks is that value stocks have a lower expected growth rate in earnings and sales, but also less risk. Value stocks are often concentrated in insurance, banking, and electric and gas utilities, for example.

For purposes of diversification and risk, it pays to keep in mind the growth/value investment style mix of your stock mutual funds.

SECTOR STOCK FUNDS

Sector funds concentrate their stock holdings in just one industry or a few related industries. They are diversified within the sector, but are not broadly diversified. They are still influenced and react to industry/sector factors as well as general stock market factors. Sector funds have greater risk than diversified common stock funds. While there are a substantial number of sectors represented by mutual funds, a handful of sector designations cover most of the sector fund offerings: energy/resources, financial/banking, gold, health, real estate, technology, telecommunications, and utilities. As is clear from this sector category list, some sectors are of greater risk than others—technology versus utilities, for example. By definition, a sector fund is a concentrated, not diversified, fund holding.

INTERNATIONAL STOCK FUNDS

International stock funds invest in the stocks of foreign firms. Some stock funds specialize in a single country, others in regions, such as the Pacific or Europe, and others invest in multiple foreign regions. In addition, some stock funds—usually termed "global funds"—invest in both foreign and U.S. securities. We have four classifications by type of investment for the international funds category—foreign stock funds, global stock funds, regional/country stock funds and emerging market stock funds.

International funds provide investors with added diversification. The most important factor when diversifying a portfolio is selecting investments whose returns are not highly correlated. Within the U.S., investors can diversify by selecting securities of firms in different industries. In the international realm, investors take the diversification process one step further by holding securities of firms in different countries. The more independently these foreign markets move in relation to the U.S. stock market, the greater the diversification benefit will be, and the lower the risk of the total portfolio.

In addition, international funds overcome some of the difficulties investors face in making foreign investments directly. For instance, individuals have to thoroughly understand the foreign brokerage process, be familiar with the various foreign marketplaces and their economies, be aware of currency fluctuation trends, and have access to reliable financial information in order to invest directly in foreign stocks. This can be a monumental task for the individual investor.

There are some risks unique to investing internationally. In addition to the risk inherent in investing in any security, there is an additional exchange rate risk. The return to a U.S. investor from a foreign security depends on both the security's return in its own currency and the rate at which that currency can be exchanged for U.S. dollars. Another uncertainty is political risk, which includes government restriction, taxation, or even total prohibition of the exchange of one currency into another. Of course, the more the mutual fund is diversified among various countries, the less the risk involved.

BALANCED STOCK/BOND FUNDS

In general, the portfolios of balanced funds consist of investments in common stocks and significant investments in bonds and convertible securities. The range as a percentage of the total portfolio of stocks and bonds is usually stated in the investment objective, and the portfolio manager has the option of allocating the proportions within the range. Some asset allocation funds—funds that have a wide latitude of portfolio composition change—can also be found in the balanced category. Also in this category are life cycle funds designed to match a particular investment objective and risk/return profile. Life cycle funds are often composed of other funds from the same fund family. A balanced fund is generally less volatile than a stock fund and provides a higher dividend yield.

BOND FUNDS

Bond mutual funds are attractive to investors because they provide diversification and liquidity, which is not as readily attainable in direct bond investments.

Bond funds have portfolios with a wide range of average maturities. Many funds use their names to characterize their maturity structure. Generally, short term means that the portfolio has a weighted average maturity of less than three years. Intermediate implies an average maturity of three to 10 years, and long term is over 10 years. The longer the maturity, the greater the change in fund value when interest rates change. Longer-term bond funds are riskier than shorter-term funds, and they usually offer higher yields.

TAXABLE BOND FUNDS

Bond funds are principally categorized by the types of bonds they hold. Corporate bond funds invest primarily in investment-grade corporate bonds of various maturities; however, corporate high-yield bond funds provide high income but invest generally in corporate bonds rated below investment grade, making them riskier.

Government bond funds invest in the bonds of the U.S. government and its agencies, while mortgage funds invest primarily in mortgage-backed bonds. General bond funds invest in a mix of government and agency bonds, corporate bonds, and mortgage-backed bonds.

MUNICIPAL BOND FUNDS

Tax-exempt municipal bond funds invest in bonds whose income is exempt from federal income tax. Some tax-exempt funds may invest in municipal bonds whose income is also exempt from the income tax of a specific state.

INTERNATIONAL BOND FUNDS

International bond funds allow mutual fund investors to hold a diversified portfolio of foreign corporate and government bonds. These foreign bonds often offer higher yields, but carry additional risks beyond those of domestic bonds. As with foreign common stocks, currency risk can be as significant as the potential default of foreign government bonds—a particular risk with the debt of emerging countries.

INDEX FUNDS

One other fund type deserves a special mention—the index fund. An example of an index fund is the Vanguard 500 Index Fund, categorized as a large-cap stock fund. This fund is designed to match the Standard & Poor's 500 stock index and does so by investing in all 500 stocks in the S&P 500; the amounts invested in each stock are proportional to the firm's market capitalization representation in the S&P 500. Statistics on index funds are quite useful for comparison with other funds, since indexes represent a widely followed segment of the market. Index funds are available covering most major segments of the bond and stock markets—domestic and international. Because they are unmanaged, they make no research efforts to select particular stocks or bonds, nor do they make timing decisions. They are always 100% invested. This passive management approach makes the expenses and the cost of managing an index fund extremely low. Lists of index funds appear at the back of this *Guide*.

Understanding Mutual Fund Statements

4

One of the advantages of mutual fund investing is the wealth of information that mutual funds provide to fund investors and prospective investors. Taken together, the various reports provide investors with vital information concerning financial matters and how the fund is managed—both key elements in the selection process. In fact, mutual fund prospectuses, annual reports, and performance statistics are key sources of information most investors will need in the selection and monitoring process.

To new mutual fund investors, the information may seem overwhelming. However, regulations governing the industry have standardized the reports: Once you know where to look for information, the location will hold true for almost all funds.

There are basically five types of statements produced by the mutual fund: the prospectus; the statement of additional information; annual, semiannual, and quarterly reports; marketing brochures; and account statements. Actually, the second report—the statement of additional information—is part of the prospectus. However, mutual funds are allowed to simplify and streamline the prospectus, if they choose, by dividing it into two parts: a prospectus that all prospective investors must receive, and the statement of additional information—which the fund must send investors if they specifically request it. Some fund families also currently offer an abbreviated or "plain English" profile prospectus.

THE PROSPECTUS

The prospectus is the single most important document produced by the mutual fund, and it is must-reading for investors before investing. Current shareholders must be sent new prospectuses when they are updated, at least once every 14 months.

The prospectus is generally organized into sections, and it must cover specific topics. The front usually gives a quick synopsis of the fund: investment category, sales or redemption charges, minimum invest-

THE PROSPECTUS FEE TABLE: AN EXAMPLE

The following table describes the fees and expenses that are incurred when you buy, hold or sell shares of the fund. The annual fund operating expenses provided below for the fund do not reflect the effect of any reduction of certain expenses during the period.

Shareholder Fees (paid by the investor directly)

Sales charge (load) on purchases and reinvested distributions.........None

Deferred sales charge (load) on redemptions ....None

Annual Fund Operating Expenses (paid from fund assets)

Management fee..0.69%

Distribution and/or Service (12b-1) fees ....None

Other Expenses 0.25%

Total annual fund operating expenses 0.94%

A portion of the brokerage commissions that the fund pays may be reimbursed and used to reduce the fund's expenses. In addition, through arrangements with the fund's custodian and transfer agent, credits realized as a result of uninvested cash balances are used to reduce custodian and transfer agent expenses. Including these reductions, the total fund operating expenses would have been 0.90%.

This **example** helps you compare the cost of investing in the fund with the cost of investing in other mutual funds.

Let's say, hypothetically, that the fund's annual return is 5% and that your shareholder fees and the fund's annual operating expenses are exactly as described in the fee table. This example illustrates the effect of fees and expenses, but is not meant to suggest actual or expected fees and expenses or returns, all of which may vary. For every $10,000 you invested, here's how much you would pay in total expenses if you sell all of your shares at the end of each time period indicated.

1 year	$96
3 years	$300
5 years	$520
10 years	$1,155

Source: Fidelity Capital Appreciation Fund prospectus, December 30, 2005.

SELECTED PER SHARE DATA AND RATIOS: AN EXAMPLE

500 Index Fund Investor Shares

	Year Ended December 31,				
	2004	2003	2002	2001	2000
Net Asset Value, Beginning of Period	$102.67	$81.15	$105.89	$121.86	$135.33
Investment Operations					
Net Investment Income	1.95*	1.44	1.32	1.260	1.29
Net Realized and Unrealized Gain (Loss) on Investments	8.97	21.51	(24.70)	(15.955)	(13.46)
Total from Investment Operations	10.92	22.95	(23.38)	(14.695)	(12.17)
Distributions					
Dividends from Net Investment Income	(1.95)	(1.43)	(1.36)	(1.275)	(1.30)
Distributions from Realized Capital Gains	—	—	—	—	—
Total Distributions	(1.95)	(1.43)	(1.36)	(1.275)	(1.30)
Net Asset Value, End of Period	**$111.64**	**$102.67**	**$ 81.15**	**$105.89**	**$121.86**
Total Return**	10.74%	28.50%	–22.15%	–12.02%	–9.06%
Ratios/Supplemental Data					
Net Assets, End of Period (Millions)	$84,167	$75,342	$56,224	$73,151	$88,240
Ratio of Total Expenses to Average Net Assets	0.18%	0.18%	0.18%	0.18%	0.18%
Ratio of Net Investment Income to Average Net Assets	1.86%*	1.61%	1.43%	1.14%	0.98%
Turnover Rate†	3%	1%	6%	3%	7%

*Net investment income per share and the ratio of net investment income to average net assets include $0.32 and 0.31%, respectively, resulting from a special dividend from Microsoft Corp. in November 2004.
**Total returns do not reflect the $10 annual account maintenance fee applied on balances under $10,000.
†Excludes the value of portfolio securities received or delivered as a result of in-kind purchases or redemptions of the Fund's capital shares.

Source: Vanguard 500 Index Fund prospectus, April 29, 2005.

ment, retirement plans available, and address and telephone number. More detailed descriptions are in the body of the prospectus.

Fee Table

All mutual fund prospectuses must include a table near the front that delineates all fees and charges to the investor (see example at top left). The table contains three sections: The first section lists shareholder fees, including all front-end and back-end loads and redemption fees; the second section lists all annual fund operating expenses, including management fees and any 12b-1 charges, as a percentage of net assets; and the third section is an illustration of the total cost of these fees and charges to an investor over time. The illustration assumes an initial investment of $10,000 and a 5% growth rate for the fund, and states the total dollar cost to an investor if shares were redeemed at the end of one year, three years, five years, and 10 years.

Selected Per Share Data and Ratios

One of the most important sections of the prospectus contains the selected per share data and ratios, which provides statistics on income and capital changes per share of the fund (see example at bottom left). The per share figures are given for the life of the fund or 10 years, whichever is less. Also included are important statistical summaries of investment activities throughout each period. These financial statements are also contained in the annual report.

The per share section summarizes the financial activity over the fund's fiscal year, which may or may not correspond to the calendar year, to arrive at the ending net asset value for the fund. The financial activity summarized includes increases in net asset value due to dividend and interest payments received and capital gains from investment activity. Decreases in net asset value are due to capital losses from investment activity, investment expenses, and payouts to fund shareholders in the form of distributions.

Potential investors may want to note the line items in this section. *Investment income* represents the dividends and interest earned by the fund during its fiscal year. *Expenses* reflect such fund costs as the management fee, legal fees, and transfer agent fees. These expenses are given in detail in the statement of operations section of the annual report.

Net investment income is investment income less expenses. This line is important for investors to note because it reflects the level and stability of net income over the time period. A high net investment income would most likely be found in funds that have income, rather than growth, as their investment category. Since net investment income must be distributed to shareholders to avoid direct taxation of the fund, a high net investment income has the potential of translating into a high tax liability for the investor.

Net realized and unrealized gain (loss) on investments is the change in the value of investments that have been sold (realized) during the period or that continue to be held (unrealized) by the fund.

Distributions to fund shareholders are also detailed. These distributions will include dividends from net investment income for the current fiscal period. Tax law requires that income earned must be distributed in the calendar year earned. Also included in distributions will be any realized net capital gains.

The last line in the per share section will be the *net asset value* at the end of the period, which reflects the value of one share of the fund. It is calculated by determining the total assets of the fund and dividing by the number of mutual fund shares outstanding. The figure will change for a variety of reasons, including changes in investment income, expenses, gains, losses, and distributions. Depending upon the source of change, a decline in net asset value may or may not be due to poor performance. For instance, a decline in net asset value may be due to a distribution of net realized gains on securities.

The financial ratios at the bottom of the per share financial data are important indicators of fund performance and strategy. The *expense ratio* relates expenses incurred by the fund to average net assets. These expenses include the investment advisory fee, legal and accounting fees, and 12b-1 charges to the fund; they do not include fund brokerage costs, loads, or redemption fees. A high expense ratio is difficult for a fund manager to overcome and detracts from your investment return. In general, common stock funds have higher expense ratios than bond funds, and smaller funds have higher expense ratios than larger funds. International funds also tend to have higher expense ratios than domestic funds. Index funds usually have the lowest expense ratios. The average expense ratio for common stock funds is 1.2%, international stock funds 1.4%, index stock funds 0.4%, and bond funds (taxable and non-taxable) about 0.7%.

The *ratio of net investment income to average net assets* is very similar to a dividend or bond yield. This, too, should reflect the investment category of the fund. Common stock funds with income as a significant part of their investment objective, such as growth and income funds, would be expected to have the highest ratios and aggressive growth funds would normally have ratios close to 0%. Bond funds would normally have the highest ratios of all funds.

The portfolio *turnover rate* is the lower of purchases or sales divided by average net assets. It reflects how frequently securities are bought and sold by the fund. For purposes of determining the turnover rate for common stock funds, fixed-income securities with a maturity of less than a year are excluded, as are all government securities, short and long term. For bond funds, however, long-term U.S. government bonds are included.

Investors should take note of the portfolio turnover rate, because the higher the turnover, the greater the brokerage costs incurred by the fund. Brokerage costs are not reflected in the expense ratio but instead are directly reflected as a decrease in net asset value. In addition, mutual funds with high turnover rates generally have higher capital gains distributions—a potential tax liability. Small-cap growth stock funds are most likely to have high turnover rates. Some bond funds may also have very high portfolio turnover rates. A 100% portfolio turnover rate indicates that the value of the portfolio was completely turned over in a year; a 200% portfolio turnover indicates that the value of the portfolio was completely turned over twice in a year. The portfolio turnover rate for the average mutual fund is around 100% but varies with market conditions and investment category.

Investment Objective/Policy

The investment objective section of the prospectus elaborates on the brief sentence or two from the prospectus cover. In this section, the fund describes the types of investments it will make—whether it is bonds, stocks, convertible securities, options, etc.—along with some general guidelines as to the proportions these securities will represent in the fund's portfolio. The investment objective statement usually indicates whether it will be oriented toward capital gains or income. In this section, the management will also briefly discuss its approach to market timing, risk assumption, and the anticipated level of portfolio turnover. Some prospectuses may indicate any investment restrictions they have placed on the fund, such as purchasing securities on margin, selling short, concentrating in firms or industries, trading foreign securities, and lending securities; this section may also state the allowable proportions in certain investment categories. The restrictions section is usually given in more detail in the statement of additional information.

Fund Management

The fund management section names the investment adviser and gives the advisory fee schedule. Most advisers charge a management fee on a sliding scale that decreases as assets under management increase. Occasionally, some portion of the fund adviser's fees is subject to the fund's performance relative to the market.

Some prospectuses will describe the fund's officers and directors with a short biography of affiliations and relevant experience. For most funds, however, this information is provided in more detail in the statement of additional information. The fund shareholders elect the board of directors; the board of directors selects the fund adviser. The adviser is usually a firm operated by or affiliated with officers of the fund. Information on fund officers and directors is not critical to fund selection. The prospectus also names the portfolio manager of the fund. The portfolio manager is responsible for the day-to-day investment decisions of the fund and is employed by the fund adviser. Who the portfolio manager is and how long the manager has been in the position can be useful in judging historical performance.

Other Important Sections

There are several other sections in a mutual fund prospectus of which investors should be aware. They will appear under various headings, depending upon the prospectus, but they are not difficult to find.

Mutual funds that have 12b-1 plans must describe them in the prospectus. A description of these plans must be prominently and clearly placed in the prospectus, usually in a section titled "Distribution Plan." The distribution plan details the marketing aspects of the fund and how they relate to fund expenses. For instance, advertising, distribution of fund literature, and any arrangements with brokers would be included in the marketing plan; the 12b-1 plan pays for these distribution expenses. The distribution plan section specifies the maximum annual 12b-1 fee that can be charged. Funds often charge less than the maximum. The actual charge to the fund of a 12b-1 plan is listed at the front of the prospectus in the fee table.

The *capital stock* section, or *fund share characteristics* section, provides shareholders with a summary of their voting rights, participation in dividends and distributions, and the number of authorized and issued shares of the fund. Often, a separate section will discuss the tax treatment that will apply to fund distributions, which may include dividends, interest, and capital gains.

The *how-to-buy-shares* section gives the minimum initial investment and any subsequent minimums; it will also list load charges or fees. In addition, information on mail, wire, and telephone purchases is provided, along with distribution reinvestment options, automatic exchange, investment and withdrawal plans, and retirement options.

The *how-to-redeem-shares* section discusses telephone, written, and wire redemption options, including automatic withdrawal plans, with a special section on signature guarantees and other documents that may be needed. Also detailed are any fees for reinvestment or redemption. Shareholder services are usually outlined here, with emphasis on exchanges among funds in a family of funds. This will include any fees for exchanging, any limits on the number of exchanges allowed, and any other exchange restrictions.

STATEMENT OF ADDITIONAL INFORMATION

This document elaborates on the prospectus. The investment objectives section is more in-depth, with a list and description of investment restrictions. The management section gives brief biographies of directors and officers, and provides the number of fund shares owned beneficially by the officers and directors named. The investment adviser section, while reiterating the major points made in the prospectus, gives all the expense items and contract provisions of the agreement between the adviser and the fund. If the fund has a 12b-1 plan, further details will likely be in the statement of additional information.

Many times, the statement of additional information will include much more information on the tax consequences of mutual fund distributions and investment. Conditions under which withholding for federal income tax will take place are also provided. The fund's financial statements are incorporated by reference to the annual report to shareholders and generally do not appear in the statement of additional information. Finally, the independent auditors give their opinion on the accuracy of the fund's financial statements.

ANNUAL, SEMIANNUAL, AND QUARTERLY REPORTS

All funds must send their shareholders audited annual and semiannual reports. Mutual funds are allowed to combine their prospectus and annual report; some do this, but many do not.

The annual report describes the fund activities over the past year and provides a listing of all investments of the fund at market value as of the end of the fiscal year. Sometimes the cost basis of each investment is also given. Looking in-depth at the individual securities held by the fund is probably not the best use of time. However, it is helpful to be aware of the overall investment categories. For instance, investors should look at the percentage invested in common stocks, bonds, convertible bonds, and any other holdings. In addition, a look at the types of common stocks held and the percentage of fund assets by industry classification gives the investor some indication of how the portfolio will fare in various market environments.

The annual report will also have a balance sheet, listing all assets and liabilities of the fund by general category. This holds little interest for investors.

The statement of operations, similar to an income statement, is of interest only in that the fund expenses are broken down. For most funds, the management fee is by far the largest expense; the expense ratio in the prospectus conveys much more useful information. The statement of changes in net assets is very close to the financial information provided in the prospectus, but the information is not on a per share basis. Per share information will, however, frequently be detailed in the annual report in a separate section. Footnotes to the financial statements elaborate on the entries, but other than any pending litigation against the fund, they are most often routine.

The quarterly or semiannual reports are current accounts of the investment portfolio and provide more timely views of the fund's investments than does the annual report.

MARKETING BROCHURES AND ADVERTISEMENTS

These will generally provide a brief description of the fund. However, the most important bit of information is the telephone number to call and request the fund prospectus and annual report, if you have not received them already. These are also usually available on-line and at the fund's Web site.

The rules regarding mutual fund advertising have been tightened and standardized. All mutual funds that use performance figures in their ads must include one-, five-, and 10-year total return figures. Bond funds that quote yields must use a standardized method for computing yield, and they must include total return figures as well. Finally, any applicable sales commissions must be mentioned in the ad.

ACCOUNT STATEMENTS

Mutual funds send out periodic account statements detailing reinvestment of dividend and capital gains distributions, new purchases or redemptions, and any other account activity such as service fees. This statement provides a running account balance by date with share accumulations, an account value to date, and a total of distributions made to date. *These statements are invaluable for tax purposes and should be saved.* The fund will also send out, in January, a Form 1099-DIV for any distributions made in the previous year and a Form 1099-B if any mutual fund shares were sold.

5

Understanding Risk

Risk tolerance refers to the level of volatility of an investment that an investor finds acceptable. The anticipated holding period of an investment is important because it should affect the investor's risk tolerance. Time is a form of diversification; longer holding periods provide greater diversification across different market environments. Investors who anticipate longer holding periods can take on more risk.

The liquidity needs of an investor similarly help define the types of funds that the investor should consider. Liquidity implies preservation of capital, and if liquidity is important, then mutual funds with smaller variations in value should be considered. A liquid mutual fund is one in which withdrawals from the fund can be made at any time with a reasonable certainty that the per share value will not have dropped sharply. Highly volatile small-cap growth funds are the least liquid, and short-term bond funds are the most liquid. The table on page 25 lists the risk characteristics for different mutual fund categories.

A LOOK AT RISK

Risk is the most difficult concept for many investors to grasp, and yet much of the mutual fund investment decision depends on an understanding of risk. There are many different ways to categorize investment risk and numerous approaches to the measurement of risk. If we can assume that the volatility of the return on your mutual fund investment is the concern you grapple with when you think of risk, the task of making decisions about risk becomes easier.

Questions about how much value a mutual fund is likely to lose in a down market or how certain it is that a fund will be worth a given amount at the end of the year are the same concerns as volatility of return. Changes in the domestic and international economies, interest rates, exchange rates, corporate profits, consumer confidence, and general expectations all combine to move markets up and down, creating volatility, or risk.

Risk Characteristics for Different Mutual Fund Categories

Stock Funds	Total Risk	Standard Deviation (%)	Beta (X)	Average Maturity (Yrs)	Bull Market Return (%)	Bear Market Return (%)
Large-Cap Stock	av	10.3	1.04	na	58.7	-35.8
Mid-Cap Stock	abv av	12.5	1.17	na	82.1	-23.6
Small-Cap Stock	high	14.9	1.36	na	93.4	-18.1
Growth Style	abv av	12.9	1.18	na	67.0	-48.9
Value Style	abv av	11.6	1.12	na	80.7	-2.8
Energy/Resources Sector	high	19.2	0.83	na	153.7	2.0
Financial/Banking Sector	abv av	12.5	1.12	na	69.9	20.6
Gold Sector	high	29.2	0.95	na	108.5	77.8
Health Sector	abv av	11.9	0.74	na	74.4	-7.3
Real Estate Sector	abv av	14.0	0.76	na	106.5	42.6
Technology Sector	high	20.7	1.74	na	72.2	-75.7
Telecommunications Sector	high	16.8	1.48	na	106.9	-72.4
Utilities Sector	av	11.0	0.81	na	80.9	-43.6
Global Stock	av	10.1	0.96	na	76.3	-30.8
Foreign Stock	abv av	12.5	1.09	na	113.9	-44.3
Regional/Country Stock	high	16.7	1.02	na	139.5	-38.8
Emerging Stock	high	16.6	1.33	na	175.0	-41.4
Balanced Stock/Bond	blw av	6.6	0.67	7.7	45.7	-10.8
Bond Funds						
Corporate Bond	low	3.6	0.03	6.9	11.6	23.4
Corporate High-Yield Bond	blw av	4.6	0.24	6.9	32.2	2.3
Mortgage-Backed Bond	low	2.2	-0.02	7.9	7.4	26.6
Gov't: Short-Term Bond	low	1.6	-0.01	3.9	3.6	21.8
Gov't: Interm-Term Bond	blw av	5.0	-0.01	7.0	7.9	32.6
Gov't: Long-Term Bond	abv av	11.9	-0.05	19.9	14.0	30.2
General Bond	low	3.3	0.00	5.7	8.4	26.6
Nat'l Muni: Short-Term Bond	low	1.0	0.00	2.0	4.8	14.1
Nat'l Muni: Interm-Term Bond	low	3.9	0.01	7.5	8.0	22.6
Nat'l Muni: Long-Term Bond	low	4.4	0.01	13.1	12.7	24.7
Nat'l Muni: High-Yield Bond	low	3.2	0.03	14.5	17.7	22.0
International Bond	blw av	6.1	0.17	8.2	28.6	25.9

Total risk for a mutual fund measures variation in return from all sources. As an example, variation in return for common stocks is caused by factors unique to the firm, industry variables, and conditions affecting all stocks. Market risk refers to the variables such as interest rates, inflation, and the business cycle that affect all stocks to some degree. In well-diversified portfolios of common stock, the firm and industry risk of the various stocks in the portfolio offset each other; thus, these portfolios tend to have lower total risk, and this total risk is usually composed almost entirely of market risk. For less diversified portfolios, funds that hold very few stocks, or sector funds that concentrate investment in one industry, total risk is usually higher and is composed of firm and industry risk in addition to market risk.

Risk levels based upon total risk are given for all funds. The five categories (high, above average, average, below average, and low) serve as a way to compare the risk inherent in common stock funds, international funds, sector funds, bond funds, or any type of mutual fund. Shorter-term bond funds would be expected to have relatively low total risk while some of the concentrated, less-diversified, small-cap stock funds would likely be ranked in the high total risk category.

The total risk measure will enable you to construct a portfolio of funds that reflects your risk tolerance and the holding period you anticipate for your portfolio. Portfolios for individuals with low risk tolerance and short holding periods should be composed predominantly of funds that are less volatile, with lower total risk. Individuals with high risk tolerances and longer holding periods can form appropriate portfolios by combining mutual funds with higher total risk.

MEASURING TOTAL RISK: STANDARD DEVIATION

Total risk is measured by the standard deviation statistic, a numerical measure of how much the return on a mutual fund has varied, no matter what the cause, from the historical average return of the fund. Higher standard deviations indicate higher total risk. The category risk rank measures the total risk of a fund to the median total risk for all funds in the same investment category. The rankings for category risk are high, above average, average, below average, and low. Funds ranked above average and high for category risk should produce returns above the average for the investment category.

The risk index indicates the magnitude of the standard deviation for a fund relative to the median standard deviation for funds in the category. A risk index of 1.2, for example, means that the standard deviation for a fund is 20% higher than the median standard deviation for the category.

MEASURING MARKET RISK:
BETA AND AVERAGE MATURITY

Market risk is a part of total risk, but measures only the sensitivity of the fund to movements in the general market. This is valuable information for the individual investor—particularly when combined with use of the total risk and category risk rank measures—to judge how a mutual fund will perform in different market situations. The market risk measure used for common stock funds is beta; for bond funds, average maturity is used.

Beta

Beta is a measure of the relative volatility inherent in a mutual fund investment. This volatility is compared to some measure of the market such as Standard & Poor's index of 500 common stocks. The market's beta is always 1.0 by definition, and a money market fund's beta is always 0. If you hold a mutual fund with a beta of 1.0, it will move, on average, in tandem with the market. If the market is up 10%, the fund will be up, on average, 10%, and if the market drops 10%, the fund will drop, on average, 10%. A mutual fund with a beta of 1.5 is 50% more volatile than the market: If the market is up 10%, the fund will be up, on average, 50% more, or 15%; conversely, if the market is down 10%, the fund, on average, will be down 15%. A negative beta, a rare occurrence, implies that the mutual fund moves in the opposite direction of the market's movement.

The higher the fund's beta, the greater the volatility of the investment in the fund and the less appropriate the fund would be for shorter holding periods or to meet liquidity needs. Remember that beta is a relative measure: A low beta only implies that the fund's movement is not volatile relative to the market. Its return, however, may be quite variable, resulting in high total risk. For instance, industry-specific sector fund moves may not be related to market volatility, but changes in the industry may cause these funds' returns to fluctuate widely. For a well-diversified stock fund, beta is a very useful measure of risk, but for concentrated funds, beta only captures a portion of the variability that the fund may experience. Betas for certain sector funds, for example, can be very misleading. Sector funds often have relatively low betas, but these funds are extremely volatile. In addition, the betas of sector funds sometimes change significantly from year to year.

Average Maturity

For all bond funds, the average maturity of the bonds in the portfolio is reported as a market risk measure, rather than beta. The volatility of a bond fund is determined by how the fund reacts primarily to changes in interest rates, although high-yield (junk) bond funds and international bond funds can be affected significantly by factors other than interest rates. When interest rates rise, bond funds fall in value; and, conversely, when interest rates fall, bond mutual funds rise in value. The longer the average maturity of the bond fund, the greater will be the variation in the return on the bond fund when interest rates change. Bond mutual fund investors with less risk tolerance and shorter holding periods should seek shorter-maturity funds, and longer-term bond fund investors who are more risk tolerant will find funds with longer maturities a better match.

In the case where a bond fund holds mortgage-backed securities, average maturity may not capture the potential for decline in effective maturity when interest rates fall and mortgages are refinanced. Some mortgage funds also use derivatives, highly leveraged financial instruments that derive their value from movements in specific interest rates or indexes, which further complicate an analysis of their risk. Bond funds that hold corporate bonds and municipal bonds also face changing effective maturities when interest rates decline and bond issuers call bonds before maturity.

Investing and Redeeming: 6
A Look at Fund Services

Mutual fund investors are usually most concerned with building and monitoring a portfolio that will deliver the best results, given their objectives. While total return and risk are crucial, services play an important role in facilitating the investment process.

A variety of useful shareholder options exist for investing and withdrawing money, both on an individual transaction and a systematic basis. By using services like those examined in this chapter, you may be able to manage your investments in a simpler, more efficient manner. This may even lead to improved results. Since our coverage is quite comprehensive, you may not find all the services discussed offered by the mutual funds you deal with. In addition, individual procedures can vary somewhat among funds.

MAKING INVESTMENTS

The traditional way of investing in a fund is simply to place a check in the mail. But it could take up to a week—or longer—for your money to arrive and be put to work. By letting a few days elapse you risk paying more per share for a volatile fund than you had expected. Of course, if you're lucky you might pay less.

It frequently makes sense to have a better idea about the price you will pay, especially if you're going to invest a fairly large sum in a more volatile fund. By taking action prior to 4 p.m. Eastern time, it's possible to buy at the price prevailing on the day you place your order. Of course, the price you'll pay is not the only consideration—putting the money to work sooner is beneficial to fixed-income investors who are placing a large amount—say $50,000 or more—into an account and don't want to wait to begin accruing dividends.

Buying at Today's Price

There are several ways to accomplish the purchase of shares at that day's net asset value:

- Transfer from a money fund. You can park your investment in the family's money market fund, wait until you're ready to invest, call the company before 4 p.m. Eastern time and request that the funds be transferred to the portfolio of your choice. Of course, you can usually also transfer from other bond and stock funds in the group.

- Wire transfer from your bank. This is the quickest way to move money and is especially recommended for large sums. You will buy in at the day's net asset value if the wire arrives at your account prior to 4 p.m. Eastern time. Your fund company will provide the instructions that you need to convey to your bank. Banks generally charge for this service but mutual funds usually do not. (Incidentally, if you invest by wire you can redeem immediately if you need to—there is no clearing period before your funds will be released.)

- Telephone purchase. Some companies allow you to place a purchase order by phone, locking in that day's price if your order is entered before 4 p.m. Eastern time. You give your instructions to the telephone representative, then send a check or wire for the cost. The payment must reach the account in five to seven business days (depending on the requirements of the company), otherwise the order will be canceled with the investor assuming any resultant losses. Some funds will only accept wires for telephone purchases. There are special conditions that need to be satisfied when you place a telephone purchase order. These requirements, which vary by company, typically include investment minimums and maximums. Minimums may or may not be higher than the fund's usual investment minimum and could be $5,000 or $10,000. The maximum may be based on the total value of your existing accounts with the family. The details should be spelled out in the prospectus. It's best to verify the information with a shareholder representative before entering your order.

- Opening a new account by wire. A number of mutual funds allow you to establish an account by wire, provided you promptly send in a completed application and wire in the cost of your shares. If your wire arrives at your new account before 4 p.m. Eastern time you will buy at the current day's price. Again, there are minimum investment requirements and other details which vary by fund. The first step is to phone for instructions.

Systematic Investments

The best way to build up your mutual fund assets is simply to put money to work on a regular basis. Modest, ongoing investments can be relatively painless and may eventually lead to significant wealth. For example, at 10% compounded annually, $100 invested at the beginning of each month would grow to $76,566 in 20 years; continuing the investments for just five additional years yields $133,780.

Systematic investment plans offer an ideal way to benefit from dollar-cost averaging. With fixed, periodic investments, you buy more shares when prices are low and fewer when they're high. This results in a lower average cost per share than a simple average of prices on your purchase dates. Dollar-cost averaging works especially well with more volatile portfolios.

There are several ways periodic investments can be made automatically, without sending in a check.

- Direct, systematic transfers. The systematic investment program, where money is taken either from your bank account or paycheck, transfers a predetermined, fixed amount at approximately the same date each month. In order for the payments to be routed directly from your bank account, your financial institution must be an Automated Clearing House (ACH) member, which most are. If you want the investment deducted directly from your paycheck, you need your employer's consent. In addition to the ACH periodic purchase you can make individual ACH purchases in varying amounts whenever you like by phoning your fund company. You would be purchasing your shares at the next business day's price if you call prior to the market's 4 p.m. closing. If you call after 4 p.m., you would buy at the price prevailing at the close of the second business day.
- Dividend transfers. By investing periodic distributions received from one mutual fund into shares of another in the same family, you can build a position in the latter. For example, the monthly dividends from a fixed-income fund could be moved into a small-cap portfolio. Although dividends from investment income are not fixed in amount like systematic purchases, they can be sufficiently stable. It wouldn't take an enormous investment in a fixed-income fund to generate $100 monthly in dividends. Another example might be the transfer of quarterly income dividends and annual capital gains distributions from

a large-cap fund into shares of a money market or short-term bond fund.

MAKING REDEMPTIONS

A variety of useful approaches are also available when you need to withdraw money from your mutual fund.

Mailing in a redemption letter is the old-fashioned way to withdraw money from a fund account. The letter must contain the necessary information—including name(s) of registered owner(s), fund name, account number and redemption amount—and be properly signed by the account owner(s). You may need a signature guarantee for your request to be processed.

There are several faster, simpler ways to redeem shares. Be sure to sign up for these additional services, if necessary.

- Requesting a check by phone. You may telephone your shareholder representative and request that a check be mailed to you or your bank. Of course, you lose interest during the mail transit time, an important consideration with larger redemptions.
- Drawing a check on a fixed-income fund. You can write a check on a money market or other fixed-income fund, perhaps on money just transferred in from another portfolio in the family. Funds generally place a minimum, commonly $100 or $500, on individual checks. If you draw your check on a fund with a fluctuating share price, it would give rise to a taxable event. Money market funds ordinarily maintain a stable $1 price, so you need not be concerned about taxable events when drawing checks on these funds.
- Wiring money from your fund. You can request your company to wire the proceeds to your bank account. This is the quickest way to make a direct transfer of money, and it is recommended for large sums. Your bank and fund will tell you about their fee policies.
- Making an ACH redemption. If you have established an Automated Clearing House linkage between your fund and bank, you can simply phone your company and request that the balance be transferred to your bank. However, it could take a few days for the money to reach your account.

Systematic Withdrawal Plans

Systematic withdrawal plans are useful for retirees and others who want to receive regular monthly or quarterly checks. The payments could be sent to someone besides the account holder, such as a student in college or another dependent. A certain minimum account balance, such as $10,000, is required to establish the program. You can change your withdrawals or discontinue them at will. Most funds offer systematic withdrawal programs.

Three key variables you need to come to grips with in establishing a withdrawal plan are:

- Your fund's expected total return;
- The expected rate of inflation; and
- Your target withdrawal percentage.

For people who may be withdrawing money over a decade or longer, a conservative stock fund can lead to the best results. Stocks have generated significantly higher long-run total returns than bonds. In fact, it may be unwise to use a withdrawal plan with a fixed-income fund if you plan on making redemptions over an extended period. For longer-term bond fund investors it's better to only take the monthly dividend checks and not disturb the corpus, since doing so can significantly deplete your capital.

For example, an income-oriented stock fund is a good withdrawal plan candidate. Because your investment in an income-oriented stock fund may not yield sufficient dividends to meet your needs, you may need to dip into principal. But your capital can still grow if your withdrawal rate is not excessive.

The best way to plan your future withdrawal stream is to make some projections. You can get a good estimate of how long your capital will last under different assumptions using annual redemptions, even though you may want to redeem more frequently. The percentage of your initial capital withdrawn annually must be realistic; you don't want to deplete your nest egg too soon.

How Long Will Your Money Last?

If the rate at which you withdraw is too close to or exceeds your fund's total return (or growth rate), you will eventually deplete your capital. The table on page 34 shows approximately how long, in years, your principal will last given the return generated by your fund and your withdrawal rate on your starting investment amount. The numbers in the body of the table are conservative estimates since they assume withdrawals are made at the beginning of the year. Thus, the first annual redemption would occur immediately. When the

Withdrawal Plans: How Long Will Your Capital Last?

Average Annual Growth[2] (%)	If the Annual Withdrawal Rate of Your Initial Capital Is[1]:											
	16%	15%	14%	13%	12%	11%	10%	9%	8%	7%	6%	5%
	The Number of Years Your Capital Will Last Is:											
1	6	6	7	7	8	9	10	11	13	15	18	22
2	6	7	7	8	9	9	11	12	14	16	19	25
3	6	7	7	8	9	10	11	13	15	18	22	29
4	7	7	8	8	9	10	12	14	16	20	26	37
5	7	7	8	9	10	11	13	15	18	23	32	62
6	7	8	8	9	10	12	14	17	21	28	49	*
7	7	8	9	10	11	13	15	19	25	40	*	*
8	8	8	9	10	12	14	17	22	33	*	*	*
9	8	9	10	11	13	16	20	28	*	*	*	*
10	8	9	10	12	14	18	25	*	*	*	*	*
11	9	10	11	13	16	22	45	*	*	*	*	*
12	9	11	12	15	19	32	*	*	*	*	*	*

[1]Assumes withdrawals are made annually at the beginning of the year.
[2]Can be expressed either as a nominal total return or real (inflation-adjusted) rate.
*Capital will last indefinitely.

portfolio's growth exceeds the withdrawal percentage by a sufficient amount, you could continue withdrawing for an indefinite period; asterisks appear in these instances.

The table can help you determine the best redemption rate. For example, if you assume your fund will grow at 9% per year in nominal terms, you could withdraw 10% of your initial investment amount annually for 20 years. If you trim your withdrawal rate back to 8%, or less, your capital would last indefinitely.

What about inflation? Suppose you expect the price level to increase by 4% per year, on average, and want to withdraw 10% in constant dollars. This means the amount you withdraw each year would need to increase by 4%. In this more realistic case, your capital would be growing at a real, or inflation-adjusted, rate of 5% (9% – 4%). You've simply reduced your 9% nominal return by the anticipated inflation percentage.

Now look in the 5% "average annual growth" row in the table. Your nest egg would last only 13 years, when inflation is factored in, with a 10% withdrawal rate. If you want the capital to last longer, you have to reduce your withdrawals. For instance, at an 8% redemption rate your capital would last 18 years; at 6% it would stretch for 32 years.

Taxes are another consideration. In addition to reducing an expected return for inflation, the careful planner can scale it back further based on an estimate of the impact of taxes on his or her results. Depending on your tax bracket and the fund you're using, your expected return after inflation and taxes could be as low as 2% to 1%, or less.

The table can also help you determine an appropriate withdrawal rate, based on how long your capital must last. Suppose your capital must last at least 20 years, during which you expect 4% inflation yearly. How much can you safely withdraw? If you estimate that your stock fund can return at least 9% annually in nominal terms (5% in real terms), you could withdraw up to 7%—in which case your principal should hold out for 23 years. It would be safer to withdraw a bit less than 7% to provide some margin for error. In fact, in a world with taxes and inflation you risk eventually depleting your capital with a withdrawal rate that exceeds 6% or so, especially if your returns don't live up to your expectations.

Comparing Fixed-Percentage and Fixed-Dollar Withdrawal Options

The most common withdrawal plan involves redeeming a fixed dollar amount over a year, often in monthly increments. The redemptions may be increased periodically for inflation. But if your withdrawal rate is too close to or exceeds the expected annual return after inflation, you would be redeeming an increasing percentage of your remaining balance each year.

Enter the fixed-percent option. As shown in the previous section, you might withdraw, say, 6% of your capital based on its value at the beginning of each year. Your annual dollar withdrawals would differ depending on the changing value of your principal. But if your withdrawal percentage is below the average total return the mutual fund generates, your dollar redemptions would gradually trend upward as your account grows. Naturally, there would be declines following years in which your fund had negative total returns. The fixed-percentage plan could be useful if you want to preserve your capital and perhaps even see it grow, but your withdrawals may not keep pace with inflation.

Fixed-Share Redemptions

Redeeming a constant number of fund shares can be advantageous for some people. Your dollar withdrawals will fluctuate with changes in the fund's share price, but fewer shares will be sold over the years to generate a given sum of withdrawals. Conversely, with a fixed-dollar withdrawal plan you sell more shares when prices are low and fewer when they are high.

The table below illustrates a fixed-share program where 2,000 shares are redeemed annually. The dollar amount withdrawn equals the net asset value multiplied by 2,000. In total, 6,000 shares are withdrawn over three years. Conversely, 6,167 shares would need to be redeemed to accommodate a $20,000 fixed yearly withdrawal. In both cases, $60,000 is redeemed over three years.

The more volatile the fund's price, the fewer shares you would have to redeem to withdraw a given sum of money. But more volatility results in greater variations in monthly withdrawals.

In any case, if you can tolerate the fluctuations you might want to consider the fixed-share withdrawal plan.

Since a number of mutual funds do not formally offer a fixed-share withdrawal option, you could simply phone in periodically and re-

Fixed-Share Withdrawal vs. Fixed-Dollar Withdrawal

Fixed-Share Plan

Year	Price ($)	Shares (No.)	Redemption ($)
1	10	2,000	20,000
2	8	2,000	16,000
3	12	2,000	24,000
Total		6,000	60,000

Fixed-Dollar Plan

Year	Price ($)	Shares (No.)	Redemption ($)
1	10	2,000	20,000
2	8	2,500	20,000
3	12	1,667	20,000
Total		6,167	60,000

quest that the shares be sold and the money transferred to your money fund or sent to you by check.

Liquidation Over a Fixed Period

You could withdraw an increasing percentage of your account balance each year in order to liquidate it within a fixed period. For example, if you want the principal paid out over a four-year period to a child attending college, you could withdraw one-fourth of the account in the first year, one-third in the second, half in the third and the remainder in the fourth.

You may be required to use this approach when making withdrawals from an IRA or other tax-qualified retirement plan. Specifically, after age 70½ you must make your withdrawals over a maximum number of years based on an IRS life expectancy table or face a penalty tax for withdrawing less than your minimum required distribution.

Important Considerations

While withdrawal plans are a useful service, they can lead to certain problems. Here are some to ponder.

- Recordkeeping for tax purposes can be a headache, especially with more frequent redemptions. Each time you make a withdrawal you're selling shares, which results in a taxable event. You need to adopt a systematic procedure for calculating gains and losses on each withdrawal.
- Volatile stock and sector stock funds are generally poor candidates for withdrawal plans. These funds can plunge as fast as they can surge. Withdrawing money when the value of your account has taken a steep decline can lead to problems if it doesn't rebound quickly.
- It's best to be conservative. Too high a withdrawal rate can deplete your capital too soon. Be sure to compare your withdrawal rate with the rate at which you expect your fund to compound, after inflation. If the former exceeds the latter by too many percentage points, your capital might not last as long as you'd like. The numbers in the table on page 34 are useful in this regard.
- Make sure you consider the impact of taxes on your investment earnings and withdrawals. Of course, the effect of taxes varies depending upon your circumstances, and tax rates are subject to change, but the tax factor is too important to overlook.

- It's a good idea to reevaluate your situation every year or so. Do some revised number crunching to see if you need to make any adjustments in your withdrawals.

What Every Investor Should Know About Mutual Funds

In mutual fund investing there are no immutable laws to guide us, as we have in physics. But the collective experience of fund investors can be distilled into a few general rules. Some of it has empirical evidence pointing its way. Most is simply common sense that investors often set aside or forget in the heat of making an investment decision.

TOP PERFORMANCE LISTS ARE DANGEROUS

Probably the single most potentially dangerous action a mutual fund investor can take is to glance at these ubiquitous lists. Funds make the top of the lists not because they are like all the rest of the funds, but because they are decidedly different in some important way. Risk is usually the first important difference. For stock funds, holding stocks that are more volatile than the average stock, holding fewer stocks, or concentrating on only a few industries, raises risk and puts a fund in position to have a greater chance at making the top of the list.

As an example, take sector funds. You can't beat the market by holding it, which is why you can always find a sector fund of one kind or another at the top of most performance lists. Call it stock picking, or industry weighting, or both, but the net effect is increased risk, and less diversification than the overall stock market.

Picking the funds at the top of the performance lists assumes that either these same stocks or sectors will continue to do well, or that the managers can continue to deftly take high risk and move money around better than all the rest.

For domestic bond funds, making the top of the list is a result of the maturity structure of the fund's portfolio. The longest maturity bond funds will be at the top of the performance lists when interest rates are falling, and at the bottom of the lists when interest rates rise. So, investing in bond funds that are at the top of the list is a forecast of interest rates—that they will stay constant or continue in the same direction, a prediction that even professional interest rate prognosticators have been woefully unsuccessful in getting right.

However, these top/bottom lists may hold a small glimmer of value. There is some empirical evidence that stock funds at the top of the heap one period have a greater likelihood to have this superior performance in the next period, on average—"hot hands" may stay hot. Why might a fund's superior performance persist? Probably because the stocks/sectors emphasized in the portfolio continue to have positive momentum into the next period. The shorter the time periods observed, the more likely this is to be true: quarter-to-quarter performance persistence is more likely than year-to-year. But be careful, this is based on performances of top funds on average, and investors don't invest in fund averages, but instead invest in individual funds.

What is more telling, however, is that bad funds tend to continue to be bad. But again, be careful. If an entire category of funds—small stock value funds or emerging market funds, for example—do poorly, then making the bottom list is probably meaningless if your fund has a lot of peer companions. But if large stock growth funds populate the top list or simply are not to be found in numbers on the bottom list, and your large stock growth fund makes an appearance at the bottom of the pile, it isn't a good sign.

And, of course, being a knee-jerk contrarian and buying funds that make the bottom list on the theory that what falls must rise, is probably a seriously flawed approach to fund selection.

SIZE MATTERS

The amount of money invested in a fund does matter, but whether larger is better than smaller depends on the investment objective of the fund. With a large stock index fund, a U.S. government bond fund or a money market fund, the more dollars under management the better. This is because they all operate in very liquid segments of the market where large block transactions are less likely to impact prices—pushing prices up when purchasing and down when selling—and large-scale transactions might prove to be cheaper to accomplish. In addition, large amounts to manage in these funds will not interfere with their investment objective. And, since some fund expenses are fixed, spreading these expenses over more investment dollars should reduce expenses as a percentage of fund assets.

On the other hand, funds with investment objectives that cover less liquid market segments—small stocks or emerging markets—can be too large. That means that individual trades will tend to be larger, which may in turn lead to higher transaction costs tied to security pricing, a wide bid-asked spread on the stocks, and making portfolio changes harder to accomplish. The classic response of funds that focus on small stocks is to migrate investments to mid-cap and large stocks when they start to achieve a large asset base.

Actively managed stock funds, when managers are picking stocks and industries and moving money around, can be flooded with new money and find themselves unable to deploy new money expeditiously or effectively. And a flood of new money usually comes after a performance that garners widespread attention and is often difficult to replicate, particularly with the surge of new investment in the fund. An index fund, passively managed and operating in a liquid segment of the market, would not be stumped by a large, sudden inflow of cash.

How large is large? When it comes to net assets, $100 billion may be just fine for an S&P 500 index fund, but $1 billion may choke an actively managed small stock fund. And beware of funds that had extraordinary performance when they had $100 million or less, a relatively small amount in net assets. In order to invest larger amounts they may have to invest money in more stocks and industries, increasing diversification and decreasing risk, dulling performance.

FUND EXPENSES CAN BE COSTLY

Fund expenses count. And they count more for some investment categories than others. The general rule is that if you invest in a fund that has a significantly higher expense ratio than the average for its category, the long-term performance drag will be costly. Few active fund managers cover the cost of the increased expenses of active management compared to the rock-bottom cost of passively managing an index fund. And if a fund manager is saddled with a relatively high expense ratio due to a small net asset base or high management/research costs, or both, the task of providing above-average category performance is all the more difficult. Some managers, when faced with this dilemma, may boost the risk level of the fund to remain competitive.

Stock funds are more expensive to manage than bond funds, international funds are more expensive than domestic funds, and funds with large asset bases are cheaper than small funds. But if the expense ratio of a bond fund is approaching 1.00%, or a stock fund 1.50%, think twice before investing. And don't forget stock index funds often charge 0.25% or less.

LOADS ARE LOADS

Whether the sales charge, or load, is up front when you buy into the fund, at the end when you sell the fund, or is an as-you-go 12b-1 charge included in the expense ratio, it will cost you. As explained in Chapter 2, loads go to sales organizations and sales personnel; they are not used to secure better portfolio managers, better research or better anything. A load reduces your return dollar for dollar. So if you are not getting financial advice worth the load, buying a loaded fund will cost you, perhaps dearly. Load funds do not outperform on average similar objective funds with no loads, and in fact, they tend to underperform by the amount of the load. How could they, given what loads are used for? Want to invest with a hot manager in a fund that is loaded? Given the iffiness of historical performance as a predictor of future performance, find a no-load fund with a similar style, performance and risk, and save the load charge.

Don't forget that almost all fund performance data is reported without adjusting for front-end or back-end loads. However, performance data does adjust for the 12b-1 charge because it is included in the expense ratio, and fund performance net of the expense ratio is accounted for in performance statistics.

MARKET TIMING DOESN'T WORK

Wouldn't it be wonderful if either you or your fund manager could time the market? You'd make a mint, but it's only a dream. Nobody, but nobody, has consistently guessed the direction of the bond or stock market over any meaningful length of time, although many will make the claim. And remember that to be successful, timing requires two calls: When to get out, and when to get back in.

One reason beyond low expense ratios that index funds are tough to beat is that they are always 100% invested in the market—they have no cash holdings—when the market takes off. Index funds always call bull markets correctly and they never miss a rally. Yet, they always fail to call a bear market or correction. However, being right on every bull market, as well as avoiding transaction costs and minimizing taxable distributions, is tough to beat.

Since returns on stock and bond funds have been distinctly positive on average annually since we have started keeping records, being ready for bull markets is more important than avoiding bear markets.

When investing in actively managed stock funds, you should hope for superior stock and industry selection, not market timing. If your actively managed portfolio is building up a large cash balance, in excess of 10% of the portfolio, your manager is either engaging in some subtle market timing or there has been a recent rush of cash into the fund. Either case may ultimately lead to poorer performance. For bond funds, when maturities are significantly shortened or lengthened, the impetus is usually market timing driven by an interest rate forecast.

GIVE NEW MANAGERS AND FUNDS TIME TO PROVE THEMSELVES BEFORE INVESTING WITH THEM

With the thousands of funds and fund managers in the investing universe that have track records of at least three years, why invest in an untried fund or manager? While finding funds that will be top performers in their category before the fact is daunting, avoiding disastrous fund investments is within reach. But it requires something upon which to base a judgment. At least a three-year performance history that can be compared to the performance of funds with similar investment objectives and assumed risk is indispensable to evaluate a fund manager or a fund. Consistently favorable performance relative to a peer group of funds over different market environments provides no guarantee of future performance, but it is infinitely better than nothing. You would be surprised how many new funds are quietly buried and new fund managers transferred after the first few disappointing years.

8 *Practical Answers to Some Common Mutual Fund Questions*

While you can easily call a mutual fund company with specific questions concerning the mechanics of your account and receive a prompt direct answer, the telephone representatives are unlikely to offer an answer to a general investment question, such as: "How many different funds should I own?"

This chapter provides practical answers to commonly asked mutual fund questions. While a series of often-asked questions and answers cannot substitute for a careful and thorough study of mutual funds, the more you know about how mutual funds operate and what contributes to performance, the better prepared you will be to make decisions when investing.

PORTFOLIO MANAGEMENT

How many different mutual funds should I own?

The number of funds suitable for an individual investor will vary depending on individual circumstances—there is no universal number that applies for everyone.

However, as a useful yardstick, consider the range of funds derived from the rationale that diversification should be one of every investor's goals. Simple but broad diversification would imply these funds: a domestic stock fund, a domestic bond fund, and an international stock fund. Dividing the domestic stock portion into these funds—one specializing in small stocks, one in mid-cap stocks, and the other in large-cap stocks—brings the count up to five. Splitting the international stock portion into funds specializing in developed economies and funds specializing in developing and emerging economies makes six. If you prefer a separate European fund and Far East fund, the total is up to seven. Building diversity in your domestic bonds by adding a junk bond fund stretches the number of funds to eight. For tax purposes, the addition of a tax-exempt bond fund would make nine funds. And if we include a money market fund, the number is 10.

The benefits of diversification are difficult to achieve with commitments of less than 10% of your portfolio to any one area, which sets the upper range at not much more than 10 funds. Thus, diversification implies a range of around four to nine funds—all unique in investment objective and security coverage.

Overdiversification results in fund investments that essentially duplicate each other; this adds nothing to performance, but it will add frustration as well as cost in keeping track of and monitoring so many funds.

Should I make sure to invest in more than one fund family, for diversification?

No—it is possible to stay within a fund family and be adequately diversified. However, there is a danger in remaining doggedly within one fund family solely for convenience—you could overlook a better-managed fund elsewhere. For instance, rather than seek out the best international fund, you may choose the one offered by the fund family you are in currently because it is most convenient.

What should I do when my fund closes?

Nothing. Many funds that close their doors to new investors will allow existing shareholders to continue to invest new money, although sometimes with limits, and most closed funds allow continuation of investments for existing IRA-type accounts.

In the long run, you may be better off if your fund closes and maintains its investment style and flexibility rather than outgrowing its past success.

Should I switch out of a fund if the portfolio manager changes?

No. The change of a portfolio manager is not reason, in and of itself, to leave a fund. Instead, monitor the fund closely to make sure the new manager is continuing the old manager's style, and that any changes won't significantly affect your investment. New portfolio managers have been known to take command of a fund and sell off securities, reflecting a change in style. A significant portfolio realignment might mean greater capital gains distributions, and therefore taxes, unless you hold the fund in a tax-sheltered account. On the other hand, if the fund is an index fund or less actively managed, the portfolio manager may not be all that important. Or the new portfolio manager may continue with the old style and perform just fine.

Switch to a fund with a similar investment objective only when the performance of your fund falls off against other funds with the same investment objective, or if your existing fund changes objectives so that it no longer reflects the objective you are seeking.

If a fund closes before I have a chance to invest and a clone is available, should I invest in the clone fund?

Most funds close because the portfolio manager feels a larger fund size will hamper his investment flexibility and style. Therefore, it is unlikely that any "clone" fund will in fact be a perfect clone of the original—what would be the point of closing the first one?

Clone funds—the Roman numeral II funds—often do not have the same portfolio manager or precisely the same investment strategy as the original. Any fund should be judged independently on its own financial merits.

PORTFOLIO EXPENSES AND CHARGES

If a fund offers class A, B, C, etc., shares, which one should I buy?

Many funds that have sales charges are offering investors a choice as to how the load will be paid. The different share classes reflect these various options, and generally the choices run somewhat like this: Class A shares have a front-end load, a sales commission on the money invested that is charged when the money is first invested; Class B shares have a back-end load, a sales charge levied on the value of the fund shares when they are sold, which sometimes decreases and eventually disappears; Class C shares might not have a front-end or back-end load, but instead contain an annual charge against your fund's value, a 12b-1 load. Other combinations of varying levels of these three loads may also be offered as an investment option.

If you intend to be invested in the fund for a long time, opt for the front-end or back-end load option, and avoid a high (greater than 0.25%) 12b-1 charge. If you intend to be in the fund only for a few years, select the fund class that does not charge a front-end or back-end load.

Of course, the best course of action is to avoid all loads, or at least high loads.

My fund just imposed a load. Should I bail out?

If your fund imposed a load, you may be grandfathered in and allowed to invest new funds without a load. But if they do charge a load on additional money you want to invest, you are faced with a dilemma. Don't sell on the news that the fund is going to impose a load, but certainly don't commit new money if you will be charged an unreasonable load.

Should I be concerned with fund expenses? After all, it's already reflected in the fund's performance numbers.

Fund expenses, including the management fee, reduce fund performance and all quoted return numbers reflect these costs. But the reason to examine past performance is to get an indication of the portfolio manager's skill. And while the performance numbers may provide some indication of the manager's past skill, the future performance of that manager remains uncertain. The only certainty about the fund's future is its expenses, which are assessed regardless of whether a fund's performance has been relatively good or bad.

Exceptionally high expenses are nearly impossible for portfolio managers to overcome relative to similar funds with average or low expenses. The lower the expenses, the better. Funds with low total assets under management, particularly if they are not part of a large family of funds, will have high expenses relative to assets under management. In addition, newly established funds have a high expense hurdle to overcome.

Should I pay any attention to mutual fund portfolio turnover rates?

The portfolio turnover rate (given in the prospectus) is the lower of purchases or sales of assets in the fund relative to the average assets in the fund for the year. A turnover ratio of 100% indicates that the dollar value of fund purchases or sales equaled the dollar value of total fund assets during the year. This doesn't mean that every single share was changed once during the year; perhaps only a small portion of the assets was transacted intensely. A portfolio turnover ratio of 200% indicates the portfolio, by value, was turned over twice during the year, and so on.

Is this important? Yes. The higher the portfolio turnover, the greater the transaction costs, which can hurt the performance of the fund; while these costs are reflected in the fund's net asset value and its performance figures, they are a concern for the future performance as noted in the question above.

Equally important for taxable investors, the higher the turnover, the more likely the fund is to make capital gains distributions; and taxes must be paid on these distributions.

What is high turnover and what is low? Stock funds average around 80% portfolio turnover, and bond funds are close to 100%.

Use portfolio turnover as a tie-breaker. If you find two funds in the same category that are equally appealing, lean toward the fund with a lower portfolio turnover.

Should I deal only with the fund family or go through some of the discount brokers that offer mutual funds?

Discount brokers such as Charles Schwab and Fidelity Brokerage offer the convenience of buying different funds without going directly to each fund family and opening separate accounts. Only one brokerage account is necessary, and all mutual fund positions are consolidated in one report. Some of these transactions incur brokerage costs; others are essentially costless.

Not all funds or fund families participate, but if convenience is important and your mutual fund transaction sizes are reasonably large, these fund services offered by discount brokers may deserve a look.

Tie-Breakers: Key Points to Consider When It's a Close Call Between Funds

9

Even when you've done your research and narrowed down your choices for a particular type of fund, sometimes it's not a clear choice between the final two funds.

Flipping a coin is one approach. But a better strategy would be to zero in on a few key points that serve as tie-breakers. While no two funds are precisely alike, top-performing funds can share almost identical investment style and return profiles. This chapter reveals fund tie-breakers to consider and when they might be most important.

AFTERTAX RETURNS

Making tax avoidance your investment focus is a formula for investment disaster. But keeping your eye on aftertax returns is simply wise investing. For example, two funds have similar compound average annual five-year pretax returns. A five-year period is probably long enough to get a picture of how the funds have performed in different market environments, but still recent enough to be relevant.

However, one fund wins on a tax-adjusted return basis for the period, producing a higher aftertax return. Why? The fund might have a lower yield, defined as income divided by net asset value, or simply made less or no distributions of capital gains. Interest earned by the fund from non-tax-exempt sources is taxable at ordinary income tax rates. Municipal bond interest is usually not taxable at the federal level and may not be taxable at the state or local level, if the fund is a state-specific municipal bond fund. Qualified dividend income from stocks held by the fund is subject to the lower long-term capital gains rate. With long-term capital gains rates (on securities sold by the fund but held by the fund for longer than one year) significantly lower than short-term capital gains tax rates, the tax penalty on short-term capital gains is serious. And no capital gains distributions means no taxes, even at the lower capital gains rate. The tax-adjusted return assumes maximum tax rates, where the disparities between capital gains tax rates and income tax rates are the greatest. For investors in lower tax brackets, the tax-adjusted rate difference might not be great.

RISK

Risk is easy to ignore when funds are on the way up, but when markets fall, risk is suddenly right in your face. There are two useful quantitative measures of risk, both calculated based upon monthly fund returns for the last three years. Beta is a measure of a fund's return sensitivity to the returns of the overall stock market, and works well as a risk measure for diversified funds. The higher the beta, the higher the volatility, and therefore risk. Beta can range from very large negative numbers to very large positive numbers, theoretically, but most stock mutual fund betas cluster in the range of 0.5 to 1.5. A zero beta would imply no sensitivity to the stock market, and would more likely belong to a money market fund than a stock fund. A negative beta indicates that, on average, the fund and the market move in opposite directions—also an unlikely figure for any stock fund. The stock market's beta is by definition always 1.0; a fund with a beta of 1.5 is expected to be 50% more volatile than the market, and a fund with a beta of 0.5 would be only half as volatile. For instance, if the market rose 20%, a fund with a beta of 1.5 would be expected to be up 30% [20% + 0.50 (20%)] and if the market fell by 20%, the fund might drop 30%. When two stock funds with similar returns are considered, give a nod to the one with the lower beta.

A second measure of risk is standard deviation, a barometer of volatility from any source, rather than just the stock market. Numerically, standard deviation is less intuitive than beta, but the higher the standard deviation, the greater the risk. Beta assumes a diversified portfolio so that other factors—such as the risk unique to individual stocks and industries—is virtually eliminated, leaving only the risk of market moves. Standard deviation works for all portfolios, diversified or not, and captures the risk from all elements.

If the two funds have similar returns, but are not well diversified, you cannot count on beta. Pick the fund with the lower standard deviation. [For more on fund risk, see Chapter 5: Understanding Risk.]

FUND SIZE

What about total assets under management by the fund? Is bigger better or is smaller better? The answer, of course, is: It depends. A U.S. government bond fund or an index fund probably can't be 'too big,' since, in general, average costs decline and size doesn't get in the way of managing the assets. On the other hand, an aggressively managed fund, particularly one concentrating in mid-cap and small-cap stocks, can lose flexibility and be less nimble when assets grow too large. A fund that is growing too fast can also pose difficulties for the manager, who may have trouble simply getting the new money invested effectively and in a timely manner. Size and rapid growth often force funds to change their investment strategies. For actively managed mid- and small-cap stock funds, give the nod to the smaller asset size fund.

EXPENSE RATIOS

Expense ratios (fund expenses per share divided by net asset value per share) are often overlooked because expenses are netted out against income, and reported returns already include the impact of expenses. So, if the return is competitive, who cares about expenses? Well, two points are important. First, expense ratios are relatively unchangeable—they are easy to forecast, whereas returns are not. Second, the higher the expense of a fund, the greater the drag that a portfolio manager must overcome in the long run in order to be consistently better than other funds in the category. Also, high expense ratios are relatively easier to overcome in fund categories that produce higher returns on average, such as stock funds, than in fixed-income fund categories where expenses have a greater effect on returns. Two municipal bond funds share the same investment objectives and almost identical performance figures, but one is hard to beat on expenses. No contest. [For more on expense ratios, see Chapter 4: Understanding Mutual Fund Statements.]

PORTFOLIO MANAGER TENURE

What better way to judge a fund manager than by the performance of the fund? But the current fund portfolio manager may not have been running the fund when the performance numbers were inked. In an uncertain world, a manager's tenure and performance record provide useful information, at least valuable enough to break a tie.

LOADS

Sales commissions, also known as loads, are probably the clearest tie-breakers. Take the case of two international European stock funds. Both have comparable performance records and even similar risk, expense ratios, size, and manager profiles. They have identical investment objectives, focusing on European stocks, and they are offered by large fund families with a long menu of services. One charges a 3.0% front-end load and a 1.0% redemption fee for all money removed in less than 90 days. Neither front- and back-end loads nor redemption fees are reflected in performance figures. And while returns going forward are always uncertain, the load is charged with perfect certainty and reduces your performance dollar-for-dollar without any beneficial effect on fund performance. Choose the no-load fund. [For more on loads, see Chapter 2: Investing in Mutual Funds.]

10

The Sell Decision: Knowing When to Walk Away

Many people hop in and out of investments all too frequently. That's due in part to the fact that mutual fund advice and information are so freely available that individuals often are persuaded to switch from their more prosaic funds to those that have been delivering more exciting short-term returns. At the opposite extreme, others take the attitude that, once bought, mutual funds can practically be held for a lifetime. That can be true in some instances, but it's often not—you really must rethink your portfolio periodically.

This chapter analyzes legitimate reasons for selling funds, as well as several reasons for staying put.

LOUSY PERFORMANCE

Continuing poor performance of a fund relative to a relevant benchmark and its peers is the number one fund-related reason for selling a mutual fund. You should focus on a fund's returns over the past one, three, and five years. Longer periods can be misleading if there have been major changes in the fund or its management.

While quarterly returns can be monitored to alert you to signs of deteriorating performance, one-year returns are the shortest relevant performance span for long-term investors to examine. However, that doesn't mean you should automatically sell if one-year returns turn up poor. Deciding how much time to give a poor performer to rebound is not easy, but you should seriously start to think about selling a fund that has lagged its benchmark and peers for the past 18 months to two years.

How do you decide on a relevant benchmark? Different benchmarks are available for different market segments and investment styles. In this *Guide*, peer and index benchmarks are provided for each investment category and investment style.

A simple way to determine which benchmark to use is to check your fund's prospectus or annual report to find out what the fund compares its performance against. Another possibility is to compare your fund's performance with an index fund that has roughly the same portfolio composition. However, you're never going to find a perfect benchmark because each fund has its own unique portfolio.

Keep the following points in mind when comparing a fund's performance with its benchmark:

- Mutual funds hold some cash, which will affect their returns relative to a fully invested index.
- Mutual funds incur expenses and trading costs, which will result in some underperformance relative to an index.
- Each fund holds its own blend of stocks and sectors, which will cause its returns to deviate from an index or benchmark.
- A mutual fund may be more or less risky than its benchmark.

A fund that trails its benchmark may be considerably less risky than another in its category that beats the yardstick. For that reason, it's often more revealing to see how a fund performed relative to its peers. You can compare a fund with several of its most similar competitors or against an average for the category.

It's always important to prune out any genuine duds. Some people tenaciously hang onto unproductive investments because they hate to admit that they made a mistake, or they may hate to deal with the tax consequences, or they are loath to expend the effort to fill out the paperwork and move to a new fund or fund family. The problem is that these individuals face a high opportunity cost by clinging to losing or mediocre funds.

OTHER REASONS TO SELL

Don't sell solely because your fund's performance has been disappointing during the past year. Rather, view a single year of underperformance as a signal to take a closer look at the fund and how it fits with your objectives. You should examine the following factors that may impact a fund's performance or its suitability for your portfolio.

- *A management change:* Management's ability is crucial for stock funds. But a management change by itself is not always a reason to sell. Perhaps the manager who left was not exceptiona!. A good replacement for a skilled manager may be waiting in the wings at a large fund company. Conversely, if a star manager leaves a fund, an equal replacement may be hard to find. So take the exit of a star manager as a warning flag, but not an automatic sell. Finally, think seriously about selling if a fund has had more than its share of management turnover, because frequent changes are not healthy and constant shifting of a portfolio creates negative tax and transaction cost consequences.

- *Rising expenses:* Significantly higher expenses can hurt performance. Perhaps a 12b-1 fee has been added or management fees have increased. A money market fund may have lifted a fee waiver, causing its yield to drop significantly relative to other similar money market funds. An increase in costs is particularly hard on bond and money market funds because they earn lower gross returns than stock funds.

- *A surge in assets:* Performance could falter if a small-stock or micro-cap fund is flooded with investor money. And the fund could experience style drift if it is forced to start investing in bigger companies. Conversely, a surge in assets may be no problem for many other types of funds, particularly for high-grade bond and money market funds or index funds that could benefit from economies of scale.

- *Shrinking assets:* Watch out if a fund is rapidly losing assets because investors are jumping ship for some reason. Sizable redemptions can force management to dump good stocks to raise cash. If gains are realized, the fund could make an unusually high capital gains distribution, saddling those who hold shares in taxable accounts with a potentially large tax bill.

- *A strategy change:* Funds change strategies in various ways. A new portfolio manager might decide to fully hedge currency risk for a foreign stock fund that previously did not hedge. An active trader might take the helm of a fund that was noted for low turnover. Or a small-cap value fund might become a mid-cap growth fund. A strategy change will not necessarily hurt a fund's performance, but it might not help a laggard either. If the new strategy does not mesh with your objectives, it may be time to move on.

Even if your funds have compared favorably to their benchmarks and peers, there can be other, compelling reasons to sell. Conversely, you may not want to walk away from a laggard just yet. That's because personal factors often dominate in the decision-making process.

TAX CONSIDERATIONS

If selling seems warranted by the performance numbers and other factors, you also need to weigh any potential tax liability you would incur by taking a large gain. On the plus side, the tax consequences may be less painful with long-term capital gains taxed at lower rates. In addition, the long-term capital gains holding period is 12 months. Nevertheless, if you would be in for a hefty tax bill it may make sense to give a lazy performer more time. This obviously is not a concern if your fund is held in an individual retirement account or other tax-advantaged plan.

On the other hand, tax considerations may argue for a sale. Do you have a paper loss in a taxable account? Perhaps you hold a fund that has done poorly because it invests in a stock-market sector, country, or region that has experienced major problems. You might expect an eventual rebound, but in the meantime you could lock in your loss to offset other gains, thereby reducing your tax bill, and then reinvest in a peer fund that has better performance.

DUMPING EXCESS BAGGAGE

Individuals who own too many funds might consider paring their holdings down to a manageable number, perhaps to as few as five or six. Money-losing investments should be pruned along with unsuitable ones. Check for redundancy in your fund portfolio: Funds with different names may in fact share the same objectives and investing style. Your performance likely will improve, and your financial life will be a lot simpler. Plus, it will be much easier to track your asset allocation.

People often make purchases that they regret later. These could include a narrowly focused fund that makes you uncomfortable due to its risk, or any gimmicky fund that really doesn't add to your portfolio.

A broad-based asset allocation fund is unnecessary if you've allocated your assets properly in the first place.

Suppose you hold a fund invested in an asset class that has done poorly even though the manager has fared better than the benchmark. In this case, you need to decide whether you still want that asset class. This is often a difficult call. It depends on factors such as your age, time horizon, and investment outlook.

Generally, mutual funds are viewed as safe because you won't lose as much as you could with an individual stock. But narrowly focused funds such as sector funds can be dicey. If you have allocated too much to a focused fund that's on the skids, think about reducing or eliminating that position before the loss becomes unmanageable. If a volatile fund plunges 50%, it must rebound 100% just to recoup its loss. Consider selling when a speculative fund has fallen 15% to 20% below your cost. Even if you have a relatively minor position, you still may want to walk away.

ALLOCATION CHANGES

Other reasons to sell may arise in your periodic asset allocation review, which should be done at least annually. This entails checking your allocations to large-cap stocks, small-cap stocks, foreign equities, bonds, money market funds, and any subcategories. Recognize that your stock funds could plunge anywhere from 20% to more than 40% within a few months during a bear market. You might want to check and see how your funds and similar ones did during down periods to get a feel for what could happen during a bear market. If you feel uncomfortable with a decline of that magnitude you should rethink your asset allocation.

However, if selling would result in large capital gains, you may wish to consider the following alternatives:

- Sell stock funds held in tax-deferred retirement plans to restore your risk balance.
- Make a more gradual change in your asset allocation by investing any new money in the underweighted categories or reinvesting distributions from your overweighted funds into your underweighted holdings. This second alternative is particularly desirable if you feel there is a good chance your overweighted funds will continue to advance and you wish to make a more modest reallocation for the time being.

STAYING THE COURSE

It's generally unwise to make a big shift from stocks to cash because you fear a bear market. Trimming your stock allocation back a moderate amount—say, from 80% to 65% of your assets—can make sense if you are uncomfortable with the risk level of your fund portfolio, but drastically reducing it because you fear a plunge is basically market timing. The stock market will fluctuate, but you can't pinpoint when it will tumble or shoot up. If you have allocated your assets properly and have sufficient emergency money, you shouldn't need to worry.

Finally, don't panic and sell just after a big plunge. You could lock in a loss and miss any rebound. Panic-selling rarely makes sense because investors tend to overreact to recent bad news, hammering prices to unrealistic lows. But even if a bear market is long and painful, it's important to remember that stocks have a bullish bias and gain a lot more in the bullish phases than they lose on the downside—that's why the long-term trend of the market is up.

Of course, this assumes you have sufficient liquid assets in money market and short-term bond funds to meet emergencies and planned big-ticket expenditures over the next several years. The following is a good rule to keep in mind: Don't have money invested in stock funds that you will need within the next five years. By following the five-year rule, you greatly reduce the risk of having to sell shares after a market tumble.

Which Funds Were Included

The funds that appear in *The Individual Investor's Guide to the Top Mutual Funds* were selected from the universe of funds. Following are the various screens we used to arrive at the final selection.

HISTORICAL RECORD

Only those funds with three full years of data that are open to new investors (not closed) are included in the *Guide* so that there is a performance record of significant length and all performance measures can be calculated.

SIZE

Funds must appear in the NASDAQ mutual fund listings and are required to have at least $50 million in assets to qualify for inclusion in the *Guide*.

LOADS

The decision as to what constitutes a significant load is difficult, but we took this approach in the *Guide*:

Funds with front-end loads, back-end loads, or redemption fees of 3% or less are included if the fund does not also have a 12b-1 charge. Funds with redemption fees that disappear after six months that also have 12b-1 charges appear in this *Guide*.

Funds with 12b-1 plans and no front- or back-end loads are included in the *Guide*; we note, however, if the fund has a 12b-1 plan and what the annual charge is. A 12b-1 fund fee greater than 0.25% is considered to be high. Investors should carefully assess these plans individually.

Funds that impose a load that exceeds 3% or increase an existing load above 3% are dropped from the *Guide*.

EXPENSES

Funds with significantly higher expense ratios than the average for their category are not included in this *Guide*.

PERFORMANCE

Funds that significantly underperformed the average performance of their category are not included in this *Guide*.

INTEREST AND AVAILABILITY

Only those funds of general interest to mutual fund investors and only those funds that are open (not closed to new investors) and available for investment by individual investors directly from the fund, without restrictions, are included in this *Guide*.

FUNDS NOT INCLUDED

AAII members who would like performance figures for no-load and low-load mutual funds that do not appear in this *Guide* can access this information on our Web site at www.aaii.com. Click on Top Mutual Funds Guide found under Publications in the left-hand menu for a complete downloadable file (covers 1,255 funds).

A Key to Terms and Statistics

Most of the information used in the mutual fund data pages and performance tables is provided by Standard & Poor's Micropal, but some may come from mutual fund reports (the prospectus and annual and quarterly reports) and solicitation of information directly from the fund. Any data source has the potential for error, however, and before investing in any mutual fund, the prospectus for the fund should be read and the annual report examined.

When *na* appears in the performance tables or on the mutual fund page, it indicates that the number was not available or does not apply in that particular instance. For example, the 10-year annual return figure would not be available for funds that have been operating for less than 10 years. We do not compile the bull and bear ratings for funds not operating during the entire bull or bear market period. Dashes (—) are used generally during years when the fund was not in operation or did not have a complete calendar year of operations. All numbers are truncated rather than rounded when necessary, unless noted otherwise in the following descriptions.

The following provides an explanation of the terms we have used in the performance tables and mutual fund data pages. The explanations are listed in the order in which the data and information appear on the mutual fund pages.

Fund Name: The funds are presented alphabetically by fund name within each category.

Ticker: The ticker symbol for each fund is given in parentheses for those investors who may want to access data with their computer or touch-tone phone. The ticker is four letters and is usually followed by an "X," indicating that it is a mutual fund. For example, the Brandywine Blue fund ticker symbol is BLUEX.

Investment Category: The fund's investment category is indicated at the top of the page below the fund's ticker symbol. After evaluating the information and statistics, we classified all mutual funds in exclusive categories by investment type. [For more complete definitions of the mutual fund investment categories used in the *Guide*, see Chapter 3: Mutual Fund Categories.]

Fund Telephone Number and Internet Address: The management company telephone number and Internet address (if applicable) that investors can call or access to have specific questions answered or to obtain a copy of the prospectus.

Fund Inception Date: The day the fund was made available to the public for purchase.

Performance
Return (%): Return percentages for the periods below.

3yr Annual: Assuming an investment on January 1, 2003, the annual total return if held through December 31, 2005.

5yr Annual: Assuming an investment on January 1, 2001, the annual total return if held through December 31, 2005.

10yr Annual: Assuming an investment on January 1, 1996, the annual total return if held through December 31, 2005.

Bull: This return reflects the fund's performance in the most recent bull market, starting March 1, 2003, and continuing through December 31, 2005.

Bear: This return reflects the fund's performance in the most recent bear market, from April 1, 2000, through February 28, 2003.

Differ From Category (+/−): The difference between the return for the fund and the average return for all funds in the same category for the *3yr Annual, 5yr Annual, 10yr Annual, Bull,* and *Bear* periods. When the difference from category is negative, the fund underperformed the average fund in its investment category for the period by the percent indicated. The rankings, with possibilities of high, above average, average, below average, and low, are relative to all other funds within the same investment category. A rank of high, for example, would indicate that the return is in the highest 20% for that time period of all funds in the investment category. (Note: State-specific muni fund averages are only calculated against other muni funds from the same state.)

Standard Deviation: A measure of total risk, expressed as an annual return, that indicates the degree of variation in return experienced relative to the average return for a fund as measured over the last three years. The higher the standard deviation, the greater the total risk of the fund. Standard deviation of any fund can be compared to any other fund. Possibilities are high, above average, average, below average, and low.

Category Risk Index: A numerical measure of relative category risk, the risk index is a ratio of the total risk of the fund to the average total risk of funds in the category as measured over the last three years. Ratios above 1.0 indicate higher than average risk and ratios below 1.0 indicate lower than average risk for the category. The possibilities are high, above average, average, below average, and low.

Beta: A risk measure that relates the fund's volatility of returns to the market. The higher the beta of a fund, the higher the market risk of the fund. The figure is based on monthly returns for 36 months. A beta of 1.0 indicates that the fund's returns will, on average, be as volatile as the market and move in the same direction; a beta higher than 1.0 indicates that if the market rises or falls, the fund will rise or fall respectively but to a greater degree; a beta of less than 1.0 indicates that if the market rises or falls, the fund will rise or fall to a lesser degree. The S&P 500 index always has a beta of 1.0 because it is the measure we selected to represent the overall stock market. Beta is a meaningful figure of risk only for well-diversified common stock portfolios. For sector funds and other concentrated portfolios, beta is less useful than total risk as a measure of risk. Beta is not calculated for bond funds since they do not react in the same way to the factors that affect the stock market. For bond funds, the average maturity of the bond portfolio is more indicative of market risk, so it is used in place of beta.

Avg Mat: For bond funds, average maturity in years is an indication of market risk. When interest rates rise, bond prices fall, and when interest rates fall, bond prices rise. The longer the average maturity of the bonds held in the portfolio, the greater the fund's sensitivity to interest rate changes will be, and thus, the greater the risk. The refinancing of mortgages and the calling of outstanding bonds can affect average maturity when interest rates decline. An *na* indicates that the mutual fund did not provide an average maturity figure.

Return (%): This is a total return figure, expressed as a percentage. All distributions were assumed to have been reinvested. Rate of return is calculated on the basis of the calendar year. Return figures do not take into account front-end and back-end loads, redemption fees, or one-time or annual account charges, if any. The 12b-1 charge, as part of the expense ratio, is reflected in the return figure.

Differ from Category (+/–): The difference between the return for the fund and average return for all funds in the same investment category for the time period.

Return, Tax-Adjusted (%): Annual return after adjusting for the maximum federal tax on income, short-term capital gains and long-term capital gains distributions. Some funds may hold portions of their portfolio in investments that receive special tax treatment; adjustments for these tax differences have not been made in this *Guide.*

Per Share Data

Dividends, Net Income ($): Per share income distributions for the calendar year. The timing of net income distributions can be found in the prospectus.

Distrib'ns, Cap Gains ($): Per share distributions for the calendar year from realized capital gains after netting out realized losses. The timing of capital gains distributions can be found in the prospectus.

Net Asset Value ($): Calendar year-end net asset value is the sum of all securities held, based on their market value, divided by the number of mutual fund shares outstanding.

Expense Ratio (%): The sum of administrative fees plus adviser management fees and 12b-1 fees divided by the average net asset value of the fund, stated as a percentage. Brokerage costs incurred by the fund are not included in the expense ratio but are instead reflected directly in net asset value. Front-end loads, back-end loads, redemption fees, and account activity charges are not included in this ratio.

Yield (%): The per share annual income distribution made by the fund divided by the sum of the year-ending net asset value plus any capital gains distributions made during the year. This ratio is similar to a dividend yield and would be higher for income-oriented funds and lower for growth-oriented funds. The figure only reflects income;

it is not total return. For some funds, the yield may be distorted if the fund reports short-term capital gains as income.

Portfolio Turnover (%): A measure of the trading activity of the fund, which is computed by dividing the lesser of purchases or sales for the year by the monthly average value of the securities owned by the fund during the year. Securities with maturities of less than one year are excluded from the calculation. The result is expressed as a percentage, with 100% implying a complete turnover within one year.

Total Assets (Millions $): Aggregate fund value in millions of dollars at the end of the calendar year.

Portfolio

Portfolio Manager: The name of the portfolio manager(s) and the year when the senior manager(s) began managing the fund are noted, providing additional information useful in evaluating past performance. (Senior managers are listed first.) Funds managed by a committee are so noted. For some funds, a recent change in the portfolio manager(s) may indicate that the long-term annual performance figures and other performance classifications are less meaningful.

Investment Style: For domestic stock funds investment style can be categorized by the size of firms the fund invests in as measured by market capitalization and the investment approach employed by the fund, either growth or value or both. The investment style attributed to the fund indicates that the historical performance of the fund most closely follows the style(s) checked (listed below). More than one size may be checked, indicating a mixture of size, and growth/value may be checked, indicating a blend of growth and value investment approaches. Style is *only* calculated for domestic stock funds.

    Style Categories: Large Cap, Mid Cap, Small Cap, Growth, Value, Grth/Val ('Cap' denotes capitalization, which is market price per share for a firm's stock times the number of common stock shares outstanding).

Portfolio: The portfolio composition classifies investments by type and gives the percentage of the total portfolio invested in each. Some funds are a "fund of funds" and their portfolio holdings are denoted by "100% other." Due to rounding of the percentages and the practice of leverage (borrowing) to buy securities, the portfolio total percentage may not equal 100.0%.

Shareholder Information
Minimum Investment and Minimum IRA Investment:
The minimum initial and subsequent investments, by mail, in the fund are detailed. Minimum investment by telephone or by wire may be different. Often, funds will have a lower minimum IRA investment; this is also indicated.

Maximum Fees:
Load: The maximum load is given, if any, and whether the load is front-end or back-end is indicated.

12b-1: If a fund has a 12b-1 plan, the percentage that the fund charges is given.

Other: Redemption fees are given along with the time period, if appropriate.

Services:
IRA: Notes whether the fund offers an individual retirement account option.

Keogh: Notes whether the fund offers a Keogh account option.

Telephone Exchange: Indicates whether telephone exchanges with other funds in the family are permitted.

Check in the prospectus to determine whether the fund allows for an automatic exchange between funds in the family; whether the fund allows for automatic investments through an investor's checking account; and whether the fund allows the automatic and systematic withdrawal of money from the fund. All funds have automatic reinvestment of distributions options.

Fund Performance Rankings and Information

When choosing among mutual funds, most investors start with performance statistics: How well have the various mutual funds performed in the past? If past performance alone could perfectly predict future performance, selection would be easy.

What past performance can tell you is how well the fund's management has handled different market environments, how consistent the fund has been, and how well the fund has done relative to its risk level, relative to other similar funds, and relative to the market.

We present performance statistics in several different forms. First, we provide an overall picture, with the average performance of each mutual fund category for the last five years, along with benchmarks for large, mid-cap and small-company domestic stocks; international stocks; bonds; and Treasury bills. The top 50 and bottom 50 mutual fund performers for the last year are given as a reference of recent performance. The list changes each year and reflects the cyclical nature of financial markets and the changing success of individual mutual fund managers. Lists of the top 50 mutual funds ranked by annual return over the last three years, five years, and 10 years are given for a long-term perspective on investment trends of performance.

Since the performance of a fund must be judged relative to similar funds, we have also classified the funds by investment category and ranked them according to their total return performance for the last year. These performance lists appear in Chapter 14 at the start of each category section. To make the comparison easier, we have also provided other data. The funds' annual returns for the last three years, five years, and 10 years give a longer-term perspective on the performance of the fund; category and total risk ranks are also given to judge performance. (To maintain ranking accuracy, funds are sorted by more decimal points of return than are shown in the *Guide*.)

Key to Fund Categories Used in Performance Tables

Stk-LC	Large-Cap Stock
Stk-MC	Mid-Cap Stock
Stk-SC	Small-Cap Stock
Sec-E	Energy/Resources Sector Stock
Sec-F	Financial/Banking Sector Stock
Sec-G	Gold Sector Stock
Sec-H	Health Sector Stock
Sec-R	Real Estate Sector Stock
Sec-T	Technology Sector Stock
Sec-TC	Telecommunications Sector Stock
Sec-U	Utilities Sector Stock
IntS-Glb	Global Stock
IntS-F	Foreign Stock
IntS-R/C	Regional/Country Stock
IntS-E	Emerging Stock
Bal	Balanced Stock/Bond
B-Corp	Corporate Bond
B-CHY	Corporate High-Yield Bond
B-MB	Mortgage-Backed Bond
B-GvST	Government: Short-Term Bond
B-GvIT	Government: Intermediate-Term Bond
B-GvLT	Government: Long-Term Bond
B-Gen	General Bond
B-MNST	National Muni: Short-Term Bond
B-MNIT	National Muni: Intermediate-Term Bond
B-MNLT	National Muni: Long-Term Bond
B-MHY	National Muni: High-Yield Bond
B-MS-AZ	Muni: Arizona Bond
B-MS-CA	Muni: California Bond
B-MS-CO	Muni: Colorado Bond
B-MS-CT	Muni: Connecticut Bond
B-MS-FL	Muni: Florida Bond
B-MS-GA	Muni: Georgia Bond
B-MS-HI	Muni: Hawaii Bond
B-MS-KY	Muni: Kentucky Bond
B-MS-MD	Muni: Maryland Bond
B-MS-MA	Muni: Massachusetts Bond
B-MS-MI	Muni: Michigan Bond
B-MS-MN	Muni: Minnesota Bond
B-MS-NJ	Muni: New Jersey Bond
B-MS-NY	Muni: New York Bond
B-MS-OH	Muni: Ohio Bond
B-MS-PA	Muni: Pennsylvania Bond
B-MS-TN	Muni: Tennessee Bond
B-MS-VA	Muni: Virginia Bond
B-MS-WV	Muni: West Virginia Bond
B-MS-WI	Muni: Wisconsin Bond
IntB	International Bond

Total Risk and Return Performances for
Different Mutual Fund Categories

Stock Funds	2005	2004	2003	2002	2001	5yr	Total Return (%) Bull	Bear	Std Dev (%)	Total Risk
Large-Cap	6.2	10.8	29.5	-21.5	-11.4	0.8	58.7	-35.8	10.3	av
Mid-Cap	9.9	15.5	37.6	-18.4	-4.3	5.9	82.1	-23.6	12.5	abv av
Small-Cap	7.3	16.4	47.0	-19.2	5.3	8.5	93.4	-18.1	14.9	high
Value Style	7.3	16.3	37.3	-14.6	6.7	8.8	80.7	-2.8	11.6	abv av
Growth Style	7.6	10.4	35.3	-25.6	-16.9	-0.8	67.0	-48.9	12.9	abv av
Energy/Resources Sector	46.8	33.7	32.1	-3.7	-12.7	16.2	153.7	2.0	19.2	high
Financial/Banking Sector	6.1	13.1	34.3	-7.5	-1.3	7.7	69.9	20.6	12.5	abv av
Gold Sector	32.8	-5.6	59.1	65.7	19.4	31.2	108.5	77.8	29.2	high
Health Sector	13.8	14.3	30.6	-23.5	-10.6	3.4	74.4	-7.3	11.9	abv av
Real Estate Sector	12.8	30.9	39.3	4.6	10.4	19.2	106.5	42.6	14.0	abv av
Technology Sector	4.2	2.4	59.2	-42.1	-30.2	-8.5	72.2	-75.7	20.7	high
Telecomm Sector	9.3	21.9	50.9	-40.8	-29.8	-1.4	106.9	-72.4	16.8	high
Utilities Sector	13.1	21.6	21.9	-25.6	-19.9	-0.2	80.9	-43.6	11.0	av
Global	11.6	13.4	31.6	-13.2	-10.9	4.8	76.3	-30.8	10.1	av
Foreign	18.0	19.6	41.9	-14.2	-18.5	6.2	113.9	-44.3	12.5	abv av
Regional/Country	27.6	19.5	49.8	-8.0	-9.9	12.9	139.5	-38.8	16.7	high
Emerging	35.7	24.7	57.1	-6.7	-3.8	18.9	175.0	-41.5	16.6	high
Balanced Stock/Bond	5.8	10.1	22.0	-8.7	-2.2	4.7	45.7	-10.8	6.6	blw av
Bond Funds										
Corporate Bond	2.1	4.1	6.7	5.4	7.4	5.1	11.6	23.4	3.6	low
Corporate High-Yield	2.4	9.4	21.4	-0.6	4.1	7.1	32.2	2.3	4.6	blw av
Mortgage-Backed	2.5	3.3	2.3	7.8	7.4	4.6	7.4	26.6	2.2	low
Gov't: Short-Term	1.6	1.1	1.4	5.8	7.2	3.4	3.6	21.8	1.6	low
Gov't: Interm-Term	2.1	4.1	3.4	11.7	6.7	5.3	7.9	32.6	5.0	blw av
Gov't: Long-Term	6.5	7.2	2.1	13.2	2.0	6.0	14.0	30.2	11.9	abv av
General Bond	2.0	3.3	4.2	7.6	7.7	5.0	8.4	26.6	3.3	low
Nat'l Muni: Short-Term	1.7	1.4	2.3	3.9	4.7	2.8	4.8	14.1	1.0	low
Nat'l Muni: Interm-Term	1.8	2.8	4.2	8.6	4.7	4.3	8.0	22.6	3.9	low
Nat'l Muni: Long-Term	3.5	4.6	5.1	9.0	4.3	5.3	12.7	24.7	4.4	low
Nat'l Muni: High-Yield	5.5	5.7	6.5	7.8	5.5	6.2	17.7	22.0	3.2	low
International	3.2	9.4	17.3	12.5	5.1	9.3	28.6	25.9	6.1	blw av
Index Comparisons										
Dow Jones Industrials	1.7	5.3	28.3	-15.0	-5.4	2.0	44.6	-23.7	9.7	av
S&P 500	4.9	10.9	28.7	-22.1	-11.9	0.6	55.9	-41.4	9.2	av
S&P Midcap 400	12.5	16.5	35.6	-14.5	-0.6	8.6	87.5	-16.0	11.7	abv av
S&P SmallCap 600	7.7	22.7	38.8	-14.6	6.5	10.8	96.1	-10.1	14.0	abv av
DJ Wilshire 5000	6.3	12.6	31.7	-20.9	-11.0	2.1	64.4	-42.0	9.7	av
S&P International 700	16.4	20.2	40.9	-15.6	-20.3	5.8	109.5	-44.6	11.9	abv av
S&P Europe 350	26.6	11.9	15.5	-30.2	-15.2	-0.7	82.2	-48.7	11.6	abv av
S&P Asia 50	24.8	20.7	40.1	-10.1	-0.5	13.6	122.8	-38.7	16.2	high
ML Corporate Bond	2.0	5.4	8.3	10.2	10.7	7.3	13.6	34.2	5.5	blw av
ML High Yield Bond	2.8	10.8	27.2	-1.1	6.3	8.8	39.0	7.1	5.4	blw av
Lehman Brothers Bond Indexes										
Interm Government	1.7	2.3	2.3	9.6	8.4	4.8	5.4	30.3	3.3	low
Mortgage-Backed	2.6	4.7	3.1	8.7	8.2	5.4	9.7	30.2	2.7	low
Municipal	3.5	4.5	5.3	9.6	5.1	5.6	12.6	26.4	4.2	low
Treasury Bills	3.3	1.4	1.0	1.6	3.4	2.1	5.6	10.0	0.3	low

The Top 50 Performers: 2005

Category	Fund (Ticker)	Annual Return (%) 2005	3yr	5yr	10yr	Category Risk	Total Risk
IntS-R/C	T Rowe Price Latin America (PRLAX)	60.0	51.7	23.3	15.5	high	high
IntS-R/C	T Rowe Price Emerg Europe & Med (TREMX)	59.0	51.8	27.3	na	abv av	high
IntS-R/C	Matthews Korea (MAKOX)	58.7	37.7	37.0	8.3	high	high
IntS-R/C	Fidelity Latin America (FLATX)	55.1	53.6	21.9	13.9	high	high
Sec-E	Fidelity Select Energy (FSENX)	51.9	34.9	13.8	15.5	blw av	high
Sec-E	US Global Inv Global Resources (PSPFX)	48.9	57.1	31.6	14.9	high	high
Sec-E	Fidelity Select Natural Gas (FSNGX)	45.7	38.0	12.9	15.6	abv av	high
Sec-E	Vanguard Energy Inv (VGENX)	44.6	38.2	20.6	17.8	low	high
IntS-E	Fidelity Emerging Market (FEMKX)	44.3	38.2	19.1	2.7	high	high
Sec-G	Vanguard Precious Metals (VGPMX)	43.7	35.3	31.3	10.5	low	high
Sec-E	RS Global Natural Resources (RSNRX)	42.2	39.5	26.1	14.2	av	high
IntS-R/C	Fidelity Japan Small Co (FJSCX)	41.3	40.6	17.5	10.0	high	high
IntS-E	Lazard Emerging Markets Open (LZOEX)	41.3	41.6	22.2	na	av	high
IntS-R/C	US Global Accolade Eastern Euro (EUROX)	40.7	51.2	40.9	na	high	high
IntS-R/C	T Rowe Price Japan (PRJPX)	40.0	33.1	5.8	2.9	abv av	high
Sec-G	Midas (MIDSX)	39.7	25.0	28.9	-3.5	av	high
Sec-G	USAA Precious Metals & Minerals (USAGX)	39.2	28.6	36.1	10.2	av	high
IntS-E	T Rowe Price Emerg Mkts Stock (PRMSX)	38.7	38.9	19.2	10.3	av	high
Sec-G	US Global Inv Gold Shares (USERX)	32.8	27.5	33.1	-4.9	high	high
IntS-R/C	Fidelity Pacific Basin (FPBFX)	32.5	27.9	9.1	6.9	blw av	abv av
IntS-F	Janus Overseas (JAOSX)	32.3	29.0	4.6	12.9	high	high
IntS-E	Vanguard Emerg Mkts Stock Index (VEIEX)	32.0	37.9	18.7	8.1	abv av	high
Sec-G	US Global Inv World Prec Minerals (UNWPX)	30.8	36.5	38.1	4.8	high	high
Sec-F	Fidelity Select Brokerage & Invest Mgmt (FSLBX)	29.8	26.0	8.5	19.7	high	high
IntS-E	Excelsior Emerging Markets (UMEMX)	29.0	40.1	20.6	na	blw av	high
Sec-H	Fidelity Select Medical Delivery (FSHCX)	29.0	34.6	15.9	11.9	high	high
IntS-F	T Rowe Price Intl Discovery (PRIDX)	27.8	37.7	10.5	15.0	abv av	abv av
IntS-R/C	Fidelity Canada (FICDX)	27.8	34.0	15.8	13.1	low	abv av
IntS-R/C	Wells Fargo Advtg Asia Pacific Inv (SASPX)	27.6	35.0	14.7	5.3	blw av	high
Sec-R	CGM Realty (CGMRX)	26.9	48.3	28.8	20.7	high	high
IntS-R/C	T Rowe Price New Asia (PRASX)	26.4	32.0	13.4	5.1	av	high
IntS-F	Thomas White International (TWWDX)	25.5	27.2	8.7	9.5	abv av	abv av
Stk-SC	CGM Focus (CGMFX)	25.2	32.8	23.2	na	high	high
IntS-F	Neuberger Berman International Inv (NBISX)	23.9	32.2	10.5	11.2	av	abv av
IntS-Glb	T Rowe Price Global Stock (PRGSX)	22.7	22.2	4.1	9.2	abv av	av
IntS-R/C	Vanguard Pacific Stock Index (VPACX)	22.5	26.3	6.1	0.9	blw av	abv av
IntS-R/C	Matthews Pacific Tiger (MAPTX)	22.5	34.2	19.5	9.2	av	high
Stk-MC	Amer Century Heritage Inv (TWHIX)	22.2	16.7	-0.1	9.2	abv av	abv av
IntS-F	Tocqueville International Value (TIVFX)	21.0	31.3	15.7	7.1	blw av	abv av
IntS-F	Bailard International Equity (BBIEX)	20.6	27.6	7.3	7.4	av	abv av
Sec-H	Schwab Health Care (SWHFX)	20.0	29.0	6.8	na	av	av
IntS-Glb	UMB Scout Worldwide (UMBWX)	19.5	23.3	7.0	10.8	av	av
IntS-F	Laudus Int'l MarketMasters Inv (SWOIX)	19.3	27.0	7.5	na	abv av	abv av
IntS-F	Fidelity Overseas (FOSFX)	19.2	25.0	4.6	7.5	abv av	abv av
IntS-F	ICAP International (ICEUX)	19.1	28.9	9.7	na	abv av	abv av
Stk-MC	Fidelity Value Discovery (FVDFX)	18.7	20.7	na	na	blw av	abv av
IntS-F	Fidelity International Discovery (FIGRX)	18.5	26.4	8.5	10.2	av	abv av
Stk-SC	Sit Small Cap Growth (SSMGX)	18.5	19.4	-2.1	9.7	av	high
IntS-R/C	Fidelity Nordic (FNORX)	18.5	29.7	5.1	14.4	abv av	high
IntS-R/C	Fidelity Europe (FIEUX)	18.1	30.8	6.9	10.9	av	high

The Bottom 50 Performers: 2005

Category	Fund (Ticker)	Annual Return (%)				Category Risk	Total Risk
		2005	3yr	5yr	10yr		
IntB	Amer Century Intl Bond Inv (BEGBX)	-8.2	7.5	8.6	4.7	high	av
IntB	T Rowe Price Intl Bond (RPIBX)	-8.1	6.7	7.4	4.2	high	blw av
Stk-LC	Thompson Plumb Growth (THPGX)	-2.4	10.2	4.9	13.4	high	abv av
Sec-F	FBR Small Cap Financial (FBRSX)	-1.5	17.2	18.8	na	blw av	av
Stk-SC	Weitz Hickory (WEHIX)	-0.2	21.8	4.0	13.2	low	abv av
Stk-MC	Meridian Growth (MERDX)	0.3	19.3	9.8	12.2	abv av	abv av
B-MS-KY	Dupree KY Tax Free Short to Med (KYSMX)	0.4	1.9	3.5	3.7	av	low
Stk-MC	Mosaic Equity Tr Mid Cap (GTSGX)	0.5	15.3	9.0	10.2	low	av
B-MS-CA	Schwab Inv CA Short Intm TF Bond (SWCSX)	0.7	1.9	3.3	3.8	low	low
Stk-LC	USAA NASDAQ 100 Index (USNQX)	0.9	17.9	-7.5	na	high	high
B-GvST	Payden US Government R (PYUSX)	1.0	1.2	4.0	4.7	high	low
B-MNST	Vanguard Limited Term TE (VMLTX)	1.1	1.8	3.4	3.9	high	low
Stk-LC	Rydex OTC Inv (RYOCX)	1.3	17.5	-8.2	10.2	high	high
B-GvIT	Amer Century Target Mat 2010 Inv (BTTNX)	1.3	2.8	6.0	6.5	high	blw av
Stk-SC	Heartland Value Plus (HRVIX)	1.3	22.1	18.7	13.0	av	high
B-MS-CA	Bernstein CA Municipal (SNCAX)	1.4	2.5	3.6	4.1	blw av	low
B-MS-FL	T Rowe Price Tx Fr Inc Tr FL Int Tx Fr (FLTFX)	1.5	2.5	4.1	4.4	blw av	low
B-MS-CO	Westcore CO Tax Exempt (WTCOX)	1.5	2.8	4.1	4.4	high	low
B-MS-NY	Bernstein NY Municipal (SNNYX)	1.6	2.7	3.9	4.3	low	low
B-MNST	Vanguard Short Term TE (VWSTX)	1.6	1.4	2.5	3.2	blw av	low
B-MS-WV	WesMark West Virginia Muni Bond (WMKMX)	1.6	2.6	4.0	na	high	low
B-MS-CT	Dreyfus CT Intm Muni Bd (DCTIX)	1.7	2.6	4.1	4.3	blw av	low
B-GvST	Excelsior Short Term Govt Sec (UMGVX)	1.7	1.5	3.7	4.4	av	low
B-Corp	T Rowe Price Short Term Bond (PRWBX)	1.7	2.3	4.1	4.7	low	low
B-Gen	Vanguard Intermediate Term Bd Idx (VBIIX)	1.7	4.1	6.5	6.3	high	blw av
B-CHY	Northern High Yield Fixed Income (NHFIX)	1.7	10.9	8.1	na	high	blw av
B-GvST	Vanguard Short Term Treasury (VFISX)	1.7	1.7	4.1	4.9	abv av	low
B-MNST	USAA Tx Ex Short Term (USSTX)	1.7	2.0	3.2	3.8	high	low
B-Gen	Janus Flexible Bond (JAFIX)	1.7	3.9	5.7	6.1	high	low
B-GvST	Vanguard Short Term Federal (VSGBX)	1.8	1.7	4.2	5.0	abv av	low
B-MS-CA	Vanguard CA Intm Term TE Inv (VCAIX)	1.8	2.9	4.4	5.1	blw av	low
B-Corp	Vanguard Int Term Invst Grade (VFICX)	1.9	4.3	6.5	6.1	abv av	blw av
B-Gen	Dodge & Cox Income (DODIX)	1.9	3.8	6.4	6.3	blw av	low
Stk-SC	Heartland Value (HRTVX)	1.9	23.7	16.7	13.8	high	high
B-MNIT	Dreyfus Intm Muni Bd (DITEX)	2.0	3.0	4.0	4.3	abv av	low
B-MNIT	Northern Intermediate Tax Exempt (NOITX)	2.0	3.2	4.7	4.7	av	low
B-MS-AZ	Northern AZ Tax Exempt (NOAZX)	2.0	3.1	4.7	na	abv av	low
Sec-T	RS Information Age (RSIFX)	2.0	29.3	-2.6	10.1	high	high
B-Corp	Westcore Plus Bond (WTIBX)	2.0	6.6	6.7	6.2	av	low
B-MNIT	TIAA-CREF Tax Exempt Bond (TCTEX)	2.1	4.1	5.6	na	high	blw av
B-GvIT	Fidelity Inflation & Protected Bonds (FINPX)	2.1	6.0	na	na	high	blw av
B-GvIT	Wells Fargo Advtg Govt Securities (STVSX)	2.1	2.7	5.4	5.6	av	low
B-Corp	Vanguard Short Term Invst Grade (VFSTX)	2.2	2.8	4.3	5.1	blw av	low
B-MS-CT	Fidelity CT Muni Inc (FICNX)	2.2	3.5	5.0	5.3	high	blw av
B-CHY	Northeast Investors (NTHEX)	2.2	10.1	6.9	6.3	blw av	low
B-MNIT	Vanguard Intermediate Term TE (VWITX)	2.2	3.3	4.5	4.8	av	low
B-MS-CA	Amer Century CA Int Tax Free Inv (BCITX)	2.2	2.7	4.2	4.7	blw av	low
B-MNIT	T Rowe Price Summit Muni Intm (PRSMX)	2.2	3.2	4.7	5.0	blw av	low
B-Gen	Fidelity US Bond Index (FBIDX)	2.2	3.8	5.9	6.1	abv av	low
B-GvST	AMF Short US Government (ASITX)	2.2	1.8	3.4	4.3	blw av	low

The Top 50 Performers: 3 Years, 2003 – 2005

Category	Fund (Ticker)	Annual Return (%)				Category Risk	Total Risk
		3yr	5yr	10yr	2005		
Sec-E	US Global Inv Global Resources (PSPFX)	57.1	31.6	14.9	48.9	high	high
IntS-R/C	Fidelity Latin America (FLATX)	53.6	21.9	13.9	55.1	high	high
IntS-R/C	T Rowe Price Emerg Europe & Med (TREMX)	51.8	27.3	na	59.0	abv av	high
IntS-R/C	T Rowe Price Latin America (PRLAX)	51.7	23.3	15.5	60.0	high	high
IntS-R/C	US Global Accolade Eastern Euro (EUROX)	51.2	40.9	na	40.7	high	high
Sec-R	CGM Realty (CGMRX)	48.3	28.8	20.7	26.9	high	high
Stk-MC	Fidelity Leveraged Company Stock (FLVCX)	42.1	23.8	na	17.4	high	high
IntS-E	Lazard Emerging Markets Open (LZOEX)	41.6	22.2	na	41.3	av	high
Sec-TC	Fidelity Select Wireless (FWRLX)	41.1	-3.9	na	17.3	abv av	high
IntS-R/C	Fidelity Japan Small Co (FJSCX)	40.6	17.5	10.0	41.3	high	high
IntS-E	Excelsior Emerging Markets (UMEMX)	40.1	20.6	na	29.0	blw av	high
Sec-E	RS Global Natural Resources (RSNRX)	39.5	26.1	14.2	42.2	av	high
IntS-E	T Rowe Price Emerg Mkts Stock (PRMSX)	38.9	19.2	10.3	38.7	av	high
Sec-E	Vanguard Energy Inv (VGENX)	38.2	20.6	17.8	44.6	low	high
IntS-E	Fidelity Emerging Market (FEMKX)	38.2	19.1	2.7	44.3	high	high
Sec-E	Fidelity Select Natural Gas (FSNGX)	38.0	12.9	15.6	45.7	abv av	high
IntS-E	Vanguard Emerg Mkts Stock Index (VEIEX)	37.9	18.7	8.1	32.0	abv av	high
IntS-F	T Rowe Price Intl Discovery (PRIDX)	37.7	10.5	15.0	27.8	abv av	abv av
IntS-R/C	Matthews Korea (MAKOX)	37.7	37.0	8.3	58.7	high	high
Stk-SC	Royce Value Plus Inv (RYVPX)	37.6	na	na	13.2	abv av	high
Sec-G	US Global Inv World Prec Minerals (UNWPX)	36.5	38.1	4.8	30.8	high	high
Sec-G	Vanguard Precious Metals (VGPMX)	35.3	31.3	10.5	43.7	low	high
IntS-R/C	Wells Fargo Advtg Asia Pacific Inv (SASPX)	35.0	14.7	5.3	27.6	blw av	high
Sec-E	Fidelity Select Energy (FSENX)	34.9	13.8	15.5	51.9	blw av	high
Sec-H	Fidelity Select Medical Delivery (FSHCX)	34.6	15.9	11.9	29.0	high	high
IntS-R/C	Matthews Pacific Tiger (MAPTX)	34.2	19.5	9.2	22.5	av	high
Stk-SC	Winslow Green Growth (WGGFX)	34.0	na	na	12.1	high	high
IntS-R/C	Fidelity Canada (FICDX)	34.0	15.8	13.1	27.8	low	abv av
Stk-SC	Oberweis Micro Cap (OBMCX)	34.0	19.7	na	12.7	high	high
Stk-MC	RS Value (RSVAX)	33.8	17.3	6.9	11.6	av	abv av
Sec-T	RS Internet Age (RIAFX)	33.3	3.5	na	7.9	high	high
Stk-SC	Royce Value Inv (RYVFX)	33.3	na	na	17.2	blw av	abv av
IntS-R/C	T Rowe Price Japan (PRJPX)	33.1	5.8	2.9	40.0	abv av	high
Stk-SC	CGM Focus (CGMFX)	32.8	23.2	na	25.2	high	high
Sec-T	Baron iOpportunity (BIOPX)	32.7	9.8	na	7.0	blw av	high
Sec-TC	T Rowe Price Media & Telecomm (PRMTX)	32.5	9.1	na	18.1	blw av	abv av
IntS-F	Neuberger Berman International Inv (NBISX)	32.2	10.5	11.2	23.9	av	abv av
IntS-F	Dodge & Cox Intl Stock (DODFX)	32.2	na	na	16.7	high	abv av
IntS-R/C	T Rowe Price New Asia (PRASX)	32.0	13.4	5.1	26.4	av	high
Stk-SC	Al Frank (VALUX)	31.8	17.0	na	11.0	high	high
IntS-F	Tocqueville International Value (TIVFX)	31.3	15.7	7.1	21.0	blw av	abv av
IntS-R/C	Fidelity Europe (FIEUX)	30.8	6.9	10.9	18.1	av	high
Stk-SC	Bridgeway Ultra Small Co Market (BRSIX)	30.5	23.6	na	4.0	abv av	high
Sec-R	Cohen & Steers Realty Shares (CSRSX)	30.0	19.0	15.6	14.9	high	high
Stk-SC	Perritt Micro Cap Opportunities (PRCGX)	29.9	24.2	14.8	14.8	blw av	abv av
IntS-R/C	Fidelity Nordic (FNORX)	29.7	5.1	14.4	18.5	abv av	high
Stk-LC	Janus Contrarian (JSVAX)	29.6	7.9	na	16.0	high	abv av
Sec-T	RS Information Age (RSIFX)	29.3	-2.6	10.1	2.0	high	high
Sec-H	Schwab Health Care (SWHFX)	29.0	6.8	na	20.0	av	av
Stk-SC	MainStay Small Cap Opportunity I (MOPIX)	29.0	18.8	14.7	11.1	av	high

The Top 50 Performers: 5 Years, 2001 – 2005

Category	Fund (Ticker)	Annual Return (%)				Category Risk	Total Risk
		5yr	10yr	3yr	2005		
IntS-R/C	US Global Accolade Eastern Euro (EUROX)	40.9	na	51.2	40.7	high	high
Sec-G	US Global Inv World Prec Minerals (UNWPX)	38.1	4.8	36.5	30.8	high	high
IntS-R/C	Matthews Korea (MAKOX)	37.0	8.3	37.7	58.7	high	high
Sec-G	USAA Precious Metals & Minerals (USAGX)	36.1	10.2	28.6	39.2	av	high
Sec-G	US Global Inv Gold Shares (USERX)	33.1	-4.9	27.5	32.8	high	high
Sec-E	US Global Inv Global Resources (PSPFX)	31.6	14.9	57.1	48.9	high	high
Sec-G	Vanguard Precious Metals (VGPMX)	31.3	10.5	35.3	43.7	low	high
Sec-G	Midas (MIDSX)	28.9	-3.5	25.0	39.7	av	high
Sec-R	CGM Realty (CGMRX)	28.8	20.7	48.3	26.9	high	high
IntS-R/C	T Rowe Price Emerging Europe & Med (TREMX)	27.3	na	51.8	59.0	abv av	high
Sec-E	RS Global Natural Resources (RSNRX)	26.1	14.2	39.5	42.2	av	high
Stk-SC	Perritt Micro Cap Opportunities (PRCGX)	24.2	14.8	29.9	14.4	blw av	abv av
Stk-MC	Fidelity Leveraged Company Stock (FLVCX)	23.8	na	42.1	17.4	high	high
Stk-SC	Bridgeway Ultra Small Co Market (BRSIX)	23.6	na	30.5	4.0	abv av	high
IntS-R/C	T Rowe Price Latin America (PRLAX)	23.3	15.5	51.7	60.0	high	high
Stk-SC	CGM Focus (CGMFX)	23.2	na	32.8	25.2	high	high
IntS-E	Lazard Emerging Markets Open (LZOEX)	22.2	na	41.6	41.3	av	high
IntS-R/C	Fidelity Latin America (FLATX)	21.9	13.9	53.6	55.1	high	high
Sec-E	Vanguard Energy Inv (VGENX)	20.6	17.8	38.2	44.6	low	high
IntS-E	Excelsior Emerging Markets (UMEMX)	20.6	na	40.1	29.0	blw av	high
Stk-SC	Berwyn (BERWX)	19.9	10.9	27.3	12.1	blw av	abv av
Stk-SC	Oberweis Micro Cap (OBMCX)	19.7	na	34.0	12.7	high	high
Sec-R	Amer Century Real Estate Inv (REACX)	19.6	15.9	28.1	15.9	av	high
IntS-R/C	Matthews Pacific Tiger (MAPTX)	19.5	9.2	34.2	22.5	av	high
Sec-R	T Rowe Price Real Estate (TRREX)	19.3	na	28.3	14.5	av	high
IntS-E	T Rowe Price Emerg Mkts Stock (PRMSX)	19.2	10.3	38.9	38.7	av	high
IntS-E	Fidelity Emerging Market (FEMKX)	19.1	2.7	38.2	44.3	high	high
Sec-R	Fidelity Real Estate Investment (FRESX)	19.0	15.3	27.2	14.8	abv av	high
Sec-R	Cohen & Steers Realty Shares (CSRSX)	19.0	15.6	30.0	14.9	high	high
Stk-SC	MainStay Small Cap Opportunity I (MOPIX)	18.8	14.7	29.0	11.1	av	high
Sec-F	FBR Small Cap Financial (FBRSX)	18.8	na	17.2	-1.5	blw av	av
Stk-SC	Heartland Value Plus (HRVIX)	18.7	13.0	22.1	1.3	av	high
IntS-E	Vanguard Emerging Mkts Stock Index (VEIEX)	18.7	8.1	37.9	32.0	abv av	high
IntS-R/C	Fidelity Japan Small Co (FJSCX)	17.5	10.0	40.6	41.3	high	high
Stk-MC	RS Value (RSVAX)	17.3	6.9	33.8	11.6	av	abv av
Stk-SC	Al Frank (VALUX)	17.0	na	31.8	11.0	high	high
Stk-MC	Delafield (DEFIX)	17.0	13.7	21.5	6.0	abv av	abv av
Stk-SC	Heartland Value (HRTVX)	16.7	13.8	23.7	1.9	high	high
Stk-SC	Stratton Small Cap Value (STSCX)	16.0	14.2	28.0	10.8	av	high
Stk-SC	Royce Micro-Cap Inv (RYOTX)	16.0	14.5	25.3	11.5	abv av	high
Sec-H	Fidelity Select Medical Delivery (FSHCX)	15.9	11.9	34.6	29.0	high	high
IntS-R/C	Fidelity Canada (FICDX)	15.8	13.1	34.0	27.8	low	abv av
IntS-F	Tocqueville International Value (TIVFX)	15.7	7.1	31.3	21.0	blw av	abv av
Stk-SC	Royce Opportunity Inv (RYPNX)	15.6	na	28.6	4.7	high	high
Stk-SC	Royce Pennsylvania Mutual Inv (PENNX)	15.3	14.1	23.8	12.5	blw av	abv av
Stk-SC	Hennessy Cornerstone Growth (HFCGX)	15.2	na	23.9	11.9	abv av	high
IntB	T Rowe Price Emerging Markets Bond (PREMX)	15.2	13.4	19.2	17.2	abv av	blw av
Stk-MC	Kinetics Paradigm (WWNPX)	15.1	na	27.5	16.1	av	abv av
Stk-SC	Royce Premier (RYPRX)	15.0	14.6	25.8	17.0	blw av	abv av
IntS-R/C	Wells Fargo Advtg Asia Pacific Inv (SASPX)	14.7	5.3	35.0	27.6	blw av	high

The Top 50 Performers: 10 Years, 1996 – 2005

Category	Fund (Ticker)	Annual Return (%)				Category Risk	Total Risk
		10yr	5yr	3yr	2005		
Sec-R	CGM Realty (CGMRX)	20.7	28.8	48.3	26.9	high	high
Sec-F	Fidelity Select Brokerage & Inv Mgmt (FSLBX)	19.7	8.5	26.0	29.8	high	high
Stk-MC	Meridian Value (MVALX)	18.7	9.0	16.8	2.9	low	av
Sec-E	Vanguard Energy Inv (VGENX)	17.8	20.6	38.2	44.6	low	high
Sec-F	Fidelity Select Insurance (FSPCX)	16.1	7.9	17.8	13.7	av	abv av
Sec-R	Amer Century Real Estate Inv (REACX)	15.9	19.6	28.1	15.9	av	high
Stk-MC	Muhlenkamp (MUHLX)	15.7	11.7	25.7	7.8	high	high
Stk-LC	Fidelity Export & Multinational (FEXPX)	15.7	7.3	20.2	15.2	abv av	av
Sec-E	Fidelity Select Natural Gas (FSNGX)	15.6	12.9	38.0	45.7	abv av	high
Sec-R	Cohen & Steers Realty Shares (CSRSX)	15.6	19.0	30.0	14.9	high	high
IntS-R/C	T Rowe Price Latin America (PRLAX)	15.5	23.3	51.7	60.0	high	high
Sec-E	Fidelity Select Energy (FSENX)	15.5	13.8	34.9	51.9	blw av	high
Sec-R	Fidelity Real Estate Investment (FRESX)	15.3	19.0	27.2	14.8	abv av	high
IntS-F	T Rowe Price Intl Discovery (PRIDX)	15.0	10.5	37.7	27.8	abv av	abv av
Sec-E	US Global Inv Global Resources (PSPFX)	14.9	31.6	57.1	48.9	high	high
IntB	Fidelity New Markets Income (FNMIX)	14.8	14.5	18.0	11.5	high	blw av
Stk-SC	Perritt Micro Cap Opportunities (PRCGX)	14.8	24.2	29.9	14.4	blw av	abv av
Stk-LC	Excelsior Value & Restructuring (UMBIX)	14.7	7.1	24.7	9.9	high	abv av
Stk-SC	MainStay Small Cap Opportunity I (MOPIX)	14.7	18.8	29.0	11.1	av	high
Stk-SC	Royce Premier (RYPRX)	14.6	15.0	25.8	17.0	blw av	abv av
Stk-SC	Royce Micro-Cap Inv (RYOTX)	14.5	16.0	25.3	11.5	abv av	high
IntS-R/C	Fidelity Nordic (FNORX)	14.4	5.1	29.7	18.5	abv av	high
Stk-SC	Hennessy Cornerstone Growth II (HENLX)	14.4	10.9	28.1	9.2	high	high
Stk-SC	Stratton Small Cap Value (STSCX)	14.2	16.0	28.0	10.8	av	high
Sec-E	RS Global Natural Resources (RSNRX)	14.2	26.1	39.5	42.2	av	high
Stk-SC	Third Avenue Value (TAVFX)	14.1	12.0	26.4	16.5	low	av
Stk-SC	Royce Pennsylvania Mutual Inv (PENNX)	14.1	15.3	23.8	12.5	blw av	abv av
Sec-H	T Rowe Price Health Sciences (PRHSX)	14.1	4.2	21.8	13.5	abv av	abv av
IntS-R/C	Fidelity Latin America (FLATX)	13.9	21.9	53.6	55.1	high	high
Stk-SC	Royce Total Return Inv (RYTRX)	13.9	13.3	18.2	8.2	low	av
Stk-LC	Mairs & Power Growth (MPGFX)	13.8	8.7	15.8	4.3	low	blw av
Stk-SC	Heartland Value (HRTVX)	13.8	16.7	23.7	1.9	high	high
Stk-MC	Delafield (DEFIX)	13.7	17.0	21.5	6.0	abv av	abv av
Stk-MC	Dreyfus Index Midcap Index (PESPX)	13.6	7.9	20.3	11.2	blw av	abv av
Stk-MC	Vanguard Strategic Equity (VSEQX)	13.5	11.7	23.9	9.9	av	abv av
Stk-LC	Thompson Plumb Growth (THPGX)	13.4	4.9	10.2	-2.4	high	abv av
IntB	T Rowe Price Emerg Markets Bond (PREMX)	13.4	15.2	19.2	17.2	abv av	blw av
Stk-SC	Value Line Emerg Opportunities (VLEOX)	13.2	8.4	18.9	8.0	low	abv av
Stk-SC	Schroder Capital US Opportunities (SCUIX)	13.2	10.6	22.2	6.4	low	abv av
Stk-SC	Weitz Hickory (WEHIX)	13.2	4.0	21.8	-0.2	low	abv av
IntS-R/C	Fidelity Canada (FICDX)	13.1	15.8	34.0	27.8	low	abv av
Stk-SC	Heartland Value Plus (HRVIX)	13.0	18.7	22.1	1.3	av	high
Stk-MC	Fidelity Mid Cap Stock (FMCSX)	13.0	1.2	19.0	16.0	abv av	abv av
Stk-SC	Skyline Special Equities (SKSEX)	12.9	13.9	22.0	10.8	blw av	abv av
Stk-MC	Marshall Mid Cap Value Inv (MRVEX)	12.9	12.9	19.3	7.1	blw av	av
Stk-SC	LKCM Small Cap Equity I (LKSCX)	12.9	12.2	23.4	14.4	blw av	abv av
IntS-F	Janus Overseas (JAOSX)	12.9	4.6	29.0	32.3	high	high
Stk-MC	Stratton Growth (STRGX)	12.8	11.7	26.2	14.4	high	high
Stk-SC	Value Line Special Situations (VALSX)	12.7	3.5	19.5	11.2	low	av
Stk-SC	Northern Small Cap Value (NOSGX)	12.6	13.2	23.3	8.0	blw av	abv av

Individual Fund Listings

DOMESTIC STOCK FUNDS

Large-Cap Stock Funds
Category Performance Ranked by 2005 Returns

Fund (Ticker)	Annual Return (%)				Category Risk	Total Risk
	2005	3Yr	5Yr	10Yr		
Neuberger Berman Partners Inv (NPRTX)	17.9	24.1	6.8	10.1	high	abv av
Janus Core Equity (JAEIX)	16.3	17.7	3.2	na	av	av
Fidelity Contra (FCNTX)	16.2	19.6	6.2	12.0	blw av	av
Janus Contrarian (JSVAX)	16.0	29.6	7.9	na	high	abv av
Fidelity Export & Multinational (FEXPX)	15.2	20.2	7.3	15.7	abv av	av
Janus Olympus (JAOLX)	14.2	17.8	-4.5	11.7	abv av	av
Fidelity Growth Company (FDGRX)	13.5	21.6	-2.3	10.2	high	abv av
Janus Growth & Income (JAGIX)	12.4	16.1	1.0	12.4	av	av
RS Growth (RSGRX)	11.3	21.5	0.7	6.9	high	abv av
Fidelity Large Cap Value (FSLVX)	11.2	18.1	na	na	av	av
ICAP Equity (ICAEX)	10.9	16.7	3.5	10.5	low	blw av
Fidelity Independence (FDFFX)	10.5	15.1	-1.4	9.3	high	abv av
Fidelity Disciplined Equity (FDEQX)	10.2	16.2	1.8	9.2	blw av	av
Excelsior Value & Restructuring (UMBIX)	9.9	24.7	7.1	14.7	high	abv av
Marsico Focus (MFOCX)	9.6	17.1	1.1	na	abv av	av
T Rowe Price Spectrum Growth (PRSGX)	9.4	19.1	4.5	9.3	abv av	av
Schwab Capital Core Equity (SWANX)	9.4	16.7	1.0	na	av	av
FMI Large Cap (FMIHX)	9.1	19.0	na	na	blw av	av
Vanguard Morgan Growth Inv (VMRGX)	9.0	17.2	1.2	9.4	abv av	av
Fidelity OTC (FOCPX)	8.9	16.9	-1.5	8.4	high	high
Brandywine Blue (BLUEX)	8.3	18.7	2.2	10.0	high	abv av
Vanguard Growth Equity (VGEQX)	7.8	16.3	-4.7	7.2	high	abv av
Marsico 21st Century (MXXIX)	7.8	25.2	7.1	na	high	abv av
Neuberger Berman Soc Responsive Inv (NBSRX)	7.5	18.0	6.4	9.4	av	av
Vanguard Tax Managed Capital Apprec (VMCAX)	7.4	16.5	0.5	9.2	av	av
Fidelity Asset Manager Aggressive (FAMRX)	7.3	21.0	-0.6	na	high	av
Amer Century Equity Growth Inv (BEQGX)	7.3	16.7	2.4	9.9	blw av	av
USAA Aggressive Growth (USAUX)	7.2	16.6	-6.1	5.5	abv av	av
Vanguard Value Index Inv (VIVAX)	7.0	17.7	2.6	9.4	abv av	av
Vanguard Windsor II Inv (VWNFX)	7.0	18.0	5.7	10.7	blw av	av
USAA Growth & Income (USGRX)	6.8	15.1	2.4	8.1	av	av
Schwab MarketTrack All Equity (SWEGX)	6.8	17.7	2.4	na	abv av	av
Sound Shore (SSHFX)	6.8	17.5	6.3	11.9	high	av

Large-Cap Stock Funds
Category Performance Ranked by 2005 Returns (cont.)

Fund (Ticker)	Annual Return (%)				Category Risk	Total Risk
	2005	3Yr	5Yr	10Yr		
Marsico Growth (MGRIX)	6.7	17.2	1.3	na	abv av	av
T Rowe Price Growth Stock (PRGFX)	6.5	15.5	1.3	9.9	av	av
Vanguard US Value (VUVLX)	6.3	16.3	6.5	na	abv av	av
T Rowe Price Value (TRVLX)	6.3	16.8	6.2	11.7	abv av	av
Schwab Inv 1000 Index I (SNXFX)	6.0	14.8	0.9	9.0	blw av	av
Vanguard Total Stock Market Index Inv (VTSMX)	5.9	16.1	1.9	9.0	av	av
Vanguard Growth & Income Inv (VQNPX)	5.8	15.2	1.2	9.6	blw av	av
Fidelity Capital Appreciation (FDCAX)	5.8	21.3	5.3	10.2	high	abv av
Fidelity Equity Income (FEQIX)	5.7	15.2	3.7	9.5	abv av	av
Nicholas (NICSX)	5.6	14.9	1.1	6.9	av	av
Vanguard Growth Index Inv (VIGRX)	5.0	12.3	-1.2	8.5	blw av	av
Vanguard Windsor Inv (VWNDX)	4.9	17.7	6.0	10.4	abv av	av
Vanguard Tax Managed Growth & Income (VTGIX)	4.8	14.3	0.5	9.0	blw av	av
Oakmark Select I (OAKLX)	4.8	14.0	10.3	na	low	blw av
Amer Century Inc & Grth Inv (BIGRX)	4.7	15.3	2.5	9.8	av	av
Vanguard 500 Index Inv (VFINX)	4.7	14.2	0.4	9.0	blw av	av
Fidelity Equity Income II (FEQTX)	4.6	15.0	3.6	9.5	abv av	av
T Rowe Price Capital Opportunity (PRCOX)	4.5	15.0	1.2	5.6	blw av	av
Gabelli Asset AAA (GABAX)	4.4	16.6	6.4	12.0	abv av	av
Mairs & Power Growth (MPGFX)	4.3	15.8	8.7	13.8	low	blw av
T Rowe Price Equity Income (PRFDX)	4.2	14.6	5.9	10.2	av	av
Vanguard Capital Value Inv (VCVLX)	4.2	19.4	na	na	high	abv av
Masters Select Value (MSVFX)	4.1	16.5	8.2	na	high	abv av
TCW Galileo Dividend Focused N (TGIGX)	2.9	16.7	7.9	11.0	abv av	av
Rydex OTC Inv (RYOCX)	1.3	17.5	-8.2	10.2	high	high
USAA NASDAQ 100 Index (USNQX)	0.9	17.9	-7.5	na	high	high
Thompson Plumb Growth (THPGX)	-2.4	10.2	4.9	13.4	high	abv av
Large-Cap Stock Category Average	**6.2**	**14.9**	**0.8**	**8.6**	**av**	**av**

Amer Century Equity Growth Inv (BEQGX)

800-345-2021
www.americancentury.com

Large-Cap Stock

PERFORMANCE

fund inception date: 5/9/91

	3yr Annual	5yr Annual	10yr Annual	Bull	Bear
Return (%)	16.7	2.4	9.9	64.3	-40.4
Differ From Category (+/-)	1.8 abv av	1.6 abv av	1.3 abv av	5.6 abv av	-4.5 av

Standard Deviation	Category Risk Index	Beta
9.4%—av	0.91—blw av	0.99

	2005	2004	2003	2002	2001	2000	1999	1998	1997	1996
Return (%)	7.3	13.9	30.2	-20.3	-11.0	-10.9	18.4	25.4	36.0	27.3
Differ From Category (+/-)	.1.1	3.1	0.7	1.2	0.4	-7.7	-8.1	1.2	8.8	6.1
Return, Tax-Adjusted (%)	7.0	13.7	30.1	-20.6	-11.2	-12.2	17.7	24.1	32.5	22.9

PER SHARE DATA

	2005	2004	2003	2002	2001	2000	1999	1998	1997	1996
Dividends, Net Income ($)	0.22	0.24	0.17	0.15	0.13	0.14	0.19	0.20	0.24	0.26
Distrib'ns, Cap Gain ($)	0.10	0.00	0.00	0.00	0.00	1.47	0.43	0.88	2.31	1.85
Net Asset Value ($)	23.37	22.08	19.60	15.19	19.24	21.77	26.23	22.71	19.04	15.96
Expense Ratio (%)	na	0.68	0.69	0.69	0.68	0.67	0.68	0.69	0.67	0.63
Yield (%)	0.91	1.09	0.85	0.98	0.67	0.58	0.70	0.84	1.14	1.46
Portfolio Turnover (%)	na	97	95	100	79	79	86	89	161	131
Total Assets (Millions $)	1,959	1,548	1,194	988	1,477	1,912	2,317	2,019	771	274

PORTFOLIO (as of 9/30/05)

Portfolio Manager: Team Managed - 1991

Investment Style
- ✔ Large Cap ✔ Growth
- Mid Cap   Value
- Small Cap Grth/Val

Portfolio
0.6% cash	0.0% corp bonds
99.4% stocks	0.0% gov't bonds
0.0% pref/conv't pref	0.0% muni bonds
0.0% conv't bds/wrnts	0.0% other

SHAREHOLDER INFORMATION

Minimum Investment
Initial: $2,500   Subsequent: $50

Minimum IRA Investment
Initial: $2,500   Subsequent: $50

Maximum Fees
Load: none   12b-1: none
Other: none

Services
- ✔ IRA
- ✔ Keogh
- ✔ Telephone Exchange

Amer Century Inc & Grth Inv (BIGRX)

800-345-2021
www.americancentury.com

Large-Cap Stock

PERFORMANCE

fund inception date: 12/17/90

	3yr Annual	5yr Annual	10yr Annual	Bull	Bear
Return (%)	15.3	2.5	9.8	60.3	-37.1
Differ From Category (+/-)	0.4 av	1.7 abv av	1.2 abv av	1.6 av	-1.2 abv av

Standard Deviation	Category Risk Index	Beta
9.8%—av	0.95—av	1.05

	2005	2004	2003	2002	2001	2000	1999	1998	1997	1996
Return (%)	4.7	12.9	29.6	-19.3	-8.3	-10.5	17.9	27.6	34.4	24.1
Differ From Category (+/-)	-1.5	2.1	0.1	2.2	3.1	-7.3	-8.6	3.4	7.2	2.9
Return, Tax-Adjusted (%)	3.9	12.6	29.3	-19.8	-8.7	-10.8	17.4	26.0	31.4	20.9

PER SHARE DATA

	2005	2004	2003	2002	2001	2000	1999	1998	1997	1996
Dividends, Net Income ($)	0.59	0.59	0.43	0.33	0.30	0.29	0.33	0.35	0.39	0.44
Distrib'ns, Cap Gain ($)	1.22	0.00	0.00	0.00	0.00	0.00	0.07	1.30	2.29	1.44
Net Asset Value ($)	30.33	30.67	27.70	21.74	27.35	30.19	34.05	29.25	24.30	20.16
Expense Ratio (%)	na	0.68	0.69	0.69	0.68	0.67	0.68	0.69	0.65	0.62
Yield (%)	1.87	1.91	1.54	1.50	1.11	0.95	0.97	1.14	1.45	2.03
Portfolio Turnover (%)	na	74	67	67	61	64	58	86	102	92
Total Assets (Millions $)	3,665	3,972	3,820	3,147	4,475	5,417	6,347	4,285	1,790	715

PORTFOLIO (as of 9/30/05)

Portfolio Manager: Team Managed - 1990

Investment Style
✔ Large Cap   Growth
   Mid Cap   Value
   Small Cap   ✔ Grth/Val

Portfolio
   0.3% cash   0.0% corp bonds
   99.6% stocks   0.0% gov't bonds
   0.1% pref/conv't pref   0.0% muni bonds
   0.0% conv't bds/wrnts   0.0% other

SHAREHOLDER INFORMATION

Minimum Investment
Initial: $2,500   Subsequent: $50

Minimum IRA Investment
Initial: $2,500   Subsequent: $50

Maximum Fees
Load: none   12b-1: none
Other: none

Services
✔ IRA
✔ Keogh
✔ Telephone Exchange

Brandywine Blue
(BLUEX)

Large-Cap Stock

800-656-3017
www.brandywinefunds.com

fund inception date: 1/10/91

PERFORMANCE

	3yr Annual	5yr Annual	10yr Annual	Bull	Bear
Return (%)	18.7	2.2	10.0	70.8	-40.4
Differ From Category (+/-)	3.8 high	1.4 abv av	1.4 abv av	12.1 high	-4.5 av

Standard Deviation	Category Risk Index	Beta
12.5%—abv av	1.21—high	1.08

	2005	2004	2003	2002	2001	2000	1999	1998	1997	1996
Return (%)	8.3	19.2	29.3	-13.4	-22.8	6.8	49.3	-0.9	19.2	23.2
Differ From Category (+/-)	.2.1	8.4	-0.2	8.1	-11.4	10.1	22.8	-25.2	-8.0	2.0
Return, Tax-Adjusted (%)	7.7	19.2	29.3	-13.4	-22.8	0.9	47.6	-1.3	15.4	23.2

PER SHARE DATA

	2005	2004	2003	2002	2001	2000	1999	1998	1997	1996
Dividends, Net Income ($)	0.00	0.00	0.00	0.00	0.00	0.00	0.00	0.20	0.00	0.00
Distrib'ns, Cap Gain ($)	1.14	0.00	0.00	0.00	0.00	10.71	2.18	0.13	5.09	0.00
Net Asset Value ($)	29.58	28.41	23.82	18.41	21.28	27.57	36.24	25.91	26.58	26.47
Expense Ratio (%)	1.13	1.09	1.14	1.13	1.09	1.07	1.08	1.06	1.08	1.13
Yield (%)	0.00	0.00	0.00	0.00	0.00	0.00	0.00	0.78	0.00	0.00
Portfolio Turnover (%)	181	279	300	311	244	245	228	299	202	196
Total Assets (Millions $)	1,352	662	379	240	257	388	399	357	590	383

PORTFOLIO (as of 9/30/05)

Portfolio Manager: Team Managed - 1991

Investment Style
✔ Large Cap   Growth
✔ Mid Cap   Value
   Small Cap   ✔ Grth/Val

Portfolio
2.7% cash
96.5% stocks
0.9% pref/conv't pref
0.0% conv't bds/wrnts

0.0% corp bonds
0.0% gov't bonds
0.0% muni bonds
0.0% other

SHAREHOLDER INFORMATION

Minimum Investment
Initial: $10,000   Subsequent: $1,000

Minimum IRA Investment
Initial: $10,000   Subsequent: $1,000

Maximum Fees
Load: none   12b-1: none
Other: none

Services
✔ IRA
✔ Keogh
✔ Telephone Exchange

Excelsior Value & Restructuring (UMBIX)

800-446-1012
www.excelsiorfunds.com

Large-Cap Stock

PERFORMANCE

fund inception date: 12/31/92

	3yr Annual	5yr Annual	10yr Annual	Bull	Bear
Return (%)	24.7	7.1	14.7	99.4	-27.9
Differ From Category (+/-)	9.8 high	6.3 high	6.1 high	40.7 high	8.0 abv av

Standard Deviation	Category Risk Index	Beta
12.5%—abv av	1.21—high	1.26

	2005	2004	2003	2002	2001	2000	1999	1998	1997	1996
Return (%).	9.9	19.3	47.7	-23.3	-4.9	7.2	41.9	10.3	33.5	25.0
Differ From Category (+/-)	.3.7	8.5	18.2	-1.8	6.5	10.5	15.4	-13.9	6.3	3.8
Return, Tax-Adjusted (%). . .	9.8	19.2	47.6	-23.4	-5.0	6.4	41.8	9.9	32.9	23.6

PER SHARE DATA

	2005	2004	2003	2002	2001	2000	1999	1998	1997	1996
Dividends, Net Income ($).	0.45	0.34	0.23	0.13	0.08	0.59	0.09	0.11	0.09	0.12
Distrib'ns, Cap Gain ($) . . .	0.00	0.00	0.00	0.00	0.00	0.00	0.00	0.14	0.27	0.47
Net Asset Value ($)	46.18	42.43	35.86	24.46	32.06	33.82	32.14	22.71	20.82	15.87
Expense Ratio (%).	1.08	0.99	0.99	0.94	0.95	0.90	0.93	0.89	0.91	0.91
Yield (%)	0.97	0.79	0.63	0.54	0.25	1.75	0.26	0.49	0.44	0.76
Portfolio Turnover (%)	8	4	16	8	15	20	43	30	62	56
Total Assets (Millions $) .	5,284	4,360	2,827	1,682	2,221	1,731	964	597	230	111

PORTFOLIO (as of 6/30/05)

Portfolio Manager: D Williams/
J McDermott/T Evnin - 1992

Investment Style
✔ Large Cap   Growth
✔ Mid Cap   ✔ Value
  Small Cap   Grth/Val

Portfolio
0.7% cash	0.0% corp bonds
96.6% stocks	0.0% gov't bonds
2.2% pref/conv't pref	0.0% muni bonds
0.0% conv't bds/wrnts	0.6% other

SHAREHOLDER INFORMATION

Minimum Investment
Initial: $500   Subsequent: $50

Minimum IRA Investment
Initial: $250   Subsequent: $50

Maximum Fees
Load: none   12b-1: none
Other: none

Services
✔ IRA
✔ Keogh
✔ Telephone Exchange

Fidelity Asset Manager Aggressive (FAMRX)

Large-Cap Stock

800-544-8544
www.fidelity.com

PERFORMANCE

fund inception date: 9/24/99

	3yr Annual	5yr Annual	10yr Annual	Bull	Bear
Return (%)	21.0	-0.6	na	75.3	-49.2
Differ From Category (+/-)	6.1 high	-1.4 blw av	na	16.6 high	-13.3 blw av

Standard Deviation	Category Risk Index	Beta
11.2%—av	1.09—high	1.09

	2005	2004	2003	2002	2001	2000	1999	1998	1997	1996
Return (%)	7.3	11.0	48.6	-34.9	-15.7	15.4	—	—	—	—
Differ From Category (+/-)	1.1	0.2	19.1	-13.4	-4.3	18.7	—	—	—	—
Return, Tax-Adjusted (%)	7.2	10.9	48.5	-35.2	-16.3	14.0	—	—	—	—

PER SHARE DATA

	2005	2004	2003	2002	2001	2000	1999	1998	1997	1996
Dividends, Net Income ($)	0.06	0.06	0.06	0.07	0.22	0.13	—	—	—	—
Distrib'ns, Cap Gain ($)	0.00	0.00	0.00	0.00	0.00	0.60	—	—	—	—
Net Asset Value ($)	12.08	11.31	10.24	6.93	10.76	13.03	—	—	—	—
Expense Ratio (%)	0.92	0.91	1.00	0.88	0.85	0.90	—	—	—	—
Yield (%)	0.49	0.53	0.58	1.01	2.04	0.95	—	—	—	—
Portfolio Turnover (%)	71	86	131	280	255	338	—	—	—	—
Total Assets (Millions $)	418	399	318	148	288	443	—	—	—	—

PORTFOLIO (as of 9/30/05)

Portfolio Manager: Habermann/Arani/Conti - 2005

Investment Style

✔ Large Cap	✔ Growth
Mid Cap	Value
Small Cap	Grth/Val

Portfolio

4.9% cash	6.4% corp bonds
83.9% stocks	0.0% gov't bonds
0.0% pref/conv't pref	0.0% muni bonds
0.0% conv't bds/wrnts	4.8% other

SHAREHOLDER INFORMATION

Minimum Investment
Initial: $2,500   Subsequent: $250

Minimum IRA Investment
Initial: $500   Subsequent: $250

Maximum Fees
Load: none   12b-1: none
Other: maint fee for low bal

Services
✔ IRA
✔ Keogh
✔ Telephone Exchange

Fidelity Capital Appreciation
(FDCAX)

Large-Cap Stock

800-544-8544
www.fidelity.com

PERFORMANCE

fund inception date: 11/26/86

	3yr Annual	5yr Annual	10yr Annual	Bull	Bear
Return (%)	21.3	5.3	10.2	78.0	-43.8
Differ From Category (+/-)	6.4 high	4.5 high	1.6 abv av	19.3 high	-7.9 blw av

Standard Deviation	Category Risk Index	Beta
12.1%—abv av	1.17—high	1.18

	2005	2004	2003	2002	2001	2000	1999	1998	1997	1996
Return (%)	5.8	11.2	51.6	-21.2	-7.5	-18.1	45.8	16.9	26.5	15.1
Differ From Category (+/-)	-0.4	0.4	22.1	0.3	3.9	-14.8	19.3	-7.3	-0.7	-6.1
Return, Tax-Adjusted (%)	4.3	10.5	51.6	-21.2	-7.5	-19.7	43.4	16.2	23.1	12.2

PER SHARE DATA

	2005	2004	2003	2002	2001	2000	1999	1998	1997	1996
Dividends, Net Income ($)	0.00	0.01	0.01	0.00	0.00	0.15	0.57	0.10	0.08	0.12
Distrib'ns, Cap Gain ($)	2.46	1.21	0.02	0.00	0.00	2.13	1.49	0.45	2.85	1.54
Net Asset Value ($)	25.10	26.03	24.51	16.18	20.55	22.23	29.87	22.07	19.38	17.64
Expense Ratio (%)	na	0.91	0.88	1.03	0.91	0.83	0.65	0.67	0.66	0.80
Yield (%)	0.00	0.03	0.04	0.00	0.00	0.61	1.81	0.44	0.35	0.62
Portfolio Turnover (%)	109	72	54	80	120	85	78	121	176	205
Total Assets (Millions $)	7,316	6,452	4,466	1,796	2,311	2,707	3,686	2,602	2,110	1,642

PORTFOLIO (as of 7/29/05)

Portfolio Manager: Fergus Shiel - 2005

Investment Style
- ✔ Large Cap Growth
- ✔ Mid Cap Value
-   Small Cap ✔ Grth/Val

Portfolio
1.6% cash	0.0% corp bonds
98.4% stocks	0.0% gov't bonds
0.0% pref/conv't pref	0.0% muni bonds
0.1% conv't bds/wrnts	0.0% other

SHAREHOLDER INFORMATION

Minimum Investment
Initial: $2,500   Subsequent: $250

Minimum IRA Investment
Initial: $500   Subsequent: $250

Maximum Fees
Load: none   12b-1: none
Other: maint fee for low bal

Services
- ✔ IRA
- ✔ Keogh
- ✔ Telephone Exchange

Fidelity Contra
(FCNTX)
Large-Cap Stock

800-544-8544
www.fidelity.com

PERFORMANCE
fund inception date: 5/17/67

	3yr Annual	5yr Annual	10yr Annual	Bull	Bear
Return (%)	19.6	6.2	12.0	78.7	-33.2
Differ From Category (+/-)	4.7 high	5.4 high	3.4 high	20.0 high	2.7 abv av

Standard Deviation	Category Risk Index	Beta
9.1%—av	0.88—blw av	0.86

	2005	2004	2003	2002	2001	2000	1999	1998	1997	1996
Return (%)	16.2	15.0	27.9	-9.6	-12.5	-6.8	25.0	31.5	23.0	21.9
Differ From Category (+/-)	10.0	4.2	-1.6	11.9	-1.1	-3.5	-1.5	7.3	-4.2	0.7
Return, Tax-Adjusted (%)	15.9	15.0	27.9	-9.6	-12.7	-9.1	21.2	29.5	20.5	19.0

PER SHARE DATA

	2005	2004	2003	2002	2001	2000	1999	1998	1997	1996
Dividends, Net Income ($)	0.23	0.05	0.04	0.05	0.22	0.24	0.28	0.30	0.35	0.38
Distrib'ns, Cap Gain ($)	0.97	0.00	0.00	0.00	0.00	6.62	10.22	4.22	4.56	3.45
Net Asset Value ($)	64.76	56.74	49.35	38.60	42.77	49.18	60.02	56.81	46.63	42.15
Expense Ratio (%)	na	0.94	0.98	0.99	0.91	0.84	0.62	0.61	0.67	0.79
Yield (%)	0.34	0.07	0.08	0.12	0.51	0.43	0.39	0.49	0.68	0.83
Portfolio Turnover (%)	na	64	67	80	154	166	177	197	144	159
Total Assets (Millions $)	60,094	44,484	36,051	27,695	32,321	40,285	46,927	38,821	30,809	23,798

PORTFOLIO (as of 9/30/05)

Portfolio Manager: William Danoff - 1990

Investment Style
- ✓ Large Cap   ✓ Growth
- ✓ Mid Cap   Value
- Small Cap   Grth/Val

Portfolio
9.8% cash	0.1% corp bonds
89.6% stocks	0.5% gov't bonds
0.0% pref/conv't pref	0.0% muni bonds
0.1% conv't bds/wrnts	0.0% other

SHAREHOLDER INFORMATION

Minimum Investment
Initial: $2,500   Subsequent: $250

Minimum IRA Investment
Initial: $500   Subsequent: $250

Maximum Fees
Load: none   12b-1: none
Other: maint fee for low bal

Services
- ✓ IRA
- ✓ Keogh
- ✓ Telephone Exchange

Fidelity Disciplined Equity
(FDEQX)
Large-Cap Stock

800-544-8544
www.fidelity.com

PERFORMANCE

fund inception date: 12/28/88

	3yr Annual	5yr Annual	10yr Annual	Bull	Bear
Return (%)	16.2	1.8	9.2	62.2	-37.6
Differ From Category (+/-)	1.3 abv av	1.0 abv av	0.6 abv av	3.5 abv av	-1.7 av

Standard Deviation	Category Risk Index	Beta
9.2%—av	0.89—blw av	0.95

	2005	2004	2003	2002	2001	2000	1999	1998	1997	1996
Return (%)	10.2	12.0	27.1	-18.5	-14.2	-3.4	22.4	21.8	33.3	15.1
Differ From Category (+/-)	.4.0	1.2	-2.4	3.0	-2.8	-0.2	-4.1	-2.4	6.1	-6.1
Return, Tax-Adjusted (%)	10.1	11.9	27.0	-18.6	-14.2	-6.0	18.7	20.0	29.8	12.6

PER SHARE DATA

	2005	2004	2003	2002	2001	2000	1999	1998	1997	1996
Dividends, Net Income ($)	0.18	0.18	0.11	0.03	0.05	0.16	0.27	0.22	0.25	0.23
Distrib'ns, Cap Gain ($)	0.00	0.00	0.00	0.00	0.00	3.57	4.90	1.82	3.30	1.49
Net Asset Value ($)	27.71	25.29	22.74	17.97	22.10	25.82	30.51	29.32	25.86	22.04
Expense Ratio (%)	na	0.90	0.90	1.00	0.84	0.79	0.62	0.64	0.69	0.81
Yield (%)	0.64	0.71	0.48	0.16	0.22	0.54	0.76	0.70	0.85	0.97
Portfolio Turnover (%)	na	64	64	68	101	118	113	125	127	297
Total Assets (Millions $)	6,104	4,951	3,987	2,752	2,992	3,393	3,614	3,145	2,557	2,099

PORTFOLIO (as of 7/29/05)

Portfolio Manager: Steven Snider - 2000

Investment Style
- ✔ Large Cap
- ✔ Mid Cap
- Small Cap
- ✔ Growth
- Value
- Grth/Val

Portfolio
- 2.5% cash
- 97.5% stocks
- 0.0% pref/conv't pref
- 0.0% conv't bds/wrnts
- 0.0% corp bonds
- 0.0% gov't bonds
- 0.0% muni bonds
- 0.0% other

SHAREHOLDER INFORMATION

Minimum Investment
Initial: $2,500   Subsequent: $250

Minimum IRA Investment
Initial: $500   Subsequent: $250

Maximum Fees
Load: none   12b-1: none
Other: maint fee for low bal

Services
- ✔ IRA
- ✔ Keogh
- ✔ Telephone Exchange

Fidelity Equity Income

800-544-8544
www.fidelity.com

(FEQIX)

Large-Cap Stock

PERFORMANCE
fund inception date: 5/16/66

	3yr Annual	5yr Annual	10yr Annual	Bull	Bear
Return (%)	15.2	3.7	9.5	62.1	-17.5
Differ From Category (+/-)	0.3 av	2.9 abv av	0.9 abv av	3.4 abv av	18.4 high

Standard Deviation	Category Risk Index	Beta
10.3%—av	1.00—abv av	1.10

	2005	2004	2003	2002	2001	2000	1999	1998	1997	1996
Return (%)...............	5.7	11.2	29.9	-17.1	-5.0	8.5	7.1	12.5	29.9	21.0
Differ From Category (+/-)	-0.5	0.4	0.4	4.4	6.4	11.8	-19.4	-11.7	2.7	-0.2
Return, Tax-Adjusted (%)...	4.8	10.5	29.3	-17.7	-6.0	6.6	4.7	10.9	28.1	18.5

PER SHARE DATA

	2005	2004	2003	2002	2001	2000	1999	1998	1997	1996
Dividends, Net Income ($).	0.84	0.81	0.71	0.68	0.76	0.87	0.81	0.85	0.96	1.02
Distrib'ns, Cap Gain ($) ...	2.13	1.66	0.93	0.14	1.18	3.32	5.14	2.39	2.04	1.84
Net Asset Value ($)	52.78	52.78	49.75	39.67	48.77	53.43	53.48	55.55	52.41	42.83
Expense Ratio (%)........	0.70	0.70	0.71	0.67	0.67	0.67	0.67	0.65	0.66	0.67
Yield (%)	1.52	1.48	1.40	1.70	1.52	1.53	1.37	1.46	1.76	2.28
Portfolio Turnover (%)	19	25	23	23	25	26	30	23	30	39
Total Assets (Millions $) .	26,058	26,372	23,520	17,734	21,832	22,353	22,829	23,707	21,178	14,259

PORTFOLIO (as of 7/29/05)

Portfolio Manager: Stephen Petersen - 1993

Investment Style

✔ Large Cap	Growth
Mid Cap	✔ Value
Small Cap	Grth/Val

Portfolio

0.2% cash	0.1% corp bonds
98.6% stocks	0.0% gov't bonds
0.7% pref/conv't pref	0.0% muni bonds
0.4% conv't bds/wrnts	0.0% other

SHAREHOLDER INFORMATION

Minimum Investment

Initial: $2,500   Subsequent: $250

Minimum IRA Investment

Initial: $500   Subsequent: $250

Maximum Fees

Load: none   12b-1: none

Other: maint fee for low bal

Services

✔ IRA

✔ Keogh

✔ Telephone Exchange

Fidelity Equity Income II
(FEQTX)

Large-Cap Stock

800-544-8544
www.fidelity.com

fund inception date: 8/21/90

	3yr Annual	5yr Annual	10yr Annual	Bull	Bear
Return (%)	15.0	3.6	9.5	59.2	-18.7
Differ From Category (+/-)	0.1 av	2.8 abv av	0.9 abv av	0.5 av	17.2 high

Standard Deviation	Category Risk Index	Beta
10.9%—av	1.06—abv av	1.15

	2005	2004	2003	2002	2001	2000	1999	1998	1997	1996
Return (%).	4.6	9.8	32.6	-15.4	-7.1	7.4	4.3	22.9	27.1	18.7
Differ From Category (+/-)	-1.6	-1.0	3.1	6.1	4.3	10.7	-22.2	-1.3	-0.1	-2.5
Return, Tax-Adjusted (%) . . .	3.2	9.2	32.3	-16.0	-8.3	3.2	1.5	20.5	24.2	16.2

PER SHARE DATA

	2005	2004	2003	2002	2001	2000	1999	1998	1997	1996
Dividends, Net Income ($).	0.34	0.37	0.24	0.24	0.33	0.42	0.36	0.33	0.43	0.51
Distrib'ns, Cap Gain ($) . . .	1.91	0.61	0.00	0.21	0.79	4.98	3.50	2.65	2.63	1.14
Net Asset Value ($)	22.86	24.01	22.78	17.39	21.03	23.86	27.37	30.01	27.01	23.75
Expense Ratio (%).	na	0.68	0.64	0.63	0.62	0.63	0.66	0.66	0.68	0.72
Yield (%)	1.37	1.50	1.05	1.36	1.51	1.45	1.16	1.01	1.45	2.04
Portfolio Turnover (%)	na	123	131	135	136	151	71	62	77	46
Total Assets (Millions $) .	12,122	12,915	12,256	9,401	12,212	13,915	17,580	19,454	16,977	15,238

PORTFOLIO (as of 8/31/05)

Portfolio Manager: Stephen Dufour - 2000

Investment Style

✔ Large Cap	Growth
Mid Cap	✔ Value
Small Cap	Grth/Val

Portfolio

0.6%	cash	0.0%	corp bonds
99.4%	stocks	0.0%	gov't bonds
0.0%	pref/conv't pref	0.0%	muni bonds
0.0%	conv't bds/wrnts	0.0%	other

SHAREHOLDER INFORMATION

Minimum Investment
Initial: $2,500   Subsequent: $250

Minimum IRA Investment
Initial: $500   Subsequent: $250

Maximum Fees
Load: none   12b-1: none
Other: maint fee for low bal

Services
✔ IRA
✔ Keogh
✔ Telephone Exchange

Fidelity Export & Multinational (FEXPX)

800-544-8544
www.fidelity.com

Large-Cap Stock

PERFORMANCE

fund inception date: 10/4/94

	3yr Annual	5yr Annual	10yr Annual	Bull	Bear
Return (%)	20.2	7.3	15.7	80.7	-22.1
Differ From Category (+/-)	5.3 high	6.5 high	7.1 high	22.0 high	13.8 abv av

Standard Deviation	Category Risk Index	Beta
10.5%—av	1.02—abv av	1.10

	2005	2004	2003	2002	2001	2000	1999	1998	1997	1996
Return (%)	15.2	13.5	32.6	-18.6	0.7	1.4	41.8	22.4	23.6	38.6
Differ From Category (+/-)	.9.0	2.7	3.1	2.9	12.2	4.7	15.3	-1.8	-3.6	17.4
Return, Tax-Adjusted (%)	14.2	12.8	32.5	-18.7	0.6	-3.4	36.8	21.5	19.1	36.7

PER SHARE DATA

	2005	2004	2003	2002	2001	2000	1999	1998	1997	1996
Dividends, Net Income ($)	0.06	0.11	0.07	0.05	0.03	0.10	0.05	0.00	0.00	0.00
Distrib'ns, Cap Gain ($)	1.30	0.82	0.00	0.00	0.00	5.21	4.80	0.77	3.79	0.86
Net Asset Value ($)	21.24	19.64	18.16	13.75	16.97	16.88	21.97	19.88	17.02	16.75
Expense Ratio (%)	0.85	0.83	0.84	0.78	0.81	0.86	0.86	0.93	0.98	1.03
Yield (%)	0.26	0.53	0.38	0.36	0.17	0.45	0.18	0.00	0.00	0.00
Portfolio Turnover (%)	68	96	129	228	170	380	265	281	429	313
Total Assets (Millions $)	4,173	1,643	1,042	675	673	495	514	412	465	398

PORTFOLIO (as of 8/31/05)

Portfolio Manager: Victor Thay - 2005

Investment Style

✔ Large Cap   Growth
✔ Mid Cap   Value
   Small Cap   ✔ Grth/Val

Portfolio

1.9% cash	0.0% corp bonds
98.1% stocks	0.0% gov't bonds
0.0% pref/conv't pref	0.0% muni bonds
0.0% conv't bds/wrnts	0.0% other

SHAREHOLDER INFORMATION

Minimum Investment
Initial: $2,500   Subsequent: $250

Minimum IRA Investment
Initial: $500   Subsequent: $250

Maximum Fees
Load: 0.75% redemption   12b-1: none
Other: redemption fee applies for 1 month

Services
✔ IRA
✔ Keogh
✔ Telephone Exchange

Fidelity Growth Company
(FDGRX)
Large-Cap Stock

800-544-8544
www.fidelity.com

Fidelity
tultinational (FEXPX)
arge-Cap Stock

PERFORMANCE   fund inception date: 1/17/83

	3yr Annual	5yr Annual	10yr Annual	Bull	Bear
Return (%)	21.6	-2.3	10.2	84.4	-61.7
Differ From Category (+/-)	6.7 high	-3.1 low	1.6 high	25.7 high	-25.8 low

Standard Deviation	Category Risk Index	Beta
13.0%—abv av	1.26—high	1.23

	2005	2004	2003	2002	2001	2000	1999	1998	1997	1996
Return (%)	13.5	12.1	41.3	-33.4	-25.3	-6.3	79.4	27.2	18.9	16.8
Differ From Category (+/-)	.7.3	1.3	11.8	-11.9	-13.9	-3.1	52.9	3.0	-8.3	-4.4
Return, Tax-Adjusted (%)	13.4	12.0	41.3	-33.4	-25.3	-8.0	77.0	25.4	16.5	15.2

PER SHARE DATA

	2005	2004	2003	2002	2001	2000	1999	1998	1997	1996
Dividends, Net Income ($)	0.01	0.07	0.00	0.00	0.00	0.00	0.00	0.09	0.22	0.28
Distrib'ns, Cap Gain ($)	0.00	0.00	0.00	0.00	0.16	7.50	6.29	3.73	4.35	1.60
Net Asset Value ($)	63.63	56.07	50.07	35.42	53.22	71.43	84.30	51.02	43.32	40.46
Expense Ratio (%)	0.84	0.82	0.83	1.08	0.95	0.85	0.74	0.65	0.71	0.85
Yield (%)	0.01	0.12	0.00	0.00	0.00	0.00	0.00	0.16	0.46	0.66
Portfolio Turnover (%)	49	49	47	63	93	69	86	76	93	78
Total Assets (Millions $)	27,415	25,180	22,609	14,798	22,742	30,397	24,337	11,440	10,509	9,273

PORTFOLIO (as of 8/31/05)

Portfolio Manager: Steven Wymer - 1997

Investment Style
✔ Large Cap   ✔ Growth
✔ Mid Cap   Value
✔ Small Cap   Grth/Val

Portfolio
0.4% cash	0.0% corp bonds
99.3% stocks	0.0% gov't bonds
0.3% pref/conv't pref	0.0% muni bonds
0.0% conv't bds/wrnts	0.0% other

SHAREHOLDER INFORMATION

Minimum Investment
Initial: $2,500   Subsequent: $250

Minimum IRA Investment
Initial: $500   Subsequent: $250

Maximum Fees
Load: none   12b-1: none
Other: maint fee for low bal

Services
✔ IRA
✔ Keogh
✔ Telephone Exchange

Fidelity Independence

(FDFFX)

Large-Cap Stock

800-544-8544
www.fidelity.com

PERFORMANCE   fund inception date: 3/24/83

	3yr Annual	5yr Annual	10yr Annual	Bull	Bear
Return (%)	15.1	-1.4	9.3	57.9	-48.7
Differ From Category (+/-)	0.2 av	-2.2 blw av	0.7 abv av	-0.8 av	-12.8 blw av

Standard Deviation	Category Risk Index	Beta
12.1%—abv av	1.17—high	1.20

	2005	2004	2003	2002	2001	2000	1999	1998	1997	1996
Return (%)..............	10.5	11.6	23.6	-15.8	-27.2	1.7	47.0	35.8	18.5	8.3
Differ From Category (+/-)	.4.3	0.8	-5.9	5.7	-15.8	5.0	20.5	11.6	-8.7	-12.9
Return, Tax-Adjusted (%)..	10.4	11.5	23.5	-16.3	-27.6	-1.6	43.3	33.0	14.2	4.4

PER SHARE DATA

	2005	2004	2003	2002	2001	2000	1999	1998	1997	1996
Dividends, Net Income ($).	0.06	0.10	0.10	0.21	0.20	0.08	0.05	0.14	0.13	0.26
Distrib'ns, Cap Gain ($) ...	0.00	0.00	0.00	0.00	0.06	4.19	3.66	2.13	3.41	2.15
Net Asset Value ($)	19.65	17.83	16.06	13.07	15.77	22.01	25.85	20.51	16.85	17.29
Expense Ratio (%).........	na	0.71	0.55	0.97	0.92	0.85	0.58	0.62	0.64	0.70
Yield (%)	0.30	0.56	0.62	1.60	1.26	0.30	0.16	0.61	0.64	1.33
Portfolio Turnover (%)	na	119	166	191	187	249	310	266	205	230
Total Assets (Millions $)..	4,742	4,705	4,726	4,240	5,486	8,474	7,268	4,946	3,932	4,046

PORTFOLIO (as of 8/31/05)

Portfolio Manager: Jason Weiner - 2003

Investment Style

° Large Cap	Growth
° Mid Cap	Value
° Small Cap	✔ Grth/Val

Portfolio

0.4%	cash	0.0%	corp bonds
99.6%	stocks	0.0%	gov't bonds
0.0%	pref/conv't pref	0.0%	muni bonds
0.0%	conv't bds/wrnts	0.0%	other

SHAREHOLDER INFORMATION

Minimum Investment

Initial: $2,500   Subsequent: $250

Minimum IRA Investment

Initial: $500   Subsequent: $250

Maximum Fees

Load: none   12b-1: none
Other: maint fee for low bal

Services

✔ IRA
✔ Keogh
✔ Telephone Exchange

Fidelity Large Cap Value

800-544-8544
www.fidelity.com

(FSLVX)

Large-Cap Stock

PERFORMANCE   fund inception date: 11/15/01

	3yr Annual	5yr Annual	10yr Annual	Bull	Bear
Return (%)	18.1	na	na	75.2	na
Differ From Category (+/-)	3.2 high	na	na	16.5 high	na

Standard Deviation	Category Risk Index	Beta
9.8%—av	0.95—av	1.01

	2005	2004	2003	2002	2001	2000	1999	1998	1997	1996
Return (%)............	11.2	17.7	25.9	-17.1	—	—	—	—	—	—
Differ From Category (+/-)	.5.0	6.9	-3.6	4.4	—	—	—	—	—	—
Return, Tax-Adjusted (%)..	10.6	17.5	25.7	-17.4	—	—	—	—	—	—

PER SHARE DATA

	2005	2004	2003	2002	2001	2000	1999	1998	1997	1996
Dividends, Net Income ($).	0.11	0.05	0.09	0.08	—	—	—	—	—	—
Distrib'ns, Cap Gain ($) ...	0.35	0.11	0.00	0.00	—	—	—	—	—	—
Net Asset Value ($)	13.13	12.22	10.52	8.43	—	—	—	—	—	—
Expense Ratio (%)........	1.06	1.18	1.19	1.20	—	—	—	—	—	—
Yield (%)	0.81	0.40	0.85	0.94	—	—	—	—	—	—
Portfolio Turnover (%)	170	72	95	81	—	—	—	—	—	—
Total Assets (Millions $)...	516	162	24	16	—	—	—	—	—	—

PORTFOLIO (as of 7/29/05)

Portfolio Manager: Bruce Dirks - 2005

Investment Style
✔ Large Cap	Growth
Mid Cap	✔ Value
Small Cap	Grth/Val

Portfolio
0.7% cash	0.0% corp bonds
96.8% stocks	0.0% gov't bonds
0.0% pref/conv't pref	0.0% muni bonds
0.0% conv't bds/wrnts	2.6% other

SHAREHOLDER INFORMATION

Minimum Investment
Initial: $2,500   Subsequent: $250

Minimum IRA Investment
Initial: $500   Subsequent: $250

Maximum Fees
Load: 0.75% redemption   12b-1: none
Other: redemption fee applies for 1 month;
maint fee for low bal

Services
✔ IRA
   Keogh
✔ Telephone Exchange

Fidelity OTC
(FOCPX)
Large-Cap Stock

800-544-8544
www.fidelity.com

	3yr Annual	5yr Annual	10yr Annual	Bull	Bear
Return (%)	16.9	-1.5	8.4	68.8	-65.2
Differ From Category (+/-)	2.0 abv av	-2.3 blw av	-0.2 av	10.1 high	-29.3 low

Standard Deviation	Category Risk Index	Beta
14.4%—high	1.40—high	1.35

	2005	2004	2003	2002	2001	2000	1999	1998	1997	1996
Return (%)	8.9	8.1	35.8	-23.2	-24.0	-26.8	72.5	40.3	9.9	23.7
Differ From Category (+/-)	.2.7	-2.7	6.3	-1.7	-12.6	-23.6	46.0	16.1	-17.3	2.5
Return, Tax-Adjusted (%)	8.9	7.9	35.8	-23.2	-24.0	-30.5	70.0	38.9	8.3	19.6

PER SHARE DATA

	2005	2004	2003	2002	2001	2000	1999	1998	1997	1996
Dividends, Net Income ($)	0.00	0.41	0.00	0.00	0.00	0.00	0.00	0.00	0.00	0.08
Distrib'ns, Cap Gain ($)	0.00	0.00	0.00	0.00	0.00	12.66	5.51	2.38	2.52	4.32
Net Asset Value ($)	37.79	34.69	32.47	23.91	31.17	41.05	67.97	43.63	33.45	32.71
Expense Ratio (%)	0.81	0.89	1.12	1.09	0.94	0.76	0.74	0.75	0.84	0.82
Yield (%)	0.00	1.18	0.00	0.00	0.00	0.00	0.00	0.00	0.00	0.21
Portfolio Turnover (%)	117	61	116	120	219	196	117	125	147	133
Total Assets (Millions $)	8,168	8,143	7,940	5,974	8,070	10,979	11,705	5,476	3,858	3,387

PORTFOLIO (as of 7/29/05)

Portfolio Manager: Shep Perkins - 2003

Investment Style
- ✔ Large Cap   ✔ Growth
- ✔ Mid Cap   Value
- ✔ Small Cap   Grth/Val

Portfolio
1.3% cash	0.0% corp bonds
98.7% stocks	0.0% gov't bonds
0.0% pref/conv't pref	0.0% muni bonds
0.0% conv't bds/wrnts	0.0% other

SHAREHOLDER INFORMATION

Minimum Investment
Initial: $2,500   Subsequent: $100

Minimum IRA Investment
Initial: $500   Subsequent: $100

Maximum Fees
Load: none   12b-1: none
Other: maint fee for low bal

Services
- ✔ IRA
- ✔ Keogh
- ✔ Telephone Exchange

FMI Large Cap
(FMIHX)

Large-Cap Stock

800-811-5311
www.fiduciarymgt.com

PERFORMANCE

fund inception date: 12/31/01

	3yr Annual	5yr Annual	10yr Annual	Bull	Bear
Return (%)	19.0	na	na	76.5	na
Differ From Category (+/-)	4.1 high	na	na	17.8 high	na

Standard Deviation	Category Risk Index	Beta
9.3%—av	0.90—blw av	0.89

	2005	2004	2003	2002	2001	2000	1999	1998	1997	1996
Return (%)	9.1	17.5	31.5	-15.0	—	—	—	—	—	—
Differ From Category (+/-)	2.9	6.7	2.0	6.6	—	—	—	—	—	—
Return, Tax-Adjusted (%)	8.6	17.1	31.2	-15.0	—	—	—	—	—	—

PER SHARE DATA

	2005	2004	2003	2002	2001	2000	1999	1998	1997	1996
Dividends, Net Income ($)	0.03	0.07	0.03	0.00	—	—	—	—	—	—
Distrib'ns, Cap Gain ($)	0.37	0.20	0.13	0.00	—	—	—	—	—	—
Net Asset Value ($)	13.39	12.66	11.02	8.50	—	—	—	—	—	—
Expense Ratio (%)	1.00	1.13	1.34	1.75	—	—	—	—	—	—
Yield (%)	0.24	0.56	0.24	0.00	—	—	—	—	—	—
Portfolio Turnover (%)	40	38	54	32	—	—	—	—	—	—
Total Assets (Millions $)	96	21	6	4	—	—	—	—	—	—

PORTFOLIO (as of 9/30/05)

Portfolio Manager: Ted Kellner/Patrick English - 2001

Investment Style

✔ Large Cap   Growth
   Mid Cap   Value
   Small Cap   ✔ Grth/Val

Portfolio

11.9% cash	0.0% corp bonds
88.2% stocks	0.0% gov't bonds
0.0% pref/conv't pref	0.0% muni bonds
0.0% conv't bds/wrnts	0.0% other

SHAREHOLDER INFORMATION

Minimum Investment
Initial: $1,000   Subsequent: $100

Minimum IRA Investment
Initial: $1,000   Subsequent: $100

Maximum Fees
Load: none   12b-1: none
Other: none

Services
✔ IRA
✔ Keogh
✔ Telephone Exchange

Gabelli Asset AAA
(GABAX)

Large-Cap Stock

800-422-3554
www.gabelli.com

	3yr Annual	5yr Annual	10yr Annual	Bull	Bear
Return (%)	16.6	6.4	12.0	68.8	-21.3
Differ From Category (+/-)	1.7 abv av	5.6 high	3.4 high	10.1 high	14.6 abv av

Standard Deviation	Category Risk Index	Beta
10.6%—av	1.03—abv av	1.10

	2005	2004	2003	2002	2001	2000	1999	1998	1997	1996
Return (%).............	4.4	16.4	30.5	-14.2	0.1	-2.3	28.4	15.9	38.0	13.3
Differ From Category (+/-)	-1.8	5.6	1.0	7.3	11.6	0.9	1.9	-8.3	10.8	-7.9
Return, Tax-Adjusted (%)...	3.6	16.1	30.2	-14.2	-0.4	-5.3	25.8	15.0	34.5	10.2

PER SHARE DATA

	2005	2004	2003	2002	2001	2000	1999	1998	1997	1996
Dividends, Net Income ($).	0.12	0.03	0.63	0.01	0.00	0.31	0.00	0.02	0.07	0.15
Distrib'ns, Cap Gain ($) ...	2.04	0.76	0.00	0.00	0.98	5.57	4.63	1.40	4.54	2.62
Net Asset Value ($)	41.13	41.45	36.26	28.25	32.97	33.90	40.84	35.47	31.85	26.42
Expense Ratio (%).........	na	1.38	1.38	1.38	1.36	1.36	1.37	1.36	1.37	1.34
Yield (%)	0.27	0.05	1.72	0.04	0.00	0.77	0.00	0.05	0.19	0.52
Portfolio Turnover (%)	na	7	7	8	15	48	32	21	22	14
Total Assets (Millions $)..	2,318	2,218	1,960	1,503	1,911	1,909	1,994	1,594	1,334	1,082

PORTFOLIO (as of 9/30/05)

Portfolio Manager: Mario Gabelli - 1986

Investment Style
✓ Large Cap   Growth
✓ Mid Cap   ✓ Value
   Small Cap   Grth/Val

Portfolio

0.0% cash	0.3% corp bonds
98.2% stocks	1.1% gov't bonds
0.2% pref/conv't pref	0.0% muni bonds
0.1% conv't bds/wrnts	0.2% other

SHAREHOLDER INFORMATION

Minimum Investment
Initial: $1,000   Subsequent: $1

Minimum IRA Investment
Initial: $250   Subsequent: $1

Maximum Fees
Load: none   12b-1: 0.25%
Other: none

Services
✓ IRA
   Keogh
✓ Telephone Exchange

ICAP Equity
(ICAEX)

Large-Cap Stock

888-221-4227
www.icapfunds.com

PERFORMANCE

fund inception date: 1/3/95

	3yr Annual	5yr Annual	10yr Annual	Bull	Bear
Return (%)	16.7	3.5	10.5	61.9	-21.7
Differ From Category (+/-)	1.8 abv av	2.7 abv av	1.9 high	3.2 abv av	14.2 abv av

Standard Deviation	Category Risk Index	Beta
8.2%—blw av	0.80—low	0.85

	2005	2004	2003	2002	2001	2000	1999	1998	1997	1996
Return (%)	10.9	11.3	28.8	-24.6	-0.6	7.8	16.2	11.4	29.0	26.2
Differ From Category (+/-)	.4.7	0.5	-0.7	-3.1	10.8	11.1	-10.3	-12.8	1.8	5.0
Return, Tax-Adjusted (%)	8.3	10.7	28.6	-24.9	-0.9	6.3	15.1	10.8	25.6	24.3

PER SHARE DATA

	2005	2004	2003	2002	2001	2000	1999	1998	1997	1996
Dividends, Net Income ($)	0.64	0.72	0.37	0.36	0.37	0.48	0.51	0.50	0.38	0.30
Distrib'ns, Cap Gain ($)	7.01	0.76	0.00	0.00	0.00	2.35	1.24	0.00	4.60	1.37
Net Asset Value ($)	41.17	44.01	40.89	32.07	43.01	43.66	43.14	38.63	35.12	31.16
Expense Ratio (%)	na	0.80	0.80	0.80	0.80	0.80	0.80	0.80	0.80	0.80
Yield (%)	1.33	1.59	0.90	1.13	0.86	1.05	1.15	1.29	0.95	0.91
Portfolio Turnover (%)	na	74	97	85	87	116	118	133	121	125
Total Assets (Millions $)	799	948	1,079	877	1,189	1,050	960	717	371	149

PORTFOLIO (as of 11/30/05)

Portfolio Manager: Team Managed - 1995

Investment Style
✔ Large Cap   Growth
  Mid Cap   Value
  Small Cap ✔ Grth/Val

Portfolio
2.6% cash	0.0% corp bonds
97.4% stocks	0.0% gov't bonds
0.0% pref/conv't pref	0.0% muni bonds
0.0% conv't bds/wrnts	0.0% other

SHAREHOLDER INFORMATION

Minimum Investment
Initial: $1,000   Subsequent: $1,000

Minimum IRA Investment
Initial: $1   Subsequent: $1

Maximum Fees
Load: none   12b-1: none
Other: none

Services
✔ IRA
✔ Keogh
✔ Telephone Exchange

Janus Contrarian
(JSVAX)

Large-Cap Stock

800-525-3713
www.janus.com

PERFORMANCE   fund inception date: 2/29/00

	3yr Annual	5yr Annual	10yr Annual	Bull	Bear
Return (%)	29.6	7.9	na	122.6	-34.3
Differ From Category (+/-)	14.7 high	7.1 high	na	63.9 high	1.6 abv av

Standard Deviation	Category Risk Index	Beta
13.7%—abv av	1.33—high	1.26

	2005	2004	2003	2002	2001	2000	1999	1998	1997	1996
Return (%)	16.0	22.6	53.2	-23.7	-11.7	—	—	—	—	—
Differ From Category (+/-)	.9.8	11.8	23.7	-2.1	-0.3	—	—	—	—	—
Return, Tax-Adjusted (%)	15.7	22.5	53.2	-23.7	-11.8	—	—	—	—	—

PER SHARE DATA

	2005	2004	2003	2002	2001	2000	1999	1998	1997	1996
Dividends, Net Income ($)	0.04	0.03	0.00	0.01	0.02	—	—	—	—	—
Distrib'ns, Cap Gain ($)	0.18	0.00	0.00	0.00	0.00	—	—	—	—	—
Net Asset Value ($)	15.14	13.24	10.82	7.06	9.26	—	—	—	—	—
Expense Ratio (%)	0.97	0.98	1.01	0.98	0.91	—	—	—	—	—
Yield (%)	0.24	0.19	0.00	0.08	0.25	—	—	—	—	—
Portfolio Turnover (%)	42	30	44	60	77	—	—	—	—	—
Total Assets (Millions $)	3,042	2,775	2,618	1,267	2,079	—	—	—	—	—

PORTFOLIO (as of 7/29/05)

Portfolio Manager: D Decker/M Ankrum - 2000

Investment Style

✔ Large Cap	Growth
Mid Cap	✔ Value
Small Cap	Grth/Val

Portfolio

0.3% cash	0.0% corp bonds
99.7% stocks	0.0% gov't bonds
0.0% pref/conv't pref	0.0% muni bonds
0.0% conv't bds/wrnts	0.0% other

SHAREHOLDER INFORMATION

Minimum Investment
Initial: $2,500   Subsequent: $100

Minimum IRA Investment
Initial: $500   Subsequent: $100

Maximum Fees
Load: none   12b-1: none
Other: none

Services
✔ IRA
✔ Keogh
✔ Telephone Exchange

Janus Core Equity
(JAEIX)

Large-Cap Stock

800-525-3713
www.janus.com

Janus Growth & Income

800-525-3713
www.janus.com

(JAGIX)

Large-Cap Stock

PERFORMANCE   fund inception date: 5/15/91

	3yr Annual	5yr Annual	10yr Annual	Bull	Bear
Return (%)	16.1	1.0	12.4	62.3	-47.2
Differ From Category (+/-)	1.2 abv av	0.2 av	3.8 high	3.6 abv av	-11.3 blw av

Standard Deviation	Category Risk Index	Beta
9.9%—av	0.96—av	0.98

	2005	2004	2003	2002	2001	2000	1999	1998	1997	1996
Return (%)	12.4	11.8	24.6	-21.5	-14.3	-11.4	51.1	34.8	34.6	26.0
Differ From Category (+/-)	.6.2	1.0	-4.9	0.0	-2.9	-8.2	24.6	10.6	7.4	4.8
Return, Tax-Adjusted (%)	12.3	11.8	24.5	-21.7	-14.6	-12.3	49.7	32.9	32.0	22.6

PER SHARE DATA

	2005	2004	2003	2002	2001	2000	1999	1998	1997	1996
Dividends, Net Income ($)	0.19	0.15	0.16	0.20	0.30	0.23	0.10	0.08	0.07	0.12
Distrib'ns, Cap Gain ($)	0.00	0.00	0.00	0.00	0.00	1.62	1.84	2.02	2.38	1.87
Net Asset Value ($)	36.01	32.19	28.91	23.34	29.97	35.35	41.94	29.10	23.15	19.05
Expense Ratio (%)	0.90	0.92	0.91	0.88	0.86	0.88	0.90	0.94	0.96	1.03
Yield (%)	0.51	0.46	0.55	0.83	1.00	0.62	0.22	0.25	0.27	0.55
Portfolio Turnover (%)	41	41	50	49	59	41	43	95	127	153
Total Assets (Millions $)	6,022	5,616	5,977	5,277	7,148	8,349	7,493	3,504	2,005	1,101

PORTFOLIO (as of 7/29/05)

Portfolio Manager: Minyoung Sohn - 2004

Investment Style

✔ Large Cap   ✔ Growth
  Mid Cap   Value
  Small Cap   Grth/Val

Portfolio

1.9% cash	0.0% corp bonds
95.1% stocks	0.0% gov't bonds
2.6% pref/conv't pref	0.0% muni bonds
0.5% conv't bds/wrnts	0.0% other

SHAREHOLDER INFORMATION

Minimum Investment
Initial: $2,500   Subsequent: $100

Minimum IRA Investment
Initial: $500   Subsequent: $100

Maximum Fees
Load: none   12b-1: none
Other: none

Services
✔ IRA
✔ Keogh
✔ Telephone Exchange

Janus Olympus
(JAOLX)

Large-Cap Stock

800-525-3713
www.janus.com

PERFORMANCE

fund inception date: 12/29/95

	3yr Annual	5yr Annual	10yr Annual	Bull	Bear
Return (%)	17.8	-4.5	11.7	67.6	-66.4
Differ From Category (+/-)	2.9 high	-5.3 low	3.1 high	8.9 abv av	-30.5 low

Standard Deviation	Category Risk Index	Beta
11.1%—av	1.08—abv av	1.04

	2005	2004	2003	2002	2001	2000	1999	1998	1997	1996
Return (%).	14.2	8.7	31.6	-28.1	-32.0	-21.6	100.1	56.9	26.7	21.7
Differ From Category (+/-)	.8.0	-2.1	2.1	-6.6	-20.6	-18.4	73.6	32.7	-0.5	0.5
Return, Tax-Adjusted (%) . .	14.2	8.7	31.6	-28.1	-32.1	-21.9	98.8	56.9	25.6	21.3

PER SHARE DATA

	2005	2004	2003	2002	2001	2000	1999	1998	1997	1996
Dividends, Net Income ($)	.0.01	0.00	0.00	0.00	0.11	0.23	0.01	0.01	0.04	0.13
Distrib'ns, Cap Gain ($) . .	.0.00	0.00	0.00	0.00	0.00	0.39	1.78	0.00	0.71	0.00
Net Asset Value ($)	32.69	28.63	26.33	20.00	27.85	41.15	53.26	27.58	17.58	14.48
Expense Ratio (%).	1.02	1.03	0.98	0.91	0.89	0.90	0.93	0.98	1.03	1.17
Yield (%)	0.02	0.00	0.00	0.00	0.38	0.55	0.02	0.04	0.21	0.89
Portfolio Turnover (%)	76	76	84	90	118	96	91	123	244	303
Total Assets (Millions $) . .	2,334	2,465	2,778	2,024	3,437	6,165	6,174	1,288	629	413

PORTFOLIO (as of 7/29/05)

Portfolio Manager: C Young/B Demain - 1997

Investment Style
- ✔ Large Cap ✔ Growth
- ✔ Mid Cap Value
- ✔ Small Cap Grth/Val

Portfolio

2.2% cash	0.2% corp bonds
97.6% stocks	0.0% gov't bonds
0.0% pref/conv't pref	0.0% muni bonds
0.0% conv't bds/wrnts	0.0% other

SHAREHOLDER INFORMATION

Minimum Investment
Initial: $2,500   Subsequent: $100

Minimum IRA Investment
Initial: $500   Subsequent: $100

Maximum Fees
Load: none   12b-1: none
Other: none

Services
- ✔ IRA
- ✔ Keogh
- ✔ Telephone Exchange

Mairs & Power Growth
(MPGFX)

Large-Cap Stock

800-304-7404
www.mairsandpower.com

	3yr Annual	5yr Annual	10yr Annual	Bull	Bear
Return (%)	15.8	8.7	13.8	61.0	18.7
Differ From Category (+/-)	0.9 abv av	7.9 high	5.2 high	2.3 abv av	54.6 high

Standard Deviation	Category Risk Index	Beta
8.4%—blw av	0.82—low	0.84

	2005	2004	2003	2002	2001	2000	1999	1998	1997	1996
Return (%)	4.3	17.9	26.3	-8.1	6.4	26.4	7.1	9.3	28.6	26.4
Differ From Category (+/-)	-1.9	7.1	-3.2	13.4	17.9	29.7	-19.4	-14.9	1.4	5.2
Return, Tax-Adjusted (%)	4.0	17.6	25.9	-8.5	5.8	23.9	5.5	8.7	27.6	25.2

PER SHARE DATA

	2005	2004	2003	2002	2001	2000	1999	1998	1997	1996
Dividends, Net Income ($)	0.78	0.68	0.53	0.45	0.71	1.09	0.93	0.72	0.78	0.71
Distrib'ns, Cap Gain ($)	0.93	0.82	0.77	0.24	2.00	9.64	5.48	1.36	1.91	1.39
Net Asset Value ($)	71.69	70.33	60.90	49.26	54.36	106.82	92.91	92.68	86.67	69.48
Expense Ratio (%)	na	0.73	0.75	0.78	0.76	0.78	0.79	0.82	0.84	0.89
Yield (%)	1.07	0.95	0.85	0.90	1.25	0.93	0.94	0.76	0.88	1.00
Portfolio Turnover (%)	na	3	2	1	8	15	5	2	5	3
Total Assets (Millions $)	2,523	2,056	1,307	772	677	582	547	580	413	150

PORTFOLIO (as of 9/30/05)

Portfolio Manager: George Mairs/William Frels - 1980

Investment Style

✔ Large Cap   Growth
✔ Mid Cap   ✔ Value
   Small Cap   Grth/Val

Portfolio

2.9% cash	0.0% corp bonds
97.1% stocks	0.0% gov't bonds
0.0% pref/conv't pref	0.0% muni bonds
0.0% conv't bds/wrnts	0.0% other

SHAREHOLDER INFORMATION

Minimum Investment
Initial: $2,500   Subsequent: $100

Minimum IRA Investment
Initial: $1,000   Subsequent: $100

Maximum Fees
Load: none   12b-1: none
Other: none

Services
✔ IRA
   Keogh
   Telephone Exchange

Marsico 21st Century
(MXXIX)
Large-Cap Stock

888-860-8686
www.marsicofunds.com

PERFORMANCE

fund inception date: 1/31/00

	3yr Annual	5yr Annual	10yr Annual	Bull	Bear
Return (%)	25.2	7.1	na	102.6	-50.1
Differ From Category (+/-)	10.3 high	6.3 high	na	43.9 high	-14.2 blw av

Standard Deviation	Category Risk Index	Beta
14.2%—abv av	1.38—high	1.32

	2005	2004	2003	2002	2001	2000	1999	1998	1997	1996
Return (%).	7.8	22.3	48.7	-10.4	-19.8	—	—	—	—	—
Differ From Category (+/-)	.1.6	11.5	19.2	11.1	-8.3	—	—	—	—	—
Return, Tax-Adjusted (%) . . .	7.8	22.3	48.7	-10.4	-19.8	—	—	—	—	—

PER SHARE DATA

	2005	2004	2003	2002	2001	2000	1999	1998	1997	1996
Dividends, Net Income ($) .	0.00	0.00	0.00	0.00	0.00	—	—	—	—	—
Distrib'ns, Cap Gain ($) . . .	0.00	0.00	0.00	0.00	0.00	—	—	—	—	—
Net Asset Value ($)	12.95	12.01	9.82	6.60	7.37	—	—	—	—	—
Expense Ratio (%).	1.39	1.50	1.55	1.60	1.50	—	—	—	—	—
Yield (%)	0.01	0.00	0.00	0.00	0.00	—	—	—	—	—
Portfolio Turnover (%)	175	191	236	388	399	—	—	—	—	—
Total Assets (Millions $) . . .	442	323	162	54	69	—	—	—	—	—

PORTFOLIO (as of 8/31/05)

Portfolio Manager: James Hillary - 2000

Investment Style
✔ Large Cap ✔ Growth
Mid Cap   Value
Small Cap Grth/Val

Portfolio
6.5% cash	0.0% corp bonds
93.5% stocks	0.0% gov't bonds
0.0% pref/conv't pref	0.0% muni bonds
0.0% conv't bds/wrnts	-0.1% other

SHAREHOLDER INFORMATION

Minimum Investment
Initial: $2,500   Subsequent: $100

Minimum IRA Investment
Initial: $1,000   Subsequent: $100

Maximum Fees
Load: 2.00% redemption   12b-1: 0.25%
Other: redemption fee applies for 1 month

Services
✔ IRA
✔ Keogh
✔ Telephone Exchange

Marsico Focus
(MFOCX)

Large-Cap Stock

888-860-8686
www.marsicofunds.com

PERFORMANCE   fund inception date: 12/31/97

	3yr Annual	5yr Annual	10yr Annual	Bull	Bear
Return (%)	17.1	1.1	na	65.7	-47.5
Differ From Category (+/-)	2.2 abv av	0.3 av	na	7.0 abv av	-11.6 blw av

Standard Deviation	Category Risk Index	Beta
10.8%—av	1.05—abv av	1.02

	2005	2004	2003	2002	2001	2000	1999	1998	1997	1996
Return (%)	9.6	11.7	31.2	-16.6	-20.8	-17.9	55.2	51.3	—	—
Differ From Category (+/-)	.3.4	0.9	1.7	4.9	-9.4	-14.7	28.7	27.1	—	—
Return, Tax-Adjusted (%)	9.6	11.7	31.2	-16.6	-20.8	-19.5	55.2	51.3	—	—

PER SHARE DATA

	2005	2004	2003	2002	2001	2000	1999	1998	1997	1996
Dividends, Net Income ($)	0.00	0.00	0.00	0.00	0.00	0.00	0.00	0.00	—	—
Distrib'ns, Cap Gain ($)	0.00	0.00	0.00	0.00	0.04	1.96	0.04	0.00	—	—
Net Asset Value ($)	18.22	16.61	14.87	11.33	13.60	17.23	23.45	15.13	—	—
Expense Ratio (%)	1.30	1.30	1.34	1.35	1.30	1.27	1.31	1.56	—	—
Yield (%)	0.00	0.00	0.00	0.00	0.00	0.00	0.00	0.00	—	—
Portfolio Turnover (%)	84	84	90	117	127	176	173	170	—	—
Total Assets (Millions $)	4,066	3,237	2,641	1,349	1,401	2,325	3,257	1,204	—	—

PORTFOLIO (as of 8/31/05)

Portfolio Manager: Thomas Marsico - 1997

Investment Style
- ✔ Large Cap ✔ Growth
- ✔ Mid Cap   Value
- ✔ Small Cap   Grth/Val

Portfolio

5.3% cash	0.0% corp bonds
94.7% stocks	0.0% gov't bonds
0.0% pref/conv't pref	0.0% muni bonds
0.0% conv't bds/wrnts	0.0% other

SHAREHOLDER INFORMATION

Minimum Investment
Initial: $2,500   Subsequent: $100

Minimum IRA Investment
Initial: $1,000   Subsequent: $100

Maximum Fees
Load: 2.00% redemption   12b-1: 0.25%
Other: redemption fee applies for 1 month

Services
- ✔ IRA
- ✔ Keogh
- ✔ Telephone Exchange

Marsico Growth
(MGRIX)

Large-Cap Stock

888-860-8686
www.marsicofunds.com

PERFORMANCE   fund inception date: 12/31/97

	3yr Annual	5yr Annual	10yr Annual	Bull	Bear
Return (%)	17.2	1.3	na	67.3	-47.7
Differ From Category (+/-)	2.3 abv av	0.5 av	na	8.6 abv av	-11.8 blw av

Standard Deviation	Category Risk Index	Beta
10.3%—av	1.00—abv av	0.98

	2005	2004	2003	2002	2001	2000	1999	1998	1997	1996
Return (%).	6.7	14.3	31.9	-16.7	-20.3	-15.8	53.3	43.4	—	—
Differ From Category (+/-)	.0.5	3.5	2.4	4.8	-8.9	-12.6	26.8	19.2	—	—
Return, Tax-Adjusted (%). . .	6.7	14.3	31.9	-16.7	-20.3	-16.4	53.1	43.4	—	—

PER SHARE DATA

	2005	2004	2003	2002	2001	2000	1999	1998	1997	1996
Dividends, Net Income ($).	0.00	0.00	0.00	0.00	0.00	0.00	0.00	0.00	—	—
Distrib'ns, Cap Gain ($) . . .	0.00	0.00	0.00	0.00	0.02	0.70	0.11	0.00	—	—
Net Asset Value ($)	18.85	17.66	15.44	11.70	14.06	17.67	21.86	14.34	—	—
Expense Ratio (%).	1.30	1.30	1.38	1.37	1.33	1.30	1.43	1.78	—	—
Yield (%)	0.00	0.00	0.00	0.00	0.00	0.00	0.00	0.00	—	—
Portfolio Turnover (%)	73	73	91	111	120	137	137	141	—	—
Total Assets (Millions $) . .	2,278	1,637	1,019	622	604	830	1,048	374	—	—

PORTFOLIO (as of 8/31/05)

Portfolio Manager: Thomas Marsico - 1997

Investment Style
✔ Large Cap   ✔ Growth
✔ Mid Cap   Value
   Small Cap   Grth/Val

Portfolio
4.9% cash	0.0% corp bonds
95.1% stocks	0.0% gov't bonds
0.0% pref/conv't pref	0.0% muni bonds
0.0% conv't bds/wrnts	0.0% other

SHAREHOLDER INFORMATION

Minimum Investment
Initial: $2,500   Subsequent: $100

Minimum IRA Investment
Initial: $1,000   Subsequent: $100

Maximum Fees
Load: 2.00% redemption   12b-1: 0.25%
Other: redemption fee applies for 1 month

Services
✔ IRA
✔ Keogh
✔ Telephone Exchange

Masters Select Value

(MSVFX)

Large-Cap Stock

800-656-8864
www.mastersfunds.com

fund inception date: 6/30/00

PERFORMANCE

	3yr Annual	5yr Annual	10yr Annual	Bull	Bear
Return (%)	16.5	8.2	na	70.0	na
Differ From Category (+/-)	1.6 abv av	7.4 high	na	11.3 high	na

Standard Deviation	Category Risk Index	Beta
11.7%—abv av	1.14—high	1.18

	2005	2004	2003	2002	2001	2000	1999	1998	1997	1996
Return (%)	4.1	14.7	32.4	-14.1	9.6	—	—	—	—	—
Differ From Category (+/-)	-2.1	3.9	2.9	7.4	21.1	—	—	—	—	—
Return, Tax-Adjusted (%)	3.2	14.7	32.4	-14.1	9.5	—	—	—	—	—

PER SHARE DATA

	2005	2004	2003	2002	2001	2000	1999	1998	1997	1996
Dividends, Net Income ($)	0.06	0.00	0.00	0.00	0.00	—	—	—	—	—
Distrib'ns, Cap Gain ($)	0.84	0.00	0.00	0.00	0.03	—	—	—	—	—
Net Asset Value ($)	14.60	14.90	12.99	9.81	11.43	—	—	—	—	—
Expense Ratio (%)	na	1.23	1.28	1.29	1.35	—	—	—	—	—
Yield (%)	0.36	0.00	0.00	0.00	0.00	—	—	—	—	—
Portfolio Turnover (%)	na	29	22	54	33	—	—	—	—	—
Total Assets (Millions $)	338	306	181	138	160	—	—	—	—	—

PORTFOLIO (as of 9/30/05)

Portfolio Manager: Team Managed - 2000

Investment Style

✔ Large Cap   Growth
Mid Cap   Value
Small Cap   ✔ Grth/Val

Portfolio

2.6% cash	0.5% corp bonds
96.1% stocks	0.0% gov't bonds
0.0% pref/conv't pref	0.0% muni bonds
0.7% conv't bds/wrnts	0.0% other

SHAREHOLDER INFORMATION

Minimum Investment
Initial: $5,000   Subsequent: $250

Minimum IRA Investment
Initial: $1,000   Subsequent: $250

Maximum Fees
Load: 2.00% redemption   12b-1: none
Other: redemption fee applies for 6 months

Services
✔ IRA
✔ Keogh
✔ Telephone Exchange

Neuberger Berman Partners Inv (NPRTX)

800-366-6264
www.nb.com

Large-Cap Stock

PERFORMANCE

fund inception date: 1/20/75

	3yr Annual	5yr Annual	10yr Annual	Bull	Bear
Return (%)	24.1	6.8	10.1	95.5	-28.6
Differ From Category (+/-)	9.2 high	6.0 high	1.5 abv av	36.8 high	7.3 abv av

Standard Deviation	Category Risk Index	Beta
12.5%—abv av	1.21—high	1.21

	2005	2004	2003	2002	2001	2000	1999	1998	1997	1996
Return (%).............	17.9	19.2	35.8	-24.8	-3.0	0.5	7.8	6.2	29.2	26.4
Differ From Category (+/-)	11.7	8.4	6.3	-3.3	8.4	3.8	-18.7	-18.0	2.0	5.2
Return, Tax-Adjusted (%)..	17.0	19.0	35.8	-24.8	-3.5	-1.3	4.9	4.4	24.2	22.7

PER SHARE DATA

	2005	2004	2003	2002	2001	2000	1999	1998	1997	1996
Dividends, Net Income ($).	0.27	0.17	0.01	0.03	0.08	0.17	0.29	0.00	0.19	0.22
Distrib'ns, Cap Gain ($) ...	1.31	0.00	0.00	0.00	0.38	1.93	3.10	2.41	5.84	2.61
Net Asset Value ($)	28.05	25.09	21.19	15.60	20.79	21.93	24.00	25.50	26.30	25.19
Expense Ratio (%).........	na	0.88	0.90	0.87	0.84	0.84	0.82	0.80	0.81	0.84
Yield (%)	0.91	0.67	0.02	0.19	0.37	0.71	1.07	0.00	0.59	0.79
Portfolio Turnover (%)	na	61	65	53	73	95	132	109	77	96
Total Assets (Millions $)..	1,995	1,456	1,327	1,083	1,666	1,991	2,668	3,250	3,230	2,218

PORTFOLIO (as of 11/30/05)

Portfolio Manager: S Basu Mullick - 1998

Investment Style
- ✔ Large Cap   Growth
- ✔ Mid Cap   ✔ Value
-    Small Cap   Grth/Val

Portfolio
3.0% cash	0.0% corp bonds
97.0% stocks	0.0% gov't bonds
0.0% pref/conv't pref	0.0% muni bonds
0.0% conv't bds/wrnts	0.0% other

SHAREHOLDER INFORMATION

Minimum Investment
Initial: $1,000   Subsequent: $100

Minimum IRA Investment
Initial: $250   Subsequent: $100

Maximum Fees
Load: none   12b-1: none
Other: none

Services
- ✔ IRA
- ✔ Keogh
- ✔ Telephone Exchange

Neuberger Berman Soc Responsive Inv (NBSRX)

800-366-6264
www.nb.com

Large-Cap Stock

PERFORMANCE

fund inception date: 3/16/94

	3yr Annual	5yr Annual	10yr Annual	Bull	Bear
Return (%)	18.0	6.4	9.4	64.6	-16.1
Differ From Category (+/-)	3.1 high	5.6 high	0.8 abv av	5.9 abv av	19.8 high

Standard Deviation	Category Risk Index	Beta
10.0%—av	0.97—av	0.98

	2005	2004	2003	2002	2001	2000	1999	1998	1997	1996
Return (%)	7.5	13.5	34.4	-14.4	-2.5	-0.4	7.0	15.0	24.4	18.5
Differ From Category (+/-)	1.3	2.7	4.9	7.1	8.9	2.8	-19.5	-9.2	-2.8	-2.7
Return, Tax-Adjusted (%)	6.9	13.1	33.5	-14.5	-4.3	-0.4	6.1	13.8	23.7	17.5

PER SHARE DATA

	2005	2004	2003	2002	2001	2000	1999	1998	1997	1996
Dividends, Net Income ($)	0.14	0.03	0.05	0.03	0.06	0.00	0.02	0.07	0.03	0.03
Distrib'ns, Cap Gain ($)	0.71	0.51	0.87	0.00	1.72	0.00	0.87	0.88	0.40	0.42
Net Asset Value ($)	22.71	21.89	19.76	15.40	18.04	20.39	20.48	20.00	18.24	15.02
Expense Ratio (%)	na	1.07	1.08	1.17	1.13	1.12	1.10	1.10	1.48	1.50
Yield (%)	0.60	0.14	0.24	0.21	0.30	0.00	0.09	0.33	0.16	0.19
Portfolio Turnover (%)	na	21	62	60	83	76	53	47	51	53
Total Assets (Millions $)	362	261	133	73	85	100	120	106	71	43

PORTFOLIO (as of 11/30/05)

Portfolio Manager: Moretti/Dyott/Ladiwala - 2001

Investment Style
✔ Large Cap   Growth
   Mid Cap   Value
   Small Cap   ✔ Grth/Val

Portfolio
3.7% cash	0.0% corp bonds
96.3% stocks	0.0% gov't bonds
0.0% pref/conv't pref	0.0% muni bonds
0.0% conv't bds/wrnts	0.0% other

SHAREHOLDER INFORMATION

Minimum Investment
Initial: $1,000   Subsequent: $100

Minimum IRA Investment
Initial: $250   Subsequent: $100

Maximum Fees
Load: none   12b-1: none
Other: none

Services
✔ IRA
✔ Keogh
✔ Telephone Exchange

Nicholas
(NICSX)

Large-Cap Stock

800-227-5987
www.nicholasfunds.com

PERFORMANCE

fund inception date: 7/14/69

	3yr Annual	5yr Annual	10yr Annual	Bull	Bear
Return (%)	14.9	1.1	6.9	61.5	-38.1
Differ From Category (+/-)	0.0 av	0.3 av	-1.7 blw av	2.8 abv av	-2.2 av

Standard Deviation	Category Risk Index	Beta
9.8%—av	0.95—av	0.94

	2005	2004	2003	2002	2001	2000	1999	1998	1997	1996
Return (%)	5.6	11.8	28.6	-21.8	-10.9	-1.4	1.7	13.1	37.0	19.7
Differ From Category (+/-)	-0.6	1.0	-0.9	-0.3	0.5	1.8	-24.8	-11.1	9.8	-1.5
Return, Tax-Adjusted (%)	4.2	11.6	28.6	-21.9	-11.1	-6.3	0.1	10.8	35.0	16.9

PER SHARE DATA

	2005	2004	2003	2002	2001	2000	1999	1998	1997	1996
Dividends, Net Income ($)	0.25	0.07	0.09	0.16	0.24	0.19	0.31	0.59	0.38	0.56
Distrib'ns, Cap Gain ($)	5.32	0.41	0.00	0.00	0.00	19.25	5.94	8.27	5.78	5.17
Net Asset Value ($)	58.20	60.42	54.47	42.41	54.47	61.45	81.15	85.82	83.80	65.94
Expense Ratio (%)	0.75	0.73	0.75	0.73	0.72	0.73	0.71	0.71	0.72	0.74
Yield (%)	0.39	0.11	0.16	0.37	0.43	0.23	0.35	0.62	0.42	0.79
Portfolio Turnover (%)	21	18	33	39	40	39	25	17	15	26
Total Assets (Millions $)	2,450	2,504	2,452	2,139	3,140	4,088	5,154	5,823	5,257	3,984

PORTFOLIO (as of 11/30/05)

Portfolio Manager: Albert Nicholas/David
Nicholas - 1969

Investment Style

✔ Large Cap   Growth
✔ Mid Cap   Value
   Small Cap   ✔ Grth/Val

Portfolio

10.8%	cash	0.0% corp bonds
87.8%	stocks	0.0% gov't bonds
0.0%	pref/conv't pref	0.0% muni bonds
0.0%	conv't bds/wrnts	1.4% other

SHAREHOLDER INFORMATION

Minimum Investment
Initial: $500   Subsequent: $100

Minimum IRA Investment
Initial: $500   Subsequent: $100

Maximum Fees
Load: none   12b-1: none
Other: none

Services
✔ IRA
✔ Keogh
✔ Telephone Exchange

Oakmark Select I
(OAKLX)
Large-Cap Stock

800-625-6275
www.oakmark.com

	3yr Annual	5yr Annual	10yr Annual	Bull	Bear
Return (%)	14.0	10.3	na	51.1	25.0
Differ From Category (+/-)	-0.9 av	9.5 high	na	-7.6 blw av	60.9 high

Standard Deviation	Category Risk Index	Beta
8.9%—blw av	0.86—low	0.79

	2005	2004	2003	2002	2001	2000	1999	1998	1997	1996
Return (%)	4.8	9.7	29.0	-12.4	26.0	25.8	14.4	16.2	55.0	—
Differ From Category (+/-)	-1.4	-1.1	-0.5	9.1	37.5	29.1	-12.1	-8.0	27.8	—
Return, Tax-Adjusted (%)	3.9	9.6	28.9	-12.5	25.9	24.1	10.2	15.2	54.7	—

PER SHARE DATA

	2005	2004	2003	2002	2001	2000	1999	1998	1997	1996
Dividends, Net Income ($)	0.29	0.24	0.10	0.02	0.05	0.09	0.20	0.05	0.00	—
Distrib'ns, Cap Gain ($)	1.79	0.00	0.00	0.00	0.00	1.36	3.72	0.71	0.17	—
Net Asset Value ($)	32.90	33.35	30.62	23.82	27.24	21.65	18.42	19.54	17.52	—
Expense Ratio (%)	1.00	1.00	1.02	1.07	1.08	1.17	1.16	1.22	1.12	—
Yield (%)	0.84	0.72	0.33	0.09	0.18	0.37	0.89	0.24	0.00	—
Portfolio Turnover (%)	21	14	20	32	21	69	67	56	—	—
Total Assets (Millions $)	6,038	5,712	5,631	4,151	4,684	2,102	1,581	1,391	982	—

PORTFOLIO (as of 6/30/05)

Portfolio Manager: Nygren/Berghoef - 1996

Investment Style
- ✔ Large Cap   Growth
- ✔ Mid Cap   Value
-    Small Cap   ✔ Grth/Val

Portfolio

0.0% cash	0.0% corp bonds
100.0% stocks	0.0% gov't bonds
0.0% pref/conv't pref	0.0% muni bonds
0.0% conv't bds/wrnts	0.0% other

SHAREHOLDER INFORMATION

Minimum Investment
Initial: $1,000   Subsequent: $100

Minimum IRA Investment
Initial: $1,000   Subsequent: $100

Maximum Fees
Load: 2.00% redemption   12b-1: none
Other: redemption fee applies for 3 months

Services
- ✔ IRA
- ✔ Keogh
- ✔ Telephone Exchange

RS Growth
(RSGRX)

Large-Cap Stock

800-766-3863
www.rsim.com

fund inception date: 5/12/92

	3yr Annual	5yr Annual	10yr Annual	Bull	Bear
Return (%)	21.5	0.7	6.9	83.9	-56.1
Differ From Category (+/-)	6.6 high	-0.1 av	-1.7 blw av	25.2 high	-20.2 low

Standard Deviation	Category Risk Index	Beta
12.7%—abv av	1.23—high	1.20

	2005	2004	2003	2002	2001	2000	1999	1998	1997	1996
Return (%).	11.3	11.9	44.2	-27.5	-20.4	-11.0	28.4	27.4	13.8	14.1
Differ From Category (+/-)	.5.1	1.1	14.7	-6.0	-9.0	-7.8	1.9	3.2	-13.4	-7.1
Return, Tax-Adjusted (%). .	.8.8	9.6	43.6	-27.5	-22.4	-12.6	26.3	24.5	10.1	11.9

PER SHARE DATA

	2005	2004	2003	2002	2001	2000	1999	1998	1997	1996
Dividends, Net Income ($).	0.00	0.00	0.00	0.00	0.00	0.00	0.00	0.00	0.00	0.00
Distrib'ns, Cap Gain ($) . .	.2.70	2.64	0.50	0.00	2.54	2.34	2.65	3.34	4.43	1.73
Net Asset Value ($)	15.85	16.66	17.32	12.37	17.07	24.62	30.43	25.92	23.18	24.16
Expense Ratio (%).	na	1.49	1.58	1.62	1.60	1.53	1.59	1.46	1.44	1.51
Yield (%)	0.00	0.00	0.00	0.00	0.00	0.00	0.00	0.00	0.00	0.00
Portfolio Turnover (%)	na	163	262	346	172	71	80	190	228	221
Total Assets (Millions $) . . .	207	218	224	170	297	482	674	678	757	643

PORTFOLIO (as of 9/30/05)

Portfolio Manager: John Wallace - 2001

Investment Style

✔ Large Cap   ✔ Growth
✔ Mid Cap   Value
   Small Cap   Grth/Val

Portfolio

1.2% cash	0.0% corp bonds
98.8% stocks	0.0% gov't bonds
0.0% pref/conv't pref	0.0% muni bonds
0.0% conv't bds/wrnts	0.0% other

SHAREHOLDER INFORMATION

Minimum Investment
Initial: $5,000   Subsequent: $1,000

Minimum IRA Investment
Initial: $1,000   Subsequent: $250

Maximum Fees
Load: none   12b-1: 0.25%
Other: none

Services
✔ IRA
  Keogh
✔ Telephone Exchange

Rydex OTC Inv
(RYOCX)

Large-Cap Stock

800-820-0888
www.rydexfunds.com

PERFORMANCE

fund inception date: 2/14/94

	3yr Annual	5yr Annual	10yr Annual	Bull	Bear
Return (%)	17.5	-8.2	10.2	58.7	-78.3
Differ From Category (+/-)	2.6 high	-9.0 low	1.6 high	0.0 av	-42.4 low

Standard Deviation	Category Risk Index	Beta
15.1%—high	1.47—high	1.37

	2005	2004	2003	2002	2001	2000	1999	1998	1997	1996
Return (%)................	1.3	9.6	46.2	-38.5	-34.6	-37.9	100.6	86.4	21.8	43.4
Differ From Category (+/-)	-4.9	-1.2	16.7	-17.0	-23.2	-34.7	74.1	62.2	-5.4	22.2
Return, Tax-Adjusted (%)...	1.2	9.6	46.2	-38.5	-34.6	-37.9	100.4	86.2	21.7	43.3

PER SHARE DATA

	2005	2004	2003	2002	2001	2000	1999	1998	1997	1996
Dividends, Net Income ($)	0.04	0.00	0.00	0.00	0.00	0.00	0.00	0.00	0.00	0.04
Distrib'ns, Cap Gain ($)...	0.00	0.00	0.00	0.00	0.00	0.17	0.47	0.27	0.10	0.00
Net Asset Value ($).....	11.00	10.89	9.93	6.79	11.05	16.91	82.36	41.36	22.36	18.43
Expense Ratio (%)........	1.20	1.22	1.27	1.08	1.16	1.15	1.15	1.13	1.27	1.33
Yield (%)...............	0.32	0.00	0.00	0.00	0.00	0.00	0.00	0.00	0.00	0.23
Portfolio Turnover (%)....	132	139	180	109	228	385	773	971	1,140	2,578
Total Assets (Millions $)...	975	1,035	940	443	926	1,743	3,010	1,109	206	175

PORTFOLIO (as of 9/30/05)

Portfolio Manager: Team Managed - 1997

Investment Style
✔ Large Cap ✔ Growth
✔ Mid Cap Value
✔ Small Cap Grth/Val

Portfolio
3.4% cash
96.6% stocks
0.0% pref/conv't pref
0.0% conv't bds/wrnts
0.0% corp bonds
0.0% gov't bonds
0.0% muni bonds
0.0% other

SHAREHOLDER INFORMATION

Minimum Investment
Initial: $25,000   Subsequent: $1

Minimum IRA Investment
Initial: $25,000   Subsequent: $1

Maximum Fees
Load: none   12b-1: none
Other: none

Services
✔ IRA
✔ Keogh
✔ Telephone Exchange

Schwab Capital Core Equity (SWANX)

Large-Cap Stock

800-435-4000
www.schwab.com/
schwabfunds

PERFORMANCE

	3yr Annual	5yr Annual	10yr Annual	Bull	Bear
Return (%)	16.7	1.0	na	67.5	-45.7
Differ From Category (+/-)	1.8 abv av	0.2 av	na	8.8 abv av	-9.8 blw av

Standard Deviation	Category Risk Index	Beta
9.6%—av	0.93—av	1.01

	2005	2004	2003	2002	2001	2000	1999	1998	1997	1996
Return (%)	9.4	13.5	28.1	-19.2	-17.8	-7.7	27.7	28.0	31.6	—
Differ From Category (+/-)	.3.2	2.7	-1.4	2.3	-6.4	-4.5	1.2	3.8	4.4	—
Return, Tax-Adjusted (%)	9.3	13.3	28.0	-19.4	-18.0	-9.3	25.8	26.9	28.7	—

PER SHARE DATA

	2005	2004	2003	2002	2001	2000	1999	1998	1997	1996
Dividends, Net Income ($)	0.09	0.16	0.11	0.07	0.08	0.07	0.04	0.09	0.12	—
Distrib'ns, Cap Gain ($)	0.00	0.00	0.00	0.00	0.00	1.44	1.47	0.57	1.33	—
Net Asset Value ($)	16.43	15.10	13.45	10.58	13.20	16.17	19.19	16.22	13.19	—
Expense Ratio (%)	0.88	0.75	0.75	0.75	0.75	0.75	0.75	0.75	0.74	—
Yield (%)	0.55	1.08	0.82	0.70	0.58	0.42	0.21	0.51	0.84	—
Portfolio Turnover (%)	86	86	73	114	106	96	99	115	120	—
Total Assets (Millions $)	643	293	256	180	218	325	361	218	160	—

PORTFOLIO (as of 7/29/05)

Portfolio Manager: J Mortimer/L Mano/
V Hsu - 1997

Investment Style

✔ Large Cap   ✔ Growth
  Mid Cap   Value
  Small Cap   Grth/Val

Portfolio

1.4% cash	0.0% corp bonds
97.6% stocks	0.0% gov't bonds
0.0% pref/conv't pref	0.0% muni bonds
0.0% conv't bds/wrnts	1.0% other

SHAREHOLDER INFORMATION

Minimum Investment
Initial: $2,500   Subsequent: $500

Minimum IRA Investment
Initial: $1,000   Subsequent: $250

Maximum Fees
Load: none   12b-1: none
Other: none

Services
✔ IRA
✔ Keogh
✔ Telephone Exchange

Schwab Inv 1000 Index I

(SNXFX)

Large-Cap Stock

800-435-4000
www.schwab.com/
schwabfunds

PERFORMANCE

fund inception date: 4/2/91

	3yr Annual	5yr Annual	10yr Annual	Bull	Bear
Return (%)	14.8	0.9	9.0	57.7	-41.2
Differ From Category (+/-)	-0.1 av	0.1 av	0.4 av	-1.0 av	-5.3 av

Standard Deviation	Category Risk Index	Beta
9.1%—av	0.88—blw av	1.00

	2005	2004	2003	2002	2001	2000	1999	1998	1997	1996
Return (%)	6.0	10.8	28.7	-21.1	-12.2	-8.2	21.0	27.1	31.9	21.5
Differ From Category (+/-)	-0.2	0.0	-0.8	0.4	-0.8	-5.0	-5.5	2.9	4.7	0.3
Return, Tax-Adjusted (%)	5.8	10.5	28.5	-21.5	-12.5	-8.4	20.6	26.7	31.4	20.9

PER SHARE DATA

	2005	2004	2003	2002	2001	2000	1999	1998	1997	1996
Dividends, Net Income ($)	0.46	0.48	0.34	0.32	0.27	0.24	0.26	0.25	0.26	0.26
Distrib'ns, Cap Gain ($)	0.00	0.00	0.00	0.00	0.00	0.00	0.00	0.00	0.00	0.00
Net Asset Value ($)	36.23	34.59	31.65	24.86	31.95	36.73	40.28	33.51	26.56	20.34
Expense Ratio (%)	0.50	0.50	0.54	0.46	0.46	0.46	0.46	0.46	0.46	0.49
Yield (%)	1.26	1.37	1.08	1.29	0.85	0.65	0.64	0.75	0.99	1.27
Portfolio Turnover (%)	6	5	5	9	8	9	3	2	0	2
Total Assets (Millions $)	4,229	4,524	4,211	3,191	4,163	4,731	5,311	4,184	2,823	1,909

PORTFOLIO (as of 7/29/05)

Portfolio Manager: J Mortimer/L Mano/
T Brown - 1997

Investment Style
✔ Large Cap   Growth
  Mid Cap   Value
  Small Cap   ✔ Grth/Val

Portfolio
  0.1% cash   0.0% corp bonds
 99.6% stocks   0.0% gov't bonds
  0.0% pref/conv't pref   0.0% muni bonds
  0.0% conv't bds/wrnts   0.3% other

SHAREHOLDER INFORMATION

Minimum Investment
Initial: $2,500   Subsequent: $500

Minimum IRA Investment
Initial: $1,000   Subsequent: $100

Maximum Fees
Load: 2.00% redemption   12b-1: none
Other: redemption fee applies for 1 month

Services
✔ IRA
✔ Keogh
✔ Telephone Exchange

Schwab MarketTrack All Equity (SWEGX)

Large-Cap Stock

800-435-4000
www.schwab.com/
schwabfunds

fund inception date: 5/19/98

	3yr Annual	5yr Annual	10yr Annual	Bull	Bear
Return (%)	17.7	2.4	na	73.1	-41.8
Differ From Category (+/-)	2.8 high	1.6 abv av	na	14.4 high	-5.9 av

Standard Deviation	Category Risk Index	Beta
10.6%—av	1.03—abv av	1.13

	2005	2004	2003	2002	2001	2000	1999	1998	1997	1996
Return (%)	6.8	13.9	33.9	-20.4	-13.0	-8.9	25.0	—	—	—
Differ From Category (+/-)	0.6	3.1	4.4	1.1	-1.6	-5.7	-1.5	—	—	—
Return, Tax-Adjusted (%)	6.6	13.8	33.7	-20.8	-13.4	-9.6	24.6	—	—	—

PER SHARE DATA

	2005	2004	2003	2002	2001	2000	1999	1998	1997	1996
Dividends, Net Income ($)	0.13	0.12	0.09	0.09	0.05	0.22	0.05	—	—	—
Distrib'ns, Cap Gain ($)	0.00	0.00	0.00	0.02	0.14	0.01	0.10	—	—	—
Net Asset Value ($)	11.94	11.30	10.02	7.55	9.62	11.29	12.66	—	—	—
Expense Ratio (%)	0.30	0.50	0.50	0.50	0.50	0.56	0.54	—	—	—
Yield (%)	1.11	1.04	0.91	1.12	0.54	1.98	0.42	—	—	—
Portfolio Turnover (%)	49	7	10	15	5	12	6	—	—	—
Total Assets (Millions $)	478	488	458	356	446	438	251	—	—	—

PORTFOLIO (as of 11/30/05)

Portfolio Manager: Team Managed - 2005

Investment Style
- ✔ Large Cap
- Mid Cap
- Small Cap
- Growth
- ✔ Value
- Grth/Val

Portfolio
0.0% cash		0.0% corp bonds
0.0% stocks		0.0% gov't bonds
0.0% pref/conv't pref		0.0% muni bonds
0.0% conv't bds/wrnts		100.0% other

SHAREHOLDER INFORMATION

Minimum Investment
Initial: $1,000   Subsequent: $500

Minimum IRA Investment
Initial: $500   Subsequent: $250

Maximum Fees
Load: 2.00% redemption   12b-1: none
Other: redemption fee applies for 1 month

Services
- ✔ IRA
- ✔ Keogh
- ✔ Telephone Exchange

Sound Shore
(SSHFX)
Large-Cap Stock

800-551-1980
www.soundshorefund.com

PERFORMANCE — fund inception date: 5/3/85

	3yr Annual	5yr Annual	10yr Annual	Bull	Bear
Return (%)	17.5	6.3	11.9	74.8	-10.6
Differ From Category (+/-)	2.6 high	5.5 high	3.3 high	16.1 high	25.3 high

Standard Deviation	Category Risk Index	Beta
11.3%—av	1.10—high	1.12

	2005	2004	2003	2002	2001	2000	1999	1998	1997	1996
Return (%)	6.8	15.3	31.7	-15.4	-0.7	20.1	0.0	3.9	36.4	33.2
Differ From Category (+/-)	0.6	4.5	2.2	6.1	10.7	23.4	-26.5	-20.3	9.2	12.0
Return, Tax-Adjusted (%)	5.7	14.4	31.4	-15.4	-2.5	18.9	-0.1	3.8	35.3	29.3

PER SHARE DATA

	2005	2004	2003	2002	2001	2000	1999	1998	1997	1996
Dividends, Net Income ($)	0.07	0.10	0.05	0.05	0.10	0.14	0.17	0.08	0.12	0.13
Distrib'ns, Cap Gain ($)	2.51	1.85	0.44	0.00	2.77	1.56	0.00	0.00	0.89	2.35
Net Asset Value ($)	36.63	36.70	33.51	25.81	30.58	33.70	29.47	29.62	28.57	21.71
Expense Ratio (%)	na	0.98	0.98	0.98	0.98	0.98	0.98	0.99	1.08	1.15
Yield (%)	0.17	0.26	0.14	0.19	0.30	0.40	0.57	0.27	0.42	0.52
Portfolio Turnover (%)	na	50	62	72	104	98	41	44	53	69
Total Assets (Millions $)	2,265	1,698	1,016	759	1,051	1,052	1,184	1,965	1,304	131

PORTFOLIO (as of 9/30/05)

Portfolio Manager: Burn/Kane/DeGulis - 1985

Investment Style

✔ Large Cap   Growth
✔ Mid Cap   ✔ Value
   Small Cap   Grth/Val

Portfolio

3.7% cash	0.0% corp bonds
96.3% stocks	0.0% gov't bonds
0.0% pref/conv't pref	0.0% muni bonds
0.0% conv't bds/wrnts	0.0% other

SHAREHOLDER INFORMATION

Minimum Investment
Initial: $10,000   Subsequent: $1

Minimum IRA Investment
Initial: $2,000   Subsequent: $1

Maximum Fees
Load: none   12b-1: none
Other: none

Services
✔ IRA
✔ Keogh
✔ Telephone Exchange

T Rowe Price Capital Opportunity (PRCOX)

800-638-5660
www.troweprice.com

Large-Cap Stock

PERFORMANCE

fund inception date: 11/30/94

	3yr Annual	5yr Annual	10yr Annual	Bull	Bear
Return (%)	15.0	1.2	5.6	58.1	-39.7
Differ From Category (+/-)	0.1 av	0.4 av	-3.0 low	-0.6 av	-3.8 av

Standard Deviation	Category Risk Index	Beta
9.3%—av	0.90—blw av	1.01

	2005	2004	2003	2002	2001	2000	1999	1998	1997	1996
Return (%)...............	4.5	11.3	30.7	-22.2	-10.1	-6.3	11.5	14.7	15.8	16.7
Differ From Category (+/-)	-1.7	0.5	1.2	-0.7	1.4	-3.1	-15.0	-9.5	-11.4	-4.5
Return, Tax-Adjusted (%)...	4.5	11.2	30.7	-22.3	-10.1	-8.2	6.7	13.6	13.8	15.2

PER SHARE DATA

	2005	2004	2003	2002	2001	2000	1999	1998	1997	1996
Dividends, Net Income ($)	0.07	0.09	0.04	0.03	0.01	0.00	0.00	0.00	0.00	0.00
Distrib'ns, Cap Gain ($)...	0.00	0.00	0.00	0.00	0.00	1.48	4.27	0.88	1.59	0.74
Net Asset Value ($).....	13.85	13.31	12.03	9.23	11.91	13.26	15.69	18.11	16.62	15.75
Expense Ratio (%).........	na	1.20	1.41	1.37	1.25	1.15	1.26	1.35	1.35	1.35
Yield (%)..............	0.50	0.67	0.33	0.32	0.08	0.00	0.00	0.00	0.00	0.00
Portfolio Turnover (%).....	na	44	48	48	54	64	133	74	85	107
Total Assets (Millions $)...	172	92	76	57	77	93	109	125	109	125

PORTFOLIO (as of 9/30/05)

Portfolio Manager: William Stromberg - 1999

Investment Style

- ✔ Large Cap
- Mid Cap
- Small Cap

- Growth
- Value
- ✔ Grth/Val

Portfolio

0.9% cash	0.0% corp bonds	
99.0% stocks	0.1% gov't bonds	
0.0% pref/conv't pref	0.0% muni bonds	
0.0% conv't bds/wrnts	0.0% other	

SHAREHOLDER INFORMATION

Minimum Investment
Initial: $2,500   Subsequent: $100

Minimum IRA Investment
Initial: $1,000   Subsequent: $50

Maximum Fees
Load: none   12b-1: none
Other: none

Services

- ✔ IRA
- ✔ Keogh
- ✔ Telephone Exchange

T Rowe Price Equity Income (PRFDX)

800-638-5660
www.troweprice.com

Large-Cap Stock

PERFORMANCE

fund inception date: 10/31/85

	3yr Annual	5yr Annual	10yr Annual	Bull	Bear
Return (%)	14.6	5.9	10.2	60.8	-3.4
Differ From Category (+/-)	-0.3 av	5.1 high	1.6 high	2.1 abv av	32.5 high

Standard Deviation	Category Risk Index	Beta
9.6%—av	0.93—av	1.02

	2005	2004	2003	2002	2001	2000	1999	1998	1997	1996
Return (%)	4.2	15.0	25.7	-13.0	1.6	13.1	3.8	9.2	28.8	20.4
Differ From Category (+/-)	-2.0	4.2	-3.8	8.5	13.1	16.4	-22.7	-15.0	1.6	-0.8
Return, Tax-Adjusted (%)	3.2	14.3	25.2	-14.0	0.2	10.1	1.5	7.1	25.7	17.9

PER SHARE DATA

	2005	2004	2003	2002	2001	2000	1999	1998	1997	1996
Dividends, Net Income ($)	0.46	0.42	0.39	0.36	0.36	0.51	0.53	0.61	0.66	0.65
Distrib'ns, Cap Gain ($)	1.33	0.72	0.27	0.45	1.01	2.64	1.97	1.49	2.14	0.84
Net Asset Value ($)	25.92	26.59	24.16	19.79	23.65	24.67	24.81	26.32	26.07	22.54
Expense Ratio (%)	na	0.74	0.78	0.79	0.80	0.60	0.77	0.77	0.79	0.81
Yield (%)	1.68	1.53	1.59	1.77	1.45	1.86	1.97	2.19	2.33	2.78
Portfolio Turnover (%)	na	16	12	15	17	21	22	23	23	25
Total Assets (Millions $)	17,958	16,034	12,160	8,954	10,128	10,187	12,321	13,495	12,771	7,818

PORTFOLIO (as of 9/30/05)

Portfolio Manager: Brian Rogers/
Team Managed - 1985

Investment Style

✔ Large Cap   Growth
✔ Mid Cap   ✔ Value
   Small Cap   Grth/Val

Portfolio

4.7%	cash	0.4%	corp bonds
94.4%	stocks	0.0%	gov't bonds
0.2%	pref/conv't pref	0.0%	muni bonds
0.3%	conv't bds/wrnts	0.0%	other

SHAREHOLDER INFORMATION

Minimum Investment
Initial: $2,500   Subsequent: $100

Minimum IRA Investment
Initial: $1,000   Subsequent: $50

Maximum Fees
Load: none   12b-1: none
Other: none

Services
✔ IRA
✔ Keogh
✔ Telephone Exchange

T Rowe Price Growth Stock (PRGFX)

800-638-5660
www.troweprice.com

Large-Cap Stock

PERFORMANCE

fund inception date: 4/11/50

	3yr Annual	5yr Annual	10yr Annual	Bull	Bear
Return (%)	15.5	1.3	9.9	58.9	-37.8
Differ From Category (+/-)	0.6 av	0.5 av	1.3 abv av	0.2 av	-1.9 av

Standard Deviation	Category Risk Index	Beta
9.8%—av	0.95—av	1.04

	2005	2004	2003	2002	2001	2000	1999	1998	1997	1996
Return (%)	6.5	10.2	31.2	-23.0	-9.7	0.2	22.1	27.4	26.5	21.7
Differ From Category (+/-)	0.3	-0.6	1.7	-1.4	1.7	3.5	-4.4	3.2	-0.7	0.5
Return, Tax-Adjusted (%)	6.5	10.1	31.1	-23.0	-10.1	-3.5	18.6	24.1	23.3	18.9

PER SHARE DATA

	2005	2004	2003	2002	2001	2000	1999	1998	1997	1996
Dividends, Net Income ($)	0.02	0.15	0.05	0.04	0.08	0.07	0.10	0.25	0.20	0.19
Distrib'ns, Cap Gain ($)	0.00	0.00	0.00	0.00	0.27	6.28	5.42	4.27	3.87	2.06
Net Asset Value ($)	28.40	26.67	24.33	18.58	24.18	27.20	33.27	32.07	28.99	26.18
Expense Ratio (%)	na	0.74	0.76	0.77	0.77	0.73	0.74	0.74	0.75	0.77
Yield (%)	0.07	0.56	0.20	0.21	0.32	0.20	0.25	0.68	0.60	0.67
Portfolio Turnover (%)	na	31	35	47	64	74	56	55	41	49
Total Assets (Millions $)	10,749	8,238	5,651	3,728	4,685	5,428	5,672	5,041	3,988	3,431

PORTFOLIO (as of 9/30/05)

Portfolio Manager: Team Managed - 1997

Investment Style
✔ Large Cap   ✔ Growth
  Mid Cap   Value
  Small Cap   Grth/Val

Portfolio

2.3% cash	0.0% corp bonds
97.7% stocks	0.0% gov't bonds
0.0% pref/conv't pref	0.0% muni bonds
0.0% conv't bds/wrnts	0.0% other

SHAREHOLDER INFORMATION

Minimum Investment
Initial: $2,500   Subsequent: $100

Minimum IRA Investment
Initial: $1,000   Subsequent: $50

Maximum Fees
Load: none   12b-1: none
Other: none

Services
✔ IRA
✔ Keogh
✔ Telephone Exchange

T Rowe Price Spectrum Growth (PRSGX)

800-638-5660
www.troweprice.com

Large-Cap Stock

PERFORMANCE

fund inception date: 6/29/90

	3yr Annual	5yr Annual	10yr Annual	Bull	Bear
Return (%)	19.1	4.5	9.3	78.2	-33.0
Differ From Category (+/-)	4.2 high	3.7 high	0.7 abv av	19.5 high	2.9 abv av

Standard Deviation	Category Risk Index	Beta
10.5%—av	1.02—abv av	1.13

	2005	2004	2003	2002	2001	2000	1999	1998	1997	1996
Return (%)	9.4	15.1	34.0	-19.8	-7.6	-0.1	21.2	13.6	17.4	20.5
Differ From Category (+/-)	.3.2	4.3	4.5	1.7	3.8	3.1	-5.3	-10.6	-9.8	-0.7
Return, Tax-Adjusted (%)	.9.2	14.9	33.9	-20.1	-8.3	-2.4	18.4	11.4	14.7	18.0

PER SHARE DATA

	2005	2004	2003	2002	2001	2000	1999	1998	1997	1996
Dividends, Net Income ($)	.0.14	0.12	0.10	0.08	0.16	0.12	0.17	0.18	0.20	0.20
Distrib'ns, Cap Gain ($)	.0.11	0.05	0.02	0.07	0.28	1.85	1.91	1.37	1.60	0.93
Net Asset Value ($)	18.22	16.87	14.80	11.13	14.07	15.72	17.71	16.45	15.93	15.13
Expense Ratio (%)	0.00	0.00	0.00	0.00	0.00	0.00	0.00	0.00	0.00	0.00
Yield (%)	0.76	0.70	0.67	0.71	1.11	0.68	0.86	1.01	1.14	1.24
Portfolio Turnover (%)	20	18	2	4	6	12	20	18	20	3
Total Assets (Millions $)	2,816	2,603	2,236	1,739	2,373	2,889	3,031	2,768	2,605	2,104

PORTFOLIO (as of 11/30/05)

Portfolio Manager: E Notzon/
Team Managed - 1998

Investment Style

✔ Large Cap	✔ Growth
✔ Mid Cap	Value
Small Cap	Grth/Val

Portfolio

0.0% cash	0.0% corp bonds
0.0% stocks	0.0% gov't bonds
0.0% pref/conv't pref	0.0% muni bonds
0.0% conv't bds/wrnts	100.0% other

SHAREHOLDER INFORMATION

Minimum Investment

Initial: $2,500   Subsequent: $100

Minimum IRA Investment

Initial: $1,000   Subsequent: $50

Maximum Fees

Load: none   12b-1: none
Other: none

Services

✔ IRA
✔ Keogh
✔ Telephone Exchange

T Rowe Price Value
(TRVLX)

Large-Cap Stock

800-638-5660
www.troweprice.com

PERFORMANCE
fund inception date: 9/30/94

	3yr Annual	5yr Annual	10yr Annual	Bull	Bear
Return (%)	16.8	6.2	11.7	71.6	-9.2
Differ From Category (+/-)	1.9 abv av	5.4 high	3.1 high	12.9 high	26.7 high

Standard Deviation	Category Risk Index	Beta
10.4%—av	1.01—abv av	1.09

	2005	2004	2003	2002	2001	2000	1999	1998	1997	1996
Return (%)...............	6.3	15.3	30.0	-16.5	1.6	15.7	9.1	6.8	29.2	28.5
Differ From Category (+/-)	.0.1	4.5	0.5	5.0	13.1	19.0	-17.4	-17.4	2.0	7.3
Return, Tax-Adjusted (%)	...5.6	15.2	29.7	-16.9	0.8	14.2	6.3	5.3	26.4	25.8

PER SHARE DATA

	2005	2004	2003	2002	2001	2000	1999	1998	1997	1996
Dividends, Net Income ($)	0.25	0.18	0.20	0.15	0.17	0.23	0.21	0.20	0.21	0.26
Distrib'ns, Cap Gain ($) ...	0.72	0.00	0.01	0.04	0.40	0.84	2.20	0.96	1.83	0.91
Net Asset Value ($)	23.38	22.90	20.01	15.56	18.88	19.15	17.50	18.31	18.24	15.76
Expense Ratio (%).........	na	0.93	0.97	0.95	0.94	1.10	0.92	0.98	1.05	1.10
Yield (%)	1.03	0.78	0.99	0.96	0.88	1.15	1.06	1.03	1.04	1.55
Portfolio Turnover (%)	na	17	31	29	42	68	68	72	67	68
Total Assets (Millions $) ..	3,072	2,429	1,482	1,140	1,322	989	851	775	546	198

PORTFOLIO (as of 9/30/05)

Portfolio Manager: J Linehan/Team Managed - 1994

Investment Style

✔ Large Cap	Growth
✔ Mid Cap	✔ Value
Small Cap	Grth/Val

Portfolio

3.7% cash	0.0% corp bonds
94.6% stocks	0.0% gov't bonds
0.7% pref/conv't pref	0.0% muni bonds
1.0% conv't bds/wrnts	0.0% other

SHAREHOLDER INFORMATION

Minimum Investment
Initial: $2,500   Subsequent: $100

Minimum IRA Investment
Initial: $1,000   Subsequent: $50

Maximum Fees
Load: none   12b-1: none
Other: none

Services
✔ IRA
✔ Keogh
✔ Telephone Exchange

TCW Galileo Dividend Focused N (TGIGX)

800-386-3829
www.tcwgalileofunds.com

Large-Cap Stock

fund inception date: 9/19/86

PERFORMANCE

	3yr Annual	5yr Annual	10yr Annual	Bull	Bear
Return (%)	16.7	7.9	11.0	69.0	18.0
Differ From Category (+/-)	1.8 abv av	7.1 high	2.4 high	10.3 high	53.9 high

Standard Deviation	Category Risk Index	Beta
10.3%—av	1.00—abv av	1.05

	2005	2004	2003	2002	2001	2000	1999	1998	1997	1996
Return (%)...............	2.9	17.4	31.5	-9.5	1.7	45.5	-4.1	0.6	22.9	13.1
Differ From Category (+/-)	-3.3	6.6	2.0	12.0	13.2	48.8	-30.7	-23.6	-4.3	-8.1
Return, Tax-Adjusted (%)...	2.7	17.1	29.9	-11.8	0.5	43.9	-5.8	-1.3	17.9	7.8

PER SHARE DATA

	2005	2004	2003	2002	2001	2000	1999	1998	1997	1996
Dividends, Net Income ($).	0.16	0.12	0.11	0.14	0.15	0.18	0.26	0.27	0.36	0.49
Distrib'ns, Cap Gain ($) ...	0.04	0.08	0.82	0.91	0.59	0.44	0.50	0.72	2.39	1.82
Net Asset Value ($)	11.59	11.45	9.93	8.29	10.32	14.37	10.34	11.58	12.51	12.52
Expense Ratio (%).........	na	1.33	1.39	1.15	1.36	1.36	1.33	1.20	1.21	1.24
Yield (%)	1.34	1.03	0.97	1.46	1.32	1.21	2.40	2.18	2.41	3.41
Portfolio Turnover (%)	na	44	33	60	73	73	71	62	75	79
Total Assets (Millions $)...	890	354	34	27	36	37	32	44	56	52

PORTFOLIO (as of 10/31/05)

Portfolio Manager: Diane Jaffee - 2001

Investment Style
- ✔ Large Cap   Growth
-    Mid Cap   ✔ Value
-    Small Cap   Grth/Val

Portfolio

8.4%	cash	0.0%	corp bonds
91.6%	stocks	0.0%	gov't bonds
0.0%	pref/conv't pref	0.0%	muni bonds
0.0%	conv't bds/wrnts	0.0%	other

SHAREHOLDER INFORMATION

Minimum Investment
Initial: $2,000   Subsequent: $250

Minimum IRA Investment
Initial: $500   Subsequent: $250

Maximum Fees
Load: none   12b-1: 0.25%
Other: none

Services
- ✔ IRA
- ✔ Keogh
- ✔ Telephone Exchange

Thompson Plumb Growth
(THPGX)
Large-Cap Stock

800-999-0887
www.thompsonplumb.com

PERFORMANCE   fund inception date: 2/10/92

	3yr Annual	5yr Annual	10yr Annual	Bull	Bear
Return (%)	10.2	4.9	13.4	44.4	7.1
Differ From Category (+/-)	-4.7 low	4.1 high	4.8 high	-14.3 low	43.0 high

Standard Deviation	Category Risk Index	Beta
11.6%—abv av	1.13—high	1.12

	2005	2004	2003	2002	2001	2000	1999	1998	1997	1996
Return (%)	-2.4	4.1	31.8	-20.4	19.1	25.6	6.4	18.4	32.3	33.0
Differ From Category (+/-)	-8.7	-6.7	2.3	1.1	30.6	28.9	-20.1	-5.8	5.1	11.8
Return, Tax-Adjusted (%)	-2.8	3.8	31.8	-20.6	17.1	21.0	5.6	16.4	30.1	30.2

PER SHARE DATA

	2005	2004	2003	2002	2001	2000	1999	1998	1997	1996
Dividends, Net Income ($)	0.27	0.44	0.14	0.25	0.02	0.00	0.00	0.00	0.00	0.00
Distrib'ns, Cap Gain ($)	1.12	0.55	0.00	0.11	4.03	9.35	1.56	3.50	3.36	2.47
Net Asset Value ($)	44.28	46.79	45.89	34.91	44.31	40.78	40.27	39.35	36.44	30.17
Expense Ratio (%)	1.06	1.05	1.07	1.11	1.20	1.29	1.32	1.41	1.52	1.58
Yield (%)	0.59	0.92	0.30	0.71	0.05	0.00	0.00	0.00	0.00	0.00
Portfolio Turnover (%)	28	29	41	74	63	64	79	67	78	102
Total Assets (Millions $)	985	1,526	1,000	512	328	85	78	72	47	24

PORTFOLIO (as of 9/30/05)

Portfolio Manager: Team Managed - 1993

Investment Style

✔ Large Cap	Growth
Mid Cap	Value
Small Cap	✔ Grth/Val

Portfolio

0.0% cash	0.0% corp bonds
100.0% stocks	0.0% gov't bonds
0.0% pref/conv't pref	0.0% muni bonds
0.0% conv't bds/wrnts	0.0% other

SHAREHOLDER INFORMATION

Minimum Investment

Initial: $2,500   Subsequent: $100

Minimum IRA Investment

Initial: $2,000   Subsequent: $50

Maximum Fees

Load: none   12b-1: none
Other: none

Services

✔ IRA
✔ Keogh
✔ Telephone Exchange

USAA Aggressive Growth
(USAUX)

Large-Cap Stock

800-531-8181
www.usaa.com

PERFORMANCE

fund inception date: 10/19/81

	3yr Annual	5yr Annual	10yr Annual	Bull	Bear
Return (%)	16.6	-6.1	5.5	62.7	-69.0
Differ From Category (+/-)	1.7 abv av	-6.9 low	-3.1 low	4.0 abv av	-33.1 low

Standard Deviation	Category Risk Index	Beta
10.2%—av	0.99—abv av	0.96

	2005	2004	2003	2002	2001	2000	1999	1998	1997	1996
Return (%)	7.2	13.0	30.7	-30.6	-33.3	-19.9	91.0	22.2	7.5	16.4
Differ From Category (+/-)	.1.0	2.2	1.2	-9.0	-21.9	-16.7	64.5	-2.0	-19.7	-4.8
Return, Tax-Adjusted (%)	7.2	13.0	30.7	-30.6	-33.3	-20.6	89.5	19.5	5.9	15.8

PER SHARE DATA

	2005	2004	2003	2002	2001	2000	1999	1998	1997	1996
Dividends, Net Income ($)	0.01	0.00	0.00	0.00	0.00	0.00	0.00	0.00	0.00	0.00
Distrib'ns, Cap Gain ($)	0.00	0.00	0.00	0.00	0.00	1.87	2.31	3.99	2.34	0.57
Net Asset Value ($)	31.34	29.24	25.87	19.78	28.50	42.78	55.15	30.69	29.73	29.81
Expense Ratio (%)	na	0.33	1.16	0.99	0.66	0.60	0.72	0.71	0.74	0.74
Yield (%)	0.04	0.00	0.00	0.00	0.00	0.00	0.00	0.00	0.00	0.00
Portfolio Turnover (%)	na	71	110	170	23	33	35	83	57	43
Total Assets (Millions $)	1,145	1,076	936	694	1,037	1,588	1,658	833	782	716

PORTFOLIO (as of 7/29/05)

Portfolio Manager: Thomas Marsico - 2002

Investment Style

✔ Large Cap   ✔ Growth
✔ Mid Cap   Value
✔ Small Cap   Grth/Val

Portfolio

2.5% cash	0.0% corp bonds
97.5% stocks	0.0% gov't bonds
0.0% pref/conv't pref	0.0% muni bonds
0.0% conv't bds/wrnts	0.0% other

SHAREHOLDER INFORMATION

Minimum Investment
Initial: $3,000   Subsequent: $50

Minimum IRA Investment
Initial: $250   Subsequent: $50

Maximum Fees
Load: none   12b-1: none
Other: none

Services
✔ IRA
✔ Keogh
✔ Telephone Exchange

USAA Growth & Income
(USGRX)
Large-Cap Stock

800-531-8181
www.usaa.com

	3yr Annual	5yr Annual	10yr Annual	Bull	Bear
Return (%)	15.1	2.4	8.1	60.1	-28.5
Differ From Category (+/-)	0.2 av	1.6 abv av	-0.5 av	1.4 av	7.4 abv av

Standard Deviation	Category Risk Index	Beta
9.7%—av	0.94—av	1.04

	2005	2004	2003	2002	2001	2000	1999	1998	1997	1996
Return (%)	6.8	10.6	29.2	-21.2	-6.1	2.9	14.3	6.4	26.0	23.0
Differ From Category (+/-)	0.6	-0.2	-0.3	0.3	5.3	6.2	-12.2	-17.8	-1.2	1.8
Return, Tax-Adjusted (%)	5.8	9.5	29.1	-21.7	-6.9	2.3	13.2	5.0	24.5	21.4

PER SHARE DATA

	2005	2004	2003	2002	2001	2000	1999	1998	1997	1996
Dividends, Net Income ($)	0.07	0.11	0.06	0.07	0.14	0.17	0.18	0.19	0.23	0.22
Distrib'ns, Cap Gain ($)	1.18	1.17	0.00	0.33	0.58	0.35	0.64	0.91	0.66	0.45
Net Asset Value ($)	18.46	18.43	17.82	13.84	18.07	20.03	19.96	18.23	18.31	15.26
Expense Ratio (%)	1.00	1.01	1.09	1.05	0.89	0.90	0.89	0.85	0.89	0.95
Yield (%)	0.36	0.54	0.31	0.46	0.72	0.81	0.87	0.99	1.18	1.40
Portfolio Turnover (%)	81	73	66	74	28	22	24	29	14	16
Total Assets (Millions $)	1,376	1,256	1,094	811	1,066	1,120	1,154	1,055	936	513

PORTFOLIO (as of 7/29/05)

Portfolio Manager: Team Managed - 2002

Investment Style
✔ Large Cap   Growth
  Mid Cap   ✔ Value
  Small Cap   Grth/Val

Portfolio
3.2% cash   0.0% corp bonds
94.6% stocks   0.0% gov't bonds
0.0% pref/conv't pref   0.0% muni bonds
0.0% conv't bds/wrnts   2.3% other

SHAREHOLDER INFORMATION

Minimum Investment
Initial: $3,000   Subsequent: $50

Minimum IRA Investment
Initial: $250   Subsequent: $50

Maximum Fees
Load: none   12b-1: none
Other: none

Services
✔ IRA
✔ Keogh
✔ Telephone Exchange

USAA NASDAQ 100 Index (USNQX)

800-531-8181
www.usaa.com

Large-Cap Stock

PERFORMANCE

fund inception date: 10/27/00

	3yr Annual	5yr Annual	10yr Annual	Bull	Bear
Return (%)	17.9	-7.5	na	60.0	na
Differ From Category (+/-)	3.0 high	-8.3 low	na	1.3 av	na

Standard Deviation	Category Risk Index	Beta
15.0%—high	1.46—high	1.37

	2005	2004	2003	2002	2001	2000	1999	1998	1997	1996
Return (%)	0.9	9.9	47.9	-37.9	-33.4	—	—	—	—	—
Differ From Category (+/-)	-5.3	-0.9	18.4	-16.3	-22.0	—	—	—	—	—
Return, Tax-Adjusted (%)	0.9	9.9	47.9	-37.9	-33.4	—	—	—	—	—

PER SHARE DATA

	2005	2004	2003	2002	2001	2000	1999	1998	1997	1996
Dividends, Net Income ($)	0.02	0.00	0.00	0.00	0.00	—	—	—	—	—
Distrib'ns, Cap Gain ($)	0.00	0.00	0.00	0.00	0.00	—	—	—	—	—
Net Asset Value ($)	5.12	5.09	4.63	3.13	5.04	—	—	—	—	—
Expense Ratio (%)	0.80	0.83	0.96	0.85	—	—	—	—	—	—
Yield (%)	0.35	0.00	0.00	0.00	0.04	—	—	—	—	—
Portfolio Turnover (%)	na	9	5	11	18	—	—	—	—	—
Total Assets (Millions $)	130	133	113	53	59	—	—	—	—	—

PORTFOLIO (as of 9/30/05)

Portfolio Manager: Chad Rakvin - 2005

Investment Style

✔ Large Cap	✔ Growth
Mid Cap	Value
Small Cap	Grth/Val

Portfolio

1.3% cash	0.0% corp bonds
97.5% stocks	0.0% gov't bonds
0.0% pref/conv't pref	0.0% muni bonds
0.0% conv't bds/wrnts	1.3% other

SHAREHOLDER INFORMATION

Minimum Investment
Initial: $3,000   Subsequent: $50

Minimum IRA Investment
Initial: $250   Subsequent: $50

Maximum Fees
Load: none   12b-1: none
Other: none

Services
✔ IRA
✔ Keogh
✔ Telephone Exchange

Vanguard 500 Index Inv

(VFINX)

Large-Cap Stock

800-662-7447
www.vanguard.com

PERFORMANCE

fund inception date: 8/31/76

	3yr Annual	5yr Annual	10yr Annual	Bull	Bear
Return (%)	14.2	0.4	9.0	55.4	-41.5
Differ From Category (+/-)	-0.7 av	-0.4 av	0.4 av	-3.3 av	-5.6 av

Standard Deviation	Category Risk Index	Beta
9.1%—av	0.88—blw av	1.00

	2005	2004	2003	2002	2001	2000	1999	1998	1997	1996
Return (%)	4.7	10.7	28.5	-22.1	-12.0	-9.0	21.0	28.6	33.2	22.8
Differ From Category (+/-)	-1.5	-0.1	-1.0	-0.6	-0.6	-5.8	-5.5	4.4	6.0	1.6
Return, Tax-Adjusted (%)	4.5	10.4	28.2	-22.6	-12.4	-9.4	20.4	27.9	32.2	21.8

PER SHARE DATA

	2005	2004	2003	2002	2001	2000	1999	1998	1997	1996
Dividends, Net Income ($)	1.98	1.95	1.43	1.36	1.28	1.30	1.41	1.33	1.32	1.28
Distrib'ns, Cap Gain ($)	0.00	0.00	0.00	0.00	0.00	0.00	1.00	0.42	0.59	0.25
Net Asset Value ($)	114.92	111.64	102.67	81.15	105.89	121.86	135.33	113.95	90.06	69.15
Expense Ratio (%)	na	0.18	0.18	0.18	0.18	0.18	0.18	0.18	0.19	0.20
Yield (%)	1.72	1.74	1.39	1.67	1.20	1.06	1.03	1.16	1.45	1.84
Portfolio Turnover (%)	na	3	2	7	4	9	6	6	5	5
Total Assets (Millions $)	69,375	84,167	75,342	56,224	73,151	88,240	104,652	74,229	49,358	30,332

PORTFOLIO (as of 9/30/05)

Portfolio Manager: George Sauter - 1987

Investment Style

✔ Large Cap	Growth
Mid Cap	Value
Small Cap	✔ Grth/Val

Portfolio

0.2% cash	0.0% corp bonds
99.8% stocks	0.0% gov't bonds
0.0% pref/conv't pref	0.0% muni bonds
0.0% conv't bds/wrnts	0.0% other

SHAREHOLDER INFORMATION

Minimum Investment
Initial: $3,000   Subsequent: $100

Minimum IRA Investment
Initial: $3,000   Subsequent: $100

Maximum Fees
Load: none   12b-1: none
Other: none

Services
✔ IRA
✔ Keogh
✔ Telephone Exchange

Vanguard Capital Value Inv (VCVLX)

800-662-7447
www.vanguard.com

Large-Cap Stock

PERFORMANCE

fund inception date: 12/17/01

	3yr Annual	5yr Annual	10yr Annual	Bull	Bear
Return (%)	19.4	na	na	79.1	na
Differ From Category (+/-)	4.5 high	na	na	20.4 high	na

Standard Deviation	Category Risk Index	Beta
12.2%—abv av	1.18—high	1.26

	2005	2004	2003	2002	2001	2000	1999	1998	1997	1996
Return (%)	4.2	15.3	41.7	-28.0	—	—	—	—	—	—
Differ From Category (+/-)	-2.0	4.5	12.2	-6.5	—	—	—	—	—	—
Return, Tax-Adjusted (%)	3.4	15.1	41.6	-28.3	—	—	—	—	—	—

PER SHARE DATA

	2005	2004	2003	2002	2001	2000	1999	1998	1997	1996
Dividends, Net Income ($)	0.10	0.13	0.06	0.07	—	—	—	—	—	—
Distrib'ns, Cap Gain ($)	0.48	0.00	0.00	0.00	—	—	—	—	—	—
Net Asset Value ($)	11.67	11.75	10.30	7.31	—	—	—	—	—	—
Expense Ratio (%)	0.59	0.53	0.53	0.54	—	—	—	—	—	—
Yield (%)	0.82	1.10	0.58	0.95	—	—	—	—	—	—
Portfolio Turnover (%)	46	40	40	40	—	—	—	—	—	—
Total Assets (Millions $)	427	449	377	199	—	—	—	—	—	—

PORTFOLIO (as of 9/30/05)

Portfolio Manager: David Fassnacht - 2004

Investment Style

✔ Large Cap	Growth
Mid Cap	✔ Value
Small Cap	Grth/Val

Portfolio

0.8%	cash	0.0%	corp bonds
99.2%	stocks	0.0%	gov't bonds
0.0%	pref/conv't pref	0.0%	muni bonds
0.0%	conv't bds/wrnts	0.0%	other

SHAREHOLDER INFORMATION

Minimum Investment
Initial: $3,000   Subsequent: $100

Minimum IRA Investment
Initial: $3,000   Subsequent: $100

Maximum Fees
Load: none   12b-1: none
Other: none

Services
✔ IRA
✔ Keogh
✔ Telephone Exchange

Vanguard Growth & Income Inv (VQNPX)

Large-Cap Stock

800-662-7447
www.vanguard.com

PERFORMANCE

fund inception date: 12/10/86

	3yr Annual	5yr Annual	10yr Annual	Bull	Bear
Return (%)	15.2	1.2	9.6	58.7	-39.6
Differ From Category (+/-)	0.3 av	0.4 av	1.0 abv av	0.0 av	-3.7 av

Standard Deviation	Category Risk Index	Beta
9.2%—av	0.89—blw av	0.99

	2005	2004	2003	2002	2001	2000	1999	1998	1997	1996
Return (%)	5.8	11.1	30.1	-21.9	-11.1	-8.9	26.0	23.9	35.5	23.0
Differ From Category (+/-)	-0.4	0.3	0.6	-0.4	0.3	-5.7	-0.5	-0.3	8.3	1.8
Return, Tax-Adjusted (%)	5.5	10.8	29.9	-22.3	-11.4	-10.1	24.7	22.4	31.9	19.7

PER SHARE DATA

	2005	2004	2003	2002	2001	2000	1999	1998	1997	1996
Dividends, Net Income ($)	0.49	0.42	0.34	0.29	0.30	0.35	0.33	0.33	0.42	0.40
Distrib'ns, Cap Gain ($)	0.00	0.00	0.00	0.00	0.00	1.47	1.28	1.28	3.18	1.82
Net Asset Value ($)	31.89	30.61	27.94	21.75	28.20	32.06	37.08	30.76	26.19	22.23
Expense Ratio (%)	0.37	0.42	0.46	0.45	0.40	0.38	0.37	0.36	0.36	0.38
Yield (%)	1.53	1.37	1.21	1.31	1.06	1.04	0.86	1.02	1.43	1.66
Portfolio Turnover (%)	84	79	88	70	41	65	54	47	66	75
Total Assets (Millions $)	5,217	6,224	5,483	4,495	6,925	8,968	8,816	5,161	2,142	1,285

PORTFOLIO (as of 9/30/05)

Portfolio Manager: John Cone - 1986

Investment Style
✔ Large Cap   Growth
  Mid Cap   Value
  Small Cap ✔ Grth/Val

Portfolio
1.5% cash   0.0% corp bonds
98.5% stocks   0.0% gov't bonds
0.0% pref/conv't pref 0.0% muni bonds
0.0% conv't bds/wrnts 0.0% other

SHAREHOLDER INFORMATION

Minimum Investment
Initial: $3,000   Subsequent: $100

Minimum IRA Investment
Initial: $3,000   Subsequent: $100

Maximum Fees
Load: none   12b-1: none
Other: none

Services
✔ IRA
✔ Keogh
  Telephone Exchange

Vanguard Growth Equity

(VGEQX)

Large-Cap Stock

800-662-7447
www.vanguard.com

PERFORMANCE

fund inception date: 3/11/92

	3yr Annual	5yr Annual	10yr Annual	Bull	Bear
Return (%)	16.3	-4.7	7.2	60.5	-66.6
Differ From Category (+/-)	1.4 abv av	-5.5 low	-1.4 blw av	1.8 av	-30.7 low

Standard Deviation	Category Risk Index	Beta
11.6%—abv av	1.13—high	1.15

	2005	2004	2003	2002	2001	2000	1999	1998	1997	1996
Return (%)	7.8	5.3	38.5	-30.9	-27.4	-23.1	53.6	38.0	31.3	19.2
Differ From Category (+/-)	1.6	-5.5	9.0	-9.4	-16.0	-19.8	27.1	13.8	4.1	-2.0
Return, Tax-Adjusted (%)	7.8	5.3	38.5	-31.0	-27.4	-23.1	47.3	35.3	23.8	10.3

PER SHARE DATA

	2005	2004	2003	2002	2001	2000	1999	1998	1997	1996
Dividends, Net Income ($)	0.00	0.01	0.02	0.02	0.00	0.00	0.00	0.00	0.00	0.01
Distrib'ns, Cap Gain ($)	0.00	0.00	0.00	0.00	0.00	0.00	4.52	1.60	4.82	4.59
Net Asset Value ($)	10.42	9.66	9.18	6.64	9.64	13.28	17.27	14.44	11.71	12.76
Expense Ratio (%)	0.72	0.61	0.42	0.43	0.77	0.74	0.92	1.04	1.02	1.06
Yield (%)	0.00	0.11	0.21	0.27	0.00	0.00	0.00	0.00	0.00	0.03
Portfolio Turnover (%)	147	162	220	273	357	303	328	249	178	147
Total Assets (Millions $)	749	787	846	541	728	916	203	124	90	90

PORTFOLIO (as of 9/30/05)

Portfolio Manager: Team Managed - 2000

Investment Style

✔ Large Cap   ✔ Growth
✔ Mid Cap   Value
Small Cap   Grth/Val

Portfolio

2.2% cash	0.0% corp bonds
97.8% stocks	0.0% gov't bonds
0.0% pref/conv't pref	0.0% muni bonds
0.0% conv't bds/wrnts	0.0% other

SHAREHOLDER INFORMATION

Minimum Investment
Initial: $10,000   Subsequent: $100

Minimum IRA Investment
Initial: $3,000   Subsequent: $100

Maximum Fees
Load: none   12b-1: none
Other: none

Services
✔ IRA
Keogh
✔ Telephone Exchange

Vanguard Growth Index Inv (VIGRX)

800-662-7447
www.vanguard.com

Large-Cap Stock

PERFORMANCE

fund inception date: 11/2/92

	3yr Annual	5yr Annual	10yr Annual	Bull	Bear
Return (%)	12.3	-1.2	8.5	45.9	-51.7
Differ From Category (+/-)	-2.6 blw av	-2.0 blw av	-0.1 av	-12.8 low	-15.8 low

Standard Deviation	Category Risk Index	Beta
9.4%—av	0.91—blw av	0.97

	2005	2004	2003	2002	2001	2000	1999	1998	1997	1996
Return (%)	5.0	7.2	25.9	-23.6	-12.9	-22.2	28.7	42.2	36.2	23.8
Differ From Category (+/-)	-1.2	-3.6	-3.6	-2.1	-1.5	-19.0	2.2	18.0	9.0	2.6
Return, Tax-Adjusted (%)	4.9	7.0	25.7	-23.9	-13.1	-22.3	27.8	41.7	35.4	22.9

PER SHARE DATA

	2005	2004	2003	2002	2001	2000	1999	1998	1997	1996
Dividends, Net Income ($)	0.21	0.30	0.18	0.23	0.19	0.13	0.23	0.22	0.23	0.22
Distrib'ns, Cap Gain ($)	0.00	0.00	0.00	0.00	0.00	0.00	1.04	0.12	0.25	0.14
Net Asset Value ($)	27.54	26.41	24.92	19.95	26.41	30.57	39.43	31.67	22.53	16.91
Expense Ratio (%)	na	0.22	0.23	0.23	0.22	0.22	0.22	0.22	0.20	0.20
Yield (%)	0.74	1.11	0.70	1.13	0.70	0.40	0.56	0.68	1.00	1.29
Portfolio Turnover (%)	na	24	44	23	31	33	33	29	26	29
Total Assets (Millions $)	6,761	7,711	7,586	6,094	8,445	11,162	15,232	6,644	2,365	787

PORTFOLIO (as of 9/30/05)

Portfolio Manager: George Sauter - 1992

Investment Style
- ✔ Large Cap   ✔ Growth
- Mid Cap   Value
- Small Cap   Grth/Val

Portfolio
0.0%	cash	0.0%	corp bonds
100.0%	stocks	0.0%	gov't bonds
0.0%	pref/conv't pref	0.0%	muni bonds
0.0%	conv't bds/wrnts	0.0%	other

SHAREHOLDER INFORMATION

Minimum Investment
Initial: $3,000   Subsequent: $100

Minimum IRA Investment
Initial: $3,000   Subsequent: $100

Maximum Fees
Load: none   12b-1: none
Other: none

Services
- ✔ IRA
- ✔ Keogh
- Telephone Exchange

Vanguard Morgan Growth Inv (VMRGX)

800-662-7447
www.vanguard.com

Large-Cap Stock

	3yr Annual	5yr Annual	10yr Annual	Bull	Bear
Return (%)	17.2	1.2	9.4	66.6	-47.7
Differ From Category (+/-)	2.3 abv av	0.4 av	0.8 abv av	7.9 abv av	-11.8 blw av

Standard Deviation	Category Risk Index	Beta
10.8%—av	1.05—abv av	1.10

	2005	2004	2003	2002	2001	2000	1999	1998	1997	1996
Return (%).............	9.0	10.4	33.7	-23.5	-13.6	-12.5	34.1	22.2	30.8	23.3
Differ From Category (+/-)	.2.8	-0.4	4.2	-2.0	-2.1	-9.3	7.6	-2.0	3.6	2.1
Return, Tax-Adjusted (%)...	9.0	10.3	33.6	-23.6	-13.8	-15.3	30.6	20.2	27.1	19.8

PER SHARE DATA

	2005	2004	2003	2002	2001	2000	1999	1998	1997	1996
Dividends, Net Income ($).	0.10	0.11	0.04	0.04	0.08	0.15	0.15	0.18	0.16	0.14
Distrib'ns, Cap Gain ($)...	0.00	0.00	0.00	0.00	0.05	2.95	3.08	1.43	2.53	1.53
Net Asset Value ($)	17.71	16.32	14.87	11.15	14.63	17.08	22.92	19.72	17.54	15.63
Expense Ratio (%)........	0.39	0.44	0.50	0.48	0.41	0.40	0.42	0.44	0.48	0.51
Yield (%)	0.53	0.64	0.26	0.35	0.51	0.74	0.57	0.85	0.79	0.81
Portfolio Turnover (%)	88	88	91	104	53	94	65	81	76	73
Total Assets (Millions $)..	4,781	4,563	3,789	2,576	3,493	4,661	5,066	3,555	2,795	2,054

PORTFOLIO (as of 9/30/05)

Portfolio Manager: Rands/Cone/Sauter/
Dickson - 1994

Investment Style
- ✔ Large Cap   ✔ Growth
- ✔ Mid Cap   Value
-    Small Cap   Grth/Val

Portfolio
5.1% cash	0.0% corp bonds
94.0% stocks	0.0% gov't bonds
0.0% pref/conv't pref	0.0% muni bonds
0.0% conv't bds/wrnts	1.0% other

SHAREHOLDER INFORMATION

Minimum Investment
Initial: $3,000   Subsequent: $100

Minimum IRA Investment
Initial: $3,000   Subsequent: $100

Maximum Fees
Load: none   12b-1: none
Other: none

Services
- ✔ IRA
- ✔ Keogh
- ✔ Telephone Exchange

Vanguard Tax Managed Capital Apprec (VMCAX)

Large-Cap Stock

800-662-7447
www.vanguard.com

PERFORMANCE

fund inception date: 9/6/94

	3yr Annual	5yr Annual	10yr Annual	Bull	Bear
Return (%)	16.5	0.5	9.2	64.0	-47.7
Differ From Category (+/-)	1.6 abv av	-0.3 av	0.6 abv av	5.3 abv av	-11.8 blw av

Standard Deviation	Category Risk Index	Beta
9.5%—av	0.92—av	1.03

	2005	2004	2003	2002	2001	2000	1999	1998	1997	1996
Return (%)...............	7.4	11.7	31.7	-23.4	-15.3	-10.1	33.5	27.9	27.2	20.9
Differ From Category (+/-)	.1.2	0.9	2.2	-1.9	-3.9	-6.9	7.0	3.7	0.0	-0.3
Return, Tax-Adjusted (%)...	7.3	11.5	31.5	-23.7	-15.5	-10.2	33.3	27.6	26.9	20.5

PER SHARE DATA

	2005	2004	2003	2002	2001	2000	1999	1998	1997	1996
Dividends, Net Income ($).	0.35	0.37	0.24	0.21	0.17	0.12	0.12	0.13	0.12	0.11
Distrib'ns, Cap Gain ($) ...	0.00	0.00	0.00	0.00	0.00	0.00	0.00	0.00	0.00	0.00
Net Asset Value ($)	29.80	28.05	25.43	19.49	25.73	30.59	34.17	25.68	20.18	15.95
Expense Ratio (%).........	na	0.14	0.17	0.17	0.18	0.19	0.19	0.19	0.17	0.20
Yield (%)	1.18	1.30	0.93	1.05	0.66	0.38	0.36	0.50	0.59	0.68
Portfolio Turnover (%)	na	5	11	10	13	17	12	5	4	12
Total Assets (Millions $)...	857	1,596	1,466	1,154	1,678	2,643	2,378	1,479	893	517

PORTFOLIO (as of 9/30/05)

Portfolio Manager: George Sauter/Team Managed - 1994

Investment Style
✔ Large Cap   Growth
  Mid Cap   Value
  Small Cap   ✔ Grth/Val

Portfolio
0.1% cash	0.0% corp bonds
100.0% stocks	0.0% gov't bonds
0.0% pref/conv't pref	0.0% muni bonds
0.0% conv't bds/wrnts	0.0% other

SHAREHOLDER INFORMATION

Minimum Investment
Initial: $10,000   Subsequent: $100

Minimum IRA Investment
Initial: $10,000   Subsequent: $100

Maximum Fees
Load: 1.00% redemption   12b-1: none
Other: redemption fee applies for 1 year

Services
✔ IRA
  Keogh
✔ Telephone Exchange

Vanguard Tax Managed Growth & Income (VTGIX)

800-662-7447
www.vanguard.com

Large-Cap Stock

PERFORMANCE

fund inception date: 9/6/94

	3yr Annual	5yr Annual	10yr Annual	Bull	Bear
Return (%)	14.3	0.5	9.0	55.7	-41.3
Differ From Category (+/-)	-0.6 av	-0.3 av	0.4 abv av	-3.0 av	-5.4 av

Standard Deviation	Category Risk Index	Beta
9.1%—av	0.88—blw av	1.00

	2005	2004	2003	2002	2001	2000	1999	1998	1997	1996
Return (%).	4.8	10.8	28.5	-21.9	-11.9	-9.0	21.1	28.6	33.3	23.0
Differ From Category (+/-)	-1.4	0.0	-1.0	-0.4	-0.5	-5.8	-5.4	4.4	6.1	1.8
Return, Tax-Adjusted (%). . .	4.5	10.5	28.2	-22.4	-12.3	-9.3	20.6	28.1	32.6	22.1

PER SHARE DATA

	2005	2004	2003	2002	2001	2000	1999	1998	1997	1996
Dividends, Net Income ($).	0.48	0.47	0.34	0.33	0.30	0.30	0.31	0.29	0.28	0.28
Distrib'ns, Cap Gain ($) . .	0.00	0.00	0.00	0.00	0.00	0.00	0.00	0.00	0.00	0.00
Net Asset Value ($)	27.15	26.36	24.23	19.15	24.93	28.66	31.81	26.55	20.88	15.89
Expense Ratio (%).	na	0.14	0.17	0.17	0.18	0.19	0.19	0.19	0.17	0.20
Yield (%)	1.76	1.78	1.40	1.69	1.19	1.03	0.98	1.09	1.34	1.76
Portfolio Turnover (%)	na	8	5	9	5	5	4	4	2	7
Total Assets (Millions $). . .	806	1,395	1,321	1,077	1,606	2,320	2,240	1,352	579	235

PORTFOLIO (as of 9/30/05)

Portfolio Manager: Corey Holeman - 2004

Investment Style
✔ Large Cap   Growth
   Mid Cap   Value
   Small Cap   ✔ Grth/Val

Portfolio
0.0% cash	0.0% corp bonds
100.0% stocks	0.0% gov't bonds
0.0% pref/conv't pref	0.0% muni bonds
0.0% conv't bds/wrnts	0.0% other

SHAREHOLDER INFORMATION

Minimum Investment
Initial: $10,000   Subsequent: $100

Minimum IRA Investment
Initial: $10,000   Subsequent: $100

Maximum Fees
Load: 1.00% redemption   12b-1: none
Other: redemption fee applies for 1 year

Services
✔ IRA
   Keogh
✔ Telephone Exchange

Vanguard Total Stock Market Index Inv (VTSMX)

800-662-7447
www.vanguard.com

Large-Cap Stock

PERFORMANCE

fund inception date: 4/27/92

	3yr Annual	5yr Annual	10yr Annual	Bull	Bear
Return (%)	16.1	1.9	9.0	63.3	-41.9
Differ From Category (+/-)	1.2 abv av	1.1 abv av	0.4 av	4.6 abv av	-6.0 av

Standard Deviation	Category Risk Index	Beta
9.7%—av	0.94—av	1.05

	2005	2004	2003	2002	2001	2000	1999	1998	1997	1996
Return (%)	5.9	12.5	31.3	-20.9	-10.9	-10.5	23.8	23.2	30.9	20.9
Differ From Category (+/-)	-0.3	1.7	1.8	0.6	0.5	-7.3	-2.7	-1.0	3.7	-0.3
Return, Tax-Adjusted (%)	5.7	12.2	31.1	-21.3	-11.3	-11.0	23.1	22.5	29.9	19.9

PER SHARE DATA

	2005	2004	2003	2002	2001	2000	1999	1998	1997	1996
Dividends, Net Income ($)	0.47	0.45	0.33	0.29	0.30	0.34	0.33	0.33	0.32	0.29
Distrib'ns, Cap Gain ($)	0.00	0.00	0.00	0.00	0.00	0.14	0.32	0.13	0.27	0.11
Net Asset Value ($)	30.00	28.77	25.99	20.07	25.74	29.26	33.22	27.42	22.64	17.77
Expense Ratio (%)	na	0.19	0.20	0.20	0.20	0.20	0.20	0.20	0.20	0.22
Yield (%)	1.57	1.54	1.25	1.45	1.15	1.14	0.98	1.19	1.40	1.62
Portfolio Turnover (%)	na	4	11	4	7	7	3	3	2	3
Total Assets (Millions $)	29,785	31,718	24,059	14,254	15,781	16,856	18,133	9,308	5,093	3,531

PORTFOLIO (as of 9/30/05)

Portfolio Manager: George Sauter - 1992

Investment Style

- ✔ Large Cap   Growth
- ✔ Mid Cap   Value
-    Small Cap   ✔ Grth/Val

Portfolio

0.7% cash	0.0% corp bonds
99.3% stocks	0.0% gov't bonds
0.0% pref/conv't pref	0.0% muni bonds
0.0% conv't bds/wrnts	0.0% other

SHAREHOLDER INFORMATION

Minimum Investment
Initial: $3,000   Subsequent: $100

Minimum IRA Investment
Initial: $3,000   Subsequent: $100

Maximum Fees
Load: none   12b-1: none
Other: none

Services
- ✔ IRA
- ✔ Keogh
-    Telephone Exchange

Vanguard US Value
(VUVLX)
Large-Cap Stock

800-662-7447
www.vanguard.com

PERFORMANCE   fund inception date: 6/29/00

	3yr Annual	5yr Annual	10yr Annual	Bull	Bear
Return (%)	16.3	6.5	na	67.2	na
Differ From Category (+/-)	1.4 abv av	5.7 high	na	8.5 abv av	na

Standard Deviation	Category Risk Index	Beta
10.5%—av	1.02—abv av	1.09

	2005	2004	2003	2002	2001	2000	1999	1998	1997	1996
Return (%)...............	6.3	13.7	30.2	-15.2	2.9	—	—	—	—	—
Differ From Category (+/-)	.0.1	2.9	0.7	6.3	14.4	—	—	—	—	—
Return, Tax-Adjusted (%)...	5.1	13.4	29.9	-15.8	2.5	—	—	—	—	—

PER SHARE DATA

	2005	2004	2003	2002	2001	2000	1999	1998	1997	1996
Dividends, Net Income ($)	0.28	0.20	0.18	0.16	0.10	—	—	—	—	—
Distrib'ns, Cap Gain ($)...	0.88	0.00	0.00	0.00	0.00	—	—	—	—	—
Net Asset Value ($).....	13.48	13.75	12.27	9.56	11.47	—	—	—	—	—
Expense Ratio (%)........	0.49	0.49	0.63	0.54	0.51	—	—	—	—	—
Yield (%)...............	1.94	1.45	1.46	1.67	0.87	—	—	—	—	—
Portfolio Turnover (%).....	52	56	50	46	54	—	—	—	—	—
Total Assets (Millions $)..	1,013	881	534	451	436	—	—	—	—	—

PORTFOLIO (as of 9/30/05)

Portfolio Manager: C Darnell/R Soucy - 2000

Investment Style

✔ Large Cap	Growth
Mid Cap	✔ Value
Small Cap	Grth/Val

Portfolio

3.5% cash	0.0% corp bonds
96.3% stocks	0.2% gov't bonds
0.0% pref/conv't pref	0.0% muni bonds
0.0% conv't bds/wrnts	0.0% other

SHAREHOLDER INFORMATION

Minimum Investment
Initial: $3,000   Subsequent: $100

Minimum IRA Investment
Initial: $3,000   Subsequent: $100

Maximum Fees
Load: none   12b-1: none
Other: none

Services
✔ IRA
✔ Keogh
✔ Telephone Exchange

Vanguard Value Index Inv

800-662-7447
www.vanguard.com

(VIVAX)

Large-Cap Stock

PERFORMANCE

fund inception date: 11/2/92

	3yr Annual	5yr Annual	10yr Annual	Bull	Bear
Return (%)	17.7	2.6	9.4	72.6	-30.2
Differ From Category (+/-)	2.8 high	1.8 abv av	0.8 abv av	13.9 high	5.7 abv av

Standard Deviation	Category Risk Index	Beta
10.2%—av	0.99—abv av	1.06

	2005	2004	2003	2002	2001	2000	1999	1998	1997	1996
Return (%)	7.0	15.2	32.2	-20.9	-11.8	6.0	12.5	14.6	29.7	21.7
Differ From Category (+/-)	0.8	4.4	2.7	0.6	-0.4	9.3	-14.0	-9.6	2.5	0.5
Return, Tax-Adjusted (%)	6.7	14.9	31.8	-21.5	-13.2	4.6	10.1	13.0	28.0	19.6

PER SHARE DATA

	2005	2004	2003	2002	2001	2000	1999	1998	1997	1996
Dividends, Net Income ($)	0.56	0.46	0.37	0.32	0.32	0.36	0.36	0.36	0.37	0.38
Distrib'ns, Cap Gain ($)	0.00	0.00	0.00	0.00	0.98	0.98	1.96	0.99	0.75	0.57
Net Asset Value ($)	22.29	21.35	18.95	14.65	18.90	22.87	22.89	22.51	20.85	17.02
Expense Ratio (%)	na	0.21	0.23	0.23	0.22	0.22	0.22	0.22	0.20	0.20
Yield (%)	2.48	2.14	1.96	2.15	1.58	1.50	1.45	1.54	1.71	2.16
Portfolio Turnover (%)	na	18	47	26	38	37	41	33	26	29
Total Assets (Millions $)	3,376	3,592	2,921	2,197	3,018	3,450	3,378	2,421	1,796	1,016

PORTFOLIO (as of 9/30/05)

Portfolio Manager: George Sauter - 1992

Investment Style

✔ Large Cap   Growth
  Mid Cap   ✔ Value
  Small Cap   Grth/Val

Portfolio

0.0% cash	0.0% corp bonds
100.0% stocks	0.0% gov't bonds
0.0% pref/conv't pref	0.0% muni bonds
0.0% conv't bds/wrnts	0.0% other

SHAREHOLDER INFORMATION

Minimum Investment
Initial: $3,000   Subsequent: $100

Minimum IRA Investment
Initial: $3,000   Subsequent: $100

Maximum Fees
Load: none   12b-1: none
Other: none

Services
✔ IRA
✔ Keogh
  Telephone Exchange

Vanguard Windsor II Inv
(VWNFX)
Large-Cap Stock

800-662-7447
www.vanguard.com

PERFORMANCE

fund inception date: 6/24/85

	3yr Annual	5yr Annual	10yr Annual	Bull	Bear
Return (%)	18.0	5.7	10.7	71.4	-9.8
Differ From Category (+/-)	3.1 high	4.9 high	2.1 high	12.7 high	26.1 high

Standard Deviation	Category Risk Index	Beta
9.3%—av	0.90—blw av	0.93

	2005	2004	2003	2002	2001	2000	1999	1998	1997	1996
Return (%)	7.0	18.3	30.0	-16.8	-3.4	16.8	-5.8	16.3	32.3	24.1
Differ From Category (+/-)	0.8	7.5	0.5	4.7	8.1	20.1	-32.4	-7.9	5.1	2.9
Return, Tax-Adjusted (%)	6.2	17.9	29.6	-17.6	-4.2	14.8	-8.3	13.6	29.4	21.4

PER SHARE DATA

	2005	2004	2003	2002	2001	2000	1999	1998	1997	1996
Dividends, Net Income ($)	0.67	0.58	0.53	0.51	0.55	0.61	0.68	0.64	0.66	0.63
Distrib'ns, Cap Gain ($)	0.88	0.00	0.00	0.00	0.15	1.24	2.50	2.67	2.19	1.16
Net Asset Value ($)	31.33	30.73	26.49	20.80	25.59	27.20	24.97	29.85	28.62	23.83
Expense Ratio (%)	0.37	0.36	0.43	0.42	0.40	0.37	0.37	0.41	0.37	0.39
Yield (%)	2.08	1.88	2.00	2.45	2.11	2.14	2.47	1.96	2.14	2.52
Portfolio Turnover (%)	28	22	29	41	33	26	26	31	30	32
Total Assets (Millions $)	29,064	29,016	22,766	17,739	22,429	25,083	26,902	31,538	24,376	15,700

PORTFOLIO (as of 9/30/05)

Portfolio Manager: Team Managed - 1985

Investment Style

✔ Large Cap	Growth
✔ Mid Cap	✔ Value
Small Cap	Grth/Val

Portfolio

3.5% cash	0.0% corp bonds
93.6% stocks	0.0% gov't bonds
0.0% pref/conv't pref	0.0% muni bonds
0.0% conv't bds/wrnts	2.9% other

SHAREHOLDER INFORMATION

Minimum Investment

Initial: $3,000   Subsequent: $100

Minimum IRA Investment

Initial: $3,000   Subsequent: $100

Maximum Fees

Load: none   12b-1: none

Other: none

Services

✔ IRA
✔ Keogh
✔ Telephone Exchange

Vanguard Windsor Inv
(VWNDX)
Large-Cap Stock

800-662-7447
www.vanguard.com

fund inception date: 10/23/58

	3yr Annual	5yr Annual	10yr Annual	Bull	Bear
Return (%)	17.7	6.0	10.4	70.8	-8.7
Differ From Category (+/-)	2.8 high	5.2 high	1.8 high	12.1 high	27.2 high

Standard Deviation	Category Risk Index	Beta
10.5%—av	1.02—abv av	1.12

	2005	2004	2003	2002	2001	2000	1999	1998	1997	1996
Return (%)	4.9	13.3	37.0	-22.2	5.7	15.8	11.5	0.8	21.9	26.3
Differ From Category (+/-)	-1.3	2.5	7.5	-0.7	17.2	19.1	-15.0	-23.4	-5.3	5.1
Return, Tax-Adjusted (%)	3.4	13.0	36.8	-22.6	4.8	12.7	8.4	-1.2	17.7	22.6

PER SHARE DATA

	2005	2004	2003	2002	2001	2000	1999	1998	1997	1996
Dividends, Net Income ($)	0.27	0.26	0.17	0.17	0.20	0.27	0.27	0.25	0.32	0.41
Distrib'ns, Cap Gain ($)	1.56	0.09	0.00	0.00	0.31	1.85	1.90	1.23	2.88	1.33
Net Asset Value ($)	17.15	18.07	16.26	12.00	15.64	15.29	15.17	15.57	16.98	16.59
Expense Ratio (%)	0.39	0.39	0.48	0.45	0.41	0.31	0.28	0.27	0.27	0.31
Yield (%)	1.41	1.43	1.01	1.41	1.24	1.57	1.58	1.48	1.61	2.28
Portfolio Turnover (%)	32	28	23	30	33	41	56	48	61	34
Total Assets (Millions $)	13,362	16,385	14,681	10,999	16,027	16,615	16,700	18,188	20,915	16,738

PORTFOLIO (as of 9/30/05)

Portfolio Manager: Team Managed - 1996

Investment Style
- ✔ Large Cap   Growth
- Mid Cap   ✔ Value
- Small Cap   Grth/Val

Portfolio
- 1.8% cash
- 97.4% stocks
- 0.0% pref/conv't pref
- 0.0% conv't bds/wrnts
- 0.0% corp bonds
- 0.0% gov't bonds
- 0.0% muni bonds
- 0.9% other

SHAREHOLDER INFORMATION

Minimum Investment
Initial: $3,000   Subsequent: $100

Minimum IRA Investment
Initial: $3,000   Subsequent: $100

Maximum Fees
Load: none   12b-1: none
Other: none

Services
- ✔ IRA
- ✔ Keogh
- ✔ Telephone Exchange

Mid-Cap Stock Funds
Category Performance Ranked by 2005 Returns

nd (Ticker)	Annual Return (%)				Category Risk	Total Risk
	2005	3Yr	5Yr	10Yr		
ner Century Heritage Inv (TWHIX)	22.2	16.7	-0.1	9.2	abv av	abv av
lelity Value Discovery (FVDFX)	18.7	20.7	na	na	blw av	abv av
inier Small/Mid Cap Equity (RIMSX)	17.5	26.3	9.1	12.5	high	high
lelity Leveraged Company Stock (FLVCX)	17.4	42.1	23.8	na	high	high
andywine Advisors (BWAFX)	16.8	18.2	2.1	na	abv av	abv av
netics Paradigm (WWNPX)	16.1	27.5	15.1	na	av	abv av
lelity Mid Cap Stock (FMCSX)	16.0	19.0	1.2	13.0	abv av	abv av
Mid Cap Growth (NBNGX)	15.2	23.1	-4.1	7.3	abv av	abv av
ratton Growth (STRGX)	14.4	26.2	11.7	12.8	high	high
andywine (BRWIX)	14.3	19.3	1.1	9.2	abv av	abv av
lelity Value (FDVLX)	14.2	23.0	13.6	12.1	blw av	abv av
nguard Mid Cap Index Inv (VIMSX)	13.9	22.5	9.3	na	av	abv av
ffalo Mid Cap (BUFMX)	13.8	24.0	na	na	high	high
irholme (FAIRX)	13.7	20.7	12.9	na	low	av
lelity Mid Cap Value (FSMVX)	13.6	22.7	na	na	blw av	av
lelity Mid Cap Growth (FSMGX)	13.5	22.8	na	na	abv av	abv av
artland Select Value (HRSVX)	13.4	21.6	12.5	na	abv av	abv av
uberger Berman Manhattan Inv (NMANX)	13.3	19.8	-3.6	6.2	abv av	abv av
ron Asset (BARAX)	12.4	22.1	5.5	10.0	av	abv av
rner Mid Cap Growth I (TMGFX)	12.0	22.9	-2.2	na	high	high
Value (RSVAX)	11.6	33.8	17.3	6.9	av	abv av
nus Enterprise (JAENX)	11.4	22.2	-4.7	7.2	blw av	abv av
eyfus Index Midcap Index (PESPX)	11.2	20.3	7.9	13.6	blw av	abv av
nguard Selected Value (VASVX)	10.6	21.6	13.3	na	blw av	av
nus Mid Cap Value Inv (JMCVX)	10.3	22.0	13.7	na	low	av
nguard Extended Market Index Inv (VEXMX)	10.2	23.3	6.9	10.0	av	abv av
nguard Strategic Equity (VSEQX)	9.9	23.9	11.7	13.5	av	abv av
vance Capital I Equity Growth (ADEGX)	9.9	19.7	2.5	11.3	av	abv av
Mid Cap Opportunities (RSMOX)	9.6	22.2	2.9	11.1	abv av	abv av
I Common Stock (FMIMX)	9.4	17.2	12.5	12.6	blw av	av
nguard Mid Cap Growth (VMGRX)	9.1	20.1	-1.6	na	high	high
ner Century Vista Inv (TWCVX)	8.8	21.6	0.6	6.5	abv av	abv av
arkman Total Return Core (MTRPX)	7.9	21.2	0.2	4.8	high	high
ells Fargo Advtg Mid Cap Disciplined Inv (SMCDX)	7.9	22.5	12.7	na	blw av	av
uhlenkamp (MUHLX)	7.8	25.7	11.7	15.7	high	high
RM Mid Cap Value Inv (CRMMX)	7.7	23.8	13.4	na	low	av
ells Fargo Advtg Discovery Inv (STDIX)	7.2	19.7	9.4	7.5	high	high
lelity Aggressive Growth (FDEGX)	7.2	16.7	-13.2	3.7	blw av	abv av
ells Fargo Advtg Opportunity Inv (SOPFX)	7.2	20.1	3.8	11.3	av	abv av
rshall Mid Cap Value Inv (MRVEX)	7.1	19.3	12.9	12.9	blw av	av
lafield (DEFIX)	6.0	21.5	17.0	13.7	abv av	abv av
cholas II Class I (NCTWX)	5.9	16.5	4.0	8.0	low	av

Mid-Cap Stock Funds
Category Performance Ranked by 2005 Returns (cont.)

Fund (Ticker)	Annual Return (%)				Category Risk	Total Risk
	2005	3Yr	5Yr	10Yr		
Fenimore Asset Management Tr Value (FAMVX)	5.5	15.6	10.9	12.0	low	blw av
Westcore MIDCO Growth (WTMGX)	4.6	18.4	4.0	9.0	abv av	abv av
Excelsior Mid Cap Val & Restructuring (UMVEX)	4.6	20.3	9.7	na	abv av	abv av
Marshall Mid Cap Growth Inv (MRMSX)	3.9	14.1	-2.0	8.3	abv av	abv av
Meridian Value (MVALX)	2.9	16.8	9.0	18.7	low	av
Fidelity Value Strategies (FSLSX)	2.7	23.8	9.7	10.7	high	high
Mosaic Equity Tr Mid Cap (GTSGX)	0.5	15.3	9.0	10.2	low	av
Meridian Growth (MERDX)	0.3	19.3	9.8	12.2	abv av	abv av
Mid-Cap Stock Category Average	**9.9**	**20.3**	**5.9**	**10.4**	**av**	**abv av**

Advance Capital I Equity Growth (ADEGX)

Mid-Cap Stock

800-345-4783
www.advancecapital
online.com

PERFORMANCE

fund inception date: 8/5/87

	3yr Annual	5yr Annual	10yr Annual	Bull	Bear
Return (%)	19.7	2.5	11.3	77.8	-43.3
Differ From Category (+/-)	-0.6 av	-3.4 blw av	0.9 av	-4.3 av	-19.6 blw av

Standard Deviation	Category Risk Index	Beta
12.3%—abv av	0.98—av	1.22

	2005	2004	2003	2002	2001	2000	1999	1998	1997	1996
Return (%)	9.9	14.4	36.6	-22.1	-15.4	7.1	50.1	16.2	17.6	17.4
Differ From Category (+/-)	.0.0	-1.1	-1.0	-3.7	-11.2	1.3	13.0	4.6	-4.6	-1.1
Return, Tax-Adjusted (%)	8.9	12.4	36.6	-22.1	-15.4	6.1	46.6	16.2	17.5	17.4

PER SHARE DATA

	2005	2004	2003	2002	2001	2000	1999	1998	1997	1996
Dividends, Net Income ($)	0.00	0.00	0.00	0.00	0.00	0.00	0.00	0.00	0.00	0.00
Distrib'ns, Cap Gain ($)	1.65	3.33	0.00	0.00	0.00	1.21	3.49	0.00	0.07	0.00
Net Asset Value ($)	25.42	24.61	24.41	17.87	22.95	27.13	26.43	20.05	17.25	14.72
Expense Ratio (%)	na	1.00	1.01	1.00	1.00	1.01	1.02	1.02	1.07	1.09
Yield (%)	0.00	0.00	0.00	0.00	0.00	0.00	0.00	0.00	0.00	0.00
Portfolio Turnover (%)	na	44	11	12	9	19	36	22	21	25
Total Assets (Millions $)	196	175	145	99	127	134	115	68	54	39

PORTFOLIO (as of 9/30/05)

Portfolio Manager: John Shoemaker/Donald Peters - 2000

Investment Style

Large Cap	✔ Growth
✔ Mid Cap	Value
Small Cap	Grth/Val

Portfolio

0.0% cash	0.0% corp bonds
100.0% stocks	0.0% gov't bonds
0.0% pref/conv't pref	0.0% muni bonds
0.0% conv't bds/wrnts	0.0% other

SHAREHOLDER INFORMATION

Minimum Investment
Initial: $10,000   Subsequent: $1,000

Minimum IRA Investment
Initial: $2,000   Subsequent: $1,000

Maximum Fees
Load: none   12b-1: 0.25%
Other: none

Services
✔ IRA
  Keogh
✔ Telephone Exchange

Amer Century Heritage Inv (TWHIX)

800-345-2021
www.americancentury.com

Mid-Cap Stock

	3yr Annual	5yr Annual	10yr Annual	Bull	Bear
Return (%)	16.7	-0.1	9.2	69.5	-41.1
Differ From Category (+/-)	-3.6 blw av	-6.0 low	-1.2 blw av	-12.6 blw av	-17.4 blw av

Standard Deviation	Category Risk Index	Beta
13.0%—abv av	1.04—abv av	1.11

	2005	2004	2003	2002	2001	2000	1999	1998	1997	1996
Return (%).............	22.2	7.0	21.6	-15.9	-25.5	17.3	51.2	-0.1	19.3	15.3
Differ From Category (+/-)	12.3	-8.5	-16.0	2.5	-21.3	11.5	14.1	-11.8	-2.9	-3.2
Return, Tax-Adjusted (%) ..	22.1	7.0	21.6	-15.9	-25.5	12.7	48.5	-0.2	14.6	13.2

PER SHARE DATA

	2005	2004	2003	2002	2001	2000	1999	1998	1997	1996
Dividends, Net Income ($)	0.00	0.00	0.00	0.00	0.00	0.00	0.04	0.02	0.07	0.09
Distrib'ns, Cap Gain ($) ...	0.09	0.00	0.00	0.00	0.00	3.64	1.48	0.00	2.70	0.71
Net Asset Value ($)	14.40	11.85	11.07	9.10	10.83	14.55	15.64	11.46	11.50	12.07
Expense Ratio (%).........	na	1.00	1.00	1.00	1.00	1.00	1.00	1.00	1.00	0.99
Yield (%)	0.00	0.00	0.00	0.00	0.00	0.00	0.25	0.18	0.50	0.72
Portfolio Turnover (%)	na	264	129	128	152	119	134	148	69	122
Total Assets (Millions $) ...	883	1,234	1,259	1,002	1,281	1,860	1,349	1,071	1,278	1,125

PORTFOLIO (as of 9/30/05)

Portfolio Manager: K Stalzer/D Rose - 2004

Investment Style

Large Cap	✔ Growth
✔ Mid Cap	Value
✔ Small Cap	Grth/Val

Portfolio

2.3% cash	0.0% corp bonds
97.7% stocks	0.0% gov't bonds
0.0% pref/conv't pref	0.0% muni bonds
0.0% conv't bds/wrnts	0.0% other

SHAREHOLDER INFORMATION

Minimum Investment
Initial: $2,500   Subsequent: $50

Minimum IRA Investment
Initial: $2,500   Subsequent: $50

Maximum Fees
Load: none   12b-1: none
Other: none

Services
✔ IRA
✔ Keogh
✔ Telephone Exchange

Amer Century Vista Inv
(TWCVX)
Mid-Cap Stock

800-345-2021
www.americancentury.com

PERFORMANCE   fund inception date: 11/25/83

	3yr Annual	5yr Annual	10yr Annual	Bull	Bear
Return (%)	21.6	0.6	6.5	85.5	-55.1
Differ From Category (+/-)	1.3 abv av	-5.3 blw av	-3.9 low	3.4 av	-31.4 low

Standard Deviation	Category Risk Index	Beta
13.6%—abv av	1.09—abv av	1.17

	2005	2004	2003	2002	2001	2000	1999	1998	1997	1996
Return (%)	8.8	15.7	42.8	-20.9	-27.5	-0.9	119.1	-14.2	-8.6	7.5
Differ From Category (+/-)	-1.1	0.2	5.2	-2.4	-23.3	-6.8	82.0	-25.9	-30.9	-11.0
Return, Tax-Adjusted (%)	8.8	15.7	42.8	-20.9	-27.5	-6.6	117.3	-14.2	-9.7	5.2

PER SHARE DATA

	2005	2004	2003	2002	2001	2000	1999	1998	1997	1996
Dividends, Net Income ($)	0.00	0.00	0.00	0.00	0.00	0.00	0.00	0.00	0.00	0.00
Distrib'ns, Cap Gain ($)	0.00	0.00	0.00	0.00	0.00	6.33	0.95	0.00	0.80	1.18
Net Asset Value ($)	15.81	14.52	12.54	8.78	11.10	15.33	22.21	10.65	12.42	14.51
Expense Ratio (%)	na	1.00	1.00	1.00	1.00	1.00	1.00	1.00	1.00	0.99
Yield (%)	0.00	0.00	0.00	0.00	0.00	0.00	0.00	0.00	0.00	0.00
Portfolio Turnover (%)	na	255	280	293	290	135	187	229	96	91
Total Assets (Millions $)	1,992	1,568	1,295	907	1,251	2,081	1,800	955	1,670	2,236

PORTFOLIO (as of 9/30/05)

Portfolio Manager: Glenn Fogle/David Rose - 1993

Investment Style

Large Cap	✔ Growth
✔ Mid Cap	Value
✔ Small Cap	Grth/Val

Portfolio

2.5% cash	0.0% corp bonds
97.5% stocks	0.0% gov't bonds
0.0% pref/conv't pref	0.0% muni bonds
0.0% conv't bds/wrnts	0.0% other

SHAREHOLDER INFORMATION

Minimum Investment
Initial: $2,500   Subsequent: $50

Minimum IRA Investment
Initial: $2,500   Subsequent: $50

Maximum Fees
Load: none   12b-1: none
Other: none

Services
✔ IRA
  Keogh
✔ Telephone Exchange

Baron Asset
(BARAX)

Mid-Cap Stock

800-992-2766
www.baronfunds.com

PERFORMANCE

fund inception date: 6/12/87

	3yr Annual	5yr Annual	10yr Annual	Bull	Bear
Return (%)	22.1	5.5	10.0	97.9	-39.8
Differ From Category (+/-)	1.8 abv av	-0.4 av	-0.4 av	15.8 high	-16.1 blw av

Standard Deviation	Category Risk Index	Beta
11.8%—abv av	0.94—av	1.09

	2005	2004	2003	2002	2001	2000	1999	1998	1997	1996
Return (%)	12.4	27.1	27.3	-19.9	-10.1	0.3	16.2	4.2	33.8	21.9
Differ From Category (+/-)	.2.5	11.6	-10.3	-1.5	-5.9	-5.5	-20.9	-7.4	11.6	3.4
Return, Tax-Adjusted (%)	11.6	26.1	27.3	-20.5	-11.6	-1.2	16.2	4.2	33.8	21.9

PER SHARE DATA

	2005	2004	2003	2002	2001	2000	1999	1998	1997	1996
Dividends, Net Income ($)	0.00	0.00	0.00	0.00	0.00	0.00	0.00	0.04	0.00	0.00
Distrib'ns, Cap Gain ($)	2.81	2.99	0.00	1.18	4.07	4.61	0.00	0.00	0.00	0.04
Net Asset Value ($)	56.29	52.52	43.83	34.42	44.46	54.39	58.77	50.54	48.51	36.23
Expense Ratio (%)	1.34	1.34	1.34	1.35	1.36	1.36	1.31	1.32	1.30	1.40
Yield (%)	0.00	0.00	0.00	0.00	0.00	0.00	0.00	0.08	0.00	0.00
Portfolio Turnover (%)	11	28	27	6	4	2	15	23	13	19
Total Assets (Millions $)	2,688	2,376	1,766	1,945	2,394	4,257	6,147	5,672	3,793	1,326

PORTFOLIO (as of 6/30/05)

Portfolio Manager: Ronald Baron/Andrew Peck - 1987

Investment Style

Large Cap	✔ Growth
✔ Mid Cap	Value
Small Cap	Grth/Val

Portfolio

1.2% cash	0.0% corp bonds
98.5% stocks	0.0% gov't bonds
0.2% pref/conv't pref	0.0% muni bonds
0.1% conv't bds/wrnts	0.0% other

SHAREHOLDER INFORMATION

Minimum Investment
Initial: $2,000   Subsequent: $1

Minimum IRA Investment
Initial: $2,000   Subsequent: $1

Maximum Fees
Load: none   12b-1: 0.25%
Other: none

Services
✔ IRA
  Keogh
✔ Telephone Exchange

Brandywine
(BRWIX)

Mid-Cap Stock

800-656-3017
www.brandywinefunds.com

PERFORMANCE

fund inception date: 12/30/85

	3yr Annual	5yr Annual	10yr Annual	Bull	Bear
Return (%)	19.3	1.1	9.2	77.0	-45.8
Differ From Category (+/-)	-1.0 av	-4.8 blw av	-1.2 blw av	-5.1 av	-22.1 blw av

Standard Deviation	Category Risk Index	Beta
13.6%—abv av	1.09—abv av	1.18

	2005	2004	2003	2002	2001	2000	1999	1998	1997	1996
Return (%)	14.3	13.1	31.4	-21.7	-20.5	7.1	53.5	-0.6	12.0	24.9
Differ From Category (+/-)	4.4	-2.4	-6.2	-3.3	-16.3	1.3	16.4	-12.3	-10.2	6.4
Return, Tax-Adjusted (%)	14.3	13.1	31.4	-21.7	-20.5	-0.4	51.4	-1.0	7.8	23.5

PER SHARE DATA

	2005	2004	2003	2002	2001	2000	1999	1998	1997	1996
Dividends, Net Income ($)	0.00	0.00	0.00	0.00	0.00	0.00	0.00	0.26	0.00	0.00
Distrib'ns, Cap Gain ($)	0.00	0.00	0.00	0.00	0.00	16.11	3.12	0.07	7.02	1.35
Net Asset Value ($)	31.09	27.18	24.03	18.28	23.35	29.39	42.88	30.28	30.89	33.69
Expense Ratio (%)	1.08	1.09	1.09	1.08	1.06	1.04	1.05	1.04	1.04	1.06
Yield (%)	0.00	0.00	0.00	0.00	0.00	0.00	0.00	0.87	0.00	0.00
Portfolio Turnover (%)	183	279	279	273	284	244	208	263	192	202
Total Assets (Millions $)	3,954	3,725	3,796	2,997	4,265	5,771	5,515	4,890	8,414	6,547

PORTFOLIO (as of 9/30/05)

Portfolio Manager: Team Managed - 1985

Investment Style

Large Cap	✔ Growth
✔ Mid Cap	Value
✔ Small Cap	Grth/Val

Portfolio

2.7% cash	0.0% corp bonds
97.3% stocks	0.0% gov't bonds
0.0% pref/conv't pref	0.0% muni bonds
0.0% conv't bds/wrnts	0.0% other

SHAREHOLDER INFORMATION

Minimum Investment
Initial: $10,000   Subsequent: $1,000

Minimum IRA Investment
Initial: $10,000   Subsequent: $1,000

Maximum Fees
Load: none   12b-1: none
Other: none

Services
✔ IRA
  Keogh
✔ Telephone Exchange

Brandywine Advisors
(BWAFX)
Mid-Cap Stock

877-636-6460
www.brandywinefunds.com

	3yr Annual	5yr Annual	10yr Annual	Bull	Bear
Return (%)	18.2	2.1	na	71.4	na
Differ From Category (+/-)	-2.1 blw av	-3.8 blw av	na	-10.7 blw av	na

Standard Deviation	Category Risk Index	Beta
13.7%—abv av	1.10—abv av	1.15

	2005	2004	2003	2002	2001	2000	1999	1998	1997	1996
Return (%)	16.8	9.8	28.8	-16.9	-19.2	—	—	—	—	—
Differ From Category (+/-)	.6.9	-5.7	-8.8	1.5	-15.0	—	—	—	—	—
Return, Tax-Adjusted (%)	14.7	9.8	28.8	-16.9	-19.2	—	—	—	—	—

PER SHARE DATA

	2005	2004	2003	2002	2001	2000	1999	1998	1997	1996
Dividends, Net Income ($)	0.00	0.00	0.00	0.00	0.00	—	—	—	—	—
Distrib'ns, Cap Gain ($)	1.40	0.00	0.00	0.00	0.00	—	—	—	—	—
Net Asset Value ($)	10.44	10.22	9.30	7.22	8.69	—	—	—	—	—
Expense Ratio (%)	119.00	1.20	1.22	1.25		—	—	—	—	—
Yield (%)	0.00	0.00	0.00	0.00	0.00	—	—	—	—	—
Portfolio Turnover (%)	207	269	269	259	278	—	—	—	—	—
Total Assets (Millions $)	191	154	143	111	125	—	—	—	—	—

PORTFOLIO (as of 9/30/05)

Portfolio Manager: Team Managed - 2000

Investment Style

Large Cap	✔ Growth
✔ Mid Cap	Value
Small Cap	Grth/Val

Portfolio

7.0% cash	0.0% corp bonds
91.6% stocks	0.0% gov't bonds
1.4% pref/conv't pref	0.0% muni bonds
0.0% conv't bds/wrnts	0.0% other

SHAREHOLDER INFORMATION

Minimum Investment
Initial: $10,000   Subsequent: $1,000

Minimum IRA Investment
Initial: $0   Subsequent: $0

Maximum Fees
Load: none   12b-1: 0.06%
Other: none

Services
  IRA
  Keogh
✔ Telephone Exchange

Buffalo Mid Cap
(BUFMX)

Mid-Cap Stock

800-492-8332
www.buffalofunds.com

PERFORMANCE   fund inception date: 12/17/01

	3yr Annual	5yr Annual	10yr Annual	Bull	Bear
Return (%)	24.0	na	na	98.9	na
Differ From Category (+/-)	3.7 high	na	na	16.8 high	na

Standard Deviation	Category Risk Index	Beta
15.0%—high	1.20—high	1.40

	2005	2004	2003	2002	2001	2000	1999	1998	1997	1996
Return (%).............	13.8	16.5	43.6	-22.1	—	—	—	—	—	—
Differ From Category (+/-)	.3.9	1.0	6.0	-3.7	—	—	—	—	—	—
Return, Tax-Adjusted (%)..	13.5	16.3	43.6	-22.1	—	—	—	—	—	—

PER SHARE DATA

	2005	2004	2003	2002	2001	2000	1999	1998	1997	1996
Dividends, Net Income ($)	.0.00	0.00	0.00	0.00	—	—	—	—	—	—
Distrib'ns, Cap Gain ($) ...	0.22	0.16	0.00	0.00	—	—	—	—	—	—
Net Asset Value ($)	14.48	12.92	11.22	7.81	—	—	—	—	—	—
Expense Ratio (%)........	1.03	1.03	1.10	1.16	—	—	—	—	—	—
Yield (%)	0.00	0.00	0.00	0.00	—	—	—	—	—	—
Portfolio Turnover (%)	21	24	8	3	—	—	—	—	—	—
Total Assets (Millions $)...	269	167	75	41	—	—	—	—	—	—

PORTFOLIO (as of 9/30/05)

Portfolio Manager: Gasaway/Male/Kornitzer - 2003

Investment Style
Large Cap	Growth
✔ Mid Cap	✔ Value
Small Cap	Grth/Val

Portfolio
9.2% cash	0.0% corp bonds
90.9% stocks	0.0% gov't bonds
0.0% pref/conv't pref	0.0% muni bonds
0.0% conv't bds/wrnts	0.0% other

SHAREHOLDER INFORMATION

Minimum Investment
Initial: $2,500   Subsequent: $100

Minimum IRA Investment
Initial: $250   Subsequent: $100

Maximum Fees
Load: none   12b-1: none
Other: none

Services
✔ IRA
Keogh
✔ Telephone Exchange

CRM Mid Cap Value Inv
(CRMMX)
Mid-Cap Stock

800-276-2883
www.crmfunds.com

PERFORMANCE   fund inception date: 9/20/00

	3yr Annual	5yr Annual	10yr Annual	Bull	Bear
Return (%)	23.8	13.4	na	97.4	na
Differ From Category (+/-)	3.5 high	7.5 high	na	15.3 high	na

Standard Deviation	Category Risk Index	Beta
10.5%—av	0.84—low	1.06

	2005	2004	2003	2002	2001	2000	1999	1998	1997	1996
Return (%)	7.7	24.6	41.6	-16.8	19.0	—	—	—	—	—
Differ From Category (+/-)	-2.2	9.1	4.0	1.6	23.3	—	—	—	—	—
Return, Tax-Adjusted (%)	7.1	23.8	41.5	-16.9	17.5	—	—	—	—	—

PER SHARE DATA

	2005	2004	2003	2002	2001	2000	1999	1998	1997	1996
Dividends, Net Income ($)	0.17	0.09	0.02	0.00	0.03	—	—	—	—	—
Distrib'ns, Cap Gain ($)	0.80	1.06	0.00	0.08	1.15	—	—	—	—	—
Net Asset Value ($)	26.69	25.68	21.54	15.23	18.42	—	—	—	—	—
Expense Ratio (%)	1.20	1.28	1.37	—	—	—	—	—	—	—
Yield (%)	0.62	0.33	0.11	0.00	0.15	—	—	—	—	—
Portfolio Turnover (%)	112	152	142	—	—	—	—	—	—	—
Total Assets (Millions $)	716	368	66	38	23	—	—	—	—	—

PORTFOLIO (as of 10/31/05)

Portfolio Manager: Jay Abramson/Robert Rewey III - 2000

Investment Style

Large Cap	Growth
✔ Mid Cap	✔ Value
Small Cap	Grth/Val

Portfolio

6.7% cash	0.0% corp bonds
93.3% stocks	0.0% gov't bonds
0.0% pref/conv't pref	0.0% muni bonds
0.0% conv't bds/wrnts	0.0% other

SHAREHOLDER INFORMATION

Minimum Investment

Initial: $2,500   Subsequent: $100

Minimum IRA Investment

Initial: $2,000   Subsequent: $100

Maximum Fees

Load: none   12b-1: none
Other: none

Services
✔ IRA
✔ Keogh
✔ Telephone Exchange

Delafield
(DEFIX)

Mid-Cap Stock

800-221-3079
www.delafieldfund.com

PERFORMANCE   fund inception date: 11/19/93

	3yr Annual	5yr Annual	10yr Annual	Bull	Bear
Return (%)	21.5	17.0	13.7	88.6	33.6
Differ From Category (+/-)	1.2 av	11.1 high	3.3 high	6.5 abv av	57.3 high

Standard Deviation	Category Risk Index	Beta
13.1%—abv av	1.05—abv av	1.31

	2005	2004	2003	2002	2001	2000	1999	1998	1997	1996
Return (%).	6.0	20.8	40.0	-7.4	32.1	13.9	8.4	-11.4	19.6	26.3
Differ From Category (+/-)	-3.9	5.3	2.4	11.0	36.4	8.1	-28.7	-23.1	-2.6	7.8
Return, Tax-Adjusted (%). . .	4.1	19.0	38.0	-7.4	30.6	13.5	8.1	-11.7	17.5	21.6

PER SHARE DATA

	2005	2004	2003	2002	2001	2000	1999	1998	1997	1996
Dividends, Net Income ($) .	0.03	0.00	0.00	0.00	0.06	0.07	0.09	0.12	0.21	0.16
Distrib'ns, Cap Gain ($) . . .	3.07	2.78	2.38	0.00	1.13	0.16	0.00	0.00	1.03	1.84
Net Asset Value ($)	23.63	25.21	23.17	18.23	19.70	15.80	14.07	13.06	14.88	13.49
Expense Ratio (%).	na	1.46	1.32	1.20	1.25	1.28	1.25	1.24	1.29	1.29
Yield (%)	0.10	0.00	0.00	0.00	0.27	0.45	0.60	0.92	1.30	1.02
Portfolio Turnover (%)	na	55	78	79	98	99	105	81	55	75
Total Assets (Millions $) . . .	372	345	247	144	199	99	86	104	147	61

PORTFOLIO (as of 3/31/05)

Portfolio Manager: D Delafield/V Sellecchia - 1993

Investment Style
Large Cap	Growth
✔ Mid Cap	✔ Value
✔ Small Cap	Grth/Val

Portfolio
0.0% cash	0.0% corp bonds
100.0% stocks	0.0% gov't bonds
0.0% pref/conv't pref	0.0% muni bonds
0.0% conv't bds/wrnts	0.0% other

SHAREHOLDER INFORMATION

Minimum Investment
Initial: $5,000   Subsequent: $1

Minimum IRA Investment
Initial: $250   Subsequent: $1

Maximum Fees
Load: 2.00% redemption   12b-1: 0.25%
Other: redemption fee applies for 3 months

Services
✔ IRA
✔ Keogh
✔ Telephone Exchange

Dreyfus Index Midcap Index (PESPX)

Mid-Cap Stock

800-645-6561
www.dreyfus.com

PERFORMANCE   fund inception date: 6/19/91

	3yr Annual	5yr Annual	10yr Annual	Bull	Bear
Return (%)	20.3	7.9	13.6	83.7	-17.2
Differ From Category (+/-)	0.0 av	2.0 av	3.2 high	1.6 av	6.5 av

Standard Deviation	Category Risk Index	Beta
11.6%—abv av	0.93—blw av	1.16

	2005	2004	2003	2002	2001	2000	1999	1998	1997	1996
Return (%).............	11.2	15.9	34.9	-15.0	-1.0	16.7	14.0	18.4	31.5	18.5
Differ From Category (+/-)	.1.3	0.4	-2.7	3.4	3.2	10.9	-23.1	6.8	9.3	0.0
Return, Tax-Adjusted (%)..	10.5	15.3	34.7	-15.5	-1.8	13.2	9.8	13.2	29.2	16.4

PER SHARE DATA

	2005	2004	2003	2002	2001	2000	1999	1998	1997	1996
Dividends, Net Income ($).	0.06	0.16	0.12	0.12	0.15	0.21	0.20	0.31	0.23	0.27
Distrib'ns, Cap Gain ($) ...	1.15	0.73	0.09	0.32	0.58	3.38	4.47	6.02	1.99	1.00
Net Asset Value ($)	27.94	26.19	23.36	17.47	21.06	22.03	21.94	23.58	25.64	21.24
Expense Ratio (%).........	na	0.50	0.51	0.50	0.50	0.50	0.50	0.50	0.50	0.50
Yield (%)	0.20	0.59	0.49	0.65	0.70	0.82	0.75	1.04	0.83	1.21
Portfolio Turnover (%)	na	14	12	19	28	45	50	67	20	14
Total Assets (Millions $) ..	2,200	1,709	1,228	735	633	493	323	273	257	184

PORTFOLIO (as of 9/30/05)

Portfolio Manager: Team Managed - 1995

Investment Style

Large Cap	Growth
✔ Mid Cap	Value
Small Cap	✔ Grth/Val

Portfolio

1.3% cash	0.0% corp bonds
98.7% stocks	0.0% gov't bonds
0.0% pref/conv't pref	0.0% muni bonds
0.0% conv't bds/wrnts	0.0% other

SHAREHOLDER INFORMATION

Minimum Investment
Initial: $2,500   Subsequent: $100

Minimum IRA Investment
Initial: $750   Subsequent: $1

Maximum Fees
Load: 1.00% redemption   12b-1: none
Other: redemption fee applies for 6 months

Services
✔ IRA
✔ Keogh
✔ Telephone Exchange

Excelsior Mid Cap Val & Restructuring (UMVEX)

Mid-Cap Stock

800-446-1012
www.excelsiorfunds.com

	3yr Annual	5yr Annual	10yr Annual	Bull	Bear
Return (%)	20.3	9.7	na	80.8	-14.4
Differ From Category (+/-)	0.0 av	3.8 abv av	na	-1.3 av	9.3 av

Standard Deviation	Category Risk Index	Beta
13.4%—abv av	1.07—abv av	1.30

	2005	2004	2003	2002	2001	2000	1999	1998	1997	1996
Return (%).	4.6	15.2	44.6	-15.7	8.4	4.2	34.4	20.1	27.5	—
Differ From Category (+/-)	-5.3	-0.3	7.0	2.7	12.7	-1.6	-2.7	8.5	5.3	—
Return, Tax-Adjusted (%) . . .	4.6	14.9	44.5	-15.8	7.7	-4.6	33.8	18.0	25.9	—

PER SHARE DATA

	2005	2004	2003	2002	2001	2000	1999	1998	1997	1996
Dividends, Net Income ($) .	0.03	0.23	0.03	0.02	0.02	0.37	0.05	0.06	0.06	—
Distrib'ns, Cap Gain ($) . . .	0.00	0.00	0.00	0.00	0.36	8.08	0.32	1.32	0.80	—
Net Asset Value ($)	18.03	17.26	15.19	10.53	12.52	11.90	19.89	15.09	13.79	—
Expense Ratio (%).	1.06	0.99	1.01	1.01	1.05	1.05	1.05	1.05	1.05	—
Yield (%)	0.16	1.35	0.21	0.18	0.12	1.84	0.23	0.39	0.43	—
Portfolio Turnover (%)	28	13	28	24	0	45	55	51	64	—
Total Assets (Millions $) . . .	220	231	184	80	25	1	0	0	0	—

PORTFOLIO (as of 6/30/05)

Portfolio Manager: Timothy Evnin/John McDermott - 1997

Investment Style
Large Cap	Growth
✔ Mid Cap	✔ Value
Small Cap	Grth/Val

Portfolio
0.0% cash	0.0% corp bonds
100.0% stocks	0.0% gov't bonds
0.0% pref/conv't pref	0.0% muni bonds
0.0% conv't bds/wrnts	0.0% other

SHAREHOLDER INFORMATION

Minimum Investment
Initial: $500   Subsequent: $50

Minimum IRA Investment
Initial: $250   Subsequent: $50

Maximum Fees
Load: none   12b-1: none
Other: none

Services
✔ IRA
✔ Keogh
✔ Telephone Exchange

Fairholme
(FAIRX)
Mid-Cap Stock

866-202-2263
www.fairholmefunds.com

PERFORMANCE   fund inception date: 12/29/99

	3yr Annual	5yr Annual	10yr Annual	Bull	Bear
Return (%)	20.7	12.9	na	90.8	35.4
Differ From Category (+/-)	0.4 av	7.0 high	na	8.7 abv av	59.1 high

Standard Deviation	Category Risk Index	Beta
9.2%—av	0.74—low	0.77

	2005	2004	2003	2002	2001	2000	1999	1998	1997	1996
Return (%)	13.7	24.9	23.9	-1.5	6.1	46.5	—	—	—	—
Differ From Category (+/-)	.3.8	9.4	-13.7	16.9	10.4	40.7	—	—	—	—
Return, Tax-Adjusted (%)	13.2	24.4	23.9	-1.7	5.9	45.9	—	—	—	—

PER SHARE DATA

	2005	2004	2003	2002	2001	2000	1999	1998	1997	1996
Dividends, Net Income ($)	0.23	0.06	0.00	0.03	0.03	0.00	—	—	—	—
Distrib'ns, Cap Gain ($)	0.48	0.53	0.01	0.10	0.09	0.28	—	—	—	—
Net Asset Value ($)	25.19	22.77	18.70	15.09	15.47	14.68	—	—	—	—
Expense Ratio (%)	na	1.00	1.00	1.00	1.00	1.00	—	—	—	—
Yield (%)	0.89	0.25	0.00	0.20	0.18	0.00	—	—	—	—
Portfolio Turnover (%)	na	23	13	48	29	39	—	—	—	—
Total Assets (Millions $)	1,439	264	93	49	26	17	—	—	—	—

PORTFOLIO (as of 5/31/05)

Portfolio Manager: Berkowitz/Pitkowsky/ Trauner - 1999

Investment Style

Large Cap	Growth
✔ Mid Cap	Value
Small Cap	✔ Grth/Val

Portfolio

5.3% cash	0.0% corp bonds
68.6% stocks	24.7% gov't bonds
1.4% pref/conv't pref	0.0% muni bonds
0.0% conv't bds/wrnts	0.0% other

SHAREHOLDER INFORMATION

Minimum Investment
Initial: $2,500   Subsequent: $1,000

Minimum IRA Investment
Initial: $1,000   Subsequent: $100

Maximum Fees
Load: 2.00% redemption   12b-1: none
Other: redemption fee applies for 2 months

Services
✔ IRA
Keogh
✔ Telephone Exchange

Fenimore Asset Management Tr Value (FAMVX)

800-932-3271
www.famfunds.com

Mid-Cap Stock

	3yr Annual	5yr Annual	10yr Annual	Bull	Bear
Return (%)	15.6	10.9	12.0	62.3	26.4
Differ From Category (+/-)	-4.7 low	5.0 abv av	1.6 av	-19.8 low	50.1 high

Standard Deviation	Category Risk Index	Beta
8.6%—blw av	0.69—low	0.84

	2005	2004	2003	2002	2001	2000	1999	1998	1997	1996
Return (%)	5.5	16.8	25.3	-5.5	15.0	19.2	-4.8	6.1	39.0	11.2
Differ From Category (+/-)	-4.4	1.3	-12.3	12.9	19.3	13.4	-42.0	-5.5	16.8	-7.3
Return, Tax-Adjusted (%)	5.1	16.3	24.8	-5.9	14.0	16.1	-5.8	4.1	38.1	10.2

PER SHARE DATA

	2005	2004	2003	2002	2001	2000	1999	1998	1997	1996
Dividends, Net Income ($)	0.37	0.07	0.09	0.11	0.17	0.36	0.29	0.20	0.08	0.18
Distrib'ns, Cap Gain ($)	0.87	1.36	0.87	0.44	1.30	4.03	1.09	3.24	1.06	0.63
Net Asset Value ($)	48.00	46.65	41.15	33.60	36.17	32.70	31.35	34.44	35.76	26.53
Expense Ratio (%)	na	1.20	1.24	1.21	1.21	1.26	1.23	1.19	1.24	1.27
Yield (%)	0.76	0.15	0.22	0.33	0.46	0.98	0.90	0.53	0.20	0.65
Portfolio Turnover (%)	na	10	9	17	10	9	16	16	9	12
Total Assets (Millions $)	1,111	920	580	470	501	367	373	376	332	254

PORTFOLIO (as of 9/30/05)

Portfolio Manager: Thomas Putnam/John Fox - 1987

Investment Style

Large Cap	Growth
✔ Mid Cap	Value
Small Cap	✔ Grth/Val

Portfolio

15.0%	cash	0.0%	corp bonds
85.0%	stocks	0.0%	gov't bonds
0.0%	pref/conv't pref	0.0%	muni bonds
0.0%	conv't bds/wrnts	0.0%	other

SHAREHOLDER INFORMATION

Minimum Investment
Initial: $500   Subsequent: $50

Minimum IRA Investment
Initial: $100   Subsequent: $50

Maximum Fees
Load: none   12b-1: none
Other: none

Services
✔ IRA
✔ Keogh
Telephone Exchange

Fidelity Aggressive Growth (FDEGX)

Mid-Cap Stock

800-544-8544
www.fidelity.com

PERFORMANCE

fund inception date: 12/28/90

	3yr Annual	5yr Annual	10yr Annual	Bull	Bear
Return (%)	16.7	-13.2	3.7	62.2	-80.6
Differ From Category (+/-)	-3.6 blw av	-19.1 low	-6.7 low	-19.9 low	-56.9 low

Standard Deviation	Category Risk Index	Beta
11.5%—abv av	0.92—blw av	1.04

	2005	2004	2003	2002	2001	2000	1999	1998	1997	1996
Return (%)............	7.2	11.1	33.4	-41.1	-47.2	-27.1	103.5	42.9	19.4	15.8
Differ From Category (+/-)	-2.7	-4.4	-4.2	-22.7	-43.0	-33.0	66.4	31.3	-2.8	-2.7
Return, Tax-Adjusted (%)...	7.2	11.1	33.4	-41.1	-47.3	-29.6	101.0	41.1	14.6	15.0

PER SHARE DATA

	2005	2004	2003	2002	2001	2000	1999	1998	1997	1996
Dividends, Net Income ($).	0.00	0.00	0.00	0.00	0.00	0.00	0.00	0.00	0.00	0.00
Distrib'ns, Cap Gain ($) ...	0.00	0.00	0.00	0.00	0.09	7.58	3.92	2.08	6.00	0.60
Net Asset Value ($)	17.80	16.60	14.93	11.19	19.02	36.17	59.63	31.69	23.75	25.19
Expense Ratio (%)........	na	0.78	0.59	0.55	0.92	0.89	0.97	1.08	1.09	1.09
Yield (%)	0.00	0.00	0.00	0.00	0.00	0.00	0.00	0.00	0.00	0.00
Portfolio Turnover (%)	na	84	176	114	118	176	186	199	212	105
Total Assets (Millions $) ..	4,329	5,054	5,278	4,131	7,410	15,220	15,199	2,897	1,982	1,854

PORTFOLIO (as of 8/31/05)

Portfolio Manager: Steven Calhoun - 2005

Investment Style
- ✔ Large Cap   ✔ Growth
- ✔ Mid Cap   Value
- ✔ Small Cap   Grth/Val

Portfolio

0.5%	cash	0.0%	corp bonds
99.5%	stocks	0.0%	gov't bonds
0.0%	pref/conv't pref	0.0%	muni bonds
0.0%	conv't bds/wrnts	0.0%	other

SHAREHOLDER INFORMATION

Minimum Investment
Initial: $2,500   Subsequent: $250

Minimum IRA Investment
Initial: $500   Subsequent: $250

Maximum Fees
Load: 1.50% redemption   12b-1: none
Other: redemption fee applies for 3 months;
maint fee for low bal

Services
- ✔ IRA
- ✔ Keogh
- ✔ Telephone Exchange

Fidelity Leveraged Company Stock (FLVCX)

Mid-Cap Stock

800-544-8544
www.fidelity.com

PERFORMANCE   fund inception date: 12/19/00

	3yr Annual	5yr Annual	10yr Annual	Bull	Bear
Return (%)	42.1	23.8	na	186.6	na
Differ From Category (+/-)	21.8 high	17.9 high	na	104.5 high	na

Standard Deviation	Category Risk Index	Beta
18.0%—high	1.44—high	1.65

	2005	2004	2003	2002	2001	2000	1999	1998	1997	1996
Return (%)	17.4	24.4	96.3	-1.7	3.2	—	—	—	—	—
Differ From Category (+/-)	.7.5	8.9	58.7	16.7	7.5	—	—	—	—	—
Return, Tax-Adjusted (%)	.17.0	23.5	95.9	-1.7	2.4	—	—	—	—	—

PER SHARE DATA

	2005	2004	2003	2002	2001	2000	1999	1998	1997	1996
Dividends, Net Income ($)	0.21	0.04	0.00	0.00	0.20	—	—	—	—	—
Distrib'ns, Cap Gain ($)	0.41	1.12	0.27	0.00	0.00	—	—	—	—	—
Net Asset Value ($)	26.02	22.68	19.33	10.00	10.18	—	—	—	—	—
Expense Ratio (%)	0.87	0.85	0.83	0.93	0.83	—	—	—	—	—
Yield (%)	0.79	0.16	0.00	0.00	1.96	—	—	—	—	—
Portfolio Turnover (%)	16	35	79	185	230	—	—	—	—	—
Total Assets (Millions $)	3,521	2,142	1,206	79	60	—	—	—	—	—

PORTFOLIO (as of 7/29/05)

Portfolio Manager: Thomas Soviero - 2000

Investment Style

Large Cap	Growth
✔ Mid Cap	Value
Small Cap	✔ Grth/Val

Portfolio

0.7% cash	0.4% corp bonds
98.6% stocks	0.0% gov't bonds
0.3% pref/conv't pref	0.0% muni bonds
0.0% conv't bds/wrnts	0.0% other

SHAREHOLDER INFORMATION

Minimum Investment
Initial: $10,000   Subsequent: $1,000

Minimum IRA Investment
Initial: $2,500   Subsequent: $1,000

Maximum Fees
Load: 1.50% redemption   12b-1: none
Other: redemption fee applies for 3 months;
maint fee for low bal

Services
✔ IRA
✔ Keogh
✔ Telephone Exchange

Fidelity Mid Cap Growth

(FSMGX)

Mid-Cap Stock

800-544-8544
www.fidelity.com

PERFORMANCE
fund inception date: 11/15/01

	3yr Annual	5yr Annual	10yr Annual	Bull	Bear
Return (%)	22.8	na	na	90.1	na
Differ From Category (+/-)	2.5 abv av	na	na	8.0 abv av	na

Standard Deviation	Category Risk Index	Beta
13.4%—abv av	1.07—abv av	1.23

	2005	2004	2003	2002	2001	2000	1999	1998	1997	1996
Return (%)	13.5	16.2	40.6	-30.4	—	—	—	—	—	—
Differ From Category (+/-)	.3.6	0.7	3.0	-12.0	—	—	—	—	—	—
Return, Tax-Adjusted (%)	13.1	15.9	40.6	-30.4	—	—	—	—	—	—

PER SHARE DATA

	2005	2004	2003	2002	2001	2000	1999	1998	1997	1996
Dividends, Net Income ($)	0.00	0.00	0.00	0.00	—	—	—	—	—	—
Distrib'ns, Cap Gain ($)	0.30	0.17	0.00	0.00	—	—	—	—	—	—
Net Asset Value ($)	13.11	11.82	10.32	7.34	—	—	—	—	—	—
Expense Ratio (%)	1.01	1.16	1.17	1.20	—	—	—	—	—	—
Yield (%)	0.00	0.00	0.00	0.00	—	—	—	—	—	—
Portfolio Turnover (%)	220	94	120	94	—	—	—	—	—	—
Total Assets (Millions $)	226	77	57	17	—	—	—	—	—	—

PORTFOLIO (as of 7/29/05)

Portfolio Manager: Bahaa Fam - 2004

Investment Style

Large Cap	✔ Growth
✔ Mid Cap	Value
Small Cap	Grth/Val

Portfolio

1.9% cash	0.0% corp bonds
98.1% stocks	0.0% gov't bonds
0.0% pref/conv't pref	0.0% muni bonds
0.0% conv't bds/wrnts	0.0% other

SHAREHOLDER INFORMATION

Minimum Investment
Initial: $2,500   Subsequent: $250

Minimum IRA Investment
Initial: $500   Subsequent: $250

Maximum Fees
Load: 0.75% redemption   12b-1: none
Other: redemption fee applies for 1 month;
maint fee for low bal

Services
✔ IRA
Keogh
✔ Telephone Exchange

Fidelity Mid Cap Stock
(FMCSX)
Mid-Cap Stock

800-544-8544
www.fidelity.com

fund inception date: 3/29/94

	3yr Annual	5yr Annual	10yr Annual	Bull	Bear
Return (%)	19.0	1.2	13.0	74.1	-34.5
Differ From Category (+/-)	-1.3 blw av	-4.7 blw av	2.6 abv av	-8.0 blw av	-10.8 blw av

Standard Deviation	Category Risk Index	Beta
13.5%—abv av	1.08—abv av	1.25

	2005	2004	2003	2002	2001	2000	1999	1998	1997	1996
Return (%)	16.0	9.0	33.2	-27.5	-12.8	32.0	39.8	15.1	27.0	18.1
Differ From Category (+/-)	.6.1	-6.5	-4.4	-9.1	-8.5	26.2	2.7	3.5	4.8	-0.4
Return, Tax-Adjusted (%)	15.6	9.0	33.1	-27.7	-13.0	29.6	36.9	13.6	24.6	15.4

PER SHARE DATA

	2005	2004	2003	2002	2001	2000	1999	1998	1997	1996
Dividends, Net Income ($)	0.04	0.07	0.09	0.09	0.16	0.10	0.01	0.00	0.01	0.03
Distrib'ns, Cap Gain ($)	0.60	0.00	0.00	0.00	0.00	2.50	2.59	1.28	1.77	1.26
Net Asset Value ($)	26.57	23.45	21.57	16.26	22.57	26.06	21.87	17.88	16.69	14.64
Expense Ratio (%)	0.71	0.65	0.66	0.87	0.84	0.86	0.74	0.86	0.96	1.00
Yield (%)	0.14	0.29	0.41	0.55	0.70	0.35	0.04	0.00	0.05	0.18
Portfolio Turnover (%)	186	137	120	200	218	205	121	132	155	179
Total Assets (Millions $)	9,949	9,093	8,049	5,132	6,547	7,011	2,286	1,784	1,763	1,695

PORTFOLIO (as of 7/29/05)

Portfolio Manager: Shep Perkins - 2005

Investment Style

Large Cap	✔ Growth
✔ Mid Cap	Value
✔ Small Cap	Grth/Val

Portfolio

1.3% cash	0.0% corp bonds
98.8% stocks	0.0% gov't bonds
0.0% pref/conv't pref	0.0% muni bonds
0.0% conv't bds/wrnts	0.0% other

SHAREHOLDER INFORMATION

Minimum Investment
Initial: $2,500   Subsequent: $250

Minimum IRA Investment
Initial: $500   Subsequent: $250

Maximum Fees
Load: 0.75% redemption   12b-1: none
Other: redemption fee applies for 1 month

Services
✔ IRA
✔ Keogh
✔ Telephone Exchange

Fidelity Mid Cap Value
(FSMVX)
Mid-Cap Stock

800-544-8544
www.fidelity.com

PERFORMANCE   fund inception date: 11/15/01

	3yr Annual	5yr Annual	10yr Annual	Bull	Bear
Return (%)	22.7	na	na	92.2	na
Differ From Category (+/-)	2.4 abv av	na	na	10.1 abv av	na

Standard Deviation	Category Risk Index	Beta
11.0%—av	0.88—blw av	1.08

	2005	2004	2003	2002	2001	2000	1999	1998	1997	1996
Return (%)	13.6	21.8	33.4	-13.5	—	—	—	—	—	—
Differ From Category (+/-)	.3.7	6.3	-4.2	4.9	—	—	—	—	—	—
Return, Tax-Adjusted (%)	12.3	21.4	33.4	-13.8	—	—	—	—	—	—

PER SHARE DATA

	2005	2004	2003	2002	2001	2000	1999	1998	1997	1996
Dividends, Net Income ($)	0.10	0.04	0.04	0.08	—	—	—	—	—	—
Distrib'ns, Cap Gain ($)	1.15	0.32	0.00	0.00	—	—	—	—	—	—
Net Asset Value ($)	15.05	14.35	12.08	9.08	—	—	—	—	—	—
Expense Ratio (%)	0.91	1.05	1.18	1.20	—	—	—	—	—	—
Yield (%)	0.58	0.27	0.33	0.88	—	—	—	—	—	—
Portfolio Turnover (%)	196	97	113	68	—	—	—	—	—	—
Total Assets (Millions $)	315	143	89	42	—	—	—	—	—	—

PORTFOLIO (as of 7/29/05)

Portfolio Manager: Bruce Dirks - 2005

Investment Style

Large Cap	Growth
✔ Mid Cap	✔ Value
Small Cap	Grth/Val

Portfolio

0.9%	cash	0.0%	corp bonds
97.5%	stocks	0.0%	gov't bonds
0.0%	pref/conv't pref	0.0%	muni bonds
0.0%	conv't bds/wrnts	1.5%	other

SHAREHOLDER INFORMATION

Minimum Investment
Initial: $2,500   Subsequent: $250

Minimum IRA Investment
Initial: $500   Subsequent: $250

Maximum Fees
Load: 0.75% redemption   12b-1: none
Other: redemption fee applies for 1 month;
maint fee for low bal

Services
✔ IRA
   Keogh
✔ Telephone Exchange

Fidelity Value
(FDVLX)

Mid-Cap Stock

800-544-8544
www.fidelity.com

PERFORMANCE

fund inception date: 12/1/78

	3yr Annual	5yr Annual	10yr Annual	Bull	Bear
Return (%)	23.0	13.6	12.1	95.2	11.7
Differ From Category (+/-)	2.7 abv av	7.7 high	1.7 av	13.1 abv av	35.4 high

Standard Deviation	Category Risk Index	Beta
11.5%—abv av	0.92—blw av	1.17

	2005	2004	2003	2002	2001	2000	1999	1998	1997	1996
Return (%)	14.2	21.2	34.4	-9.2	12.2	8.1	8.5	0.1	21.0	16.8
Differ From Category (+/-)	4.3	5.7	-3.2	9.2	16.5	2.3	-28.6	-11.5	-1.2	-1.7
Return, Tax-Adjusted (%)	13.0	20.2	34.3	-9.5	11.8	7.2	5.5	-2.8	17.6	13.0

PER SHARE DATA

	2005	2004	2003	2002	2001	2000	1999	1998	1997	1996
Dividends, Net Income ($)	0.43	0.16	0.23	0.36	0.51	0.95	0.73	0.55	0.48	0.53
Distrib'ns, Cap Gain ($)	5.14	3.71	0.05	0.00	0.00	0.00	5.62	7.15	7.95	5.92
Net Asset Value ($)	75.88	71.29	62.07	46.39	51.51	46.35	43.81	46.35	54.04	51.54
Expense Ratio (%)	na	0.98	0.98	0.95	0.77	0.48	0.54	0.61	0.66	0.88
Yield (%)	0.53	0.21	0.37	0.77	0.99	2.04	1.47	1.02	0.77	0.92
Portfolio Turnover (%)	na	40	40	42	49	48	50	36	56	112
Total Assets (Millions $)	14,328	10,279	6,984	5,092	5,238	3,522	4,383	5,523	7,914	7,080

PORTFOLIO (as of 7/29/05)

Portfolio Manager: Richard Fentin - 1996

Investment Style
✔ Large Cap   Growth
✔ Mid Cap   ✔ Value
    Small Cap   Grth/Val

Portfolio
6.2% cash	0.2% corp bonds
93.1% stocks	0.0% gov't bonds
0.3% pref/conv't pref	0.0% muni bonds
0.2% conv't bds/wrnts	0.0% other

SHAREHOLDER INFORMATION

Minimum Investment
Initial: $2,500   Subsequent: $100

Minimum IRA Investment
Initial: $500   Subsequent: $100

Maximum Fees
Load: none   12b-1: none
Other: maint fee for low bal

Services
✔ IRA
✔ Keogh
✔ Telephone Exchange

Fidelity Value Discovery

(FVDFX)

Mid-Cap Stock

800-544-8544
www.fidelity.com

PERFORMANCE

fund inception date: 12/10/02

	3yr Annual	**5yr Annual**	**10yr Annual**	**Bull**	**Bear**
Return (%)	20.7	na	na	84.3	na
Differ From Category (+/-)	0.4 av	na	na	2.2 av	na

Standard Deviation	**Category Risk Index**	**Beta**
11.7%—abv av	0.94—blw av	1.18

	2005	2004	2003	2002	2001	2000	1999	1998	1997	1996
Return (%)	18.7	14.5	29.5	—	—	—	—	—	—	—
Differ From Category (+/-)	8.8	-1.0	-8.1	—	—	—	—	—	—	—
Return, Tax-Adjusted (%)	18.0	13.8	29.1	—	—	—	—	—	—	—

PER SHARE DATA

	2005	2004	2003	2002	2001	2000	1999	1998	1997	1996
Dividends, Net Income ($)	0.03	0.02	0.00	—	—	—	—	—	—	—
Distrib'ns, Cap Gain ($)	0.54	0.54	0.29	—	—	—	—	—	—	—
Net Asset Value ($)	15.65	13.68	12.49	—	—	—	—	—	—	—
Expense Ratio (%)	0.96	1.08	1.44	—	—	—	—	—	—	—
Yield (%)	0.18	0.14	0.00	—	—	—	—	—	—	—
Portfolio Turnover (%)	113	164	158	—	—	—	—	—	—	—
Total Assets (Millions $)	293	77	47	—	—	—	—	—	—	—

PORTFOLIO (as of 7/29/05)

Portfolio Manager: Scott Offen - 2002

Investment Style

Large Cap	Growth
✔ Mid Cap	✔ Value
Small Cap	Grth/Val

Portfolio

0.6% cash	0.0% corp bonds
99.4% stocks	0.0% gov't bonds
0.0% pref/conv't pref	0.0% muni bonds
0.0% conv't bds/wrnts	0.0% other

SHAREHOLDER INFORMATION

Minimum Investment
Initial: $2,500   Subsequent: $100

Minimum IRA Investment
Initial: $500   Subsequent: $100

Maximum Fees
Load: none   12b-1: none
Other: maint fee for low bal

Services
✔ IRA
✔ Keogh
✔ Telephone Exchange

Fidelity Value Strategies

(FSLSX)

Mid-Cap Stock

800-544-8544
www.fidelity.com

PERFORMANCE

fund inception date: 12/27/83

	3yr Annual	5yr Annual	10yr Annual	Bull	Bear
Return (%)	23.8	9.7	10.7	102.4	-21.8
Differ From Category (+/-)	3.5 high	3.8 abv av	0.3 av	20.3 high	1.9 av

Standard Deviation	Category Risk Index	Beta
18.8%—high	1.50—high	1.78

	2005	2004	2003	2002	2001	2000	1999	1998	1997	1996
Return (%)	2.7	14.8	61.0	-25.8	12.7	11.8	19.4	1.2	26.7	2.0
Differ From Category (+/-)	-7.2	-0.7	23.4	-7.3	17.0	6.0	-17.7	-10.4	4.5	-16.5
Return, Tax-Adjusted (%)	-0.1	14.8	61.0	-25.8	12.5	10.5	14.5	0.7	23.9	-1.0

PER SHARE DATA

	2005	2004	2003	2002	2001	2000	1999	1998	1997	1996
Dividends, Net Income ($)	0.11	0.00	0.00	0.00	0.02	0.02	0.00	0.03	0.32
Distrib'ns, Cap Gain ($)	7.16	0.15	0.00	0.07	0.30	1.52	6.16	0.65	3.13	2.35
Net Asset Value ($)	31.28	37.53	32.80	20.37	27.52	24.69	23.54	25.22	25.58	22.91
Expense Ratio (%)	na	0.87	0.76	0.73	0.77	0.58	0.61	0.69	0.76	0.81
Yield (%)	0.29	0.00	0.00	0.00	0.00	0.07	0.06	0.00	0.10	1.26
Portfolio Turnover (%)	na	26	32	49	31	48	60	—	—	—
Total Assets (Millions $)	171	207	22	14	20	20	19	19	21	20

PORTFOLIO (as of 8/31/05)

Portfolio Manager: Rich Fentin - 2005

Investment Style

Large Cap	Growth
✔ Mid Cap	✔ Value
Small Cap	Grth/Val

Portfolio

7.8% cash	0.0% corp bonds
92.2% stocks	0.0% gov't bonds
0.0% pref/conv't pref	0.0% muni bonds
0.0% conv't bds/wrnts	0.0% other

SHAREHOLDER INFORMATION

Minimum Investment
Initial: $2,500   Subsequent: $250

Minimum IRA Investment
Initial: $500   Subsequent: $100

Maximum Fees
Load: none   12b-1: none
Other: maint fee for low bal

Services
✔ IRA
✔ Keogh
✔ Telephone Exchange

FMI Common Stock
(FMIMX)

Mid-Cap Stock

800-811-5311
www.fiduciarymgt.com

PERFORMANCE

fund inception date: 12/18/81

	3yr Annual	5yr Annual	10yr Annual	Bull	Bear
Return (%)	17.2	12.5	12.6	72.4	17.1
Differ From Category (+/-)	-3.1 blw av	6.6 high	2.2 abv av	-9.7 blw av	40.8 high

Standard Deviation	Category Risk Index	Beta
10.8%—av	0.86—blw av	1.03

	2005	2004	2003	2002	2001	2000	1999	1998	1997	1996
Return (%)	9.4	18.7	24.0	-5.7	18.6	19.0	6.5	-5.0	29.2	17.1
Differ From Category (+/-)	-0.5	3.2	-13.6	12.7	22.9	13.2	-30.6	-16.7	7.0	-1.4
Return, Tax-Adjusted (%)	7.6	17.9	23.6	-5.7	15.8	17.8	5.9	-9.1	25.4	13.3

PER SHARE DATA

	2005	2004	2003	2002	2001	2000	1999	1998	1997	1996
Dividends, Net Income ($)	0.02	0.00	0.00	0.00	0.00	0.00	0.00	0.00	0.01	0.15
Distrib'ns, Cap Gain ($)	2.95	1.21	0.48	0.00	2.68	1.07	0.43	4.71	3.86	2.50
Net Asset Value ($)	24.36	25.15	22.27	18.36	19.48	18.92	16.89	16.32	22.66	20.73
Expense Ratio (%)	1.23	1.25	1.25	1.10	1.20	1.20	1.30	1.20	1.20	1.20
Yield (%)	0.05	0.00	0.00	0.00	0.00	0.00	0.00	0.00	0.04	0.64
Portfolio Turnover (%)	34	34	34	29	46	46	75	54	60	43
Total Assets (Millions $)	446	436	328	111	64	50	41	42	52	44

PORTFOLIO (as of 9/30/05)

Portfolio Manager: T Kellner/P English - 1981

Investment Style

Large Cap	Growth
✔ Mid Cap	✔ Value
✔ Small Cap	Grth/Val

Portfolio

3.3% cash	0.0% corp bonds
96.7% stocks	0.0% gov't bonds
0.0% pref/conv't pref	0.0% muni bonds
0.0% conv't bds/wrnts	0.0% other

SHAREHOLDER INFORMATION

Minimum Investment
Initial: $1,000   Subsequent: $100

Minimum IRA Investment
Initial: $1,000   Subsequent: $100

Maximum Fees
Load: none   12b-1: none
Other: none

Services
✔ IRA
✔ Keogh
Telephone Exchange

Heartland Select Value

(HRSVX)

Mid-Cap Stock

800-432-7856
www.heartlandfunds.com

PERFORMANCE

fund inception date: 10/11/96

	3yr Annual	5yr Annual	10yr Annual	Bull	Bear
Return (%)	21.6	12.5	na	90.3	18.8
Differ From Category (+/-)	1.3 abv av	6.6 high	na	8.2 abv av	42.5 high

Standard Deviation	Category Risk Index	Beta
13.0%—abv av	1.04—abv av	1.30

	2005	2004	2003	2002	2001	2000	1999	1998	1997	1996
Return (%)	13.4	17.0	35.6	-13.8	16.4	30.6	1.9	1.7	22.9	—
Differ From Category (+/-)	.3.5	1.5	-2.0	4.6	20.7	24.8	-35.2	-9.9	0.7	—
Return, Tax-Adjusted (%)	12.8	16.8	35.6	-13.9	16.1	29.9	0.5	0.3	21.5	—

PER SHARE DATA

	2005	2004	2003	2002	2001	2000	1999	1998	1997	1996
Dividends, Net Income ($)	0.06	0.01	0.01	0.03	0.02	0.14	0.42	0.30	0.11	—
Distrib'ns, Cap Gain ($)	0.91	0.21	0.00	0.00	0.16	0.14	0.00	0.26	0.48	—
Net Asset Value ($)	25.56	23.37	20.16	14.87	17.30	15.03	11.73	11.94	12.30	—
Expense Ratio (%)	na	1.33	1.47	1.46	1.48	1.22	0.74	1.36	2.73	—
Yield (%)	0.21	0.05	0.06	0.22	0.08	0.89	3.54	2.49	0.84	—
Portfolio Turnover (%)	na	72	47	39	108	120	160	48	30	—
Total Assets (Millions $)	155	110	76	56	29	10	7	8	8	—

PORTFOLIO (as of 9/30/05)

Portfolio Manager: Team Managed - 1999

Investment Style

Large Cap   Growth
✔ Mid Cap   ✔ Value
Small Cap   Grth/Val

Portfolio

5.3% cash	0.0% corp bonds
94.7% stocks	0.0% gov't bonds
0.0% pref/conv't pref	0.0% muni bonds
0.0% conv't bds/wrnts	0.0% other

SHAREHOLDER INFORMATION

Minimum Investment

Initial: $1,000   Subsequent: $100

Minimum IRA Investment

Initial: $500   Subsequent: $100

Maximum Fees

Load: 2.00% redemption   12b-1: 0.25%
Other: redemption fee applies for 10 days

Services

✔ IRA
✔ Keogh
✔ Telephone Exchange

Janus Enterprise
(JAENX)

Mid-Cap Stock

800-525-3713
www.janus.com

PERFORMANCE   fund inception date: 9/1/92

	3yr Annual	5yr Annual	10yr Annual	Bull	Bear
Return (%)	22.2	-4.7	7.2	86.0	-73.6
Differ From Category (+/-)	1.9 abv av	-10.6 low	-3.2 low	3.9 av	-49.9 low

Standard Deviation	Category Risk Index	Beta
11.5%—abv av	0.92—blw av	1.10

	2005	2004	2003	2002	2001	2000	1999	1998	1997	1996
Return (%)............	11.4	20.6	35.8	-28.2	-39.9	-30.5	121.9	33.7	10.8	11.6
Differ From Category (+/-)	.1.5	5.1	-1.8	-9.8	-35.7	-36.4	84.8	22.1	-11.4	-6.9
Return, Tax-Adjusted (%)..	11.4	20.6	35.8	-28.2	-39.9	-30.5	120.0	30.9	9.4	10.3

PER SHARE DATA

	2005	2004	2003	2002	2001	2000	1999	1998	1997	1996
Dividends, Net Income ($)	0.00	0.00	0.00	0.00	0.00	0.00	0.00	0.00	0.00	0.00
Distrib'ns, Cap Gain ($) ...	0.00	0.00	0.00	0.00	0.00	0.00	3.33	4.30	1.96	1.28
Net Asset Value ($)	41.91	37.62	31.17	22.95	32.00	53.27	76.67	36.22	30.48	29.34
Expense Ratio (%)........	1.03	0.90	0.89	0.90	0.90	0.88	0.95	1.06	1.04	1.12
Yield (%)	0.00	0.00	0.00	0.00	0.00	0.00	0.00	0.00	0.00	0.00
Portfolio Turnover (%)	27	21	22	64	85	80	98	134	111	93
Total Assets (Millions $)..	1,795	1,835	1,884	1,626	3,209	6,267	4,435	728	573	722

PORTFOLIO (as of 7/29/05)

Portfolio Manager: Jonathan Coleman - 2002

Investment Style

Large Cap	✔ Growth
✔ Mid Cap	Value
✔ Small Cap	Grth/Val

Portfolio

2.1% cash	0.0% corp bonds
97.9% stocks	0.0% gov't bonds
0.0% pref/conv't pref	0.0% muni bonds
0.0% conv't bds/wrnts	0.0% other

SHAREHOLDER INFORMATION

Minimum Investment
Initial: $2,500   Subsequent: $100

Minimum IRA Investment
Initial: $500   Subsequent: $100

Maximum Fees
Load: none   12b-1: none
Other: none

Services
✔ IRA
✔ Keogh
✔ Telephone Exchange

Janus Mid Cap Value Inv
(JMCVX)
Mid-Cap Stock

800-525-3713
www.janus.com

fund inception date: 8/12/98

	3yr Annual	5yr Annual	10yr Annual	Bull	Bear
Return (%)	22.0	13.7	na	87.9	18.1
Differ From Category (+/-)	1.7 abv av	7.8 high	na	5.8 abv av	41.8 high

Standard Deviation	Category Risk Index	Beta
10.5%—av	0.84—low	1.05

	2005	2004	2003	2002	2001	2000	1999	1998	1997	1996
Return (%)	10.3	18.3	39.3	-13.0	20.5	27.3	21.5	—	—	—
Differ From Category (+/-)	0.4	2.8	1.7	5.4	24.8	21.5	-15.6	—	—	—
Return, Tax-Adjusted (%)	8.9	16.8	39.2	-13.1	19.9	24.8	19.2	—	—	—

PER SHARE DATA

	2005	2004	2003	2002	2001	2000	1999	1998	1997	1996
Dividends, Net Income ($)	0.24	0.08	0.10	0.03	0.03	0.10	0.04	—	—	—
Distrib'ns, Cap Gain ($)	1.83	1.93	0.00	0.00	0.35	1.36	1.24	—	—	—
Net Asset Value ($)	22.32	22.09	20.39	14.71	16.96	14.39	12.51	—	—	—
Expense Ratio (%)	0.94	0.94	1.08	1.15	1.22	1.59	1.62	—	—	—
Yield (%)	1.00	0.35	0.50	0.20	0.16	0.63	0.31	—	—	—
Portfolio Turnover (%)	86	91	97	39	116	129	154	—	—	—
Total Assets (Millions $)	4,408	3,453	1,747	948	265	51	25	—	—	—

PORTFOLIO (as of 7/29/05)

Portfolio Manager: T Perkins/R Perkins/ J Kautz - 1998

Investment Style

Large Cap	Growth
✔ Mid Cap	✔ Value
Small Cap	Grth/Val

Portfolio

11.6%	cash	0.0%	corp bonds
88.4%	stocks	0.0%	gov't bonds
0.0%	pref/conv't pref	0.0%	muni bonds
0.0%	conv't bds/wrnts	0.0%	other

SHAREHOLDER INFORMATION

Minimum Investment
Initial: $2,500   Subsequent: $100

Minimum IRA Investment
Initial: $500   Subsequent: $100

Maximum Fees
Load: none   12b-1: none
Other: none

Services
✔ IRA
✔ Keogh
✔ Telephone Exchange

Kinetics Paradigm
(WWNPX)

Mid-Cap Stock

800-930-3828
www.kineticsfunds.com

fund inception date: 12/31/99

	3yr Annual	5yr Annual	10yr Annual	Bull	Bear
Return (%)	27.5	15.1	na	114.4	-4.0
Differ From Category (+/-)	7.2 high	9.2 high	na	32.3 high	19.7 abv av

Standard Deviation	Category Risk Index	Beta
11.8%—abv av	0.94—av	1.06

	2005	2004	2003	2002	2001	2000	1999	1998	1997	1996
Return (%).	16.1	20.9	47.7	-4.6	2.1	3.9	—	—	—	—
Differ From Category (+/-)	.6.2	5.4	10.1	13.8	6.4	-1.9	—	—	—	—
Return, Tax-Adjusted (%) . .	16.0	20.4	47.6	-4.6	2.1	3.9	—	—	—	—

PER SHARE DATA

	2005	2004	2003	2002	2001	2000	1999	1998	1997	1996
Dividends, Net Income ($)	0.01	0.01	0.05	0.00	0.00	0.00	—	—	—	—
Distrib'ns, Cap Gain ($) . . .	0.02	0.46	0.00	0.00	0.00	0.00	—	—	—	—
Net Asset Value ($)	20.33	17.54	14.90	10.12	10.61	10.39	—	—	—	—
Expense Ratio (%).	na	1.74	1.74	2.74	2.74	2.00	—	—	—	—
Yield (%)	0.05	0.08	0.36	0.00	0.00	0.00	—	—	—	—
Portfolio Turnover (%)	na	52	20	40	41	89	—	—	—	—
Total Assets (Millions $) . . .	418	89	58	5	5	4	—	—	—	—

PORTFOLIO (as of 9/30/05)

Portfolio Manager: Peter Doyle - 1999

Investment Style

Large Cap	Growth
✔ Mid Cap	✔ Value
Small Cap	Grth/Val

Portfolio

14.0% cash	0.0% corp bonds
85.9% stocks	0.0% gov't bonds
0.0% pref/conv't pref	0.0% muni bonds
0.0% conv't bds/wrnts	0.1% other

SHAREHOLDER INFORMATION

Minimum Investment
Initial: $2,500   Subsequent: $100

Minimum IRA Investment
Initial: $2,500   Subsequent: $100

Maximum Fees
Load: none   12b-1: none
Other: none

Services
✔ IRA
  Keogh
✔ Telephone Exchange

Markman Total Return Core (MTRPX)

800-707-2771
www.markman.com

Mid-Cap Stock

Markman Total Cap Growth Inv (MNMSX)
Mid-Cap Stock

PERFORMANCE

fund inception date: 1/26/95

	3yr Annual	5yr Annual	10yr Annual	Bull	Bear
Return (%)	21.2	0.2	4.8	86.3	-59.9
Differ From Category (+/-)	0.9 av	-5.7 blw av	-5.6 low	4.2 abv av	-36.2 low

Standard Deviation	Category Risk Index	Beta
14.6%—high	1.17—high	1.36

	2005	2004	2003	2002	2001	2000	1999	1998	1997	1996
Return (%)	7.9	14.3	44.4	-25.6	-23.5	-25.3	35.4	18.3	19.3	11.1
Differ From Category (+/-)	-2.0	-1.2	6.8	-7.2	-19.3	-31.2	-1.7	6.7	-2.9	-7.4
Return, Tax-Adjusted (%)	7.8	14.1	44.2	-26.3	-24.3	-26.4	32.9	16.8	15.4	8.1

PER SHARE DATA

	2005	2004	2003	2002	2001	2000	1999	1998	1997	1996
Dividends, Net Income ($)	0.05	0.07	0.08	0.17	0.23	0.10	0.29	0.16	0.47	0.31
Distrib'ns, Cap Gain ($)	0.00	0.00	0.00	0.00	0.00	0.68	1.11	0.57	1.34	0.76
Net Asset Value ($)	11.00	10.24	9.02	6.30	8.69	11.67	16.69	13.35	11.90	11.49
Expense Ratio (%)	na	1.44	1.50	0.96	0.95	0.95	0.95	—	—	—
Yield (%)	0.48	0.69	0.85	2.62	2.68	0.81	1.61	1.14	3.57	2.56
Portfolio Turnover (%)	na	472	228	145	162	142	68	—	—	—
Total Assets (Millions $)	56	60	59	20	37	65	101	84	86	79

PORTFOLIO (as of 11/30/05)

Portfolio Manager: Robert Markman - 1995

Investment Style
✔ Large Cap   ✔ Growth
✔ Mid Cap   Value
✔ Small Cap   Grth/Val

Portfolio

0.0%	cash	0.0%	corp bonds
94.8%	stocks	0.0%	gov't bonds
1.5%	pref/conv't pref	0.0%	muni bonds
0.0%	conv't bds/wrnts	3.7%	other

SHAREHOLDER INFORMATION

Minimum Investment
Initial: $25,000   Subsequent: $500

Minimum IRA Investment
Initial: $25,000   Subsequent: $500

Maximum Fees
Load: none   12b-1: none
Other: none

Services
✔ IRA
✔ Keogh
✔ Telephone Exchange

Marshall Mid Cap Growth Inv (MRMSX)

Mid-Cap Stock

800-236-3863
www.marshallfunds.com

PERFORMANCE

fund inception date: 9/30/93

	3yr Annual	5yr Annual	10yr Annual	Bull	Bear
Return (%)	14.1	-2.0	8.3	52.6	-56.7
Differ From Category (+/-)	-6.2 low	-7.9 low	-2.1 blw av	-29.5 low	-33.0 low

Standard Deviation	Category Risk Index	Beta
13.3%—abv av	1.06—abv av	1.23

	2005	2004	2003	2002	2001	2000	1999	1998	1997	1996
Return (%).	3.9	11.9	27.6	-31.7	-10.5	-11.2	61.1	15.7	22.7	20.6
Differ From Category (+/-)	-6.0	-3.6	-10.0	-13.3	-6.3	-17.0	24.0	4.1	0.5	2.1
Return, Tax-Adjusted (%). . .	3.9	11.9	27.6	-31.7	-10.5	-15.5	58.9	14.5	19.9	17.7

PER SHARE DATA

	2005	2004	2003	2002	2001	2000	1999	1998	1997	1996
Dividends, Net Income ($).	0.00	0.00	0.00	0.00	0.00	0.00	0.00	0.00	0.00	0.00
Distrib'ns, Cap Gain ($) . . .	0.00	0.00	0.00	0.00	0.04	4.97	1.69	0.82	1.81	1.22
Net Asset Value ($)	14.09	13.55	12.10	9.48	13.89	15.57	23.06	15.50	14.21	13.10
Expense Ratio (%).	0.54	1.24	1.28	1.24	1.19	1.18	1.21	1.23	1.24	1.01
Yield (%)	0.00	0.00	0.00	0.00	0.00	0.00	0.00	0.00	0.00	0.00
Portfolio Turnover (%)	188	240	121	167	118	108	173	167	211	189
Total Assets (Millions $) . . .	173	188	246	196	319	401	424	263	216	161

PORTFOLIO (as of 11/30/05)

Portfolio Manager: Team Managed - 2004

Investment Style

Large Cap	✔ Growth
✔ Mid Cap	Value
✔ Small Cap	Grth/Val

Portfolio

3.9% cash	0.0% corp bonds
96.1% stocks	0.0% gov't bonds
0.0% pref/conv't pref	0.0% muni bonds
0.0% conv't bds/wrnts	0.0% other

SHAREHOLDER INFORMATION

Minimum Investment
Initial: $1,000   Subsequent: $50

Minimum IRA Investment
Initial: $1,000   Subsequent: $50

Maximum Fees
Load: 2.00% redemption   12b-1: none
Other: redemption fee applies for 1 month

Services
✔ IRA
  Keogh
✔ Telephone Exchange

Marshall Mid Cap Value Inv (MRVEX)

800-236-3863
www.marshallfunds.com

Mid-Cap Stock

PERFORMANCE
fund inception date: 9/30/93

	3yr Annual	5yr Annual	10yr Annual	Bull	Bear
Return (%)	19.3	12.9	12.9	78.4	24.3
Differ From Category (+/-)	-1.0 blw av	7.0 high	2.5 abv av	-3.7 av	48.0 high

Standard Deviation	Category Risk Index	Beta
11.0%—av	0.88—blw av	1.10

	2005	2004	2003	2002	2001	2000	1999	1998	1997	1996
Return (%)	7.1	16.6	35.8	-11.5	22.1	17.3	6.1	5.1	23.3	13.9
Differ From Category (+/-)	-2.8	1.1	-1.8	6.9	26.4	11.5	-31.0	-6.5	1.1	-4.6
Return, Tax-Adjusted (%)	5.6	15.5	35.2	-11.6	19.0	15.6	3.3	3.0	19.4	8.7

PER SHARE DATA

	2005	2004	2003	2002	2001	2000	1999	1998	1997	1996
Dividends, Net Income ($)	0.05	0.06	0.01	0.01	0.02	0.08	0.08	0.14	0.12	0.19
Distrib'ns, Cap Gain ($)	1.50	0.96	0.45	0.00	1.68	0.70	1.38	0.94	1.95	1.89
Net Asset Value ($)	14.60	15.06	13.81	10.52	11.91	11.16	10.22	11.08	11.57	11.09
Expense Ratio (%)	1.20	1.22	1.27	1.26	1.30	1.33	1.25	1.25	1.23	0.98
Yield (%)	0.29	0.37	0.09	0.08	0.11	0.63	0.68	1.18	0.88	1.44
Portfolio Turnover (%)	37	33	39	44	104	94	90	59	55	67
Total Assets (Millions $)	651	544	347	210	190	115	116	144	185	175

PORTFOLIO (as of 11/30/05)

Portfolio Manager: Matthew Fahey - 1997

Investment Style

Large Cap	Growth
✔ Mid Cap	✔ Value
Small Cap	Grth/Val

Portfolio

2.9% cash	0.0% corp bonds
97.1% stocks	0.0% gov't bonds
0.0% pref/conv't pref	0.0% muni bonds
0.0% conv't bds/wrnts	0.0% other

SHAREHOLDER INFORMATION

Minimum Investment
Initial: $1,000   Subsequent: $50

Minimum IRA Investment
Initial: $1,000   Subsequent: $50

Maximum Fees
Load: 2.00% redemption   12b-1: none
Other: redemption fee applies for 1 month

Services
✔ IRA
✔ Keogh
✔ Telephone Exchange

Meridian Growth
(MERDX)

Mid-Cap Stock

800-446-6662
www.meridianfund.com

PERFORMANCE   fund inception date: 8/2/84

	3yr Annual	5yr Annual	10yr Annual	Bull	Bear
Return (%)	19.3	9.8	12.2	77.9	1.5
Differ From Category (+/-)	-1.0 blw av	3.9 abv av	1.8 abv av	-4.2 av	25.2 abv av

Standard Deviation	Category Risk Index	Beta
14.1%—abv av	1.13—abv av	1.35

	2005	2004	2003	2002	2001	2000	1999	1998	1997	1996
Return (%)	0.3	14.4	47.9	-17.8	14.7	28.2	13.3	3.0	19.2	11.1
Differ From Category (+/-)	-9.6	-1.1	10.3	0.6	19.0	22.4	-23.8	-8.6	-3.0	-7.4
Return, Tax-Adjusted (%)	0.0	14.2	47.3	-18.3	12.7	22.9	11.6	-1.3	15.6	8.1

PER SHARE DATA

	2005	2004	2003	2002	2001	2000	1999	1998	1997	1996
Dividends, Net Income ($)	0.00	0.00	0.00	0.06	0.00	2.44	0.15	0.14	0.32	0.36
Distrib'ns, Cap Gain ($)	0.80	0.56	0.92	0.61	2.84	1.86	1.78	6.50	4.81	2.76
Net Asset Value ($)	36.57	37.24	33.03	22.98	28.79	28.06	25.40	24.29	30.73	30.08
Expense Ratio (%)	0.88	0.88	0.95	1.02	1.04	1.09	1.01	0.95	0.96	0.96
Yield (%)	0.00	0.00	0.00	0.24	0.00	8.14	0.55	0.89	1.10
Portfolio Turnover (%)	32	19	27	26	43	28	51	38	37	34
Total Assets (Millions $)	1,636	1,632	746	317	208	152	138	231	332	378

PORTFOLIO (as of 6/30/05)

Portfolio Manager: Richard Aster - 1984

Investment Style

Large Cap	Growth
✔ Mid Cap	Value
Small Cap	✔ Grth/Val

Portfolio

1.7% cash	0.0% corp bonds
98.3% stocks	0.0% gov't bonds
0.0% pref/conv't pref	0.0% muni bonds
0.0% conv't bds/wrnts	0.0% other

SHAREHOLDER INFORMATION

Minimum Investment
Initial: $1,000   Subsequent: $50

Minimum IRA Investment
Initial: $1,000   Subsequent: $50

Maximum Fees
Load: 2.00% redemption   12b-1: none
Other: redemption fee applies for 2 months

Services
✔ IRA
✔ Keogh
✔ Telephone Exchange

Meridian Value
(MVALX)

Mid-Cap Stock

800-446-6662
www.meridianfund.com

	3yr Annual	5yr Annual	10yr Annual	Bull	Bear
Return (%)	16.8	9.0	18.7	64.2	11.0
Differ From Category (+/-)	-3.5 blw av	3.1 abv av	8.3 high	-17.9 low	34.7 high

Standard Deviation	Category Risk Index	Beta
10.5%—av	0.84—low	1.00

	2005	2004	2003	2002	2001	2000	1999	1998	1997	1996
Return (%).............	2.9	15.1	34.7	-13.3	11.7	37.1	38.2	18.9	21.3	32.3
Differ From Category (+/-)	-7.0	-0.4	-2.9	5.1	16.0	31.3	1.1	7.3	-0.9	13.8
Return, Tax-Adjusted (%)...	1.1	12.9	34.7	-13.3	11.6	34.6	34.9	18.3	16.7	29.4

PER SHARE DATA

	2005	2004	2003	2002	2001	2000	1999	1998	1997	1996
Dividends, Net Income ($).	0.32	0.28	0.00	0.00	0.04	1.09	0.68	0.00	1.23	0.86
Distrib'ns, Cap Gain ($) ...	4.28	5.11	0.00	0.00	0.04	0.68	1.68	0.47	0.99	0.00
Net Asset Value ($)	34.63	38.09	37.84	28.09	32.42	29.11	22.69	18.32	15.86	14.85
Expense Ratio (%)........	1.09	1.09	1.11	1.12	1.10	1.41	1.42	1.38	1.48	1.51
Yield (%)	0.81	0.65	0.00	0.00	0.11	3.66	2.80	0.00	7.32	5.75
Portfolio Turnover (%)	59	81	60	54	77	86	124	133	144	125
Total Assets (Millions $)..	1,903	2,406	1,916	1,185	1,135	286	35	18	9	5

PORTFOLIO (as of 6/30/05)

Portfolio Manager: Richard Aster - 1994

Investment Style

Large Cap	Growth
✔ Mid Cap	✔ Value
Small Cap	Grth/Val

Portfolio

1.7% cash	0.0% corp bonds
98.4% stocks	0.0% gov't bonds
0.0% pref/conv't pref	0.0% muni bonds
0.0% conv't bds/wrnts	0.0% other

SHAREHOLDER INFORMATION

Minimum Investment
Initial: $1,000   Subsequent: $50

Minimum IRA Investment
Initial: $1,000   Subsequent: $50

Maximum Fees
Load: 2.00% redemption   12b-1: none
Other: redemption fee applies for 2 months

Services
✔ IRA
✔ Keogh
✔ Telephone Exchange

Mosaic Equity Tr Mid Cap
(GTSGX)
Mid-Cap Stock

800-670-3600
www.mosaicfunds.com

fund inception date: 7/21/83

	3yr Annual	5yr Annual	10yr Annual	Bull	Bear
Return (%)	15.3	9.0	10.2	59.8	13.9
Differ From Category (+/-)	-5.0 low	3.1 abv av	-0.2 av	-22.3 low	37.6 high

Standard Deviation	Category Risk Index	Beta
10.1%—av	0.81—low	1.00

	2005	2004	2003	2002	2001	2000	1999	1998	1997	1996
Return (%).............	0.5	18.9	28.5	-12.8	15.3	18.4	9.5	6.8	17.0	6.0
Differ From Category (+/-)	-9.4	3.4	-9.1	5.6	19.6	12.6	-27.6	-4.8	-5.2	-12.5
Return, Tax-Adjusted (%) . .	-0.1	18.0	28.3	-12.9	13.7	14.2	9.5	4.3	11.9	-8.3

PER SHARE DATA

	2005	2004	2003	2002	2001	2000	1999	1998	1997	1996
Dividends, Net Income ($).	0.00	0.00	0.00	0.00	0.01	0.04	0.00	0.00	0.00	0.02
Distrib'ns, Cap Gain ($) . . .	0.60	0.63	0.11	0.06	0.72	1.95	0.00	1.14	2.73	10.10
Net Asset Value ($)	11.99	12.52	11.06	8.69	10.04	9.36	9.57	8.74	9.25	10.64
Expense Ratio (%).........	na	1.25	1.25	1.24	1.25	1.25	1.25	1.26	1.27	1.41
Yield (%)	0.00	0.00	0.00	0.00	0.09	0.32	0.00	0.00	0.00	0.08
Portfolio Turnover (%)	na	38	25	35	47	75	65	88	80	21
Total Assets (Millions $) . . .	146	115	55	26	13	9	9	9	11	13

PORTFOLIO (as of 11/30/05)

Portfolio Manager: Jay Sekelsky/
Frank Burgess - 1996

Investment Style

Large Cap	Growth
✔ Mid Cap	Value
Small Cap	✔ Grth/Val

Portfolio

6.9% cash	0.0% corp bonds
93.1% stocks	0.0% gov't bonds
0.0% pref/conv't pref	0.0% muni bonds
0.0% conv't bds/wrnts	0.0% other

SHAREHOLDER INFORMATION

Minimum Investment
Initial: $1,000   Subsequent: $50

Minimum IRA Investment
Initial: $500   Subsequent: $50

Maximum Fees
Load: none   12b-1: none
Other: none

Services
✔ IRA
✔ Keogh
✔ Telephone Exchange

Muhlenkamp
(MUHLX)
Mid-Cap Stock

800-860-3863
www.muhlenkamp.com

PERFORMANCE   fund inception date: 11/1/88

	3yr Annual	5yr Annual	10yr Annual	Bull	Bear
Return (%)	25.7	11.7	15.7	109.2	-7.8
Differ From Category (+/-)	5.4 high	5.8 high	5.3 high	27.1 high	15.9 ab av

Standard Deviation	Category Risk Index	Beta
15.0%—high	1.20—high	1.47

	2005	2004	2003	2002	2001	2000	1999	1998	1997	1996
Return (%)	7.8	24.5	48.0	-19.9	9.3	25.3	11.4	3.2	32.8	29.9
Differ From Category (+/-)	-2.1	9.0	10.4	-1.5	13.6	19.5	-25.7	-8.4	10.6	11.4
Return, Tax-Adjusted (%)	7.7	24.4	48.0	-19.9	9.3	24.1	10.9	3.1	32.8	29.7

PER SHARE DATA

	2005	2004	2003	2002	2001	2000	1999	1998	1997	1996
Dividends, Net Income ($)	0.76	0.11	0.00	0.00	0.00	0.00	0.00	0.08	0.01	0.11
Distrib'ns, Cap Gain ($)	0.00	0.00	0.00	0.00	0.00	2.33	0.80	0.00	0.00	0.00
Net Asset Value ($)	84.44	78.97	63.51	42.89	53.56	48.98	41.11	37.65	36.55	27.52
Expense Ratio (%)	na	1.14	1.18	1.17	1.17	1.28	1.35	1.32	1.33	1.55
Yield (%)	0.89	0.13	0.00	0.00	0.00	0.00	0.00	0.19	0.03	0.40
Portfolio Turnover (%)	na	7	9	11	11	32	14	27	13	16
Total Assets (Millions $)	3,083	1,985	1,157	601	539	266	177	195	125	42

PORTFOLIO (as of 9/30/05)

Portfolio Manager: Ronald Muhlenkamp - 1988

Investment Style

Large Cap	Growth
✔ Mid Cap	Value
✔ Small Cap	✔ Grth/Val

Portfolio

0.0% cash	0.0% corp bonds
100.0% stocks	0.0% gov't bonds
0.0% pref/conv't pref	0.0% muni bonds
0.0% conv't bds/wrnts	0.0% other

SHAREHOLDER INFORMATION

Minimum Investment
Initial: $1,500   Subsequent: $50

Minimum IRA Investment
Initial: $1   Subsequent: $1

Maximum Fees
Load: none   12b-1: none
Other: none

Services
✔ IRA
✔ Keogh
  Telephone Exchange

Neuberger Berman Manhattan Inv (NMANX)

Mid-Cap Stock

800-366-6264
www.nb.com

PERFORMANCE   fund inception date: 3/1/79

	3yr Annual	5yr Annual	10yr Annual	Bull	Bear
Return (%)	19.8	-3.6	6.2	77.0	-66.6
Differ From Category (+/-)	-0.5 av	-9.5 low	-4.2 low	-5.1 av	-42.9 low

Standard Deviation	Category Risk Index		Beta
13.5%—abv av	1.08—abv av		1.24

	2005	2004	2003	2002	2001	2000	1999	1998	1997	1996
Return (%).............	13.3	16.2	30.5	-31.2	-29.6	-11.4	50.7	16.3	29.2	9.8
Differ From Category (+/-)	.3.4	0.7	-7.1	-12.8	-25.4	-17.3	13.6	4.7	7.0	-8.7
Return, Tax-Adjusted (%)	.13.3	16.2	30.5	-31.2	-29.7	-17.8	48.7	14.8	22.6	6.0

PER SHARE DATA

	2005	2004	2003	2002	2001	2000	1999	1998	1997	1996
Dividends, Net Income ($)	.0.00	0.00	0.00	0.00	0.00	0.00	0.00	0.00	0.00	0.00
Distrib'ns, Cap Gain ($) ...	0.00	0.00	0.00	0.00	0.05	5.36	1.20	0.83	3.84	1.66
Net Asset Value ($)	7.88	6.95	5.98	4.58	6.66	9.54	16.69	11.95	11.01	11.68
Expense Ratio (%).........	na	1.09	1.12	1.05	0.95	0.92	1.00	0.94	0.98	0.98
Yield (%)	.0.00	0.00	0.00	0.00	0.00	0.00	0.00	0.00	0.00	0.00
Portfolio Turnover (%)	na	65	145	98	102	105	115	90	89	53
Total Assets (Millions $) ...	350	343	335	280	497	767	822	628	571	532

PORTFOLIO (as of 11/30/05)

Portfolio Manager: J Brorson/K Turek - 2003

Investment Style
Large Cap	✔ Growth
✔ Mid Cap	Value
✔ Small Cap	Grth/Val

Portfolio
0.0% cash	0.0% corp bonds
100.0% stocks	0.0% gov't bonds
0.0% pref/conv't pref	0.0% muni bonds
0.0% conv't bds/wrnts	0.0% other

SHAREHOLDER INFORMATION

Minimum Investment
Initial: $1,000   Subsequent: $100

Minimum IRA Investment
Initial: $250   Subsequent: $100

Maximum Fees
Load: none   12b-1: none
Other: none

Services
✔ IRA
✔ Keogh
✔ Telephone Exchange

Nicholas II Class I
(NCTWX)
Mid-Cap Stock

800-227-5987
www.nicholasfunds.com

	3yr Annual	5yr Annual	10yr Annual	Bull	Bear
Return (%)	16.5	4.0	8.0	64.5	-26.4
Differ From Category (+/-)	-3.8 low	-1.9 blw av	-2.4 blw av	-17.6 low	-2.7 av

Standard Deviation	Category Risk Index	Beta
10.2%—av	0.82—low	1.01

	2005	2004	2003	2002	2001	2000	1999	1998	1997	1996
Return (%)	5.9	12.0	33.3	-20.3	-3.1	-2.0	1.1	9.2	37.0	19.3
Differ From Category (+/-)	-4.0	-3.5	-4.3	-1.9	1.1	-7.9	-36.0	-2.4	14.8	0.8
Return, Tax-Adjusted (%)	4.5	11.3	33.2	-20.3	-3.6	-9.3	0.8	6.9	33.5	16.1

PER SHARE DATA

	2005	2004	2003	2002	2001	2000	1999	1998	1997	1996
Dividends, Net Income ($)	0.02	0.00	0.00	0.00	0.00	0.00	0.01	0.13	0.07	0.22
Distrib'ns, Cap Gain ($)	2.13	0.91	0.00	0.00	0.58	13.12	0.47	4.00	5.24	3.02
Net Asset Value ($)	22.20	22.98	21.34	16.01	20.09	21.34	35.96	36.03	36.94	30.99
Expense Ratio (%)	0.70	0.63	0.65	0.65	0.62	0.62	0.61	0.59	0.61	0.62
Yield (%)	0.08	0.00	0.00	0.00	0.00	0.00	0.02	0.33	0.16	0.64
Portfolio Turnover (%)	21	15	26	47	49	65	21	20	30	24
Total Assets (Millions $)	565	557	522	417	578	690	941	1,109	1,025	784

PORTFOLIO (as of 10/31/05)

Portfolio Manager: David Nicholas - 1993

Investment Style

✔ Large Cap   ✔ Growth
✔ Mid Cap   Value
  Small Cap   Grth/Val

Portfolio

5.9%	cash	0.0% corp bonds
93.2%	stocks	0.0% gov't bonds
0.9%	pref/conv't pref	0.0% muni bonds
0.0%	conv't bds/wrnts	0.0% other

SHAREHOLDER INFORMATION

Minimum Investment
Initial: $100,000   Subsequent: $100

Minimum IRA Investment
Initial: $500   Subsequent: $100

Maximum Fees
Load: none   12b-1: none
Other: none

Services
✔ IRA
✔ Keogh
✔ Telephone Exchange

Rainier Small/Mid Cap Equity (RIMSX)

Mid-Cap Stock

800-248-6314
www.rainierfunds.com

PERFORMANCE

fund inception date: 5/10/94

	3yr Annual	5yr Annual	10yr Annual	Bull	Bear
Return (%)	26.3	9.1	12.5	108.0	-27.7
Differ From Category (+/-)	6.0 high	3.2 abv av	2.1 abv av	25.9 high	-4.0 av

Standard Deviation	Category Risk Index	Beta
14.9%—high	1.19—high	1.37

	2005	2004	2003	2002	2001	2000	1999	1998	1997	1996
Return (%).............	17.5	17.3	46.2	-20.0	-3.9	7.0	17.6	2.9	32.2	22.5
Differ From Category (+/-)	.7.6	1.8	8.6	-1.6	0.3	1.2	-19.5	-8.7	10.0	4.0
Return, Tax-Adjusted (%)..	17.0	16.7	46.2	-20.0	-4.7	4.0	17.6	2.2	29.7	19.4

PER SHARE DATA

	2005	2004	2003	2002	2001	2000	1999	1998	1997	1996
Dividends, Net Income ($).	0.00	0.00	0.00	0.00	0.00	0.00	0.00	0.00	0.00	0.06
Distrib'ns, Cap Gain ($) ...	0.99	1.05	0.00	0.00	1.02	3.87	0.00	0.85	2.31	1.77
Net Asset Value ($)	33.15	29.04	25.65	17.54	21.93	23.92	26.11	22.19	22.45	18.78
Expense Ratio (%)........	1.25	1.28	1.32	1.26	1.25	1.25	1.25	1.26	1.40	1.48
Yield (%)	0.00	0.00	0.00	0.00	0.00	0.00	0.00	0.00	0.00	0.27
Portfolio Turnover (%)	115	135	140	162	166	199	143	107	130	151
Total Assets (Millions $)..	1,545	539	258	167	312	445	440	542	353	125

PORTFOLIO (as of 6/30/05)

Portfolio Manager: Team Managed - 1994

Investment Style

Large Cap	Growth
✔ Mid Cap	Value
✔ Small Cap	✔ Grth/Val

Portfolio

0.0% cash	0.0% corp bonds
100.0% stocks	0.0% gov't bonds
0.0% pref/conv't pref	0.0% muni bonds
0.0% conv't bds/wrnts	0.0% other

SHAREHOLDER INFORMATION

Minimum Investment
Initial: $25,000   Subsequent: $1,000

Minimum IRA Investment
Initial: $25,000   Subsequent: $1,000

Maximum Fees
Load: none   12b-1: 0.25%
Other: none

Services
✔ IRA
✔ Keogh
✔ Telephone Exchange

RS Mid Cap Opportunities

(RSMOX)

Mid-Cap Stock

800-766-3863
www.rsim.com

PERFORMANCE

fund inception date: 7/12/95

	3yr Annual	5yr Annual	10yr Annual	Bull	Bear
Return (%)	22.2	2.9	11.1	85.8	-50.6
Differ From Category (+/-)	1.9 abv av	-3.0 blw av	0.7 av	3.7 av	-26.9 blw av

Standard Deviation	Category Risk Index	Beta
13.3%—abv av	1.06—abv av	1.23

	2005	2004	2003	2002	2001	2000	1999	1998	1997	1996
Return (%)	9.6	12.3	48.4	-26.4	-14.0	-6.2	56.1	11.7	22.3	24.1
Differ From Category (+/-)	-0.3	-3.2	10.8	-8.0	-9.8	-12.1	19.0	0.1	0.1	5.6
Return, Tax-Adjusted (%)	9.6	12.3	48.4	-26.4	-14.3	-10.2	48.7	10.0	17.7	23.2

PER SHARE DATA

	2005	2004	2003	2002	2001	2000	1999	1998	1997	1996
Dividends, Net Income ($)	0.00	0.00	0.00	0.00	0.10	0.02	0.05	0.19	0.04	0.02
Distrib'ns, Cap Gain ($)	0.00	0.00	0.00	0.00	0.00	3.14	5.06	0.77	3.04	0.32
Net Asset Value ($)	13.35	12.18	10.84	7.30	9.92	11.65	15.92	14.04	13.51	13.62
Expense Ratio (%)	na	1.45	1.53	1.53	1.47	1.39	1.59	1.30	1.30	1.71
Yield (%)	0.00	0.00	0.00	0.00	0.99	0.12	0.22	1.30	0.22	0.14
Portfolio Turnover (%)	na	184	253	401	409	542	408	212	236	212
Total Assets (Millions $)	219	209	141	89	156	198	227	184	298	310

PORTFOLIO (as of 9/30/05)

Portfolio Manager: John Wallace - 1995

Investment Style

Large Cap	✔ Growth
✔ Mid Cap	Value
✔ Small Cap	Grth/Val

Portfolio

3.6% cash	0.0% corp bonds
96.4% stocks	0.0% gov't bonds
0.0% pref/conv't pref	0.0% muni bonds
0.0% conv't bds/wrnts	0.0% other

SHAREHOLDER INFORMATION

Minimum Investment
Initial: $5,000   Subsequent: $1,000

Minimum IRA Investment
Initial: $1,000   Subsequent: $250

Maximum Fees
Load: none   12b-1: 0.25%
Other: none

Services
✔ IRA
  Keogh
✔ Telephone Exchange

RS Value
(RSVAX)

Mid-Cap Stock

800-766-3863
www.rsim.com

PERFORMANCE

fund inception date: 6/30/93

	3yr Annual	5yr Annual	10yr Annual	Bull	Bear
Return (%)	33.8	17.3	6.9	131.2	9.6
Differ From Category (+/-)	13.5 high	11.4 high	-3.5 low	49.1 high	33.3 high

Standard Deviation	Category Risk Index	Beta
11.9%—abv av	0.95—av	0.91

	2005	2004	2003	2002	2001	2000	1999	1998	1997	1996
Return (%)	11.6	29.3	65.9	1.3	-8.2	10.3	38.3	-32.6	-29.5	21.6
Differ From Category (+/-)	.1.7	13.8	28.3	19.8	-4.0	4.5	1.2	-44.3	-51.8	3.1
Return, Tax-Adjusted (%)	11.6	29.2	65.9	1.3	-8.2	10.3	38.3	-33.6	-29.6	21.2

PER SHARE DATA

	2005	2004	2003	2002	2001	2000	1999	1998	1997	1996
Dividends, Net Income ($)	0.01	0.03	0.00	0.00	0.00	0.00	0.00	0.00	0.00	0.00
Distrib'ns, Cap Gain ($)	0.00	0.00	0.00	0.00	0.00	0.00	0.00	0.58	0.07	0.20
Net Asset Value ($)	24.55	21.99	17.03	10.26	10.12	11.03	10.00	7.23	11.61	16.57
Expense Ratio (%)	na	1.49	1.54	1.67	2.22	2.22	2.17	2.83	2.48	2.46
Yield (%)	0.02	0.13	0.00	0.00	0.00	0.00	0.00	0.00	0.00	0.00
Portfolio Turnover (%)	na	147	129	125	131	117	86	39	36	44
Total Assets (Millions $)	1,570	625	374	57	67	92	116	126	403	1,063

PORTFOLIO (as of 9/30/05)

Portfolio Manager: Kelley/Pilara/Wolf - 2001

Investment Style

Large Cap	Growth
✔ Mid Cap	✔ Value
Small Cap	Grth/Val

Portfolio

24.6% cash	0.0% corp bonds
75.4% stocks	0.0% gov't bonds
0.0% pref/conv't pref	0.0% muni bonds
0.0% conv't bds/wrnts	0.0% other

SHAREHOLDER INFORMATION

Minimum Investment
Initial: $5,000   Subsequent: $1,000

Minimum IRA Investment
Initial: $1,000   Subsequent: $250

Maximum Fees
Load: none   12b-1: 0.25%
Other: none

Services
✔ IRA
 Keogh
✔ Telephone Exchange

Sit Mid Cap Growth
(NBNGX)

Mid-Cap Stock

800-332-5580
www.sitfunds.com

PERFORMANCE
fund inception date: 9/2/82

	3yr Annual	5yr Annual	10yr Annual	Bull	Bear
Return (%)	23.1	-4.1	7.3	87.3	-66.2
Differ From Category (+/-)	2.8 abv av	-10.0 low	-3.1 low	5.2 abv av	-42.5 low

Standard Deviation	Category Risk Index	Beta
12.9%—abv av	1.03—abv av	1.12

	2005	2004	2003	2002	2001	2000	1999	1998	1997	1996
Return (%)	15.2	17.0	38.5	-34.6	-33.3	-4.3	70.6	6.8	17.7	21.8
Differ From Category (+/-)	.5.3	1.5	0.9	-16.2	-29.1	-10.2	33.5	-4.8	-4.5	3.3
Return, Tax-Adjusted (%)	15.2	17.0	38.5	-34.6	-33.6	-8.2	68.7	3.3	14.8	16.5

PER SHARE DATA

	2005	2004	2003	2002	2001	2000	1999	1998	1997	1996
Dividends, Net Income ($)	0.00	0.00	0.00	0.00	0.00	0.00	0.00	0.00	0.00	0.00
Distrib'ns, Cap Gain ($)	0.00	0.00	0.00	0.00	0.23	4.07	1.23	2.54	2.02	2.62
Net Asset Value ($)	12.76	11.07	9.46	6.83	10.45	16.03	20.69	12.94	14.69	14.27
Expense Ratio (%)	1.25	1.15	1.15	1.15	1.06	1.00	1.00	1.00	0.92	0.77
Yield (%)	0.00	0.00	0.00	0.00	0.00	0.00	0.00	0.00	0.00	0.00
Portfolio Turnover (%)	40	65	53	61	56	62	68	52	38	50
Total Assets (Millions $)	218	211	192	147	253	474	510	364	382	375

PORTFOLIO (as of 9/30/05)

Portfolio Manager: Eugene Sit/
Team Managed - 1982

Investment Style

Large Cap	✔ Growth
✔ Mid Cap	Value
✔ Small Cap	Grth/Val

Portfolio

3.6% cash	0.0% corp bonds
96.5% stocks	0.0% gov't bonds
0.0% pref/conv't pref	0.0% muni bonds
0.0% conv't bds/wrnts	0.0% other

SHAREHOLDER INFORMATION

Minimum Investment
Initial: $5,000   Subsequent: $100

Minimum IRA Investment
Initial: $2,000   Subsequent: $100

Maximum Fees
Load: 2.00% redemption   12b-1: none
Other: redemption fee applies for 1 month

Services
✔ IRA
✔ Keogh
✔ Telephone Exchange

Stratton Growth
(STRGX)

Mid-Cap Stock

800-634-5726
www.strattonmgt.com/
mutualmain.html

PERFORMANCE

fund inception date: 9/29/72

	3yr Annual	5yr Annual	10yr Annual	Bull	Bear
Return (%)	26.2	11.7	12.8	111.6	4.3
Differ From Category (+/-)	5.9 high	5.8 high	2.4 abv av	29.5 high	28.0 high

Standard Deviation	Category Risk Index	Beta
14.3%—high	1.14—high	1.29

	2005	2004	2003	2002	2001	2000	1999	1998	1997	1996
Return (%).............	14.4	23.5	42.1	-21.3	10.1	22.0	-9.2	11.4	36.0	14.1
Differ From Category (+/-)	.4.5	8.0	4.5	-2.9	14.4	16.2	-46.4	-0.2	13.8	-4.4
Return, Tax-Adjusted (%)..	13.6	22.6	41.3	-21.6	8.1	19.9	-10.5	9.3	33.4	11.9

PER SHARE DATA

	2005	2004	2003	2002	2001	2000	1999	1998	1997	1996
Dividends, Net Income ($).	0.07	0.04	0.09	0.15	0.26	0.33	0.41	0.59	0.54	0.58
Distrib'ns, Cap Gain ($) ...	2.07	1.99	1.32	0.23	2.75	2.44	1.33	2.43	2.52	1.21
Net Asset Value ($)	44.35	40.69	34.69	25.46	32.81	32.61	29.23	34.07	33.39	27.00
Expense Ratio (%).........	na	1.15	1.28	1.28	1.21	1.24	1.13	1.07	1.11	1.17
Yield (%)	0.15	0.08	0.25	0.59	0.73	0.94	1.34	1.61	1.50	2.05
Portfolio Turnover (%)	na	44	38	41	14	49	39	38	34	20
Total Assets (Millions $) ...	173	110	57	38	49	47	44	63	60	45

PORTFOLIO (as of 9/30/05)

Portfolio Manager: James Stratton - 1972

Investment Style

Large Cap	Growth
✔ Mid Cap	✔ Value
Small Cap	Grth/Val

Portfolio

0.0% cash	0.0% corp bonds
94.5% stocks	0.0% gov't bonds
0.0% pref/conv't pref	0.0% muni bonds
0.0% conv't bds/wrnts	5.5% other

SHAREHOLDER INFORMATION

Minimum Investment
Initial: $2,000   Subsequent: $100

Minimum IRA Investment
Initial: $0   Subsequent: $0

Maximum Fees
Load: 1.50% redemption   12b-1: none
Other: redemption fee applies for 4 months

Services
IRA
✔ Keogh
✔ Telephone Exchange

Turner Mid Cap Growth I

800-224-6312
www.turnerinvestments.com

(TMGFX)

Mid-Cap Stock

PERFORMANCE

fund inception date: 10/1/96

	3yr Annual	5yr Annual	10yr Annual	Bull	Bear
Return (%)	22.9	-2.2	na	88.0	-63.4
Differ From Category (+/-)	2.6 abv av	-8.1 low	na	5.9 abv av	-39.7 low

Standard Deviation	Category Risk Index	Beta
15.0%—high	1.20—high	1.35

	2005	2004	2003	2002	2001	2000	1999	1998	1997	1996
Return (%).............	12.0	11.0	49.5	-32.8	-28.3	-8.0	125.4	26.5	40.5	—
Differ From Category (+/-)	.2.1	-4.5	11.9	-14.4	-24.1	-13.8	88.3	14.9	18.3	—
Return, Tax-Adjusted (%)	..12.0	11.0	49.5	-32.8	-28.3	-9.6	122.3	26.5	39.5	—

PER SHARE DATA

	2005	2004	2003	2002	2001	2000	1999	1998	1997	1996
Dividends, Net Income ($)	0.00	0.00	0.00	0.00	0.00	0.00	0.00	0.00	0.00	—
Distrib'ns, Cap Gain ($) ...	0.00	0.00	0.00	0.00	0.00	3.07	2.70	0.00	0.50	—
Net Asset Value ($)	27.37	24.43	22.00	14.71	21.91	30.59	36.45	17.51	13.84	—
Expense Ratio (%)........	1.20	1.16	1.15	1.05	1.04	1.03	1.03	1.23	1.25	—
Yield (%)	0.00	0.00	0.00	0.00	0.00	0.00	0.00	0.00	0.00	—
Portfolio Turnover (%)	152	167	209	260	335	307	291	304	—	—
Total Assets (Millions $) ..	1,022	998	877	509	749	937	333	35	13	—

PORTFOLIO (as of 9/30/05)

Portfolio Manager: McHugh/McVail/Turner - 1996

Investment Style

Large Cap	✔ Growth
✔ Mid Cap	Value
Small Cap	Grth/Val

Portfolio

1.1%	cash	0.0%	corp bonds
98.9%	stocks	0.0%	gov't bonds
0.0%	pref/conv't pref	0.0%	muni bonds
0.0%	conv't bds/wrnts	0.0%	other

SHAREHOLDER INFORMATION

Minimum Investment
Initial: $2,500   Subsequent: $50

Minimum IRA Investment
Initial: $2,000   Subsequent: $50

Maximum Fees
Load: none   12b-1: none
Other: none

Services
✔ IRA
Keogh
✔ Telephone Exchange

Vanguard Extended Market Index Inv (VEXMX)

800-662-7447
www.vanguard.com

Mid-Cap Stock

fund inception date: 12/21/87

PERFORMANCE

	3yr Annual	5yr Annual	10yr Annual	Bull	Bear
Return (%)	23.3	6.9	10.0	97.0	-45.3
Differ From Category (+/-)	3.0 high	1.0 av	-0.4 av	14.9 high	-21.6 blw av

Standard Deviation	Category Risk Index	Beta
12.7%—abv av	1.02—av	1.26

	2005	2004	2003	2002	2001	2000	1999	1998	1997	1996
Return (%).	10.2	18.7	43.4	-18.0	-9.1	-15.5	36.2	8.3	26.7	17.6
Differ From Category (+/-)	.0.3	3.2	5.8	0.4	-4.9	-21.4	-0.9	-3.3	4.5	-0.9
Return, Tax-Adjusted (%). .	10.1	18.5	43.2	-18.3	-10.0	-18.1	33.4	6.4	24.7	15.0

PER SHARE DATA

	2005	2004	2003	2002	2001	2000	1999	1998	1997	1996
Dividends, Net Income ($)	0.33	0.29	0.21	0.18	0.21	0.26	0.32	0.37	0.36	0.34
Distrib'ns, Cap Gain ($) . . .	0.00	0.00	0.00	0.00	0.81	4.43	3.64	2.17	1.91	1.72
Net Asset Value ($)	34.26	31.36	26.66	18.74	23.09	26.62	37.07	30.62	30.75	26.19
Expense Ratio (%).	na	0.25	0.26	0.26	0.25	0.25	0.25	0.23	0.23	0.25
Yield (%)	0.96	0.90	0.79	0.96	0.87	0.84	0.78	1.13	1.10	1.21
Portfolio Turnover (%)	na	17	8	17	20	33	26	27	15	22
Total Assets (Millions $) . .	5,441	5,484	4,259	2,629	3,115	3,881	4,221	2,939	2,723	2,099

PORTFOLIO (as of 9/30/05)

Portfolio Manager: George Sauter - 1987

Investment Style

Large Cap	Growth
✔ Mid Cap	Value
✔ Small Cap	✔ Grth/Val

Portfolio

0.7% cash	0.0% corp bonds
99.3% stocks	0.0% gov't bonds
0.0% pref/conv't pref	0.0% muni bonds
0.0% conv't bds/wrnts	0.0% other

SHAREHOLDER INFORMATION

Minimum Investment
Initial: $3,000   Subsequent: $100

Minimum IRA Investment
Initial: $3,000   Subsequent: $100

Maximum Fees
Load: none   12b-1: none
Other: none

Services
✔ IRA
✔ Keogh
Telephone Exchange

Vanguard Mid Cap Growth

800-662-7447
www.vanguard.com

(VMGRX)

Mid-Cap Stock

fund inception date: 12/31/97

	3yr Annual	5yr Annual	10yr Annual	Bull	Bear
Return (%)	20.1	-1.6	na	76.8	-53.2
Differ From Category (+/-)	-0.2 av	-7.5 low	na	-5.3 av	-29.5 blw av

Standard Deviation	Category Risk Index	Beta
14.5%—high	1.16—high	1.26

	2005	2004	2003	2002	2001	2000	1999	1998	1997	1996
Return (%)	9.1	11.3	42.8	-28.5	-25.3	12.9	83.3	26.3	—	—
Differ From Category (+/-)	-0.8	-4.2	5.2	-10.1	-21.1	7.1	46.2	14.7	—	—
Return, Tax-Adjusted (%)	9.1	11.3	42.8	-28.5	-25.3	6.8	81.8	26.3	—	—

PER SHARE DATA

	2005	2004	2003	2002	2001	2000	1999	1998	1997	1996
Dividends, Net Income ($)	0.01	0.00	0.00	0.00	0.00	0.00	0.00	0.00	—	—
Distrib'ns, Cap Gain ($)	0.00	0.00	0.00	0.00	0.00	6.71	0.94	0.00	—	—
Net Asset Value ($)	17.51	16.05	14.41	10.09	14.12	18.92	22.09	12.63	—	—
Expense Ratio (%)	0.45	0.34	0.48	1.24	1.39	2.14	1.39	1.04	—	—
Yield (%)	0.02	0.00	0.00	0.00	0.00	0.00	0.00	0.00	—	—
Portfolio Turnover (%)	80	102	106	221	149	206	174	167	—	—
Total Assets (Millions $)	619	512	304	35	33	29	19	7	—	—

PORTFOLIO (as of 9/30/05)

Portfolio Manager: Evelyn Lapham/John Yoon 1998

Investment Style

Large Cap	✔ Growth
Mid Cap	Value
Small Cap	Grth/Val

Portfolio

2.3%	cash	0.0%	corp bonds
97.7%	stocks	0.0%	gov't bonds
0.0%	pref/conv't pref	0.0%	muni bonds
0.0%	conv't bds/wrnts	0.0%	other

SHAREHOLDER INFORMATION

Minimum Investment
Initial: $10,000   Subsequent: $100

Minimum IRA Investment
Initial: $3,000   Subsequent: $100

Maximum Fees
Load: none   12b-1: none
Other: none

Services
✔ IRA
✔ Keogh
✔ Telephone Exchange

Vanguard Mid Cap Index Inv (VIMSX)

Mid-Cap Stock

800-662-7447
www.vanguard.com

PERFORMANCE

	3yr Annual	5yr Annual	10yr Annual	Bull	Bear
Return (%)	22.5	9.3	na	94.0	-15.8
Differ From Category (+/-)	2.2 abv av	3.4 abv av	na	11.9 abv av	7.9 av

Standard Deviation	Category Risk Index	Beta
11.9%—abv av	0.95—av	1.19

	2005	2004	2003	2002	2001	2000	1999	1998	1997	1996
Return (%)	13.9	20.3	34.1	-14.6	-0.5	18.2	15.4	—	—	—
Differ From Category (+/-)	4.0	4.8	-3.5	3.8	3.8	12.4	-21.7	—	—	—
Return, Tax-Adjusted (%)	13.7	20.1	33.9	-15.1	-1.1	16.1	13.4	—	—	—

PER SHARE DATA

	2005	2004	2003	2002	2001	2000	1999	1998	1997	1996
Dividends, Net Income ($)	0.19	0.16	0.12	0.09	0.07	0.08	0.08	—	—	—
Distrib'ns, Cap Gain ($)	0.00	0.00	0.00	0.13	0.25	0.98	0.94	—	—	—
Net Asset Value ($)	17.63	15.64	13.13	9.88	11.81	12.21	11.29	—	—	—
Expense Ratio (%)	na	0.22	0.26	0.26	0.25	0.25	0.25	—	—	—
Yield (%)	1.08	1.02	0.92	0.92	0.58	0.59	0.62	—	—	—
Portfolio Turnover (%)	na	16	73	20	24	51	38	—	—	—
Total Assets (Millions $)	6,399	5,234	3,610	2,267	2,049	1,614	605	—	—	—

PORTFOLIO (as of 9/30/05)

Portfolio Manager: George Sauter - 1998

Investment Style

Large Cap	Growth
✔ Mid Cap	Value
Small Cap	✔ Grth/Val

Portfolio

0.2% cash	0.0% corp bonds
99.8% stocks	0.0% gov't bonds
0.0% pref/conv't pref	0.0% muni bonds
0.0% conv't bds/wrnts	0.0% other

SHAREHOLDER INFORMATION

Minimum Investment
Initial: $3,000   Subsequent: $100

Minimum IRA Investment
Initial: $3,000   Subsequent: $100

Maximum Fees
Load: none   12b-1: none
Other: none

Services
✔ IRA
✔ Keogh
✔ Telephone Exchange

Vanguard Selected Value

(VASVX)

Mid-Cap Stock

800-662-7447
www.vanguard.com

PERFORMANCE

fund inception date: 2/15/96

	3yr Annual	5yr Annual	10yr Annual	Bull	Bear
Return (%)	21.6	13.3	na	90.9	13.5
Differ From Category (+/-)	1.3 abv av	7.4 high	na	8.8 abv av	37.2 high

Standard Deviation	Category Risk Index	Beta
11.1%—av	0.89—blw av	1.06

	2005	2004	2003	2002	2001	2000	1999	1998	1997	1996
Return (%)	10.6	20.3	35.2	-9.7	15.0	17.3	-2.7	-11.7	17.4	—
Differ From Category (+/-)	0.7	4.8	-2.4	8.7	19.3	11.5	-39.9	-23.4	-4.8	—
Return, Tax-Adjusted (%)	9.7	20.1	34.8	-10.5	14.5	16.3	-3.3	-12.5	16.3	—

PER SHARE DATA

	2005	2004	2003	2002	2001	2000	1999	1998	1997	1996
Dividends, Net Income ($)	0.29	0.26	0.26	0.24	0.17	0.24	0.16	0.08	0.05	—
Distrib'ns, Cap Gain ($)	0.85	0.00	0.00	0.00	0.00	0.00	0.00	0.33	0.46	—
Net Asset Value ($)	18.86	18.07	15.23	11.46	12.97	11.42	9.94	10.39	12.28	—
Expense Ratio (%)	na	0.60	0.78	0.74	0.70	0.63	0.73	0.47	0.32	—
Yield (%)	1.47	1.43	1.70	2.09	1.31	2.10	1.60	0.74	0.39	—
Portfolio Turnover (%)	28	35	40	50	67	40	102	47	32	—
Total Assets (Millions $)	3,933	2,300	1,422	1,094	995	196	187	149	191	—

PORTFOLIO (as of 9/30/05)

Portfolio Manager: James Barrow/Mark Giambrone - 1999

Investment Style

Large Cap	Growth
Mid Cap	✔ Value
Small Cap	Grth/Val

Portfolio

8.2%	cash	0.0% corp bonds
91.8%	stocks	0.0% gov't bonds
0.0%	pref/conv't pref	0.0% muni bonds
0.0%	conv't bds/wrnts	0.0% other

SHAREHOLDER INFORMATION

Minimum Investment

Initial: $25,000 Subsequent: $100

Minimum IRA Investment

Initial: $25,000 Subsequent: $100

Maximum Fees

Load: 1.00% redemption 12b-1: none
Other: redemption fee applies for 1 year

Services

✔ IRA
✔ Keogh
✔ Telephone Exchange

Vanguard Strategic Equity

800-662-7447
www.vanguard.com

(VSEQX)

Mid-Cap Stock

PERFORMANCE

fund inception date: 8/14/95

	3yr Annual	5yr Annual	10yr Annual	Bull	Bear
Return (%)	23.9	11.7	13.5	95.6	-6.2
Differ From Category (+/-)	3.6 high	5.8 high	3.1 abv av	13.5 high	17.5 abv av

Standard Deviation	Category Risk Index	Beta
12.5%—abv av	1.00—av	1.19

	2005	2004	2003	2002	2001	2000	1999	1998	1997	1996
Return (%).	9.9	20.4	43.8	-13.1	5.4	7.4	19.3	0.5	26.1	25.1
Differ From Category (+/-)	.0.0	4.9	6.2	5.3	9.7	1.6	-17.8	-11.1	3.9	6.6
Return, Tax-Adjusted (%). . .	8.8	19.6	43.6	-13.4	5.0	3.3	18.3	0.1	23.9	22.6

PER SHARE DATA

	2005	2004	2003	2002	2001	2000	1999	1998	1997	1996
Dividends, Net Income ($).	0.21	0.14	0.13	0.13	0.14	0.21	0.16	0.15	0.14	0.18
Distrib'ns, Cap Gain ($) , . .	1.44	0.96	0.00	0.00	0.00	3.03	0.37	0.00	1.08	0.71
Net Asset Value ($)	21.93	21.43	18.71	13.10	15.23	14.58	16.76	14.52	14.60	12.57
Expense Ratio (%).	0.45	0.45	0.50	0.50	0.54	0.49	0.46	0.43	0.40	0.38
Yield (%)	0.89	0.62	0.69	0.99	0.91	1.19	0.93	1.03	0.89	1.35
Portfolio Turnover (%)	75	66	100	73	82	83	51	71	85	106
Total Assets (Millions $). .	5,614	3,746	1,980	914	879	745	626	535	474	153

PORTFOLIO (as of 9/30/05)

Portfolio Manager: G Sauter/J Dickson - 1995

Investment Style
Large Cap	Growth
✔ Mid Cap	Value
Small Cap	✔ Grth/Val

Portfolio
0.1% cash	0.0% corp bonds
99.9% stocks	0.0% gov't bonds
0.0% pref/conv't pref	0.0% muni bonds
0.0% conv't bds/wrnts	0.0% other

SHAREHOLDER INFORMATION

Minimum Investment
Initial: $3,000   Subsequent: $100

Minimum IRA Investment
Initial: $3,000   Subsequent: $100

Maximum Fees
Load: none   12b-1: none
Other: none

Services
✔ IRA
✔ Keogh
✔ Telephone Exchange

Wells Fargo Advtg Discovery Inv (STDIX)

Mid-Cap Stock

800-368-3863
www.wellsfargofunds.com

fund inception date: 12/31/87

	3yr Annual	5yr Annual	10yr Annual	Bull	Bear
Return (%)	19.7	9.4	7.5	76.8	-17.1
Differ From Category (+/-)	-0.6 av	3.5 abv av	-2.9 low	-5.3 blw av	6.6 av

Standard Deviation	Category Risk Index	Beta
15.5%—high	1.24—high	1.35

	2005	2004	2003	2002	2001	2000	1999	1998	1997	1996
Return (%)	7.2	15.6	38.3	-12.1	4.1	3.9	5.2	7.0	10.8	1.4
Differ From Category (+/-)	-2.7	0.1	0.7	6.3	8.4	-1.9	-31.9	-4.6	-11.4	-17.1
Return, Tax-Adjusted (%)	5.5	14.7	38.1	-12.6	3.8	0.9	5.0	6.7	8.2	-1.7

PER SHARE DATA

	2005	2004	2003	2002	2001	2000	1999	1998	1997	1996
Dividends, Net Income ($)	0.00	0.00	0.00	0.00	0.00	0.04	0.00	0.00	0.00	1.12
Distrib'ns, Cap Gain ($)	2.49	1.21	0.21	0.45	0.23	2.78	0.22	0.24	2.29	0.59
Net Asset Value ($)	20.47	21.53	19.73	14.42	16.84	16.39	18.64	17.95	17.00	17.45
Expense Ratio (%)	na	1.40	1.40	1.50	1.50	1.50	1.40	1.30	1.40	1.40
Yield (%)	0.00	0.00	0.00	0.00	0.00	0.18	0.00	0.00	0.00	6.19
Portfolio Turnover (%)	na	171	302	420	502	481	214	186	169	792
Total Assets (Millions $)	208	191	167	133	158	165	187	322	383	514

PORTFOLIO (as of 10/31/05)

Portfolio Manager: Thomas Pence/James Tsch - 2001

Investment Style

Large Cap	✔ Growth
Mid Cap	Value
Small Cap	Grth/Val

Portfolio

0.0% cash	0.0% corp bonds
0.0% stocks	0.0% gov't bonds
0.0% pref/conv't pref	0.0% muni bonds
0.0% conv't bds/wrnts	0.0% other

SHAREHOLDER INFORMATION

Minimum Investment
Initial: $2,500   Subsequent: $100

Minimum IRA Investment
Initial: $1,000   Subsequent: $100

Maximum Fees
Load: none   12b-1: none
Other: none

Services
✔ IRA
✔ Keogh
✔ Telephone Exchange

Wells Fargo Advtg Mid Cap Disciplined Inv (SMCDX)

800-368-3863
www.wellsfargofunds.com

Mid-Cap Stock

PERFORMANCE   fund inception date: 12/31/98

	3yr Annual	5yr Annual	10yr Annual	Bull	Bear
Return (%)	22.5	12.7	na	96.7	-1.2
Differ From Category (+/-)	2.2 abv av	6.8 high	na	14.6 high	22.5 abv a

Standard Deviation	Category Risk Index	Beta
10.8%—av	0.86—blw av	0.99

	2005	2004	2003	2002	2001	2000	1999	1998	1997	199
Return (%)...............	7.9	21.1	40.6	-11.7	12.4	22.8	35.2	—	—	—
Differ From Category (+/-)	-2.0	5.6	3.0	6.7	16.7	17.0	-1.9	—	—	—
Return, Tax-Adjusted (%)...	5.5	19.7	39.9	-12.3	12.4	21.1	35.2	—	—	—

PER SHARE DATA

	2005	2004	2003	2002	2001	2000	1999	1998	1997	199
Dividends, Net Income ($).	0.00	0.05	0.02	0.00	0.00	0.06	0.00	—	—	—
Distrib'ns, Cap Gain ($) ...	3.59	1.80	0.72	0.52	0.00	0.96	0.00	—	—	—
Net Asset Value ($)	20.51	22.34	20.13	14.85	17.42	15.50	13.52	—	—	—
Expense Ratio (%).........	na	1.30	1.50	1.50	1.50	1.50	—	—	—	—
Yield (%)	0.00	0.20	0.07	0.00	0.00	0.39	0.00	—	—	—
Portfolio Turnover (%)	na	62	252	431	648	301	—	—	—	—
Total Assets (Millions $)...	545	675	315	155	92	18	6	—	—	—

PORTFOLIO (as of 10/31/05)

Portfolio Manager: Robert Costomiris - 2001

Investment Style

Large Cap	Growth
✔ Mid Cap	✔ Value
Small Cap	Grth/Val

Portfolio

0.0%	cash	0.0%	corp bonds
100.0%	stocks	0.0%	gov't bonds
0.0%	pref/conv't pref	0.0%	muni bonds
0.0%	conv't bds/wrnts	0.0%	other

SHAREHOLDER INFORMATION

Minimum Investment
Initial: $2,500   Subsequent: $100

Minimum IRA Investment
Initial: $1,000   Subsequent: $100

Maximum Fees
Load: none   12b-1: none
Other: none

Services
✔ IRA
✔ Keogh
✔ Telephone Exchange

Wells Fargo Advtg Opportunity Inv (SOPFX)

800-368-3863
www.wellsfargofunds.com

Mid-Cap Stock

	3yr Annual	5yr Annual	10yr Annual	Bull	Bear
Return (%)	20.1	3.8	11.3	79.0	-32.2
Differ From Category (+/-)	-0.2 av	-2.1 blw av	0.9 av	-3.1 av	-8.5 blw av

Standard Deviation	Category Risk Index	Beta
11.8%—abv av	0.94—av	1.18

	2005	2004	2003	2002	2001	2000	1999	1998	1997	1996
Return (%)...............	7.2	17.6	37.4	-26.9	-4.8	8.5	33.3	15.4	23.4	18.1
Differ From Category (+/-)	-2.7	2.1	-0.2	-8.5	-0.5	2.7	-3.8	3.8	1.2	-0.4
Return, Tax-Adjusted (%)...	5.6	17.6	37.4	-26.9	-5.3	5.8	30.0	13.0	20.0	14.6

PER SHARE DATA

	2005	2004	2003	2002	2001	2000	1999	1998	1997	1996
Dividends, Net Income ($)	0.00	0.00	0.00	0.00	0.07	0.17	0.08	0.05	0.10	0.25
Distrib'ns, Cap Gain ($) ...	4.93	0.00	0.00	0.00	0.95	5.64	6.35	4.47	5.75	3.82
Net Asset Value ($)	44.87	46.40	39.45	28.70	39.29	42.35	44.69	38.62	37.41	35.26
Expense Ratio (%).........	na	1.35	1.40	1.40	1.30	1.20	1.20	1.20	1.30	1.30
Yield (%)	0.00	0.00	0.00	0.00	0.17	0.34	0.16	0.11	0.24	0.65
Portfolio Turnover (%)	na	42	60	70	88	87	81	86	93	103
Total Assets (Millions $)..	1,965	2,406	2,709	2,507	3,664	3,337	2,537	2,038	1,925	1,770

PORTFOLIO (as of 10/31/05)

Portfolio Manager: R Weiss/A Miletti - 2001

Investment Style
✔ Large Cap   Growth
✔ Mid Cap   ✔ Value
  Small Cap   Grth/Val

Portfolio
0.0% cash	0.0% corp bonds
95.5% stocks	0.0% gov't bonds
1.3% pref/conv't pref	0.0% muni bonds
0.0% conv't bds/wrnts	3.3% other

SHAREHOLDER INFORMATION

Minimum Investment
Initial: $2,500   Subsequent: $100

Minimum IRA Investment
Initial: $1,000   Subsequent: $100

Maximum Fees
Load: none   12b-1: none
Other: none

Services
✔ IRA
✔ Keogh
✔ Telephone Exchange

Westcore MIDCO Growth
(WTMGX)
Mid-Cap Stock

800-392-2673
www.westcore.com

PERFORMANCE

fund inception date: 8/1/86

	3yr Annual	5yr Annual	10yr Annual	Bull	Bear
Return (%)	18.4	4.0	9.0	66.1	-47.0
Differ From Category (+/-)	-1.9 blw av	-1.9 blw av	-1.4 blw av	-16.0 blw av	-23.3 blw av

Standard Deviation	Category Risk Index	Beta
13.5%—abv av	1.08—abv av	1.25

	2005	2004	2003	2002	2001	2000	1999	1998	1997	1996
Return (%)	4.6	12.4	41.1	-17.9	-10.4	-17.5	59.3	10.4	14.8	16.9
Differ From Category (+/-)	-5.3	-3.1	3.5	0.5	-6.2	-23.4	22.2	-1.2	-7.4	-1.6
Return, Tax-Adjusted (%)	4.6	12.4	41.1	-17.9	-10.4	-27.4	49.9	7.8	11.6	12.7

PER SHARE DATA

	2005	2004	2003	2002	2001	2000	1999	1998	1997	1996
Dividends, Net Income ($)	0.00	0.00	0.00	0.00	0.00	0.00	0.00	0.00	0.00	0.00
Distrib'ns, Cap Gain ($)	0.02	0.00	0.00	0.00	0.00	9.96	8.85	2.50	3.24	3.02
Net Asset Value ($)	7.81	7.48	6.65	4.71	5.74	6.41	20.06	18.92	19.66	20.06
Expense Ratio (%)	1.11	1.14	1.15	1.15	1.15	1.15	1.15	1.13	1.14	1.08
Yield (%)	0.00	0.00	0.00	0.00	0.00	0.00	0.00	0.00	0.00	0.00
Portfolio Turnover (%)	84	53	49	67	190	117	116	75	60	62
Total Assets (Millions $)	195	194	168	89	119	176	300	491	603	570

PORTFOLIO (as of 9/30/05)

Portfolio Manager: William Chester/Team Managed - 1986

Investment Style

Large Cap	✔ Growth
✔ Mid Cap	Value
✔ Small Cap	Grth/Val

Portfolio

7.2% cash	0.0% corp bonds
92.8% stocks	0.0% gov't bonds
0.0% pref/conv't pref	0.0% muni bonds
0.0% conv't bds/wrnts	0.0% other

SHAREHOLDER INFORMATION

Minimum Investment
Initial: $2,500   Subsequent: $100

Minimum IRA Investment
Initial: $1,000   Subsequent: $100

Maximum Fees
Load: 2.00% redemption   12b-1: none
Other: redemption fee applies for 3 months

Services
✔ IRA
✔ Keogh
✔ Telephone Exchange

Small-Cap Stock Funds
Category Performance Ranked by 2005 Returns

Fund (Ticker)	Annual Return (%)				Category Risk	Total Risk
	2005	3Yr	5Yr	10Yr		
CGM Focus (CGMFX)	25.2	32.8	23.2	na	high	high
Sit Small Cap Growth (SSMGX)	18.5	19.4	-2.1	9.7	av	high
Royce Value Inv (RYVFX)	17.2	33.3	na	na	blw av	abv av
Royce Premier (RYPRX)	17.0	25.8	15.0	14.6	blw av	abv av
Third Avenue Value (TAVFX)	16.5	26.4	12.0	14.1	low	av
Perritt Micro Cap Opportunities (PRCGX)	14.4	29.9	24.2	14.8	blw av	abv av
LKCM Small Cap Equity I (LKSCX)	14.4	23.4	12.2	12.9	blw av	abv av
Royce Value Plus Inv (RYVPX)	13.2	37.6	na	na	abv av	high
Oberweis Micro Cap (OBMCX)	12.7	34.0	19.7	na	high	high
Royce Pennsylvania Mutual Inv (PENNX)	12.5	23.8	15.3	14.1	blw av	abv av
Berwyn (BERWX)	12.1	27.3	19.9	10.9	blw av	abv av
Winslow Green Growth (WGGFX)	12.1	34.0	na	na	high	high
Hennessy Cornerstone Growth (HFCGX)	11.9	23.9	15.2	na	abv av	high
T Rowe Price New Horizons (PRNHX)	11.9	25.3	7.0	9.5	av	high
Royce Micro-Cap Inv (RYOTX)	11.5	25.3	16.0	14.5	abv av	high
Value Line Special Situations (VALSX)	11.2	19.5	3.5	12.7	low	av
MainStay Small Cap Opportunity I (MOPIX)	11.1	29.0	18.8	14.7	av	high
Third Avenue Small Cap Value (TASCX)	11.0	23.2	13.9	na	low	av
Al Frank (VALUX)	11.0	31.8	17.0	na	high	high
Skyline Special Equities (SKSEX)	10.8	22.0	13.9	12.9	blw av	abv av
Stratton Small Cap Value (STSCX)	10.8	28.0	16.0	14.2	av	high
Managers Small Cap (MSSCX)	10.8	20.9	-1.6	na	av	abv av
T Rowe Price Diversified Small Cap Grth (PRDSX)	10.4	19.5	2.2	na	av	high
Vanguard Explorer (VEXPX)	9.2	21.5	6.3	10.6	av	high
Hennessy Cornerstone Growth II (HENLX)	9.2	28.1	10.9	14.4	high	high
Laudus Rosenberg US Discovery Inv (RDIVX)	8.6	21.9	na	na	blw av	abv av
Marshall Small Cap Growth Inv (MRSCX)	8.6	23.5	7.9	na	high	high
Vanguard Small Cap Growth Inv (VISGX)	8.6	21.6	8.6	na	av	high
USAA Capital Growth (USCGX)	8.5	25.1	-0.6	na	abv av	high
Royce Total Return Inv (RYTRX)	8.2	18.2	13.3	13.9	low	av
Fidelity Small Cap Stock (FSLCX)	8.0	21.5	10.0	na	blw av	abv av
Northern Small Cap Value (NOSGX)	8.0	23.3	13.2	12.6	blw av	abv av
Value Line Emerging Opportunities (VLEOX)	8.0	18.9	8.4	13.2	low	abv av
Vanguard Tax Managed Small Cap (VTMSX)	7.7	22.3	10.5	na	av	abv av
Vanguard Small Cap Index Inv (NAESX)	7.4	23.3	9.1	10.2	av	abv av
RS Smaller Co Growth (RSSGX)	6.7	25.6	5.5	na	high	high
Schroder Capital US Opportunities Inv (SCUIX)	6.4	22.2	10.6	13.2	low	abv av
Preferred Small Cap Growth (PSMCX)	6.2	23.6	0.3	1.3	high	high
Vanguard Small Cap Value Inv (VISVX)	6.0	21.6	11.8	na	blw av	abv av
UMB Scout Small Cap (UMBHX)	5.6	22.0	12.3	11.4	low	abv av
n/i numeric investors Growth (NISGX)	5.5	23.2	5.1	na	av	high
Royce Opportunity Inv (RYPNX)	4.7	28.6	15.6	na	high	high

Small-Cap Stock Funds
Category Performance Ranked by 2005 Returns (cont.)

Fund (Ticker)	Annual Return (%)				Category Risk	Total Risk
	2005	3Yr	5Yr	10Yr		
Bridgeway Ultra Small Company Market (BRSIX)	4.0	30.5	23.6	na	abv av	high
TIAA-CREF Instl Sm Cap Eq Retail (TCSEX)	3.2	22.3	na	na	abv av	high
Oberweis Emerging Growth (OBEGX)	2.7	22.3	6.8	7.5	high	high
Excelsior Small Cap Retail (UMLCX)	2.6	23.2	9.0	6.8	abv av	high
Laudus Small Cap MarketMasters (SWOSX)	2.6	23.4	6.8	na	abv av	high
Heartland Value (HRTVX)	1.9	23.7	16.7	13.8	high	high
Heartland Value Plus (HRVIX)	1.3	22.1	18.7	13.0	av	high
Weitz Hickory (WEHIX)	-0.2	21.8	4.0	13.2	low	abv av
Small-Cap Stock Category Average	**7.3**	**22.0**	**8.5**	**11.4**	**av**	**high**

Al Frank
(VALUX)

Small-Cap Stock

888-263-6443
www.alfrank.com

PERFORMANCE   fund inception date: 1/2/98

	3yr Annual	5yr Annual	10yr Annual	Bull	Bear
Return (%)	31.8	17.0	na	138.2	-17.6
Differ From Category (+/-)	9.8 high	8.5 high	na	44.8 high	0.6 av

Standard Deviation	Category Risk Index	Beta
17.5%—high	1.17—high	1.67

	2005	2004	2003	2002	2001	2000	1999	1998	1997	1996
Return (%)	11.0	15.8	77.9	-25.9	29.8	6.9	60.4	—	—	—
Differ From Category (+/-)	.3.7	-0.6	30.9	-6.7	24.5	1.3	22.1	—	—	—
Return, Tax-Adjusted (%)	10.4	15.8	77.9	-26.0	29.6	5.4	60.4	—	—	—

PER SHARE DATA

	2005	2004	2003	2002	2001	2000	1999	1998	1997	1996
Dividends, Net Income ($)	0.00	0.00	0.00	0.00	0.00	0.00	0.00	—	—	—
Distrib'ns, Cap Gain ($)	1.12	0.01	0.00	0.09	0.15	1.07	0.00	—	—	—
Net Asset Value ($)	30.46	28.44	24.56	13.80	18.77	14.58	14.55	—	—	—
Expense Ratio (%)	na	1.61	1.79	2.25	2.25	2.25	1.70	—	—	—
Yield (%)	0.00	0.00	0.00	0.00	0.00	0.00	0.00	—	—	—
Portfolio Turnover (%)	na	25	14	28	17	30	19	—	—	—
Total Assets (Millions $)	264	259	179	49	47	20	8	—	—	—

PORTFOLIO (as of 9/30/05)

Portfolio Manager: John Buckingham - 1998

Investment Style

Large Cap	Growth
✔ Mid Cap	✔ Value
✔ Small Cap	Grth/Val

Portfolio

2.4% cash	0.0% corp bonds
97.6% stocks	0.0% gov't bonds
0.0% pref/conv't pref	0.0% muni bonds
0.0% conv't bds/wrnts	0.0% other

SHAREHOLDER INFORMATION

Minimum Investment
Initial: $1,000   Subsequent: $100

Minimum IRA Investment
Initial: $1,000   Subsequent: $100

Maximum Fees
Load: 2.00% redemption   12b-1: 0.25%
Other: redemption fee applies for 2 months

Services
✔ IRA
✔ Keogh
✔ Telephone Exchange

Berwyn
(BERWX)

Small-Cap Stock

800-992-6757
www.theberwynfunds.com

PERFORMANCE   fund inception date: 5/4/84

	3yr Annual	5yr Annual	10yr Annual	Bull	Bear
Return (%)	27.3	19.9	10.9	115.6	24.6
Differ From Category (+/-)	5.3 high	11.4 high	-0.5 blw av	22.2 high	42.8 high

Standard Deviation	Category Risk Index	Beta
12.5%—abv av	0.83—blw av	1.18

	2005	2004	2003	2002	2001	2000	1999	1998	1997	1996
Return (%).............	12.1	22.8	50.0	-6.8	28.9	2.1	-4.6	-18.9	26.0	14.2
Differ From Category (+/-)	.4.8	6.4	3.0	12.4	23.6	-3.5	-42.9	-20.3	2.7	-7.0
Return, Tax-Adjusted (%)..	10.7	21.9	49.0	-9.6	27.1	2.1	-4.6	-19.6	23.2	10.6

PER SHARE DATA

	2005	2004	2003	2002	2001	2000	1999	1998	1997	1996
Dividends, Net Income ($).	0.02	0.00	1.08	1.46	0.24	0.00	0.00	0.00	0.00	0.00
Distrib'ns, Cap Gain ($) ...	2.83	1.48	0.00	0.00	0.97	0.00	0.00	0.85	2.74	2.50
Net Asset Value ($)	29.67	28.96	24.78	17.23	20.07	16.52	16.18	16.96	22.01	19.69
Expense Ratio (%).........	na	1.20	1.41	1.29	1.24	1.64	1.39	1.20	1.20	1.21
Yield (%)	0.05	0.00	4.35	8.44	1.12	0.00	0.00	0.00	0.00	0.00
Portfolio Turnover (%)	na	23	23	32	37	16	6	19	26	33
Total Assets (Millions $) ...	184	110	52	33	44	27	39	63	100	94

PORTFOLIO (as of 9/30/05)

Portfolio Manager: Team Managed - 2005

Investment Style

Large Cap	Growth
Mid Cap	✔ Value
✔ Small Cap	Grth/Val

Portfolio

16.1% cash	0.0% corp bonds
83.9% stocks	0.0% gov't bonds
0.0% pref/conv't pref	0.0% muni bonds
0.0% conv't bds/wrnts	0.0% other

SHAREHOLDER INFORMATION

Minimum Investment
Initial: $3,000   Subsequent: $250

Minimum IRA Investment
Initial: $1,000   Subsequent: $250

Maximum Fees
Load: 1.00% redemption   12b-1: none
Other: redemption fee applies for 6 months

Services
✔ IRA
Keogh
✔ Telephone Exchange

Bridgeway Ultra Small Company Market (BRSIX)

800-661-3550
www.bridgewayfund.com

Small-Cap Stock

PERFORMANCE

fund inception date: 7/31/97

	3yr Annual	5yr Annual	10yr Annual	Bull	Bear
Return (%)	30.5	23.6	na	125.3	17.5
Differ From Category (+/-)	8.5 high	15.1 high	na	31.9 high	35.7 high

Standard Deviation	Category Risk Index	Beta
16.6%—high	1.11—abv av	1.49

	2005	2004	2003	2002	2001	2000	1999	1998	1997	1996
Return (%)	4.0	19.1	79.4	4.9	23.9	0.6	31.4	-1.8	—	—
Differ From Category (+/-)	-3.3	2.7	32.4	24.2	18.6	-5.0	-6.9	-3.3	—	—
Return, Tax-Adjusted (%)	3.6	19.1	79.3	4.9	23.9	0.4	31.4	-1.8	—	—

PER SHARE DATA

	2005	2004	2003	2002	2001	2000	1999	1998	1997	1996
Dividends, Net Income ($)	0.03	0.03	0.00	0.00	0.01	0.04	0.00	0.00	—	—
Distrib'ns, Cap Gain ($)	0.53	0.00	0.04	0.00	0.00	0.00	0.00	0.00	—	—
Net Asset Value ($)	17.94	17.77	14.94	8.35	7.96	6.43	6.43	4.89	—	—
Expense Ratio (%)	0.73	0.67	0.75	0.75	0.75	0.75	0.75	0.75	—	—
Yield (%)	0.15	0.15	0.00	0.00	0.14	0.66	0.00	0.00	—	—
Portfolio Turnover (%)	13	19	18	56	215	40	48	68	—	—
Total Assets (Millions $)	758	806	752	100	39	3	2	1	—	—

PORTFOLIO (as of 9/30/05)

Portfolio Manager: John Montgomery - 1997

Investment Style

Large Cap	Growth
Mid Cap	Value
✔ Small Cap	✔ Grth/Val

Portfolio

2.0% cash	0.0% corp bonds
97.4% stocks	0.0% gov't bonds
0.0% pref/conv't pref	0.0% muni bonds
0.0% conv't bds/wrnts	0.6% other

SHAREHOLDER INFORMATION

Minimum Investment
Initial: $2,000   Subsequent: $500

Minimum IRA Investment
Initial: $2,000   Subsequent: $500

Maximum Fees
Load: 2.00% redemption   12b-1: none
Other: redemption fee applies for 6 months

Services
✔ IRA
✔ Keogh
✔ Telephone Exchange

CGM Focus
(CGMFX)

Small-Cap Stock

800-345-4048
www.cgmfunds.com

	3yr Annual	5yr Annual	10yr Annual	Bull	Bear
Return (%)	32.8	23.2	na	154.7	74.5
Differ From Category (+/-)	10.8 high	14.7 high	na	61.3 high	92.7 high

Standard Deviation	Category Risk Index	Beta
21.0%—high	1.40—high	1.45

	2005	2004	2003	2002	2001	2000	1999	1998	1997	1996
Return (%)..............	25.2	12.4	66.4	-17.7	47.6	53.9	8.4	3.5	—	—
Differ From Category (+/-)	17.9	-4.0	19.4	1.5	42.3	48.3	-29.9	2.1	—	—
Return, Tax-Adjusted (%) ..	23.4	10.3	66.4	-17.7	45.8	52.5	8.3	3.5	—	—

PER SHARE DATA

	2005	2004	2003	2002	2001	2000	1999	1998	1997	1996
Dividends, Net Income ($).	0.44	0.04	0.00	0.00	0.01	0.36	0.03	0.00	—	—
Distrib'ns, Cap Gain ($) ...	3.12	4.07	0.00	0.00	1.44	0.00	0.00	0.00	—	—
Net Asset Value ($)	33.41	29.51	29.93	17.98	21.87	15.80	10.50	9.71	—	—
Expense Ratio (%).........	na	1.12	1.18	1.20	1.20	1.21	1.21	1.20	—	—
Yield (%)	1.20	0.11	0.00	0.00	0.04	2.27	0.28	0.00	—	—
Portfolio Turnover (%)	na	327	204	155	254	551	288	340	—	—
Total Assets (Millions $) ..	1,636	925	774	384	250	79	69	110	—	—

PORTFOLIO (as of 9/30/05)

Portfolio Manager: G Kenneth Heebner - 1997

Investment Style

Large Cap	Growth
Mid Cap	✔ Value
✔ Small Cap	Grth/Val

Portfolio

1.8% cash	0.0% corp bonds
98.1% stocks	0.1% gov't bonds
0.0% pref/conv't pref	0.0% muni bonds
0.0% conv't bds/wrnts	0.0% other

SHAREHOLDER INFORMATION

Minimum Investment

Initial: $2,500   Subsequent: $50

Minimum IRA Investment

Initial: $1,000   Subsequent: $50

Maximum Fees

Load: none   12b-1: none
Other: none

Services

✔ IRA
✔ Keogh
✔ Telephone Exchange

Excelsior Small Cap Retail

(UMLCX)

Small-Cap Stock

800-446-1012
www.excelsiorfunds.com

PERFORMANCE

fund inception date: 12/31/92

	3yr Annual	5yr Annual	10yr Annual	Bull	Bear
Return (%)	23.2	9.0	6.8	107.4	-40.2
Differ From Category (+/-)	1.2 abv av	0.5 av	-4.6 low	14.0 abv av	-22.0 blw av

Standard Deviation	Category Risk Index	Beta
16.3%—high	1.09—abv av	1.58

	2005	2004	2003	2002	2001	2000	1999	1998	1997	1996
Return (%).	2.6	22.6	48.7	-19.3	1.9	-1.1	29.7	-12.3	14.2	-2.3
Differ From Category (+/-)	-4.7	6.2	1.7	-0.1	-3.4	-6.7	-8.6	-13.8	-9.1	-23.5
Return, Tax-Adjusted (%). . .	1.9	22.6	48.7	-19.3	1.8	-2.7	29.7	-12.5	14.2	-3.6

PER SHARE DATA

	2005	2004	2003	2002	2001	2000	1999	1998	1997	1996
Dividends, Net Income ($).	0.00	0.00	0.00	0.00	0.04	0.07	0.00	0.00	0.00	0.00
Distrib'ns, Cap Gain ($) . . .	0.89	0.00	0.00	0.00	0.00	0.92	0.00	0.12	0.00	0.49
Net Asset Value ($)	16.59	17.00	13.86	9.32	11.56	11.38	12.53	9.66	11.17	9.78
Expense Ratio (%).	1.55	0.83	0.83	0.84	0.89	0.92	0.94	0.94	0.94	0.90
Yield (%)	0.00	0.00	0.00	0.00	0.32	0.55	0.00	0.00	0.00	0.00
Portfolio Turnover (%)	61	82	105	144	132	134	115	73	55	38
Total Assets (Millions $) . . .	511	531	329	173	119	96	63	47	66	70

PORTFOLIO (as of 6/30/05)

Portfolio Manager: Douglas Pyle/Jennifer Byrne - 1999

Investment Style

Large Cap	Growth
Mid Cap	Value
✔ Small Cap	✔ Grth/Val

Portfolio

1.8% cash	0.0% corp bonds
98.2% stocks	0.0% gov't bonds
0.0% pref/conv't pref	0.0% muni bonds
0.0% conv't bds/wrnts	0.0% other

SHAREHOLDER INFORMATION

Minimum Investment

Initial: $500   Subsequent: $50

Minimum IRA Investment

Initial: $250   Subsequent: $50

Maximum Fees

Load: none   12b-1: none
Other: none

Services

✔ IRA
✔ Keogh
✔ Telephone Exchange

Fidelity Small Cap Stock

800-544-8544
www.fidelity.com

(FSLCX)

Small-Cap Stock

PERFORMANCE

fund inception date: 3/12/98

	3yr Annual	5yr Annual	10yr Annual	Bull	Bear
Return (%)	21.5	10.0	na	92.0	-16.6
Differ From Category (+/-)	-0.5 av	1.5 av	na	-1.4 av	1.6 av

Standard Deviation	Category Risk Index	Beta
13.0%—abv av	0.87—blw av	1.22

	2005	2004	2003	2002	2001	2000	1999	1998	1997	1996
Return (%)	8.0	14.5	45.0	-15.7	6.4	11.8	42.6	—	—	—
Differ From Category (+/-)	0.7	-1.9	-2.0	3.5	1.1	6.2	4.3	—	—	—
Return, Tax-Adjusted (%)	7.0	13.4	44.9	-16.1	6.3	10.6	42.6	—	—	—

PER SHARE DATA

	2005	2004	2003	2002	2001	2000	1999	1998	1997	1996
Dividends, Net Income ($)	0.00	0.00	0.00	0.00	0.02	0.04	0.00	—	—	—
Distrib'ns, Cap Gain ($)	1.26	1.33	0.07	0.31	0.00	0.65	0.00	—	—	—
Net Asset Value ($)	18.30	18.16	17.10	11.84	14.36	13.51	12.71	—	—	—
Expense Ratio (%)	1.07	1.08	1.10	1.07	1.05	1.17	1.04	—	—	—
Yield (%)	0.00	0.00	0.00	0.00	0.13	0.28	0.00	—	—	—
Portfolio Turnover (%)	99	96	116	132	126	120	170	—	—	—
Total Assets (Millions $)	4,253	4,159	2,505	1,419	1,354	1,142	688	—	—	—

PORTFOLIO (as of 7/29/05)

Portfolio Manager: Paul Antico - 2005

Investment Style

Large Cap	Growth
Mid Cap	Value
✔ Small Cap	✔ Grth/Val

Portfolio

0.3% cash	0.0% corp bonds
99.6% stocks	0.0% gov't bonds
0.1% pref/conv't pref	0.0% muni bonds
0.0% conv't bds/wrnts	0.0% other

SHAREHOLDER INFORMATION

Minimum Investment
Initial: $2,500   Subsequent: $250

Minimum IRA Investment
Initial: $500   Subsequent: $250

Maximum Fees
Load: 2.00% redemption   12b-1: none
Other: redemption fee applies for 3 months

Services
✔ IRA
✔ Keogh
✔ Telephone Exchange

Heartland Value
(HRTVX)

Small-Cap Stock

800-432-7856
www.heartlandfunds.com

PERFORMANCE · fund inception date: 12/28/84

	3yr Annual	5yr Annual	10yr Annual	Bull	Bear
Return (%)	23.7	16.7	13.8	100.2	12.7
Differ From Category (+/-)	1.7 abv av	8.2 high	2.4 abv av	6.8 abv av	30.9 high

Standard Deviation	Category Risk Index	Beta
16.8%—high	1.12—high	1.53

	2005	2004	2003	2002	2001	2000	1999	1998	1997	1996
Return (%)................	1.9	9.1	70.1	-11.4	29.4	2.0	25.0	-11.4	23.1	20.9
Differ From Category (+/-)	-5.4	-7.3	23.1	7.8	24.1	-3.6	-13.3	-12.9	-0.2	-0.3
Return, Tax-Adjusted (%)...	0.1	7.4	69.0	-12.3	26.2	-0.1	24.9	-11.8	19.8	18.8

PER SHARE DATA

	2005	2004	2003	2002	2001	2000	1999	1998	1997	1996
Dividends, Net Income ($).	0.00	0.00	0.00	0.00	0.00	0.00	0.00	0.06	0.17	0.07
Distrib'ns, Cap Gain ($)...	6.03	5.67	2.36	1.53	5.20	4.03	0.10	0.63	4.87	2.08
Net Asset Value ($).....	44.80	49.81	51.14	31.46	37.25	32.98	36.50	29.29	33.87	31.65
Expense Ratio (%).........	na	1.20	1.28	1.29	1.29	1.22	1.34	1.15	1.12	1.23
Yield (%)...............	0.00	0.00	0.00	0.00	0.00	0.00	0.00	0.18	0.44	0.19
Portfolio Turnover (%).....	na	32	48	49	56	48	23	36	55	31
Total Assets (Millions $)..	1,552	1,876	2,185	924	1,093	896	1,195	1,545	2,127	1,627

PORTFOLIO (as of 9/30/05)

Portfolio Manager: Team Managed - 1984

Investment Style

Large Cap	Growth
Mid Cap	✔ Value
✔ Small Cap	Grth/Val

Portfolio

6.6% cash	0.2% corp bonds
93.0% stocks	0.0% gov't bonds
0.0% pref/conv't pref	0.0% muni bonds
0.2% conv't bds/wrnts	0.0% other

SHAREHOLDER INFORMATION

Minimum Investment
Initial: $5,000   Subsequent: $100

Minimum IRA Investment
Initial: $500   Subsequent: $100

Maximum Fees
Load: 2.00% redemption   12b-1: 0.25%
Other: redemption fee applies for 10 days

Services
✔ IRA
✔ Keogh
✔ Telephone Exchange

Heartland Value Plus
(HRVIX)
Small-Cap Stock

800-432-7856
www.heartlandfunds.com

PERFORMANCE

fund inception date: 10/26/93

	3yr Annual	5yr Annual	10yr Annual	Bull	Bear
Return (%)	22.1	18.7	13.0	94.3	1.8
Differ From Category (+/-)	0.1 av	10.2 high	1.6 av	0.9 av	20.0 abv av

Standard Deviation	Category Risk Index	Beta
14.8%—high	0.99—av	1.40

	2005	2004	2003	2002	2001	2000	1999	1998	1997	1996
Return (%)	1.3	16.9	53.5	-3.7	34.7	-8.8	1.6	-10.7	30.6	33.8
Differ From Category (+/-)	-6.0	0.5	6.5	15.5	29.4	-14.5	-36.7	-12.2	7.3	12.6
Return, Tax-Adjusted (%)	0.5	16.5	53.5	-4.0	34.1	-9.6	0.4	-12.2	27.3	30.5

PER SHARE DATA

	2005	2004	2003	2002	2001	2000	1999	1998	1997	1996
Dividends, Net Income ($)	0.16	0.07	0.05	0.12	0.18	0.29	0.44	0.60	0.48	0.39
Distrib'ns, Cap Gain ($)	1.20	0.65	0.00	0.00	0.00	0.00	0.00	0.03	1.26	0.77
Net Asset Value ($)	25.85	26.85	23.57	15.39	16.12	12.11	13.57	13.80	16.13	13.73
Expense Ratio (%)	na	1.23	1.34	1.44	1.48	1.36	1.39	1.21	1.12	1.45
Yield (%)	0.59	0.24	0.21	0.80	1.09	2.40	3.21	4.32	2.75	2.66
Portfolio Turnover (%)	na	57	68	65	80	121	82	64	74	73
Total Assets (Millions $)	275	417	219	58	60	44	87	174	336	67

PORTFOLIO (as of 9/30/05)

Portfolio Manager: Team Managed - 1993

Investment Style

Large Cap	Growth
✔ Mid Cap	✔ Value
✔ Small Cap	Grth/Val

Portfolio

5.3% cash	0.0% corp bonds
94.0% stocks	0.0% gov't bonds
0.0% pref/conv't pref	0.0% muni bonds
0.7% conv't bds/wrnts	0.0% other

SHAREHOLDER INFORMATION

Minimum Investment
Initial: $1,000   Subsequent: $100

Minimum IRA Investment
Initial: $500   Subsequent: $100

Maximum Fees
Load: 2.00% redemption   12b-1: 0.25%
Other: redemption fee applies for 10 days

Services
✔ IRA
✔ Keogh
✔ Telephone Exchange

Hennessy Cornerstone Growth (HFCGX)

Small-Cap Stock

800-966-4354
www.hennessy-funds.com

PERFORMANCE

fund inception date: 11/1/96

	3yr Annual	5yr Annual	10yr Annual	Bull	Bear
Return (%)	23.9	15.2	na	100.9	-3.5
Differ From Category (+/-)	1.9 abv av	6.7 high	na	7.5 abv av	14.7 abv av

Standard Deviation	Category Risk Index	Beta
16.7%—high	1.11—abv av	1.41

	2005	2004	2003	2002	2001	2000	1999	1998	1997	1996
Return (%)	11.9	16.6	45.8	-4.7	12.1	5.3	37.7	3.6	31.3	—
Differ From Category (+/-)	4.6	0.2	-1.2	14.5	6.8	-0.3	-0.6	2.2	8.0	—
Return, Tax-Adjusted (%)	10.9	13.6	45.8	-5.3	10.6	-3.2	37.7	3.6	24.3	—

PER SHARE DATA

	2005	2004	2003	2002	2001	2000	1999	1998	1997	1996
Dividends, Net Income ($)	0.00	0.00	0.00	0.00	0.00	3.50	0.00	0.00	1.78	—
Distrib'ns, Cap Gain ($)	1.23	3.88	0.00	0.48	1.03	0.00	0.00	0.00	0.00	—
Net Asset Value ($)	19.36	18.43	19.35	13.27	14.41	13.85	16.32	11.85	11.43	—
Expense Ratio (%)	1.25	1.25	1.27	1.10	1.11	1.18	1.15	1.16	1.56	—
Yield (%)	0.00	0.00	0.00	0.00	0.00	25.29	0.00	0.00	15.58	—
Portfolio Turnover (%)	3	107	74	70	103	95	125	119	—	—
Total Assets (Millions $)	1,138	996	914	459	168	156	157	117	54	—

PORTFOLIO (as of 9/30/05)

Portfolio Manager: Neil Hennessy - 1996

Investment Style

✔ Large Cap ✔ Growth
✔ Mid Cap   Value
✔ Small Cap   Grth/Val

Portfolio

2.8% cash	0.0% corp bonds
97.2% stocks	0.0% gov't bonds
0.0% pref/conv't pref	0.0% muni bonds
0.0% conv't bds/wrnts	0.0% other

SHAREHOLDER INFORMATION

Minimum Investment
Initial: $2,500   Subsequent: $100

Minimum IRA Investment
Initial: $250   Subsequent: $100

Maximum Fees
Load: 1.50% redemption   12b-1: none
Other: redemption fee applies for 3 months

Services
✔ IRA
✔ Keogh
✔ Telephone Exchange

Hennessy Cornerstone Growth II (HENLX)

800-966-4354
www.hennessy-funds.com

Small-Cap Stock

PERFORMANCE

fund inception date: 12/2/92

	3yr Annual	5yr Annual	10yr Annual	Bull	Bear
Return (%)	28.1	10.9	14.4	123.0	-52.2
Differ From Category (+/-)	6.1 high	2.4 av	3.0 abv av	29.6 high	-34.0 low

Standard Deviation	Category Risk Index	Beta
18.2%—high	1.21—high	1.38

	2005	2004	2003	2002	2001	2000	1999	1998	1997	1996
Return (%).	9.2	16.7	64.9	-20.8	0.7	-18.5	62.1	16.7	22.6	21.3
Differ From Category (+/-)	.1.9	0.3	17.9	-1.6	-4.6	-24.2	23.8	15.3	-0.7	0.1
Return, Tax-Adjusted (%)	. . .7.3	16.7	64.9	-20.8	0.7	-19.4	60.5	16.7	18.1	17.1

PER SHARE DATA

	2005	2004	2003	2002	2001	2000	1999	1998	1997	1996
Dividends, Net Income ($)	.0.00	0.01	0.00	0.00	0.00	0.00	0.00	0.00	0.00	0.00
Distrib'ns, Cap Gain ($) . . .	3.68	0.00	0.00	0.00	0.04	1.23	1.38	0.00	3.31	2.14
Net Asset Value ($)	29.39	30.47	26.10	15.82	19.99	19.89	26.08	17.28	14.80	14.89
Expense Ratio (%).	1.25	1.38	1.58	1.40	1.30	1.40	1.50	1.50	1.60	1.80
Yield (%)	0.00	0.03	0.00	0.00	0.00	0.00	0.00	0.00	0.00	0.00
Portfolio Turnover (%)	192	113	90	132	288	157	162	116	141	178
Total Assets (Millions $) . . .	257	329	161	77	143	185	113	44	33	31

PORTFOLIO (as of 9/30/05)

Portfolio Manager: Neil Hennessy - 2005

Investment Style

Large Cap	✔ Growth
Mid Cap	Value
✔ Small Cap	Grth/Val

Portfolio

2.0% cash	0.0% corp bonds
98.0% stocks	0.0% gov't bonds
0.0% pref/conv't pref	0.0% muni bonds
0.0% conv't bds/wrnts	0.0% other

SHAREHOLDER INFORMATION

Minimum Investment
Initial: $2,500   Subsequent: $100

Minimum IRA Investment
Initial: $250   Subsequent: $100

Maximum Fees
Load: none   12b-1: none
Other: none

Services
✔ IRA
✔ Keogh
Telephone Exchange

Laudus Rosenberg US Discovery Inv (RDIVX)

800-447-3332
www.laudusfunds.com

Small-Cap Stock

PERFORMANCE

fund inception date: 10/3/01

	3yr Annual	5yr Annual	10yr Annual	Bull	Bear
Return (%)	21.9	na	na	87.9	na
Differ From Category (+/-)	-0.1 av	na	na	-5.5 av	na

Standard Deviation	Category Risk Index	Beta
13.1%—abv av	0.87—blw av	1.24

	2005	2004	2003	2002	2001	2000	1999	1998	1997	1996
Return (%)	8.6	18.3	40.9	-4.2	—	—	—	—	—	—
Differ From Category (+/-)	.1.3	1.9	-6.1	15.1	—	—	—	—	—	—
Return, Tax-Adjusted (%)	8.3	18.1	40.7	-4.2	—	—	—	—	—	—

PER SHARE DATA

	2005	2004	2003	2002	2001	2000	1999	1998	1997	1996
Dividends, Net Income ($)	0.00	0.02	0.00	0.00	—	—	—	—	—	—
Distrib'ns, Cap Gain ($)	0.33	0.18	0.12	0.00	—	—	—	—	—	—
Net Asset Value ($)	17.06	16.00	13.69	9.80	—	—	—	—	—	—
Expense Ratio (%)	1.49	1.40	1.40	1.40	—	—	—	—	—	—
Yield (%)	0.00	0.14	0.00	0.00	—	—	—	—	—	—
Portfolio Turnover (%)	63	93	99	—	—	—	—	—	—	—
Total Assets (Millions $)	239	22	3	0	—	—	—	—	—	—

PORTFOLIO (as of 9/30/05)

Portfolio Manager: Team Managed - 2001

Investment Style

Large Cap	Growth
Mid Cap	Value
✔ Small Cap	✔ Grth/Val

Portfolio

5.1% cash	0.0% corp bonds
94.6% stocks	0.0% gov't bonds
0.0% pref/conv't pref	0.0% muni bonds
0.0% conv't bds/wrnts	0.3% other

SHAREHOLDER INFORMATION

Minimum Investment
Initial: $2,500   Subsequent: $500

Minimum IRA Investment
Initial: $1,000   Subsequent: $500

Maximum Fees
Load: 2.00% redemption   12b-1: 0.25%
Other: redemption fee applies for 1 month

Services
✔ IRA
  Keogh
✔ Telephone Exchange

Laudus Small Cap MarketMasters (SWOSX)

800-435-4000
www.schwab.com/
schwabfunds

Small-Cap Stock

PERFORMANCE

fund inception date: 9/16/97

	3yr Annual	5yr Annual	10yr Annual	Bull	Bear
Return (%)	23.4	6.8	na	96.9	-40.7
Differ From Category (+/-)	1.4 abv av	-1.7 blw av	na	3.5 abv av	-22.5 blw av

Standard Deviation	Category Risk Index	Beta
16.6%—high	1.11—abv av	1.58

	2005	2004	2003	2002	2001	2000	1999	1998	1997	1996
Return (%)	2.6	15.3	58.6	-25.9	0.0	-11.3	37.8	0.6	—	—
Differ From Category (+/-)	-4.7	-1.1	11.6	-6.7	-5.4	-17.0	-0.5	-0.8	—	—
Return, Tax-Adjusted (%)	1.4	15.3	58.6	-25.9	-0.2	-14.1	35.9	0.4	—	—

PER SHARE DATA

	2005	2004	2003	2002	2001	2000	1999	1998	1997	1996
Dividends, Net Income ($)	0.00	0.00	0.00	0.00	0.03	0.55	0.46	0.05	—	—
Distrib'ns, Cap Gain ($)	1.13	0.00	0.00	0.00	0.02	0.72	0.00	0.00	—	—
Net Asset Value ($)	12.85	13.60	11.79	7.43	10.03	10.09	12.80	9.62	—	—
Expense Ratio (%)	1.64	1.55	1.55	0.84	0.50	0.50	0.50	0.50	—	—
Yield (%)	0.00	0.00	0.00	0.00	0.26	5.12	3.57	0.48	—	—
Portfolio Turnover (%)	94	140	94	324	172	91	145	166	—	—
Total Assets (Millions $)	108	138	126	83	126	146	150	138	—	—

PORTFOLIO (as of 7/31/05)

Portfolio Manager: Team Managed - 2000

Investment Style

Large Cap	✔ Growth
Mid Cap	Value
✔ Small Cap	Grth/Val

Portfolio

13.6% cash	0.0% corp bonds
85.6% stocks	0.0% gov't bonds
0.0% pref/conv't pref	0.0% muni bonds
0.0% conv't bds/wrnts	0.8% other

SHAREHOLDER INFORMATION

Minimum Investment
Initial: $2,500   Subsequent: $500

Minimum IRA Investment
Initial: $1,000   Subsequent: $250

Maximum Fees
Load: 2.00% redemption   12b-1: none
Other: redemption fee applies for 1 month

Services
✔ IRA
✔ Keogh
✔ Telephone Exchange

LKCM Small Cap Equity I

800-688-5526
www.lkcm.com

(LKSCX)

Small-Cap Stock

PERFORMANCE

fund inception date: 7/14/94

	3yr Annual	5yr Annual	10yr Annual	Bull	Bear
Return (%)	23.4	12.2	12.9	100.3	-6.8
Differ From Category (+/-)	1.4 abv av	3.7 abv av	1.5 av	6.9 abv av	11.4 av

Standard Deviation	Category Risk Index	Beta
12.6%—abv av	0.84—blw av	1.19

	2005	2004	2003	2002	2001	2000	1999	1998	1997	1996
Return (%).	14.4	22.0	34.7	-11.7	7.5	11.3	16.7	-6.2	23.0	25.6
Differ From Category (+/-)	.7.1	5.6	-12.3	7.5	2.2	5.7	-21.6	-7.7	-0.3	4.4
Return, Tax-Adjusted (%). .	12.0	20.2	33.7	-11.8	6.2	7.8	16.3	-6.4	19.6	23.7

PER SHARE DATA

	2005	2004	2003	2002	2001	2000	1999	1998	1997	1996
Dividends, Net Income ($).	0.00	0.00	0.00	0.01	0.07	0.05	0.03	0.07	0.07	0.07
Distrib'ns, Cap Gain ($) . . .	3.46	2.40	1.00	0.01	0.92	3.10	0.25	0.05	2.64	0.88
Net Asset Value ($)	21.12	21.46	19.54	15.24	17.29	17.00	18.08	15.72	16.89	16.20
Expense Ratio (%).	na	0.96	0.97	0.94	0.92	0.93	0.90	0.91	0.95	1.00
Yield (%)	0.00	0.00	0.00	0.03	0.40	0.24	0.15	0.41	0.36	0.39
Portfolio Turnover (%)	na	53	43	52	62	79	48	35	34	66
Total Assets (Millions $) . . .	370	344	267	207	221	211	230	246	255	199

PORTFOLIO (as of 9/30/05)

Portfolio Manager: J King - 1994

Investment Style

Large Cap	Growth
Mid Cap	Value
✔ Small Cap	✔ Grth/Val

Portfolio

4.6% cash	0.0% corp bonds
95.5% stocks	0.0% gov't bonds
0.0% pref/conv't pref	0.0% muni bonds
0.0% conv't bds/wrnts	0.0% other

SHAREHOLDER INFORMATION

Minimum Investment
Initial: $10,000   Subsequent: $1,000

Minimum IRA Investment
Initial: $10,000   Subsequent: $1,000

Maximum Fees
Load: none   12b-1: none
Other: none

Services
✔ IRA
✔ Keogh
✔ Telephone Exchange

MainStay Small Cap Opportunity I (MOPIX)

Small-Cap Stock

800-624-6782
www.nylim.com/
mainstayfunds

PERFORMANCE
fund inception date: 1/12/87

	3yr Annual	5yr Annual	10yr Annual	Bull	Bear
Return (%)	29.0	18.8	14.7	120.1	-1.2
Differ From Category (+/-)	7.0 high	10.3 high	3.3 high	26.7 high	17.0 abv av

Standard Deviation	Category Risk Index	Beta
14.6%—high	0.97—av	1.24

	2005	2004	2003	2002	2001	2000	1999	1998	1997	1996
Return (%)	11.1	25.7	53.7	-3.3	13.9	-9.5	3.0	3.4	33.3	29.8
Differ From Category (+/-)	3.8	9.3	6.7	16.0	8.6	-15.2	-35.3	2.0	10.0	8.6
Return, Tax-Adjusted (%)	9.6	23.1	52.6	-3.7	13.5	-9.5	2.1	-0.3	27.8	21.2

PER SHARE DATA

	2005	2004	2003	2002	2001	2000	1999	1998	1997	1996
Dividends, Net Income ($)	0.00	0.00	0.05	0.13	0.11	0.00	0.01	0.00	0.00	0.14
Distrib'ns, Cap Gain ($)	1.80	2.91	0.81	0.00	0.00	0.00	0.52	2.68	3.66	3.98
Net Asset Value ($)	18.45	18.19	16.80	11.49	12.02	10.64	11.76	11.93	14.19	13.47
Expense Ratio (%)	na	1.16	1.27	1.26	1.15	1.21	1.18	1.14	1.14	1.15
Yield (%)	0.00	0.00	0.27	1.15	0.90	0.00	0.04	0.00	0.00	0.78
Portfolio Turnover (%)	na	132	135	103	77	104	56	73	55	82
Total Assets (Millions $)	340	229	197	111	115	159	250	200	193	171

PORTFOLIO (as of 10/31/05)

Portfolio Manager: K O'Connor/J Sanders - 1987

Investment Style

Large Cap	Growth
Mid Cap	✔ Value
✔ Small Cap	Grth/Val

Portfolio

-9.1%	cash	0.0%	corp bonds
109.0%	stocks	0.0%	gov't bonds
0.0%	pref/conv't pref	0.0%	muni bonds
0.0%	conv't bds/wrnts	0.1%	other

SHAREHOLDER INFORMATION

Minimum Investment
Initial: $5,000,000   Subsequent: $1

Minimum IRA Investment
Initial: $5,000,000   Subsequent: $1

Maximum Fees
Load: none   12b-1: none
Other: none

Services
✔ IRA
✔ Keogh
✔ Telephone Exchange

Managers Small Cap

(MSSCX)

Small-Cap Stock

800-835-3879
www.managersfunds.com

PERFORMANCE

fund inception date: 9/24/97

	3yr Annual	5yr Annual	10yr Annual	Bull	Bear
Return (%)	20.9	-1.6	na	86.1	-65.7
Differ From Category (+/-)	-1.1 blw av	-10.1 low	na	-7.3 blw av	-47.5 low

Standard Deviation	Category Risk Index	Beta
14.0%—abv av	0.93—av	1.34

	2005	2004	2003	2002	2001	2000	1999	1998	1997	1996
Return (%)	10.8	10.5	44.3	-39.8	-13.2	-26.8	125.2	17.6	—	—
Differ From Category (+/-)	.3.5	-5.9	-2.7	-20.6	-18.6	-32.5	86.9	16.2	—	—
Return, Tax-Adjusted (%)	10.8	10.5	44.3	-39.8	-13.2	-29.3	123.9	17.6	—	—

PER SHARE DATA

	2005	2004	2003	2002	2001	2000	1999	1998	1997	1996
Dividends, Net Income ($)	0.00	0.00	0.00	0.00	0.00	0.00	0.00	0.00	—	—
Distrib'ns, Cap Gain ($)	0.00	0.00	0.00	0.00	0.00	2.96	0.71	0.00	—	—
Net Asset Value ($)	13.65	12.32	11.14	7.72	12.84	14.80	24.15	11.21	—	—
Expense Ratio (%)	1.65	1.60	1.60	1.56	1.50	1.50	1.50	1.50	—	—
Yield (%)	0.00	0.00	0.00	0.00	0.00	0.00	0.00	0.00	—	—
Portfolio Turnover (%)	67	54	207	108	134	148	161	273	—	—
Total Assets (Millions $)	70	66	49	37	56	62	65	10	—	—

PORTFOLIO (as of 10/31/05)

Portfolio Manager: Y Bockstein/G Babyak - 2002

Investment Style

Large Cap	✔ Growth
Mid Cap	Value
✔ Small Cap	Grth/Val

Portfolio

5.5% cash	0.0% corp bonds
94.5% stocks	0.0% gov't bonds
0.0% pref/conv't pref	0.0% muni bonds
0.0% conv't bds/wrnts	0.0% other

SHAREHOLDER INFORMATION

Minimum Investment
Initial: $2,000   Subsequent: $100

Minimum IRA Investment
Initial: $1,000   Subsequent: $100

Maximum Fees
Load: none   12b-1: none
Other: none

Services
✔ IRA
✔ Keogh
✔ Telephone Exchange

Marshall Small Cap Growth Inv (MRSCX)

800-236-3863
www.marshallfunds.com

Small-Cap Stock

PERFORMANCE

fund inception date: 9/4/96

	3yr Annual	5yr Annual	10yr Annual	Bull	Bear
Return (%)	23.5	7.9	na	106.3	-51.5
Differ From Category (+/-)	1.5 abv av	-0.6 blw av	na	12.9 abv av	-33.3 low

Standard Deviation	Category Risk Index	Beta
17.8%—high	1.19—high	1.60

	2005	2004	2003	2002	2001	2000	1999	1998	1997	1996
Return (%)	8.6	16.6	48.6	-28.7	8.9	-19.6	34.7	3.4	23.1	—
Differ From Category (+/-)	1.3	0.2	1.6	-9.5	3.6	-25.3	-3.6	2.0	-0.2	—
Return, Tax-Adjusted (%)	7.3	16.6	48.6	-28.7	8.0	-21.5	34.1	3.3	22.2	—

PER SHARE DATA

	2005	2004	2003	2002	2001	2000	1999	1998	1997	1996
Dividends, Net Income ($)	0.00	0.00	0.00	0.00	0.00	0.00	0.00	0.00	0.00	—
Distrib'ns, Cap Gain ($)	1.37	0.00	0.00	0.00	0.58	1.63	0.41	0.02	0.49	—
Net Asset Value ($)	15.77	15.75	13.50	9.08	12.75	12.25	17.27	13.16	12.75	—
Expense Ratio (%)	1.55	1.58	1.72	1.63	1.58	1.59	1.59	1.60	1.80	—
Yield (%)	0.00	0.00	0.00	0.00	0.00	0.00	0.00	0.00	0.00	—
Portfolio Turnover (%)	195	267	248	292	287	105	219	139	—	—
Total Assets (Millions $)	162	154	111	77	112	114	144	112	70	—

PORTFOLIO (as of 11/30/05)

Portfolio Manager: Team Managed - 2004

Investment Style

Large Cap	✔ Growth
Mid Cap	Value
✔ Small Cap	Grth/Val

Portfolio

4.1% cash	0.0% corp bonds
95.8% stocks	0.0% gov't bonds
0.0% pref/conv't pref	0.0% muni bonds
0.0% conv't bds/wrnts	0.1% other

SHAREHOLDER INFORMATION

Minimum Investment
Initial: $1,000   Subsequent: $50

Minimum IRA Investment
Initial: $1,000   Subsequent: $50

Maximum Fees
Load: 2.00% redemption   12b-1: none
Other: redemption fee applies for 1 month

Services
✔ IRA
  Keogh
✔ Telephone Exchange

n/i numeric investors Growth (NISGX)

800-348-5031
www.numeric.com

Small-Cap Stock

PERFORMANCE

fund inception date: 5/31/96

	3yr Annual	5yr Annual	10yr Annual	Bull	Bear
Return (%)	23.2	5.1	na	92.1	-47.0
Differ From Category (+/-)	1.2 abv av	-3.4 blw av	na	-1.3 av	-28.8 blw av

Standard Deviation	Category Risk Index	Beta
14.9%—high	0.99—av	1.34

	2005	2004	2003	2002	2001	2000	1999	1998	1997	1996
Return (%)	5.5	17.4	51.1	-19.4	-14.9	-4.3	49.4	2.2	15.6	—
Differ From Category (+/-)	-1.8	1.0	4.1	-0.2	-20.3	-10.0	11.1	0.8	-7.7	—
Return, Tax-Adjusted (%)	4.2	17.4	51.1	-19.4	-14.9	-11.0	48.9	2.2	11.8	—

PER SHARE DATA

	2005	2004	2003	2002	2001	2000	1999	1998	1997	1996
Dividends, Net Income ($)	0.00	0.00	0.00	0.00	0.00	0.00	0.00	0.00	0.00	—
Distrib'ns, Cap Gain ($)	1.42	0.00	0.00	0.00	0.00	6.52	0.36	0.01	2.49	—
Net Asset Value ($)	14.96	15.58	13.27	8.78	10.90	12.81	19.23	13.19	12.91	—
Expense Ratio (%)	na	1.49	1.49	1.35	1.08	1.00	1.00	1.00	1.00	—
Yield (%)	0.00	0.00	0.00	0.00	0.00	0.00	0.00	0.00	0.00	—
Portfolio Turnover (%)	na	238	237	241	271	228	309	338	266	—
Total Assets (Millions $)	45	41	39	33	40	53	74	99	116	—

PORTFOLIO (as of 10/31/05)

Portfolio Manager: Team Managed - 1996

Investment Style

Large Cap	✔ Growth
Mid Cap	Value
✔ Small Cap	Grth/Val

Portfolio

2.3% cash	0.0% corp bonds
97.7% stocks	0.0% gov't bonds
0.0% pref/conv't pref	0.0% muni bonds
0.0% conv't bds/wrnts	0.0% other

SHAREHOLDER INFORMATION

Minimum Investment
Initial: $3,000   Subsequent: $100

Minimum IRA Investment
Initial: $1,000   Subsequent: $100

Maximum Fees
Load: 2.00% redemption   12b-1: none
Other: redemption fee applies for 1 year

Services
✔ IRA
✔ Keogh
✔ Telephone Exchange

Northern Small Cap Value (NOSGX)

800-595-9111
www.northernfunds.com

Small-Cap Stock

PERFORMANCE

fund inception date: 4/1/94

	3yr Annual	5yr Annual	10yr Annual	Bull	Bear
Return (%)	23.3	13.2	12.6	98.6	-1.9
Differ From Category (+/-)	1.3 abv av	4.7 abv av	1.2 av	5.2 abv av	16.3 abv av

Standard Deviation	Category Risk Index	Beta
13.3%—abv av	0.89—blw av	1.26

	2005	2004	2003	2002	2001	2000	1999	1998	1997	1996
Return (%)	8.0	22.5	41.5	-6.2	5.9	8.4	12.1	-5.9	29.8	18.9
Differ From Category (+/-)	0.7	6.1	-5.5	13.0	0.6	2.8	-26.2	-7.4	6.5	-2.3
Return, Tax-Adjusted (%)	6.8	21.5	41.3	-6.3	4.8	1.7	10.1	-6.7	28.5	17.0

PER SHARE DATA

	2005	2004	2003	2002	2001	2000	1999	1998	1997	1996
Dividends, Net Income ($)	0.08	0.14	0.10	0.04	0.01	0.06	0.11	0.01	0.04	0.06
Distrib'ns, Cap Gain ($)	1.18	0.80	0.00	0.00	0.51	4.66	1.14	0.54	0.68	0.65
Net Asset Value ($)	15.45	15.46	13.40	9.54	10.22	10.15	14.10	13.78	15.26	12.33
Expense Ratio (%)	1.00	1.00	1.00	1.00	1.00	1.00	1.00	1.00	1.00	1.00
Yield (%)	0.46	0.88	0.76	0.45	0.11	0.37	0.73	0.07	0.24	0.45
Portfolio Turnover (%)	23	51	69	77	16	18	18	18	18	47
Total Assets (Millions $)	513	484	383	258	247	154	240	314	336	193

PORTFOLIO (as of 9/30/05)

Portfolio Manager: Robert Bergson - 2001

Investment Style

Large Cap	Growth
Mid Cap	Value
✔ Small Cap	✔ Grth/Val

Portfolio

3.8% cash	0.0% corp bonds
95.4% stocks	0.0% gov't bonds
0.0% pref/conv't pref	0.0% muni bonds
0.0% conv't bds/wrnts	0.8% other

SHAREHOLDER INFORMATION

Minimum Investment
Initial: $2,500   Subsequent: $50

Minimum IRA Investment
Initial: $500   Subsequent: $50

Maximum Fees
Load: none   12b-1: none
Other: none

Services
✔ IRA
✔ Keogh
✔ Telephone Exchange

Oberweis Emerging Growth (OBEGX)

Small-Cap Stock

800-323-6166
www.oberweisfunds.com

PERFORMANCE   **fund inception date: 1/7/87**

	3yr Annual	5yr Annual	10yr Annual	Bull	Bear
Return (%)	22.3	6.8	7.5	101.7	-51.2
Differ From Category (+/-)	0.3 av	-1.7 blw av	-3.9 low	8.3 abv av	-33.0 low

Standard Deviation	Category Risk Index	Beta
22.1%—high	1.47—high	1.83

	2005	2004	2003	2002	2001	2000	1999	1998	1997	1996
Return (%)	2.7	6.2	67.7	-24.2	0.4	-10.6	53.1	-3.1	-8.5	22.4
Differ From Category (+/-)	-4.6	-10.2	20.7	-5.0	-4.9	-16.3	14.8	-4.5	-31.9	1.2
Return, Tax-Adjusted (%)	1.8	5.8	67.7	-24.2	0.4	-17.9	53.1	-3.9	-11.3	19.9

PER SHARE DATA

	2005	2004	2003	2002	2001	2000	1999	1998	1997	1996
Dividends, Net Income ($)	0.00	0.00	0.00	0.00	0.00	0.00	0.00	0.00	0.00	0.00
Distrib'ns, Cap Gain ($)	1.74	0.76	0.00	0.00	0.00	13.11	0.00	1.15	4.64	2.64
Net Asset Value ($)	26.95	27.93	27.05	16.13	21.29	21.19	36.15	23.60	25.71	32.86
Expense Ratio (%)	na	1.44	1.37	1.57	1.65	1.42	1.59	1.55	1.44	1.48
Yield (%)	0.00	0.00	0.00	0.00	0.00	0.00	0.00	0.00	0.00	0.00
Portfolio Turnover (%)	na	55	56	66	66	73	63	49	75	64
Total Assets (Millions $)	184	173	244	62	80	84	105	94	140	186

PORTFOLIO (as of 9/30/05)

Portfolio Manager: J W Oberweis/
D Oberweis - 1987

Investment Style

Large Cap	✔ Growth
Mid Cap	Value
✔ Small Cap	Grth/Val

Portfolio

1.7% cash	0.0% corp bonds
98.3% stocks	0.0% gov't bonds
0.0% pref/conv't pref	0.0% muni bonds
0.0% conv't bds/wrnts	0.0% other

SHAREHOLDER INFORMATION

Minimum Investment
Initial: $1,000   Subsequent: $100

Minimum IRA Investment
Initial: $500   Subsequent: $100

Maximum Fees
Load: 1.00% redemption   12b-1: 0.25%
Other: redemption fee applies for 6 months

Services
✔ IRA
✔ Keogh
✔ Telephone Exchange

Individual Fund Listings   **209**

Oberweis Micro Cap

(OBMCX)

Small-Cap Stock

800-323-6166
www.oberweisfunds.com

PERFORMANCE

fund inception date: 1/1/96

	3yr Annual	5yr Annual	10yr Annual	Bull	Bear
Return (%)	34.0	19.7	na	138.3	-27.8
Differ From Category (+/-)	12.0 high	11.2 high	na	44.9 high	-9.6 av

Standard Deviation	Category Risk Index	Beta
24.2%—high	1.61—high	1.93

	2005	2004	2003	2002	2001	2000	1999	1998	1997	1996
Return (%)	12.7	2.1	108.9	-17.3	23.8	-8.0	19.3	4.4	10.6	—
Differ From Category (+/-)	.5.4	-14.3	61.9	1.9	18.5	-13.6	-19.0	3.0	-12.7	—
Return, Tax-Adjusted (%)	10.7	-2.3	106.0	-17.3	23.8	-10.7	19.3	4.4	10.6	—

PER SHARE DATA

	2005	2004	2003	2002	2001	2000	1999	1998	1997	1996
Dividends, Net Income ($)	0.00	0.00	0.00	0.00	0.00	0.00	0.00	0.00	0.00	—
Distrib'ns, Cap Gain ($)	2.31	7.91	2.70	0.00	0.00	2.33	0.00	0.00	0.00	—
Net Asset Value ($)	17.31	17.50	26.26	13.86	16.77	13.54	16.94	14.19	13.59	—
Expense Ratio (%)	na	1.70	1.60	1.93	1.98	2.00	2.00	1.99	1.81	—
Yield (%)	0.00	0.00	0.00	0.00	0.00	0.00	0.00	0.00	0.00	—
Portfolio Turnover (%)	na	58	87	81	82	79	46	41	89	—
Total Assets (Millions $)	68	47	100	22	49	20	21	28	37	—

PORTFOLIO (as of 9/30/05)

Portfolio Manager: J W Oberweis/
J D Oberweis - 1996

Investment Style

Large Cap	✔ Growth
Mid Cap	Value
✔ Small Cap	Grth/Val

Portfolio

3.8% cash	0.0% corp bonds
96.2% stocks	0.0% gov't bonds
0.0% pref/conv't pref	0.0% muni bonds
0.0% conv't bds/wrnts	0.0% other

SHAREHOLDER INFORMATION

Minimum Investment
Initial: $1,000   Subsequent: $100

Minimum IRA Investment
Initial: $500   Subsequent: $100

Maximum Fees
Load: 1.00% redemption   12b-1: 0.25%
Other: redemption fee applies for 6 months

Services
✔ IRA
✔ Keogh
✔ Telephone Exchange

Guide to the Top Mutual Funds

Perritt Micro Cap Opportunities (PRCGX)

800-331-8936
www.perrittcap.com

Small-Cap Stock

PERFORMANCE

fund inception date: 5/2/88

	3yr Annual	5yr Annual	10yr Annual	Bull	Bear
Return (%)	29.9	24.2	14.8	127.5	5.6
Differ From Category (+/-)	7.9 high	15.7 high	3.4 high	34.1 high	23.8 abv av

Standard Deviation	Category Risk Index	Beta
13.5%—abv av	0.90—blw av	1.14

	2005	2004	2003	2002	2001	2000	1999	1998	1997	1996
Return (%)	14.4	17.1	63.4	0.4	34.4	6.2	-8.1	-4.2	22.1	17.9
Differ From Category (+/-)	.7.1	0.7	16.4	19.7	29.1	0.6	-46.5	-5.7	-1.2	-3.3
Return, Tax-Adjusted (%)	13.6	16.7	62.6	0.0	34.2	0.0	-8.1	-4.2	18.7	15.0

PER SHARE DATA

	2005	2004	2003	2002	2001	2000	1999	1998	1997	1996
Dividends, Net Income ($)	0.00	0.00	0.49	0.09	0.00	1.95	0.00	0.00	0.00	0.04
Distrib'ns, Cap Gain ($)	1.46	0.60	0.34	0.14	0.11	0.00	0.00	0.00	2.26	1.27
Net Asset Value ($)	29.51	27.06	23.63	14.96	15.12	11.33	12.59	13.71	14.32	13.47
Expense Ratio (%)	na	1.25	1.44	1.60	1.60	1.75	1.72	1.81	1.52	1.92
Yield (%)	0.00	0.00	2.02	0.58	0.00	17.23	0.00	0.00	0.00	0.25
Portfolio Turnover (%)	24	30	32	118	94	89	53	24	83	58
Total Assets (Millions $)	535	258	170	19	16	9	9	12	14	8

PORTFOLIO (as of 9/30/05)

Portfolio Manager: Michael Corbett - 1999

Investment Style

Large Cap	✔ Growth
Mid Cap	Value
✔ Small Cap	Grth/Val

Portfolio

3.5% cash	0.0% corp bonds
96.5% stocks	0.0% gov't bonds
0.0% pref/conv't pref	0.0% muni bonds
0.0% conv't bds/wrnts	0.0% other

SHAREHOLDER INFORMATION

Minimum Investment
Initial: $1,000   Subsequent: $50

Minimum IRA Investment
Initial: $250   Subsequent: $50

Maximum Fees
Load: 2.00% redemption   12b-1: none
Other: redemption fee applies for 3 months

Services
✔ IRA
Keogh
Telephone Exchange

Preferred Small Cap Growth (PSMCX)

Small-Cap Stock

800-662-4769
www.preferredgroup.com

PERFORMANCE

fund inception date: 11/1/95

	3yr Annual	5yr Annual	10yr Annual	Bull	Bear
Return (%)	23.6	0.3	1.3	96.4	-62.0
Differ From Category (+/-)	1.6 abv av	-8.2 low	-10.1 low	3.0 abv av	-43.8 low

Standard Deviation	Category Risk Index	Beta
17.3%—high	1.15—high	1.55

	2005	2004	2003	2002	2001	2000	1999	1998	1997	1996
Return (%)	6.2	11.8	59.0	-32.7	-19.9	-16.8	-10.6	-4.7	31.8	20.4
Differ From Category (+/-)	-1.1	-4.6	12.0	-13.5	-25.2	-22.5	-48.9	-6.2	8.5	-0.8
Return, Tax-Adjusted (%)	6.2	11.8	59.0	-32.7	-19.9	-16.8	-10.6	-5.6	28.6	19.9

PER SHARE DATA

	2005	2004	2003	2002	2001	2000	1999	1998	1997	1996
Dividends, Net Income ($)	0.00	0.00	0.00	0.00	0.00	0.00	0.03	0.02	0.08	0.03
Distrib'ns, Cap Gain ($)	0.00	0.00	0.00	0.00	0.00	0.00	0.00	0.57	1.83	0.16
Net Asset Value ($)	9.92	9.34	8.35	5.25	7.81	9.75	11.72	13.14	14.45	12.45
Expense Ratio (%)	1.28	1.35	1.50	1.37	1.26	1.11	0.92	0.90	0.88	0.88
Yield (%)	0.00	0.00	0.00	0.00	0.00	0.00	0.21	0.12	0.52	0.20
Portfolio Turnover (%)	140	167	189	194	183	236	121	105	104	—
Total Assets (Millions $)	116	123	105	39	58	97	96	124	122	69

PORTFOLIO (as of 9/30/05)

Portfolio Manager: Bill McVail/
Team Managed - 2000

Investment Style

Large Cap	✔ Growth
Mid Cap	Value
✔ Small Cap	Grth/Val

Portfolio

1.7% cash	0.0%	corp bonds
98.3% stocks	0.0%	gov't bonds
0.0% pref/conv't pref	0.0%	muni bonds
0.0% conv't bds/wrnts	0.0%	other

SHAREHOLDER INFORMATION

Minimum Investment
Initial: $1,000   Subsequent: $50

Minimum IRA Investment
Initial: $250   Subsequent: $50

Maximum Fees
Load: none   12b-1: none
Other: none

Services
✔ IRA
✔ Keogh
✔ Telephone Exchange

Royce Micro-Cap Inv
(RYOTX)
Small-Cap Stock

800-221-4268
www.roycefunds.com

PERFORMANCE

fund inception date: 12/31/91

	3yr Annual	5yr Annual	10yr Annual	Bull	Bear
Return (%)	25.3	16.0	14.5	112.6	3.4
Differ From Category (+/-)	3.3 abv av	7.5 high	3.1 abv av	19.2 high	21.6 abv av

Standard Deviation	Category Risk Index	Beta
15.4%—high	1.03—abv av	1.35

	2005	2004	2003	2002	2001	2000	1999	1998	1997	1996
Return (%).............	11.5	15.7	52.6	-13.4	23.1	16.7	13.6	-3.3	24.6	15.5
Differ From Category (+/-)	.4.2	-0.7	5.6	5.8	17.8	11.1	-24.7	-4.8	1.3	-5.7
Return, Tax-Adjusted (%)...	9.9	14.2	51.7	-13.5	22.7	14.0	13.1	-4.4	22.8	13.4

PER SHARE DATA

	2005	2004	2003	2002	2001	2000	1999	1998	1997	1996
Dividends, Net Income ($).	0.13	0.00	0.00	0.00	0.00	0.00	0.00	0.00	0.00	0.00
Distrib'ns, Cap Gain ($) ...	1.48	1.54	0.57	0.10	0.19	1.28	0.21	0.51	0.75	0.55
Net Asset Value ($)	15.90	15.71	14.93	10.16	11.85	9.78	9.50	8.55	9.40	8.14
Expense Ratio (%).........	na	1.46	1.48	1.49	1.75	1.49	1.35	1.49	1.50	1.79
Yield (%)	0.73	0.00	0.00	0.00	0.00	0.00	0.00	0.04	0.00	0.04
Portfolio Turnover (%)	na	44	44	10	30	74	102	56	38	70
Total Assets (Millions $)...	491	482	433	263	202	140	112	165	200	141

PORTFOLIO (as of 9/30/05)

Portfolio Manager: Whitney George - 1991

Investment Style

Large Cap	Growth
Mid Cap	✔ Value
✔ Small Cap	Grth/Val

Portfolio

11.7% cash	0.0% corp bonds
82.7% stocks	0.0% gov't bonds
0.0% pref/conv't pref	0.0% muni bonds
0.0% conv't bds/wrnts	5.6% other

SHAREHOLDER INFORMATION

Minimum Investment
Initial: $2,000   Subsequent: $50

Minimum IRA Investment
Initial: $500   Subsequent: $50

Maximum Fees
Load: 1.00% redemption   12b-1: none
Other: redemption fee applies for 6 months

Services
✔ IRA
✔ Keogh
✔ Telephone Exchange

Royce Opportunity Inv

(RYPNX)

Small-Cap Stock

800-221-4268
www.roycefunds.com

fund inception date: 11/20/96

PERFORMANCE

	3yr Annual	5yr Annual	10yr Annual	Bull	Bear
Return (%)	28.6	15.6	na	124.6	-8.2
Differ From Category (+/-)	6.6 high	7.1 high	na	31.2 high	10.0 av

Standard Deviation	Category Risk Index	Beta
18.2%—high	1.21—high	1.69

	2005	2004	2003	2002	2001	2000	1999	1998	1997	1996
Return (%)	4.7	17.5	72.8	-17.0	17.3	19.8	32.3	4.9	20.8	—
Differ From Category (+/-)	-2.6	1.1	25.8	2.2	12.0	14.2	-6.0	3.5	-2.5	—
Return, Tax-Adjusted (%)	2.8	16.3	71.6	-17.2	17.0	17.5	29.8	4.3	18.8	—

PER SHARE DATA

	2005	2004	2003	2002	2001	2000	1999	1998	1997	1996
Dividends, Net Income ($)	0.00	0.00	0.00	0.00	0.00	0.00	0.00	0.00	0.08	—
Distrib'ns, Cap Gain ($)	1.67	0.93	0.58	0.11	0.11	0.81	0.74	0.18	0.36	—
Net Asset Value ($)	12.29	13.31	12.14	7.37	9.01	7.78	7.19	6.02	5.92	—
Expense Ratio (%)	na	1.14	1.15	1.17	1.19	1.24	1.46	1.25	0.99	—
Yield (%)	0.00	0.00	0.00	0.00	0.00	0.00	0.00	0.00	1.27	—
Portfolio Turnover (%)	na	47	55	46	44	56	122	120	77	—
Total Assets (Millions $)	1,514	1,678	1,310	636	576	297	60	33	22	—

PORTFOLIO (as of 9/30/05)

Portfolio Manager: Boniface Zaino - 1998

Investment Style

Large Cap	Growth
Mid Cap	✔ Value
✔ Small Cap	Grth/Val

Portfolio

6.9%	cash	0.0%	corp bonds
88.3%	stocks	0.0%	gov't bonds
0.0%	pref/conv't pref	0.0%	muni bonds
0.0%	conv't bds/wrnts	4.8%	other

SHAREHOLDER INFORMATION

Minimum Investment
Initial: $2,000   Subsequent: $50

Minimum IRA Investment
Initial: $500   Subsequent: $50

Maximum Fees
Load: 1.00% redemption   12b-1: none
Other: redemption fee applies for 6 months

Services
✔ IRA
✔ Keogh
✔ Telephone Exchange

Royce Pennsylvania Mutual Inv (PENNX)

800-221-4268
www.roycefunds.com

Small-Cap Stock

PERFORMANCE

fund inception date: 10/3/68

	3yr Annual	5yr Annual	10yr Annual	Bull	Bear
Return (%)	23.8	15.3	14.1	100.3	17.2
Differ From Category (+/-)	1.8 abv av	6.8 high	2.7 abv av	6.9 abv av	35.4 high

Standard Deviation	Category Risk Index	Beta
12.7%—abv av	0.85—blw av	1.17

	2005	2004	2003	2002	2001	2000	1999	1998	1997	1996
Return (%)	12.5	20.2	40.2	-9.2	18.3	18.3	5.9	4.1	24.9	12.8
Differ From Category (+/-)	.5.2	3.8	-6.8	10.0	13.0	12.7	-32.4	2.7	1.6	-8.4
Return, Tax-Adjusted (%)	11.5	19.3	39.4	-9.5	16.2	13.7	4.5	2.1	21.8	7.0

PER SHARE DATA

	2005	2004	2003	2002	2001	2000	1999	1998	1997	1996
Dividends, Net Income ($)	0.00	0.00	0.00	0.00	0.02	0.05	0.04	0.05	0.06	0.11
Distrib'ns, Cap Gain ($)	0.63	0.53	0.36	0.12	0.70	1.59	0.45	0.71	1.00	1.44
Net Asset Value ($)	10.78	10.14	8.88	6.59	7.39	6.88	7.28	7.35	7.82	7.11
Expense Ratio (%)	na	0.89	0.93	0.94	0.99	1.03	1.04	1.01	1.05	0.99
Yield (%)	0.00	0.00	0.00	0.00	0.28	0.59	0.51	0.62	0.69	1.28
Portfolio Turnover (%)	na	32	30	33	39	45	21	29	18	29
Total Assets (Millions $)	1,803	1,242	839	462	445	370	371	467	508	456

PORTFOLIO (as of 9/30/05)

Portfolio Manager: Charles Royce - 1968

Investment Style

Large Cap	Growth
✔ Mid Cap	✔ Value
✔ Small Cap	Grth/Val

Portfolio

9.9% cash	0.0% corp bonds
86.5% stocks	0.0% gov't bonds
0.0% pref/conv't pref	0.0% muni bonds
0.0% conv't bds/wrnts	3.6% other

SHAREHOLDER INFORMATION

Minimum Investment
Initial: $2,000   Subsequent: $50

Minimum IRA Investment
Initial: $500   Subsequent: $50

Maximum Fees
Load: 1.00% redemption   12b-1: none
Other: redemption fee applies for 6 months

Services
✔ IRA
✔ Keogh
✔ Telephone Exchange

Royce Premier
(RYPRX)

Small-Cap Stock

800-221-4268
www.roycefunds.com

PERFORMANCE

fund inception date: 12/31/91

	3yr Annual	5yr Annual	10yr Annual	Bull	Bear
Return (%)	25.8	15.0	14.6	109.9	8.8
Differ From Category (+/-)	3.8 high	6.5 high	3.2 high	16.5 high	27.0 high

Standard Deviation	Category Risk Index	Beta
12.4%—abv av	0.83—blw av	1.13

	2005	2004	2003	2002	2001	2000	1999	1998	1997	1996
Return (%)............	17.0	22.8	38.7	-7.7	9.6	17.1	11.4	6.7	18.4	18.1
Differ From Category (+/-)	.9.7	6.4	-8.3	11.5	4.3	11.5	-26.9	5.3	-4.9	-3.1
Return, Tax-Adjusted (%) ..	16.2	21.9	38.5	-8.3	9.1	14.3	10.1	6.3	16.7	15.6

PER SHARE DATA

	2005	2004	2003	2002	2001	2000	1999	1998	1997	1996
Dividends, Net Income ($).	0.00	0.00	0.00	0.00	0.00	0.03	0.01	0.05	0.09	0.10
Distrib'ns, Cap Gain ($) ...	0.84	0.71	0.13	0.34	0.23	1.27	0.58	0.09	0.46	0.49
Net Asset Value ($)	16.86	15.12	12.90	9.39	10.54	9.83	9.56	9.14	8.70	7.81
Expense Ratio (%)........	na	1.14	1.16	1.17	1.19	1.20	1.35	1.23	1.24	1.25
Yield (%)	0.00	0.00	0.00	0.00	0.00	0.27	0.09	0.54	0.96	1.20
Portfolio Turnover (%)	na	24	26	33	41	40	70	46	18	34
Total Assets (Millions $) ..	3,276	2,974	1,711	849	799	674	568	572	534	317

PORTFOLIO (as of 9/30/05)

Portfolio Manager: Charles Royce - 1991

Investment Style

Large Cap	Growth
✔ Mid Cap	✔ Value
✔ Small Cap	Grth/Val

Portfolio

12.1% cash	0.0% corp bonds
87.0% stocks	0.0% gov't bonds
0.0% pref/conv't pref	0.0% muni bonds
0.0% conv't bds/wrnts	0.9% other

SHAREHOLDER INFORMATION

Minimum Investment
Initial: $2,000   Subsequent: $50

Minimum IRA Investment
Initial: $500   Subsequent: $50

Maximum Fees
Load: 1.00% redemption   12b-1: none
Other: redemption fee applies for 6 months

Services
✔ IRA
✔ Keogh
✔ Telephone Exchange

Royce Total Return Inv

(RYTRX)

Small-Cap Stock

800-221-4268
www.roycefunds.com

PERFORMANCE

fund inception date: 12/15/93

	3yr Annual	5yr Annual	10yr Annual	Bull	Bear
Return (%)	18.2	13.3	13.9	73.7	27.0
Differ From Category (+/-)	-3.8 low	4.8 abv av	2.5 abv av	-19.7 low	45.2 high

Standard Deviation	Category Risk Index	Beta
10.2%—av	0.68—low	1.02

	2005	2004	2003	2002	2001	2000	1999	1998	1997	1996
Return (%)	8.2	17.5	29.9	-1.6	14.7	19.4	1.5	4.7	23.7	25.4
Differ From Category (+/-)	0.9	1.1	-17.1	17.7	9.4	13.8	-36.8	3.3	0.4	4.2
Return, Tax-Adjusted (%)	7.4	17.1	29.6	-1.9	13.7	17.0	-0.2	3.5	22.5	20.8

PER SHARE DATA

	2005	2004	2003	2002	2001	2000	1999	1998	1997	1996
Dividends, Net Income ($)	0.13	0.12	0.09	0.08	0.11	0.15	0.16	0.15	0.11	0.16
Distrib'ns, Cap Gain ($)	0.55	0.17	0.08	0.01	0.21	0.57	0.35	0.16	0.15	0.73
Net Asset Value ($)	12.60	12.26	10.69	8.37	8.59	7.77	7.15	7.56	7.52	6.29
Expense Ratio (%)	na	1.15	1.18	1.20	1.24	1.25	1.25	1.25	1.25	1.25
Yield (%)	0.95	0.95	0.86	0.89	1.19	1.79	2.13	1.94	1.46	2.27
Portfolio Turnover (%)	na	22	20	22	24	24	39	66	26	111
Total Assets (Millions $)	4,274	3,738	2,794	1,113	511	277	249	244	121	6

PORTFOLIO (as of 9/30/05)

Portfolio Manager: Charles Royce - 1993

Investment Style

Large Cap	Growth
✔ Mid Cap	✔ Value
✔ Small Cap	Grth/Val

Portfolio

11.0% cash	1.3% corp bonds
80.6% stocks	3.0% gov't bonds
0.8% pref/conv't pref	0.0% muni bonds
0.1% conv't bds/wrnts	3.3% other

SHAREHOLDER INFORMATION

Minimum Investment
Initial: $2,000   Subsequent: $50

Minimum IRA Investment
Initial: $500   Subsequent: $50

Maximum Fees
Load: 1.00% redemption   12b-1: none
Other: redemption fee applies for 6 months

Services
✔ IRA
✔ Keogh
✔ Telephone Exchange

Royce Value Inv
(RYVFX)

800-221-4268
www.roycefunds.com

Small-Cap Stock

fund inception date: 6/14/01

PERFORMANCE

	3yr Annual	5yr Annual	10yr Annual	Bull	Bear
Return (%)	33.3	na	na	140.6	na
Differ From Category (+/-)	11.3 high	na	na	47.2 high	na

Standard Deviation	Category Risk Index	Beta
12.6%—abv av	0.84—blw av	1.14

	2005	2004	2003	2002	2001	2000	1999	1998	1997	1996
Return (%)	17.2	30.9	54.3	-23.5	—	—	—	—	—	—
Differ From Category (+/-)	.9.9	14.5	7.3	-4.3	—	—	—	—	—	—
Return, Tax-Adjusted (%)	16.9	30.4	53.8	-24.5	—	—	—	—	—	—

PER SHARE DATA

	2005	2004	2003	2002	2001	2000	1999	1998	1997	1996
Dividends, Net Income ($)	0.00	0.00	0.00	0.16	—	—	—	—	—	—
Distrib'ns, Cap Gain ($)	0.16	0.19	0.15	0.00	—	—	—	—	—	—
Net Asset Value ($)	9.67	8.39	6.56	4.35	—	—	—	—	—	—
Expense Ratio (%)	na	1.49	1.49	1.49	—	—	—	—	—	—
Yield (%)	0.00	0.00	0.00	3.67	—	—	—	—	—	—
Portfolio Turnover (%)	na	83	181	—	—	—	—	—	—	—
Total Assets (Millions $)	102	38	4	1	—	—	—	—	—	—

PORTFOLIO (as of 9/30/05)

Portfolio Manager: W George/J Kaplan - 2004

Investment Style

Large Cap	Growth
Mid Cap	✔ Value
✔ Small Cap	Grth/Val

Portfolio

14.8%	cash	0.0%	corp bonds
83.7%	stocks	0.0%	gov't bonds
0.0%	pref/conv't pref	0.0%	muni bonds
0.0%	conv't bds/wrnts	1.5%	other

SHAREHOLDER INFORMATION

Minimum Investment
Initial: $2,000   Subsequent: $50

Minimum IRA Investment
Initial: $500   Subsequent: $50

Maximum Fees
Load: 1.00% redemption   12b-1: 0.25%
Other: redemption fee applies for 6 months

Services
✔ IRA
✔ Keogh
✔ Telephone Exchange

Royce Value Plus Inv
(RYVPX)

Small-Cap Stock

800-221-4268
www.roycefunds.com

PERFORMANCE

fund inception date: 6/14/01

	3yr Annual	5yr Annual	10yr Annual	Bull	Bear
Return (%)	37.6	na	na	169.6	na
Differ From Category (+/-)	15.6 high	na	na	76.2 high	na

Standard Deviation	Category Risk Index	Beta
16.8%—high	1.12—abv av	1.48

	2005	2004	2003	2002	2001	2000	1999	1998	1997	1996
Return (%)	13.2	28.1	79.8	-14.7	—	—	—	—	—	—
Differ From Category (+/-)	.5.9	11.7	32.8	4.5	—	—	—	—	—	—
Return, Tax-Adjusted (%)	12.7	28.1	78.8	-15.5	—	—	—	—	—	—

PER SHARE DATA

	2005	2004	2003	2002	2001	2000	1999	1998	1997	1996
Dividends, Net Income ($)	0.00	0.00	0.00	0.12	—	—	—	—	—	—
Distrib'ns, Cap Gain ($)	0.35	0.04	0.36	0.00	—	—	—	—	—	—
Net Asset Value ($)	12.03	10.94	8.57	4.97	—	—	—	—	—	—
Expense Ratio (%)	na	1.30	1.49	1.49	—	—	—	—	—	—
Yield (%)	0.00	0.00	0.00	2.41	—	—	—	—	—	—
Portfolio Turnover (%)	na	56	161	—	—	—	—	—	—	—
Total Assets (Millions $)	270	209	20	4	—	—	—	—	—	—

PORTFOLIO (as of 9/30/05)

Portfolio Manager: Whitney George/Chip Skinner - 2001

Investment Style

Large Cap	Growth
Mid Cap	✔ Value
✔ Small Cap	Grth/Val

Portfolio

8.9% cash	0.0% corp bonds
86.4% stocks	0.0% gov't bonds
0.0% pref/conv't pref	0.0% muni bonds
0.0% conv't bds/wrnts	4.8% other

SHAREHOLDER INFORMATION

Minimum Investment
Initial: $2,000   Subsequent: $50

Minimum IRA Investment
Initial: $500   Subsequent: $50

Maximum Fees
Load: 1.00% redemption   12b-1: 0.25%
Other: redemption fee applies for 6 months

Services
✔ IRA
Keogh
✔ Telephone Exchange

RS Smaller Co Growth
(RSSGX)
Small-Cap Stock

800-766-3863
www.rsim.com

fund inception date: 8/15/96

	3yr Annual	5yr Annual	10yr Annual	Bull	Bear
Return (%)	25.6	5.5	na	116.3	-52.7
Differ From Category (+/-)	3.6 high	-3.0 blw av	na	22.9 high	-34.5 low

Standard Deviation	Category Risk Index	Beta
16.9%—high	1.13—high	1.46

	2005	2004	2003	2002	2001	2000	1999	1998	1997	1996
Return (%)	6.7	15.3	60.9	-39.0	8.3	4.4	56.6	-0.6	30.4	—
Differ From Category (+/-)	-0.6	-1.1	13.9	-19.8	3.0	-1.2	18.3	-2.1	7.1	—
Return, Tax-Adjusted (%)	4.7	14.5	60.9	-39.5	7.7	2.1	56.6	-0.6	30.4	—

PER SHARE DATA

	2005	2004	2003	2002	2001	2000	1999	1998	1997	1996
Dividends, Net Income ($)	0.00	0.00	0.00	0.00	0.00	0.00	0.00	0.00	0.00	—
Distrib'ns, Cap Gain ($)	3.02	1.12	0.00	0.49	0.60	2.56	0.00	0.00	0.00	—
Net Asset Value ($)	21.11	22.57	20.58	12.79	21.78	20.69	22.34	14.26	14.35	—
Expense Ratio (%)	na	1.59	1.73	1.81	1.66	1.67	1.92	1.91	1.95	—
Yield (%)	0.00	0.00	0.00	0.00	0.00	0.00	0.00	0.00	0.00	—
Portfolio Turnover (%)	na	163	220	128	167	126	90	108	170	—
Total Assets (Millions $)	242	214	200	111	116	106	103	93	103	—

PORTFOLIO (as of 9/30/05)

Portfolio Manager: William Wolfenden - 2001

Investment Style

Large Cap	✔ Growth
Mid Cap	Value
✔ Small Cap	Grth/Val

Portfolio

7.4% cash	0.0% corp bonds
92.6% stocks	0.0% gov't bonds
0.0% pref/conv't pref	0.0% muni bonds
0.0% conv't bds/wrnts	0.0% other

SHAREHOLDER INFORMATION

Minimum Investment
Initial: $5,000   Subsequent: $1,000

Minimum IRA Investment
Initial: $1,000   Subsequent: $250

Maximum Fees
Load: none   12b-1: 0.25%
Other: none

Services
✔ IRA
  Keogh
✔ Telephone Exchange

Schroder Capital US Opportunities Inv (SCUIX)

800-464-3108
www.schroders.com/us

Small-Cap Stock

PERFORMANCE

fund inception date: 8/5/93

	3yr Annual	5yr Annual	10yr Annual	Bull	Bear
Return (%)	22.2	10.6	13.2	94.3	-5.4
Differ From Category (+/-)	0.2 av	2.1 av	1.8 abv av	0.9 av	12.8 abv av

Standard Deviation	Category Risk Index	Beta
12.2%—abv av	0.81—low	1.10

	2005	2004	2003	2002	2001	2000	1999	1998	1997	1996
Return (%)	6.4	25.2	37.1	-18.8	11.5	31.2	13.1	-9.2	26.8	22.2
Differ From Category (+/-)	-0.9	8.8	-9.9	0.4	6.2	25.6	-25.2	-10.7	3.5	1.0
Return, Tax-Adjusted (%)	5.8	23.5	37.1	-19.2	9.8	26.6	13.1	-9.2	24.7	11.1

PER SHARE DATA

	2005	2004	2003	2002	2001	2000	1999	1998	1997	1996
Dividends, Net Income ($)	0.00	0.00	0.00	0.00	0.00	0.00	0.00	0.00	0.00	0.00
Distrib'ns, Cap Gain ($)	0.75	2.03	0.00	0.34	1.35	3.30	0.00	0.03	1.26	5.83
Net Asset Value ($)	19.79	19.29	17.06	12.44	15.74	15.34	14.33	12.67	13.99	12.05
Expense Ratio (%)	na	1.62	1.93	1.49	1.49	1.18	1.35	1.37	1.49	1.49
Yield (%)	0.00	0.00	0.00	0.00	0.00	0.00	0.00	0.00	0.00	0.00
Portfolio Turnover (%)	107	144	162	81	105	172	52	55	34	59
Total Assets (Millions $)	147	103	49	41	39	56	45	52	42	14

PORTFOLIO (as of 6/30/05)

Portfolio Manager: Jenny Jones - 2003

Investment Style

Large Cap	Growth
✔ Mid Cap	Value
✔ Small Cap	✔ Grth/Val

Portfolio

7.8% cash	0.0% corp bonds
90.5% stocks	0.0% gov't bonds
0.0% pref/conv't pref	0.0% muni bonds
0.0% conv't bds/wrnts	1.7% other

SHAREHOLDER INFORMATION

Minimum Investment
Initial: $10,000   Subsequent: $1,000

Minimum IRA Investment
Initial: $2,000   Subsequent: $250

Maximum Fees
Load: 2.00% redemption   12b-1: none
Other: redemption fee applies for 2 months

Services
✔ IRA
✔ Keogh
✔ Telephone Exchange

Sit Small Cap Growth
(SSMGX)
Small-Cap Stock

800-332-5580
www.sitfunds.com

	3yr Annual	5yr Annual	10yr Annual	Bull	Bear
Return (%)	19.4	-2.1	9.7	79.3	-57.6
Differ From Category (+/-)	-2.6 blw av	-10.6 low	-1.7 blw av	-14.1 blw av	-39.4 low

Standard Deviation	Category Risk Index	Beta
15.1%—high	1.01—av	1.36

	2005	2004	2003	2002	2001	2000	1999	1998	1997	1996
Return (%)	18.5	6.7	34.5	-26.2	-28.1	6.2	108.6	1.9	7.6	14.9
Differ From Category (+/-)	11.2	-9.7	-12.5	-7.0	-33.5	0.6	70.3	0.5	-15.7	-6.3
Return, Tax-Adjusted (%)	18.5	6.7	34.5	-26.2	-28.2	5.9	108.6	-1.2	6.8	13.6

PER SHARE DATA

	2005	2004	2003	2002	2001	2000	1999	1998	1997	1996
Dividends, Net Income ($)	0.00	0.00	0.00	0.00	0.00	0.00	0.00	0.00	0.00	0.00
Distrib'ns, Cap Gain ($)	0.00	0.00	0.00	0.00	0.04	0.58	0.00	3.09	0.68	0.81
Net Asset Value ($)	31.68	26.73	25.03	18.60	25.21	35.16	33.61	16.11	19.13	18.43
Expense Ratio (%)	1.50	1.50	1.50	1.50	1.50	1.50	1.50	1.50	1.50	1.50
Yield (%)	0.00	0.00	0.00	0.00	0.00	0.00	0.00	0.00	0.00	0.00
Portfolio Turnover (%)	34	66	59	65	39	39	71	79	58	69
Total Assets (Millions $)	241	192	219	153	206	264	103	48	66	58

PORTFOLIO (as of 9/30/05)

Portfolio Manager: Eugene Sit/
Team Managed - 1994

Investment Style

Large Cap	✔ Growth
Mid Cap	Value
✔ Small Cap	Grth/Val

Portfolio

0.0%	cash	0.0%	corp bonds
100.0%	stocks	0.0%	gov't bonds
0.0%	pref/conv't pref	0.0%	muni bonds
0.0%	conv't bds/wrnts	0.0%	other

SHAREHOLDER INFORMATION

Minimum Investment
Initial: $5,000   Subsequent: $100

Minimum IRA Investment
Initial: $2,000   Subsequent: $100

Maximum Fees
Load: 2.00% redemption   12b-1: none
Other: redemption fee applies for 1 month

Services
✔ IRA
✔ Keogh
✔ Telephone Exchange

Skyline Special Equities
(SKSEX)
Small-Cap Stock

800-828-2759
www.skylinefunds.com

	3yr Annual	5yr Annual	10yr Annual	Bull	Bear
Return (%)	22.0	13.9	12.9	94.2	18.3
Differ From Category (+/-)	0.0 av	5.4 abv av	1.5 av	0.8 av	36.5 high

Standard Deviation	Category Risk Index	Beta
12.8%—abv av	0.85—blw av	1.26

	2005	2004	2003	2002	2001	2000	1999	1998	1997	1996
Return (%)............	10.8	16.6	40.7	-7.2	13.9	24.2	-13.2	-7.1	35.4	30.3
Differ From Category (+/-)	.3.5	0.2	-6.3	12.0	8.6	18.6	-51.6	-8.6	12.1	9.1
Return, Tax-Adjusted (%)...	7.5	14.6	39.5	-7.2	13.9	24.2	-14.5	-7.4	32.2	24.3

PER SHARE DATA

	2005	2004	2003	2002	2001	2000	1999	1998	1997	1996
Dividends, Net Income ($).	0.00	0.00	0.00	0.00	0.00	0.00	0.00	0.00	0.00	0.00
Distrib'ns, Cap Gain ($) ...	6.42	3.69	1.56	0.00	0.00	0.00	1.23	0.32	2.89	3.61
Net Asset Value ($)	25.43	28.64	27.78	20.86	22.50	19.75	15.90	19.78	21.66	18.16
Expense Ratio (%)........	na	1.47	1.48	1.48	1.49	1.51	1.48	1.47	1.48	1.51
Yield (%)	0.00	0.00	0.00	0.00	0.00	0.00	0.00	0.00	0.00	0.00
Portfolio Turnover (%)	na	47	52	81	93	92	81	68	62	130
Total Assets (Millions $)...	519	567	527	383	374	287	223	446	467	219

PORTFOLIO (as of 9/30/05)

Portfolio Manager: Team Managed - 1987

Investment Style

Large Cap	Growth
✔ Mid Cap	✔ Value
✔ Small Cap	Grth/Val

Portfolio

0.0% cash	0.0% corp bonds
100.0% stocks	0.0% gov't bonds
0.0% pref/conv't pref	0.0% muni bonds
0.0% conv't bds/wrnts	0.0% other

SHAREHOLDER INFORMATION

Minimum Investment
Initial: $1,000   Subsequent: $100

Minimum IRA Investment
Initial: $1,000   Subsequent: $100

Maximum Fees
Load: 2.00% redemption   12b-1: none
Other: redemption fee applies for 1 month

Services
✔ IRA
✔ Keogh
✔ Telephone Exchange

Stratton Small Cap Value

(STSCX)

Small-Cap Stock

800-634-5726
www.strattonmgt.com/
mutualmain.html

	3yr Annual	5yr Annual	10yr Annual	Bull	Bear
Return (%)	28.0	16.0	14.2	119.6	22.4
Differ From Category (+/-)	6.0 high	7.5 high	2.8 abv av	26.2 high	40.6 high

Standard Deviation	Category Risk Index	Beta
14.8%—high	0.99—av	1.34

	2005	2004	2003	2002	2001	2000	1999	1998	1997	1996
Return (%)	10.8	26.4	49.6	-9.5	10.8	23.9	-1.9	-9.5	42.4	14.9
Differ From Category (+/-)	3.5	10.0	2.6	9.7	5.5	18.3	-40.3	-11.0	19.1	-6.3
Return, Tax-Adjusted (%)	10.3	25.8	48.8	-9.5	10.4	22.9	-2.5	-9.9	40.5	12.4

PER SHARE DATA

	2005	2004	2003	2002	2001	2000	1999	1998	1997	1996
Dividends, Net Income ($)	0.00	0.00	0.00	0.00	0.00	0.27	0.27	0.18	0.41	0.70
Distrib'ns, Cap Gain ($)	1.43	1.23	1.24	0.01	0.52	0.44	0.00	0.04	2.26	1.83
Net Asset Value ($)	43.28	40.33	32.96	22.88	25.30	23.32	19.44	20.11	22.47	33.58
Expense Ratio (%)	na	1.47	1.67	1.68	1.74	0.98	1.08	1.62	1.29	—
Yield (%)	0.00	0.00	0.00	0.00	0.00	1.13	1.38	0.89	1.65	1.97
Portfolio Turnover (%)	na	17	26	18	38	53	43	26	—	—
Total Assets (Millions $)	356	116	62	45	44	40	36	43	39	22

PORTFOLIO (as of 9/30/05)

Portfolio Manager: James Stratton/Gerald Van Horn - 2000

Investment Style

Large Cap	Growth
Mid Cap	✔ Value
✔ Small Cap	Grth/Val

Portfolio

0.0%	cash	0.0%	corp bonds
100.0%	stocks	0.0%	gov't bonds
0.0%	pref/conv't pref	0.0%	muni bonds
0.0%	conv't bds/wrnts	0.0%	other

SHAREHOLDER INFORMATION

Minimum Investment
Initial: $2,000   Subsequent: $100

Minimum IRA Investment
Initial: $0   Subsequent: $0

Maximum Fees
Load: 1.50% redemption   12b-1: none
Other: redemption fee applies for 4 months

Services
  IRA
✔ Keogh
✔ Telephone Exchange

T Rowe Price Diversified Small Cap Grth (PRDSX)

800-638-5660
www.troweprice.com

Small-Cap Stock

PERFORMANCE

fund inception date: 6/30/97

	3yr Annual	5yr Annual	10yr Annual	Bull	Bear
Return (%)	19.5	2.2	na	82.1	-50.1
Differ From Category (+/-)	-2.5 blw av	-6.3 low	na	-11.3 blw av	-31.9 blw av

Standard Deviation	Category Risk Index	Beta
14.5%—high	0.97—av	1.35

	2005	2004	2003	2002	2001	2000	1999	1998	1997	1996
Return (%)	10.4	10.2	40.2	-27.5	-9.8	-8.2	27.6	3.5	—	—
Differ From Category (+/-)	.3.1	-6.2	-6.8	-8.2	-15.2	-13.9	-10.7	2.1	—	—
Return, Tax-Adjusted (%)	10.4	10.2	40.2	-27.5	-9.8	-8.8	27.6	3.5	—	—

PER SHARE DATA

	2005	2004	2003	2002	2001	2000	1999	1998	1997	1996
Dividends, Net Income ($)	0.00	0.00	0.00	0.00	0.00	0.00	0.00	0.00	—	—
Distrib'ns, Cap Gain ($)	0.00	0.00	0.00	0.00	0.00	0.40	0.00	0.03	—	—
Net Asset Value ($)	14.01	12.68	11.50	8.20	11.31	12.54	14.11	11.05	—	—
Expense Ratio (%)	na	1.25	1.25	1.25	1.35	1.25	1.25	1.25	—	—
Yield (%)	0.00	0.00	0.00	0.00	0.00	0.00	0.00	0.00	—	—
Portfolio Turnover (%)	na	26	23	43	30	66	49	40	—	—
Total Assets (Millions $)	88	83	75	50	72	85	75	70	—	—

PORTFOLIO (as of 9/30/05)

Portfolio Manager: P Wojcik/Team Managed 1997

Investment Style

Large Cap	✔ Growth
Mid Cap	Value
✔ Small Cap	Grth/Val

Portfolio

2.3% cash	0.0% corp bonds
97.8% stocks	0.0% gov't bonds
0.0% pref/conv't pref	0.0% muni bonds
0.0% conv't bds/wrnts	0.0% other

SHAREHOLDER INFORMATION

Minimum Investment

Initial: $2,500   Subsequent: $100

Minimum IRA Investment

Initial: $1,000   Subsequent: $50

Maximum Fees

Load: 1.00% redemption   12b-1: none

Other: redemption fee applies for 6 months

Services

✔ IRA
✔ Keogh
✔ Telephone Exchange

T Rowe Price New Horizons (PRNHX)

800-638-5660
www.troweprice.com

Small-Cap Stock

	3yr Annual	5yr Annual	10yr Annual	Bull	Bear
Return (%)	25.3	7.0	9.5	105.5	-41.3
Differ From Category (+/-)	3.3 abv av	-1.5 blw av	-1.9 blw av	12.1 abv av	-23.1 blw av

Standard Deviation	Category Risk Index	Beta
14.6%—high	0.97—av	1.37

	2005	2004	2003	2002	2001	2000	1999	1998	1997	1996
Return (%)	11.9	17.9	49.3	-26.6	-2.8	-1.8	32.5	6.2	9.7	17.0
Differ From Category (+/-)	.4.6	1.5	2.3	-7.3	-8.2	-7.5	-5.8	4.8	-13.6	-4.2
Return, Tax-Adjusted (%)	11.3	17.9	49.3	-26.6	-3.3	-4.1	29.9	5.1	9.2	14.0

PER SHARE DATA

	2005	2004	2003	2002	2001	2000	1999	1998	1997	1996
Dividends, Net Income ($)	0.00	0.00	0.00	0.00	0.00	0.00	0.00	0.00	0.00	0.00
Distrib'ns, Cap Gain ($)	1.00	0.00	0.00	0.00	0.56	3.14	3.02	1.27	0.58	2.19
Net Asset Value ($)	31.74	29.24	24.80	16.61	22.63	23.89	27.53	23.34	23.30	21.77
Expense Ratio (%)	na	0.87	0.91	0.92	0.91	0.88	0.90	0.89	0.88	0.90
Yield (%)	0.00	0.00	0.00	0.00	0.00	0.00	0.00	0.00	0.00	0.00
Portfolio Turnover (%)	na	25	29	23	27	47	45	41	45	41
Total Assets (Millions $)	6,530	5,741	4,955	3,359	5,583	6,122	6,022	5,228	5,104	4,363

PORTFOLIO (as of 9/30/05)

Portfolio Manager: J Laporte/Team Managed - 1988

Investment Style

Large Cap	✔ Growth
Mid Cap	Value
✔ Small Cap	Grth/Val

Portfolio

1.6% cash	0.0% corp bonds
98.4% stocks	0.0% gov't bonds
0.0% pref/conv't pref	0.0% muni bonds
0.0% conv't bds/wrnts	0.0% other

SHAREHOLDER INFORMATION

Minimum Investment
Initial: $2,500   Subsequent: $100

Minimum IRA Investment
Initial: $1,000   Subsequent: $50

Maximum Fees
Load: none   12b-1: none
Other: none

Services
✔ IRA
✔ Keogh
✔ Telephone Exchange

Third Avenue Small Cap Value (TASCX)

800-443-1021
www.thirdave.com

Small-Cap Stock

PERFORMANCE

fund inception date: 4/1/97

Return (%)	3yr Annual	5yr Annual	10yr Annual	Bull	Bear
Return (%)	23.2	13.9	na	96.7	7.9
Differ From Category (+/-)	1.2 abv av	5.4 abv av	na	3.3 abv av	26.1 abv av

Standard Deviation	Category Risk Index	Beta
10.9%—av	0.73—low	1.04

	2005	2004	2003	2002	2001	2000	1999	1998	1997	1996
Return (%)..............	11.0	21.2	39.0	-10.8	15.2	17.1	11.2	-2.7	—	—
Differ From Category (+/-)	.3.7	4.8	-8.0	8.4	9.9	11.5	-27.1	-4.2	—	—
Return, Tax-Adjusted (%)..	10.6	21.1	38.9	-11.2	14.6	15.3	10.9	-3.0	—	—

PER SHARE DATA

	2005	2004	2003	2002	2001	2000	1999	1998	1997	1996
Dividends, Net Income ($).	0.30	0.09	0.03	0.14	0.12	0.21	0.10	0.09	—	—
Distrib'ns, Cap Gain ($) ...	0.33	0.08	0.08	0.00	0.17	0.69	0.00	0.00	—	—
Net Asset Value ($)	24.45	22.57	18.75	13.56	15.37	13.59	12.40	11.23	—	—
Expense Ratio (%).........	na	1.14	1.17	1.17	1.23	1.30	1.28	1.28	—	—
Yield (%)	1.22	0.40	0.13	1.01	0.75	1.48	0.79	0.78	—	—
Portfolio Turnover (%)	11	10	22	19	18	19	10	6	—	—
Total Assets (Millions $)..	2,069	1,134	602	395	332	151	127	144	—	—

PORTFOLIO (as of 10/31/05)

Portfolio Manager: Curtis Jensen - 2001

Investment Style

Large Cap	Growth
✓ Mid Cap	Value
✓ Small Cap	✓ Grth/Val

Portfolio

28.1% cash	0.0% corp bonds
67.9% stocks	1.5% gov't bonds
0.5% pref/conv't pref	0.0% muni bonds
0.0% conv't bds/wrnts	2.0% other

SHAREHOLDER INFORMATION

Minimum Investment
Initial: $1,000   Subsequent: $1,000

Minimum IRA Investment
Initial: $500   Subsequent: $200

Maximum Fees
Load: 1.00% redemption   12b-1: none
Other: redemption fee applies for 1 year

Services
✓ IRA
✓ Keogh
✓ Telephone Exchange

Third Avenue Value
(TAVFX)

800-443-1021
www.thirdave.com

Small-Cap Stock

	3yr Annual	5yr Annual	10yr Annual	Bull	Bear
Return (%)	26.4	12.0	14.1	110.3	-13.8
Differ From Category (+/-)	4.4 high	3.5 abv av	2.7 abv av	16.9 high	4.4 av

Standard Deviation	Category Risk Index	Beta
9.9%—av	0.66—low	0.85

	2005	2004	2003	2002	2001	2000	1999	1998	1997	1996
Return (%).............	16.5	26.6	37.0	-15.1	2.8	20.7	12.8	3.9	23.8	21.9
Differ From Category (+/-)	.9.2	10.2	-10.0	4.1	-2.5	15.1	-25.5	2.5	0.5	0.7
Return, Tax-Adjusted (%)..	14.9	26.3	36.9	-15.6	2.0	14.4	12.5	3.4	23.1	20.6

PER SHARE DATA

	2005	2004	2003	2002	2001	2000	1999	1998	1997	1996
Dividends, Net Income ($).	1.61	0.78	0.32	0.39	0.62	4.68	0.00	0.40	0.41	0.57
Distrib'ns, Cap Gain ($) ...	3.87	0.00	0.00	0.04	0.19	2.16	0.42	0.00	0.16	0.15
Net Asset Value ($)	54.78	51.70	41.45	30.47	36.43	36.22	35.99	32.29	31.46	25.86
Expense Ratio (%).........	na	1.12	1.11	1.07	1.07	1.09	1.10	1.08	1.13	1.21
Yield (%)	2.74	1.49	0.75	1.29	1.67	12.19	0.00	1.24	1.29	2.20
Portfolio Turnover (%)	16	8	11	19	16	30	5	24	10	14
Total Assets (Millions $)..	6,891	4,321	3,098	2,233	2,632	1,940	1,379	1,600	1,676	645

PORTFOLIO (as of 10/31/05)

Portfolio Manager: Martin Whitman - 1990

Investment Style

Large Cap	Growth
✔ Mid Cap	✔ Value
✔ Small Cap	Grth/Val

Portfolio

13.8% cash	3.9% corp bonds
70.4% stocks	9.1% gov't bonds
0.5% pref/conv't pref	1.5% muni bonds
0.2% conv't bds/wrnts	0.5% other

SHAREHOLDER INFORMATION

Minimum Investment
Initial: $1,000   Subsequent: $1,000

Minimum IRA Investment
Initial: $500   Subsequent: $200

Maximum Fees
Load: 1.00% redemption   12b-1: none
Other: redemption fee applies for 2 months

Services
✔ IRA
✔ Keogh
✔ Telephone Exchange

TIAA-CREF Instl Sm Cap Eq Retail (TCSEX)

800-223-1200
www.tiaa-cref.org

Small-Cap Stock

PERFORMANCE

fund inception date: 10/1/02

	3yr Annual	5yr Annual	10yr Annual	Bull	Bear
Return (%)	22.3	na	na	93.5	na
Differ From Category (+/-)	0.3 av	na	na	0.1 av	na

Standard Deviation	Category Risk Index	Beta
15.2%—high	1.01—abv av	1.46

	2005	2004	2003	2002	2001	2000	1999	1998	1997	1996
Return (%)	3.2	20.4	47.1	—	—	—	—	—	—	—
Differ From Category (+/-)	-4.1	4.0	0.1	—	—	—	—	—	—	—
Return, Tax-Adjusted (%)	1.8	19.5	45.5	—	—	—	—	—	—	—

PER SHARE DATA

	2005	2004	2003	2002	2001	2000	1999	1998	1997	1996
Dividends, Net Income ($)	0.12	0.13	0.13	—	—	—	—	—	—	—
Distrib'ns, Cap Gain ($)	1.33	0.70	0.93	—	—	—	—	—	—	—
Net Asset Value ($)	14.42	15.35	13.43	—	—	—	—	—	—	—
Expense Ratio (%)	0.30	0.30	0.30	—	—	—	—	—	—	—
Yield (%)	0.76	0.79	0.91	—	—	—	—	—	—	—
Portfolio Turnover (%)	273	295	328	—	—	—	—	—	—	—
Total Assets (Millions $)	73	70	31	—	—	—	—	—	—	—

PORTFOLIO (as of 9/30/05)

Portfolio Manager: Team Managed - 2002

Investment Style

Large Cap	Growth
Mid Cap	✔ Value
✔ Small Cap	Grth/Val

Portfolio

0.0% cash	0.0% corp bonds
97.2% stocks	0.0% gov't bonds
0.0% pref/conv't pref	0.0% muni bonds
0.0% conv't bds/wrnts	2.8% other

SHAREHOLDER INFORMATION

Minimum Investment
Initial: $2,500   Subsequent: $50

Minimum IRA Investment
Initial: $2,000   Subsequent: $50

Maximum Fees
Load: none   12b-1: none
Other: none

Services
✔ IRA
Keogh
✔ Telephone Exchange

UMB Scout Small Cap

(UMBHX)

Small-Cap Stock

800-996-2862
www.scoutfunds.com

	3yr Annual	5yr Annual	10yr Annual	Bull	Bear
Return (%)	22.0	12.3	11.4	84.4	15.6
Differ From Category (+/-)	0.0 av	3.8 abv av	0.0 av	-9.0 blw av	33.8 high

Standard Deviation	Category Risk Index	Beta
11.5%—abv av	0.77—low	1.01

	2005	2004	2003	2002	2001	2000	1999	1998	1997	1996
Return (%)	5.6	24.7	38.1	-11.6	11.3	21.8	1.2	-3.6	23.0	12.5
Differ From Category (+/-)	-1.7	8.3	-8.9	7.6	6.0	16.2	-37.1	-5.1	-0.3	-8.7
Return, Tax-Adjusted (%)	5.1	24.0	37.7	-11.9	7.7	20.6	-0.3	-5.6	20.9	9.7

PER SHARE DATA

	2005	2004	2003	2002	2001	2000	1999	1998	1997	1996
Dividends, Net Income ($)	0.00	0.00	0.00	0.03	0.14	0.17	0.15	0.20	0.22	0.21
Distrib'ns, Cap Gain ($)	0.41	0.60	0.28	0.11	1.82	0.23	0.57	0.78	0.67	0.72
Net Asset Value ($)	15.85	15.39	12.83	9.49	10.89	11.59	9.87	10.46	11.89	10.43
Expense Ratio (%)	1.07	0.89	0.87	0.88	0.99	0.91	0.89	0.85	0.87	0.86
Yield (%)	0.00	0.00	0.00	0.27	1.07	1.47	1.42	1.79	1.74	1.83
Portfolio Turnover (%)	66	109	89	105	122	16	13	13	20	29
Total Assets (Millions $)	432	196	60	38	37	30	37	46	50	48

PORTFOLIO (as of 9/30/05)

Portfolio Manager: David Bagby/
Team Managed - 1986

Investment Style

Large Cap	Growth
✔ Mid Cap	✔ Value
✔ Small Cap	Grth/Val

Portfolio

17.7% cash	0.0% corp bonds
82.3% stocks	0.0% gov't bonds
0.0% pref/conv't pref	0.0% muni bonds
0.0% conv't bds/wrnts	0.0% other

SHAREHOLDER INFORMATION

Minimum Investment
Initial: $1,000   Subsequent: $100

Minimum IRA Investment
Initial: $100   Subsequent: $100

Maximum Fees
Load: 2.00% redemption   12b-1: none
Other: redemption fee applies for 2 months

Services
✔ IRA
✔ Keogh
✔ Telephone Exchange

USAA Capital Growth

(USCGX)

800-531-8181
www.usaa.com

Small-Cap Stock

PERFORMANCE

fund inception date: 10/27/00

	3yr Annual	5yr Annual	10yr Annual	Bull	Bear
Return (%)	25.1	-0.6	na	101.1	na
Differ From Category (+/-)	3.1 abv av	-9.1 low	na	7.7 abv av	na

Standard Deviation	Category Risk Index	Beta
15.2%—high	1.01—abv av	1.32

	2005	2004	2003	2002	2001	2000	1999	1998	1997	1996
Return (%)	8.5	16.2	55.2	-27.6	-31.2	—	—	—	—	—
Differ From Category (+/-)	1.2	-0.2	8.2	-8.4	-36.6	—	—	—	—	—
Return, Tax-Adjusted (%)	8.1	16.2	55.2	-27.6	-31.2	—	—	—	—	—

PER SHARE DATA

	2005	2004	2003	2002	2001	2000	1999	1998	1997	1996
Dividends, Net Income ($)	0.00	0.00	0.00	0.00	0.00	—	—	—	—	—
Distrib'ns, Cap Gain ($)	0.17	0.00	0.00	0.00	0.00	—	—	—	—	—
Net Asset Value ($)	7.98	7.51	6.46	4.16	5.75	—	—	—	—	—
Expense Ratio (%)	1.00	1.00	1.00	1.00	—	—	—	—	—	—
Yield (%)	0.00	0.00	0.00	0.00	0.00	—	—	—	—	—
Portfolio Turnover (%)	166	195	151	188	8	—	—	—	—	—
Total Assets (Millions $)	125	97	67	29	30	—	—	—	—	—

PORTFOLIO (as of 7/29/05)

Portfolio Manager: W Elcock - 2002

Investment Style

Large Cap	✔ Growth
Mid Cap	Value
✔ Small Cap	Grth/Val

Portfolio

2.3% cash	0.0% corp bonds
97.7% stocks	0.0% gov't bonds
0.0% pref/conv't pref	0.0% muni bonds
0.0% conv't bds/wrnts	0.0% other

SHAREHOLDER INFORMATION

Minimum Investment

Initial: $3,000   Subsequent: $50

Minimum IRA Investment

Initial: $250   Subsequent: $50

Maximum Fees

Load: none   12b-1: none
Other: none

Services

✔ IRA
Keogh
✔ Telephone Exchange

Value Line Emerging Opportunities (VLEOX)

800-223-0818
www.valueline.com

Small-Cap Stock

fund inception date: 6/23/93

PERFORMANCE

	3yr Annual	5yr Annual	10yr Annual	Bull	Bear
Return (%)	18.9	8.4	13.2	74.2	-22.3
Differ From Category (+/-)	-3.1 low	-0.1 av	1.8 abv av	-19.2 low	-4.1 av

Standard Deviation	Category Risk Index	Beta
11.4%—abv av	0.76—low	1.03

	2005	2004	2003	2002	2001	2000	1999	1998	1997	1996
Return (%)	8.0	16.6	33.6	-14.1	3.8	5.5	70.6	4.6	11.5	10.3
Differ From Category (+/-)	0.7	0.2	-13.4	5.1	-1.5	-0.1	32.3	3.2	-11.8	-10.9
Return, Tax-Adjusted (%)	7.8	16.6	33.6	-14.3	3.7	2.7	69.8	4.2	7.8	5.9

PER SHARE DATA

	2005	2004	2003	2002	2001	2000	1999	1998	1997	1996
Dividends, Net Income ($)	0.00	0.00	0.00	0.00	0.00	0.00	0.00	0.00	0.00	0.00
Distrib'ns, Cap Gain ($)	0.39	0.00	0.00	0.16	0.10	2.99	0.51	0.23	2.49	2.23
Net Asset Value ($)	28.05	26.32	22.56	16.88	19.85	19.21	21.31	12.82	12.50	13.54
Expense Ratio (%)	1.14	1.19	1.35	1.48	1.46	1.34	1.34	1.81	1.83	2.09
Yield (%)	0.00	0.00	0.00	0.00	0.00	0.00	0.00	0.00	0.00	0.00
Portfolio Turnover (%)	44	55	79	130	111	104	203	149	100	57
Total Assets (Millions $)	526	372	214	110	58	50	40	22	22	18

PORTFOLIO (as of 6/30/05)

Portfolio Manager: Team Managed - 1993

Investment Style

Large Cap	✔ Growth
Mid Cap	Value
✔ Small Cap	Grth/Val

Portfolio

11.9% cash	0.0% corp bonds
88.0% stocks	0.0% gov't bonds
0.0% pref/conv't pref	0.0% muni bonds
0.0% conv't bds/wrnts	0.1% other

SHAREHOLDER INFORMATION

Minimum Investment
Initial: $1,000   Subsequent: $100

Minimum IRA Investment
Initial: $0   Subsequent: $0

Maximum Fees
Load: none   12b-1: 0.25%
Other: none

Services
  IRA
✔ Keogh
✔ Telephone Exchange

Value Line Special Situations (VALSX)

Small-Cap Stock

800-223-0818
www.valueline.com

PERFORMANCE
fund inception date: 5/30/56

	3yr Annual	5yr Annual	10yr Annual	Bull	Bear
Return (%)	19.5	3.5	12.7	76.5	-43.8
Differ From Category (+/-)	-2.5 blw av	-5.0 blw av	1.3 av	-16.9 low	-25.6 blw av

Standard Deviation	Category Risk Index	Beta
10.3%—av	0.69—low	0.93

	2005	2004	2003	2002	2001	2000	1999	1998	1997	1996
Return (%)	11.2	18.4	29.6	-15.1	-17.6	-6.7	61.6	29.8	32.1	7.2
Differ From Category (+/-)	.3.9	2.0	-17.4	4.1	-23.0	-12.4	23.3	28.4	8.8	-14.0
Return, Tax-Adjusted (%)	10.3	18.1	29.6	-15.1	-18.0	-8.0	60.0	28.4	27.6	0.1

PER SHARE DATA

	2005	2004	2003	2002	2001	2000	1999	1998	1997	1996
Dividends, Net Income ($)	0.00	0.00	0.00	0.00	0.00	0.00	0.00	0.00	0.00	0.26
Distrib'ns, Cap Gain ($)	1.42	0.44	0.00	0.00	0.44	1.71	1.40	1.04	2.99	3.75
Net Asset Value ($)	25.60	24.23	20.84	16.08	18.95	23.55	27.09	17.70	14.48	13.34
Expense Ratio (%)	na	1.15	1.18	1.20	1.14	1.01	0.89	1.02	1.08	1.08
Yield (%)	0.00	0.00	0.00	0.00	0.00	0.00	0.00	0.00	0.00	1.53
Portfolio Turnover (%)	na	54	52	66	88	78	85	183	240	146
Total Assets (Millions $)	431	384	310	242	262	388	420	191	117	90

PORTFOLIO (as of 6/30/05)

Portfolio Manager: Team Managed - 1990

Investment Style

Large Cap	✔ Growth
✔ Mid Cap	Value
✔ Small Cap	Grth/Val

Portfolio

4.3% cash	0.0% corp bonds
95.5% stocks	0.0% gov't bonds
0.0% pref/conv't pref	0.0% muni bonds
0.0% conv't bds/wrnts	0.2% other

SHAREHOLDER INFORMATION

Minimum Investment
Initial: $1,000   Subsequent: $100

Minimum IRA Investment
Initial: $1,000   Subsequent: $100

Maximum Fees
Load: none   12b-1: 0.25%
Other: none

Services
✔ IRA
✔ Keogh
✔ Telephone Exchange

Vanguard Explorer
(VEXPX)
Small-Cap Stock

800-662-7447
www.vanguard.com

	3yr Annual	5yr Annual	10yr Annual	Bull	Bear
Return (%)	21.5	6.3	10.6	89.9	-32.5
Differ From Category (+/-)	-0.5 av	-2.2 blw av	-0.8 blw av	-3.5 av	-14.3 blw av

Standard Deviation	Category Risk Index	Beta
14.8%—high	0.99—av	1.43

	2005	2004	2003	2002	2001	2000	1999	1998	1997	1996
Return (%)	9.2	13.7	44.2	-24.5	0.5	9.2	37.2	3.5	14.5	14.0
Differ From Category (+/-)	.1.9	-2.7	-2.8	-5.3	-4.8	3.6	-1.1	2.1	-8.8	-7.2
Return, Tax-Adjusted (%)	7.9	13.7	44.2	-24.5	0.4	5.0	34.2	3.2	12.2	12.2

PER SHARE DATA

	2005	2004	2003	2002	2001	2000	1999	1998	1997	1996
Dividends, Net Income ($)	0.23	0.00	0.00	0.01	0.11	0.25	0.23	0.20	0.25	0.27
Distrib'ns, Cap Gain ($)	6.21	0.07	0.00	0.00	0.00	13.91	8.03	0.30	5.85	2.83
Net Asset Value ($)	75.11	74.57	65.62	45.49	60.31	60.09	68.62	56.71	55.30	53.83
Expense Ratio (%)	na	0.57	0.72	0.70	0.72	0.71	0.74	0.62	0.62	0.63
Yield (%)	0.28	0.00	0.00	0.01	0.17	0.33	0.30	0.35	0.40	0.47
Portfolio Turnover (%)	81	82	77	69	77	123	79	72	84	51
Total Assets (Millions $)	8,295	8,230	6,126	3,508	4,648	4,488	3,136	2,464	2,541	2,264

PORTFOLIO (as of 9/30/05)

Portfolio Manager: G Sauter/J Dickson - 1994

Investment Style

Large Cap	✔ Growth
Mid Cap	Value
✔ Small Cap	Grth/Val

Portfolio

4.8% cash	0.0% corp bonds
93.6% stocks	0.0% gov't bonds
0.0% pref/conv't pref	0.0% muni bonds
0.0% conv't bds/wrnts	1.6% other

SHAREHOLDER INFORMATION

Minimum Investment
Initial: $3,000   Subsequent: $100

Minimum IRA Investment
Initial: $3,000   Subsequent: $100

Maximum Fees
Load: none   12b-1: none
Other: none

Services
✔ IRA
✔ Keogh
✔ Telephone Exchange

Vanguard Small Cap Growth Inv (VISGX)

800-662-7447
www.vanguard.com

Small-Cap Stock

PERFORMANCE

fund inception date: 5/21/98

	3yr Annual	5yr Annual	10yr Annual	Bull	Bear
Return (%)	21.6	8.6	na	90.4	-26.1
Differ From Category (+/-)	-0.4 av	0.1 av	na	-3.0 av	-7.9 av

Standard Deviation	Category Risk Index	Beta
15.0%—high	1.00—av	1.38

	2005	2004	2003	2002	2001	2000	1999	1998	1997	1996
Return (%)	8.6	16.0	42.8	-15.4	-0.7	1.5	19.8	—	—	—
Differ From Category (+/-)	.1.3	-0.4	-4.2	3.8	-6.1	-4.1	-18.5	—	—	—
Return, Tax-Adjusted (%)	8.6	16.0	42.8	-15.4	-0.8	0.5	19.6	—	—	—

PER SHARE DATA

	2005	2004	2003	2002	2001	2000	1999	1998	1997	1996
Dividends, Net Income ($)	0.04	0.02	0.02	0.03	0.02	0.00	0.04	—	—	—
Distrib'ns, Cap Gain ($)	0.00	0.00	0.00	0.00	0.00	0.57	0.00	—	—	—
Net Asset Value ($)	16.43	15.16	13.08	9.17	10.87	10.97	11.38	—	—	—
Expense Ratio (%)	na	0.23	0.27	0.27	0.27	0.27	0.25	—	—	—
Yield (%)	0.24	0.13	0.16	0.27	0.13	0.02	0.30	—	—	—
Portfolio Turnover (%)	na	41	108	61	74	136	82	—	—	—
Total Assets (Millions $)	1,726	1,435	907	388	357	356	167	—	—	—

PORTFOLIO (as of 9/30/05)

Portfolio Manager: Gerald O'Reilly - 2004

Investment Style

Large Cap	✔ Growth
Mid Cap	Value
✔ Small Cap	Grth/Val

Portfolio

0.1% cash	0.0% corp bonds
99.9% stocks	0.0% gov't bonds
0.0% pref/conv't pref	0.0% muni bonds
0.0% conv't bds/wrnts	0.0% other

SHAREHOLDER INFORMATION

Minimum Investment
Initial: $3,000   Subsequent: $100

Minimum IRA Investment
Initial: $3,000   Subsequent: $100

Maximum Fees
Load: none   12b-1: none
Other: none

Services
✔ IRA
✔ Keogh
   Telephone Exchange

Vanguard Small Cap Index Inv (NAESX)

800-662-7447
www.vanguard.com

Small-Cap Stock

PERFORMANCE
fund inception date: 10/3/60

	3yr Annual	5yr Annual	10yr Annual	Bull	Bear
Return (%)	23.3	9.1	10.2	98.7	-29.1
Differ From Category (+/-)	1.3 abv av	0.6 av	-1.2 blw av	5.3 abv av	-10.9 blw av

Standard Deviation	Category Risk Index	Beta
14.0%—abv av	0.93—av	1.38

	2005	2004	2003	2002	2001	2000	1999	1998	1997	1996
Return (%)	7.4	19.8	45.6	-20.0	3.1	-2.6	23.1	-2.6	24.5	18.1
Differ From Category (+/-)	0.1	3.4	-1.4	-0.8	-2.2	-8.3	-15.2	-4.1	1.2	-3.1
Return, Tax-Adjusted (%)	7.2	19.6	45.4	-20.3	2.6	-5.6	20.6	-4.4	22.9	15.3

PER SHARE DATA

	2005	2004	2003	2002	2001	2000	1999	1998	1997	1996
Dividends, Net Income ($)	0.29	0.27	0.20	0.19	0.23	0.26	0.27	0.30	0.27	0.27
Distrib'ns, Cap Gain ($)	0.00	0.00	0.00	0.00	0.00	3.03	2.08	1.55	1.12	1.44
Net Asset Value ($)	28.52	26.82	22.60	15.66	19.82	19.44	23.60	21.20	23.75	20.23
Expense Ratio (%)	na	0.23	0.27	0.27	0.27	0.27	0.25	0.24	0.23	0.25
Yield (%)	1.01	0.98	0.90	1.22	1.13	1.15	1.03	1.33	1.10	1.24
Portfolio Turnover (%)	na	19	39	32	39	49	42	35	29	28
Total Assets (Millions $)	5,902	6,247	4,871	2,943	3,545	3,577	3,553	2,768	2,652	1,713

PORTFOLIO (as of 9/30/05)

Portfolio Manager: George Sauter - 1989

Investment Style

Large Cap	Growth
Mid Cap	Value
✔ Small Cap	✔ Grth/Val

Portfolio

0.4% cash	0.0% corp bonds
99.7% stocks	0.0% gov't bonds
0.0% pref/conv't pref	0.0% muni bonds
0.0% conv't bds/wrnts	0.0% other

SHAREHOLDER INFORMATION

Minimum Investment
Initial: $3,000   Subsequent: $100

Minimum IRA Investment
Initial: $3,000   Subsequent: $100

Maximum Fees
Load: none   12b-1: none
Other: none

Services
✔ IRA
✔ Keogh
  Telephone Exchange

Vanguard Small Cap Value Inv (VISVX)

800-662-7447
www.vanguard.com

Small-Cap Stock

PERFORMANCE

fund inception date: 5/21/98

	3yr Annual	5yr Annual	10yr Annual	Bull	Bear
Return (%)	21.6	11.8	na	94.5	6.6
Differ From Category (+/-)	-0.4 av	3.3 abv av	na	1.1 av	24.8 abv av

Standard Deviation	Category Risk Index	Beta
13.1%—abv av	0.87—blw av	1.29

	2005	2004	2003	2002	2001	2000	1999	1998	1997	1996
Return (%)	6.0	23.5	37.1	-14.2	13.7	21.8	2.8	—	—	—
Differ From Category (+/-)	-1.3	7.1	-9.9	5.1	8.4	16.2	-35.5	—	—	—
Return, Tax-Adjusted (%)	5.7	23.2	36.8	-15.0	12.3	20.3	1.4	—	—	—

PER SHARE DATA

	2005	2004	2003	2002	2001	2000	1999	1998	1997	1996
Dividends, Net Income ($)	0.26	0.23	0.20	0.09	0.07	0.08	0.07	—	—	—
Distrib'ns, Cap Gain ($)	0.00	0.00	0.00	0.28	0.55	0.50	0.46	—	—	—
Net Asset Value ($)	14.56	13.97	11.49	8.52	10.29	9.65	8.45	—	—	—
Expense Ratio (%)	na	0.23	0.27	0.27	0.27	0.27	0.25	—	—	—
Yield (%)	1.79	1.61	1.72	1.02	0.59	0.80	0.78	—	—	—
Portfolio Turnover (%)	na	30	109	57	59	82	80	—	—	—
Total Assets (Millions $)	3,446	2,947	1,730	1,176	802	317	204	—	—	—

PORTFOLIO (as of 9/30/05)

Portfolio Manager: George Sauter - 1998

Investment Style

Large Cap	Growth
Mid Cap	✔ Value
✔ Small Cap	Grth/Val

Portfolio

0.4% cash	0.0% corp bonds
99.7% stocks	0.0% gov't bonds
0.0% pref/conv't pref	0.0% muni bonds
0.0% conv't bds/wrnts	0.0% other

SHAREHOLDER INFORMATION

Minimum Investment
Initial: $3,000   Subsequent: $100

Minimum IRA Investment
Initial: $3,000   Subsequent: $100

Maximum Fees
Load: none   12b-1: none
Other: none

Services
✔ IRA
✔ Keogh
Telephone Exchange

Vanguard Tax Managed Small Cap (VTMSX)

Small-Cap Stock

800-662-7447
www.vanguard.com

fund inception date: 3/25/99

	3yr Annual	5yr Annual	10yr Annual	Bull	Bear
Return (%)	22.3	10.5	na	96.1	-9.9
Differ From Category (+/-)	0.3 av	2.0 av	na	2.7 av	8.3 av

Standard Deviation		Category Risk Index		Beta
13.9%—abv av		0.93—av		1.32

	2005	2004	2003	2002	2001	2000	1999	1998	1997	1996
Return (%)	7.7	22.8	38.5	-14.4	5.4	13.4	—	—	—	—
Differ From Category (+/-)	0.4	6.4	-8.5	4.8	0.1	7.8	—	—	—	—
Return, Tax-Adjusted (%)	7.6	22.6	38.3	-14.6	5.2	13.2	—	—	—	—

PER SHARE DATA

	2005	2004	2003	2002	2001	2000	1999	1998	1997	1996
Dividends, Net Income ($)	0.20	0.17	0.11	0.10	0.09	0.07	—	—	—	—
Distrib'ns, Cap Gain ($)	0.00	0.00	0.00	0.00	0.00	0.00	—	—	—	—
Net Asset Value ($)	22.70	21.25	17.44	12.67	14.92	14.23	—	—	—	—
Expense Ratio (%)	na	0.14	0.17	0.17	0.20	0.20	—	—	—	—
Yield (%)	0.86	0.81	0.62	0.74	0.56	0.52	—	—	—	—
Portfolio Turnover (%)	na	19	21	21	25	64	—	—	—	—
Total Assets (Millions $)	1,458	1,282	929	601	568	368	—	—	—	—

PORTFOLIO (as of 9/30/05)

Portfolio Manager: Team Managed - 1999

Investment Style

Large Cap	Growth
Mid Cap	Value
✔ Small Cap	✔ Grth/Val

Portfolio

0.0%	cash	0.0%	corp bonds
100.0%	stocks	0.0%	gov't bonds
0.0%	pref/conv't pref	0.0%	muni bonds
0.0%	conv't bds/wrnts	0.0%	other

SHAREHOLDER INFORMATION

Minimum Investment
Initial: $10,000   Subsequent: $100

Minimum IRA Investment
Initial: $10,000   Subsequent: $100

Maximum Fees
Load: 1.00% redemption   12b-1: none
Other: redemption fee applies for 1 year

Services
✔ IRA
   Keogh
✔ Telephone Exchange

Weitz Hickory
(WEHIX)
Small-Cap Stock

800-232-4161
www.weitzfunds.com

PERFORMANCE

fund inception date: 4/1/93

	3yr Annual	5yr Annual	10yr Annual	Bull	Bear
Return (%)	21.8	4.0	13.2	89.2	-38.3
Differ From Category (+/-)	-0.2 av	-4.5 blw av	1.8 abv av	-4.2 av	-20.1 blw av

Standard Deviation	Category Risk Index	Beta
12.0%—abv av	0.80—low	1.09

	2005	2004	2003	2002	2001	2000	1999	1998	1997	1996
Return (%).............	-0.2	22.6	47.9	-29.3	-4.6	-17.2	36.6	33.0	39.1	35.3
Differ From Category (+/-)	-7.6	6.2	0.9	-10.1	-10.0	-22.9	-1.7	31.6	15.8	14.1
Return, Tax-Adjusted (%)..	-0.2	22.4	47.7	-29.5	-4.6	-19.9	35.0	32.4	36.9	33.3

PER SHARE DATA

	2005	2004	2003	2002	2001	2000	1999	1998	1997	1996
Dividends, Net Income ($)	0.08	0.23	0.25	0.14	0.00	0.00	0.01	0.10	0.07	0.00
Distrib'ns, Cap Gain ($) ...	0.00	0.00	0.00	0.00	0.01	5.29	2.56	0.45	1.91	1.04
Net Asset Value ($)	32.71	32.86	26.99	18.42	26.26	27.55	39.65	30.98	23.70	18.80
Expense Ratio (%)........	1.21	1.30	1.32	1.25	1.22	1.23	1.30	1.46	1.50	1.50
Yield (%)	0.23	0.69	0.94	0.76	0.00	0.00	0.02	0.30	0.28	0.00
Portfolio Turnover (%)	58	50	64	18	22	46	40	29	28	28
Total Assets (Millions $) ...	341	344	247	195	359	469	913	539	22	10

PORTFOLIO (as of 6/30/05)

Portfolio Manager: Wallace Weitz - 1993

Investment Style
- ✔ Large Cap   Growth
- ✔ Mid Cap   ✔ Value
- ✔ Small Cap   Grth/Val

Portfolio
6.6% cash	0.0% corp bonds
93.4% stocks	0.0% gov't bonds
0.0% pref/conv't pref	0.0% muni bonds
0.0% conv't bds/wrnts	0.0% other

SHAREHOLDER INFORMATION

Minimum Investment
Initial: $10,000   Subsequent: $1

Minimum IRA Investment
Initial: $4,000   Subsequent: $1

Maximum Fees
Load: none   12b-1: none
Other: none

Services
- ✔ IRA
- Keogh
- ✔ Telephone Exchange

Winslow Green Growth
(WGGFX)
Small-Cap Stock

888-314-9049
www.forumfunds.com

PERFORMANCE   fund inception date: 3/30/01

	3yr Annual	5yr Annual	10yr Annual	Bull	Bear
Return (%)	34.0	na	na	149.9	na
Differ From Category (+/-)	12.0 high	na	na	56.5 high	na

Standard Deviation	Category Risk Index	Beta
24.5%—high	1.63—high	1.76

	2005	2004	2003	2002	2001	2000	1999	1998	1997	1996
Return (%).	12.1	12.0	91.7	-37.5	—	—	—	—	—	—
Differ From Category (+/-)	.4.8	-4.4	44.7	-18.3	—	—	—	—	—	—
Return, Tax-Adjusted (%). .	11.9	11.8	91.7	-37.5	—	—	—	—	—	—

PER SHARE DATA

	2005	2004	2003	2002	2001	2000	1999	1998	1997	1996
Dividends, Net Income ($).	0.00	0.00	0.00	0.00	—	—	—	—	—	—
Distrib'ns, Cap Gain ($) . . .	0.22	0.24	0.00	0.00	—	—	—	—	—	—
Net Asset Value ($)	17.62	15.90	14.40	7.51	—	—	—	—	—	—
Expense Ratio (%).	na	1.45	1.45	1.45	—	—	—	—	—	—
Yield (%)	0.00	0.00	0.00	0.00	—	—	—	—	—	—
Portfolio Turnover (%)	na	102	202	114	—	—	—	—	—	—
Total Assets (Millions $) . . .	152	48	55	11	—	—	—	—	—	—

PORTFOLIO (as of 9/30/05)

Portfolio Manager: J Robinson/M Patsky - 2001

Investment Style

Large Cap	✔ Growth
Mid Cap	Value
✔ Small Cap	Grth/Val

Portfolio

7.8% cash	0.0% corp bonds
92.3% stocks	0.0% gov't bonds
0.0% pref/conv't pref	0.0% muni bonds
0.0% conv't bds/wrnts	0.0% other

SHAREHOLDER INFORMATION

Minimum Investment
Initial: $5,000   Subsequent: $250

Minimum IRA Investment
Initial: $2,000   Subsequent: $250

Maximum Fees
Load: none   12b-1: none
Other: none

Services
✔ IRA
   Keogh
✔ Telephone Exchange

SECTOR STOCK FUNDS

Energy/Resources Sector Stock Funds
Category Performance Ranked by 2005 Returns

Fund (Ticker)	Annual Return (%)				Category Risk	Total Risk
	2005	3Yr	5Yr	10Yr		
Fidelity Select Energy (FSENX)	51.9	34.9	13.8	15.5	blw av	high
US Global Inv Global Resources (PSPFX)	48.9	57.1	31.6	14.9	high	high
Fidelity Select Natural Gas (FSNGX)	45.7	38.0	12.9	15.6	abv av	high
Vanguard Energy Inv (VGENX)	44.6	38.2	20.6	17.8	low	high
RS Global Natural Resources (RSNRX)	42.2	39.5	26.1	14.2	av	high
Energy/Resources Sector Category Average	**46.8**	**36.5**	**16.2**	**16.2**	**av**	**high**

Fidelity Select Energy
(FSENX)

Energy/Resources Sector

800-544-8544
www.fidelity.com

PERFORMANCE

fund inception date: 7/14/81

	3yr Annual	5yr Annual	10yr Annual	Bull	Bear
Return (%)	34.9	13.8	15.5	144.6	-10.1
Differ From Category (+/-)	-1.6 av	-2.4 av	-0.7 av	-9.1 av	-12.1 blw av

Standard Deviation	Category Risk Index	Beta
17.8%—high	0.93—blw av	0.62

	2005	2004	2003	2002	2001	2000	1999	1998	1997	1996
Return (%)	51.9	31.7	22.8	-11.4	-11.9	31.8	34.2	-14.7	10.2	32.4
Differ From Category (+/-)	.5.1	-2.0	-9.3	-7.7	0.8	-8.2	0.9	10.5	-0.6	-3.9
Return, Tax-Adjusted (%)	50.8	31.4	22.7	-11.7	-12.5	29.0	33.7	-15.1	6.6	30.2

PER SHARE DATA

	2005	2004	2003	2002	2001	2000	1999	1998	1997	1996
Dividends, Net Income ($)	0.09	0.17	0.14	0.14	0.04	0.14	0.09	0.01	0.09	0.13
Distrib'ns, Cap Gain ($)	2.44	0.28	0.00	0.00	0.69	2.97	0.29	0.41	4.09	1.31
Net Asset Value ($)	46.76	32.53	25.06	20.52	23.33	27.29	23.35	17.70	21.15	23.21
Expense Ratio (%)	0.97	1.17	1.21	1.12	1.12	1.25	1.42	1.58	1.57	1.63
Yield (%)	0.18	0.51	0.55	0.68	0.16	0.46	0.38	0.05	0.35	0.53
Portfolio Turnover (%)	91	33	73	119	117	124	138	115	87	97
Total Assets (Millions $)	2,281	570	255	198	226	273	194	123	158	240

PORTFOLIO (as of 8/31/05)

Portfolio Manager: Matthew Friedman - 2004

Investment Style

Large Cap	Growth
Mid Cap	Value
Small Cap	Grth/Val

Portfolio

7.9% cash	0.0% corp bonds
92.2% stocks	0.0% gov't bonds
0.0% pref/conv't pref	0.0% muni bonds
0.0% conv't bds/wrnts	0.0% other

SHAREHOLDER INFORMATION

Minimum Investment

Initial: $2,500   Subsequent: $250

Minimum IRA Investment

Initial: $500   Subsequent: $250

Maximum Fees

Load: 0.75% redemption   12b-1: none
Other: redemption fee applies for 1 month

Services

✔ IRA
✔ Keogh
✔ Telephone Exchange

Fidelity Select Natural Gas (FSNGX)

800-544-8544
www.fidelity.com

Energy/Resources Sector

PERFORMANCE

fund inception date: 4/21/93

	3yr Annual	5yr Annual	10yr Annual	Bull	Bear
Return (%)	38.0	12.9	15.6	153.1	1.5
Differ From Category (+/-)	1.5 abv av	-3.3 blw av	-0.6 av	-0.6 av	-0.5 av

Standard Deviation	Category Risk Index	Beta
19.8%—high	1.03—abv av	0.66

	2005	2004	2003	2002	2001	2000	1999	1998	1997	1996
Return (%).............	45.7	40.2	28.6	-9.5	-22.7	71.2	26.1	-12.4	-8.0	34.3
Differ From Category (+/-)	-1.1	6.5	-3.5	-5.8	-10.0	31.2	-7.2	12.9	-18.9	-2.0
Return, Tax-Adjusted (%)..	43.6	39.9	28.6	-9.7	-22.9	70.7	25.8	-12.6	-8.5	33.5

PER SHARE DATA

	2005	2004	2003	2002	2001	2000	1999	1998	1997	1996
Dividends, Net Income ($).	0.00	0.02	0.00	0.10	0.03	0.04	0.09	0.10	0.00	0.01
Distrib'ns, Cap Gain ($) ...	4.08	0.44	0.00	0.00	0.13	0.30	0.00	0.00	0.33	0.29
Net Asset Value ($)	38.82	29.79	21.58	16.77	18.65	24.31	14.43	11.52	13.27	14.84
Expense Ratio (%)........	0.98	1.14	1.24	1.13	1.10	1.39	1.52	1.82	1.70	1.67
Yield (%)	0.00	0.06	0.00	0.59	0.15	0.16	0.62	0.86	0.00	0.06
Portfolio Turnover (%)	190	171	108	68	94	85	107	118	283	79
Total Assets (Millions $) ..	1,809	615	241	154	197	446	52	44	69	153

PORTFOLIO (as of 8/31/05)

Portfolio Manager: James McElligot - 2005

Investment Style

Large Cap	Growth
Mid Cap	Value
Small Cap	Grth/Val

Portfolio

4.6%	cash	0.0%	corp bonds
95.4%	stocks	0.0%	gov't bonds
0.0%	pref/conv't pref	0.0%	muni bonds
0.0%	conv't bds/wrnts	0.0%	other

SHAREHOLDER INFORMATION

Minimum Investment
Initial: $2,500   Subsequent: $250

Minimum IRA Investment
Initial: $500   Subsequent: $250

Maximum Fees
Load: 0.75% redemption   12b-1: none
Other: redemption fee applies for 1 month

Services
✔ IRA
Keogh
✔ Telephone Exchange

RS Global Natural Resources (RSNRX)

Energy/Resources Sector

800-766-3863
www.rsim.com

fund inception date: 11/15/95

	3yr Annual	5yr Annual	10yr Annual	Bull	Bear
Return (%)	39.5	26.1	14.2	162.2	48.1
Differ From Category (+/-)	3.0 high	9.9 high	-2.0 blw av	8.5 high	46.1 high

Standard Deviation	Category Risk Index	Beta
18.1%—high	0.94—av	0.91

	2005	2004	2003	2002	2001	2000	1999	1998	1997	1996
Return (%).............	42.2	34.4	42.1	17.0	0.6	25.8	22.3	-34.4	-17.1	41.2
Differ From Category (+/-)	-4.6	0.7	10.0	20.8	13.4	-14.2	-11.0	-9.2	-28.0	4.9
Return, Tax-Adjusted (%)..	40.6	33.5	42.1	17.0	0.6	25.8	22.3	-34.7	-17.3	41.2

PER SHARE DATA

	2005	2004	2003	2002	2001	2000	1999	1998	1997	1996
Dividends, Net Income ($).	0.69	0.04	0.00	0.00	0.00	0.00	0.00	0.00	0.00	0.00
Distrib'ns, Cap Gain ($) ...	1.84	1.03	0.00	0.00	0.00	0.00	0.00	0.19	0.18	0.00
Net Asset Value ($)	32.65	24.72	19.23	13.53	11.56	11.49	9.13	7.46	11.67	14.29
Expense Ratio (%)........	na	1.49	1.69	1.77	1.86	1.98	2.09	1.95	1.81	1.94
Yield (%)	1.98	0.14	0.00	0.00	0.00	0.00	0.00	0.00	0.00	0.00
Portfolio Turnover (%)	na	97	117	159	167	159	140	63	97	82
Total Assets (Millions $)..	1,713	626	142	39	22	29	23	24	79	121

PORTFOLIO (as of 6/30/05)

Portfolio Manager: Andrew Pilara/
MacKenzie Davis - 1995

Investment Style

Large Cap	Growth
Mid Cap	Value
Small Cap	Grth/Val

Portfolio

12.2% cash	0.0% corp bonds
87.8% stocks	0.0% gov't bonds
0.0% pref/conv't pref	0.0% muni bonds
0.0% conv't bds/wrnts	0.0% other

SHAREHOLDER INFORMATION

Minimum Investment
Initial: $5,000   Subsequent: $1,000

Minimum IRA Investment
Initial: $1,000   Subsequent: $250

Maximum Fees
Load: none   12b-1: 0.25%
Other: none

Services
✔ IRA
  Keogh
✔ Telephone Exchange

US Global Inv Global Resources (PSPFX)

800-873-8637
www.usfunds.com

Energy/Resources Sector

PERFORMANCE

fund inception date: 8/3/83

	3yr Annual	5yr Annual	10yr Annual	Bull	Bear
Return (%)	57.1	31.6	14.9	259.4	19.9
Differ From Category (+/-)	20.6 high	15.4 high	-1.3 blw av	105.7 high	17.9 high

Standard Deviation	Category Risk Index	Beta
22.9%—high	1.19—high	1.00

	2005	2004	2003	2002	2001	2000	1999	1998	1997	1996
Return (%).	48.9	30.4	99.5	17.7	-13.5	10.6	14.5	-38.5	-2.7	34.1
Differ From Category (+/-)	.2.1	-3.3	67.4	21.5	-0.8	-29.4	-18.8	-13.3	-13.6	-2.2
Return, Tax-Adjusted (%). .	47.0	29.2	99.1	16.8	-13.5	10.6	14.5	-39.3	-5.4	28.9

PER SHARE DATA

	2005	2004	2003	2002	2001	2000	1999	1998	1997	1996
Dividends, Net Income ($).	0.32	0.34	0.13	0.09	0.00	0.00	0.00	0.00	0.07	0.37
Distrib'ns, Cap Gain ($) . . .	1.05	0.30	0.00	0.00	0.00	0.00	0.00	0.24	0.84	0.57
Net Asset Value ($)	14.29	10.51	8.55	4.35	3.77	4.36	3.94	3.44	5.98	7.08
Expense Ratio (%).	1.30	1.54	3.75	3.83	3.61	3.79	4.43	2.38	2.30	2.57
Yield (%)	2.05	3.15	1.47	2.02	0.00	0.00	0.00	0.00	0.95	4.83
Portfolio Turnover (%) . . .	116	140	101	96	65	55	153	192	52	117
Total Assets (Millions $) . . .	718	260	215	12	11	14	15	15	25	26

PORTFOLIO (as of 9/30/05)

Portfolio Manager: F Holmes/B Hicks/
E Smith - 1999

Investment Style

Large Cap	Growth
Mid Cap	Value
Small Cap	Grth/Val

Portfolio

8.6% cash	0.0% corp bonds
90.5% stocks	0.0% gov't bonds
0.0% pref/conv't pref	0.0% muni bonds
0.0% conv't bds/wrnts	0.9% other

SHAREHOLDER INFORMATION

Minimum Investment
Initial: $5,000   Subsequent: $50

Minimum IRA Investment
Initial: $1   Subsequent: $1

Maximum Fees
Load: 0.25% redemption   12b-1: none
Other: redemption fee applies for 1 month

Services
✔ IRA
✔ Keogh
✔ Telephone Exchange

Vanguard Energy Inv
(VGENX)

Energy/Resources Sector

800-662-7447
www.vanguard.com

fund inception date: 5/23/84

	3yr Annual	5yr Annual	10yr Annual	Bull	Bear
Return (%)	38.2	20.6	17.8	161.8	18.9
Differ From Category (+/-)	1.7 high	4.4 high	1.6 abv av	8.1 abv av	16.9 abv av

Standard Deviation	Category Risk Index	Beta
16.2%—high	0.84—low	0.69

	2005	2004	2003	2002	2001	2000	1999	1998	1997	1996
Return (%).	44.6	36.6	33.8	-0.6	-2.5	36.4	20.9	-20.5	14.8	34.0
Differ From Category (+/-)	-2.2	2.9	1.7	3.1	10.2	-3.6	-12.4	4.7	4.0	-2.3
Return, Tax-Adjusted (%). .	43.9	36.2	33.0	-2.4	-4.2	34.5	20.2	-21.4	13.1	32.8

PER SHARE DATA

	2005	2004	2003	2002	2001	2000	1999	1998	1997	1996
Dividends, Net Income ($).	0.74	0.52	0.39	0.36	0.40	0.36	0.36	0.35	0.32	0.24
Distrib'ns, Cap Gain ($) . . .	1.03	0.20	0.74	1.59	1.54	1.38	0.00	0.42	1.33	0.40
Net Asset Value ($)	56.05	40.00	29.85	23.20	25.29	28.07	21.92	18.42	24.14	22.54
Expense Ratio (%).	0.33	0.38	0.40	0.39	0.41	0.48	0.41	0.38	0.39	0.51
Yield (%)	1.29	1.30	1.27	1.45	1.49	1.22	1.61	1.85	1.25	1.04
Portfolio Turnover (%)	1	26	23	28	24	18	22	19	15	21
Total Assets (Millions $) . .	5,650	4,706	2,219	1,305	1,282	1,351	1,018	820	1,181	848

PORTFOLIO (as of 9/30/05)

Portfolio Manager: Karl Bandtel - 2002

Investment Style

Large Cap	Growth
Mid Cap	Value
Small Cap	Grth/Val

Portfolio

7.9% cash	0.0% corp bonds
91.9% stocks	0.0% gov't bonds
0.1% pref/conv't pref	0.0% muni bonds
0.1% conv't bds/wrnts	0.0% other

SHAREHOLDER INFORMATION

Minimum Investment
Initial: $25,000   Subsequent: $100

Minimum IRA Investment
Initial: $25,000   Subsequent: $100

Maximum Fees
Load: 1.00% redemption   12b-1: none
Other: redemption fee applies for 1 year

Services
✔ IRA
✔ Keogh
✔ Telephone Exchange

Financial/Banking Sector Stock Funds
Category Performance Ranked by 2005 Returns

Fund (Ticker)	Annual Return (%)				Category Risk	Total Risk
	2005	3Yr	5Yr	10Yr		
Fidelity Select Brokerage & Investment Mgmt (FSLBX)	29.8	26.0	8.5	19.7	high	high
Fidelity Select Insurance (FSPCX)	13.7	17.8	7.9	16.1	av	abv av
T Rowe Price Financial Services (PRISX)	5.1	17.2	7.0	na	abv av	abv av
ICON Financial (ICFSX)	2.4	19.3	7.4	na	high	abv av
FBR Small Cap Financial (FBRSX)	-1.5	17.2	18.8	na	blw av	av
Financial/Banking Sector Category Average	**6.1**	**17.1**	**7.7**	**14.2**	**av**	**abv av**

FBR Small Cap Financial

888-888-0025
www.fbrfunds.com

(FBRSX)

Financial/Banking Sector

PERFORMANCE

fund inception date: 1/2/97

	3yr Annual	5yr Annual	10yr Annual	Bull	Bear
Return (%)	17.2	18.8	na	60.5	112.2
Differ From Category (+/-)	0.1 abv av	11.1 high	na	-9.4 av	91.6 high

Standard Deviation	Category Risk Index	Beta
11.1%—av	0.89—blw av	0.76

	2005	2004	2003	2002	2001	2000	1999	1998	1997	1996
Return (%)	-1.5	16.0	41.0	18.6	23.8	32.4	-5.4	-13.5	—	—
Differ From Category (+/-)	-7.7	2.9	6.7	26.1	25.2	-3.6	-5.3	-19.7	—	—
Return, Tax-Adjusted (%)	-3.2	14.0	40.5	17.8	22.4	32.1	-5.4	-15.7	—	—

PER SHARE DATA

	2005	2004	2003	2002	2001	2000	1999	1998	1997	1996
Dividends, Net Income ($)	0.14	0.18	0.07	0.13	0.47	0.10	0.02	0.07	—	—
Distrib'ns, Cap Gain ($)	3.70	4.35	0.66	0.64	0.34	0.00	0.00	1.93	—	—
Net Asset Value ($)	29.95	34.28	33.48	24.26	21.09	17.69	13.44	14.23	—	—
Expense Ratio (%)	na	1.55	1.57	1.56	1.53	1.90	1.89	1.63	—	—
Yield (%)	0.42	0.47	0.21	0.52	2.18	0.57	0.12	0.43	—	—
Portfolio Turnover (%)	na	36	17	44	68	82	25	94	—	—
Total Assets (Millions $)	463	662	612	353	153	69	27	50	—	—

PORTFOLIO (as of 11/30/05)

Portfolio Manager: David Ellison - 1997

Investment Style

Large Cap	Growth
Mid Cap	Value
Small Cap	Grth/Val

Portfolio

15.7%	cash	0.0%	corp bonds
84.3%	stocks	0.0%	gov't bonds
0.0%	pref/conv't pref	0.0%	muni bonds
0.0%	conv't bds/wrnts	0.0%	other

SHAREHOLDER INFORMATION

Minimum Investment
Initial: $2,000   Subsequent: $100

Minimum IRA Investment
Initial: $1,000   Subsequent: $100

Maximum Fees
Load: 1.00% redemption   12b-1: 0.25%
Other: redemption fee applies for 3 months

Services
✔ IRA
✔ Keogh
✔ Telephone Exchange

Fidelity Select Brokerage & Investment Mgmt (FSLBX)

800-544-8544
www.fidelity.com

Financial/Banking Sector

PERFORMANCE

fund inception date: 7/29/85

	3yr Annual	5yr Annual	10yr Annual	Bull	Bear
Return (%)	26.0	8.5	19.7	120.1	-23.6
Differ From Category (+/-)	8.9 high	0.8 high	5.5 high	50.2 high	-44.2 low

Standard Deviation	Category Risk Index	Beta
16.2%—high	1.30—high	1.47

	2005	2004	2003	2002	2001	2000	1999	1998	1997	1996
Return (%)	29.8	12.9	36.4	-17.2	-8.9	27.9	30.6	5.6	62.3	39.6
Differ From Category (+/-)	23.7	-0.2	2.1	-9.8	-7.6	-8.1	30.8	-0.5	16.0	6.6
Return, Tax-Adjusted (%)	28.9	12.8	36.4	-17.4	-10.3	25.1	28.9	5.3	61.6	38.4

PER SHARE DATA

	2005	2004	2003	2002	2001	2000	1999	1998	1997	1996
Dividends, Net Income ($)	0.19	0.24	0.16	0.23	0.12	0.00	0.05	0.01	0.09	0.06
Distrib'ns, Cap Gain ($)	3.45	0.00	0.00	0.00	3.41	6.49	3.13	0.52	0.61	0.65
Net Asset Value ($)	68.95	55.87	49.68	36.54	44.42	53.14	46.83	38.47	36.86	23.17
Expense Ratio (%)	0.98	1.10	1.16	1.11	1.08	1.28	1.24	1.33	1.94	1.61
Yield (%)	0.26	0.42	0.32	0.62	0.25	0.00	0.10	0.02	0.24	0.25
Portfolio Turnover (%)	98	64	64	74	105	47	59	100	16	166
Total Assets (Millions $)	1,020	436	407	349	462	636	469	550	648	111

PORTFOLIO (as of 8/31/05)

Portfolio Manager: Brian Kennedy - 2003

Investment Style

Large Cap	Growth
Mid Cap	Value
Small Cap	Grth/Val

Portfolio

3.4%	cash	0.0%	corp bonds
96.6%	stocks	0.0%	gov't bonds
0.0%	pref/conv't pref	0.0%	muni bonds
0.0%	conv't bds/wrnts	0.0%	other

SHAREHOLDER INFORMATION

Minimum Investment
Initial: $2,500   Subsequent: $250

Minimum IRA Investment
Initial: $500   Subsequent: $250

Maximum Fees
Load: 0.75% redemption   12b-1: none
Other: redemption fee applies for 1 month

Services
✔ IRA
✔ Keogh
✔ Telephone Exchange

Fidelity Select Insurance

(FSPCX)

Financial/Banking Sector

800-544-8544
www.fidelity.com

PERFORMANCE

fund inception date: 12/16/85

	3yr Annual	5yr Annual	10yr Annual	Bull	Bear
Return (%)	17.8	7.9	16.1	77.5	27.4
Differ From Category (+/-)	0.7 abv av	0.2 abv av	1.9 high	7.6 abv av	6.8 abv av

Standard Deviation	Category Risk Index	Beta
12.5%—abv av	1.00—av	1.19

	2005	2004	2003	2002	2001	2000	1999	1998	1997	1996
Return (%)..............	13.7	12.8	27.4	-5.6	-4.9	53.2	-6.0	20.3	42.4	23.7
Differ From Category (+/-)	.7.6	-0.3	-6.9	1.8	-3.5	17.2	-5.8	14.2	-3.9	-9.3
Return, Tax-Adjusted (%) .	.13.3	12.6	26.9	-6.3	-5.0	52.7	-9.0	18.3	40.1	22.1

PER SHARE DATA

	2005	2004	2003	2002	2001	2000	1999	1998	1997	1996
Dividends, Net Income ($).	0.60	0.10	0.08	0.09	0.03	0.12	0.00	0.00	0.00	0.03
Distrib'ns, Cap Gain ($) ...	1.26	0.59	1.29	1.55	0.30	0.65	6.60	3.98	3.54	1.45
Net Asset Value ($)	68.38	61.80	55.42	44.59	48.86	51.75	34.30	43.30	39.49	30.67
Expense Ratio (%)........	1.05	1.23	1.24	1.17	1.16	1.36	1.31	1.45	1.82	1.74
Yield (%)	0.86	0.16	0.14	0.19	0.06	0.22	0.00	0.00	0.00	0.09
Portfolio Turnover (%)	50	59	95	104	175	107	72	157	142	164
Total Assets (Millions $) ...	208	171	109	107	115	211	46	100	112	35

PORTFOLIO (as of 8/31/05)

Portfolio Manager: Charles Hebard - 2004

Investment Style
Large Cap   Growth
Mid Cap   Value
Small Cap   Grth/Val

Portfolio

0.1% cash	0.0% corp bonds
99.9% stocks	0.0% gov't bonds
0.0% pref/conv't pref	0.0% muni bonds
0.0% conv't bds/wrnts	0.0% other

SHAREHOLDER INFORMATION

Minimum Investment
Initial: $2,500   Subsequent: $250

Minimum IRA Investment
Initial: $500   Subsequent: $250

Maximum Fees
Load: 0.75% redemption   12b-1: none
Other: redemption fee applies for 1 month

Services
✔ IRA
✔ Keogh
✔ Telephone Exchange

ICON Financial
(ICFSX)

Financial/Banking Sector

888-389-4266
www.iconfunds.com

	3yr Annual	5yr Annual	10yr Annual	Bull	Bear
Return (%)	19.3	7.4	na	82.4	15.1
Differ From Category (+/-)	2.2 high	-0.3 abv av	na	12.5 high	-5.5 abv av

Standard Deviation	Category Risk Index	Beta
14.2%—abv av	1.14—high	1.34

	2005	2004	2003	2002	2001	2000	1999	1998	1997	1996
Return (%)	2.4	18.3	40.2	-17.7	2.6	50.0	-1.7	7.0	—	—
Differ From Category (+/-)	-3.7	5.2	5.9	-10.3	4.0	14.0	-1.6	0.9	—	—
Return, Tax-Adjusted (%)	1.4	17.0	40.1	-17.8	-0.7	46.8	-1.9	-4.1	—	—

PER SHARE DATA

	2005	2004	2003	2002	2001	2000	1999	1998	1997	1996
Dividends, Net Income ($)	0.09	0.03	0.06	0.03	0.00	0.12	0.00	0.06	—	—
Distrib'ns, Cap Gain ($)	0.86	1.02	0.00	0.00	2.11	1.29	0.12	1.39	—	—
Net Asset Value ($)	13.10	13.71	12.48	8.94	10.91	12.76	9.49	9.78	—	—
Expense Ratio (%)	1.26	1.32	1.34	1.36	1.41	1.33	1.58	1.33	—	—
Yield (%)	0.66	0.19	0.45	0.33	0.00	0.82	0.00	0.50	—	—
Portfolio Turnover (%)	171	115	143	70	174	29	53	88	—	—
Total Assets (Millions $)	268	207	127	119	57	111	6	17	—	—

PORTFOLIO (as of 3/31/05)

Portfolio Manager: Derek Rollingson - 2003

Investment Style
Large Cap	Growth
Mid Cap	Value
Small Cap	Grth/Val

Portfolio
1.6% cash	0.0% corp bonds
98.4% stocks	0.0% gov't bonds
0.0% pref/conv't pref	0.0% muni bonds
0.0% conv't bds/wrnts	0.0% other

SHAREHOLDER INFORMATION

Minimum Investment
Initial: $1,000   Subsequent: $100

Minimum IRA Investment
Initial: $1,000   Subsequent: $100

Maximum Fees
Load: none   12b-1: none
Other: none

Services
✔ IRA
✔ Keogh
✔ Telephone Exchange

T Rowe Price Financial Services (PRISX)

800-638-5660
www.troweprice.com

Financial/Banking Sector

PERFORMANCE

fund inception date: 9/30/96

	3yr Annual	5yr Annual	10yr Annual	Bull	Bear
Return (%)	17.2	7.0	na	71.8	5.0
Differ From Category (+/-)	0.1 av	-0.7 av	na	1.9 abv av	-15.6 av

Standard Deviation	Category Risk Index	Beta
12.7%—abv av	1.02—abv av	1.23

	2005	2004	2003	2002	2001	2000	1999	1998	1997	1996
Return (%)	5.1	13.4	35.0	-10.1	-3.1	36.7	1.7	11.5	41.4	—
Differ From Category (+/-)	-1.0	0.3	0.7	-2.6	-1.8	0.7	1.9	5.4	-4.9	—
Return, Tax-Adjusted (%)	2.8	12.5	34.4	-10.4	-4.9	35.8	0.4	10.7	40.5	—

PER SHARE DATA

	2005	2004	2003	2002	2001	2000	1999	1998	1997	1996
Dividends, Net Income ($)	0.32	0.17	0.23	0.13	0.15	0.09	0.10	0.16	0.10	—
Distrib'ns, Cap Gain ($)	3.28	1.10	0.51	0.06	1.68	0.55	0.85	0.34	0.33	—
Net Asset Value ($)	21.14	23.50	21.86	16.75	18.84	21.38	16.12	16.82	15.56	—
Expense Ratio (%)	na	0.93	0.97	1.00	0.97	1.00	1.14	1.19	1.25	—
Yield (%)	1.31	0.69	1.02	0.77	0.73	0.41	0.58	0.93	0.62	—
Portfolio Turnover (%)	na	36	51	49	55	32	37	47	46	—
Total Assets (Millions $)	395	411	372	265	309	337	159	224	177	—

PORTFOLIO (as of 9/30/05)

Portfolio Manager: A Dopkin/
Team Managed - 2000

Investment Style

Large Cap	Growth
Mid Cap	Value
Small Cap	Grth/Val

Portfolio

0.6% cash	0.0% corp bonds
99.4% stocks	0.0% gov't bonds
0.0% pref/conv't pref	0.0% muni bonds
0.0% conv't bds/wrnts	0.0% other

SHAREHOLDER INFORMATION

Minimum Investment
Initial: $2,500   Subsequent: $100

Minimum IRA Investment
Initial: $1,000   Subsequent: $50

Maximum Fees
Load: none   12b-1: none
Other: none

Services
✔ IRA
✔ Keogh
✔ Telephone Exchange

Gold Sector Stock Funds
Category Performance Ranked by 2005 Returns

Fund (Ticker)	Annual Return (%)				Category Risk	Total Risk
	2005	3Yr	5Yr	10Yr		
Vanguard Precious Metals (VGPMX)	43.7	35.3	31.3	10.5	low	high
Midas (MIDSX)	39.7	25.0	28.9	-3.5	av	high
USAA Precious Metals & Minerals (USAGX)	39.2	28.6	36.1	10.2	av	high
US Global Inv Gold Shares (USERX)	32.8	27.5	33.1	-4.9	high	high
US Global Inv World Prec Minerals (UNWPX)	30.8	36.5	38.1	4.8	high	high
Gold Sector Category Average	**32.8**	**25.6**	**31.2**	**4.2**	**av**	**high**

Midas
(MIDSX)
Gold Sector

800-400-6432
www.midasfunds.com

PERFORMANCE

fund inception date: 1/8/86

	3yr Annual	5yr Annual	10yr Annual	Bull	Bear
Return (%)	25.0	28.9	-3.5	113.5	34.6
Differ From Category (+/-)	-0.6 av	-2.3 blw av	-7.7 blw av	5.0 av	-43.2 low

Standard Deviation	Category Risk Index	Beta
29.9%—high	1.02—av	0.98

	2005	2004	2003	2002	2001	2000	1999	1998	1997	1996
Return (%)	39.7	-2.7	43.7	61.0	13.1	-38.2	-9.9	-28.4	-59.0	21.1
Differ From Category (+/-)	6.9	2.9	-15.4	-4.7	-6.3	-17.8	-13.4	-13.0	-14.1	11.0
Return, Tax-Adjusted (%)	39.7	-2.7	43.7	61.0	13.1	-38.2	-9.9	-28.4	-59.0	21.1

PER SHARE DATA

	2005	2004	2003	2002	2001	2000	1999	1998	1997	1996
Dividends, Net Income ($)	0.00	0.00	0.00	0.00	0.00	0.00	0.00	0.00	0.00	0.00
Distrib'ns, Cap Gain ($)	0.00	0.00	0.00	0.00	0.00	0.00	0.00	0.00	0.00	0.00
Net Asset Value ($)	2.99	2.14	2.20	1.53	0.95	0.84	1.36	1.51	2.11	5.15
Expense Ratio (%)	na	2.58	2.44	2.58	2.83	3.40	2.81	2.33	1.90	1.63
Yield (%)	0.00	0.00	0.00	0.00	0.00	0.00	0.00	0.00	0.00	0.00
Portfolio Turnover (%)	na	34	54	45	61	109	74	27	50	23
Total Assets (Millions $)	75	57	68	55	39	35	72	88	101	201

PORTFOLIO (as of 6/30/05)

Portfolio Manager: Thomas Winmill - 1999

Investment Style

Large Cap	Growth
Mid Cap	Value
Small Cap	Grth/Val

Portfolio

0.0% cash	0.0% corp bonds
99.9% stocks	0.0% gov't bonds
0.0% pref/conv't pref	0.0% muni bonds
0.1% conv't bds/wrnts	0.0% other

SHAREHOLDER INFORMATION

Minimum Investment
Initial: $1,000   Subsequent: $100

Minimum IRA Investment
Initial: $1,000   Subsequent: $100

Maximum Fees
Load: 1.00% redemption   12b-1: 0.25%
Other: redemption fee applies for 1 month

Services
✔ IRA
✔ Keogh
✔ Telephone Exchange

US Global Inv Gold Shares
(USERX)
Gold Sector

800-873-8637
www.usfunds.com

PERFORMANCE

fund inception date: 7/1/74

	3yr Annual	5yr Annual	10yr Annual	Bull	Bear
Return (%)	27.5	33.1	-4.9	116.2	66.1
Differ From Category (+/-)	1.9 abv av	1.9 abv av	-9.1 low	7.7 abv av	-11.7 blw av

Standard Deviation	Category Risk Index		Beta
32.5%—high	1.11—high		0.92

	2005	2004	2003	2002	2001	2000	1999	1998	1997	1996
Return (%).............	32.8	-6.4	67.0	81.3	11.1	-29.8	-2.6	-32.9	-57.3	-25.4
Differ From Category (+/-)	.0.0	-0.8	7.9	15.6	-8.3	-9.4	-6.1	-17.5	-12.4	-35.6
Return, Tax-Adjusted (%)	..32.5	-6.5	67.0	81.3	11.1	-29.8	-2.6	-32.9	-57.8	-26.2

PER SHARE DATA

	2005	2004	2003	2002	2001	2000	1999	1998	1997	1996
Dividends, Net Income ($)	.0.12	0.05	0.03	0.00	0.00	0.00	0.00	0.00	0.00	0.00
Distrib'ns, Cap Gain ($) ...	0.00	0.00	0.00	0.00	0.00	0.00	0.00	0.00	0.04	0.05
Net Asset Value ($)	10.70	8.15	8.76	5.26	2.90	2.61	3.72	3.82	0.57	1.40
Expense Ratio (%)........	1.97	1.93	2.64	3.57	5.79	5.74	5.24	2.47	1.80	1.54
Yield (%)	1.10	0.56	0.29	0.00	0.00	0.00	0.00	0.00	0.00	0.00
Portfolio Turnover (%)	66	85	138	164	95	82	388	220	44	24
Total Assets (Millions $)....	90	76	86	48	23	22	34	38	66	153

PORTFOLIO (as of 9/30/05)

Portfolio Manager: Frank Holmes - 1999

Investment Style

Large Cap	Growth
Mid Cap	Value
Small Cap	Grth/Val

Portfolio

16.6% cash	0.0% corp bonds
82.9% stocks	0.0% gov't bonds
0.0% pref/conv't pref	0.0% muni bonds
0.2% conv't bds/wrnts	0.3% other

SHAREHOLDER INFORMATION

Minimum Investment
Initial: $5,000   Subsequent: $50

Minimum IRA Investment
Initial: $1   Subsequent: $1

Maximum Fees
Load: 0.50% redemption   12b-1: none
Other: redemption fee applies for 1 month

Services
✔ IRA
✔ Keogh
✔ Telephone Exchange

US Global Inv World Prec Minerals (UNWPX)

800-873-8637
www.usfunds.com

Gold Sector

PERFORMANCE   fund inception date: 11/27/85

	3yr Annual	5yr Annual	10yr Annual	Bull	Bear
Return (%)	36.5	38.1	4.8	154.6	46.4
Differ From Category (+/-)	10.9 high	6.9 high	0.6 abv av	46.1 high	-31.4 low

Standard Deviation	Category Risk Index		Beta
32.1%—high	1.10—high		1.07

	2005	2004	2003	2002	2001	2000	1999	1998	1997	1996
Return (%)	30.8	0.9	92.7	83.4	7.5	-38.0	-12.6	-15.7	-41.0	19.5
Differ From Category (+/-)	-2.0	6.6	33.6	17.7	-11.9	-17.6	-16.1	-0.3	3.9	9.4
Return, Tax-Adjusted (%)	29.9	0.5	89.8	81.6	7.5	-38.1	-12.6	-15.8	-41.3	16.9

PER SHARE DATA

	2005	2004	2003	2002	2001	2000	1999	1998	1997	1996
Dividends, Net Income ($)	0.67	0.46	1.86	0.25	0.00	0.02	0.00	0.01	0.14	1.11
Distrib'ns, Cap Gain ($)	0.37	0.00	0.00	0.00	0.00	0.00	0.00	0.00	0.00	0.00
Net Asset Value ($)	20.32	16.36	16.66	9.70	5.43	5.05	8.19	9.38	11.15	19.16
Expense Ratio (%)	1.48	1.47	1.92	2.27	2.86	2.50	2.12	1.74	1.52	1.51
Yield (%)	3.23	2.79	11.17	2.61	0.00	0.41	0.00	0.12	1.24	5.79
Portfolio Turnover (%)	55	65	141	104	68	93	252	43	40	25
Total Assets (Millions $)	327	292	288	90	41	41	81	109	131	226

PORTFOLIO (as of 9/30/05)

Portfolio Manager: Frank Holmes - 1999

Investment Style

Large Cap	Growth
Mid Cap	Value
Small Cap	Grth/Val

Portfolio

7.8% cash	0.0% corp bonds
91.8% stocks	0.0% gov't bonds
0.0% pref/conv't pref	0.0% muni bonds
0.3% conv't bds/wrnts	0.2% other

SHAREHOLDER INFORMATION

Minimum Investment

Initial: $5,000   Subsequent: $50

Minimum IRA Investment

Initial: $1   Subsequent: $1

Maximum Fees

Load: 0.50% redemption   12b-1: none

Other: redemption fee applies for 1 month

Services

✔ IRA
✔ Keogh
✔ Telephone Exchange

USAA Precious Metals & Minerals (USAGX)

800-531-8181
www.usaa.com

Gold Sector

PERFORMANCE

fund inception date: 8/15/84

	3yr Annual	5yr Annual	10yr Annual	Bull	Bear
Return (%)	28.6	36.1	10.2	124.8	106.4
Differ From Category (+/-)	3.0 abv av	4.9 high	6.0 high	16.3 high	28.6 high

Standard Deviation	Category Risk Index	Beta
29.0%—high	0.99—av	0.94

	2005	2004	2003	2002	2001	2000	1999	1998	1997	1996
Return (%)............	39.2	-10.7	71.4	67.6	30.9	-14.9	7.1	1.0	-38.1	0.0
Differ From Category (+/-)	.6.4	-5.1	12.3	1.9	11.5	5.5	3.7	16.5	6.8	-10.1
Return, Tax-Adjusted (%)..	39.0	-10.8	70.2	65.3	30.6	-15.1	7.1	1.0	-38.1	0.0

PER SHARE DATA

	2005	2004	2003	2002	2001	2000	1999	1998	1997	1996
Dividends, Net Income ($).	0.00	0.00	0.86	0.38	0.05	0.02	0.00	0.00	0.00	0.00
Distrib'ns, Cap Gain ($) ...	0.16	0.15	0.00	0.00	0.00	0.00	0.00	0.00	0.00	0.00
Net Asset Value ($)	21.18	15.33	17.35	10.62	6.58	5.06	5.98	5.58	5.52	8.93
Expense Ratio (%).......	1.23	1.26	1.47	1.56	1.68	1.58	1.52	1.46	1.31	1.33
Yield (%)	0.00	0.00	4.94	3.60	0.70	0.47	0.00	0.00	0.00	0.00
Portfolio Turnover (%)	27	27	31	41	52	27	33	19	26	16
Total Assets (Millions $)...	394	325	331	144	78	69	88	91	84	130

PORTFOLIO (as of 8/31/05)

Portfolio Manager: Mark Johnson - 1994

Investment Style
Large Cap   Growth
Mid Cap   Value
Small Cap   Grth/Val

Portfolio
4.0% cash	0.0% corp bonds
95.9% stocks	0.0% gov't bonds
0.0% pref/conv't pref	0.0% muni bonds
0.1% conv't bds/wrnts	0.0% other

SHAREHOLDER INFORMATION

Minimum Investment
Initial: $3,000   Subsequent: $50

Minimum IRA Investment
Initial: $250   Subsequent: $50

Maximum Fees
Load: none   12b-1: none
Other: none

Services
✔ IRA
✔ Keogh
✔ Telephone Exchange

Vanguard Precious Metals
(VGPMX)
Gold Sector

800-662-7447
www.vanguard.com

	3yr Annual	5yr Annual	10yr Annual	Bull	Bear
Return (%)	35.3	31.3	10.5	153.0	77.0
Differ From Category (+/-)	9.7 high	0.1 av	6.3 high	44.5 high	-0.8 av

Standard Deviation		Category Risk Index		Beta
23.2%—high		0.79—low		0.95

	2005	2004	2003	2002	2001	2000	1999	1998	1997	1996
Return (%).............	43.7	8.0	59.4	33.3	18.3	-7.3	28.8	-3.9	-38.9	-0.7
Differ From Category (+/-)	10.9	13.7	0.3	-32.4	-1.1	13.1	25.4	11.5	6.0	-10.9
Return, Tax-Adjusted (%)..	43.0	7.1	58.1	31.1	16.3	-8.2	28.2	-4.4	-39.3	-1.6

PER SHARE DATA

	2005	2004	2003	2002	2001	2000	1999	1998	1997	1996
Dividends, Net Income ($).	0.24	0.14	0.93	0.49	0.39	0.20	0.10	0.09	0.13	0.21
Distrib'ns, Cap Gain ($) ...	0.56	0.86	0.00	0.00	0.00	0.00	0.00	0.00	0.00	0.07
Net Asset Value ($)	23.20	16.69	16.38	10.89	8.55	7.58	8.41	6.61	6.97	11.63
Expense Ratio (%)........	0.48	0.55	0.60	0.63	0.65	0.77	0.77	0.62	0.50	0.60
Yield (%)	1.01	0.82	5.70	4.49	4.56	2.63	1.18	1.36	1.86	1.79
Portfolio Turnover (%)	36	15	43	52	17	28	23	26	19	5
Total Assets (Millions $) ..	2,485	894	669	527	371	315	382	311	293	497

PORTFOLIO (as of 9/30/05)

Portfolio Manager: Graham French - 1996

Investment Style

Large Cap	Growth
Mid Cap	Value
Small Cap	Grth/Val

Portfolio

4.0% cash	0.0% corp bonds
95.9% stocks	0.0% gov't bonds
0.0% pref/conv't pref	0.0% muni bonds
0.0% conv't bds/wrnts	0.1% other

SHAREHOLDER INFORMATION

Minimum Investment
Initial: $10,000   Subsequent: $100

Minimum IRA Investment
Initial: $10,000   Subsequent: $100

Maximum Fees
Load: 1.00% redemption   12b-1: none
Other: redemption fee applies for 1 year

Services
✔ IRA
✔ Keogh
✔ Telephone Exchange

Health Sector Stock Funds
Category Performance Ranked by 2005 Returns

Fund (Ticker)	Annual Return (%)				Category Risk	Total Risk
	2005	3Yr	5Yr	10Yr		
Fidelity Select Medical Delivery (FSHCX)	29.0	34.6	15.9	11.9	high	high
Schwab Health Care (SWHFX)	20.0	29.0	6.8	na	av	av
ICON Healthcare (ICHCX)	13.9	20.7	9.1	na	av	abv av
T Rowe Price Health Sciences (PRHSX)	13.5	21.8	4.2	14.1	abv av	abv av
Fidelity Select Medical Systems & Equip (FSMEX)	7.4	18.9	9.6	na	av	av
Health Sector Category Average	**13.8**	**19.2**	**3.4**	**13.0**	**av**	**abv av**

Fidelity Select Medical Delivery (FSHCX)

Health Sector

800-544-8544
www.fidelity.com

PERFORMANCE   **fund inception date: 6/30/86**

	3yr Annual	5yr Annual	10yr Annual	Bull	Bear
Return (%)	34.6	15.9	11.9	153.1	48.2
Differ From Category (+/-)	15.4 high	12.5 high	-1.1 abv av	78.7 high	55.6 high

Standard Deviation	Category Risk Index	Beta
16.1%—high	1.35—high	0.54

	2005	2004	2003	2002	2001	2000	1999	1998	1997	1996
Return (%)	29.0	45.4	30.1	-12.1	-2.3	67.8	-29.5	-6.1	20.1	11.0
Differ From Category (+/-)	15.2	31.1	-0.5	11.4	8.3	24.2	-51.4	-30.0	-2.8	-5.0
Return, Tax-Adjusted (%)	28.0	45.4	30.1	-12.1	-2.3	67.8	-29.5	-7.1	16.1	7.4

PER SHARE DATA

	2005	2004	2003	2002	2001	2000	1999	1998	1997	1996
Dividends, Net Income ($)	0.00	0.00	0.00	0.00	0.00	0.00	0.00	0.00	0.00	0.00
Distrib'ns, Cap Gain ($)	2.94	0.00	0.00	0.00	0.00	0.00	0.00	1.34	5.23	3.45
Net Asset Value ($)	54.56	44.83	30.82	23.68	26.95	27.59	16.44	23.35	26.05	26.42
Expense Ratio (%)	1.03	1.24	1.13	1.19	1.22	1.67	1.37	1.57	1.57	1.62
Yield (%)	0.00	0.00	0.00	0.00	0.00	0.00	0.00	0.00	0.00	0.00
Portfolio Turnover (%)	244	196	269	106	113	154	67	109	78	132
Total Assets (Millions $)	1,706	447	222	133	132	311	51	146	142	183

PORTFOLIO (as of 8/31/05)

Portfolio Manager: Matthew Sabel - 2005

Investment Style

Large Cap	Growth
Mid Cap	Value
Small Cap	Grth/Val

Portfolio

2.8% cash	0.0% corp bonds
97.2% stocks	0.0% gov't bonds
0.0% pref/conv't pref	0.0% muni bonds
0.0% conv't bds/wrnts	0.0% other

SHAREHOLDER INFORMATION

Minimum Investment
Initial: $2,500   Subsequent: $250

Minimum IRA Investment
Initial: $500   Subsequent: $250

Maximum Fees
Load: 0.75% redemption   12b-1: none
Other: redemption fee applies for 1 month

Services
✔ IRA
   Keogh
✔ Telephone Exchange

Fidelity Select Medical Systems & Equipment (FSMEX)

Health Sector

800-544-8544
www.fidelity.com

PERFORMANCE

fund inception date: 4/28/98

	3yr Annual	5yr Annual	10yr Annual	Bull	Bear
Return (%)	18.9	9.6	na	66.0	26.1
Differ From Category (+/-)	-0.3 abv av	6.2 high	na	-8.4 av	33.5 high

Standard Deviation	Category Risk Index	Beta
9.7%—av	0.82—av	0.68

	2005	2004	2003	2002	2001	2000	1999	1998	1997	1996
Return (%)	7.4	17.4	33.3	-6.2	0.3	50.3	10.7	—	—	—
Differ From Category (+/-)	-6.4	3.1	2.7	17.3	11.0	6.7	-11.1	—	—	—
Return, Tax-Adjusted (%)	6.9	17.3	32.8	-6.3	0.0	46.8	10.0	—	—	—

PER SHARE DATA

	2005	2004	2003	2002	2001	2000	1999	1998	1997	1996
Dividends, Net Income ($)	0.00	0.00	0.00	0.00	0.00	0.00	0.00	—	—	—
Distrib'ns, Cap Gain ($)	0.84	0.11	0.53	0.11	0.34	2.31	0.42	—	—	—
Net Asset Value ($)	24.33	23.40	20.02	15.42	16.56	16.91	13.12	—	—	—
Expense Ratio (%)	1.00	1.15	1.29	1.23	1.23	1.65	2.38	—	—	—
Yield (%)	0.00	0.00	0.00	0.00	0.00	0.00	0.00	—	—	—
Portfolio Turnover (%)	28	33	82	87	64	101	85	—	—	—
Total Assets (Millions $)	1,185	866	440	145	148	155	39	—	—	—

PORTFOLIO (as of 8/31/05)

Portfolio Manager: Aaron Cooper - 2005

Investment Style

Large Cap	Growth
Mid Cap	Value
Small Cap	Grth/Val

Portfolio

0.7% cash	0.0% corp bonds
99.3% stocks	0.0% gov't bonds
0.0% pref/conv't pref	0.0% muni bonds
0.0% conv't bds/wrnts	0.0% other

SHAREHOLDER INFORMATION

Minimum Investment

Initial: $2,500   Subsequent: $500

Minimum IRA Investment

Initial: $500   Subsequent: $250

Maximum Fees

Load: 0.75% redemption   12b-1: none
Other: redemption fee applies for 1 month

Services

✔ IRA
✔ Keogh
✔ Telephone Exchange

ICON Healthcare
(ICHCX)
Health Sector

888-389-4266
www.iconfunds.com

PERFORMANCE   fund inception date: 2/21/97

	3yr Annual	5yr Annual	10yr Annual	Bull	Bear
Return (%)	20.7	9.1	na	81.0	11.8
Differ From Category (+/-)	1.5 abv av	5.7 high	na	6.6 abv av	19.2 high

Standard Deviation	Category Risk Index	Beta
11.5%—abv av	0.97—av	0.76

	2005	2004	2003	2002	2001	2000	1999	1998	1997	1996
Return (%)............	13.9	17.9	31.1	-9.2	-3.1	43.0	3.8	15.3	—	—
Differ From Category (+/-)	.0.1	3.6	0.5	14.3	7.5	-0.6	-18.0	-8.5	—	—
Return, Tax-Adjusted (%)	..13.6	17.8	31.1	-9.2	-4.1	41.3	3.1	9.4	—	—

PER SHARE DATA

	2005	2004	2003	2002	2001	2000	1999	1998	1997	1996
Dividends, Net Income ($)	.0.00	0.00	0.00	0.00	0.00	0.00	0.00	0.00	—	—
Distrib'ns, Cap Gain ($)	..0.27	0.04	0.00	0.00	0.61	0.77	0.31	3.16	—	—
Net Asset Value ($)	17.90	15.95	13.56	10.34	11.39	12.41	9.25	9.26	—	—
Expense Ratio (%)........	1.22	1.29	1.34	1.39	1.45	1.38	1.40	1.24	—	—
Yield (%)	0.00	0.00	0.00	0.00	0.00	0.00	0.00	0.00	—	—
Portfolio Turnover (%)	48	53	86	105	145	115	86	52	—	—
Total Assets (Millions $) ...	705	341	217	128	41	79	29	27	—	—

PORTFOLIO (as of 3/31/05)

Portfolio Manager: J Waller - 2003

Investment Style

Large Cap	Growth
Mid Cap	Value
Small Cap	Grth/Val

Portfolio

2.6%	cash	0.0%	corp bonds
97.5%	stocks	0.0%	gov't bonds
0.0%	pref/conv't pref	0.0%	muni bonds
0.0%	conv't bds/wrnts	0.0%	other

SHAREHOLDER INFORMATION

Minimum Investment
Initial: $1,000   Subsequent: $100

Minimum IRA Investment
Initial: $1,000   Subsequent: $100

Maximum Fees
Load: none   12b-1: none
Other: none

Services
✔ IRA
✔ Keogh
✔ Telephone Exchange

Schwab Health Care
(SWHFX)
Health Sector

800-435-4000
www.schwab.com/
schwabfunds

	3yr Annual	5yr Annual	10yr Annual	Bull	Bear
Return (%)	29.0	6.8	na	122.4	na
Differ From Category (+/-)	9.8 high	3.4 abv av	na	48.0 high	na

Standard Deviation	Category Risk Index	Beta
10.0%—av	0.84—av	0.66

	2005	2004	2003	2002	2001	2000	1999	1998	1997	1996
Return (%).............	20.0	31.0	36.7	-24.3	-14.4	—	—	—	—	—
Differ From Category (+/-)	.6.2	16.7	6.1	-0.8	-3.7	—	—	—	—	—
Return, Tax-Adjusted (%)..	20.0	31.0	36.7	-24.5	-14.4	—	—	—	—	—

PER SHARE DATA

	2005	2004	2003	2002	2001	2000	1999	1998	1997	1996
Dividends, Net Income ($).	0.00	0.00	0.00	0.03	0.01	—	—	—	—	—
Distrib'ns, Cap Gain ($) ...	0.00	0.00	0.00	0.00	0.00	—	—	—	—	—
Net Asset Value ($)	14.86	12.38	9.45	6.91	9.18	—	—	—	—	—
Expense Ratio (%).......	1.07	1.04	1.04	0.89	—	—	—	—	—	—
Yield (%)	0.00	0.00	0.00	0.47	0.05	—	—	—	—	—
Portfolio Turnover (%)	42	105	200	99	92	—	—	—	—	—
Total Assets (Millions $) ...	499	77	29	20	33	—	—	—	—	—

PORTFOLIO (as of 7/29/05)

Portfolio Manager: J Mortimer/L Mano/
V Hsu - 2000

Investment Style
Large Cap   Growth
Mid Cap   Value
Small Cap   Grth/Val

Portfolio

1.8% cash	0.0% corp bonds
97.6% stocks	0.0% gov't bonds
0.0% pref/conv't pref	0.0% muni bonds
0.0% conv't bds/wrnts	0.6% other

SHAREHOLDER INFORMATION

Minimum Investment
Initial: $5,000   Subsequent: $500

Minimum IRA Investment
Initial: $5,000   Subsequent: $500

Maximum Fees
Load: 2.00% redemption   12b-1: none
Other: redemption fee applies for 1 month

Services
✔ IRA
✔ Keogh
✔ Telephone Exchange

T Rowe Price Health Sciences (PRHSX)

800-638-5660
www.troweprice.com

Health Sector

PERFORMANCE

fund inception date: 12/29/95

	3yr Annual	5yr Annual	10yr Annual	Bull	Bear
Return (%)	21.8	4.2	14.1	82.1	-9.0
Differ From Category (+/-)	2.6 high	0.8 av	1.1 high	7.7 high	-1.6 abv av

Standard Deviation	Category Risk Index	Beta
12.7%—abv av	1.07—abv av	0.87

	2005	2004	2003	2002	2001	2000	1999	1998	1997	1996
Return (%)	13.5	15.8	37.4	-27.7	-5.9	52.1	7.9	22.3	19.4	26.7
Differ From Category (+/-)	-0.3	1.5	6.8	-4.2	4.7	8.5	-13.9	-1.5	-3.5	10.7
Return, Tax-Adjusted (%)	12.7	15.8	37.4	-27.7	-6.2	49.0	6.3	21.4	17.8	25.6

PER SHARE DATA

	2005	2004	2003	2002	2001	2000	1999	1998	1997	1996
Dividends, Net Income ($)	0.00	0.00	0.00	0.00	0.00	0.00	0.00	0.00	0.00	0.00
Distrib'ns, Cap Gain ($)	1.16	0.00	0.00	0.00	0.31	2.48	1.26	0.66	0.97	0.40
Net Asset Value ($)	25.07	23.11	19.95	14.51	20.08	21.70	15.93	16.01	13.66	12.27
Expense Ratio (%)	na	0.93	1.00	1.04	0.95	0.98	1.11	1.16	1.18	1.35
Yield (%)	0.00	0.00	0.00	0.00	0.00	0.00	0.00	0.00	0.00	0.00
Portfolio Turnover (%)	na	44	45	62	63	111	82	86	104	133
Total Assets (Millions $)	1,434	1,329	1,027	678	961	972	303	317	271	194

PORTFOLIO (as of 9/30/05)

Portfolio Manager: K Jenner/Team Managed - 2000

Investment Style

Large Cap	Growth
Mid Cap	Value
Small Cap	Grth/Val

Portfolio

0.2%	cash	0.0%	corp bonds
99.8%	stocks	0.0%	gov't bonds
0.0%	pref/conv't pref	0.0%	muni bonds
0.0%	conv't bds/wrnts	0.0%	other

SHAREHOLDER INFORMATION

Minimum Investment
Initial: $2,500   Subsequent: $100

Minimum IRA Investment
Initial: $1,000   Subsequent: $50

Maximum Fees
Load: none   12b-1: none
Other: none

Services
✔ IRA
✔ Keogh
✔ Telephone Exchange

Real Estate Sector Stock Funds
Category Performance Ranked by 2005 Returns

Fund (Ticker)	Annual Return (%)				Category Risk	Total Risk
	2005	3Yr	5Yr	10Yr		
CGM Realty (CGMRX)	26.9	48.3	28.8	20.7	high	high
Amer Century Real Estate Inv (REACX)	15.9	28.1	19.6	15.9	av	high
Cohen & Steers Realty Shares (CSRSX)	14.9	30.0	19.0	15.6	high	high
Fidelity Real Estate Investment (FRESX)	14.8	27.2	19.0	15.3	abv av	high
T Rowe Price Real Estate (TRREX)	14.5	28.3	19.3	na	av	high
Real Estate Sector Category Average	**12.8**	**27.7**	**19.2**	**15.5**	**av**	**abv av**

Amer Century Real Estate Inv (REACX)

800-345-2021
www.americancentury.com

Real Estate Sector

	3yr Annual	5yr Annual	10yr Annual	Bull	Bear
Return (%)	28.1	19.6	15.9	109.8	46.6
Differ From Category (+/-)	0.4 abv av	0.4 high	0.4 high	3.3 abv av	4.0 high

Standard Deviation	Category Risk Index	Beta
14.6%—high	1.04—av	0.70

	2005	2004	2003	2002	2001	2000	1999	1998	1997	1996
Return (%)	15.9	29.6	39.7	5.5	10.5	27.1	-2.7	-18.1	25.2	40.8
Differ From Category (+/-)	.3.1	-1.3	0.4	0.9	0.1	-1.5	-1.4	-2.3	3.4	6.4
Return, Tax-Adjusted (%)	13.6	27.6	38.4	4.1	8.9	25.1	-4.8	-19.3	23.3	38.2

PER SHARE DATA

	2005	2004	2003	2002	2001	2000	1999	1998	1997	1996
Dividends, Net Income ($)	0.50	0.49	0.53	0.54	0.58	0.61	0.70	0.45	0.40	0.46
Distrib'ns, Cap Gain ($)	2.72	1.64	0.15	0.00	0.00	0.00	0.00	0.12	0.52	0.29
Net Asset Value ($)	25.45	24.75	20.80	15.42	15.12	14.22	11.71	12.77	16.26	13.80
Expense Ratio (%)	1.16	1.17	1.18	1.20	1.19	1.20	1.20	1.15	1.17	1.00
Yield (%)	1.76	1.85	2.52	3.52	3.83	4.25	5.95	3.46	2.40	3.22
Portfolio Turnover (%)	171	158	162	156	242	102	66	28	69	86
Total Assets (Millions $)	769	548	286	128	88	90	96	121	119	10

PORTFOLIO (as of 9/30/05)

Portfolio Manager: S Blasdell/P Davidson - 1995

Investment Style

Large Cap	Growth
Mid Cap	Value
Small Cap	Grth/Val

Portfolio

4.0% cash	0.0% corp bonds
96.0% stocks	0.0% gov't bonds
0.0% pref/conv't pref	0.0% muni bonds
0.0% conv't bds/wrnts	0.0% other

SHAREHOLDER INFORMATION

Minimum Investment
Initial: $2,500   Subsequent: $50

Minimum IRA Investment
Initial: $2,500   Subsequent: $50

Maximum Fees
Load: none   12b-1: none
Other: none

Services
✓ IRA
  Keogh
✓ Telephone Exchange

CGM Realty
(CGMRX)
Real Estate Sector

800-345-4048
www.cgmfunds.com

PERFORMANCE

fund inception date: 5/13/94

	3yr Annual	5yr Annual	10yr Annual	Bull	Bear
Return (%)	48.3	28.8	20.7	220.6	40.5
Differ From Category (+/-)	20.6 high	9.6 high	5.2 high	114.1 high	-2.1 blw av

Standard Deviation	Category Risk Index	Beta
22.0%—high	1.57—high	1.48

	2005	2004	2003	2002	2001	2000	1999	1998	1997	1996
Return (%)	26.9	35.5	89.7	3.5	5.1	29.1	2.6	-21.1	23.3	44.0
Differ From Category (+/-)	14.1	4.6	50.4	-1.1	-5.3	0.5	4.0	-5.4	1.5	9.6
Return, Tax-Adjusted (%)	21.4	33.0	88.9	1.8	3.0	26.5	0.1	-22.8	19.3	40.6

PER SHARE DATA

	2005	2004	2003	2002	2001	2000	1999	1998	1997	1996
Dividends, Net Income ($)	0.46	0.18	0.07	0.58	0.71	0.73	0.65	0.59	0.64	0.65
Distrib'ns, Cap Gain ($)	9.85	3.75	0.53	0.00	0.00	0.00	0.16	0.16	1.59	0.41
Net Asset Value ($)	27.19	29.56	24.75	13.38	13.47	13.53	11.08	11.59	15.60	14.50
Expense Ratio (%)	na	0.96	1.02	1.03	1.00	1.02	1.06	1.04	1.00	1.00
Yield (%)	1.24	0.54	0.27	4.33	5.27	5.39	5.76	4.99	3.69	4.32
Portfolio Turnover (%)	na	43	68	173	131	78	49	86	128	57
Total Assets (Millions $)	1,030	785	645	340	383	500	372	419	490	162

PORTFOLIO (as of 9/30/05)

Portfolio Manager: G Kenneth Heebner - 1994

Investment Style

Large Cap	Growth
Mid Cap	Value
Small Cap	Grth/Val

Portfolio

0.4% cash	0.0% corp bonds
99.6% stocks	0.0% gov't bonds
0.0% pref/conv't pref	0.0% muni bonds
0.0% conv't bds/wrnts	0.0% other

SHAREHOLDER INFORMATION

Minimum Investment
Initial: $2,500   Subsequent: $50

Minimum IRA Investment
Initial: $1,000   Subsequent: $50

Maximum Fees
Load: none   12b-1: none
Other: none

Services
✔ IRA
✔ Keogh
✔ Telephone Exchange

Cohen & Steers Realty Shares (CSRSX)

Real Estate Sector

800-437-9912
www.cohenandsteers.com

PERFORMANCE

fund inception date: 7/1/9 ▌

	3yr Annual	5yr Annual	10yr Annual	Bull	Bear
Return (%)	30.0	19.0	15.6	123.7	33.2
Differ From Category (+/-)	2.3 high	-0.2 abv av	0.1 abv av	17.2 high	-9.4 low

Standard Deviation	Category Risk Index	Beta
15.4%—high	1.10—high	0.78

	2005	2004	2003	2002	2001	2000	1999	1998	1997	1996
Return (%).............	14.9	38.4	38.0	2.7	5.7	26.6	2.6	-18.0	21.1	38.4
Differ From Category (+/-)	.2.1	7.5	-1.3	-1.9	-4.7	-2.0	4.0	-2.3	-0.7	4.0
Return, Tax-Adjusted (%)..	12.6	35.8	35.4	0.7	3.6	24.2	0.6	-20.1	18.4	35.8

PER SHARE DATA

	2005	2004	2003	2002	2001	2000	1999	1998	1997	1996
Dividends, Net Income ($).	2.26	2.24	2.77	2.38	2.27	2.24	1.98	1.88	1.88	1.88
Distrib'ns, Cap Gain ($) ...	5.04	4.67	1.04	0.00	0.00	0.00	0.00	1.40	2.30	0.55
Net Asset Value ($)	72.59	69.66	55.64	43.34	44.41	44.26	36.91	37.98	50.18	45.09
Expense Ratio (%).........	na	1.06	1.07	1.08	1.09	1.07	1.06	1.04	1.05	1.08
Yield (%)	2.90	3.01	4.88	5.49	5.11	5.06	5.36	4.77	3.58	4.11
Portfolio Turnover (%)	na	29	37	37	45	33	21	30	40	33
Total Assets (Millions $)..	2,451	2,265	1,681	1,255	1,387	1,312	1,465	1,933	3,433	2,036

PORTFOLIO (as of 9/30/05)

Portfolio Manager: Cohen/Steers/Harvey/Corl - 1991

Investment Style

Large Cap	Growth
Mid Cap	Value
Small Cap	Grth/Val

Portfolio

0.0% cash	0.0% corp bonds
93.8% stocks	0.0% gov't bonds
0.0% pref/conv't pref	0.0% muni bonds
0.0% conv't bds/wrnts	6.2% other

SHAREHOLDER INFORMATION

Minimum Investment
Initial: $10,000   Subsequent: $500

Minimum IRA Investment
Initial: $0   Subsequent: $0

Maximum Fees
Load: 1.00% redemption   12b-1: none
Other: redemption fee applies for 6 months

Services
  IRA
  Keogh
  ✔ Telephone Exchange

Fidelity Real Estate Investment (FRESX)

Real Estate Sector

800-544-8544
www.fidelity.com

PERFORMANCE
fund inception date: 11/14/86

	3yr Annual	5yr Annual	10yr Annual	Bull	Bear
Return (%)	27.2	19.0	15.3	107.6	46.6
Differ From Category (+/-)	-0.5 abv av	-0.2 av	-0.2 av	1.1 abv av	4.0 high

Standard Deviation	Category Risk Index	Beta
14.8%—high	1.06—abv av	0.73

	2005	2004	2003	2002	2001	2000	1999	1998	1997	1996
Return (%).............	14.8	34.1	33.7	5.7	9.5	31.3	-0.9	-18.6	21.3	36.2
Differ From Category (+/-)	.2.0	3.2	-5.6	1.1	-0.9	2.7	0.4	-2.8	-0.5	1.8
Return, Tax-Adjusted (%)..	12.9	32.3	32.5	3.7	6.8	29.4	-2.7	-20.4	19.0	34.1

PER SHARE DATA

	2005	2004	2003	2002	2001	2000	1999	1998	1997	1996
Dividends, Net Income ($)	.0.73	0.67	0.54	0.77	0.78	0.73	0.69	0.77	0.79	0.72
Distrib'ns, Cap Gain ($) ...	1.99	1.34	0.26	0.43	0.89	0.00	0.00	0.41	0.56	0.00
Net Asset Value ($)	31.16	29.54	23.71	18.39	18.52	18.50	14.70	15.54	20.45	18.03
Expense Ratio (%)........	0.84	0.83	0.84	0.79	0.82	0.88	0.89	0.84	0.90	0.95
Yield (%)	2.20	2.16	2.25	4.09	4.01	3.94	4.69	4.82	3.76	3.99
Portfolio Turnover (%)	33	54	32	71	71	32	28	76	55	85
Total Assets (Millions $) ..	5,835	4,557	2,712	1,720	1,245	1,037	724	1,239	2,480	1,722

PORTFOLIO (as of 7/29/05)

Portfolio Manager: Steve Buller - 1998

Investment Style

Large Cap	Growth
Mid Cap	Value
Small Cap	Grth/Val

Portfolio

2.7%	cash	0.0% corp bonds
97.3%	stocks	0.0% gov't bonds
0.0%	pref/conv't pref	0.0% muni bonds
0.0%	conv't bds/wrnts	0.0% other

SHAREHOLDER INFORMATION

Minimum Investment
Initial: $2,500   Subsequent: $100

Minimum IRA Investment
Initial: $500   Subsequent: $100

Maximum Fees
Load: 0.75% redemption   12b-1: none
Other: redemption fee applies for 3 months; maint fee for low bal

Services
✔ IRA
✔ Keogh
✔ Telephone Exchange

T Rowe Price Real Estate
(TRREX)
Real Estate Sector

800-638-5660
www.troweprice.com

fund inception date: 10/31/97

PERFORMANCE

	3yr Annual	5yr Annual	10yr Annual	Bull	Bear
Return (%)	28.3	19.3	na	112.5	45.3
Differ From Category (+/-)	0.6 high	0.1 abv av	na	6.0 high	2.7 abv av

Standard Deviation	Category Risk Index	Beta
14.8%—high	1.06—av	0.72

	2005	2004	2003	2002	2001	2000	1999	1998	1997	1996
Return (%)	14.5	36.8	34.8	5.3	8.8	31.9	-1.2	-14.8	—	—
Differ From Category (+/-)	.1.7	5.9	-4.5	0.7	-1.6	3.3	0.1	0.9	—	—
Return, Tax-Adjusted (%)	.12.9	35.2	32.8	3.5	6.8	29.6	-3.2	-16.4	—	—

PER SHARE DATA

	2005	2004	2003	2002	2001	2000	1999	1998	1997	1996
Dividends, Net Income ($)	.0.70	0.60	0.59	0.49	0.53	0.47	0.45	0.44	—	—
Distrib'ns, Cap Gain ($)	.0.24	0.07	0.00	0.00	0.00	0.00	0.00	0.00	—	—
Net Asset Value ($)	19.49	17.90	13.65	10.62	10.54	10.19	8.11	8.68	—	—
Expense Ratio (%)	na	0.90	1.00	1.00	1.00	1.00	1.00	1.00	—	—
Yield (%)	3.54	3.33	4.32	4.61	5.02	4.61	5.54	5.06	—	—
Portfolio Turnover (%)	na	8	5	10	37	19	27	57	—	—
Total Assets (Millions $)	930	641	291	132	69	54	25	28	—	—

PORTFOLIO (as of 9/30/05)

Portfolio Manager: D Lee/Team Managed - 1997

Investment Style

Large Cap	Growth
Mid Cap	Value
Small Cap	Grth/Val

Portfolio

2.8% cash	0.0% corp bonds
97.2% stocks	0.0% gov't bonds
0.0% pref/conv't pref	0.0% muni bonds
0.0% conv't bds/wrnts	0.0% other

SHAREHOLDER INFORMATION

Minimum Investment
Initial: $2,500   Subsequent: $100

Minimum IRA Investment
Initial: $1,000   Subsequent: $50

Maximum Fees
Load: 1.00% redemption   12b-1: none
Other: redemption fee applies for 6 months

Services
✔ IRA
✔ Keogh
✔ Telephone Exchange

Technology Sector Stock Funds
Category Performance Ranked by 2005 Returns

Fund (Ticker)	Annual Return (%)				Category Risk	Total Risk
	2005	3Yr	5Yr	10Yr		
Fidelity Select Electronics (FSELX)	15.7	21.5	-5.5	12.1	high	high
T Rowe Price Glbl Technology (PRGTX)	10.9	22.3	-3.9	na	low	high
RS Internet Age (RIAFX)	7.9	33.3	3.5	na	high	high
Baron iOpportunity (BIOPX)	7.0	32.7	9.8	na	blw av	high
Buffalo Science & Technology (BUFTX)	6.9	26.2	na	na	blw av	high
RS Information Age (RSIFX)	2.0	29.3	-2.6	10.1	high	high
Technology Sector Category Average	**4.2**	**19.1**	**-8.5**	**8.4**	**av**	**high**

Baron iOpportunity
(BIOPX)

Technology Sector

800-992-2766
www.baronfunds.com

PERFORMANCE

fund inception date: 2/29/00

	3yr Annual	5yr Annual	10yr Annual	Bull	Bear
Return (%)	32.7	9.8	na	139.9	-58.7
Differ From Category (+/-)	13.6 high	18.3 high	na	67.7 high	17.1 high

Standard Deviation	Category Risk Index	Beta
17.9%—high	0.86—blw av	1.53

	2005	2004	2003	2002	2001	2000	1999	1998	1997	1996
Return (%)	7.0	25.5	73.8	-29.0	-3.6	—	—	—	—	—
Differ From Category (+/-)	2.8	23.1	14.6	13.1	26.6	—	—	—	—	—
Return, Tax-Adjusted (%)	7.0	25.5	73.8	-29.0	-3.6	—	—	—	—	—

PER SHARE DATA

	2005	2004	2003	2002	2001	2000	1999	1998	1997	1996
Dividends, Net Income ($)	0.00	0.00	0.00	0.00	0.00	—	—	—	—	—
Distrib'ns, Cap Gain ($)	0.00	0.00	0.00	0.00	0.00	—	—	—	—	—
Net Asset Value ($)	9.72	9.08	7.23	4.16	5.86	—	—	—	—	—
Expense Ratio (%)	1.50	1.50	1.50	1.50	—	—	—	—	—	—
Yield (%)	0.00	0.00	0.00	0.00	0.00	—	—	—	—	—
Portfolio Turnover (%)	84	86	90	96	123	—	—	—	—	—
Total Assets (Millions $)	146	168	167	63	101	—	—	—	—	—

PORTFOLIO (as of 9/30/05)

Portfolio Manager: Mitch Rubin - 2000

Investment Style

Large Cap	Growth
Mid Cap	Value
Small Cap	Grth/Val

Portfolio

0.0% cash	0.0% corp bonds
100.0% stocks	0.0% gov't bonds
0.0% pref/conv't pref	0.0% muni bonds
0.0% conv't bds/wrnts	0.0% other

SHAREHOLDER INFORMATION

Minimum Investment
Initial: $2,000   Subsequent: $1

Minimum IRA Investment
Initial: $2,000   Subsequent: $1

Maximum Fees
Load: none   12b-1: 0.25%
Other: none

Services
✔ IRA
Keogh
✔ Telephone Exchange

Buffalo Science & Technology (BUFTX)

Technology Sector

800-492-8332
www.buffalofunds.com

PERFORMANCE

fund inception date: 4/16/01

	3yr Annual	5yr Annual	10yr Annual	Bull	Bear
Return (%)	26.2	na	na	102.8	na
Differ From Category (+/-)	7.1 high	na	na	30.6 high	na

Standard Deviation	Category Risk Index	Beta
17.6%—high	0.85—blw av	1.52

	2005	2004	2003	2002	2001	2000	1999	1998	1997	1996
Return (%)	6.9	15.6	62.6	-39.0	—	—	—	—	—	—
Differ From Category (+/-)	2.7	13.2	3.4	3.1	—	—	—	—	—	—
Return, Tax-Adjusted (%)	6.8	15.6	62.6	-39.0	—	—	—	—	—	—

PER SHARE DATA

	2005	2004	2003	2002	2001	2000	1999	1998	1997	1996
Dividends, Net Income ($)	0.00	0.00	0.00	0.00	—	—	—	—	—	—
Distrib'ns, Cap Gain ($)	0.05	0.00	0.00	0.00	—	—	—	—	—	—
Net Asset Value ($)	12.41	11.65	10.07	6.19	—	—	—	—	—	—
Expense Ratio (%)	1.05	1.03	1.23	1.17	—	—	—	—	—	—
Yield (%)	0.00	0.00	0.00	0.00	—	—	—	—	—	—
Portfolio Turnover (%)	25	38	26	4	—	—	—	—	—	—
Total Assets (Millions $)	88	69	30	14	—	—	—	—	—	—

PORTFOLIO (as of 9/30/05)

Portfolio Manager: Team Managed - 2001

Investment Style

Large Cap	Growth
Mid Cap	Value
Small Cap	Grth/Val

Portfolio

5.2%	cash	0.0%	corp bonds
94.8%	stocks	0.0%	gov't bonds
0.0%	pref/conv't pref	0.0%	muni bonds
0.0%	conv't bds/wrnts	0.0%	other

SHAREHOLDER INFORMATION

Minimum Investment

Initial: $2,500   Subsequent: $100

Minimum IRA Investment

Initial: $250   Subsequent: $100

Maximum Fees

Load: none   12b-1: none

Other: none

Services

✔ IRA

Keogh

✔ Telephone Exchange

Fidelity Select Electronics

(FSELX)

Technology Sector

800-544-8544
www.fidelity.com

fund inception date: 7/29/85

	3yr Annual	5yr Annual	10yr Annual	Bull	Bear
Return (%)	21.5	-5.5	12.1	75.5	-75.0
Differ From Category (+/-)	2.4 abv av	3.0 abv av	3.7 high	3.3 abv av	0.8 abv av

Standard Deviation	Category Risk Index	Beta
25.4%—high	1.23—high	2.04

	2005	2004	2003	2002	2001	2000	1999	1998	1997	1996
Return (%)	15.7	-9.8	71.8	-50.5	-14.7	-17.6	106.6	51.1	13.7	41.7
Differ From Category (+/-)	11.5	-12.3	12.6	-8.4	15.5	10.3	-27.1	-14.5	4.6	12.5
Return, Tax-Adjusted (%)	15.7	-9.8	71.8	-50.5	-14.7	-21.8	103.8	51.1	8.1	41.7

PER SHARE DATA

	2005	2004	2003	2002	2001	2000	1999	1998	1997	1996
Dividends, Net Income ($)	0.00	0.00	0.00	0.00	0.00	0.00	0.00	0.00	0.00	0.00
Distrib'ns, Cap Gain ($)	0.00	0.00	0.00	0.00	0.00	18.68	6.62	0.00	10.20	0.00
Net Asset Value ($)	43.73	37.78	41.89	24.37	49.27	57.78	88.88	46.56	30.81	36.48
Expense Ratio (%)	0.96	1.06	1.06	0.97	0.87	0.98	1.15	1.18	1.33	1.22
Yield (%)	0.00	0.00	0.00	0.00	0.00	0.00	0.00	0.00	0.00	0.00
Portfolio Turnover (%)	119	50	70	57	100	125	160	435	341	366
Total Assets (Millions $)	2,687	2,921	3,932	2,214	5,106	6,350	6,781	2,723	2,302	1,565

PORTFOLIO (as of 8/31/05)

Portfolio Manager: James Morrow - 2004

Investment Style
- Large Cap   Growth
- Mid Cap   Value
- Small Cap   Grth/Val

Portfolio

2.0% cash	0.0% corp bonds
97.9% stocks	0.0% gov't bonds
0.0% pref/conv't pref	0.0% muni bonds
0.1% conv't bds/wrnts	0.0% other

SHAREHOLDER INFORMATION

Minimum Investment
Initial: $2,500   Subsequent: $250

Minimum IRA Investment
Initial: $500   Subsequent: $250

Maximum Fees
Load: 0.75% redemption   12b-1: none
Other: redemption fee applies for 1 month

Services
✓ IRA
✓ Keogh
✓ Telephone Exchange

RS Information Age
(RSIFX)

Technology Sector

800-766-3863
www.rsim.com

PERFORMANCE

fund inception date: 11/15/95

	3yr Annual	5yr Annual	10yr Annual	Bull	Bear
Return (%)	29.3	-2.6	10.1	109.0	-76.8
Differ From Category (+/-)	10.2 high	5.9 high	1.7 abv av	36.8 high	-1.0 av

Standard Deviation	Category Risk Index	Beta
25.6%—high	1.24—high	2.07

	2005	2004	2003	2002	2001	2000	1999	1998	1997	1996
Return (%)	2.0	7.3	97.7	-48.0	-22.1	-35.0	126.2	52.2	6.1	26.7
Differ From Category (+/-)	-2.2	4.9	38.5	-5.9	8.1	-7.1	-7.5	-13.4	-3.0	-2.5
Return, Tax-Adjusted (%)	2.0	7.3	97.7	-48.0	-22.4	-37.5	121.8	52.2	5.3	25.8

PER SHARE DATA

	2005	2004	2003	2002	2001	2000	1999	1998	1997	1996
Dividends, Net Income ($)	0.00	0.00	0.00	0.00	0.00	0.00	0.00	0.00	0.00	0.00
Distrib'ns, Cap Gain ($)	0.00	0.00	0.00	0.00	0.29	4.33	3.89	0.00	0.44	0.27
Net Asset Value ($)	16.35	16.02	14.93	7.55	14.53	19.01	35.79	17.96	11.80	11.51
Expense Ratio (%)	na	1.64	1.57	1.74	1.67	1.54	1.68	1.74	1.82	2.03
Yield (%)	0.00	0.00	0.00	0.00	0.00	0.00	0.00	0.00	0.00	0.00
Portfolio Turnover (%)	na	143	194	219	318	185	182	224	369	452
Total Assets (Millions $)	90	133	242	50	125	202	355	158	119	106

PORTFOLIO (as of 9/30/05)

Portfolio Manager: Bishop/Laidley/Thacker - 2001

Investment Style

Large Cap	Growth
Mid Cap	Value
Small Cap	Grth/Val

Portfolio

2.8%	cash	0.0%	corp bonds
97.2%	stocks	0.0%	gov't bonds
0.0%	pref/conv't pref	0.0%	muni bonds
0.0%	conv't bds/wrnts	0.0%	other

SHAREHOLDER INFORMATION

Minimum Investment
Initial: $5,000   Subsequent: $1,000

Minimum IRA Investment
Initial: $1,000   Subsequent: $250

Maximum Fees
Load: none   12b-1: 0.25%
Other: none

Services
✔ IRA
  Keogh
✔ Telephone Exchange

RS Internet Age
(RIAFX)

Technology Sector

800-766-3863
www.rsim.com

	3yr Annual	5yr Annual	10yr Annual	Bull	Bear
Return (%)	33.3	3.5	na	132.2	-76.6
Differ From Category (+/-)	14.2 high	12.0 high	na	60.0 high	-0.8 abv av

Standard Deviation	Category Risk Index	Beta
25.9%—high	1.25—high	2.08

	2005	2004	2003	2002	2001	2000	1999	1998	1997	1996
Return (%)	7.9	9.2	101.2	-43.2	-11.7	-46.3	—	—	—	—
Differ From Category (+/-)	3.7	6.8	42.0	-1.1	18.5	-18.4	—	—	—	—
Return, Tax-Adjusted (%)	7.9	9.2	101.2	-43.2	-11.7	-46.3	—	—	—	—

PER SHARE DATA

	2005	2004	2003	2002	2001	2000	1999	1998	1997	1996
Dividends, Net Income ($)	0.00	0.00	0.00	0.00	0.00	0.00	—	—	—	—
Distrib'ns, Cap Gain ($)	0.00	0.00	0.00	0.00	0.00	0.00	—	—	—	—
Net Asset Value ($)	7.76	7.19	6.58	3.27	5.76	6.53	—	—	—	—
Expense Ratio (%)	na	1.72	1.82	2.08	1.78	1.76	—	—	—	—
Yield (%)	0.00	0.00	0.00	0.00	0.00	0.00	—	—	—	—
Portfolio Turnover (%)	na	139	208	203	315	238	—	—	—	—
Total Assets (Millions $)	86	107	126	36	69	100	—	—	—	—

PORTFOLIO (as of 9/30/05)

Portfolio Manager: Bishop/Laidley/Thacker - 1999

Investment Style

Large Cap	Growth
Mid Cap	Value
Small Cap	Grth/Val

Portfolio

0.2% cash	0.0% corp bonds
99.8% stocks	0.0% gov't bonds
0.0% pref/conv't pref	0.0% muni bonds
0.0% conv't bds/wrnts	0.0% other

SHAREHOLDER INFORMATION

Minimum Investment
Initial: $5,000   Subsequent: $1,000

Minimum IRA Investment
Initial: $1,000   Subsequent: $250

Maximum Fees
Load: none   12b-1: 0.25%
Other: none

Services
✓ IRA
  Keogh
✓ Telephone Exchange

T Rowe Price Glbl Technology (PRGTX)

Technology Sector

800-638-5660
www.troweprice.com

PERFORMANCE

fund inception date: 9/29/00

	3yr Annual	5yr Annual	10yr Annual	Bull	Bear
Return (%)	22.3	-3.9	na	87.0	na
Differ From Category (+/-)	3.2 high	4.6 abv av	na	14.8 abv av	na

Standard Deviation	Category Risk Index	Beta
15.7%—high	0.76—low	1.42

	2005	2004	2003	2002	2001	2000	1999	1998	1997	1996
Return (%)	10.9	10.2	49.8	-29.8	-36.0	—	—	—	—	—
Differ From Category (+/-)	.6.7	7.8	-9.4	12.3	-5.8	—	—	—	—	—
Return, Tax-Adjusted (%)	10.9	10.2	49.8	-29.8	-36.0	—	—	—	—	—

PER SHARE DATA

	2005	2004	2003	2002	2001	2000	1999	1998	1997	1996
Dividends, Net Income ($)	0.00	0.00	0.00	0.00	0.00	—	—	—	—	—
Distrib'ns, Cap Gain ($)	0.00	0.00	0.00	0.00	0.00	—	—	—	—	—
Net Asset Value ($)	6.10	5.50	4.99	3.33	4.75	—	—	—	—	—
Expense Ratio (%)	na	1.50	1.50	1.50	1.50	—	—	—	—	—
Yield (%)	0.00	0.00	0.00	0.00	0.00	—	—	—	—	—
Portfolio Turnover (%)	na	137	151	211	189	—	—	—	—	—
Total Assets (Millions $)	117	92	85	55	84	—	—	—	—	—

PORTFOLIO (as of 9/30/05)

Portfolio Manager: R Gensler/Team Managed 2002

Investment Style

Large Cap	Growth
Mid Cap	Value
Small Cap	Grth/Val

Portfolio

0.0% cash	0.0% corp bonds
100.0% stocks	0.0% gov't bonds
0.0% pref/conv't pref	0.0% muni bonds
0.0% conv't bds/wrnts	0.0% other

SHAREHOLDER INFORMATION

Minimum Investment
Initial: $2,500   Subsequent: $100

Minimum IRA Investment
Initial: $1,000   Subsequent: $50

Maximum Fees
Load: none   12b-1: none
Other: none

Services
✔ IRA
✔ Keogh
✔ Telephone Exchange

Telecommunications Sector Stock Funds
Category Performance Ranked by 2005 Returns

Fund (Ticker)	Annual Return (%)				Category Risk	Total Risk
	2005	3Yr	5Yr	10Yr		
T Rowe Price Media & Telecomm (PRMTX)	18.1	32.5	9.1	na	blw av	abv av
Fidelity Select Wireless (FWRLX)	17.3	41.1	-3.9	na	abv av	high
Fidelity Select Developing Communications (FSDCX)	3.5	26.5	-7.6	7.9	high	high
Gabelli Global Telecommunications AAA (GABTX)	2.8	21.8	0.2	10.3	low	abv av
Telecommunications Sector Category Average	**9.3**	**27.5**	**-1.4**	**6.5**	**av**	**high**

Fidelity Select Developing Communications (FSDCX)

800-544-8544
www.fidelity.com

Telecommunications Sector

PERFORMANCE

fund inception date: 6/29/90

	3yr Annual	5yr Annual	10yr Annual	Bull	Bear
Return (%)	26.5	-7.6	7.9	99.4	-81.2
Differ From Category (+/-)	-1.0 abv av	-6.2 blw av	1.4 abv av	-7.5 abv av	-8.7 av

Standard Deviation	Category Risk Index	Beta
23.6%—high	1.44—high	1.86

	2005	2004	2003	2002	2001	2000	1999	1998	1997	1996
Return (%)	3.5	16.5	68.0	-47.7	-36.1	-29.7	122.5	67.6	6.0	14.5
Differ From Category (+/-)	-5.8	-5.4	17.1	-6.9	-6.3	2.3	1.3	26.7	-10.7	-6.3
Return, Tax-Adjusted (%)	3.5	16.5	68.0	-47.7	-36.1	-34.6	120.4	67.6	1.9	14.5

PER SHARE DATA

	2005	2004	2003	2002	2001	2000	1999	1998	1997	1996
Dividends, Net Income ($)	0.00	0.00	0.00	0.00	0.00	0.00	0.00	0.00	0.00	0.00
Distrib'ns, Cap Gain ($)	0.00	0.00	0.00	0.00	0.00	15.45	3.07	0.07	4.35	0.00
Net Asset Value ($)	20.01	19.33	16.59	9.87	18.90	29.59	62.88	30.08	18.00	21.26
Expense Ratio (%)	1.07	1.23	1.58	1.22	0.98	1.11	1.34	1.61	1.64	1.51
Yield (%)	0.00	0.00	0.00	0.00	0.00	0.00	0.00	0.00	0.00	0.00
Portfolio Turnover (%)	226	205	111	198	368	112	299	383	202	249
Total Assets (Millions $)	438	782	606	321	788	1,677	2,261	445	204	275

PORTFOLIO (as of 8/31/05)

Portfolio Manager: Charlie Chai - 2003

Investment Style
Large Cap   Growth
Mid Cap   Value
Small Cap   Grth/Val

Portfolio
0.0% cash   0.0% corp bonds
100.0% stocks   0.0% gov't bonds
0.0% pref/conv't pref 0.0% muni bonds
0.0% conv't bds/wrnts 0.0% other

SHAREHOLDER INFORMATION

Minimum Investment
Initial: $2,500   Subsequent: $250

Minimum IRA Investment
Initial: $500   Subsequent: $250

Maximum Fees
Load: 0.75% redemption   12b-1: none
Other: redemption fee applies for 1 month

Services
✔ IRA
✔ Keogh
✔ Telephone Exchange

Fidelity Select Wireless
(FWRLX)

Telecommunications Sector

800-544-8544
www.fidelity.com

PERFORMANCE

fund inception date: 9/21/00

	3yr Annual	5yr Annual	10yr Annual	Bull	Bear
Return (%)	41.1	-3.9	na	182.4	na
Differ From Category (+/-)	13.6 high	-2.5 abv av	na	75.5 high	na

Standard Deviation	Category Risk Index	Beta
17.2%—high	1.05—abv av	1.52

	2005	2004	2003	2002	2001	2000	1999	1998	1997	1996
Return (%).	17.3	42.5	68.3	-55.2	-34.7	—	—	—	—	—
Differ From Category (+/-)	.8.0	20.6	17.4	-14.4	-4.9	—	—	—	—	—
Return, Tax-Adjusted (%). .	17.3	42.5	68.3	-55.2	-34.7	—	—	—	—	—

PER SHARE DATA

	2005	2004	2003	2002	2001	2000	1999	1998	1997	1996
Dividends, Net Income ($).	0.00	0.00	0.00	0.00	0.00	—	—	—	—	—
Distrib'ns, Cap Gain ($) . . .	0.00	0.00	0.00	0.00	0.00	—	—	—	—	—
Net Asset Value ($)	6.84	5.83	4.09	2.43	5.43	—	—	—	—	—
Expense Ratio (%).	1.04	1.43	2.01	1.54	1.48	—	—	—	—	—
Yield (%)	0.00	0.00	0.00	0.00	0.00	—	—	—	—	—
Portfolio Turnover (%)	96	79	110	148	153	—	—	—	—	—
Total Assets (Millions $) . . .	475	489	150	56	116	—	—	—	—	—

PORTFOLIO (as of 8/31/05)

Portfolio Manager: Brian Younger - 2000

Investment Style

Large Cap	Growth
Mid Cap	Value
Small Cap	Grth/Val

Portfolio

0.8% cash	0.0% corp bonds
99.2% stocks	0.0% gov't bonds
0.0% pref/conv't pref	0.0% muni bonds
0.0% conv't bds/wrnts	0.0% other

SHAREHOLDER INFORMATION

Minimum Investment
Initial: $2,500   Subsequent: $250

Minimum IRA Investment
Initial: $500   Subsequent: $250

Maximum Fees
Load: 0.75% redemption   12b-1: none
Other: redemption fee applies for 1 month

Services
✔ IRA
✔ Keogh
✔ Telephone Exchange

Gabelli Global Telecommunications AAA (GABTX)

800-422-3554
www.gabelli.com

Telecommunications Sector

PERFORMANCE
fund inception date: 11/1/93

	3yr Annual	5yr Annual	10yr Annual	Bull	Bear
Return (%)	21.8	0.2	10.3	83.6	-60.1
Differ From Category (+/-)	-5.7 av	1.6 high	3.8 high	-23.3 av	12.4 high

Standard Deviation	Category Risk Index		Beta
12.1%—abv av	0.74—low		1.15

	2005	2004	2003	2002	2001	2000	1999	1998	1997	1996
Return (%)	2.8	23.3	42.7	-29.5	-20.7	-24.0	80.2	34.7	31.8	8.9
Differ From Category (+/-)	-6.5	1.4	-8.2	11.3	9.1	8.0	-41.0	-6.2	15.1	-11.9
Return, Tax-Adjusted (%)	2.6	23.2	42.7	-29.5	-20.7	-26.6	76.6	32.7	29.1	6.8

PER SHARE DATA

	2005	2004	2003	2002	2001	2000	1999	1998	1997	1996
Dividends, Net Income ($)	0.19	0.08	0.00	0.00	0.00	0.63	0.05	0.01	0.00	0.05
Distrib'ns, Cap Gain ($)	0.00	0.00	0.00	0.00	0.02	2.15	2.90	1.30	1.55	0.79
Net Asset Value ($)	17.53	17.23	14.03	9.83	13.96	17.63	26.95	16.62	13.32	11.28
Expense Ratio (%)	na	1.62	1.62	1.66	1.52	1.46	1.48	1.60	1.78	1.72
Yield (%)	1.08	0.45	0.00	0.00	0.00	3.18	0.15	0.06	0.00	0.38
Portfolio Turnover (%)	na	15	11	8	15	49	60	20	9	7
Total Assets (Millions $)	195	209	186	139	234	332	459	170	118	109

PORTFOLIO (as of 9/30/05)

Portfolio Manager: Mario Gabelli/
Team Managed - 1993

Investment Style

Large Cap	Growth
Mid Cap	Value
Small Cap	Grth/Val

Portfolio

0.0% cash	0.0% corp bonds
99.2% stocks	0.8% gov't bonds
0.0% pref/conv't pref	0.0% muni bonds
0.0% conv't bds/wrnts	0.0% other

SHAREHOLDER INFORMATION

Minimum Investment
Initial: $1,000   Subsequent: $1

Minimum IRA Investment
Initial: $250   Subsequent: $1

Maximum Fees
Load: none   12b-1: 0.25%
Other: none

Services
✔ IRA
　 Keogh
✔ Telephone Exchange

Individual Fund Listings   281

T Rowe Price Media & Telecommunications (PRMTX)

800-638-5660
www.troweprice.com

Telecommunications Sector

PERFORMANCE

fund inception date: 7/28/97

	3yr Annual	5yr Annual	10yr Annual	Bull	Bear
Return (%)	32.5	9.1	na	141.2	-56.1
Differ From Category (+/-)	5.0 high	10.5 high	na	34.3 high	16.4 high

Standard Deviation	Category Risk Index	Beta
14.0%—abv av	0.85—blw av	1.41

	2005	2004	2003	2002	2001	2000	1999	1998	1997	1996
Return (%)	18.1	26.3	55.9	-28.3	-6.9	-25.1	93.0	35.1	—	—
Differ From Category (+/-)	.8.8	4.4	5.0	12.5	22.9	6.9	-28.2	-5.8	—	—
Return, Tax-Adjusted (%)	18.1	26.3	55.9	-28.3	-6.9	-29.7	90.2	34.1	—	—

PER SHARE DATA

	2005	2004	2003	2002	2001	2000	1999	1998	1997	1996
Dividends, Net Income ($)	0.00	0.00	0.00	0.00	0.00	0.37	0.00	0.00	—	—
Distrib'ns, Cap Gain ($)	0.00	0.00	0.00	0.00	0.00	8.60	3.22	0.86	—	—
Net Asset Value ($)	33.59	28.43	22.51	14.43	20.15	21.65	39.99	22.54	—	—
Expense Ratio (%)	na	0.96	1.10	1.15	1.08	0.94	0.93	1.03	—	—
Yield (%)	0.00	0.00	0.00	0.00	0.00	1.22	0.00	0.00	—	—
Portfolio Turnover (%)	na	108	124	184	241	197	58	49	—	—
Total Assets (Millions $)	1,009	876	665	421	675	798	930	246	—	—

PORTFOLIO (as of 9/30/05)

Portfolio Manager: R Gensler/Team Managed - 2000

Investment Style

Large Cap	Growth
Mid Cap	Value
Small Cap	Grth/Val

Portfolio

0.0%	cash	0.0%	corp bonds
100.0%	stocks	0.0%	gov't bonds
0.0%	pref/conv't pref	0.0%	muni bonds
0.0%	conv't bds/wrnts	0.0%	other

SHAREHOLDER INFORMATION

Minimum Investment
Initial: $2,500   Subsequent: $100

Minimum IRA Investment
Initial: $1,000   Subsequent: $50

Maximum Fees
Load: none   12b-1: none
Other: none

Services
✔ IRA
✔ Keogh
✔ Telephone Exchange

Utilities Sector Stock Funds
Category Performance Ranked by 2005 Returns

Fund (Ticker)	Annual Return (%)				Category Risk	Total Risk
	2005	3Yr	5Yr	10Yr		
Amer Century Utilities Inv (BULIX)	14.3	20.6	0.1	7.7	low	av
FBR Gas Utility Index (GASFX)	13.5	19.9	2.2	10.2	abv av	av
Fidelity Utilities (FIUIX)	9.9	17.1	0.0	6.6	av	av
Fidelity Select Utilities Growth (FSUTX)	9.3	19.7	-1.4	7.7	high	abv av
Utilities Sector Category Average	13.1	18.7	-0.2	7.8	av	av

Amer Century Utilities Inv
(BULIX)
Utilities Sector

800-345-2021
www.americancentury.com

PERFORMANCE

fund inception date: 3/1/93

	3yr Annual	5yr Annual	10yr Annual	Bull	Bear
Return (%)	20.6	0.1	7.7	84.9	-46.8
Differ From Category (+/-)	1.9 high	0.3 abv av	-0.1 abv av	4.0 abv av	-3.1 av

Standard Deviation	Category Risk Index	Beta
10.0%—av	0.91—low	0.72

	2005	2004	2003	2002	2001	2000	1999	1998	1997	1996
Return (%).	14.3	23.8	23.9	-27.4	-20.9	3.9	11.4	27.4	35.8	4.8
Differ From Category (+/-)	.1.2	2.2	2.0	-1.8	-1.0	-4.9	-3.9	3.5	6.7	-7.6
Return, Tax-Adjusted (%) . .	13.8	23.3	23.5	-28.3	-21.6	0.5	9.4	24.0	32.9	3.2

PER SHARE DATA

	2005	2004	2003	2002	2001	2000	1999	1998	1997	1996
Dividends, Net Income ($) .	0.40	0.29	0.25	0.27	0.25	0.98	0.35	0.38	0.42	0.46
Distrib'ns, Cap Gain ($) . . .	0.00	0.00	0.00	0.00	0.02	0.83	0.93	1.66	0.85	0.00
Net Asset Value ($) . . . : .	13.40	12.08	10.02	8.31	11.81	15.26	16.46	15.96	14.24	11.51
Expense Ratio (%)	na	0.68	0.69	0.69	0.68	0.67	0.68	0.69	0.72	0.71
Yield (%)	2.97	2.38	2.53	3.25	2.10	6.09	1.99	2.13	2.78	3.96
Portfolio Turnover (%)	na	31	34	26	10	32	50	98	92	93
Total Assets (Millions $) . . .	293	194	144	119	200	296	319	307	207	145

PORTFOLIO (as of 9/30/05)

Portfolio Manager: Team Managed - 1996

Investment Style

Large Cap	Growth
Mid Cap	Value
Small Cap	Grth/Val

Portfolio

2.9%	cash	0.0%	corp bonds
97.1%	stocks	0.0%	gov't bonds
0.0%	pref/conv't pref	0.0%	muni bonds
0.0%	conv't bds/wrnts	0.0%	other

SHAREHOLDER INFORMATION

Minimum Investment
Initial: $2,500   Subsequent: $50

Minimum IRA Investment
Initial: $2,500   Subsequent: $50

Maximum Fees
Load: none   12b-1: none
Other: none

Services
✔ IRA
✔ Keogh
✔ Telephone Exchange

FBR Gas Utility Index

(GASFX)

Utilities Sector

888-888-0025
www.fbrfunds.com

	3yr Annual	5yr Annual	10yr Annual	Bull	Bear
Return (%)	19.9	2.2	10.2	88.7	-16.8
Differ From Category (+/-)	1.2 high	2.4 high	2.4 high	7.8 high	26.9 high

Standard Deviation	Category Risk Index	Beta
11.2%—av	1.02—abv av	0.77

	2005	2004	2003	2002	2001	2000	1999	1998	1997	1996
Return (%).	13.5	23.0	23.4	-23.9	-14.7	55.8	-3.7	5.2	24.1	20.7
Differ From Category (+/-)	.0.4	1.4	1.5	1.7	5.2	47.0	-19.1	-18.7	-5.0	8.3
Return, Tax-Adjusted (%). .	13.0	22.5	22.9	-25.0	-17.7	51.2	-6.4	3.4	22.8	19.3

PER SHARE DATA

	2005	2004	2003	2002	2001	2000	1999	1998	1997	1996
Dividends, Net Income ($).	0.53	0.40	0.37	0.44	0.51	0.52	0.51	0.51	0.46	0.45
Distrib'ns, Cap Gain ($) . .	0.00	0.00	0.00	0.00	2.03	2.51	1.42	0.68	0.12	0.00
Net Asset Value ($)	17.33	15.74	13.16	10.99	14.97	20.67	15.37	17.98	18.25	15.22
Expense Ratio (%).	na	0.85	0.85	0.85	0.85	0.85	0.85	0.85	0.85	0.85
Yield (%)	3.06	2.55	2.80	4.01	3.02	2.22	3.05	2.71	2.50	2.95
Portfolio Turnover (%)	na	34	39	29	38	16	10	12	8	10
Total Assets (Millions $) . . .	286	239	212	159	229	318	184	230	246	229

PORTFOLIO (as of 11/30/05)

Portfolio Manager: Team Managed - 1989

Investment Style

Large Cap	Growth
Mid Cap	Value
Small Cap	Grth/Val

Portfolio

0.9% cash	0.0% corp bonds
99.1% stocks	0.0% gov't bonds
0.0% pref/conv't pref	0.0% muni bonds
0.0% conv't bds/wrnts	0.0% other

SHAREHOLDER INFORMATION

Minimum Investment
Initial: $2,000   Subsequent: $100

Minimum IRA Investment
Initial: $1,000   Subsequent: $100

Maximum Fees
Load: 1.00% redemption   12b-1: none
Other: redemption fee applies for 3 months

Services
✔ IRA
✔ Keogh
✔ Telephone Exchange

Fidelity Select Utilities Growth (FSUTX)

Utilities Sector

800-544-8544
www.fidelity.com

PERFORMANCE

fund inception date: 12/10/81

	3yr Annual	5yr Annual	10yr Annual	Bull	Bear
Return (%)	19.7	-1.4	7.7	85.4	-61.3
Differ From Category (+/-)	1.0 av	-1.2 blw av	-0.1 av	4.5 high	-17.6 low

Standard Deviation	Category Risk Index	Beta
11.9%—abv av	1.08—high	0.98

	2005	2004	2003	2002	2001	2000	1999	1998	1997	1996
Return (%)	9.3	24.2	26.4	-30.4	-21.8	-13.5	25.9	43.1	30.3	11.3
Differ From Category (+/-)	-3.8	2.6	4.5	-4.7	-1.9	-22.4	10.6	19.2	1.2	-1.1
Return, Tax-Adjusted (%)	9.0	23.9	26.1	-30.8	-22.4	-16.1	22.5	39.7	26.4	8.4

PER SHARE DATA

	2005	2004	2003	2002	2001	2000	1999	1998	1997	1996
Dividends, Net Income ($)	0.93	0.62	0.40	0.48	0.26	1.97	0.42	0.25	0.58	0.70
Distrib'ns, Cap Gain ($)	0.00	0.00	0.00	0.00	0.93	4.85	9.30	7.93	7.30	3.54
Net Asset Value ($)	43.10	40.26	32.94	26.40	38.59	50.80	66.10	60.94	48.88	43.90
Expense Ratio (%)	1.02	1.19	1.17	1.09	0.99	1.04	1.16	1.33	1.47	1.38
Yield (%)	2.15	1.53	1.21	1.81	0.65	3.53	0.55	0.36	1.03	1.47
Portfolio Turnover (%)	51	76	139	54	80	93	113	78	31	65
Total Assets (Millions $)	276	345	207	183	320	539	626	504	359	256

PORTFOLIO (as of 8/31/05)

Portfolio Manager: Brian Younger - 2002

Investment Style
Large Cap	Growth
Mid Cap	Value
Small Cap	Grth/Val

Portfolio
2.0%	cash	0.0%	corp bonds
98.0%	stocks	0.0%	gov't bonds
0.0%	pref/conv't pref	0.0%	muni bonds
0.0%	conv't bds/wrnts	0.0%	other

SHAREHOLDER INFORMATION

Minimum Investment
Initial: $2,500   Subsequent: $250

Minimum IRA Investment
Initial: $500   Subsequent: $250

Maximum Fees
Load: 0.75% redemption   12b-1: none
Other: redemption fee applies for 1 month

Services
✔ IRA
✔ Keogh
✔ Telephone Exchange

Fidelity Utilities
(FIUIX)

Utilities Sector

800-544-8544
www.fidelity.com

PERFORMANCE **fund inception date: 11/27/87**

	3yr Annual	5yr Annual	10yr Annual	Bull	Bear
Return (%)	17.1	0.0	6.6	70.9	-58.1
Differ From Category (+/-)	-1.6 blw av	0.2 av	-1.2 low	-10.0 low	-14.4 blw av

Standard Deviation	Category Risk Index	Beta
10.9%—av	0.99—av	0.86

	2005	2004	2003	2002	2001	2000	1999	1998	1997	1996
Return (%)	9.9	21.1	20.8	-26.6	-15.1	-20.4	26.7	28.5	31.6	11.4
Differ From Category (+/-)	-3.2	-0.5	-1.1	-1.0	4.8	-29.3	11.4	4.6	2.5	-1.0
Return, Tax-Adjusted (%)	9.6	20.7	20.5	-27.2	-15.5	-24.2	23.8	26.5	27.9	9.3

PER SHARE DATA

	2005	2004	2003	2002	2001	2000	1999	1998	1997	1996
Dividends, Net Income ($)	0.26	0.29	0.22	0.20	0.16	0.09	0.18	0.35	0.44	0.48
Distrib'ns, Cap Gain ($)	0.00	0.00	0.00	0.00	0.00	4.73	3.05	1.29	2.20	0.54
Net Asset Value ($)	14.67	13.59	11.48	9.70	13.49	16.09	25.77	23.18	19.46	16.91
Expense Ratio (%)	0.89	0.73	0.95	0.89	0.78	0.80	0.85	0.85	0.81	0.77
Yield (%)	1.77	2.13	1.91	2.06	1.18	0.43	0.62	1.43	2.03	2.75
Portfolio Turnover (%)	57	21	32	58	126	50	55	57	56	98
Total Assets (Millions $)	1,014	962	857	820	1,427	2,125	2,885	2,128	1,709	1,268

PORTFOLIO (as of 7/29/05)

Portfolio Manager: Douglas Simmons - 2005

Investment Style

Large Cap	Growth
Mid Cap	Value
Small Cap	Grth/Val

Portfolio

1.6%	cash	0.0%	corp bonds
98.4%	stocks	0.0%	gov't bonds
0.0%	pref/conv't pref	0.0%	muni bonds
0.0%	conv't bds/wrnts	0.0%	other

SHAREHOLDER INFORMATION

Minimum Investment
Initial: $2,500   Subsequent: $250

Minimum IRA Investment
Initial: $500   Subsequent: $250

Maximum Fees
Load: none   12b-1: none
Other: maint fee for low bal

Services
✔ IRA
✔ Keogh
✔ Telephone Exchange

INTERNATIONAL STOCK FUNDS

Global Stock Funds
Category Performance Ranked by 2005 Returns

Fund (Ticker)	Annual Return (%)				Category Risk	Total Risk
	2005	3Yr	5Yr	10Yr		
T Rowe Price Global Stock (PRGSX)	22.7	22.2	4.1	9.2	abv av	av
UMB Scout Worldwide (UMBWX)	19.5	23.3	7.0	10.8	av	av
Amer Century Global Growth Inv (TWGGX)	18.1	22.2	1.6	na	abv av	av
Gabelli Global Growth AAA (GICPX)	13.7	20.7	0.0	10.7	high	abv av
Fidelity Worldwide (FWWFX)	13.5	20.8	6.0	8.7	high	av
Vanguard Global Equity (VHGEX)	11.7	24.7	12.0	11.6	high	av
Global Stock Category Average	**11.6**	**18.5**	**4.8**	**8.8**	**av**	**av**

Amer Century Global Growth Inv (TWGGX)

800-345-2021
www.americancentury.com

Global Stock

fund inception date: 12/1/98

PERFORMANCE

	3yr Annual	5yr Annual	10yr Annual	Bull	Bear
Return (%)	22.2	1.6	na	91.1	-51.9
Differ From Category (+/-)	3.7 abv av	-3.2 blw av	na	14.8 abv av	-21.0 blw av

Standard Deviation	Category Risk Index	Beta
11.1%—av	1.10—abv av	1.10

	2005	2004	2003	2002	2001	2000	1999	1998	1997	1996
Return (%)	18.1	15.1	34.5	-20.2	-25.6	-5.7	86.0	—	—	—
Differ From Category (+/-)	.6.5	1.7	2.9	-7.0	-14.7	0.7	44.4	—	—	—
Return, Tax-Adjusted (%)	.17.7	15.0	34.5	-20.2	-25.6	-7.2	85.1	—	—	—

PER SHARE DATA

	2005	2004	2003	2002	2001	2000	1999	1998	1997	1996
Dividends, Net Income ($)	0.07	0.01	0.00	0.00	0.00	0.00	0.00	—	—	—
Distrib'ns, Cap Gain ($)	0.00	0.00	0.00	0.00	0.00	0.75	0.26	—	—	—
Net Asset Value ($)	9.13	7.79	6.78	5.04	6.32	8.50	9.81	—	—	—
Expense Ratio (%)	na	1.30	1.31	1.32	1.30	1.30	1.30	—	—	—
Yield (%)	0.76	0.17	0.00	0.00	0.00	0.00	0.00	—	—	—
Portfolio Turnover (%)	na	79	152	278	232	123	133	—	—	—
Total Assets (Millions $)	394	312	262	201	275	452	318	—	—	—

PORTFOLIO (as of 9/30/05)

Portfolio Manager: Matthew Hudson - 2002

Investment Style

Large Cap	Growth
Mid Cap	Value
Small Cap	Grth/Val

Portfolio

1.0% cash	0.0% corp bonds
99.0% stocks	0.0% gov't bonds
0.0% pref/conv't pref	0.0% muni bonds
0.0% conv't bds/wrnts	0.0% other

SHAREHOLDER INFORMATION

Minimum Investment
Initial: $2,500   Subsequent: $50

Minimum IRA Investment
Initial: $2,500   Subsequent: $50

Maximum Fees
Load: 2.00% redemption   12b-1: none
Other: redemption fee applies for 2 months

Services
✔ IRA
✔ Keogh
✔ Telephone Exchange

Fidelity Worldwide
(FWWFX)

Global Stock

800-544-8544
www.fidelity.com

PERFORMANCE

fund inception date: 5/30/90

	3yr Annual	5yr Annual	10yr Annual	Bull	Bear
Return (%)	20.8	6.0	8.7	86.3	-35.2
Differ From Category (+/-)	2.3 abv av	1.2 abv av	-0.1 av	10.0 av	-4.3 av

Standard Deviation	Category Risk Index	Beta
11.3%—av	1.12—high	1.16

	2005	2004	2003	2002	2001	2000	1999	1998	1997	1996
Return (%).............	13.5	12.2	38.4	-18.8	-6.2	-8.0	30.8	7.1	12.0	18.7
Differ From Category (+/-)	.1.9	-1.2	6.8	-5.6	4.7	-1.6	-10.8	-7.2	-5.1	1.9
Return, Tax-Adjusted (%)..	12.5	12.0	38.2	-18.8	-6.2	-11.0	28.7	6.3	10.2	17.4

PER SHARE DATA

	2005	2004	2003	2002	2001	2000	1999	1998	1997	1996
Dividends, Net Income ($).	0.10	0.10	0.07	0.02	0.00	0.40	0.10	0.10	0.11	0.17
Distrib'ns, Cap Gain ($) ...	1.04	0.02	0.00	0.00	0.00	2.25	1.52	0.44	1.16	0.38
Net Asset Value ($)	19.57	18.25	16.37	11.88	14.66	15.63	19.90	16.53	15.95	15.39
Expense Ratio (%)........	na	1.28	1.28	1.20	1.05	1.04	1.07	1.12	1.16	1.18
Yield (%)	0.48	0.54	0.42	0.16	0.00	2.23	0.46	0.58	0.64	1.07
Portfolio Turnover (%)	na	106	106	120	152	235	164	100	85	49
Total Assets (Millions $)..	1,278	1,169	957	642	807	928	1,125	1,014	1,145	926

PORTFOLIO (as of 7/29/05)

Portfolio Manager: Richard Mace - 2002

Investment Style

Large Cap	Growth
Mid Cap	Value
Small Cap	Grth/Val

Portfolio

0.9% cash	0.0% corp bonds
99.1% stocks	0.0% gov't bonds
0.0% pref/conv't pref	0.0% muni bonds
0.0% conv't bds/wrnts	0.0% other

SHAREHOLDER INFORMATION

Minimum Investment
Initial: $2,500   Subsequent: $250

Minimum IRA Investment
Initial: $500   Subsequent: $250

Maximum Fees
Load: 1.00% redemption   12b-1: none
Other: redemption fee applies for 1 month;
maint fee for low bal

Services
✔ IRA
✔ Keogh
✔ Telephone Exchange

Gabelli Global Growth AAA (GICPX)

800-422-3554
www.gabelli.com

Global Stock

PERFORMANCE

fund inception date: 2/7/94

	3yr Annual	5yr Annual	10yr Annual	Bull	Bear
Return (%)	20.7	0.0	10.7	83.0	-66.8
Differ From Category (+/-)	2.2 av	-4.8 blw av	1.9 abv av	6.7 av	-35.9 low

Standard Deviation	Category Risk Index	Beta
11.8%—abv av	1.17—high	1.10

	2005	2004	2003	2002	2001	2000	1999	1998	1997	1996
Return (%)	13.7	9.4	41.3	-24.7	-24.1	-37.4	116.0	28.9	41.7	12.5
Differ From Category (+/-)	.2.1	-4.0	9.7	-11.5	-13.2	-31.0	74.4	14.6	24.6	-4.3
Return, Tax-Adjusted (%)	13.6	9.4	41.3	-24.7	-24.1	-38.3	114.3	26.8	37.6	9.0

PER SHARE DATA

	2005	2004	2003	2002	2001	2000	1999	1998	1997	1996
Dividends, Net Income ($)	0.02	0.00	0.00	0.00	0.00	0.00	0.00	0.11	0.00	0.00
Distrib'ns, Cap Gain ($)	0.00	0.00	0.00	0.00	0.00	1.59	1.46	1.27	2.37	1.44
Net Asset Value ($)	20.43	17.98	16.43	11.62	15.45	20.37	35.17	16.99	14.28	11.75
Expense Ratio (%)	na	1.82	1.71	1.75	1.75	1.60	1.58	1.66	1.78	2.06
Yield (%)	0.08	0.00	0.00	0.00	0.00	0.00	0.00	0.60	0.00	0.00
Portfolio Turnover (%)	na	100	63	82	102	93	63	105	68	47
Total Assets (Millions $)	106	114	133	105	182	285	446	74	41	32

PORTFOLIO (as of 9/30/05)

Portfolio Manager: Team Managed - 1994

Investment Style

Large Cap	Growth
Mid Cap	Value
Small Cap	Grth/Val

Portfolio

0.0% cash	0.0% corp bonds
98.9% stocks	1.1% gov't bonds
0.0% pref/conv't pref	0.0% muni bonds
0.0% conv't bds/wrnts	0.0% other

SHAREHOLDER INFORMATION

Minimum Investment
Initial: $1,000   Subsequent: $1

Minimum IRA Investment
Initial: $250   Subsequent: $1

Maximum Fees
Load: none   12b-1: 0.25%
Other: none

Services
✔ IRA
Keogh
✔ Telephone Exchange

T Rowe Price Global Stock

(PRGSX)

Global Stock

800-638-5660
www.troweprice.com

PERFORMANCE

fund inception date: 12/28/95

	3yr Annual	5yr Annual	10yr Annual	Bull	Bear
Return (%)	22.2	4.1	9.2	92.4	-43.6
Differ From Category (+/-)	3.7 abv av	-0.7 av	0.4 abv av	16.1 abv av	-12.7 blw av

Standard Deviation	Category Risk Index	Beta
10.5%—av	1.04—abv av	1.05

	2005	2004	2003	2002	2001	2000	1999	1998	1997	1996
Return (%)..............	22.7	14.4	30.0	-20.7	-15.3	-7.9	28.7	22.5	13.2	20.0
Differ From Category (+/-)	11.1	1.0	-1.6	-7.5	-4.4	-1.5	-12.9	8.2	-3.9	3.2
Return, Tax-Adjusted (%) ..	22.3	14.2	29.9	-20.8	-15.6	-8.8	27.9	21.4	12.1	19.2

PER SHARE DATA

	2005	2004	2003	2002	2001	2000	1999	1998	1997	1996
Dividends, Net Income ($).	0.02	0.08	0.04	0.03	0.12	0.02	0.06	0.10	0.06	0.06
Distrib'ns, Cap Gain ($) ...	0.32	0.00	0.01	0.00	0.00	0.79	0.49	0.45	0.54	0.18
Net Asset Value ($)	19.37	16.06	14.11	10.89	13.78	16.43	18.72	15.00	12.72	11.76
Expense Ratio (%).........	na	1.00	1.20	1.20	1.20	1.20	1.20	1.20	1.30	1.30
Yield (%)	0.10	0.49	0.28	0.27	0.87	0.11	0.31	0.64	0.45	0.50
Portfolio Turnover (%)	na	72	39	48	52	72	47	47	42	50
Total Assets (Millions $) ...	150	86	82	63	77	99	90	49	34	17

PORTFOLIO (as of 9/30/05)

Portfolio Manager: D Tenerelli/R Smith - 1995

Investment Style

Large Cap	Growth
Mid Cap	Value
Small Cap	Grth/Val

Portfolio

0.0%	cash	0.0%	corp bonds
100.0%	stocks	0.0%	gov't bonds
0.0%	pref/conv't pref	0.0%	muni bonds
0.0%	conv't bds/wrnts	0.0%	other

SHAREHOLDER INFORMATION

Minimum Investment
Initial: $2,500   Subsequent: $100

Minimum IRA Investment
Initial: $1,000   Subsequent: $50

Maximum Fees
Load: 2.00% redemption   12b-1: none
Other: redemption fee applies for 3 months

Services
✔ IRA
✔ Keogh
✔ Telephone Exchange

UMB Scout Worldwide

(UMBWX)

Global Stock

800-996-2862
www.scoutfunds.com

PERFORMANCE

fund inception date: 9/14/93

	3yr Annual	5yr Annual	10yr Annual	Bull	Bear
Return (%)	23.3	7.0	10.8	96.2	-35.1
Differ From Category (+/-)	4.8 high	2.2 abv av	2.0 high	19.9 high	-4.2 av

Standard Deviation	Category Risk Index	Beta
10.4%—av	1.03—av	0.96

	2005	2004	2003	2002	2001	2000	1999	1998	1997	1996
Return (%)	19.5	18.0	33.1	-15.8	-11.0	-8.1	31.4	17.9	18.3	18.3
Differ From Category (+/-)	7.9	4.6	1.5	-2.6	0.0	-1.7	-10.2	3.6	1.2	1.5
Return, Tax-Adjusted (%)	19.0	17.7	32.7	-16.1	-11.4	-8.7	30.5	17.1	17.3	17.3

PER SHARE DATA

	2005	2004	2003	2002	2001	2000	1999	1998	1997	1996
Dividends, Net Income ($)	0.23	0.17	0.14	0.14	0.23	0.05	0.21	0.31	0.24	0.23
Distrib'ns, Cap Gain ($)	0.30	0.00	0.00	0.00	0.01	0.56	0.36	0.02	0.22	0.11
Net Asset Value ($)	28.26	24.10	20.58	15.58	18.67	21.24	23.77	18.56	16.02	13.94
Expense Ratio (%)	1.15	1.10	1.14	1.12	0.91	0.91	0.86	0.87	0.86	0.85
Yield (%)	0.79	0.70	0.66	0.87	1.22	0.22	0.88	1.69	1.49	1.64
Portfolio Turnover (%)	19	12	12	13	10	8	8	3	18	5
Total Assets (Millions $)	1,980	1,023	593	354	358	307	268	108	57	43

PORTFOLIO (as of 9/30/05)

Portfolio Manager: Moffett/Anderson/
Fogarty - 1993

Investment Style

Large Cap	Growth
Mid Cap	Value
Small Cap	Grth/Val

Portfolio

4.5% cash	0.0% corp bonds
91.9% stocks	0.0% gov't bonds
3.6% pref/conv't pref	0.0% muni bonds
0.0% conv't bds/wrnts	0.0% other

SHAREHOLDER INFORMATION

Minimum Investment
Initial: $1,000   Subsequent: $100

Minimum IRA Investment
Initial: $100   Subsequent: $100

Maximum Fees
Load: 2.00% redemption   12b-1: none
Other: redemption fee applies for 2 months

Services
✓ IRA
✓ Keogh
✓ Telephone Exchange

Vanguard Global Equity

(VHGEX)

Global Stock

800-662-7447
www.vanguard.com

PERFORMANCE   fund inception date: 8/14/95

	3yr Annual	5yr Annual	10yr Annual	Bull	Bear
Return (%)	24.7	12.0	11.6	100.3	-11.1
Differ From Category (+/-)	6.2 high	7.2 high	2.8 high	24.0 high	19.8 high

Standard Deviation	Category Risk Index	Beta
11.3%—av	1.12—high	1.07

	2005	2004	2003	2002	2001	2000	1999	1998	1997	1996
Return (%)............	11.7	20.0	44.5	-5.6	-3.7	-0.1	25.9	9.3	6.9	15.5
Differ From Category (+/-)	.0.1	6.6	12.9	7.6	7.2	6.3	-15.7	-5.0	-10.2	-1.3
Return, Tax-Adjusted (%)..	10.9	19.3	43.9	-5.9	-4.7	-2.5	23.9	7.2	5.3	14.5

PER SHARE DATA

	2005	2004	2003	2002	2001	2000	1999	1998	1997	1996
Dividends, Net Income ($)	0.24	0.21	0.13	0.08	0.12	0.26	0.18	0.26	0.23	0.14
Distrib'ns, Cap Gain ($) ...	0.44	0.27	0.07	0.02	0.44	1.17	0.84	0.75	0.44	0.19
Net Asset Value ($)	19.51	18.06	15.45	10.83	11.58	12.62	14.14	12.06	11.98	11.84
Expense Ratio (%)........	0.80	0.90	1.05	1.11	1.08	0.70	0.71	0.68	0.71	0.85
Yield (%)	1.20	1.14	0.83	0.73	0.99	1.88	1.20	2.02	1.85	1.16
Portfolio Turnover (%)	83	19	13	14	27	31	36	34	24	29
Total Assets (Millions $) ..	2,676	1,270	826	251	158	143	145	128	126	107

PORTFOLIO (as of 9/30/05)

Portfolio Manager: Jeremy Hosking - 1995

Investment Style

Large Cap	Growth
Mid Cap	Value
Small Cap	Grth/Val

Portfolio

5.2% cash	0.1% corp bonds
94.7% stocks	0.0% gov't bonds
0.0% pref/conv't pref	0.0% muni bonds
0.0% conv't bds/wrnts	0.0% other

SHAREHOLDER INFORMATION

Minimum Investment
Initial: $3,000   Subsequent: $100

Minimum IRA Investment
Initial: $3,000   Subsequent: $100

Maximum Fees
Load: none   12b-1: none
Other: none

Services
✔ IRA
✔ Keogh
✔ Telephone Exchange

Foreign Stock Funds
Category Performance Ranked by 2005 Returns

Fund (Ticker)	Annual Return (%)				Category Risk	Total Risk
	2005	3Yr	5Yr	10Yr		
Janus Overseas (JAOSX)	32.3	29.0	4.6	12.9	high	high
T Rowe Price Intl Discovery (PRIDX)	27.8	37.7	10.5	15.0	abv av	abv av
Thomas White International (TWWDX)	25.5	27.2	8.7	9.5	abv av	abv av
Neuberger Berman International Inv (NBISX)	23.9	32.2	10.5	11.2	av	abv av
Tocqueville International Value (TIVFX)	21.0	31.3	15.7	7.1	blw av	abv av
Bailard International Equity (BBIEX)	20.6	27.6	7.3	7.4	av	abv av
Laudus International MarketMasters Inv (SWOIX)	19.3	27.0	7.5	na	abv av	abv av
Fidelity Overseas (FOSFX)	19.2	25.0	4.6	7.5	abv av	abv av
ICAP International (ICEUX)	19.1	28.9	9.7	na	abv av	abv av
Fidelity International Discovery (FIGRX)	18.5	26.4	8.5	10.2	av	abv av
Vanguard International Value (VTRIX)	17.9	26.0	8.3	7.7	abv av	abv av
Excelsior International (UMINX)	17.6	26.7	2.9	5.6	abv av	abv av
SSgA International Stock Selection (SSAIX)	17.0	26.5	6.8	5.0	blw av	abv av
Dodge & Cox Intl Stock (DODFX)	16.7	32.2	na	na	high	abv av
T Rowe Price Intl Growth & Income (TRIGX)	15.7	25.7	7.6	na	low	abv av
Vanguard Total Intl Stock Index (VGTSX)	15.5	25.1	5.8	na	blw av	abv av
Vanguard International Growth (VWIGX)	14.9	22.5	4.1	7.0	blw av	abv av
Bernstein International Value II (SIMTX)	14.6	23.7	8.4	na	av	abv av
Vanguard Tax Managed International (VTMGX)	13.6	23.7	4.5	na	blw av	abv av
Vanguard Developing Markets Index (VDMIX)	13.3	23.6	4.4	na	blw av	abv av
Foreign Stock Category Average	**18.0**	**26.0**	**6.2**	**8.6**	**av**	**abv av**

Bailard International Equity (BBIEX)

800-882-8383
www.bailard.com

Foreign Stock

PERFORMANCE

fund inception date: 9/4/79

	3yr Annual	5yr Annual	10yr Annual	Bull	Bear
Return (%)	27.6	7.3	7.4	116.5	-47.0
Differ From Category (+/-)	1.6 abv av	1.1 abv av	-1.2 av	2.6 abv av	-2.6 av

Standard Deviation	Category Risk Index	Beta
12.0%—abv av	0.96—av	1.05

	2005	2004	2003	2002	2001	2000	1999	1998	1997	1996
Return (%)	20.6	19.7	43.8	-12.7	-21.5	-19.2	32.4	12.0	9.9	9.5
Differ From Category (+/-)	.2.6	0.1	1.9	1.6	-2.9	-6.1	-19.5	-1.4	6.2	-7.0
Return, Tax-Adjusted (%)	.19.4	19.3	43.4	-12.8	-21.5	-20.8	30.2	10.1	8.6	7.5

PER SHARE DATA

	2005	2004	2003	2002	2001	2000	1999	1998	1997	1996
Dividends, Net Income ($)	.0.15	0.05	0.05	0.02	0.00	0.01	0.02	0.06	0.13	0.05
Distrib'ns, Cap Gain ($)	.0.19	0.00	0.00	0.00	0.00	0.60	0.65	0.46	0.14	0.36
Net Asset Value ($)	7.63	6.60	5.56	3.90	4.49	5.72	7.84	6.47	6.26	5.94
Expense Ratio (%)	1.35	1.35	1.37	1.34	1.44	1.37	1.49	1.41	1.44	1.54
Yield (%)	1.86	0.80	0.86	0.49	0.00	0.14	0.21	0.86	2.09	0.79
Portfolio Turnover (%)	74	69	39	69	90	101	85	78	67	103
Total Assets (Millions $)	169	194	159	92	99	138	173	127	132	119

PORTFOLIO (as of 9/30/05)

Portfolio Manager: Rosemary Macedo - 1995

Investment Style

Large Cap	Growth
Mid Cap	Value
Small Cap	Grth/Val

Portfolio

0.0% cash	0.0% corp bonds
96.1% stocks	0.0% gov't bonds
0.1% pref/conv't pref	0.0% muni bonds
0.0% conv't bds/wrnts	3.7% other

SHAREHOLDER INFORMATION

Minimum Investment
Initial: $5,000   Subsequent: $100

Minimum IRA Investment
Initial: $5,000   Subsequent: $100

Maximum Fees
Load: 2.00% redemption   12b-1: none
Other: redemption fee applies for 1 month

Services
✔ IRA
  Keogh
✔ Telephone Exchange

Bernstein International Value II (SIMTX)

212-756-4097
www.bernstein.com

Foreign Stock

PERFORMANCE

fund inception date: 4/30/99

	3yr Annual	5yr Annual	10yr Annual	Bull	Bear
Return (%)	23.7	8.4	na	95.0	-24.5
Differ From Category (+/-)	-2.3 av	2.2 abv av	na	-18.9 blw av	19.9 high

Standard Deviation	Category Risk Index	Beta
12.3%—abv av	0.98—av	1.08

	2005	2004	2003	2002	2001	2000	1999	1998	1997	1996
Return (%)	14.6	18.4	39.3	-8.8	-12.9	-2.9	—	—	—	—
Differ From Category (+/-)	-3.4	-1.2	-2.6	5.4	5.6	10.2	—	—	—	—
Return, Tax-Adjusted (%)	14.1	18.1	38.9	-9.2	-13.9	-6.8	—	—	—	—

PER SHARE DATA

	2005	2004	2003	2002	2001	2000	1999	1998	1997	1996
Dividends, Net Income ($)	0.31	0.17	0.17	0.16	0.45	0.79	—	—	—	—
Distrib'ns, Cap Gain ($)	0.00	0.00	0.00	0.00	0.00	2.56	—	—	—	—
Net Asset Value ($)	24.03	21.23	18.07	13.09	14.53	17.20	—	—	—	—
Expense Ratio (%)	1.27	1.28	1.29	1.29	1.28	1.25	—	—	—	—
Yield (%)	1.28	0.80	0.91	1.18	3.09	3.97	—	—	—	—
Portfolio Turnover (%)	61	92	28	67	45	24	—	—	—	—
Total Assets (Millions $)	2,785	2,458	2,022	1,468	1,541	1,814	—	—	—	—

PORTFOLIO (as of 6/30/05)

Portfolio Manager: Team Managed - 1999

Investment Style

Large Cap	Growth
Mid Cap	Value
Small Cap	Grth/Val

Portfolio

1.6% cash	0.0% corp bonds
98.4% stocks	0.0% gov't bonds
0.0% pref/conv't pref	0.0% muni bonds
0.0% conv't bds/wrnts	0.0% other

SHAREHOLDER INFORMATION

Minimum Investment
Initial: $25,000   Subsequent: $5,000

Minimum IRA Investment
Initial: $25,000   Subsequent: $5,000

Maximum Fees
Load: none   12b-1: none
Other: none

Services
✔ IRA
✔ Keogh
   Telephone Exchange

Dodge & Cox Intl Stock
(DODFX)
Foreign Stock

800-621-3979
www.dodgeandcox.com

fund inception date: 5/1/01

	3yr Annual	5yr Annual	10yr Annual	Bull	Bear
Return (%)	32.2	na	na	153.9	na
Differ From Category (+/-)	6.2 high	na	na	40.0 high	na

Standard Deviation	Category Risk Index	Beta
13.7%—abv av	1.10—high	1.21

	2005	2004	2003	2002	2001	2000	1999	1998	1997	1996
Return (%)	16.7	32.4	49.4	-13.1	—	—	—	—	—	—
Differ From Category (+/-)	-1.3	12.8	7.5	1.1	—	—	—	—	—	—
Return, Tax-Adjusted (%)	16.1	31.9	49.1	-13.4	—	—	—	—	—	—

PER SHARE DATA

	2005	2004	2003	2002	2001	2000	1999	1998	1997	1996
Dividends, Net Income ($)	0.35	0.24	0.14	0.13	—	—	—	—	—	—
Distrib'ns, Cap Gain ($)	0.39	0.22	0.00	0.06	—	—	—	—	—	—
Net Asset Value ($)	35.03	30.64	23.48	15.81	—	—	—	—	—	—
Expense Ratio (%)	na	0.77	0.82	0.90	—	—	—	—	—	—
Yield (%)	0.98	0.77	0.60	0.83	—	—	—	—	—	—
Portfolio Turnover (%)	na	6	11	12	—	—	—	—	—	—
Total Assets (Millions $)	12,056	4,203	655	117	—	—	—	—	—	—

PORTFOLIO (as of 9/30/05)

Portfolio Manager: Team Managed - 2001

Investment Style

Large Cap	Growth
Mid Cap	Value
Small Cap	Grth/Val

Portfolio

5.4%	cash	0.0%	corp bonds
94.6%	stocks	0.0%	gov't bonds
0.0%	pref/conv't pref	0.0%	muni bonds
0.0%	conv't bds/wrnts	0.0%	other

SHAREHOLDER INFORMATION

Minimum Investment
Initial: $2,500   Subsequent: $100

Minimum IRA Investment
Initial: $1,000   Subsequent: $100

Maximum Fees
Load: none   12b-1: none
Other: none

Services
✔ IRA
✔ Keogh
✔ Telephone Exchange

Excelsior International

(UMINX)

Foreign Stock

800-446-1012
www.excelsiorfunds.com

PERFORMANCE

fund inception date: 7/21/87

	3yr Annual	5yr Annual	10yr Annual	Bull	Bear
Return (%)	26.7	2.9	5.6	117.4	-60.7
Differ From Category (+/-)	0.7 abv av	-3.3 blw av	-3.0 low	3.5 abv av	-16.3 low

Standard Deviation	Category Risk Index		Beta
12.5%—abv av	1.00—abv av		1.12

	2005	2004	2003	2002	2001	2000	1999	1998	1997	1996
Return (%).	17.6	21.7	42.2	-21.7	-27.4	-23.9	56.2	7.9	9.2	7.2
Differ From Category (+/-)	-0.4	2.1	0.3	-7.5	-8.9	-10.8	4.3	-5.5	5.5	-9.3
Return, Tax-Adjusted (%). .	17.2	21.7	41.8	-21.9	-28.3	-24.8	56.1	7.6	8.2	6.3

PER SHARE DATA

	2005	2004	2003	2002	2001	2000	1999	1998	1997	1996
Dividends, Net Income ($).	0.12	0.00	0.08	0.03	0.08	0.13	0.00	0.07	0.06	0.10
Distrib'ns, Cap Gain ($) . . .	0.00	0.00	0.00	0.00	0.52	0.60	0.04	0.00	0.43	0.19
Net Asset Value ($)	15.09	12.95	10.64	7.54	9.67	14.08	19.42	12.46	11.61	11.07
Expense Ratio (%).	1.50	1.38	1.40	1.23	1.41	1.40	1.42	1.44	1.43	1.40
Yield (%)	0.81	0.01	0.78	0.38	0.76	0.86	0.00	0.55	0.46	0.89
Portfolio Turnover (%)	66	58	73	50	55	25	50	37	116	38
Total Assets (Millions $) . . .	375	209	119	109	177	362	373	230	178	106

PORTFOLIO (as of 6/30/05)

Portfolio Manager: R Tritsch/D Linehan/
D Elefson - 1996

Investment Style
Large Cap   Growth
Mid Cap   Value
Small Cap   Grth/Val

Portfolio
2.5% cash   0.0% corp bonds
94.2% stocks   0.0% gov't bonds
1.0% pref/conv't pref 0.0% muni bonds
0.0% conv't bds/wrnts 2.3% other

SHAREHOLDER INFORMATION

Minimum Investment
Initial: $500   Subsequent: $50

Minimum IRA Investment
Initial: $250   Subsequent: $50

Maximum Fees
Load: 2.00% redemption   12b-1: none
Other: redemption fee applies for 1 month

Services
✔ IRA
✔ Keogh
✔ Telephone Exchange

Fidelity International Discovery (FIGRX)

800-544-8544
www.fidelity.com

Foreign Stock

PERFORMANCE
fund inception date: 12/29/86

	3yr Annual	5yr Annual	10yr Annual	Bull	Bear
Return (%)	26.4	8.5	10.2	115.9	-40.8
Differ From Category (+/-)	0.4 abv av	2.3 abv av	1.6 abv av	2.0 abv av	3.6 abv av

Standard Deviation	Category Risk Index		Beta
12.2%—abv av	0.98—av		1.10

	2005	2004	2003	2002	2001	2000	1999	1998	1997	1996
Return (%).............	18.5	19.0	43.3	-9.8	-17.4	-14.0	53.7	9.9	7.1	12.6
Differ From Category (+/-)	.0.5	-0.6	1.4	4.4	1.1	-0.9	1.8	-3.5	3.4	-3.9
Return, Tax-Adjusted (%)..	17.4	18.7	42.9	-10.0	-17.4	-16.4	51.6	9.1	5.4	11.4

PER SHARE DATA

	2005	2004	2003	2002	2001	2000	1999	1998	1997	1996
Dividends, Net Income ($).	0.31	0.15	0.18	0.09	0.00	0.51	0.33	0.09	0.37	0.29
Distrib'ns, Cap Gain ($) ...	1.40	0.12	0.00	0.00	0.00	2.66	1.50	0.63	0.88	0.37
Net Asset Value ($)	31.66	28.20	23.92	16.82	18.76	22.72	30.10	20.91	19.70	19.55
Expense Ratio (%)........	na	1.11	1.11	1.12	1.09	1.05	1.10	1.13	1.15	1.14
Yield (%)	0.92	0.52	0.75	0.53	0.00	2.00	1.04	0.41	1.79	1.45
Portfolio Turnover (%)	na	81	81	63	81	104	94	143	70	95
Total Assets (Millions $)..	4,657	2,504	1,498	907	941	1,183	1,395	871	1,030	1,081

PORTFOLIO (as of 7/29/05)

Portfolio Manager: William Kennedy - 2004

Investment Style

Large Cap	Growth
Mid Cap	Value
Small Cap	Grth/Val

Portfolio

2.3%	cash	0.0%	corp bonds
96.3%	stocks	0.0%	gov't bonds
1.4%	pref/conv't pref	0.0%	muni bonds
0.0%	conv't bds/wrnts	0.0%	other

SHAREHOLDER INFORMATION

Minimum Investment
Initial: $2,500   Subsequent: $250

Minimum IRA Investment
Initial: $500   Subsequent: $250

Maximum Fees
Load: 1.00% redemption   12b-1: none
Other: redemption fee applies for 1 month;
maint fee for low bal

Services
✔ IRA
  Keogh
✔ Telephone Exchange

Fidelity Overseas
(FOSFX)
Foreign Stock

800-544-8544
www.fidelity.com

fund inception date: 12/4/84

	3yr Annual	5yr Annual	10yr Annual	Bull	Bear
Return (%)	25.0	4.6	7.5	108.6	-51.0
Differ From Category (+/-)	-1.0 av	-1.6 av	-1.1 av	-5.3 av	-6.6 blw av

Standard Deviation	Category Risk Index	Beta
13.3%—abv av	1.06—abv av	1.18

	2005	2004	2003	2002	2001	2000	1999	1998	1997	1996
Return (%).............	19.2	13.5	44.3	-19.4	-20.2	-18.3	42.8	12.8	10.9	13.1
Differ From Category (+/-)	.1.2	-6.1	2.4	-5.2	-1.7	-5.2	-9.1	-0.6	7.2	-3.4
Return, Tax-Adjusted (%)..	18.8	13.2	43.8	-19.5	-20.2	-20.7	40.9	12.2	9.6	11.0

PER SHARE DATA

	2005	2004	2003	2002	2001	2000	1999	1998	1997	1996
Dividends, Net Income ($).	0.41	0.19	0.30	0.09	0.00	0.86	0.44	0.20	0.34	0.37
Distrib'ns, Cap Gain ($) ...	0.16	0.11	0.00	0.00	0.00	4.12	2.64	0.51	1.34	1.63
Net Asset Value ($)	41.61	35.38	31.43	22.00	27.42	34.37	48.01	35.98	32.54	30.84
Expense Ratio (%).........	na	1.00	1.00	1.16	1.12	1.16	1.23	1.24	1.20	1.12
Yield (%)	0.98	0.53	0.95	0.40	0.00	2.23	0.86	0.54	1.00	1.13
Portfolio Turnover (%)	na	104	104	72	95	132	85	69	68	82
Total Assets (Millions $) ..	5,371	4,687	3,961	2,843	3,481	4,653	5,404	3,847	3,705	3,247

PORTFOLIO (as of 7/29/05)

Portfolio Manager: Richard Mace - 1996

Investment Style

Large Cap	Growth
Mid Cap	Value
Small Cap	Grth/Val

Portfolio

2.8% cash	0.0% corp bonds
97.2% stocks	0.0% gov't bonds
0.0% pref/conv't pref	0.0% muni bonds
0.0% conv't bds/wrnts	0.0% other

SHAREHOLDER INFORMATION

Minimum Investment
Initial: $2,500   Subsequent: $250

Minimum IRA Investment
Initial: $500   Subsequent: $250

Maximum Fees
Load: 1.00% redemption   12b-1: none
Other: redemption fee applies for 1 month;
maint fee for low bal

Services
✔ IRA
✔ Keogh
✔ Telephone Exchange

ICAP International
(ICEUX)

Foreign Stock

888-221-4227
www.icapfunds.com

PERFORMANCE

fund inception date: 12/31/97

	3yr Annual	5yr Annual	10yr Annual	Bull	Bear
Return (%)	28.9	9.7	na	129.9	-35.6
Differ From Category (+/-)	2.9 abv av	3.5 high	na	16.0 abv av	8.8 abv av

Standard Deviation	Category Risk Index	Beta
12.5%—abv av	1.00—abv av	1.15

	2005	2004	2003	2002	2001	2000	1999	1998	1997	1996
Return (%)	19.1	26.8	41.8	-18.3	-8.9	-4.8	20.3	27.4	—	—
Differ From Category (+/-)	.1.1	7.2	-0.1	-4.1	9.6	8.3	-31.6	14.0	—	—
Return, Tax-Adjusted (%)	.17.2	26.3	41.0	-18.8	-9.3	-6.7	19.1	25.9	—	—

PER SHARE DATA

	2005	2004	2003	2002	2001	2000	1999	1998	1997	1996
Dividends, Net Income ($)	0.54	0.30	0.41	0.29	0.20	0.37	0.10	0.37	—	—
Distrib'ns, Cap Gain ($)	2.50	0.18	0.00	0.00	0.13	2.04	1.22	0.73	—	—
Net Asset Value ($)	32.89	30.18	24.20	17.45	21.69	24.19	27.91	24.32	—	—
Expense Ratio (%)	na	0.80	0.80	0.80	0.95	0.80	1.00	1.00	—	—
Yield (%)	1.53	0.98	1.70	1.67	0.92	1.40	0.33	1.45	—	—
Portfolio Turnover (%)	na	122	218	276	267	370	245	272	—	—
Total Assets (Millions $)	179	93	45	18	21	33	32	28	—	—

PORTFOLIO (as of 11/30/05)

Portfolio Manager: Team Managed - 1997

Investment Style

Large Cap	Growth
Mid Cap	Value
Small Cap	Grth/Val

Portfolio

4.7% cash	0.0% corp bonds
95.3% stocks	0.0% gov't bonds
0.0% pref/conv't pref	0.0% muni bonds
0.0% conv't bds/wrnts	0.0% other

SHAREHOLDER INFORMATION

Minimum Investment
Initial: $1,000   Subsequent: $1,000

Minimum IRA Investment
Initial: $1   Subsequent: $1

Maximum Fees
Load: 2.00% redemption   12b-1: none
Other: redemption fee applies for 1 month

Services
✔ IRA
✔ Keogh
✔ Telephone Exchange

Janus Overseas
(JAOSX)

Foreign Stock

800-525-3713
www.janus.com

fund inception date: 5/2/94

	3yr Annual	5yr Annual	10yr Annual	Bull	Bear
Return (%)	29.0	4.6	12.9	134.4	-61.9
Differ From Category (+/-)	3.0 abv av	-1.6 av	4.3 high	20.5 abv av	-17.5 low

Standard Deviation	Category Risk Index	Beta
15.4%—high	1.23—high	1.24

	2005	2004	2003	2002	2001	2000	1999	1998	1997	1996
Return (%)............	32.3	18.5	36.7	-23.8	-23.1	-18.5	86.0	16.0	18.2	28.8
Differ From Category (+/-)	14.3	-1.1	-5.2	-9.6	-4.6	-5.4	34.1	2.6	14.5	12.3
Return, Tax-Adjusted (%)..	31.9	18.1	36.2	-24.1	-23.2	-20.7	85.9	15.8	17.3	28.0

PER SHARE DATA

	2005	2004	2003	2002	2001	2000	1999	1998	1997	1996
Dividends, Net Income ($).	0.28	0.23	0.24	0.16	0.10	0.20	0.00	0.10	0.10	0.04
Distrib'ns, Cap Gain ($) ...	0.00	0.00	0.00	0.00	0.00	3.66	0.14	0.00	0.50	0.26
Net Asset Value ($)	31.83	24.26	20.66	15.29	20.30	26.54	37.20	20.08	17.39	15.22
Expense Ratio (%)........	0.92	0.93	0.94	0.89	0.85	0.88	0.91	0.94	1.01	1.23
Yield (%)	0.87	0.93	1.17	1.06	0.50	0.64	0.00	0.48	0.53	0.27
Portfolio Turnover (%)	57	58	104	63	65	62	92	105	72	71
Total Assets (Millions $)..	2,779	2,331	2,768	3,092	5,278	8,157	8,765	4,329	3,241	955

PORTFOLIO (as of 7/29/05)

Portfolio Manager: B Lynn/G Yettick - 2001

Investment Style
Large Cap   Growth
Mid Cap   Value
Small Cap   Grth/Val

Portfolio

0.5% cash	0.0% corp bonds
96.1% stocks	0.0% gov't bonds
3.5% pref/conv't pref	0.0% muni bonds
0.0% conv't bds/wrnts	0.0% other

SHAREHOLDER INFORMATION

Minimum Investment
Initial: $2,500   Subsequent: $100

Minimum IRA Investment
Initial: $500   Subsequent: $100

Maximum Fees
Load: 2.00% redemption   12b-1: none
Other: redemption fee applies for 3 months

Services
✔ IRA
✔ Keogh
✔ Telephone Exchange

Laudus International MarketMasters Inv (SWOIX)

800-435-4000
www.schwab.com/
schwabfunds

Foreign Stock

PERFORMANCE

fund inception date: 10/16/96

	3yr Annual	5yr Annual	10yr Annual	Bull	Bear
Return (%)	27.0	7.5	na	121.6	-48.1
Differ From Category (+/-)	1.0 abv av	1.3 abv av	na	7.7 abv av	-3.7 av

Standard Deviation	Category Risk Index	Beta
12.5%—abv av	1.00—abv av	1.19

	2005	2004	2003	2002	2001	2000	1999	1998	1997	1996
Return (%)	19.3	19.3	43.9	-18.3	-14.1	-14.4	74.8	13.2	6.8	—
Differ From Category (+/-)	.1.3	-0.3	2.0	-4.1	4.4	-1.3	22.9	-0.2	3.1	—
Return, Tax-Adjusted (%)	18.9	19.2	43.8	-18.3	-15.3	-17.0	69.8	12.7	4.8	—

PER SHARE DATA

	2005	2004	2003	2002	2001	2000	1999	1998	1997	1996
Dividends, Net Income ($)	0.16	0.02	0.04	0.00	0.07	0.77	0.49	0.13	0.34	—
Distrib'ns, Cap Gain ($)	0.00	0.00	0.00	0.00	0.66	0.79	1.84	0.00	0.30	—
Net Asset Value ($)	17.94	15.17	12.73	8.87	10.86	13.50	17.60	11.41	10.19	—
Expense Ratio (%)	na	1.78	1.65	0.93	0.50	0.50	0.50	0.50	0.50	—
Yield (%)	0.90	0.14	0.28	0.00	0.61	5.36	2.54	1.17	3.20	—
Portfolio Turnover (%)	na	69	99	158	51	80	249	236	179	—
Total Assets (Millions $)	884	637	358	211	231	269	156	79	77	—

PORTFOLIO (as of 7/31/05)

Portfolio Manager: Federico Laffan - 2005

Investment Style

Large Cap	Growth
Mid Cap	Value
Small Cap	Grth/Val

Portfolio

4.7% cash	0.0% corp bonds
93.4% stocks	0.0% gov't bonds
0.0% pref/conv't pref	0.0% muni bonds
0.0% conv't bds/wrnts	1.9% other

SHAREHOLDER INFORMATION

Minimum Investment
Initial: $2,500   Subsequent: $500

Minimum IRA Investment
Initial: $1,000   Subsequent: $250

Maximum Fees
Load: 2.00% redemption   12b-1: none
Other: redemption fee applies for 1 month

Services
✔ IRA
✔ Keogh
✔ Telephone Exchange

Neuberger Berman International Inv (NBISX)

800-366-6264
www.nb.com

Foreign Stock

PERFORMANCE

fund inception date: 6/15/94

	3yr Annual	5yr Annual	10yr Annual	Bull	Bear
Return (%)	32.2	10.5	11.2	144.5	-50.3
Differ From Category (+/-)	6.2 high	4.3 high	2.6 abv av	30.6 high	-5.9 blw av

Standard Deviation	Category Risk Index	Beta
12.2%—abv av	0.98—av	1.01

	2005	2004	2003	2002	2001	2000	1999	1998	1997	1996
Return (%)...............	23.9	30.3	43.3	-13.1	-18.0	-24.3	65.8	2.3	11.2	23.6
Differ From Category (+/-)	.5.9	10.7	1.4	1.2	0.5	-11.2	13.9	-11.1	7.5	7.1
Return, Tax-Adjusted (%)..	23.0	30.0	42.7	-13.2	-18.1	-27.9	65.5	2.3	10.9	23.6

PER SHARE DATA

	2005	2004	2003	2002	2001	2000	1999	1998	1997	1996
Dividends, Net Income ($).	0.13	0.11	0.16	0.03	0.02	0.00	0.01	0.00	0.00	0.02
Distrib'ns, Cap Gain ($) ...	0.75	0.00	0.00	0.00	0.04	4.32	0.21	0.01	0.14	0.00
Net Asset Value ($)	21.67	18.20	14.05	9.92	11.45	14.04	24.31	14.80	14.47	13.14
Expense Ratio (%).........	na	1.40	1.70	1.69	1.56	1.43	1.61	1.62	1.70	1.70
Yield (%)	0.57	0.58	1.13	0.30	0.17	0.00	0.04	0.00	0.00	0.15
Portfolio Turnover (%)	na	38	90	63	61	80	94	46	37	45
Total Assets (Millions $)...	634	235	103	70	90	137	192	127	112	73

PORTFOLIO (as of 11/30/05)

Portfolio Manager: Benjamin Segal - 2000

Investment Style
Large Cap   Growth
Mid Cap   Value
Small Cap   Grth/Val

Portfolio
3.7% cash	0.0% corp bonds
96.4% stocks	0.0% gov't bonds
0.0% pref/conv't pref	0.0% muni bonds
0.0% conv't bds/wrnts	0.0% other

SHAREHOLDER INFORMATION

Minimum Investment
Initial: $1,000   Subsequent: $100

Minimum IRA Investment
Initial: $250   Subsequent: $100

Maximum Fees
Load: 2.00% redemption   12b-1: none
Other: redemption fee applies for 6 months

Services
✔ IRA
✔ Keogh
✔ Telephone Exchange

SSgA International Stock Selection (SSAIX)

800-997-7327
www.ssgafunds.com

Foreign Stock

PERFORMANCE

fund inception date: 3/7/95

	3yr Annual	5yr Annual	10yr Annual	Bull	Bear
Return (%)	26.5	6.8	5.0	113.1	-45.0
Differ From Category (+/-)	0.5 abv av	0.6 av	-3.6 low	-0.8 abv av	-0.6 abv av

Standard Deviation	Category Risk Index	Beta
11.8%—abv av	0.94—blw av	1.07

	2005	2004	2003	2002	2001	2000	1999	1998	1997	1996
Return (%).............	17.0	21.0	42.8	-13.7	-20.4	-16.3	32.5	13.5	-10.1	3.9
Differ From Category (+/-)	-1.0	1.4	0.9	0.6	-1.9	-3.2	-19.4	0.1	-13.8	-12.6
Return, Tax-Adjusted (%)..	16.0	20.2	42.1	-14.0	-20.6	-18.4	31.9	10.3	-11.5	3.1

PER SHARE DATA

	2005	2004	2003	2002	2001	2000	1999	1998	1997	1996
Dividends, Net Income ($).	0.15	0.19	0.13	0.07	0.04	0.00	0.13	0.39	0.15	0.18
Distrib'ns, Cap Gain ($) ...	0.33	0.00	0.00	0.00	0.00	1.26	0.00	0.69	0.49	0.06
Net Asset Value ($)	11.03	9.87	8.33	5.93	6.95	8.79	12.06	9.21	9.17	10.84
Expense Ratio (%).........	na	1.24	1.00	1.00	1.00	1.00	1.00	1.00	1.00	1.00
Yield (%)	1.31	1.91	1.52	1.13	0.57	0.00	1.04	3.89	1.52	1.64
Portfolio Turnover (%)	na	59	70	50	85	64	62	74	48	22
Total Assets (Millions $) ...	394	156	123	82	72	93	120	98	142	67

PORTFOLIO (as of 5/31/05)

Portfolio Manager: Team Managed - 2001

Investment Style

Large Cap	Growth
Mid Cap	Value
Small Cap	Grth/Val

Portfolio

0.0% cash	0.0% corp bonds
100.0% stocks	0.0% gov't bonds
0.0% pref/conv't pref	0.0% muni bonds
0.0% conv't bds/wrnts	0.0% other

SHAREHOLDER INFORMATION

Minimum Investment
Initial: $1,000   Subsequent: $100

Minimum IRA Investment
Initial: $250   Subsequent: $100

Maximum Fees
Load: 2.00% redemption   12b-1: 0.07%
Other: redemption fee applies for 2 months

Services
✔ IRA
  Keogh
✔ Telephone Exchange

T Rowe Price Intl Discovery (PRIDX)

Foreign Stock

800-638-5660
www.troweprice.com

PERFORMANCE

fund inception date: 12/30/88

	3yr Annual	5yr Annual	10yr Annual	Bull	Bear
Return (%)	37.7	10.5	15.0	169.8	-58.4
Differ From Category (+/-)	11.7 high	4.3 high	6.4 high	55.9 high	-14.0 low

Standard Deviation	Category Risk Index	Beta
13.4%—abv av	1.07—abv av	1.07

	2005	2004	2003	2002	2001	2000	1999	1998	1997	1996
Return (%)	27.8	23.7	65.2	-16.2	-24.6	-15.6	155.0	6.1	-5.6	13.8
Differ From Category (+/-)	.9.8	4.1	23.3	-2.0	-6.1	-2.4	103.1	-7.3	-9.4	-2.7
Return, Tax-Adjusted (%)	27.6	23.7	65.0	-16.2	-24.6	-18.7	151.4	5.6	-5.9	13.5

PER SHARE DATA

	2005	2004	2003	2002	2001	2000	1999	1998	1997	1996
Dividends, Net Income ($)	0.15	0.01	0.08	0.00	0.00	0.00	0.00	0.01	0.00	0.07
Distrib'ns, Cap Gain ($)	0.21	0.03	0.06	0.00	0.00	5.83	2.81	0.30	0.25	0.06
Net Asset Value ($)	41.36	32.63	26.40	16.06	19.18	25.45	36.77	15.65	15.05	16.22
Expense Ratio (%)	na	1.32	1.41	1.44	1.38	1.27	1.42	1.47	1.41	1.45
Yield (%)	0.36	0.03	0.30	0.00	0.00	0.00	0.00	0.06	0.00	0.42
Portfolio Turnover (%)	na	106	116	93	59	81	98	34	72	52
Total Assets (Millions $)	1,382	1,002	705	370	486	765	687	193	228	322

PORTFOLIO (as of 9/30/05)

Portfolio Manager: Team Managed - 1988

Investment Style

Large Cap	Growth
Mid Cap	Value
Small Cap	Grth/Val

Portfolio

4.5% cash	0.0% corp bonds
95.5% stocks	0.0% gov't bonds
0.0% pref/conv't pref	0.0% muni bonds
0.0% conv't bds/wrnts	0.0% other

SHAREHOLDER INFORMATION

Minimum Investment
Initial: $2,500   Subsequent: $100

Minimum IRA Investment
Initial: $1,000   Subsequent: $50

Maximum Fees
Load: 2.00% redemption   12b-1: none
Other: redemption fee applies for 1 year

Services
✓ IRA
✓ Keogh
✓ Telephone Exchange

T Rowe Price Intl Growth & Income (TRIGX)

800-638-5660
www.troweprice.com

Foreign Stock

PERFORMANCE **fund inception date: 12/21/98**

	3yr Annual	5yr Annual	10yr Annual	Bull	Bear
Return (%)	25.7	7.6	na	111.2	-32.4
Differ From Category (+/-)	-0.3 av	1.4 abv av	na	-2.7 av	12.0 high

Standard Deviation	Category Risk Index	Beta
11.4%—abv av	0.91—low	0.99

	2005	2004	2003	2002	2001	2000	1999	1998	1997	1996
Return (%)...............	15.7	23.1	39.4	-11.6	-17.5	-4.3	19.6	—	—	—
Differ From Category (+/-)	-2.3	3.5	-2.5	2.6	1.0	8.8	-32.3	—	—	—
Return, Tax-Adjusted (%)..	14.9	22.7	39.2	-12.0	-17.9	-5.8	18.4	—	—	—

PER SHARE DATA

	2005	2004	2003	2002	2001	2000	1999	1998	1997	1996
Dividends, Net Income ($)	0.21	0.11	0.04	0.08	0.10	0.13	0.19	—	—	—
Distrib'ns, Cap Gain ($) ...	0.15	0.01	0.00	0.01	0.00	0.64	0.23	—	—	—
Net Asset Value ($)	14.14	12.53	10.28	7.40	8.48	10.41	11.71	—	—	—
Expense Ratio (%).........	na	1.25	1.25	1.44	1.25	1.25	1.25	—	—	—
Yield (%)	1.46	0.87	0.38	1.07	1.17	1.17	1.59	—	—	—
Portfolio Turnover (%)	na	46	53	25	9	32	36	—	—	—
Total Assets (Millions $) ...	909	552	144	12	10	10	11	—	—	—

PORTFOLIO (as of 9/30/05)

Portfolio Manager: Team Managed - 1998

Investment Style

Large Cap	Growth
Mid Cap	Value
Small Cap	Grth/Val

Portfolio

1.6% cash	0.0% corp bonds
98.4% stocks	0.0% gov't bonds
0.0% pref/conv't pref	0.0% muni bonds
0.0% conv't bds/wrnts	0.0% other

SHAREHOLDER INFORMATION

Minimum Investment
Initial: $2,500   Subsequent: $100

Minimum IRA Investment
Initial: $1,000   Subsequent: $50

Maximum Fees
Load: 2.00% redemption   12b-1: none
Other: redemption fee applies for 3 months

Services
✓ IRA
✓ Keogh
✓ Telephone Exchange

Thomas White International (TWWDX)

800-811-0535
www.thomaswhite.com

Foreign Stock

PERFORMANCE

fund inception date: 6/28/94

	3yr Annual	5yr Annual	10yr Annual	Bull	Bear
Return (%)	27.2	8.7	9.5	122.0	-40.2
Differ From Category (+/-)	1.2 abv av	2.5 abv av	0.9 abv av	8.1 abv av	4.2 abv av

Standard Deviation	Category Risk Index		Beta
12.5%—abv av	1.00—abv av		1.10

	2005	2004	2003	2002	2001	2000	1999	1998	1997	1996
Return (%)	25.5	20.4	36.3	-11.3	-16.7	-14.6	26.3	16.5	11.7	16.5
Differ From Category (+/-)	.7.5	0.8	-5.6	2.9	1.8	-1.5	-25.6	3.1	8.0	0.0
Return, Tax-Adjusted (%)	23.9	19.9	35.7	-11.6	-16.9	-15.4	22.5	14.7	10.1	13.9

PER SHARE DATA

	2005	2004	2003	2002	2001	2000	1999	1998	1997	1996
Dividends, Net Income ($)	0.18	0.15	0.13	0.07	0.06	0.01	0.07	0.13	0.19	0.19
Distrib'ns, Cap Gain ($)	1.07	0.00	0.00	0.00	0.00	0.55	2.49	0.91	0.54	0.76
Net Asset Value ($)	15.92	13.79	11.59	8.61	9.79	11.84	14.54	13.82	12.76	12.09
Expense Ratio (%)	na	1.50	1.50	1.50	1.50	1.50	1.44	1.42	1.47	1.50
Yield (%)	1.05	1.09	1.12	0.79	0.65	0.05	0.38	0.87	1.44	1.44
Portfolio Turnover (%)	na	46	26	50	35	38	67	51	48	51
Total Assets (Millions $)	75	46	44	26	29	34	42	63	49	42

PORTFOLIO (as of 6/30/05)

Portfolio Manager: Thomas White - 1994

Investment Style
Large Cap	Growth
Mid Cap	Value
Small Cap	Grth/Val

Portfolio
2.7% cash	0.0% corp bonds
96.3% stocks	0.0% gov't bonds
0.0% pref/conv't pref	0.0% muni bonds
0.0% conv't bds/wrnts	1.0% other

SHAREHOLDER INFORMATION

Minimum Investment
Initial: $2,500   Subsequent: $100

Minimum IRA Investment
Initial: $1,000   Subsequent: $100

Maximum Fees
Load: 2.00% redemption   12b-1: none
Other: redemption fee applies for 2 months

Services
✔ IRA
   Keogh
✔ Telephone Exchange

Individual Fund Listings   **309**

Tocqueville International Value (TIVFX)

800-697-3863
www.tocquevillefunds.com

Foreign Stock

PERFORMANCE

fund inception date: 8/1/94

	3yr Annual	5yr Annual	10yr Annual	Bull	Bear
Return (%)	31.3	15.7	7.1	141.2	-27.5
Differ From Category (+/-)	5.3 abv av	9.5 high	-1.5 av	27.3 high	16.9 high

Standard Deviation	Category Risk Index	Beta
11.8%—abv av	0.94—blw av	0.96

	2005	2004	2003	2002	2001	2000	1999	1998	1997	1996
Return (%)...............	21.0	21.7	53.7	1.5	-9.8	-19.7	31.0	6.1	-30.8	24.4
Differ From Category (+/-)	.3.0	2.1	11.8	15.8	8.7	-6.5	-20.9	-7.3	-34.6	7.9
Return, Tax-Adjusted (%)..	18.9	21.5	53.5	1.5	-9.8	-19.8	28.1	6.1	-31.2	22.6

PER SHARE DATA

	2005	2004	2003	2002	2001	2000	1999	1998	1997	1996
Dividends, Net Income ($).	0.05	0.08	0.04	0.01	0.00	0.03	0.05	0.00	0.11	0.06
Distrib'ns, Cap Gain ($) ...	1.86	0.00	0.00	0.00	0.00	0.00	1.22	0.00	0.00	0.62
Net Asset Value ($)	15.31	14.26	11.78	7.69	7.58	8.41	10.51	9.02	8.50	12.45
Expense Ratio (%).........	na	1.71	1.77	1.73	1.77	1.72	1.67	2.00	1.99	1.98
Yield (%)	0.30	0.54	0.33	0.10	0.00	0.35	0.42	0.00	1.29	0.45
Portfolio Turnover (%)	35	43	55	61	54	45	78	77	70	135
Total Assets (Millions $) ...	238	210	144	84	70	84	100	76	54	27

PORTFOLIO (as of 9/30/05)

Portfolio Manager: Francois Sicart - 1994

Investment Style

Large Cap	Growth
Mid Cap	Value
Small Cap	Grth/Val

Portfolio

2.6% cash	0.0% corp bonds
95.7% stocks	0.0% gov't bonds
0.0% pref/conv't pref	0.0% muni bonds
1.8% conv't bds/wrnts	0.0% other

SHAREHOLDER INFORMATION

Minimum Investment
Initial: $1,000   Subsequent: $100

Minimum IRA Investment
Initial: $250   Subsequent: $100

Maximum Fees
Load: 2.00% redemption   12b-1: 0.25%
Other: redemption fee applies for 4 months

Services
✔ IRA
✔ Keogh
✔ Telephone Exchange

Vanguard Developing Markets Index (VDMIX)

Foreign Stock

800-662-7447
www.vanguard.com

	3yr Annual	5yr Annual	10yr Annual	Bull	Bear
Return (%)	23.6	4.4	na	101.4	na
Differ From Category (+/-)	-2.4 av	-1.8 blw av	na	-12.5 av	na

Standard Deviation	Category Risk Index	Beta
11.6%—abv av	0.93—blw av	1.05

	2005	2004	2003	2002	2001	2000	1999	1998	1997	1996
Return (%)	13.3	20.2	38.6	-15.7	-22.0	—	—	—	—	—
Differ From Category (+/-)	-4.7	0.6	-3.3	-1.4	-3.5	—	—	—	—	—
Return, Tax-Adjusted (%)	12.5	19.3	37.7	-16.3	-22.5	—	—	—	—	—

PER SHARE DATA

	2005	2004	2003	2002	2001	2000	1999	1998	1997	1996
Dividends, Net Income ($)	0.22	0.19	0.14	0.12	0.12	—	—	—	—	—
Distrib'ns, Cap Gain ($)	0.00	0.00	0.00	0.00	0.00	—	—	—	—	—
Net Asset Value ($)	10.21	9.20	7.81	5.74	6.95	—	—	—	—	—
Expense Ratio (%)	na	0.00	0.00	0.00	0.00	—	—	—	—	—
Yield (%)	2.14	2.06	1.83	2.02	1.72	—	—	—	—	—
Portfolio Turnover (%)	na	4	7	5	3	—	—	—	—	—
Total Assets (Millions $)	1,780	1,198	734	399	189	—	—	—	—	—

PORTFOLIO (as of 9/30/05)

Portfolio Manager: George Sauter/Team
Managed - 2000

Investment Style

Large Cap	Growth
Mid Cap	Value
Small Cap	Grth/Val

Portfolio

0.3% cash	0.0% corp bonds
97.5% stocks	0.0% gov't bonds
0.0% pref/conv't pref	0.0% muni bonds
0.0% conv't bds/wrnts	2.2% other

SHAREHOLDER INFORMATION

Minimum Investment
Initial: $3,000   Subsequent: $100

Minimum IRA Investment
Initial: $3,000   Subsequent: $100

Maximum Fees
Load: 2.00% redemption   12b-1: none
Other: redemption fee applies for 2 months

Services
✔ IRA
  Keogh
  Telephone Exchange

Vanguard International Growth (VWIGX)

800-662-7447
www.vanguard.com

Foreign Stock

PERFORMANCE

fund inception date: 9/30/81

	3yr Annual	5yr Annual	10yr Annual	Bull	Bear
Return (%)	22.5	4.1	7.0	96.5	-46.2
Differ From Category (+/-)	-3.5 blw av	-2.1 blw av	-1.6 blw av	-17.4 blw av	-1.8 av

Standard Deviation	Category Risk Index	Beta
11.4%—abv av	0.91—blw av	1.04

	2005	2004	2003	2002	2001	2000	1999	1998	1997	1996
Return (%).............	14.9	18.9	34.4	-17.7	-18.9	-8.6	26.3	16.9	4.1	14.6
Differ From Category (+/-)	-3.1	-0.7	-7.5	-3.5	-0.4	4.6	-25.6	3.5	0.4	-1.9
Return, Tax-Adjusted (%)..	14.0	18.2	33.8	-18.2	-19.4	-10.2	24.8	16.2	2.9	13.1

PER SHARE DATA

	2005	2004	2003	2002	2001	2000	1999	1998	1997	1996
Dividends, Net Income ($).	0.37	0.32	0.21	0.18	0.24	0.22	0.26	0.22	0.21	0.19
Distrib'ns, Cap Gain ($) ...	0.32	0.00	0.00	0.00	0.04	1.42	0.90	0.16	0.52	0.55
Net Asset Value ($)	21.00	18.86	16.13	12.16	15.01	18.87	22.49	18.77	16.39	16.46
Expense Ratio (%)........	0.58	0.63	0.69	0.67	0.61	0.53	0.58	0.59	0.57	0.56
Yield (%)	1.73	1.67	1.30	1.48	1.59	1.08	1.11	1.16	1.24	1.11
Portfolio Turnover (%)	48	45	59	40	48	48	37	37	22	22
Total Assets (Millions $) ..	8,871	8,097	6,424	4,768	6,088	8,900	9,681	7,723	6,809	5,569

PORTFOLIO (as of 9/30/05)

Portfolio Manager: Richard Foulkes/James Anderson - 1981

Investment Style

Large Cap	Growth
Mid Cap	Value
Small Cap	Grth/Val

Portfolio

4.7%	cash	0.0%	corp bonds
93.3%	stocks	0.0%	gov't bonds
1.0%	pref/conv't pref	0.0%	muni bonds
1.0%	conv't bds/wrnts	0.0%	other

SHAREHOLDER INFORMATION

Minimum Investment
Initial: $3,000   Subsequent: $100

Minimum IRA Investment
Initial: $3,000   Subsequent: $100

Maximum Fees
Load: 2.00% redemption   12b-1: none
Other: redemption fee applies for 2 months

Services
✓ IRA
✓ Keogh
✓ Telephone Exchange

Vanguard International Value (VTRIX)

Foreign Stock

800-662-7447
www.vanguard.com

PERFORMANCE

	3yr Annual	5yr Annual	10yr Annual	Bull	Bear
Return (%)	26.0	8.3	7.7	114.3	-31.6
Differ From Category (+/-)	0.0 abv av	2.1 abv av	-0.9 av	0.4 abv av	12.8 high

Standard Deviation	Category Risk Index	Beta
12.4%—abv av	0.99—abv av	1.13

	2005	2004	2003	2002	2001	2000	1999	1998	1997	1996
Return (%)	17.9	19.7	41.9	-13.3	-14.0	-7.4	21.7	19.5	-4.5	10.2
Differ From Category (+/-)	-0.1	0.1	0.0	0.9	4.5	5.7	-30.2	6.1	-8.3	-6.3
Return, Tax-Adjusted (%)	16.7	19.1	41.0	-13.8	-14.5	-8.5	20.1	16.8	-7.7	3.9

PER SHARE DATA

	2005	2004	2003	2002	2001	2000	1999	1998	1997	1996
Dividends, Net Income ($)	0.56	0.48	0.46	0.29	0.30	0.73	0.66	1.06	0.69	0.82
Distrib'ns, Cap Gain ($)	1.10	0.00	0.00	0.00	0.00	0.19	0.73	0.91	2.96	5.77
Net Asset Value ($)	34.82	30.93	26.24	18.83	22.07	26.03	29.12	25.09	22.64	27.54
Expense Ratio (%)	na	0.56	0.62	0.65	0.64	0.53	0.59	0.52	0.49	0.50
Yield (%)	1.55	1.55	1.75	1.54	1.35	2.78	2.21	4.07	2.69	2.46
Portfolio Turnover (%)	32	74	27	26	37	78	41	39	37	82
Total Assets (Millions $)	4,127	2,663	1,704	1,104	895	835	1,045	806	777	917

PORTFOLIO (as of 9/30/05)

Portfolio Manager: Team Managed - 2000

Investment Style

Large Cap	Growth
Mid Cap	Value
Small Cap	Grth/Val

Portfolio

3.8%	cash	0.0%	corp bonds
94.7%	stocks	0.0%	gov't bonds
1.5%	pref/conv't pref	0.0%	muni bonds
0.0%	conv't bds/wrnts	0.0%	other

SHAREHOLDER INFORMATION

Minimum Investment
Initial: $3,000   Subsequent: $100

Minimum IRA Investment
Initial: $3,000   Subsequent: $100

Maximum Fees
Load: 2.00% redemption   12b-1: none
Other: redemption fee applies for 2 months

Services
✔ IRA
✔ Keogh
✔ Telephone Exchange

Vanguard Tax Managed International (VTMGX)

800-662-7447
www.vanguard.com

Foreign Stock

PERFORMANCE

fund inception date: 8/17/99

	3yr Annual	5yr Annual	10yr Annual	Bull	Bear
Return (%)	23.7	4.5	na	102.2	-47.0
Differ From Category (+/-)	-2.3 av	-1.7 av	na	-11.7 av	-2.6 av

Standard Deviation	Category Risk Index	Beta
11.6%—abv av	0.93—blw av	1.05

	2005	2004	2003	2002	2001	2000	1999	1998	1997	1996
Return (%)	13.6	20.2	38.6	-15.6	-21.9	-14.2	—	—	—	—
Differ From Category (+/-)	-4.4	0.6	-3.3	-1.4	-3.4	-1.1	—	—	—	—
Return, Tax-Adjusted (%)	12.7	19.4	37.8	-16.3	-22.4	-14.6	—	—	—	—

PER SHARE DATA

	2005	2004	2003	2002	2001	2000	1999	1998	1997	1996
Dividends, Net Income ($)	0.26	0.20	0.15	0.14	0.13	0.11	—	—	—	—
Distrib'ns, Cap Gain ($)	0.00	0.00	0.00	0.00	0.00	0.00	—	—	—	—
Net Asset Value ($)	11.48	10.33	8.76	6.43	7.79	10.14	—	—	—	—
Expense Ratio (%)	na	0.23	0.28	0.31	0.35	0.35	—	—	—	—
Yield (%)	2.23	1.95	1.74	2.17	1.60	1.08	—	—	—	—
Portfolio Turnover (%)	na	5	9	7	20	5	—	—	—	—
Total Assets (Millions $)	1,119	825	514	334	327	241	—	—	—	—

PORTFOLIO (as of 9/30/05)

Portfolio Manager: Team Managed - 1999

Investment Style

Large Cap   Growth
Mid Cap   Value
Small Cap   Grth/Val

Portfolio

0.0% cash	0.0% corp bonds
99.8% stocks	0.0% gov't bonds
0.2% pref/conv't pref	0.0% muni bonds
0.0% conv't bds/wrnts	0.0% other

SHAREHOLDER INFORMATION

Minimum Investment
Initial: $10,000   Subsequent: $100

Minimum IRA Investment
Initial: $10,000   Subsequent: $100

Maximum Fees
Load: 1.00% redemption   12b-1: none
Other: redemption fee applies for 1 year

Services
✔ IRA
   Keogh
✔ Telephone Exchange

Vanguard Total Intl Stock Index (VGTSX)

800-662-7447
www.vanguard.com

Foreign Stock

	3yr Annual	5yr Annual	10yr Annual	Bull	Bear
Return (%)	25.1	5.8	na	108.6	-46.1
Differ From Category (+/-)	-0.9 av	-0.4 av	na	-5.3 av	-1.7 abv av

Standard Deviation	Category Risk Index	Beta
11.9%—abv av	0.95—blw av	1.09

	2005	2004	2003	2002	2001	2000	1999	1998	1997	1996
Return (%)	15.5	20.8	40.3	-15.0	-20.1	-15.6	29.9	15.6	-0.7	—
Differ From Category (+/-)	-2.5	1.2	-1.6	-0.8	-1.6	-2.5	-22.0	2.2	-4.5	—
Return, Tax-Adjusted (%)	14.7	20.0	39.4	-15.7	-20.6	-16.2	29.1	14.7	-1.4	—

PER SHARE DATA

	2005	2004	2003	2002	2001	2000	1999	1998	1997	1996
Dividends, Net Income ($)	0.29	0.26	0.19	0.16	0.17	0.20	0.21	0.21	0.17	—
Distrib'ns, Cap Gain ($)	0.00	0.00	0.00	0.00	0.00	0.05	0.01	0.01	0.02	—
Net Asset Value ($)	14.27	12.60	10.64	7.72	9.28	11.83	14.31	11.19	9.87	—
Expense Ratio (%)	na	0.00	0.00	0.00	0.00	0.00	0.00	0.00	0.00	—
Yield (%)	2.06	2.02	1.78	2.03	1.77	1.68	1.46	1.87	1.71	—
Portfolio Turnover (%)	na	3	2	5	2	3	1	2	6	—
Total Assets (Millions $)	12,696	8,516	5,279	2,994	2,900	2,920	2,570	1,375	903	—

PORTFOLIO (as of 9/30/05)

Portfolio Manager: Team Managed - 1996

Investment Style

Large Cap	Growth
Mid Cap	Value
Small Cap	Grth/Val

Portfolio

0.4% cash	0.0% corp bonds
97.0% stocks	0.0% gov't bonds
0.0% pref/conv't pref	0.0% muni bonds
0.0% conv't bds/wrnts	2.6% other

SHAREHOLDER INFORMATION

Minimum Investment
Initial: $3,000   Subsequent: $100

Minimum IRA Investment
Initial: $3,000   Subsequent: $100

Maximum Fees
Load: 2.00% redemption   12b-1: none
Other: redemption fee applies for 2 months

Services
✔ IRA
✔ Keogh
   Telephone Exchange

Regional/Country Stock Funds
Category Performance Ranked by 2005 Returns

Fund (Ticker)	Annual Return (%)				Category Risk	Total Risk
	2005	3Yr	5Yr	10Yr		
T Rowe Price Latin America (PRLAX)	60.0	51.7	23.3	15.5	high	high
T Rowe Price Emerging Europe & Med (TREMX)	59.0	51.8	27.3	na	abv av	high
Matthews Korea (MAKOX)	58.7	37.7	37.0	8.3	high	high
Fidelity Latin America (FLATX)	55.1	53.6	21.9	13.9	high	high
Fidelity Japan Small Co (FJSCX)	41.3	40.6	17.5	10.0	high	high
US Global Accolade Eastern European (EUROX)	40.7	51.2	40.9	na	high	high
T Rowe Price Japan (PRJPX)	40.0	33.1	5.8	2.9	abv av	high
Fidelity Pacific Basin (FPBFX)	32.5	27.9	9.1	6.9	blw av	abv av
Fidelity Canada (FICDX)	27.8	34.0	15.8	13.1	low	abv av
Wells Fargo Advtg Asia Pacific Inv (SASPX)	27.6	35.0	14.7	5.3	blw av	high
T Rowe Price New Asia (PRASX)	26.4	32.0	13.4	5.1	av	high
Vanguard Pacific Stock Index (VPACX)	22.5	26.3	6.1	0.9	blw av	abv av
Matthews Pacific Tiger (MAPTX)	22.5	34.2	19.5	9.2	av	high
Fidelity Nordic (FNORX)	18.5	29.7	5.1	14.4	abv av	high
Fidelity Europe (FIEUX)	18.1	30.8	6.9	10.9	av	high
Fidelity China Region (FHKCX)	14.4	22.9	7.1	8.3	blw av	abv av
Vanguard European Stock Index (VEURX)	9.2	22.3	3.6	9.5	low	abv av
Regional/Country Stock Category Average	**27.6**	**31.5**	**12.9**	**8.2**	**av**	**high**

Fidelity Canada
(FICDX)
Regional/Country Stock

800-544-8544
www.fidelity.com

fund inception date: 11/17/87

	3yr Annual	5yr Annual	10yr Annual	Bull	Bear
Return (%)	34.0	15.8	13.1	129.8	-9.8
Differ From Category (+/-)	2.5 abv av	2.9 abv av	4.9 high	-9.7 av	29.0 high

Standard Deviation	Category Risk Index	Beta
13.5%—abv av	0.81—low	0.91

	2005	2004	2003	2002	2001	2000	1999	1998	1997	1996
Return (%)............	27.8	23.9	51.9	-4.2	-9.6	12.2	40.5	-14.9	6.1	15.9
Differ From Category (+/-)	.0.2	4.4	2.1	3.8	0.3	34.4	-31.9	-16.9	17.0	2.5
Return, Tax-Adjusted (%)	..27.7	23.8	51.6	-4.3	-9.6	10.1	40.4	-15.0	3.6	9.3

PER SHARE DATA

	2005	2004	2003	2002	2001	2000	1999	1998	1997	1996
Dividends, Net Income ($)	.0.16	0.08	0.13	0.04	0.03	1.04	0.03	0.07	0.05	0.13
Distrib'ns, Cap Gain ($) ...0.01		0.00	0.00	0.00	0.00	0.00	0.00	0.00	2.08	4.29
Net Asset Value ($)	43.13	33.86	27.39	18.12	18.97	21.02	19.63	13.99	16.53	17.62
Expense Ratio (%).........	na	1.37	1.37	1.46	1.20	1.06	1.06	0.80	0.92	0.98
Yield (%)	0.37	0.23	0.47	0.22	0.15	4.94	0.15	0.50	0.26	0.59
Portfolio Turnover (%)	na	52	52	98	93	1	286	215	139	139
Total Assets (Millions $) ..2,106		646	226	78	86	150	58	48	88	130

PORTFOLIO (as of 7/29/05)

Portfolio Manager: Maxime LeMieux - 2002

Investment Style

Large Cap	Growth
Mid Cap	Value
Small Cap	Grth/Val

Portfolio

5.0% cash	0.0% corp bonds
92.1% stocks	0.0% gov't bonds
0.0% pref/conv't pref	0.0% muni bonds
0.0% conv't bds/wrnts	2.9% other

SHAREHOLDER INFORMATION

Minimum Investment
Initial: $2,500   Subsequent: $250

Minimum IRA Investment
Initial: $500   Subsequent: $250

Maximum Fees
Load: 1.50% redemption   12b-1: none
Other: redemption fee applies for 3 months; maint fee for low bal

Services
✔ IRA
✔ Keogh
✔ Telephone Exchange

Fidelity China Region

(FHKCX)

Regional/Country Stock

800-544-8544
www.fidelity.com

PERFORMANCE

fund inception date: 11/1/95

	3yr Annual	5yr Annual	10yr Annual	Bull	Bear
Return (%)	22.9	7.1	8.3	89.3	-42.1
Differ From Category (+/-)	-8.6 low	-5.8 av	0.1 av	-50.2 low	-3.3 abv av

Standard Deviation	Category Risk Index	Beta
14.2%—abv av	0.85—blw av	0.99

	2005	2004	2003	2002	2001	2000	1999	1998	1997	1996
Return (%).	14.4	11.5	45.4	-15.0	-10.4	-17.5	84.9	-5.3	-22.0	40.9
Differ From Category (+/-)	-13.2	-8.0	-4.4	-7.0	-0.5	4.6	12.5	-7.3	-11.2	27.5
Return, Tax-Adjusted (%) . .	14.0	10.9	44.6	-15.6	-10.9	-18.7	84.2	-6.4	-22.2	40.2

PER SHARE DATA

	2005	2004	2003	2002	2001	2000	1999	1998	1997	1996
Dividends, Net Income ($).	0.22	0.26	0.26	0.19	0.16	0.56	0.17	0.32	0.06	0.14
Distrib'ns, Cap Gain ($) . . .	0.00	0.00	0.00	0.00	0.00	0.00	0.00	0.00	0.00	0.08
Net Asset Value ($)	19.30	17.06	15.53	10.86	13.00	14.70	18.51	10.11	11.02	14.21
Expense Ratio (%).	na	1.30	1.30	1.31	1.30	1.21	1.32	1.40	1.31	1.62
Yield (%)	1.13	1.52	1.67	1.74	1.23	3.80	0.91	3.16	0.54	0.97
Portfolio Turnover (%)	na	39	39	53	75	103	84	109	174	118
Total Assets (Millions $) . . .	443	335	274	110	137	175	274	133	180	197

PORTFOLIO (as of 7/29/05)

Portfolio Manager: K Lee - 2005

Investment Style

Large Cap	Growth
Mid Cap	Value
Small Cap	Grth/Val

Portfolio

4.8% cash	0.0% corp bonds
95.2% stocks	0.0% gov't bonds
0.0% pref/conv't pref	0.0% muni bonds
0.0% conv't bds/wrnts	0.0% other

SHAREHOLDER INFORMATION

Minimum Investment
Initial: $2,500   Subsequent: $250

Minimum IRA Investment
Initial: $500   Subsequent: $250

Maximum Fees
Load: 1.50% redemption   12b-1: none
Other: redemption fee applies for 3 months; maint fee for low bal

Services
✔ IRA
✔ Keogh
✔ Telephone Exchange

Fidelity Europe
(FIEUX)
Regional/Country Stock

800-544-8544
www.fidelity.com

PERFORMANCE

fund inception date: 10/1/86

	3yr Annual	5yr Annual	10yr Annual	Bull	Bear
Return (%)	30.8	6.9	10.9	146.6	-51.7
Differ From Category (+/-)	-0.7 abv av	-6.0 blw av	2.7 abv av	7.1 abv av	-12.9 blw av

Standard Deviation	Category Risk Index	Beta
15.8%—high	0.95—av	1.38

	2005	2004	2003	2002	2001	2000	1999	1998	1997	1996
Return (%)	18.1	28.9	46.9	-25.4	-16.0	-9.1	18.6	20.7	22.8	25.6
Differ From Category (+/-)	-9.5	9.4	-2.9	-17.4	-6.1	13.0	-53.8	18.8	33.7	12.2
Return, Tax-Adjusted (%)	16.1	28.7	46.3	-25.6	-16.3	-11.4	17.3	18.8	20.5	23.0

PER SHARE DATA

	2005	2004	2003	2002	2001	2000	1999	1998	1997	1996
Dividends, Net Income ($)	0.30	0.09	0.29	0.14	0.24	0.12	0.18	0.28	0.39	0.24
Distrib'ns, Cap Gain ($)	3.97	0.08	0.00	0.00	0.00	4.09	1.94	2.25	2.35	1.73
Net Asset Value ($)	35.97	34.15	26.62	18.32	24.76	29.77	37.47	33.48	29.94	26.61
Expense Ratio (%)	na	0.98	0.98	1.13	0.99	1.06	0.89	1.09	1.18	1.27
Yield (%)	0.75	0.26	1.08	0.76	0.96	0.35	0.45	0.78	1.20	0.84
Portfolio Turnover (%)	na	162	162	127	123	144	106	114	57	45
Total Assets (Millions $)	2,766	2,208	1,476	896	1,153	1,407	1,478	1,623	951	773

PORTFOLIO (as of 7/29/05)

Portfolio Manager: David Baverez - 2003

Investment Style

Large Cap	Growth
Mid Cap	Value
Small Cap	Grth/Val

Portfolio

0.3% cash	0.0% corp bonds
97.4% stocks	0.0% gov't bonds
0.0% pref/conv't pref	0.0% muni bonds
2.3% conv't bds/wrnts	0.0% other

SHAREHOLDER INFORMATION

Minimum Investment
Initial: $2,500   Subsequent: $250

Minimum IRA Investment
Initial: $500   Subsequent: $250

Maximum Fees
Load: 1.00% redemption   12b-1: none
Other: redemption fee applies for 1 month;
maint fee for low bal

Services
✔ IRA
✔ Keogh
✔ Telephone Exchange

Fidelity Japan Small Co

(FJSCX)

Regional/Country Stock

800-544-8544
www.fidelity.com

PERFORMANCE

fund inception date: 11/1/95

	3yr Annual	5yr Annual	10yr Annual	Bull	Bear
Return (%)	40.6	17.5	10.0	182.0	-57.9
Differ From Category (+/-)	9.1 high	4.6 abv av	1.8 abv av	42.5 high	-19.1 low

Standard Deviation	Category Risk Index	Beta
22.3%—high	1.34—high	0.49

	2005	2004	2003	2002	2001	2000	1999	1998	1997	1996
Return (%).	41.3	22.2	60.8	0.9	-20.0	-50.2	237.4	31.1	-30.3	-24.5
Differ From Category (+/-)	13.7	2.7	11.0	9.0	-10.1	-28.1	165.0	29.2	-19.5	-38.0
Return, Tax-Adjusted (%) . .	40.3	22.1	60.7	0.9	-20.0	-53.9	236.5	31.1	-30.3	-24.6

PER SHARE DATA

	2005	2004	2003	2002	2001	2000	1999	1998	1997	1996
Dividends, Net Income ($) .	0.02	0.01	0.02	0.00	0.00	0.00	0.15	0.00	0.01	0.00
Distrib'ns, Cap Gain ($) . . .	0.83	0.05	0.00	0.00	0.00	4.46	0.00	0.00	0.00	0.04
Net Asset Value ($)	16.82	12.58	10.34	6.44	6.38	7.98	24.27	7.24	5.52	7.94
Expense Ratio (%)	na	1.12	1.12	1.19	1.19	1.06	1.07	1.23	1.34	1.34
Yield (%)	0.11	0.07	0.19	0.00	0.00	0.00	0.61	0.00	0.18	0.00
Portfolio Turnover (%)	na	43	43	50	52	39	39	39	101	66
Total Assets (Millions $) . .	1,971	1,312	882	361	286	422	2,114	130	76	78

PORTFOLIO (as of 7/29/05)

Portfolio Manager: Kenichi Mizushita - 1996

Investment Style

Large Cap	Growth
Mid Cap	Value
Small Cap	Grth/Val

Portfolio

1.9% cash	0.0% corp bonds
98.1% stocks	0.0% gov't bonds
0.0% pref/conv't pref	0.0% muni bonds
0.0% conv't bds/wrnts	0.0% other

SHAREHOLDER INFORMATION

Minimum Investment
Initial: $2,500 Subsequent: $250

Minimum IRA Investment
Initial: $500 Subsequent: $250

Maximum Fees
Load: 1.50% redemption 12b-1: none
Other: redemption fee applies for 3 months;
maint fee for low bal

Services
✓ IRA
✓ Keogh
✓ Telephone Exchange

Fidelity Latin America
(FLATX)
Regional/Country Stock

800-544-8544
www.fidelity.com

	3yr Annual	5yr Annual	10yr Annual	Bull	Bear
Return (%)	53.6	21.9	13.9	289.5	-45.2
Differ From Category (+/-)	22.1 high	9.0 high	5.7 high	150.0 high	-6.4 av

Standard Deviation	Category Risk Index	Beta
20.0%—high	1.20—high	1.47

	2005	2004	2003	2002	2001	2000	1999	1998	1997	1996
Return (%)	55.1	41.1	65.7	-20.8	-6.0	-17.4	54.9	-38.3	32.8	30.7
Differ From Category (+/-)	27.5	21.6	15.9	-12.8	3.9	4.7	-17.5	-40.3	43.7	17.3
Return, Tax-Adjusted (%)	54.1	40.4	64.9	-21.3	-6.7	-17.6	54.3	-38.9	32.2	29.8

PER SHARE DATA

	2005	2004	2003	2002	2001	2000	1999	1998	1997	1996
Dividends, Net Income ($)	0.46	0.30	0.23	0.17	0.25	0.07	0.14	0.25	0.20	0.23
Distrib'ns, Cap Gain ($)	0.38	0.00	0.00	0.00	0.00	0.00	0.00	0.00	0.00	0.00
Net Asset Value ($)	31.98	21.15	15.22	9.33	12.01	13.06	15.91	10.37	17.22	13.11
Expense Ratio (%)	na	1.31	1.31	1.41	1.35	1.23	1.30	1.33	1.29	1.32
Yield (%)	1.42	1.41	1.51	1.82	2.08	0.53	0.87	2.41	1.16	1.75
Portfolio Turnover (%)	na	28	28	128	96	51	49	31	64	70
Total Assets (Millions $)	1,851	501	270	149	210	268	410	307	861	535

PORTFOLIO (as of 7/29/05)

Portfolio Manager: B Bottamini/A Kutas - 2005

Investment Style

Large Cap	Growth
Mid Cap	Value
Small Cap	Grth/Val

Portfolio

2.9% cash	0.0% corp bonds
77.5% stocks	0.0% gov't bonds
19.6% pref/conv't pref	0.0% muni bonds
0.0% conv't bds/wrnts	0.0% other

SHAREHOLDER INFORMATION

Minimum Investment
Initial: $2,500   Subsequent: $250

Minimum IRA Investment
Initial: $500   Subsequent: $250

Maximum Fees
Load: 1.50% redemption   12b-1: none
Other: redemption fee applies for 3 months;
maint fee for low bal

Services
✔ IRA
✔ Keogh
✔ Telephone Exchange

Fidelity Nordic
(FNORX)

Regional/Country Stock

800-544-8544
www.fidelity.com

fund inception date: 11/1/95

PERFORMANCE

	3yr Annual	5yr Annual	10yr Annual	Bull	Bear
Return (%)	29.7	5.1	14.4	145.1	-57.8
Differ From Category (+/-)	-1.8 av	-7.8 low	6.2 high	5.6 abv av	-19.0 low

Standard Deviation	Category Risk Index	Beta
17.6%—high	1.05—abv av	1.55

	2005	2004	2003	2002	2001	2000	1999	1998	1997	1996
Return (%)	18.5	32.7	38.8	-18.2	-27.8	-8.4	59.5	29.5	12.1	41.6
Differ From Category (+/-)	-9.1	13.2	-11.0	-10.2	-17.9	13.7	-12.9	27.6	23.0	28.2
Return, Tax-Adjusted (%)	16.7	32.3	38.4	-18.5	-27.9	-8.6	58.8	29.5	10.1	41.2

PER SHARE DATA

	2005	2004	2003	2002	2001	2000	1999	1998	1997	1996
Dividends, Net Income ($)	0.35	0.22	0.15	0.12	0.06	0.03	0.06	0.00	0.07	0.05
Distrib'ns, Cap Gain ($)	2.49	0.00	0.00	0.00	0.00	0.22	0.45	0.00	1.18	0.10
Net Asset Value ($)	29.87	27.63	20.99	15.23	18.78	26.13	28.83	18.42	14.22	13.80
Expense Ratio (%)	na	1.40	1.40	1.30	1.20	1.15	1.23	1.35	1.42	2.00
Yield (%)	1.08	0.79	0.71	0.78	0.31	0.11	0.20	0.00	0.45	0.35
Portfolio Turnover (%)	na	96	96	106	88	80	70	69	74	35
Total Assets (Millions $)	187	158	88	73	104	187	168	110	65	44

PORTFOLIO (as of 7/29/05)

Portfolio Manager: Trygve Toraasen - 1998

Investment Style

Large Cap	Growth
Mid Cap	Value
Small Cap	Grth/Val

Portfolio

5.0% cash	0.0% corp bonds
95.0% stocks	0.0% gov't bonds
0.0% pref/conv't pref	0.0% muni bonds
0.0% conv't bds/wrnts	0.0% other

SHAREHOLDER INFORMATION

Minimum Investment
Initial: $2,500   Subsequent: $250

Minimum IRA Investment
Initial: $500   Subsequent: $250

Maximum Fees
Load: 1.50% redemption   12b-1: none
Other: redemption fee applies for 3 months;
maint fee for low bal

Services
✔ IRA
✔ Keogh
✔ Telephone Exchange

Fidelity Pacific Basin
(FPBFX)

800-544-8544
www.fidelity.com

Regional/Country Stock

PERFORMANCE

fund inception date: 10/1/86

	3yr Annual	5yr Annual	10yr Annual	Bull	Bear
Return (%)	27.9	9.1	6.9	119.7	-52.1
Differ From Category (+/-)	-3.6 blw av	-3.8 av	-1.3 av	-19.8 av	-13.3 blw av

Standard Deviation	Category Risk Index	Beta
14.2%—abv av	0.85—blw av	0.77

	2005	2004	2003	2002	2001	2000	1999	1998	1997	1996
Return (%)	32.5	14.0	38.6	-7.8	-19.9	-35.3	119.6	8.2	-15.1	-2.7
Differ From Category (+/-)	4.9	-5.5	-11.2	0.2	-9.9	-13.2	47.2	6.3	-4.2	-16.2
Return, Tax-Adjusted (%)	31.9	13.8	38.2	-7.8	-19.9	-37.0	118.8	8.1	-15.7	-2.9

PER SHARE DATA

	2005	2004	2003	2002	2001	2000	1999	1998	1997	1996
Dividends, Net Income ($)	0.18	0.08	0.16	0.00	0.00	1.12	0.26	0.02	0.25	0.08
Distrib'ns, Cap Gain ($)	0.32	0.13	0.00	0.00	0.00	0.23	0.00	0.00	0.00	0.00
Net Asset Value ($)	25.67	19.77	17.53	12.76	13.85	17.29	28.74	13.22	12.23	14.70
Expense Ratio (%)	na	1.17	1.17	1.50	1.45	1.22	1.36	1.72	1.31	1.24
Yield (%)	0.69	0.40	0.91	0.00	0.00	6.39	0.90	0.15	2.04	0.54
Portfolio Turnover (%)	na	97	97	98	123	144	101	57	42	85
Total Assets (Millions $)	852	497	430	297	331	447	989	227	214	447

PORTFOLIO (as of 7/29/05)

Portfolio Manager: Dale Nicholls - 2004

Investment Style

Large Cap	Growth
Mid Cap	Value
Small Cap	Grth/Val

Portfolio

0.1% cash	0.0% corp bonds
99.7% stocks	0.0% gov't bonds
0.2% pref/conv't pref	0.0% muni bonds
0.0% conv't bds/wrnts	0.0% other

SHAREHOLDER INFORMATION

Minimum Investment
Initial: $2,500   Subsequent: $250

Minimum IRA Investment
Initial: $500   Subsequent: $250

Maximum Fees
Load: 1.50% redemption   12b-1: none
Other: redemption fee applies for 3 months;
maint fee for low bal

Services
✔ IRA
✔ Keogh
✔ Telephone Exchange

Individual Fund Listings   323

Matthews Korea
(MAKOX)
Regional/Country Stock

800-789-2742
www.matthewsfunds.com

	3yr Annual	5yr Annual	10yr Annual	Bull	Bear
Return (%)	37.7	37.0	8.3	186.4	-3.0
Differ From Category (+/-)	6.2 high	24.1 high	0.1 av	46.9 high	35.8 high

Standard Deviation	Category Risk Index	Beta
22.7%—high	1.36—high	1.74

	2005	2004	2003	2002	2001	2000	1999	1998	1997	1996
Return (%)	58.7	23.4	33.2	8.1	71.0	-52.8	108.0	96.1	-64.7	-31.7
Differ From Category (+/-)	31.1	3.9	-16.6	16.2	81.0	-30.7	35.6	94.2	-53.9	-45.2
Return, Tax-Adjusted (%)	58.3	19.9	31.2	6.0	69.1	-56.7	103.7	96.1	-64.7	-31.7

PER SHARE DATA

	2005	2004	2003	2002	2001	2000	1999	1998	1997	1996
Dividends, Net Income ($)	0.00	0.01	0.00	0.00	0.01	0.00	0.00	0.00	0.00	0.00
Distrib'ns, Cap Gain ($)	0.11	0.99	0.46	0.39	0.20	1.50	0.88	0.00	0.00	0.00
Net Asset Value ($)	6.37	4.08	4.21	3.52	3.58	2.24	7.63	4.08	2.08	5.90
Expense Ratio (%)	1.31	1.51	1.72	1.75	1.78	1.75	1.77	2.06	2.50	2.23
Yield (%)	0.00	0.17	0.04	0.00	0.24	0.00	0.00	0.00	0.00	0.00
Portfolio Turnover (%)	7	18	29	47	81	47	57	94	112	139
Total Assets (Millions $)	229	128	221	189	181	73	213	131	26	3

PORTFOLIO (as of 9/30/05)

Portfolio Manager: Mark Headley/G Paul
Matthews - 1995

Investment Style

Large Cap	Growth
Mid Cap	Value
Small Cap	Grth/Val

Portfolio

0.0%	cash	0.0%	corp bonds
97.0%	stocks	0.0%	gov't bonds
3.0%	pref/conv't pref	0.0%	muni bonds
0.0%	conv't bds/wrnts	0.0%	other

SHAREHOLDER INFORMATION

Minimum Investment
Initial: $2,500   Subsequent: $250

Minimum IRA Investment
Initial: $500   Subsequent: $50

Maximum Fees
Load: 2.00% redemption   12b-1: none
Other: redemption fee applies for 3 months

Services
✔ IRA
  Keogh
✔ Telephone Exchange

Matthews Pacific Tiger

(MAPTX)

Regional/Country Stock

800-789-2742
www.matthewsfunds.com

PERFORMANCE

fund inception date: 9/12/94

	3yr Annual	5yr Annual	10yr Annual	Bull	Bear
Return (%)	34.2	19.5	9.2	149.5	-33.2
Differ From Category (+/-)	2.7 abv av	6.6 high	1.0 abv av	10.0 abv av	5.6 high

Standard Deviation	Category Risk Index	Beta
15.9%—high	0.95—av	1.31

	2005	2004	2003	2002	2001	2000	1999	1998	1997	1996
Return (%)	22.5	23.3	60.1	-6.4	7.9	-24.0	83.0	-2.8	-40.8	24.1
Differ From Category (+/-)	-5.1	3.8	10.3	1.6	17.9	-1.8	10.6	-4.8	-30.0	10.7
Return, Tax-Adjusted (%)	22.1	22.8	59.9	-6.4	7.7	-26.6	81.9	-3.1	-40.9	24.1

PER SHARE DATA

	2005	2004	2003	2002	2001	2000	1999	1998	1997	1996
Dividends, Net Income ($)	0.12	0.10	0.04	0.00	0.01	0.41	0.19	0.01	0.01	0.00
Distrib'ns, Cap Gain ($)	0.09	0.21	0.00	0.00	0.03	0.84	0.00	0.06	0.02	0.00
Net Asset Value ($)	19.27	15.90	13.15	8.24	8.81	8.20	12.32	6.84	7.15	12.12
Expense Ratio (%)	1.36	1.50	1.75	1.79	1.90	1.81	1.90	1.90	1.90	1.90
Yield (%)	0.62	0.59	0.33	0.00	0.12	4.53	1.53	0.20	0.08	0.00
Portfolio Turnover (%)	4	15	28	57	63	52	98	73	71	125
Total Assets (Millions $)	1,814	852	456	107	87	71	119	52	37	33

PORTFOLIO (as of 9/30/05)

Portfolio Manager: Mark Headley/G Paul Matthews - 1994

Investment Style

Large Cap	Growth
Mid Cap	Value
Small Cap	Grth/Val

Portfolio

0.4% cash	0.0% corp bonds
99.6% stocks	0.0% gov't bonds
0.0% pref/conv't pref	0.0% muni bonds
0.0% conv't bds/wrnts	0.0% other

SHAREHOLDER INFORMATION

Minimum Investment
Initial: $2,500   Subsequent: $250

Minimum IRA Investment
Initial: $500   Subsequent: $50

Maximum Fees
Load: 2.00% redemption   12b-1: none
Other: redemption fee applies for 3 months

Services
✔ IRA
  Keogh
✔ Telephone Exchange

T Rowe Price Emerging Europe & Mediterranean (TREMX)

800-638-5660
www.troweprice.com

Regional/Country Stock

fund inception date: 8/31/00

	3yr Annual	5yr Annual	10yr Annual	Bull	Bear
Return (%)	51.8	27.3	na	246.3	na
Differ From Category (+/-)	20.3 high	14.4 high	na	106.8 high	na

Standard Deviation	Category Risk Index	Beta
19.6%—high	1.17—abv av	1.26

	2005	2004	2003	2002	2001	2000	1999	1998	1997	1996
Return (%)	59.0	30.0	69.2	3.7	-7.6	—	—	—	—	—
Differ From Category (+/-)	31.4	10.5	19.4	11.8	2.3	—	—	—	—	—
Return, Tax-Adjusted (%)	58.8	30.0	69.1	3.7	-7.6	—	—	—	—	—

PER SHARE DATA

	2005	2004	2003	2002	2001	2000	1999	1998	1997	1996
Dividends, Net Income ($)	0.04	0.00	0.02	0.00	0.00	—	—	—	—	—
Distrib'ns, Cap Gain ($)	0.03	0.00	0.00	0.00	0.00	—	—	—	—	—
Net Asset Value ($)	25.21	15.90	12.23	7.24	6.98	—	—	—	—	—
Expense Ratio (%)	1.75	1.75	1.75	1.75	1.75	—	—	—	—	—
Yield (%)	0.15	0.00	0.16	0.00	0.00	—	—	—	—	—
Portfolio Turnover (%)	28	68	54	94	83	—	—	—	—	—
Total Assets (Millions $)	974	153	57	23	20	—	—	—	—	—

PORTFOLIO (as of 9/30/05)

Portfolio Manager: D Warren/C Alderson - 2000

Investment Style

Large Cap	Growth
Mid Cap	Value
Small Cap	Grth/Val

Portfolio

9.8%	cash	0.0%	corp bonds
90.2%	stocks	0.0%	gov't bonds
0.0%	pref/conv't pref	0.0%	muni bonds
0.0%	conv't bds/wrnts	0.0%	other

SHAREHOLDER INFORMATION

Minimum Investment
Initial: $2,500   Subsequent: $100

Minimum IRA Investment
Initial: $1,000   Subsequent: $50

Maximum Fees
Load: 2.00% redemption   12b-1: none
Other: redemption fee applies for 1 year

Services
✔ IRA
✔ Keogh
✔ Telephone Exchange

T Rowe Price Japan
(PRJPX)

800-638-5660
www.troweprice.com

Regional/Country Stock

fund inception date: 12/27/91

PERFORMANCE

	3yr Annual	5yr Annual	10yr Annual	Bull	Bear
Return (%)	33.1	5.8	2.9	149.1	-65.6
Differ From Category (+/-)	1.6 abv av	-7.1 blw av	-5.3 low	9.6 abv av	-26.8 low

Standard Deviation	Category Risk Index	Beta
17.9%—high	1.07—abv av	0.50

	2005	2004	2003	2002	2001	2000	1999	1998	1997	1996
Return (%).............	40.0	16.8	44.1	-16.8	-32.2	-37.2	112.7	9.1	-22.0	-10.9
Differ From Category (+/-)	12.4	-2.7	-5.7	-8.8	-22.3	-15.1	40.3	7.2	-11.2	-24.4
Return, Tax-Adjusted (%)..	39.9	16.8	44.1	-16.8	-32.2	-38.7	112.5	9.1	-22.0	-10.9

PER SHARE DATA

	2005	2004	2003	2002	2001	2000	1999	1998	1997	1996
Dividends, Net Income ($).	0.00	0.00	0.00	0.00	0.00	0.00	0.00	0.00	0.00	0.00
Distrib'ns, Cap Gain ($) ...	0.04	0.00	0.00	0.00	0.00	1.20	0.05	0.00	0.00	0.00
Net Asset Value ($)	11.82	8.47	7.25	5.03	6.05	8.93	15.92	7.51	6.88	8.83
Expense Ratio (%).........	na	1.21	1.38	1.35	1.25	1.09	1.14	1.32	1.24	1.32
Yield (%)	0.00	0.00	0.00	0.00	0.00	0.00	0.00	0.00	0.00	0.00
Portfolio Turnover (%)	na	212	255	104	46	59	58	66	32	29
Total Assets (Millions $)...	377	209	162	100	133	243	596	181	152	147

PORTFOLIO (as of 9/30/05)

Portfolio Manager: D Warren/M Gunn - 1991

Investment Style

Large Cap	Growth
Mid Cap	Value
Small Cap	Grth/Val

Portfolio

8.9% cash	0.0% corp bonds
91.1% stocks	0.0% gov't bonds
0.0% pref/conv't pref	0.0% muni bonds
0.0% conv't bds/wrnts	0.0% other

SHAREHOLDER INFORMATION

Minimum Investment
Initial: $2,500   Subsequent: $100

Minimum IRA Investment
Initial: $1,000   Subsequent: $50

Maximum Fees
Load: 2.00% redemption   12b-1: none
Other: redemption fee applies for 3 months

Services
✔ IRA
✔ Keogh
✔ Telephone Exchange

T Rowe Price Latin America (PRLAX)

800-638-5660
www.troweprice.com

Regional/Country Stock

PERFORMANCE

fund inception date: 12/29/93

	3yr Annual	5yr Annual	10yr Annual	Bull	Bear
Return (%)	51.7	23.3	15.5	280.9	-38.7
Differ From Category (+/-)	20.2 high	10.4 high	7.3 high	141.4 high	0.1 abv av

Standard Deviation	Category Risk Index	Beta
20.1%—high	1.20—high	1.47

	2005	2004	2003	2002	2001	2000	1999	1998	1997	1996
Return (%).............	60.0	38.3	57.9	-18.1	-0.2	-11.2	59.3	-35.4	31.8	23.3
Differ From Category (+/-)	32.4	18.8	8.1	-10.0	9.7	11.0	-13.1	-37.4	42.7	9.9
Return, Tax-Adjusted (%) . .	59.6	37.7	57.1	-18.1	-1.2	-11.3	59.1	-35.9	31.3	22.5

PER SHARE DATA

	2005	2004	2003	2002	2001	2000	1999	1998	1997	1996
Dividends, Net Income ($) .	0.20	0.21	0.16	0.00	0.15	0.04	0.04	0.14	0.12	0.11
Distrib'ns, Cap Gain ($) . . .	0.01	0.00	0.00	0.00	0.20	0.00	0.00	0.00	0.00	0.03
Net Asset Value ($)	25.32	15.95	11.69	7.51	9.17	9.56	10.81	6.81	10.77	8.26
Expense Ratio (%)	na	1.41	1.55	1.53	1.49	1.46	1.62	1.53	1.47	1.66
Yield (%)	0.78	1.31	1.36	0.00	1.60	0.41	0.37	2.05	1.11	1.32
Portfolio Turnover (%)	na	35	27	21	30	27	43	19	32	22
Total Assets (Millions $) . .	1,019	311	201	129	177	207	268	182	433	211

PORTFOLIO (as of 9/30/05)

Portfolio Manager: D Warren/G Ngaro - 1993

Investment Style

Large Cap	Growth
Mid Cap	Value
Small Cap	Grth/Val

Portfolio

7.1% cash	0.0% corp bonds
92.9% stocks	0.0% gov't bonds
0.0% pref/conv't pref	0.0% muni bonds
0.0% conv't bds/wrnts	0.0% other

SHAREHOLDER INFORMATION

Minimum Investment
Initial: $2,500   Subsequent: $100

Minimum IRA Investment
Initial: $1,000   Subsequent: $50

Maximum Fees
Load: 2.00% redemption   12b-1: none
Other: redemption fee applies for 1 year

Services
✔ IRA
✔ Keogh
✔ Telephone Exchange

T Rowe Price New Asia
(PRASX)
Regional/Country Stock

800-638-5660
www.troweprice.com

800-638-5660
www.troweprice.com

PERFORMANCE
fund inception date: 9/28/90

	3yr Annual	5yr Annual	10yr Annual	Bull	Bear
Return (%)	32.0	13.4	5.1	136.9	-49.5
Differ From Category (+/-)	0.5 abv av	0.5 av	-3.1 blw av	-2.6 abv av	-10.7 av

Standard Deviation	Category Risk Index	Beta
16.2%—high	0.97—av	1.17

	2005	2004	2003	2002	2001	2000	1999	1998	1997	1996
Return (%)	26.4	18.6	53.5	-9.3	-10.0	-30.7	99.8	-11.1	-37.1	13.5
Differ From Category (+/-)	-1.2	-0.9	3.7	-1.3	0.0	-8.6	27.4	-13.1	-26.3	0.1
Return, Tax-Adjusted (%)	24.9	18.5	53.1	-9.6	-10.0	-30.7	99.5	-11.7	-37.4	13.1

PER SHARE DATA

	2005	2004	2003	2002	2001	2000	1999	1998	1997	1996
Dividends, Net Income ($)	0.12	0.00	0.06	0.04	0.00	0.00	0.04	0.09	0.08	0.06
Distrib'ns, Cap Gain ($)	0.72	0.05	0.01	0.00	0.00	0.00	0.00	0.00	0.00	0.01
Net Asset Value ($)	11.83	10.04	8.51	5.59	6.21	6.90	9.97	5.01	5.74	9.26
Expense Ratio (%)	na	1.09	1.17	1.17	1.22	1.08	1.21	1.29	1.10	1.11
Yield (%)	0.95	0.00	0.70	0.71	0.00	0.00	0.40	1.79	1.39	0.64
Portfolio Turnover (%)	na	72	72	72	49	52	69	68	41	42
Total Assets (Millions $)	1,378	997	886	543	639	800	1,375	622	782	2,182

PORTFOLIO (as of 9/30/05)

Portfolio Manager: D Warren/F Dydasco/
M Edwards - 1990

Investment Style

Large Cap	Growth
Mid Cap	Value
Small Cap	Grth/Val

Portfolio

3.0% cash	0.0% corp bonds
97.0% stocks	0.0% gov't bonds
0.0% pref/conv't pref	0.0% muni bonds
0.0% conv't bds/wrnts	0.0% other

SHAREHOLDER INFORMATION

Minimum Investment
Initial: $2,500   Subsequent: $100

Minimum IRA Investment
Initial: $1,000   Subsequent: $50

Maximum Fees
Load: 2.00% redemption   12b-1: none
Other: redemption fee applies for 1 year

Services
✔ IRA
✔ Keogh
✔ Telephone Exchange

US Global Accolade
Eastern European (EUROX)

800-873-8637
www.usfunds.com

Regional/Country Stock

PERFORMANCE

fund inception date: 3/31/97

	3yr Annual	5yr Annual	10yr Annual	Bull	Bear
Return (%)	51.2	40.9	na	245.7	4.1
Differ From Category (+/-)	19.7 high	28.0 high	na	106.2 high	42.9 high

Standard Deviation	Category Risk Index		Beta
21.6%—high	1.29—high		1.38

	2005	2004	2003	2002	2001	2000	1999	1998	1997	1996
Return (%)..............	40.7	52.3	61.3	34.6	19.3	-21.4	29.7	-25.3	—	—
Differ From Category (+/-)	13.1	32.8	11.5	42.7	29.3	0.7	-42.7	-27.3	—	—
Return, Tax-Adjusted (%)..	38.9	51.2	60.0	34.6	19.3	-21.4	29.7	-25.3	—	—

PER SHARE DATA

	2005	2004	2003	2002	2001	2000	1999	1998	1997	1996
Dividends, Net Income ($).	0.00	0.27	0.06	0.00	0.00	0.00	0.00	0.00	—	—
Distrib'ns, Cap Gain ($) ...	3.66	0.95	1.06	0.00	0.00	0.00	0.00	0.00	—	—
Net Asset Value ($)	39.50	30.66	20.93	13.68	10.16	8.51	10.83	8.35	—	—
Expense Ratio (%)........	2.08	2.03	2.90	4.63	6.43	5.14	4.36	4.55	—	—
Yield (%)	0.00	0.85	0.25	0.00	0.00	0.00	0.00	0.00	—	—
Portfolio Turnover (%)	95	89	109	214	58	30	29	97	—	—
Total Assets (Millions $)..	1,031	459	68	12	4	4	6	6	—	—

PORTFOLIO (as of 9/30/05)

Portfolio Manager: Team Managed - 1997

Investment Style
Large Cap   Growth
Mid Cap   Value
Small Cap   Grth/Val

Portfolio

3.7% cash	0.0% corp bonds
92.6% stocks	0.0% gov't bonds
3.7% pref/conv't pref	0.0% muni bonds
0.0% conv't bds/wrnts	0.0% other

SHAREHOLDER INFORMATION

Minimum Investment
Initial: $5,000   Subsequent: $50

Minimum IRA Investment
Initial: $0   Subsequent: $0

Maximum Fees
Load: 2.00% redemption   12b-1: 0.25%
Other: redemption fee applies for 6 months

Services
    IRA
    Keogh
✔ Telephone Exchange

Vanguard European Stock Index (VEURX)

800-662-7447
www.vanguard.com

Regional/Country Stock

PERFORMANCE

	3yr Annual	5yr Annual	10yr Annual	Bull	Bear
Return (%)	22.3	3.6	9.5	98.6	-44.7
Differ From Category (+/-)	-9.2 low	-9.3 low	1.3 abv av	-40.9 blw av	-5.9 av

Standard Deviation	Category Risk Index	Beta
13.2%—abv av	0.79—low	1.24

	2005	2004	2003	2002	2001	2000	1999	1998	1997	1996
Return (%).............	9.2	20.8	38.7	-17.9	-20.3	-8.2	16.6	28.8	24.2	21.2
Differ From Category (+/-)	-18.4	1.3	-11.1	-9.9	-10.3	13.9	-55.8	26.9	35.1	7.8
Return, Tax-Adjusted (%)...	8.3	19.9	37.7	-18.7	-20.9	-8.8	15.7	27.6	23.2	20.1

PER SHARE DATA

	2005	2004	2003	2002	2001	2000	1999	1998	1997	1996
Dividends, Net Income ($).	0.70	0.58	0.46	0.40	0.45	0.42	0.50	0.52	0.37	0.36
Distrib'ns, Cap Gain ($) ...	0.00	0.00	0.00	0.00	0.00	0.05	0.15	0.14	0.08	0.06
Net Asset Value ($)	27.70	25.99	22.00	16.21	20.25	25.99	28.83	25.28	20.13	16.57
Expense Ratio (%).........	na	0.27	0.32	0.33	0.30	0.29	0.29	0.29	0.31	0.35
Yield (%)	2.52	2.23	2.09	2.46	2.22	1.62	1.72	2.04	1.83	2.16
Portfolio Turnover (%)	5	5	6	15	3	8	7	7	3	4
Total Assets (Millions $)	11,580	9,220	6,252	3,998	4,405	5,611	6,106	4,479	2,432	1,595

PORTFOLIO (as of 9/30/05)

Portfolio Manager: George Sauter - 1990

Investment Style

Large Cap	Growth
Mid Cap	Value
Small Cap	Grth/Val

Portfolio

0.4% cash	0.0% corp bonds
99.4% stocks	0.0% gov't bonds
0.2% pref/conv't pref	0.0% muni bonds
0.0% conv't bds/wrnts	0.0% other

SHAREHOLDER INFORMATION

Minimum Investment
Initial: $3,000   Subsequent: $100

Minimum IRA Investment
Initial: $3,000   Subsequent: $100

Maximum Fees
Load: 2.00% redemption   12b-1: none
Other: redemption fee applies for 2 months

Services
✔ IRA
✔ Keogh
✔ Telephone Exchange

Vanguard Pacific Stock Index (VPACX)

800-662-7447
www.vanguard.com

Regional/Country Stock

	3yr Annual	5yr Annual	10yr Annual	Bull	Bear
Return (%)	26.3	6.1	0.9	107.2	-51.6
Differ From Category (+/-)	-5.2 blw av	-6.8 blw av	-7.3 low	-32.3 blw av	-12.8 blw av

Standard Deviation	Category Risk Index	Beta
14.1%—abv av	0.84—blw av	0.61

	2005	2004	2003	2002	2001	2000	1999	1998	1997	1996
Return (%).	22.5	18.8	38.4	-9.3	-26.3	-25.7	57.0	2.4	-25.6	-7.8
Differ From Category (+/-)	-5.1	-0.7	-11.4	-1.3	-16.4	-3.6	-15.4	0.5	-14.8	-21.3
Return, Tax-Adjusted (%) . .	21.9	18.1	37.7	-9.7	-26.4	-26.1	56.5	2.0	-26.0	-8.1

PER SHARE DATA

	2005	2004	2003	2002	2001	2000	1999	1998	1997	1996
Dividends, Net Income ($) .	0.16	0.16	0.11	0.07	0.03	0.13	0.09	0.07	0.09	0.09
Distrib'ns, Cap Gain ($) . . .	0.00	0.00	0.00	0.00	0.00	0.00	0.00	0.00	0.00	0.00
Net Asset Value ($)	11.34	9.38	8.03	5.88	6.56	8.95	12.22	7.84	7.72	10.51
Expense Ratio (%)	na	0.34	0.30	0.40	0.37	0.38	0.37	0.40	0.35	0.35
Yield (%)	1.41	1.67	1.30	1.13	0.48	1.39	0.73	0.82	1.16	0.85
Portfolio Turnover (%)	7	3	3	20	2	6	6	4	8	9
Total Assets (Millions $) . .	6,031	3,945	2,469	1,432	1,327	1,924	2,526	1,033	827	978

PORTFOLIO (as of 9/30/05)

Portfolio Manager: George Sauter - 1990

Investment Style
Large Cap   Growth
Mid Cap   Value
Small Cap   Grth/Val

Portfolio

0.2%	cash	0.0% corp bonds
99.9%	stocks	0.0% gov't bonds
0.0%	pref/conv't pref	0.0% muni bonds
0.0%	conv't bds/wrnts	0.0% other

SHAREHOLDER INFORMATION

Minimum Investment
Initial: $3,000   Subsequent: $100

Minimum IRA Investment
Initial: $3,000   Subsequent: $100

Maximum Fees
Load: 2.00% redemption   12b-1: none
Other: redemption fee applies for 2 months

Services
✔ IRA
✔ Keogh
✔ Telephone Exchange

Wells Fargo Advtg Asia Pacific Inv (SASPX)

800-368-3863
www.wellsfargofunds.com

Regional/Country Stock

	3yr Annual	5yr Annual	10yr Annual	Bull	Bear
Return (%)	35.0	14.7	5.3	153.9	-50.9
Differ From Category (+/-)	3.5 high	1.8 abv av	-2.9 blw av	14.4 high	-12.1 blw av

Standard Deviation	Category Risk Index	Beta
14.8%—high	0.89—blw av	0.79

	2005	2004	2003	2002	2001	2000	1999	1998	1997	1996
Return (%)............	27.6	20.4	60.2	-7.7	-12.5	-36.9	96.0	-3.1	-30.9	2.1
Differ From Category (+/-)	.0.0	0.9	10.4	0.3	-2.5	-14.8	23.6	-5.1	-20.1	-11.3
Return, Tax-Adjusted (%)	..25.5	19.4	59.6	-8.0	-12.8	-38.1	93.4	-3.4	-31.2	1.0

	2005	2004	2003	2002	2001	2000	1999	1998	1997	1996
Dividends, Net Income ($)	.0.11	0.03	0.09	0.04	0.06	0.36	0.40	0.05	0.07	0.17
Distrib'ns, Cap Gain ($) ...	1.19	0.53	0.00	0.00	0.00	0.00	0.00	0.00	0.00	0.12
Net Asset Value ($)	11.64	10.22	8.98	5.66	6.18	7.13	11.88	6.27	6.52	9.54
Expense Ratio (%)........	1.69	1.70	1.70	2.00	2.00	2.00	1.70	2.00	2.00	2.30
Yield (%)	0.86	0.29	0.99	0.69	0.94	5.04	3.39	0.78	1.13	1.79
Portfolio Turnover (%)	117	153	286	158	166	22	206	192	96	91
Total Assets (Millions $) ...	224	126	93	57	38	56	140	27	25	70

Portfolio Manager: Anthony Cragg - 1993

Investment Style

Large Cap	Growth
Mid Cap	Value
Small Cap	Grth/Val

Portfolio

0.0% cash	0.0% corp bonds
100.0% stocks	0.0% gov't bonds
0.0% pref/conv't pref	0.0% muni bonds
0.0% conv't bds/wrnts	0.0% other

Minimum Investment
Initial: $2,500   Subsequent: $100

Minimum IRA Investment
Initial: $1,000   Subsequent: $100

Maximum Fees
Load: 1.00% redemption   12b-1: none
Other: redemption fee applies for 1 month

Services
✔ IRA
✔ Keogh
✔ Telephone Exchange

Emerging Stock Funds
Category Performance Ranked by 2005 Returns

Fund (Ticker)	Annual Return (%)				Category Risk	Total Risk
	2005	3Yr	5Yr	10Yr		
Fidelity Emerging Market (FEMKX)	44.3	38.2	19.1	2.7	high	high
Lazard Emerging Markets Open (LZOEX)	41.3	41.6	22.2	na	av	high
T Rowe Price Emerging Markets Stock (PRMSX)	38.7	38.9	19.2	10.3	av	high
Vanguard Emerging Mkts Stock Index (VEIEX)	32.0	37.9	18.7	8.1	abv av	high
Excelsior Emerging Markets (UMEMX)	29.0	40.1	20.6	na	blw av	high
Emerging Stock Category Average	**35.7**	**38.4**	**18.9**	**7.5**	**av**	**high**

Excelsior Emerging Markets (UMEMX)

Emerging Stock

800-446-1012
www.excelsiorfunds.com

fund inception date: 1/2/98

PERFORMANCE

	3yr Annual	5yr Annual	10yr Annual	Bull	Bear
Return (%)	40.1	20.6	na	174.3	-41.5
Differ From Category (+/-)	1.7 high	1.7 high	na	-0.7 abv av	0.0 abv av

Standard Deviation	Category Risk Index	Beta
15.9%—high	0.96—blw av	1.26

	2005	2004	2003	2002	2001	2000	1999	1998	1997	1996
Return (%).	29.0	30.0	63.9	-5.3	-1.8	-31.5	67.3	—	—	—
Differ From Category (+/-)	-6.7	5.3	6.8	1.4	2.1	-2.2	-4.4	—	—	—
Return, Tax-Adjusted (%). .	28.6	29.2	63.4	-5.4	-1.9	-31.5	67.1	—	—	—

PER SHARE DATA

	2005	2004	2003	2002	2001	2000	1999	1998	1997	1996
Dividends, Net Income ($).	0.10	0.08	0.05	0.01	0.02	0.00	0.02	—	—	—
Distrib'ns, Cap Gain ($) . . .	0.00	0.16	0.00	0.00	0.00	0.00	0.00	—	—	—
Net Asset Value ($)	11.19	8.76	6.93	4.26	4.51	4.61	6.73	—	—	—
Expense Ratio (%).	1.70	1.65	1.61	1.59	1.65	1.65	—	—	—	—
Yield (%)	0.90	0.89	0.71	0.18	0.37	0.00	0.33	—	—	—
Portfolio Turnover (%)	21	14	43	11	30	57	—	—	—	—
Total Assets (Millions $) . . .	710	350	139	21	16	11	12	—	—	—

PORTFOLIO (as of 6/30/05)

Portfolio Manager: Donald Elefson - 1999

Investment Style
Large Cap   Growth
Mid Cap   Value
Small Cap   Grth/Val

Portfolio

2.1% cash	0.0% corp bonds
93.0% stocks	0.0% gov't bonds
2.7% pref/conv't pref	0.0% muni bonds
0.0% conv't bds/wrnts	2.3% other

SHAREHOLDER INFORMATION

Minimum Investment
Initial: $500   Subsequent: $50

Minimum IRA Investment
Initial: $250   Subsequent: $50

Maximum Fees
Load: 2.00% redemption   12b-1: none
Other: redemption fee applies for 1 month

Services
✔ IRA
  Keogh
✔ Telephone Exchange

Fidelity Emerging Market
(FEMKX)
Emerging Stock

800-544-8544
www.fidelity.com

PERFORMANCE   fund inception date: 11/1/90

	3yr Annual	5yr Annual	10yr Annual	Bull	Bear
Return (%)	38.2	19.1	2.7	176.1	-42.7
Differ From Category (+/-)	-0.2 abv av	0.2 av	-4.8 blw av	1.1 abv av	-1.2 blw av

Standard Deviation	Category Risk Index	Beta
17.6%—high	1.06—high	1.34

	2005	2004	2003	2002	2001	2000	1999	1998	1997	1996
Return (%).............	44.3	22.9	48.8	-6.9	-2.4	-32.9	70.5	-26.5	-40.7	10.0
Differ From Category (+/-)	.8.6	-1.8	-8.3	-0.2	1.4	-3.7	-1.2	-4.9	-29.9	-3.8
Return, Tax-Adjusted (%)	.43.7	22.5	48.2	-7.1	-2.6	-33.0	70.5	-26.5	-41.3	9.3

PER SHARE DATA

	2005	2004	2003	2002	2001	2000	1999	1998	1997	1996
Dividends, Net Income ($)	.0.21	0.11	0.12	0.05	0.03	0.03	0.00	0.00	0.23	0.25
Distrib'ns, Cap Gain ($) ...	0.00	0.00	0.00	0.00	0.00	0.00	0.00	0.00	0.00	0.00
Net Asset Value ($)	18.44	12.93	10.61	7.21	7.80	8.03	12.02	7.05	9.60	16.62
Expense Ratio (%)........	na	1.36	1.36	1.39	1.45	1.35	1.42	1.56	1.35	1.29
Yield (%)	1.13	0.81	1.08	0.69	0.38	0.37	0.00	0.00	2.39	1.50
Portfolio Turnover (%)	na	105	105	120	113	100	94	87	69	77
Total Assets (Millions $) ..	1,990	760	484	265	243	270	555	270	446	1,161

PORTFOLIO (as of 7/29/05)

Portfolio Manager: Robert von Rekowsky - 2004

Investment Style

Large Cap	Growth
Mid Cap	Value
Small Cap	Grth/Val

Portfolio

3.3% cash	0.0% corp bonds
92.0% stocks	0.0% gov't bonds
4.7% pref/conv't pref	0.0% muni bonds
0.0% conv't bds/wrnts	0.0% other

SHAREHOLDER INFORMATION

Minimum Investment
Initial: $2,500   Subsequent: $250

Minimum IRA Investment
Initial: $500   Subsequent: $250

Maximum Fees
Load: 1.50% redemption   12b-1: none
Other: redemption fee applies for 3 months;
maint fee for low bal

Services
✔ IRA
✔ Keogh
✔ Telephone Exchange

Lazard Emerging Markets Open (LZOEX)

Emerging Stock

800-823-6300
www.lazardnet.com

fund inception date: 1/7/97

PERFORMANCE

	3yr Annual	5yr Annual	10yr Annual	Bull	Bear
Return (%)	41.6	22.2	na	202.5	-35.7
Differ From Category (+/-)	3.2 high	3.3 high	na	27.5 high	5.8 high

Standard Deviation	Category Risk Index	Beta
16.5%—high	0.99—av	1.33

	2005	2004	2003	2002	2001	2000	1999	1998	1997	1996
Return (%)	41.3	30.1	54.5	-0.6	-3.5	-29.8	55.2	-23.3	—	—
Differ From Category (+/-)	.5.6	5.4	-2.6	6.1	0.3	-0.5	-16.5	-1.7	—	—
Return, Tax-Adjusted (%)	39.1	29.8	53.9	-0.9	-3.7	-29.8	54.8	-23.6	—	—

PER SHARE DATA

	2005	2004	2003	2002	2001	2000	1999	1998	1997	1996
Dividends, Net Income ($)	0.14	0.10	0.14	0.06	0.03	0.00	0.08	0.08	—	—
Distrib'ns, Cap Gain ($)	1.67	0.00	0.00	0.00	0.00	0.00	0.00	0.00	—	—
Net Asset Value ($)	17.99	14.06	10.88	7.13	7.24	7.54	10.74	6.97	—	—
Expense Ratio (%)	na	1.60	1.60	1.60	1.60	1.60	1.60	0.60	—	—
Yield (%)	0.69	0.71	1.24	0.88	0.45	0.00	0.71	1.14	—	—
Portfolio Turnover (%)	na	43	29	31	43	72	46	36	—	—
Total Assets (Millions $)	145	31	19	9	7	6	11	8	—	—

PORTFOLIO (as of 9/30/05)

Portfolio Manager: Reinsberg/Donald - 1997

Investment Style

Large Cap	Growth
Mid Cap	Value
Small Cap	Grth/Val

Portfolio

5.2% cash	0.0% corp bonds
94.8% stocks	0.0% gov't bonds
0.0% pref/conv't pref	0.0% muni bonds
0.0% conv't bds/wrnts	0.0% other

SHAREHOLDER INFORMATION

Minimum Investment
Initial: $10,000   Subsequent: $1

Minimum IRA Investment
Initial: $10,000   Subsequent: $1

Maximum Fees
Load: 1.00% redemption   12b-1: 0.25%
Other: redemption fee applies for 1 month

Services
✔ IRA
✔ Keogh
✔ Telephone Exchange

T Rowe Price Emerging Markets Stock (PRMSX)

Emerging Stock

800-638-5660
www.troweprice.com

fund inception date: 3/31/95

PERFORMANCE

	3yr Annual	5yr Annual	10yr Annual	Bull	Bear
Return (%)	38.9	19.2	10.3	181.4	-42.1
Differ From Category (+/-)	0.5 abv av	0.3 abv av	2.8 high	6.4 high	-0.6 blw av

Standard Deviation	Category Risk Index	Beta
16.6%—high	1.00—av	1.35

	2005	2004	2003	2002	2001	2000	1999	1998	1997	1996
Return (%)	38.7	26.9	52.3	-4.9	-5.6	-26.3	87.4	-28.7	1.2	11.8
Differ From Category (+/-)	3.0	2.2	-4.8	1.8	-1.8	2.9	15.7	-7.1	12.1	-2.0
Return, Tax-Adjusted (%)	37.6	26.7	51.9	-4.9	-5.7	-26.3	87.4	-28.8	0.9	10.8

PER SHARE DATA

	2005	2004	2003	2002	2001	2000	1999	1998	1997	1996
Dividends, Net Income ($)	0.18	0.04	0.09	0.02	0.01	0.00	0.00	0.04	0.00	0.04
Distrib'ns, Cap Gain ($)	1.05	0.18	0.00	0.00	0.00	0.00	0.00	0.00	0.15	0.30
Net Asset Value ($)	25.68	19.41	15.47	10.22	10.77	11.43	15.52	8.28	11.68	11.69
Expense Ratio (%)	na	1.33	1.43	1.51	1.58	1.50	1.75	1.75	1.75	1.75
Yield (%)	0.67	0.20	0.58	0.19	0.09	0.00	0.00	0.48	0.00	0.33
Portfolio Turnover (%)	53	70	66	70	70	56	59	54	84	41
Total Assets (Millions $)	1,465	755	440	170	155	152	162	72	124	73

PORTFOLIO (as of 9/30/05)

Portfolio Manager: Team Managed - 1995

Investment Style

Large Cap	Growth
Mid Cap	Value
Small Cap	Grth/Val

Portfolio

5.4% cash	0.0% corp bonds
92.7% stocks	0.0% gov't bonds
0.0% pref/conv't pref	0.0% muni bonds
0.0% conv't bds/wrnts	1.9% other

SHAREHOLDER INFORMATION

Minimum Investment
Initial: $2,500   Subsequent: $100

Minimum IRA Investment
Initial: $1,000   Subsequent: $50

Maximum Fees
Load: 2.00% redemption   12b-1: none
Other: redemption fee applies for 1 year

Services
✔ IRA
✔ Keogh
✔ Telephone Exchange

Vanguard Emerging Mkts Stock Index (VEIEX)

800-662-7447
www.vanguard.com

Emerging Stock

BALANCED STOCK/BOND FUNDS

Category Performance Ranked by 2005 Returns

Fund (Ticker)	Annual Return (%)				Category Risk	Total Risk
	2005	3Yr	5Yr	10Yr		
Fidelity Balanced (FBALX)	10.6	16.3	8.0	10.6	high	blw av
Fidelity Freedom 2040 (FFFFX)	9.0	16.7	2.0	na	high	av
Fidelity Freedom 2030 (FFFEX)	8.8	15.5	2.4	na	high	blw av
T Rowe Price Retirement 2040 (TRRDX)	8.1	17.0	na	na	high	av
T Rowe Price Retirement 2030 (TRRCX)	8.1	17.0	na	na	high	av
Fidelity Freedom 2020 (FFFDX)	7.7	13.8	2.9	na	abv av	blw av
Janus Balanced (JABAX)	7.7	10.0	3.4	10.1	blw av	blw av
T Rowe Price Personal Strategy Growth (TRSGX)	7.6	16.9	5.6	9.6	high	blw av
Exeter Pro Blend Extended Term A (MNBAX)	7.5	13.3	6.3	9.2	abv av	blw av
Vanguard STAR (VGSTX)	7.4	13.7	5.9	9.6	av	blw av
T Rowe Price Retirement 2020 (TRRBX)	7.1	15.4	na	na	high	blw av
Vanguard LifeStrategy Growth (VASGX)	6.8	15.6	3.4	8.4	high	blw av
T Rowe Price Capital Appreciation (PRWCX)	6.8	15.6	11.3	12.4	abv av	blw av
Vanguard Wellington Inv (VWELX)	6.8	12.7	6.8	9.9	abv av	blw av
Fidelity Four-In-One Index (FFNOX)	6.4	15.3	3.0	na	high	blw av
T Rowe Price Personal Strategy Balanced (TRPBX)	6.4	14.2	6.0	8.8	av	blw av
T Rowe Price Retirement 2010 (TRRAX)	6.2	13.4	na	na	abv av	blw av
Vanguard LifeStrategy Moderate Growth (VSMGX)	5.6	12.6	4.1	8.1	av	blw av
Schwab MarketTrack Growth (SWHGX)	5.6	14.4	3.0	7.7	high	blw av
T Rowe Price Balanced (RPBAX)	5.5	12.3	4.4	8.2	av	blw av
Vanguard Asset Allocation Inv (VAAPX)	5.0	13.8	3.4	9.2	high	blw av
Schwab MarketTrack Balanced (SWBGX)	4.8	11.6	3.7	7.3	av	blw av
Fidelity Puritan (FPURX)	4.6	11.8	4.9	8.7	abv av	blw av
Vanguard Balanced Index Inv (VBINX)	4.6	11.1	3.7	8.2	blw av	blw av
Vanguard LifeStrategy Conservative Growth (VSCGX)	4.4	9.5	4.4	7.5	low	blw av
Balanced Stock/Bond Category Average	**5.8**	**12.4**	**4.7**	**8.6**	**av**	**blw av**

Exeter Pro Blend Extended Term A (MNBAX)

Balanced Stock/Bond

800-466-3863
www.manningnapier
advisors.com/www/
exeter_fund.asp

PERFORMANCE

fund inception date: 10/12/93

	3yr Annual	5yr Annual	10yr Annual	Bull	Bear
Return (%)	13.3	6.3	9.2	46.9	5.3
Differ From Category (+/-)	0.9 abv av	1.6 high	0.6 abv av	1.2 abv av	16.2 high

Standard Deviation	Category Risk Index	Beta
6.8%—blw av	1.03—abv av	0.60

	2005	2004	2003	2002	2001	2000	1999	1998	1997	1996
Return (%)	7.5	13.1	19.7	-9.9	3.9	16.3	11.0	2.8	17.5	14.1
Differ From Category (+/-)	1.7	3.0	-2.3	-1.2	6.2	12.9	-0.6	-11.1	-1.5	0.2
Return, Tax-Adjusted (%)	6.3	12.4	19.2	-10.5	2.1	14.1	8.8	0.7	13.8	12.1

PER SHARE DATA

	2005	2004	2003	2002	2001	2000	1999	1998	1997	1996
Dividends, Net Income ($)	0.14	0.11	0.10	0.19	0.31	0.31	0.33	0.30	0.33	0.28
Distrib'ns, Cap Gain ($)	0.95	0.36	0.09	0.00	0.62	0.78	0.69	0.80	1.73	0.47
Net Asset Value ($)	15.05	15.00	13.68	11.59	13.08	13.50	12.57	12.26	13.01	12.86
Expense Ratio (%)	na	1.17	1.17	1.19	1.20	1.20	1.15	1.15	1.15	—
Yield (%)	0.84	0.72	0.75	1.59	2.26	2.17	2.48	2.28	2.21	2.12
Portfolio Turnover (%)	na	50	67	82	75	95	78	61	63	—
Total Assets (Millions $)	368	302	225	162	153	92	65	68	68	35

PORTFOLIO (as of 11/30/05)

Portfolio Manager: Team Managed - 1993

Investment Style

Large Cap	Growth
Mid Cap	Value
Small Cap	Grth/Val

Portfolio

11.9%	cash	3.1%	corp bonds
67.9%	stocks	17.0%	gov't bonds
0.0%	pref/conv't pref	0.0%	muni bonds
0.0%	conv't bds/wrnts	0.0%	other

SHAREHOLDER INFORMATION

Minimum Investment
Initial: $2,000   Subsequent: $100

Minimum IRA Investment
Initial: $2,000   Subsequent: $100

Maximum Fees
Load: none   12b-1: none
Other: none

Services
✔ IRA
✔ Keogh
✔ Telephone Exchange

Fidelity Balanced
(FBALX)

Balanced Stock/Bond

800-544-8544
www.fidelity.com

PERFORMANCE

fund inception date: 11/6/86

	3yr Annual	5yr Annual	10yr Annual	Bull	Bear
Return (%)	16.3	8.0	10.6	60.5	-5.5
Differ From Category (+/-)	3.9 high	3.3 high	2.0 high	14.8 high	5.4 abv av

Standard Deviation	Category Risk Index	Beta
8.5%—blw av	1.29—high	0.87

	2005	2004	2003	2002	2001	2000	1999	1998	1997	1996
Return (%).............	10.6	10.9	28.2	-8.4	2.2	5.3	8.8	20.2	23.4	9.3
Differ From Category (+/-)	.4.8	0.8	6.2	0.3	4.5	1.9	-2.8	6.3	4.4	-4.6
Return, Tax-Adjusted (%)...	9.5	10.0	27.5	-9.4	0.8	3.4	5.3	17.3	19.8	7.4

PER SHARE DATA

	2005	2004	2003	2002	2001	2000	1999	1998	1997	1996
Dividends, Net Income ($).	0.30	0.26	0.26	0.36	0.45	0.48	0.46	0.46	0.56	0.65
Distrib'ns, Cap Gain ($) ...	0.63	0.44	0.00	0.00	0.17	0.49	1.98	1.27	1.46	0.00
Net Asset Value ($)	18.76	17.82	16.75	13.29	14.90	15.19	15.36	16.36	15.27	14.08
Expense Ratio (%)........	0.65	0.66	0.67	0.66	0.64	0.67	0.65	0.67	0.74	0.79
Yield (%)	1.54	1.42	1.55	2.70	2.98	3.06	2.65	2.60	3.34	4.61
Portfolio Turnover (%)	82	99	137	150	115	139	157	135	70	247
Total Assets (Millions $)..	16,603	12,577	9,808	6,550	7,005	6,096	6,123	5,316	4,284	3,919

PORTFOLIO (as of 7/29/05)

Portfolio Manager: George Fischer - 2004

Investment Style

Large Cap	Growth
Mid Cap	Value
Small Cap	Grth/Val

Portfolio

7.2%	cash	9.3% corp bonds
67.8%	stocks	15.3% gov't bonds
0.1%	pref/conv't pref	0.0% muni bonds
0.2%	conv't bds/wrnts	0.1% other

SHAREHOLDER INFORMATION

Minimum Investment
Initial: $2,500   Subsequent: $100

Minimum IRA Investment
Initial: $500   Subsequent: $100

Maximum Fees
Load: none   12b-1: none
Other: maint fee for low bal

Services
✔ IRA
✔ Keogh
✔ Telephone Exchange

Fidelity Four-In-One Index

800-544-8544
www.fidelity.com

(FFNOX)

Balanced Stock/Bond

PERFORMANCE

fund inception date: 6/29/99

	3yr Annual	5yr Annual	10yr Annual	Bull	Bear
Return (%)	15.3	3.0	na	59.3	-34.9
Differ From Category (+/-)	2.9 high	-1.7 blw av	na	13.6 high	-24.0 low

Standard Deviation	Category Risk Index	Beta
8.3%—blw av	1.26—high	0.90

	2005	2004	2003	2002	2001	2000	1999	1998	1997	1996
Return (%)	6.4	12.3	28.2	-15.9	-10.0	-7.6	—	—	—	—
Differ From Category (+/-)	0.6	2.2	6.2	-7.2	-7.8	-11.1	—	—	—	—
Return, Tax-Adjusted (%)	5.8	11.6	27.5	-16.6	-10.7	-8.5	—	—	—	—

PER SHARE DATA

	2005	2004	2003	2002	2001	2000	1999	1998	1997	1996
Dividends, Net Income ($)	0.45	0.42	0.34	0.38	0.45	0.57	—	—	—	—
Distrib'ns, Cap Gain ($)	0.01	0.02	0.00	0.00	0.03	0.10	—	—	—	—
Net Asset Value ($)	26.34	25.17	22.80	18.05	21.93	24.91	—	—	—	—
Expense Ratio (%)	0.28	0.08	0.08	0.08	0.08	0.08	—	—	—	—
Yield (%)	1.70	1.66	1.49	2.10	2.04	2.27	—	—	—	—
Portfolio Turnover (%)	3	7	18	21	23	2	—	—	—	—
Total Assets (Millions $)	1,071	795	477	267	289	325	—	—	—	—

PORTFOLIO (as of 8/31/05)

Portfolio Manager: Derek Young/
Christopher Sharp - 2005

Investment Style

Large Cap	Growth
Mid Cap	Value
Small Cap	Grth/Val

Portfolio

0.0% cash	0.0% corp bonds
0.0% stocks	0.0% gov't bonds
0.0% pref/conv't pref	0.0% muni bonds
0.0% conv't bds/wrnts	100.0% other

SHAREHOLDER INFORMATION

Minimum Investment
Initial: $10,000   Subsequent: $1,000

Minimum IRA Investment
Initial: $500   Subsequent: $250

Maximum Fees
Load: 0.50% redemption   12b-1: none
Other: redemption fee applies for 3 months;
maint fee for low bal

Services
✔ IRA
✔ Keogh
✔ Telephone Exchange

Fidelity Freedom 2020

(FFFDX)

Balanced Stock/Bond

800-544-8544
www.fidelity.com

fund inception date: 10/17/96

	3yr Annual	5yr Annual	10yr Annual	Bull	Bear
Return (%)	13.8	2.9	na	50.4	-29.3
Differ From Category (+/-)	1.4 abv av	-1.8 blw av	na	4.7 abv av	-18.4 low

Standard Deviation	Category Risk Index	Beta
7.1%—blw av	1.08—abv av	0.76

	2005	2004	2003	2002	2001	2000	1999	1998	1997	1996
Return (%)...............	7.7	9.5	24.9	-13.7	-9.0	-3.0	25.3	21.6	21.2	—
Differ From Category (+/-)	.1.9	-0.6	2.9	-5.0	-6.8	-6.5	13.7	7.7	2.2	—
Return, Tax-Adjusted (%)...	7.0	8.8	24.1	-14.3	-10.3	-5.1	23.2	20.2	19.6	—

PER SHARE DATA

	2005	2004	2003	2002	2001	2000	1999	1998	1997	1996
Dividends, Net Income ($).	0.23	0.26	0.22	0.22	0.26	0.39	0.45	0.28	0.34	—
Distrib'ns, Cap Gain ($) ...	0.10	0.04	0.04	0.00	0.43	0.96	0.57	0.27	0.13	—
Net Asset Value ($)	14.71	13.96	13.02	10.64	12.58	14.56	16.38	13.95	11.93	—
Expense Ratio (%)........	0.75	0.08	0.08	0.07	0.06	0.08	0.07	0.08	0.08	—
Yield (%)	1.55	1.85	1.68	2.06	1.99	2.51	2.65	1.96	2.81	—
Portfolio Turnover (%)	0	3	6	10	50	28	18	15	21	—
Total Assets (Millions $) .	12,265	9,338	6,736	3,735	2,796	1,893	1,560	860	84	—

PORTFOLIO (as of 11/30/05)

Portfolio Manager: Ren Cheng - 1996

Investment Style
Large Cap   Growth
Mid Cap   Value
Small Cap   Grth/Val

Portfolio

0.0% cash	0.0% corp bonds
0.0% stocks	0.0% gov't bonds
0.0% pref/conv't pref	0.0% muni bonds
0.0% conv't bds/wrnts	100.0% other

SHAREHOLDER INFORMATION

Minimum Investment
Initial: $2,500   Subsequent: $250

Minimum IRA Investment
Initial: $500   Subsequent: $250

Maximum Fees
Load: none   12b-1: none
Other: maint fee for low bal

Services
✔ IRA
✔ Keogh
✔ Telephone Exchange

Fidelity Freedom 2030
(FFFEX)
Balanced Stock/Bond

800-544-8544
www.fidelity.com

PERFORMANCE

fund inception date: 10/17/96

	3yr Annual	5yr Annual	10yr Annual	Bull	Bear
Return (%)	15.5	2.4	na	58.7	-36.2
Differ From Category (+/-)	3.1 high	-2.3 low	na	13.0 high	-25.3 low

Standard Deviation	Category Risk Index	Beta
8.3%—blw av	1.26—high	0.88

	2005	2004	2003	2002	2001	2000	1999	1998	1997	1996
Return (%)	8.8	10.4	28.4	-17.3	-11.6	-5.0	28.5	22.1	21.4	—
Differ From Category (+/-)	.3.0	0.3	6.4	-8.6	-9.4	-8.5	16.9	8.2	2.4	—
Return, Tax-Adjusted (%)	8.2	9.8	27.7	-17.7	-12.9	-6.7	26.6	20.5	19.9	—

PER SHARE DATA

	2005	2004	2003	2002	2001	2000	1999	1998	1997	1996
Dividends, Net Income ($)	0.19	0.22	0.19	0.15	0.20	0.34	0.41	0.24	0.31	—
Distrib'ns, Cap Gain ($)	0.11	0.00	0.00	0.00	0.53	0.71	0.48	0.48	0.12	—
Net Asset Value ($)	15.02	14.08	12.95	10.24	12.56	15.00	16.88	13.89	11.99	—
Expense Ratio (%)	0.77	0.08	0.08	0.07	0.06	0.08	0.07	0.08	0.08	—
Yield (%)	1.22	1.56	1.46	1.46	1.52	2.16	2.36	1.67	2.55	—
Portfolio Turnover (%)	0	2	4	5	37	26	16	34	19	—
Total Assets (Millions $)	7,400	5,500	3,899	2,091	1,708	1,273	788	282	57	—

PORTFOLIO (as of 11/30/05)

Portfolio Manager: Ren Cheng - 1996

Investment Style

Large Cap	Growth
Mid Cap	Value
Small Cap	Grth/Val

Portfolio

0.0%	cash	0.0%	corp bonds
0.0%	stocks	0.0%	gov't bonds
0.0%	pref/conv't pref	0.0%	muni bonds
0.0%	conv't bds/wrnts	100.0%	other

SHAREHOLDER INFORMATION

Minimum Investment
Initial: $2,500   Subsequent: $250

Minimum IRA Investment
Initial: $500   Subsequent: $250

Maximum Fees
Load: none   12b-1: none
Other: maint fee for low bal

Services
✔ IRA
✔ Keogh
✔ Telephone Exchange

Fidelity Freedom 2040

800-544-8544
www.fidelity.com

(FFFFX)

Balanced Stock/Bond

PERFORMANCE

fund inception date: 9/6/00

	3yr Annual	5yr Annual	10yr Annual	Bull	Bear
Return (%)	16.7	2.0	na	64.5	na
Differ From Category (+/-)	4.3 high	-2.7 low	na	18.8 high	na

Standard Deviation	Category Risk Index	Beta
9.0%—av	1.36—high	0.97

	2005	2004	2003	2002	2001	2000	1999	1998	1997	1996
Return (%)	9.0	11.3	31.1	-19.6	-13.5	—	—	—	—	—
Differ From Category (+/-)	.3.2	1.2	9.1	-10.9	-11.2	—	—	—	—	—
Return, Tax-Adjusted (%)	8.4	10.7	30.5	-20.0	-14.0	—	—	—	—	—

PER SHARE DATA

	2005	2004	2003	2002	2001	2000	1999	1998	1997	1996
Dividends, Net Income ($)	0.10	0.13	0.09	0.07	0.07	—	—	—	—	—
Distrib'ns, Cap Gain ($)	0.09	0.02	0.03	0.01	0.12	—	—	—	—	—
Net Asset Value ($)	8.83	8.27	7.56	5.86	7.39	—	—	—	—	—
Expense Ratio (%)	0.79	0.08	0.08	0.08	0.08	—	—	—	—	—
Yield (%)	1.06	1.50	1.18	1.19	0.93	—	—	—	—	—
Portfolio Turnover (%)	1	3	4	5	38	—	—	—	—	—
Total Assets (Millions $)	3,118	1,864	1,034	342	161	—	—	—	—	—

PORTFOLIO (as of 11/30/05)

Portfolio Manager: Ren Cheng - 2000

Investment Style

Large Cap	Growth
Mid Cap	Value
Small Cap	Grth/Val

Portfolio

0.0% cash	0.0% corp bonds
0.0% stocks	0.0% gov't bonds
0.0% pref/conv't pref	0.0% muni bonds
0.0% conv't bds/wrnts	100.0% other

SHAREHOLDER INFORMATION

Minimum Investment
Initial: $2,500   Subsequent: $250

Minimum IRA Investment
Initial: $500   Subsequent: $250

Maximum Fees
Load: none   12b-1: none
Other: maint fee for low bal

Services
✔ IRA
✔ Keogh
✔ Telephone Exchange

Fidelity Puritan
(FPURX)

Balanced Stock/Bond

800-544-8544
www.fidelity.com

PERFORMANCE
fund inception date: 4/16/47

	3yr Annual	5yr Annual	10yr Annual	Bull	Bear
Return (%)	11.8	4.9	8.7	44.0	-4.6
Differ From Category (+/-)	-0.6 av	0.2 abv av	0.1 abv av	-1.7 av	6.3 abv av

Standard Deviation	Category Risk Index	Beta
7.0%—blw av	1.06—abv av	0.74

	2005	2004	2003	2002	2001	2000	1999	1998	1997	1996
Return (%)	4.6	9.2	22.2	-7.9	-1.0	7.7	2.8	16.5	22.3	15.1
Differ From Category (+/-)	-1.2	-0.9	0.2	0.8	1.2	4.3	-8.8	2.6	3.3	1.2
Return, Tax-Adjusted (%)	3.2	7.8	20.9	-9.0	-2.6	5.4	0.6	13.6	19.6	11.1

PER SHARE DATA

	2005	2004	2003	2002	2001	2000	1999	1998	1997	1996
Dividends, Net Income ($)	0.49	0.45	0.45	0.50	0.60	0.61	0.64	0.67	0.68	0.62
Distrib'ns, Cap Gain ($)	0.59	0.72	0.30	0.00	0.35	1.01	0.97	1.56	0.96	1.54
Net Asset Value ($)	18.73	18.95	18.47	15.79	17.67	18.83	19.03	20.07	19.38	17.24
Expense Ratio (%)	0.63	0.64	0.66	0.64	0.63	0.64	0.63	0.63	0.66	0.72
Yield (%)	2.53	2.28	2.39	3.16	3.32	3.07	3.19	3.09	3.34	3.30
Portfolio Turnover (%)	75	67	86	79	67	62	80	84	80	139
Total Assets (Millions $)	24,079	23,935	21,964	18,031	20,315	21,369	24,371	25,682	22,822	18,502

PORTFOLIO (as of 7/29/05)

Portfolio Manager: Stephen Petersen - 2000

Investment Style
Large Cap   Growth
Mid Cap   Value
Small Cap   Grth/Val

Portfolio

11.3% cash	20.0% corp bonds
56.5% stocks	11.2% gov't bonds
0.5% pref/conv't pref	0.0% muni bonds
0.2% conv't bds/wrnts	0.3% other

SHAREHOLDER INFORMATION

Minimum Investment
Initial: $2,500   Subsequent: $100

Minimum IRA Investment
Initial: $500   Subsequent: $100

Maximum Fees
Load: none   12b-1: none
Other: maint fee for low bal

Services
✔ IRA
✔ Keogh
✔ Telephone Exchange

Janus Balanced
(JABAX)

Balanced Stock/Bond

800-525-3713
www.janus.com

PERFORMANCE

fund inception date: 9/1/92

	3yr Annual	5yr Annual	10yr Annual	Bull	Bear
Return (%)	10.0	3.4	10.1	35.3	-17.9
Differ From Category (+/-)	-2.4 blw av	-1.3 av	1.5 high	-10.4 blw av	-7.0 av

Standard Deviation	Category Risk Index	Beta
5.5%—blw av	0.83—blw av	0.55

	2005	2004	2003	2002	2001	2000	1999	1998	1997	1996
Return (%)	7.7	8.7	13.7	-6.5	-5.0	-2.1	23.5	31.2	21.8	15.3
Differ From Category (+/-)	1.9	-1.4	-8.3	2.2	-2.8	-5.6	11.9	17.3	2.8	1.4
Return, Tax-Adjusted (%)	7.0	7.9	13.0	-7.4	-6.0	-4.1	22.2	30.1	18.7	11.6

PER SHARE DATA

	2005	2004	2003	2002	2001	2000	1999	1998	1997	1996
Dividends, Net Income ($)	0.40	0.41	0.37	0.47	0.53	0.63	0.46	0.35	0.36	0.32
Distrib'ns, Cap Gain ($)	0.00	0.00	0.00	0.00	0.00	1.03	0.32	0.11	1.49	1.35
Net Asset Value ($)	22.48	21.25	19.94	17.88	19.63	21.24	23.39	19.61	15.33	14.14
Expense Ratio (%)	0.80	0.87	0.88	0.84	0.83	0.85	0.91	1.01	1.10	1.21
Yield (%)	1.78	1.92	1.85	2.62	2.69	2.82	1.92	1.78	2.11	2.06
Portfolio Turnover (%)	47	45	73	88	117	87	64	73	139	151
Total Assets (Millions $)	2,571	2,901	3,750	3,902	4,472	4,739	3,420	1,137	389	220

PORTFOLIO (as of 6/30/05)

Portfolio Manager: Gibson Smith/Marc Pinto - 2005

Investment Style

Large Cap	Growth
Mid Cap	Value
Small Cap	Grth/Val

Portfolio

4.2%	cash	18.1%	corp bonds
60.2%	stocks	17.6%	gov't bonds
0.0%	pref/conv't pref	0.0%	muni bonds
0.0%	conv't bds/wrnts	0.0%	other

SHAREHOLDER INFORMATION

Minimum Investment
Initial: $2,500   Subsequent: $100

Minimum IRA Investment
Initial: $500   Subsequent: $100

Maximum Fees
Load: none   12b-1: none
Other: none

Services
✔ IRA
✔ Keogh
✔ Telephone Exchange

Schwab MarketTrack Balanced (SWBGX)

Balanced Stock/Bond

800-435-4000
www.schwab.com/
schwabfunds

	3yr Annual	5yr Annual	10yr Annual	Bull	Bear
Return (%)	11.6	3.7	7.3	43.2	-18.9
Differ From Category (+/-)	-0.8 av	-1.0 av	-1.3 blw av	-2.5 av	-8.0 blw av

Standard Deviation	Category Risk Index	Beta
6.4%—blw av	0.97—av	0.67

	2005	2004	2003	2002	2001	2000	1999	1998	1997	1996
Return (%)	4.8	9.6	21.0	-9.8	-4.4	-1.0	14.0	15.1	17.7	11.1
Differ From Category (+/-)	-1.0	-0.5	-1.0	-1.1	-2.1	-4.5	2.4	1.2	-1.3	-2.8
Return, Tax-Adjusted (%)	4.0	8.9	20.1	-10.6	-5.6	-2.4	13.0	13.7	16.3	10.2

PER SHARE DATA

	2005	2004	2003	2002	2001	2000	1999	1998	1997	1996
Dividends, Net Income ($)	0.34	0.28	0.29	0.29	0.40	0.49	0.28	0.33	0.23	0.23
Distrib'ns, Cap Gain ($)	0.05	0.00	0.00	0.00	0.12	0.10	0.09	0.26	0.31	0.00
Net Asset Value ($)	15.56	15.20	14.12	11.91	13.53	14.70	15.46	13.89	12.58	11.15
Expense Ratio (%)	0.36	0.50	0.50	0.50	0.50	0.56	0.58	0.59	0.78	0.89
Yield (%)	2.17	1.83	2.06	2.42	2.89	3.32	1.80	2.35	1.80	2.09
Portfolio Turnover (%)	11	11	17	31	21	18	7	32	104	44
Total Assets (Millions $)	526	553	531	472	521	544	436	298	162	98

PORTFOLIO (as of 11/30/05)

Portfolio Manager: Team Managed - 2005

Investment Style

Large Cap	Growth
Mid Cap	Value
Small Cap	Grth/Val

Portfolio

0.0% cash	0.0% corp bonds
0.0% stocks	0.0% gov't bonds
0.0% pref/conv't pref	0.0% muni bonds
0.0% conv't bds/wrnts	100.0% other

SHAREHOLDER INFORMATION

Minimum Investment
Initial: $1,000   Subsequent: $500

Minimum IRA Investment
Initial: $500   Subsequent: $250

Maximum Fees
Load: 2.00% redemption   12b-1: none
Other: redemption fee applies for 1 month

Services
✔ IRA
✔ Keogh
✔ Telephone Exchange

Schwab MarketTrack Growth (SWHGX)

Balanced Stock/Bond

800-435-4000
www.schwab.com/
schwabfunds

PERFORMANCE

fund inception date: 11/17/95

	3yr Annual	5yr Annual	10yr Annual	Bull	Bear
Return (%)	14.4	3.0	7.7	56.5	-31.0
Differ From Category (+/-)	2.0 abv av	-1.7 blw av	-0.9 blw av	10.8 abv av	-20.1 low

Standard Deviation	Category Risk Index	Beta
8.4%—blw av	1.27—high	0.90

	2005	2004	2003	2002	2001	2000	1999	1998	1997	1996
Return (%)...............	5.6	11.6	27.0	-15.4	-8.4	-4.8	19.3	15.1	21.0	14.4
Differ From Category (+/-)	-0.2	1.5	5.0	-6.7	-6.2	-8.3	7.7	1.2	2.0	0.5
Return, Tax-Adjusted (%)...	5.0	11.0	26.4	-16.0	-9.2	-5.9	18.7	14.4	19.3	13.7

PER SHARE DATA

	2005	2004	2003	2002	2001	2000	1999	1998	1997	1996
Dividends, Net Income ($).	0.28	0.23	0.21	0.20	0.24	0.44	0.18	0.22	0.16	0.20
Distrib'ns, Cap Gain ($) ...	0.00	0.00	0.00	0.00	0.16	0.09	0.13	0.03	0.62	0.00
Net Asset Value ($)	17.16	16.50	14.99	11.96	14.39	16.15	17.53	14.95	13.20	11.56
Expense Ratio (%)........	0.30	0.50	0.50	0.50	0.50	0.56	0.58	0.60	0.75	0.89
Yield (%)	1.63	1.37	1.37	1.69	1.63	2.69	1.04	1.48	1.15	1.72
Portfolio Turnover (%)	33	9	9	21	10	12	7	14	113	46
Total Assets (Millions $)...	686	673	611	511	553	557	493	311	184	113

PORTFOLIO (as of 11/30/05)

Portfolio Manager: Team Managed - 2005

Investment Style

Large Cap	Growth
Mid Cap	Value
Small Cap	Grth/Val

Portfolio

0.0% cash	0.0% corp bonds
0.0% stocks	0.0% gov't bonds
0.0% pref/conv't pref	0.0% muni bonds
0.0% conv't bds/wrnts	100.0% other

SHAREHOLDER INFORMATION

Minimum Investment
Initial: $1,000   Subsequent: $500

Minimum IRA Investment
Initial: $500   Subsequent: $250

Maximum Fees
Load: 2.00% redemption   12b-1: none
Other: redemption fee applies for 1 month

Services
✔ IRA
✔ Keogh
✔ Telephone Exchange

T Rowe Price Balanced

(RPBAX)

Balanced Stock/Bond

800-638-5660
www.troweprice.com

PERFORMANCE

fund inception date: 12/29/39

	3yr Annual	5yr Annual	10yr Annual	Bull	Bear
Return (%)	12.3	4.4	8.2	44.7	-14.4
Differ From Category (+/-)	-0.1 av	-0.3 abv av	-0.4 av	-1.0 av	-3.5 av

Standard Deviation		Category Risk Index		Beta	
6.3%—blw av		0.95—av		0.65	

	2005	2004	2003	2002	2001	2000	1999	1998	1997	1996
Return (%)	5.5	10.3	21.7	-8.5	-3.9	2.0	10.2	15.9	18.9	14.5
Differ From Category (+/-)	-0.3	0.2	-0.3	0.2	-1.7	-1.4	-1.4	2.0	-0.1	0.6
Return, Tax-Adjusted (%)	4.2	9.3	20.7	-9.6	-5.4	0.6	8.8	14.6	17.3	12.7

PER SHARE DATA

	2005	2004	2003	2002	2001	2000	1999	1998	1997	1996
Dividends, Net Income ($)	0.49	0.46	0.42	0.47	0.52	0.53	0.54	0.52	0.53	0.50
Distrib'ns, Cap Gain ($)	0.50	0.12	0.00	0.03	0.38	0.40	0.23	0.04	0.12	0.13
Net Asset Value ($)	19.77	19.70	18.41	15.51	17.49	19.17	19.69	18.59	16.54	14.48
Expense Ratio (%)	na	0.71	0.78	0.79	0.83	0.79	0.79	0.78	0.81	0.87
Yield (%)	2.41	2.32	2.28	3.02	2.90	2.70	2.71	2.79	3.18	3.42
Portfolio Turnover (%)	na	23	38	49	36	16	21	13	15	22
Total Assets (Millions $)	2,502	2,325	2,048	1,582	1,791	1,896	2,091	1,650	1,219	876

PORTFOLIO (as of 9/30/05)

Portfolio Manager: R Whitney/
Team Managed - 1994

Investment Style

Large Cap	Growth
Mid Cap	Value
Small Cap	Grth/Val

Portfolio

1.0% cash	8.4% corp bonds
64.0% stocks	22.9% gov't bonds
0.0% pref/conv't pref	0.0% muni bonds
0.0% conv't bds/wrnts	3.8% other

SHAREHOLDER INFORMATION

Minimum Investment
Initial: $2,500   Subsequent: $100

Minimum IRA Investment
Initial: $1,000   Subsequent: $50

Maximum Fees
Load: none   12b-1: none
Other: none

Services
✓ IRA
  Keogh
✓ Telephone Exchange

T Rowe Price Capital Appreciation (PRWCX)

800-638-5660
www.troweprice.com

Balanced Stock/Bond

PERFORMANCE

fund inception date: 6/30/86

	3yr Annual	5yr Annual	10yr Annual	Bull	Bear
Return (%)	15.6	11.3	12.4	58.5	31.0
Differ From Category (+/-)	3.2 high	6.6 high	3.8 high	12.8 high	41.9 high

Standard Deviation	Category Risk Index	Beta
7.4%—blw av	1.12—abv av	0.74

	2005	2004	2003	2002	2001	2000	1999	1998	1997	1996
Return (%).	6.8	15.2	25.4	0.5	10.2	22.1	7.0	5.7	16.2	16.8
Differ From Category (+/-)	.1.0	5.1	3.4	9.3	12.5	18.7	-4.6	-8.2	-2.8	2.9
Return, Tax-Adjusted (%) . .	.5.9	14.3	24.7	-0.5	8.6	19.4	3.8	1.9	12.6	13.2

PER SHARE DATA

	2005	2004	2003	2002	2001	2000	1999	1998	1997	1996
Dividends, Net Income ($).	0.30	0.29	0.26	0.28	0.38	0.45	0.50	0.50	0.50	0.60
Distrib'ns, Cap Gain ($) . .	.0.47	0.39	0.06	0.23	0.35	0.82	1.13	1.82	1.58	0.90
Net Asset Value ($)	20.06	19.49	17.50	14.21	14.64	13.95	12.51	13.22	14.71	14.47
Expense Ratio (%).	na	0.78	0.83	0.85	0.86	0.87	0.88	0.62	0.64	0.76
Yield (%)	1.46	1.45	1.48	1.93	2.53	3.04	3.66	3.32	3.06	3.90
Portfolio Turnover (%)	na	18	18	17	25	32	28	53	48	44
Total Assets (Millions $) . .	7,280	4,962	2,942	1,853	1,405	914	856	1,004	1,060	960

PORTFOLIO (as of 9/30/05)

Portfolio Manager: Stephen Boesel - 2001

Investment Style

Large Cap	Growth
Mid Cap	Value
Small Cap	Grth/Val

Portfolio

23.6% cash	6.6% corp bonds
60.8% stocks	0.1% gov't bonds
4.5% pref/conv't pref	0.0% muni bonds
3.9% conv't bds/wrnts	0.5% other

SHAREHOLDER INFORMATION

Minimum Investment
Initial: $2,500   Subsequent: $100

Minimum IRA Investment
Initial: $1,000   Subsequent: $50

Maximum Fees
Load: none   12b-1: none
Other: none

Services
✓ IRA
✓ Keogh
✓ Telephone Exchange

T Rowe Price Personal Strategy Balanced (TRPBX)

800-638-5660
www.troweprice.com

Balanced Stock/Bond

PERFORMANCE

fund inception date: 7/29/94

	3yr Annual	5yr Annual	10yr Annual	Bull	Bear
Return (%)	14.2	6.0	8.8	52.1	-8.4
Differ From Category (+/-)	1.8 abv av	1.3 high	0.2 abv av	6.4 abv av	2.5 abv av

Standard Deviation	Category Risk Index	Beta
6.7%—blw av	1.02—av	0.71

	2005	2004	2003	2002	2001	2000	1999	1998	1997	1996
Return (%)	6.4	12.5	24.3	-7.7	-2.4	5.6	7.9	13.9	17.4	14.2
Differ From Category (+/-)	.0.6	2.4	2.3	1.0	-0.2	2.2	-3.7	0.0	-1.6	0.3
Return, Tax-Adjusted (%) . . .	5.5	11.7	23.5	-8.6	-3.5	3.5	6.2	12.0	15.6	12.2

PER SHARE DATA

	2005	2004	2003	2002	2001	2000	1999	1998	1997	1996
Dividends, Net Income ($)	.0.34	0.34	0.31	0.36	0.41	0.50	0.49	0.45	0.44	0.39
Distrib'ns, Cap Gain ($) . .	.0.24	0.04	0.01	0.00	0.01	0.71	0.40	0.49	0.31	0.32
Net Asset Value ($)	18.77	18.19	16.52	13.57	15.09	15.92	16.24	15.90	14.82	13.29
Expense Ratio (%).	0.90	0.86	0.90	1.02	0.90	0.98	1.00	1.05	1.05	1.05
Yield (%)	1.78	1.86	1.87	2.65	2.71	3.00	2.94	2.74	2.90	2.86
Portfolio Turnover (%)	74	73	87	97	78	48	34	41	54	47
Total Assets (Millions $) . .	1,238	975	863	603	660	620	619	421	281	180

PORTFOLIO (as of 9/30/05)

Portfolio Manager: Team Managed - 1998

Investment Style

Large Cap	Growth
Mid Cap	Value
Small Cap	Grth/Val

Portfolio

6.7%	cash	4.6%	corp bonds
66.7%	stocks	19.3%	gov't bonds
0.0%	pref/conv't pref	0.0%	muni bonds
0.0%	conv't bds/wrnts	2.7%	other

SHAREHOLDER INFORMATION

Minimum Investment
Initial: $2,500   Subsequent: $100

Minimum IRA Investment
Initial: $1,000   Subsequent: $50

Maximum Fees
Load: none   12b-1: none
Other: none

Services
✔ IRA
✔ Keogh
✔ Telephone Exchange

T Rowe Price Personal Strategy Growth (TRSGX)

800-638-5660
www.troweprice.com

Balanced Stock/Bond

PERFORMANCE

fund inception date: 7/29/94

	3yr Annual	5yr Annual	10yr Annual	Bull	Bear
Return (%)	16.9	5.6	9.6	65.6	-18.1
Differ From Category (+/-)	4.5 high	0.9 abv av	1.0 high	19.9 high	-7.2 av

Standard Deviation	Category Risk Index	Beta
8.5%—blw av	1.29—high	0.91

	2005	2004	2003	2002	2001	2000	1999	1998	1997	1996
Return (%)	7.6	14.9	29.2	-12.3	-6.0	4.7	11.2	15.6	20.2	17.6
Differ From Category (+/-)	1.8	4.8	7.2	-3.6	-3.7	1.3	-0.4	1.7	1.2	3.7
Return, Tax-Adjusted (%)	7.1	14.4	28.7	-12.8	-6.5	2.8	9.9	14.3	19.3	15.0

PER SHARE DATA

	2005	2004	2003	2002	2001	2000	1999	1998	1997	1996
Dividends, Net Income ($)	0.21	0.27	0.23	0.24	0.27	0.35	0.32	0.32	0.26	0.24
Distrib'ns, Cap Gain ($)	0.29	0.02	0.01	0.00	0.00	1.08	0.52	0.45	0.15	0.89
Net Asset Value ($)	23.09	21.91	19.31	15.13	17.54	18.95	19.48	18.30	16.52	14.08
Expense Ratio (%)	1.00	0.98	1.00	1.10	1.10	1.10	1.10	1.10	1.10	1.10
Yield (%)	0.89	1.23	1.19	1.58	1.53	1.74	1.60	1.70	1.55	1.60
Portfolio Turnover (%)	52	47	52	68	54	42	36	33	39	39
Total Assets (Millions $)	919	662	541	322	316	284	262	194	98	42

PORTFOLIO (as of 9/30/05)

Portfolio Manager: Team Managed - 1998

Investment Style

Large Cap	Growth
Mid Cap	Value
Small Cap	Grth/Val

Portfolio

2.7% cash	2.5% corp bonds
86.0% stocks	7.5% gov't bonds
0.0% pref/conv't pref	0.2% muni bonds
0.0% conv't bds/wrnts	1.1% other

SHAREHOLDER INFORMATION

Minimum Investment
Initial: $2,500   Subsequent: $100

Minimum IRA Investment
Initial: $1,000   Subsequent: $50

Maximum Fees
Load: none   12b-1: none
Other: none

Services
✔ IRA
✔ Keogh
✔ Telephone Exchange

T Rowe Price Retirement 2010 (TRRAX)

800-638-5660
www.troweprice.com

Balanced Stock/Bond

PERFORMANCE

fund inception date: 9/30/02

	3yr Annual	5yr Annual	10yr Annual	Bull	Bear
Return (%)	13.4	na	na	50.0	na
Differ From Category (+/-)	1.0 abv av	na	na	4.3 abv av	na

Standard Deviation	Category Risk Index	Beta
6.9%—blw av	1.05—abv av	0.74

	2005	2004	2003	2002	2001	2000	1999	1998	1997	1996
Return (%)	6.2	11.1	23.7	—	—	—	—	—	—	—
Differ From Category (+/-)	0.4	1.0	1.7	—	—	—	—	—	—	—
Return, Tax-Adjusted (%)	5.5	10.4	23.3	—	—	—	—	—	—	—

PER SHARE DATA

	2005	2004	2003	2002	2001	2000	1999	1998	1997	1996
Dividends, Net Income ($)	0.26	0.20	0.13	—	—	—	—	—	—	—
Distrib'ns, Cap Gain ($)	0.09	0.09	0.01	—	—	—	—	—	—	—
Net Asset Value ($)	14.57	14.04	12.90	—	—	—	—	—	—	—
Expense Ratio (%)	0.68	0.00	0.00	—	—	—	—	—	—	—
Yield (%)	1.77	1.41	1.00	—	—	—	—	—	—	—
Portfolio Turnover (%)	6	1	13	—	—	—	—	—	—	—
Total Assets (Millions $)	1,304	752	151	—	—	—	—	—	—	—

PORTFOLIO (as of 11/30/05)

Portfolio Manager: Jerome Clark - 2002

Investment Style

Large Cap	Growth
Mid Cap	Value
Small Cap	Grth/Val

Portfolio

0.0% cash	0.0% corp bonds
0.0% stocks	0.0% gov't bonds
0.0% pref/conv't pref	0.0% muni bonds
0.0% conv't bds/wrnts	100.0% other

SHAREHOLDER INFORMATION

Minimum Investment
Initial: $2,500   Subsequent: $100

Minimum IRA Investment
Initial: $1,000   Subsequent: $50

Maximum Fees
Load: none   12b-1: none
Other: none

Services
✔ IRA
✔ Keogh
✔ Telephone Exchange

T Rowe Price Retirement 2020 (TRRBX)

800-638-5660
www.troweprice.com

Balanced Stock/Bond

PERFORMANCE

fund inception date: 9/30/02

	3yr Annual	5yr Annual	10yr Annual	Bull	Bear
Return (%)	15.4	na	na	59.6	na
Differ From Category (+/-)	3.0 high	na	na	13.9 high	na

Standard Deviation	Category Risk Index	Beta
8.1%—blw av	1.23—high	0.88

	2005	2004	2003	2002	2001	2000	1999	1998	1997	1996
Return (%)	7.1	12.8	27.4	—	—	—	—	—	—	—
Differ From Category (+/-)	.1.3	2.7	5.4	—	—	—	—	—	—	—
Return, Tax-Adjusted (%)	6.5	12.2	26.9	—	—	—	—	—	—	—

PER SHARE DATA

	2005	2004	2003	2002	2001	2000	1999	1998	1997	1996
Dividends, Net Income ($)	0.22	0.18	0.12	—	—	—	—	—	—	—
Distrib'ns, Cap Gain ($)	0.11	0.10	0.02	—	—	—	—	—	—	—
Net Asset Value ($)	15.63	14.89	13.45	—	—	—	—	—	—	—
Expense Ratio (%)	0.76	0.00	0.00	—	—	—	—	—	—	—
Yield (%)	1.39	1.20	0.89	—	—	—	—	—	—	—
Portfolio Turnover (%)	1	0	4	—	—	—	—	—	—	—
Total Assets (Millions $)	1,636	907	177	—	—	—	—	—	—	—

PORTFOLIO (as of 11/30/05)

Portfolio Manager: Jerome Clark - 2002

Investment Style

Large Cap	Growth
Mid Cap	Value
Small Cap	Grth/Val

Portfolio

0.0%	cash	0.0%	corp bonds
0.0%	stocks	0.0%	gov't bonds
0.0%	pref/conv't pref	0.0%	muni bonds
0.0%	conv't bds/wrnts	100.0%	other

SHAREHOLDER INFORMATION

Minimum Investment
Initial: $2,500   Subsequent: $100

Minimum IRA Investment
Initial: $1,000   Subsequent: $50

Maximum Fees
Load: none   12b-1: none
Other: none

Services
✔ IRA
✔ Keogh
✔ Telephone Exchange

T Rowe Price Retirement 2030 (TRRCX)

800-638-5660
www.troweprice.com

Balanced Stock/Bond

PERFORMANCE

fund inception date: 9/30/02

	3yr Annual	5yr Annual	10yr Annual	Bull	Bear
Return (%)	17.0	na	na	68.0	na
Differ From Category (+/-)	4.6 high	na	na	22.3 high	na

Standard Deviation	Category Risk Index	Beta
9.3%—av	1.41—high	1.01

	2005	2004	2003	2002	2001	2000	1999	1998	1997	1996
Return (%)	8.1	14.1	29.9	—	—	—	—	—	—	—
Differ From Category (+/-)	2.3	4.0	7.9	—	—	—	—	—	—	—
Return, Tax-Adjusted (%)	7.6	13.6	29.6	—	—	—	—	—	—	—

PER SHARE DATA

	2005	2004	2003	2002	2001	2000	1999	1998	1997	1996
Dividends, Net Income ($)	0.16	0.14	0.10	—	—	—	—	—	—	—
Distrib'ns, Cap Gain ($)	0.11	0.12	0.02	—	—	—	—	—	—	—
Net Asset Value ($)	16.49	15.50	13.81	—	—	—	—	—	—	—
Expense Ratio (%)	0.80	0.00	0.00	—	—	—	—	—	—	—
Yield (%)	0.96	0.89	0.72	—	—	—	—	—	—	—
Portfolio Turnover (%)	1	9	3	—	—	—	—	—	—	—
Total Assets (Millions $)	974	498	104	—	—	—	—	—	—	—

PORTFOLIO (as of 11/30/05)

Portfolio Manager: Jerome Clark - 2002

Investment Style

Large Cap	Growth
Mid Cap	Value
Small Cap	Grth/Val

Portfolio

0.0% cash	0.0% corp bonds
0.0% stocks	0.0% gov't bonds
0.0% pref/conv't pref	0.0% muni bonds
0.0% conv't bds/wrnts	100.0% other

SHAREHOLDER INFORMATION

Minimum Investment
Initial: $2,500   Subsequent: $100

Minimum IRA Investment
Initial: $1,000   Subsequent: $50

Maximum Fees
Load: none   12b-1: none
Other: none

Services
✔ IRA
✔ Keogh
✔ Telephone Exchange

T Rowe Price Retirement 2040 (TRRDX)

800-638-5660
www.troweprice.com

Balanced Stock/Bond

PERFORMANCE

fund inception date: 9/30/02

	3yr Annual	5yr Annual	10yr Annual	Bull	Bear
Return (%)	17.0	na	na	68.1	na
Differ From Category (+/-)	4.6 high	na	na	22.4 high	na

Standard Deviation	Category Risk Index	Beta
9.4%—av	1.42—high	1.01

	2005	2004	2003	2002	2001	2000	1999	1998	1997	1996
Return (%)	8.1	14.1	29.9	—	—	—	—	—	—	—
Differ From Category (+/-)	2.3	4.0	7.9	—	—	—	—	—	—	—
Return, Tax-Adjusted (%)	7.6	13.6	29.6	—	—	—	—	—	—	—

PER SHARE DATA

	2005	2004	2003	2002	2001	2000	1999	1998	1997	1996
Dividends, Net Income ($)	0.16	0.14	0.10	—	—	—	—	—	—	—
Distrib'ns, Cap Gain ($)	0.11	0.09	0.02	—	—	—	—	—	—	—
Net Asset Value ($)	16.57	15.57	13.85	—	—	—	—	—	—	—
Expense Ratio (%)	0.80	0.00	0.00	—	—	—	—	—	—	—
Yield (%)	0.95	0.89	0.72	—	—	—	—	—	—	—
Portfolio Turnover (%)	1	1	19	—	—	—	—	—	—	—
Total Assets (Millions $)	438	203	36	—	—	—	—	—	—	—

PORTFOLIO (as of 11/30/05)

Portfolio Manager: Jerome Clark - 2002

Investment Style

Large Cap	Growth
Mid Cap	Value
Small Cap	Grth/Val

Portfolio

0.0% cash	0.0% corp bonds
0.0% stocks	0.0% gov't bonds
0.0% pref/conv't pref	0.0% muni bonds
0.0% conv't bds/wrnts	100.0% other

SHAREHOLDER INFORMATION

Minimum Investment
Initial: $2,500   Subsequent: $100

Minimum IRA Investment
Initial: $1,000   Subsequent: $50

Maximum Fees
Load: none   12b-1: none
Other: none

Services
✔ IRA
✔ Keogh
✔ Telephone Exchange

Vanguard Asset Allocation Inv (VAAPX)

Balanced Stock/Bond

800-662-7447
www.vanguard.com

PERFORMANCE

fund inception date: 11/3/88

	3yr Annual	5yr Annual	10yr Annual	Bull	Bear
Return (%)	13.8	3.4	9.2	53.8	-23.7
Differ From Category (+/-)	1.4 abv av	-1.3 blw av	0.6 abv av	8.1 abv av	-12.8 blw av

Standard Deviation	Category Risk Index	Beta
8.5%—blw av	1.29—high	0.92

	2005	2004	2003	2002	2001	2000	1999	1998	1997	1996
Return (%)..............	5.0	11.0	26.4	-15.4	-5.3	4.9	5.2	25.4	27.3	15.7
Differ From Category (+/-)	-0.8	0.9	4.4	-6.7	-3.0	1.5	-6.4	11.5	8.3	1.8
Return, Tax-Adjusted (%)...	4.3	10.3	25.9	-16.1	-6.3	2.9	2.9	22.8	24.5	12.3

PER SHARE DATA

	2005	2004	2003	2002	2001	2000	1999	1998	1997	1996
Dividends, Net Income ($)	0.45	0.48	0.28	0.40	0.61	1.02	0.88	0.76	0.74	0.72
Distrib'ns, Cap Gain ($) ...	0.00	0.00	0.00	0.00	0.00	0.27	0.96	1.18	1.01	1.05
Net Asset Value ($)	25.33	24.56	22.56	18.07	21.81	23.67	23.80	24.38	21.05	17.94
Expense Ratio (%)........	0.38	0.38	0.43	0.42	0.44	0.44	0.49	0.49	0.49	0.47
Yield (%)	1.77	1.95	1.24	2.18	2.79	4.26	3.55	2.97	3.35	3.79
Portfolio Turnover (%)	6	34	43	54	77	29	11	60	10	47
Total Assets (Millions $) .	9,350	9,724	8,445	6,513	7,750	8,889	8,597	6,974	4,099	2,597

PORTFOLIO (as of 9/30/05)

Portfolio Manager: Thomas Loeb - 1988

Investment Style

Large Cap	Growth
Mid Cap	Value
Small Cap	Grth/Val

Portfolio

18.4%	cash	0.0%	corp bonds
81.7%	stocks	0.0%	gov't bonds
0.0%	pref/conv't pref	0.0%	muni bonds
0.0%	conv't bds/wrnts	0.0%	other

SHAREHOLDER INFORMATION

Minimum Investment
Initial: $3,000   Subsequent: $100

Minimum IRA Investment
Initial: $3,000   Subsequent: $100

Maximum Fees
Load: none   12b-1: none
Other: none

Services
✔ IRA
✔ Keogh
✔ Telephone Exchange

Vanguard Balanced Index Inv (VBINX)

Balanced Stock/Bond

800-662-7447
www.vanguard.com

PERFORMANCE

fund inception date: 9/28/92

	3yr Annual	5yr Annual	10yr Annual	Bull	Bear
Return (%)	11.1	3.7	8.2	39.6	-18.2
Differ From Category (+/-)	-1.3 av	-1.0 av	-0.4 av	-6.1 av	-7.3 av

Standard Deviation	Category Risk Index	Beta
5.9%—blw av	0.89—blw av	0.62

	2005	2004	2003	2002	2001	2000	1999	1998	1997	1996
Return (%)............	4.6	9.3	19.8	-9.5	-3.0	-2.0	13.6	17.8	22.2	13.9
Differ From Category (+/-)	-1.2	-0.8	-2.2	-0.8	-0.8	-5.5	2.0	3.9	3.2	0.0
Return, Tax-Adjusted (%)...	3.6	8.3	18.8	-10.6	-4.2	-3.4	12.2	16.3	20.5	12.1

PER SHARE DATA

	2005	2004	2003	2002	2001	2000	1999	1998	1997	1996
Dividends, Net Income ($).	0.53	0.50	0.45	0.52	0.60	0.65	0.58	0.54	0.53	0.49
Distrib'ns, Cap Gain ($) ...	0.00	0.00	0.00	0.00	0.03	0.10	0.14	0.14	0.15	0.12
Net Asset Value ($)	19.81	19.45	18.27	15.65	17.86	19.08	20.22	18.48	16.29	13.92
Expense Ratio (%)........	na	0.20	0.22	0.22	0.22	0.22	0.20	0.21	0.20	0.20
Yield (%)	2.67	2.57	2.46	3.32	3.33	3.37	2.84	2.90	3.22	3.49
Portfolio Turnover (%)	na	26	27	40	33	28	29	25	18	37
Total Assets (Millions $) ..	4,098	4,674	3,895	2,990	3,117	3,586	3,128	2,004	1,260	826

PORTFOLIO (as of 9/30/05)

Portfolio Manager: G Sauter/C Alwine - 2002

Investment Style

Large Cap   Growth
Mid Cap   Value
Small Cap   Grth/Val

Portfolio

2.0%	cash	11.3%	corp bonds
60.4%	stocks	26.3%	gov't bonds
0.0%	pref/conv't pref	0.0%	muni bonds
0.0%	conv't bds/wrnts	0.0%	other

SHAREHOLDER INFORMATION

Minimum Investment
Initial: $3,000   Subsequent: $100

Minimum IRA Investment
Initial: $3,000   Subsequent: $100

Maximum Fees
Load: none   12b-1: none
Other: none

Services
✔ IRA
✔ Keogh
Telephone Exchange

Vanguard LifeStrategy Conservative Growth (VSCGX)

Balanced Stock/Bond

800-662-7447
www.vanguard.com

PERFORMANCE

fund inception date: 9/30/94

	3yr Annual	5yr Annual	10yr Annual	Bull	Bear
Return (%)	9.5	4.4	7.5	33.4	-6.8
Differ From Category (+/-)	-2.9 blw av	-0.3 abv av	-1.1 blw av	-12.3 blw av	4.1 abv av

Standard Deviation	Category Risk Index	Beta
4.8%—blw av	0.73—low	0.48

	2005	2004	2003	2002	2001	2000	1999	1998	1997	1996
Return (%)	4.4	8.0	16.5	-5.3	0.0	3.1	7.8	15.8	16.8	10.3
Differ From Category (+/-)	-1.4	-2.1	-5.5	3.4	2.2	-0.3	-3.8	1.9	-2.2	-3.6
Return, Tax-Adjusted (%)	3.4	6.9	15.5	-6.7	-1.6	1.0	6.0	13.8	14.6	8.0

PER SHARE DATA

	2005	2004	2003	2002	2001	2000	1999	1998	1997	1996
Dividends, Net Income ($)	0.44	0.43	0.38	0.49	0.58	0.70	0.63	0.59	0.56	0.53
Distrib'ns, Cap Gain ($)	0.00	0.00	0.00	0.00	0.04	0.16	0.11	0.20	0.19	0.20
Net Asset Value ($)	15.49	15.26	14.54	12.82	14.06	14.71	15.10	14.71	13.40	12.14
Expense Ratio (%)	na	0.00	0.00	0.00	0.00	0.00	0.00	0.14	0.00	0.00
Yield (%)	2.84	2.81	2.61	3.82	4.11	4.70	4.14	3.95	4.12	4.29
Portfolio Turnover (%)	na	5	5	12	14	9	5	3	1	2
Total Assets (Millions $)	4,324	3,650	2,924	2,193	2,026	1,897	1,748	1,416	803	462

PORTFOLIO (as of 11/30/05)

Portfolio Manager: Team Managed - 1994

Investment Style

Large Cap	Growth
Mid Cap	Value
Small Cap	Grth/Val

Portfolio

0.0% cash	0.0% corp bonds
0.0% stocks	0.0% gov't bonds
0.0% pref/conv't pref	0.0% muni bonds
0.0% conv't bds/wrnts	100.0% other

SHAREHOLDER INFORMATION

Minimum Investment
Initial: $3,000   Subsequent: $100

Minimum IRA Investment
Initial: $3,000   Subsequent: $100

Maximum Fees
Load: none   12b-1: none
Other: none

Services
✔ IRA
✔ Keogh
✔ Telephone Exchange

Vanguard LifeStrategy Growth (VASGX)

800-662-7447
www.vanguard.com

Balanced Stock/Bond

fund inception date: 9/30/94

PERFORMANCE

	3yr Annual	5yr Annual	10yr Annual	Bull	Bear
Return (%)	15.6	3.4	8.4	60.7	-32.6
Differ From Category (+/-)	3.2 high	-1.3 av	-0.2 av	15.0 high	-21.7 low

Standard Deviation	Category Risk Index	Beta
8.4%—blw av	1.27—high	0.91

	2005	2004	2003	2002	2001	2000	1999	1998	1997	1996
Return (%).............	6.8	12.5	28.5	-15.8	-8.8	-5.4	17.3	21.4	22.2	15.4
Differ From Category (+/-)	.1.0	2.4	6.5	-7.1	-6.6	-8.9	5.7	7.5	3.2	1.5
Return, Tax-Adjusted (%)...	6.1	11.8	27.8	-16.5	-9.6	-6.5	16.2	20.0	20.7	13.7

PER SHARE DATA

	2005	2004	2003	2002	2001	2000	1999	1998	1997	1996
Dividends, Net Income ($)	.0.41	0.39	0.28	0.32	0.37	0.51	0.45	0.41	0.38	0.35
Distrib'ns, Cap Gain ($) ...	0.00	0.00	0.00	0.00	0.06	0.17	0.16	0.27	0.29	0.23
Net Asset Value ($)	21.00	20.04	18.16	14.36	17.43	19.59	21.41	18.79	16.04	13.68
Expense Ratio (%)........	na	0.00	0.00	0.00	0.00	0.00	0.00	0.14	0.00	0.00
Yield (%)	1.95	1.94	1:54	2.22	2.11	2.58	2.08	2.15	2.32	2.51
Portfolio Turnover (%)	na	5	2	7	7	9	1	2	1	0
Total Assets (Millions $) ..	7,001	6,040	4,754	3,281	3,726	3,738	3,177	1,924	1,184	629

PORTFOLIO (as of 11/30/05)

Portfolio Manager: Team Managed - 1994

Investment Style

Large Cap	Growth
Mid Cap	Value
Small Cap	Grth/Val

Portfolio

0.0% cash	0.0% corp bonds
0.0% stocks	0.0% gov't bonds
0.0% pref/conv't pref	0.0% muni bonds
0.0% conv't bds/wrnts	100.0% other

SHAREHOLDER INFORMATION

Minimum Investment
Initial: $3,000   Subsequent: $100

Minimum IRA Investment
Initial: $3,000   Subsequent: $100

Maximum Fees
Load: none   12b-1: none
Other: none

Services
✔ IRA
✔ Keogh
✔ Telephone Exchange

Vanguard LifeStrategy Moderate Growth (VSMGX)

800-662-7447
www.vanguard.com

Balanced Stock/Bond

PERFORMANCE

fund inception date: 9/30/94

	3yr Annual	5yr Annual	10yr Annual	Bull	Bear
Return (%)	12.6	4.1	8.1	46.8	-20.0
Differ From Category (+/-)	0.2 av	-0.6 av	-0.5 av	1.1 av	-9.1 blw av

Standard Deviation	Category Risk Index	Beta
6.6%—blw av	1.00—av	0.70

	2005	2004	2003	2002	2001	2000	1999	1998	1997	1996
Return (%)	5.6	10.5	22.4	-10.3	-4.4	-0.8	12.0	19.0	19.7	12.7
Differ From Category (+/-)	-0.2	0.4	0.4	-1.6	-2.2	-4.3	0.4	5.1	0.7	-1.2
Return, Tax-Adjusted (%)	4.8	9.6	21.5	-11.3	-5.6	-2.4	10.5	17.3	17.9	10.7

PER SHARE DATA

	2005	2004	2003	2002	2001	2000	1999	1998	1997	1996
Dividends, Net Income ($)	0.45	0.44	0.35	0.43	0.49	0.64	0.55	0.51	0.49	0.44
Distrib'ns, Cap Gain ($)	0.00	0.00	0.00	0.00	0.06	0.14	0.13	0.25	0.22	0.23
Net Asset Value ($)	18.47	17.91	16.61	13.87	15.93	17.25	18.18	16.86	14.81	12.97
Expense Ratio (%)	na	0.00	0.00	0.00	0.00	0.00	0.00	0.14	0.00	0.00
Yield (%)	2.43	2.45	2.10	3.06	3.06	3.68	3.00	2.98	3.26	3.33
Portfolio Turnover (%)	na	6	5	15	16	12	3	5	2	3
Total Assets (Millions $)	8,023	7,002	5,649	3,985	4,243	3,911	3,441	2,202	1,358	826

PORTFOLIO (as of 11/30/05)

Portfolio Manager: Team Managed - 1994

Investment Style

Large Cap	Growth
Mid Cap	Value
Small Cap	Grth/Val

Portfolio

0.0%	cash	0.0%	corp bonds
0.0%	stocks	0.0%	gov't bonds
0.0%	pref/conv't pref	0.0%	muni bonds
0.0%	conv't bds/wrnts	100.0%	other

SHAREHOLDER INFORMATION

Minimum Investment
Initial: $3,000   Subsequent: $100

Minimum IRA Investment
Initial: $3,000   Subsequent: $100

Maximum Fees
Load: none   12b-1: none
Other: none

Services
✔ IRA
✔ Keogh
✔ Telephone Exchange

Vanguard STAR
(VGSTX)

Balanced Stock/Bond

800-662-7447
www.vanguard.com

PERFORMANCE
fund inception date: 3/29/85

	3yr Annual	5yr Annual	10yr Annual	Bull	Bear
Return (%)	13.7	5.9	9.6	50.1	-5.1
Differ From Category (+/-)	1.3 abv av	1.2 abv av	1.0 abv av	4.4 abv av	5.8 abv av

Standard Deviation	Category Risk Index	Beta
6.5%—blw av	0.98—av	0.67

	2005	2004	2003	2002	2001	2000	1999	1998	1997	1996
Return (%)	7.4	11.6	22.7	-9.8	0.5	10.9	7.1	12.3	21.1	16.1
Differ From Category (+/-)	1.6	1.5	0.7	-1.1	2.8	7.5	-4.5	-1.6	2.1	2.2
Return, Tax-Adjusted (%)	6.5	10.7	21.7	-10.9	-1.6	7.7	5.3	9.9	18.1	12.8

PER SHARE DATA

	2005	2004	2003	2002	2001	2000	1999	1998	1997	1996
Dividends, Net Income ($)	0.47	0.44	0.39	0.48	0.55	0.64	0.61	0.58	0.59	0.59
Distrib'ns, Cap Gain ($)	0.06	0.00	0.00	0.00	0.87	1.65	0.40	0.98	1.20	0.98
Net Asset Value ($)	19.60	18.74	17.20	14.35	16.44	17.81	18.21	17.96	17.38	15.86
Expense Ratio (%)	na	0.00	0.00	0.00	0.00	0.00	0.00	0.00	0.00	0.00
Yield (%)	2.39	2.34	2.26	3.34	3.17	3.28	3.27	3.06	3.17	3.50
Portfolio Turnover (%)	na	6	15	12	6	17	10	16	15	18
Total Assets (Millions $)	12,168	10,763	9,134	7,217	8,242	8,119	8,087	8,083	7,355	5,863

PORTFOLIO (as of 11/30/05)

Portfolio Manager: Team Managed - 1985

Investment Style

Large Cap	Growth
Mid Cap	Value
Small Cap	Grth/Val

Portfolio

0.0% cash	0.0% corp bonds
0.0% stocks	0.0% gov't bonds
0.0% pref/conv't pref	0.0% muni bonds
0.0% conv't bds/wrnts	100.0% other

SHAREHOLDER INFORMATION

Minimum Investment
Initial: $1,000   Subsequent: $100

Minimum IRA Investment
Initial: $1,000   Subsequent: $100

Maximum Fees
Load: none   12b-1: none
Other: none

Services
✔ IRA
✔ Keogh
✔ Telephone Exchange

Vanguard Wellington Inv
(VWELX)

Balanced Stock/Bond

800-662-7447
www.vanguard.com

PERFORMANCE

fund inception date: 7/1/29

	3yr Annual	5yr Annual	10yr Annual	Bull	Bear
Return (%)	12.7	6.8	9.9	48.2	5.0
Differ From Category (+/-)	0.3 abv av	2.1 high	1.3 high	2.5 abv av	15.9 high

Standard Deviation	Category Risk Index	Beta
6.8%—blw av	1.03—abv av	0.69

	2005	2004	2003	2002	2001	2000	1999	1998	1997	1996
Return (%)	6.8	11.1	20.7	-6.9	4.1	10.4	4.4	12.0	23.2	16.1
Differ From Category (+/-)	.1.0	1.0	-1.3	1.9	6.4	7.0	-7.2	-1.9	4.2	2.2
Return, Tax-Adjusted (%)	5.2	9.6	19.6	-8.0	2.0	7.8	1.8	8.8	20.3	13.1

PER SHARE DATA

	2005	2004	2003	2002	2001	2000	1999	1998	1997	1996
Dividends, Net Income ($)	0.90	0.88	0.77	0.84	0.95	1.07	1.14	1.13	1.12	1.06
Distrib'ns, Cap Gain ($)	0.97	0.91	0.00	0.00	1.12	1.48	1.50	2.44	1.57	1.11
Net Asset Value ($)	30.35	30.19	28.81	24.56	27.26	28.21	27.96	29.35	29.45	26.15
Expense Ratio (%)	na	0.31	0.36	0.36	0.36	0.31	0.30	0.31	0.29	0.31
Yield (%)	2.87	2.81	2.65	3.42	3.34	3.60	3.86	3.55	3.61	3.88
Portfolio Turnover (%)	na	24	28	25	33	33	22	29	27	30
Total Assets (Millions $)	26,251	28,328	24,326	19,495	21,724	22,799	25,529	25,761	21,812	16,190

PORTFOLIO (as of 9/30/05)

Portfolio Manager: Paul Kaplan/Edward Bousa - 1994

Investment Style

Large Cap	Growth
Mid Cap	Value
Small Cap	Grth/Val

Portfolio

3.9% cash	23.9% corp bonds
65.3% stocks	7.0% gov't bonds
0.0% pref/conv't pref	0.0% muni bonds
0.0% conv't bds/wrnts	0.0% other

SHAREHOLDER INFORMATION

Minimum Investment
Initial: $3,000   Subsequent: $100

Minimum IRA Investment
Initial: $3,000   Subsequent: $100

Maximum Fees
Load: none   12b-1: none
Other: none

Services
✔ IRA
✔ Keogh
✔ Telephone Exchange

TAXABLE BOND FUNDS

Corporate Bond Funds
Category Performance Ranked by 2005 Returns

Fund (Ticker)	Annual Return (%)				Category Risk	Total Risk
	2005	3Yr	5Yr	10Yr		
Vanguard Long Term Invst Grade (VWESX)	5.1	6.7	8.5	7.1	high	av
Schwab Inv Yield Plus Investor (SWYPX)	3.3	2.8	3.3	na	low	low
USAA Intermediate Term Bond (USIBX)	2.7	4.7	5.6	na	av	low
T Rowe Price Corporate Income (PRPIX)	2.5	7.4	7.2	6.2	high	blw av
Vanguard Short Term Invst Grade (VFSTX)	2.2	2.8	4.3	5.1	blw av	low
Westcore Plus Bond (WTIBX)	2.0	6.6	6.7	6.2	av	low
Vanguard Intermediate Term Invst Grade (VFICX)	1.9	4.3	6.5	6.1	abv av	blw av
T Rowe Price Short Term Bond (PRWBX)	1.7	2.3	4.1	4.7	low	low
Corporate Bond Category Average	**2.1**	**4.2**	**5.1**	**5.5**	**av**	**low**

Schwab Inv Yield Plus Investor (SWYPX)

800-435-4000
www.schwab.com/
schwabfunds

Corporate Bond

PERFORMANCE AND PER SHARE DATA   fund inception date: 10/1/99

	3yr Annual	5yr Annual	10yr Annual	Category Risk Index	
Return (%)	2.8	3.3	na	0.11—low	
Differ From Category (+/-)	-1.4 blw av	-1.8 blw av	na	Avg Mat	0.5 yrs

	2005	2004	2003	2002	2001	2000	1999	1998	1997	1996
Return (%)	3.3	2.2	2.9	2.6	5.8	5.6	—	—	—	—
Differ From Category (+/-)	1.2	-1.9	-3.8	-2.8	-1.6	-3.2	—	—	—	—
Return, Tax-Adjusted (%)	2.0	1.3	1.8	1.0	3.6	2.9	—	—	—	—
Dividends, Net Income ($)	0.35	0.24	0.29	0.41	0.55	0.68	—	—	—	—
Expense Ratio (%)	0.59	0.60	0.56	0.55	0.55	0.55	—	—	—	—
Yield (%)	3.61	2.52	2.97	4.17	5.53	6.89	—	—	—	—
Total Assets (Millions $)	727	745	422	370	293	64	—	—	—	—

SHAREHOLDER INFORMATION

Minimum Investment
Initial: $2,500   IRA: $1,000
Subsequent: $500   IRA: $500

Maximum Fees
Load: none   12b-1: none
Other: none

T Rowe Price Corporate Income (PRPIX)

800-638-5660
www.troweprice.com

Corporate Bond

PERFORMANCE AND PER SHARE DATA   fund inception date: 10/31/95

	3yr Annual	5yr Annual	10yr Annual	Category Risk Index	
Return (%)	7.4	7.2	6.2	1.50—high	
Differ From Category (+/-)	3.2 high	2.1 high	0.7 abv av	Avg Mat	11.1 yrs

	2005	2004	2003	2002	2001	2000	1999	1998	1997	1996
Return (%)	2.5	7.0	13.0	4.2	9.7	7.9	-0.8	2.2	12.5	4.6
Differ From Category (+/-)	0.4	2.9	6.3	-1.2	2.3	-0.9	-1.8	-4.0	3.5	0.4
Return, Tax-Adjusted (%)	0.8	5.3	11.0	1.6	6.9	5.0	-3.5	-0.5	9.5	1.8
Dividends, Net Income ($)	0.46	0.49	0.53	0.62	0.65	0.68	0.67	0.74	0.76	0.73
Expense Ratio (%)	0.80	0.75	0.80	0.80	0.80	0.80	0.80	0.80	0.80	0.80
Yield (%)	4.78	4.91	5.46	6.87	7.00	7.49	7.33	7.47	7.26	7.34
Total Assets (Millions $)	209	216	102	84	73	50	51	55	33	16

SHAREHOLDER INFORMATION

Minimum Investment
Initial: $2,500   IRA: $1,000
Subsequent: $100   IRA: $50

Maximum Fees
Load: none   12b-1: none
Other: none

T Rowe Price Short Term Bond (PRWBX)

800-638-5660
www.troweprice.com

Corporate Bond

PERFORMANCE AND PER SHARE DATA   fund inception date: 3/2/84

	3yr Annual	5yr Annual	10yr Annual	Category Risk Index
Return (%)	2.3	4.1	4.7	0.44—low
Differ From Category (+/-)	-1.9 low	-1.0 blw av	-0.8 blw av	**Avg Mat** 2.1 yrs

	2005	2004	2003	2002	2001	2000	1999	1998	1997	1996
Return (%)	1.7	1.4	3.7	5.3	8.4	8.4	2.2	6.1	6.2	3.9
Differ From Category (+/-)	-0.4	-2.7	-3.0	-0.1	1.0	-0.4	1.3	-0.1	-2.8	-0.3
Return, Tax-Adjusted (%)	0.5	0.5	2.5	3.5	6.2	6.1	0.1	3.9	3.9	1.5
Dividends, Net Income ($)	0.16	0.13	0.16	0.22	0.27	0.27	0.25	0.26	0.28	0.28
Expense Ratio (%)	0.55	0.55	0.55	0.55	0.59	0.72	0.73	0.72	0.74	0.72
Yield (%)	3.44	2.75	3.24	4.52	5.56	5.87	5.60	5.58	5.88	5.97
Total Assets (Millions $)	1,265	1,517	1,294	904	599	467	305	347	345	447

SHAREHOLDER INFORMATION

Minimum Investment
Initial: $2,500   IRA: $1,000
Subsequent: $100   IRA: $50

Maximum Fees
Load: none   12b-1: none
Other: none

USAA Intermediate Term Bond (USIBX)

800-531-8181
www.usaa.com

Corporate Bond

PERFORMANCE AND PER SHARE DATA   fund inception date: 8/2/99

	3yr Annual	5yr Annual	10yr Annual	Category Risk Index
Return (%)	4.7	5.6	na	1.08—av
Differ From Category (+/-)	0.5 abv av	0.5 abv av	na	**Avg Mat** 5.1 yrs

	2005	2004	2003	2002	2001	2000	1999	1998	1997	1996
Return (%)	2.7	3.9	7.5	5.7	8.3	9.0	—	—	—	—
Differ From Category (+/-)	0.6	-0.2	0.8	0.3	0.9	0.2	—	—	—	—
Return, Tax-Adjusted (%)	1.0	2.3	5.8	3.3	5.6	6.0	—	—	—	—
Dividends, Net Income ($)	0.47	0.47	0.50	0.62	0.70	0.74	—	—	—	—
Expense Ratio (%)	0.65	0.65	0.65	0.65	0.65	—	—	—	—	—
Yield (%)	4.68	4.55	4.84	6.15	6.90	7.40	—	—	—	—
Total Assets (Millions $)	395	315	245	203	183	72	—	—	—	—

SHAREHOLDER INFORMATION

Minimum Investment
Initial: $3,000   IRA: $250
Subsequent: $50   IRA: $50

Maximum Fees
Load: none   12b-1: none
Other: none

Vanguard Intermediate Term Invst Grade (VFICX)

800-662-7447
www.vanguard.com

Corporate Bond

	3yr Annual	5yr Annual	10yr Annual	Category Risk Index	
Return (%)	4.3	6.5	6.1	1.31—abv av	
Differ From Category (+/-)	0.1 av	1.4 abv av	0.6 abv av	**Avg Mat**	6.7 yrs

	2005	2004	2003	2002	2001	2000	1999	1998	1997	1996
Return (%)	1.9	4.7	6.2	10.2	9.4	10.7	-1.5	8.3	8.9	2.7
Differ From Category (+/-) . .	-0.2	0.6	-0.5	4.8	2.0	1.9	-2.5	2.1	-0.1	-1.5
Return, Tax-Adjusted (%)	0.3	3.0	4.3	7.9	6.8	7.8	-4.0	5.6	6.3	0.2
Dividends, Net Income ($) .	0.47	0.47	0.52	0.59	0.63	0.66	0.62	0.63	0.64	0.64
Expense Ratio (%)	0.20	0.20	0.20	0.21	0.22	0.25	0.27	0.26	0.25	0.28
Yield (%)	4.75	4.67	5.13	5.79	6.51	6.96	6.71	6.22	6.41	6.52
Total Assets (Millions $) . . .	2,451	3,145	2,747	2,498	2,015	1,920	1,457	1,181	868	621

SHAREHOLDER INFORMATION

Minimum Investment
Initial: $3,000   IRA: $3,000
Subsequent: $100   IRA: $100

Maximum Fees
Load: none   12b-1: none
Other: none

Vanguard Long Term Invst Grade (VWESX)

800-662-7447
www.vanguard.com

Corporate Bond

	3yr Annual	5yr Annual	10yr Annual	Category Risk Index	
Return (%)	6.7	8.5	7.1	2.64—high	
Differ From Category (+/-)	2.5 high	3.4 high	1.6 high	**Avg Mat**	20.9 yrs

	2005	2004	2003	2002	2001	2000	1999	1998	1997	1996
Return (%)	5.1	8.9	6.2	13.2	9.5	11.7	-6.2	9.2	13.7	1.2
Differ From Category (+/-) . . .	3.0	4.8	-0.5	7.8	2.1	2.9	-7.2	3.0	4.7	-3.0
Return, Tax-Adjusted (%)	3.2	6.9	4.2	10.7	6.9	8.9	-8.7	6.2	10.8	-1.8
Dividends, Net Income ($) . .	0.52	0.52	0.53	0.56	0.56	0.57	0.56	0.59	0.61	0.62
Expense Ratio (%)	0.25	0.28	0.31	0.32	0.30	0.30	0.30	0.32	0.28	0.31
Yield (%)	5.41	5.46	5.67	6.02	6.47	6.78	6.87	6.16	6.57	6.91
Total Assets (Millions $)	4,224	4,213	3,851	3,753	3,550	3,704	3,724	4,153	3,637	3,461

SHAREHOLDER INFORMATION

Minimum Investment
Initial: $3,000   IRA: $3,000
Subsequent: $100   IRA: $100

Maximum Fees
Load: none   12b-1: none
Other: none

Vanguard Short Term Invst Grade (VFSTX)

800-662-7447
www.vanguard.com

Corporate Bond

PERFORMANCE AND PER SHARE DATA   fund inception date: 10/29/82

	3yr Annual	5yr Annual	10yr Annual	Category Risk Index	
Return (%)	2.8	4.3	5.1	0.47—blw av	
Differ From Category (+/-)	-1.4 blw av	-0.8 av	-0.4 blw av	**Avg Mat**	2.8 yrs

	2005	2004	2003	2002	2001	2000	1999	1998	1997	1996
Return (%)	2.2	2.1	4.2	5.2	8.1	8.1	3.3	6.5	6.9	4.7
Differ From Category (+/-)	0.1	-2.0	-2.5	-0.2	0.7	-0.7	2.4	0.3	-2.1	0.5
Return, Tax-Adjusted (%)	0.9	0.9	2.7	3.1	5.6	5.5	0.8	4.1	4.5	2.3
Dividends, Net Income ($)	0.38	0.37	0.44	0.58	0.68	0.71	0.66	0.66	0.67	0.66
Expense Ratio (%)	0.18	0.21	0.23	0.24	0.24	0.25	0.27	0.28	0.25	0.27
Yield (%)	3.61	3.44	4.03	5.36	6.26	6.64	6.24	6.10	6.15	6.16
Total Assets (Millions $)	10,409	13,122	11,120	8,668	7,383	7,341	6,799	5,428	4,601	4,609

SHAREHOLDER INFORMATION

Minimum Investment
Initial: $3,000   IRA: $3,000
Subsequent: $100   IRA: $100

Maximum Fees
Load: none   12b-1: none
Other: none

Westcore Plus Bond (WTIBX)

800-392-2673
www.westcore.com

Corporate Bond

PERFORMANCE AND PER SHARE DATA   fund inception date: 6/1/88

	3yr Annual	5yr Annual	10yr Annual	Category Risk Index	
Return (%)	6.6	6.7	6.2	1.06—av	
Differ From Category (+/-)	2.4 high	1.6 high	0.7 abv av	**Avg Mat**	8.3 yrs

	2005	2004	2003	2002	2001	2000	1999	1998	1997	1996
Return (%)	2.0	6.3	11.5	7.1	6.7	10.3	0.4	6.4	8.2	3.7
Differ From Category (+/-)	-0.1	2.2	4.8	1.7	-0.7	1.5	-0.5	0.2	-0.8	-0.5
Return, Tax-Adjusted (%)	-0.2	4.4	9.3	4.5	4.2	7.7	-1.8	4.1	5.8	1.5
Dividends, Net Income ($)	0.58	0.59	0.64	0.70	0.67	0.64	0.61	0.60	0.62	0.59
Expense Ratio (%)	0.55	0.55	0.55	0.55	0.62	0.85	0.85	0.85	0.85	0.81
Yield (%)	5.49	5.35	5.84	6.72	6.53	6.20	6.15	5.71	5.93	5.73
Total Assets (Millions $)	379	164	60	51	55	54	37	44	51	68

SHAREHOLDER INFORMATION

Minimum Investment
Initial: $2,500   IRA: $1,000
Subsequent: $100   IRA: $100

Maximum Fees
Load: 2.00% redemption   12b-1: none
Other: redemption fee applies for 3 months

Corporate High-Yield Bond Funds
Category Performance Ranked by 2005 Returns

Fund (Ticker)	Annual Return (%)				Category Risk	Total Risk
	2005	3Yr	5Yr	10Yr		
Fidelity Capital & Income (FAGIX)	5.4	18.2	9.4	7.9	high	blw av
Fidelity High Income (SPHIX)	3.8	13.2	6.9	5.9	abv av	blw av
Wells Fargo Advtg High Income Inv (STHYX)	3.3	12.4	5.6	7.1	av	blw av
USAA High Yield Opportunities (USHYX)	3.3	13.0	8.2	na	abv av	blw av
Vanguard High Yield Corp Inv (VWEHX)	2.7	9.3	6.4	6.0	blw av	low
TIAA-CREF High Yield Bond (TCHYX)	2.7	11.3	7.8	na	abv av	blw av
Northeast Investors (NTHEX)	2.2	10.1	6.9	6.3	blw av	low
Northern High Yield Fixed Income (NHFIX)	1.7	10.9	8.1	na	high	blw av
Corporate High-Yield Bond Category Average	**2.4**	**10.7**	**7.1**	**6.4**	**av**	**blw av**

Fidelity Capital & Income
(FAGIX)

800-544-8544
www.fidelity.com

Corporate High-Yield Bond

	3yr Annual	5yr Annual	10yr Annual	Category Risk Index	
Return (%)	18.2	9.4	7.9	1.56—high	
Differ From Category (+/-)	7.5 high	2.3 high	1.5 high	**Avg Mat**	8.9 yrs

	2005	2004	2003	2002	2001	2000	1999	1998	1997	1996
Return (%)	5.4	12.5	39.1	-0.4	-4.6	-9.4	13.3	4.7	14.7	11.4
Differ From Category (+/-) . .	3.0	3.1	17.7	0.2	-8.8	-4.7	7.8	2.5	0.4	-3.4
Return, Tax-Adjusted (%). . . .	3.1	10.1	35.7	-2.9	-7.7	-12.5	9.2	0.5	11.8	7.9
Dividends, Net Income ($). .	0.54	0.56	0.61	0.44	0.61	0.74	0.73	0.95	0.68	0.80
Expense Ratio (%).	0.78	0.78	0.83	0.81	0.78	0.82	0.81	0.82	0.86	0.98
Yield (%)	6.50	6.58	7.61	7.06	9.02	9.58	7.46	9.92	6.76	8.52
Total Assets (Millions $) . . .	5,411	4,912	4,260	2,802	2,875	2,837	2,846	2,196	2,096	2,163

SHAREHOLDER INFORMATION

Minimum Investment
Initial: $2,500   IRA: $500
Subsequent: $250   IRA: $250

Maximum Fees
Load: 1.00% redemption   12b-1: none
Other: redemp fee applies for 3 mos; maint fee for low bal

Fidelity High Income
(SPHIX)

800-544-8544
www.fidelity.com

Corporate High-Yield Bond

	3yr Annual	5yr Annual	10yr Annual	Category Risk Index	
Return (%)	13.2	6.9	5.9	1.13—abv av	
Differ From Category (+/-)	2.5 high	-0.2 av	-0.5 blw av	**Avg Mat**	6.4 yrs

	2005	2004	2003	2002	2001	2000	1999	1998	1997	1996
Return (%)	3.8	9.6	27.4	1.4	-4.8	-14.2	8.9	2.1	15.9	14.3
Differ From Category (+/-) . . .	1.4	0.2	6.0	2.1	-9.0	-9.4	3.4	-0.1	1.6	-0.5
Return, Tax-Adjusted (%).	1.3	7.0	24.3	-1.5	-8.5	-17.2	5.2	-1.1	11.9	10.2
Dividends, Net Income ($) .	0.64	0.68	0.69	0.63	0.89	0.92	1.07	0.92	1.11	1.09
Expense Ratio (%)	0.77	0.77	0.79	0.76	0.74	0.74	0.80	0.80	0.80	0.80
Yield (%)	7.29	7.48	7.68	8.28	10.99	9.77	8.83	7.44	8.35	8.49
Total Assets (Millions $) . . .	3,355	3,114	2,902	1,741	1,551	2,131	3,262	2,862	2,447	1,717

SHAREHOLDER INFORMATION

Minimum Investment
Initial: $2,500   IRA: $500
Subsequent: $250   IRA: $250

Maximum Fees
Load: 1.00% redemption   12b-1: none
Other: redemp fee applies for 3 mos; maint fee for low bal

Northeast Investors
(NTHEX)

Corporate High-Yield Bond

800-225-6704
www.northeastinvestors.com

fund inception date: 3/1/50

PERFORMANCE AND PER SHARE DATA

	3yr Annual	5yr Annual	10yr Annual	Category Risk Index
Return (%)	10.1	6.9	6.3	0.87—blw av
Differ From Category (+/-)	-0.6 av	-0.2 blw av	-0.1 av	Avg Mat 6.0 yrs

	2005	2004	2003	2002	2001	2000	1999	1998	1997	1996
Return (%)	2.2	14.3	14.3	3.2	1.3	-6.0	3.5	-0.2	13.8	20.1
Differ From Category (+/-)	-0.2	4.9	-7.1	3.9	-2.8	-1.3	-2.0	-2.5	-0.5	5.3
Return, Tax-Adjusted (%)	-0.5	11.7	11.3	0.0	-2.8	-10.3	-0.5	-3.9	10.4	16.2
Dividends, Net Income ($)	0.62	0.56	0.60	0.62	0.87	1.06	1.06	1.00	0.96	1.00
Expense Ratio (%)	0.67	0.67	0.65	0.70	0.21	0.61	0.61	0.61	0.64	0.66
Yield (%)	8.28	7.11	8.09	8.79	11.70	12.97	10.90	9.39	8.24	8.99
Total Assets (Millions $)	1,352	2,019	1,761	1,730	1,292	1,208	1,854	2,314	2,161	1,355

SHAREHOLDER INFORMATION

Minimum Investment
Initial: $1,000   IRA: $500
Subsequent: $50   IRA: $50

Maximum Fees
Load: none   12b-1: none
Other: none

Northern High Yield Fixed Income (NHFIX)

Corporate High-Yield Bond

800-595-9111
www.northernfunds.com

fund inception date: 12/31/98

PERFORMANCE AND PER SHARE DATA

	3yr Annual	5yr Annual	10yr Annual	Category Risk Index
Return (%)	10.9	8.1	na	1.16—high
Differ From Category (+/-)	0.2 av	1.0 abv av	na	Avg Mat 7.7 yrs

	2005	2004	2003	2002	2001	2000	1999	1998	1997	1996
Return (%)	1.7	8.5	23.5	1.3	7.0	-6.8	4.8	—	—	—
Differ From Category (+/-)	-0.7	-0.9	2.1	2.0	2.9	-2.1	-0.7	—	—	—
Return, Tax-Adjusted (%)	-0.5	5.9	20.3	-1.8	3.2	-10.6	1.8	—	—	—
Dividends, Net Income ($)	0.57	0.62	0.67	0.66	0.81	0.93	0.75	—	—	—
Expense Ratio (%)	0.90	0.90	0.90	0.90	0.90	0.90	0.90	—	—	—
Yield (%)	7.11	7.30	8.00	8.91	10.24	11.39	7.69	—	—	—
Total Assets (Millions $)	1,060	943	711	330	248	177	127	—	—	—

SHAREHOLDER INFORMATION

Minimum Investment
Initial: $2,500   IRA: $500
Subsequent: $50   IRA: $50

Maximum Fees
Load: 2.00% redemption   12b-1: none
Other: redemption fee applies for 1 month

TIAA-CREF High Yield Bond (TCHYX)

800-223-1200
www.tiaa-cref.org

Corporate High-Yield Bond

	3yr Annual	5yr Annual	10yr Annual	Category Risk Index
Return (%)	11.3	7.8	na	1.13—abv av
Differ From Category (+/-)	0.6 av	0.7 abv av	na	**Avg Mat** 7.7 yrs

	2005	2004	2003	2002	2001	2000	1999	1998	1997	1996
Return (%)	2.7	9.2	23.1	0.4	4.8	—	—	—	—	—
Differ From Category (+/-)	0.3	-0.2	1.7	1.1	0.7	—	—	—	—	—
Return, Tax-Adjusted (%)	0.2	6.8	20.0	-2.8	1.0	—	—	—	—	—
Dividends, Net Income ($)	0.65	0.66	0.72	0.77	0.93	—	—	—	—	—
Expense Ratio (%)	na	0.34	0.34	0.34	0.34	—	—	—	—	—
Yield (%)	7.20	6.94	7.68	9.35	10.41	—	—	—	—	—
Total Assets (Millions $)	280	279	227	104	92	—	—	—	—	—

SHAREHOLDER INFORMATION

Minimum Investment
Initial: $2,500   IRA: $2,000
Subsequent: $50   IRA: $50

Maximum Fees
Load: none   12b-1: none
Other: none

USAA High Yield Opportunities (USHYX)

800-531-8181
www.usaa.com

Corporate High-Yield Bond

	3yr Annual	5yr Annual	10yr Annual	Category Risk Index
Return (%)	13.0	8.2	na	1.07—abv av
Differ From Category (+/-)	2.3 high	1.1 abv av	na	**Avg Mat** 7.6 yrs

	2005	2004	2003	2002	2001	2000	1999	1998	1997	1996
Return (%)	3.3	10.5	26.5	-4.6	7.8	-1.9	—	—	—	—
Differ From Category (+/-)	0.9	1.1	5.1	-4.0	3.7	2.8	—	—	—	—
Return, Tax-Adjusted (%)	0.9	8.0	23.3	-8.0	3.6	-6.0	—	—	—	—
Dividends, Net Income ($)	0.61	0.62	0.67	0.76	0.96	1.04	—	—	—	—
Expense Ratio (%)	0.95	0.99	1.00	1.00	0.75	—	—	—	—	—
Yield (%)	7.10	6.90	7.71	10.20	11.16	11.73	—	—	—	—
Total Assets (Millions $)	379	238	162	64	55	43	—	—	—	—

SHAREHOLDER INFORMATION

Minimum Investment
Initial: $3,000   IRA: $250
Subsequent: $50   IRA: $50

Maximum Fees
Load: none   12b-1: none
Other: none

Vanguard High Yield Corp Inv (VWEHX)

800-662-7447
www.vanguard.com

Corporate High-Yield Bond

PERFORMANCE AND PER SHARE DATA — fund inception date: 12/27/78

	3yr Annual	5yr Annual	10yr Annual	Category Risk Index	
Return (%)	9.3	6.4	6.0	0.93—blw av	
Differ From Category (+/-)	-1.4 blw av	-0.7 blw av	-0.4 blw av	**Avg Mat**	8.0 yrs

	2005	2004	2003	2002	2001	2000	1999	1998	1997	1996
Return (%)	2.7	8.5	17.2	1.7	2.9	-0.8	2.5	5.6	11.9	9.5
Differ From Category (+/-) ...	-0.3	-0.9	-4.2	2.4	-1.2	3.9	-3.0	3.4	-2.4	-5.3
Return, Tax-Adjusted (%).....	-0.3	5.9	14.3	-1.3	-0.5	-4.3	-0.6	2.2	8.4	6.0
Dividends, Net Income ($) .	0.44	0.46	0.48	0.51	0.60	0.64	0.63	0.66	0.69	0.69
Expense Ratio (%)	0.22	0.23	0.26	0.27	0.27	0.28	0.29	0.28	0.29	0.34
Yield (%)	7.11	7.14	7.46	8.63	9.47	9.55	8.54	8.46	8.50	8.72
Total Assets (Millions $)...	5,212	7,317	7,095	5,433	5,160	5,270	5,699	5,380	4,571	3,583

SHAREHOLDER INFORMATION

Minimum Investment

Initial: $3,000   IRA: $3,000
Subsequent: $100   IRA: $100

Maximum Fees

Load: 1.00% redemption   12b-1: none
Other: redemption fee applies for 1 year

Wells Fargo Advtg High Income Inv (STHYX)

800-368-3863
www.wellsfargofunds.com

Corporate High-Yield Bond

PERFORMANCE AND PER SHARE DATA — fund inception date: 12/28/95

	3yr Annual	5yr Annual	10yr Annual	Category Risk Index	
Return (%)	12.4	5.6	7.1	1.02—av	
Differ From Category (+/-)	1.7 abv av	-1.5 low	0.7 abv av	**Avg Mat**	6.0 yrs

	2005	2004	2003	2002	2001	2000	1999	1998	1997	1996
Return (%)	3.3	10.2	24.7	-6.6	-0.7	-7.0	7.8	3.0	15.9	26.8
Differ From Category (+/-) ...	0.9	0.8	3.3	-6.0	-4.9	-2.3	2.3	0.8	1.6	12.0
Return, Tax-Adjusted (%)	1.0	7.7	21.8	-10.2	-5.0	-11.2	3.9	-0.6	11.8	22.4
Dividends, Net Income ($) ..	0.52	0.54	0.56	0.74	0.99	1.14	1.09	1.06	1.04	1.02
Expense Ratio (%)	na	0.86	0.90	1.00	0.90	0.90	0.80	0.80	0.60	0.00
Yield (%).................	6.83	6.76	7.20	11.01	12.44	12.72	10.07	9.48	8.57	8.83
Total Assets (Millions $).....	220	290	405	448	938	623	631	551	569	283

SHAREHOLDER INFORMATION

Minimum Investment

Initial: $2,500   IRA: $1,000
Subsequent: $100   IRA: $100

Maximum Fees

Load: 1.00% redemption   12b-1: none
Other: redemption fee applies for 6 months

Mortgage-Backed Bond Funds
Category Performance Ranked by 2005 Returns

Fund (Ticker)	Annual Return (%)				Category Risk	Total Risk
	2005	3Yr	5Yr	10Yr		
Dreyfus BASIC US Mortgage Securities (DIGFX)	3.4	3.2	5.2	5.8	abv av	low
Vanguard GNMA (VFIIX)	3.3	3.3	5.4	6.0	high	low
Fidelity Ginnie Mae (FGMNX)	3.1	3.1	5.0	5.7	blw av	low
Payden GNMA R (PYGNX)	2.9	3.3	5.5	na	high	low
Amer Century Ginnie Mae Inv (BGNMX)	2.8	2.6	4.7	5.5	av	low
T Rowe Price GNMA (PRGMX)	2.7	2.9	5.0	5.5	abv av	low
USAA GNMA Tr (USGNX)	2.7	2.7	4.8	5.2	av	low
Fidelity Mortgage Securities (FMSFX)	2.4	3.4	5.4	6.0	abv av	low
Mortgage-Backed Bond Category Average	**2.5**	**2.7**	**4.6**	**5.3**	**av**	**low**

Amer Century Ginnie Mae Inv (BGNMX)

800-345-2021
www.americancentury.com

Mortgage-Backed Bond

PERFORMANCE AND PER SHARE DATA

fund inception date: 9/23/85

	3yr Annual	5yr Annual	10yr Annual	Category Risk Index	
Return (%)	2.6	4.7	5.5	1.09—av	
Differ From Category (+/-)	-0.1 av	0.1 av	0.2 abv av	**Avg Mat**	4.7 yrs

	2005	2004	2003	2002	2001	2000	1999	1998	1997	1996
Return (%)	2.8	3.1	2.0	8.3	7.4	10.4	0.9	6.3	8.7	5.2
Differ From Category (+/-)	-0.3	-0.2	-0.3	0.5	0.0	0.2	-0.3	0.0	0.2	0.7
Return, Tax-Adjusted (%)	1.2	1.5	0.4	6.2	5.0	7.8	-1.4	3.9	6.1	2.5
Dividends, Net Income ($)	0.48	0.48	0.50	0.59	0.64	0.67	0.65	0.65	0.70	0.72
Expense Ratio (%)	0.58	0.59	0.59	0.59	0.59	0.59	0.59	0.58	0.55	0.58
Yield (%)	4.65	4.60	4.74	5.39	6.01	6.42	6.41	6.05	6.55	6.85
Total Assets (Millions $)	1,400	1,517	1,732	2,069	1,646	1,288	1,298	1,377	1,233	1,131

SHAREHOLDER INFORMATION

Minimum Investment		Maximum Fees	
Initial: $2,500	IRA: $2,500	Load: none	12b-1: none
Subsequent: $50	IRA: $50	Other: none	

Dreyfus BASIC US Mortgage Securities (DIGFX)

800-645-6561
www.dreyfus.com

Mortgage-Backed Bond

PERFORMANCE AND PER SHARE DATA

fund inception date: 8/5/87

	3yr Annual	5yr Annual	10yr Annual	Category Risk Index	
Return (%)	3.2	5.2	5.8	1.18—abv av	
Differ From Category (+/-)	0.5 high	0.6 high	0.5 high	**Avg Mat**	5.5 yrs

	2005	2004	2003	2002	2001	2000	1999	1998	1997	1996
Return (%)	3.4	2.8	3.5	8.8	7.6	11.0	2.8	4.7	9.5	4.8
Differ From Category (+/-)	0.9	-0.5	1.2	1.0	0.2	0.8	1.6	-1.6	1.0	0.3
Return, Tax-Adjusted (%)	2.0	1.0	2.1	6.7	5.4	8.4	0.1	2.1	6.6	2.2
Dividends, Net Income ($)	0.61	0.71	0.60	0.68	0.87	0.91	0.96	0.97	0.99	0.99
Expense Ratio (%)	na	0.66	0.68	0.65	0.65	0.65	0.65	0.65	0.65	0.65
Yield (%)	4.08	4.67	3.83	4.26	5.69	6.08	6.63	6.44	6.34	6.50
Total Assets (Millions $)	209	232	259	267	160	122	112	96	76	57

SHAREHOLDER INFORMATION

Minimum Investment		Maximum Fees	
Initial: $10,000	IRA: $5,000	Load: none	12b-1: none
Subsequent: $1,000	IRA: $1,000	Other: none	

Fidelity Ginnie Mae
(FGMNX)

Mortgage-Backed Bond

800-544-8544
www.fidelity.com

PERFORMANCE AND PER SHARE DATA   fund inception date: 11/8/85

	3yr Annual	5yr Annual	10yr Annual	Category Risk Index	
Return (%)	3.1	5.0	5.7	1.09—blw av	
Differ From Category (+/-)	0.4 abv av	0.4 abv av	0.4 high	**Avg Mat** 5.3 yrs	

	2005	2004	2003	2002	2001	2000	1999	1998	1997	1996
Return (%)	3.1	4.2	2.2	8.6	7.2	10.7	1.2	6.3	8.7	4.8
Differ From Category (+/-)	0.6	0.9	-0.1	0.8	-0.2	0.5	0.0	0.0	0.2	0.3
Return, Tax-Adjusted (%)	1.3	2.7	1.1	6.7	4.9	8.0	-1.1	3.9	6.0	2.3
Dividends, Net Income ($)	0.55	0.46	0.31	0.54	0.63	0.70	0.66	0.68	0.71	0.69
Expense Ratio (%)	0.45	0.60	0.57	0.60	0.62	0.63	0.64	0.72	0.75	0.75
Yield (%)	5.06	4.11	2.81	4.80	5.81	6.53	6.38	6.21	6.51	6.49
Total Assets (Millions $)	3,789	4,036	4,505	6,808	3,901	1,890	1,758	1,093	862	793

SHAREHOLDER INFORMATION

Minimum Investment
Initial: $2,500   IRA: $500
Subsequent: $100   IRA: $100

Maximum Fees
Load: none   12b-1: none
Other: maint fee for low bal

Fidelity Mortgage Securities
(FMSFX)

Mortgage-Backed Bond

800-544-8544
www.fidelity.com

PERFORMANCE AND PER SHARE DATA   fund inception date: 12/31/84

	3yr Annual	5yr Annual	10yr Annual	Category Risk Index	
Return (%)	3.4	5.4	6.0	1.18—abv av	
Differ From Category (+/-)	0.7 high	0.8 high	0.7 high	**Avg Mat** 4.5 yrs	

	2005	2004	2003	2002	2001	2000	1999	1998	1997	1996
Return (%)	2.4	4.4	3.5	9.1	7.6	11.2	1.8	5.8	9.1	5.4
Differ From Category (+/-)	-0.1	1.1	1.2	1.3	0.2	1.0	0.6	-0.5	0.6	0.9
Return, Tax-Adjusted (%)	1.0	3.0	2.4	7.1	5.2	8.5	-0.5	3.1	6.4	2.6
Dividends, Net Income ($)	0.45	0.41	0.28	0.52	0.66	0.71	0.67	0.69	0.68	0.70
Expense Ratio (%)	na	0.62	0.60	0.63	0.66	0.67	0.70	0.71	0.72	0.73
Yield (%)	4.10	3.63	2.50	4.58	6.02	6.62	6.47	6.29	6.15	6.40
Total Assets (Millions $)	1,764	1,618	1,311	1,339	417	377	391	448	484	521

SHAREHOLDER INFORMATION

Minimum Investment
Initial: $2,500   IRA: $500
Subsequent: $100   IRA: $100

Maximum Fees
Load: none   12b-1: none
Other: maint fee for low bal

Payden GNMA R
(PYGNX)

Mortgage-Backed Bond

800-572-9336
www.payden.com

PERFORMANCE AND PER SHARE DATA   fund inception date: 8/27/99

	3yr Annual	5yr Annual	10yr Annual	Category Risk Index	
Return (%)	3.3	5.5	na	1.23—high	
Differ From Category (+/-)	0.6 high	0.9 high	na	**Avg Mat**	5.6 yrs

	2005	2004	2003	2002	2001	2000	1999	1998	1997	1996
Return (%)	2.9	4.1	3.0	9.9	7.7	11.2	—	—	—	—
Differ From Category (+/-)	0.4	0.8	0.7	2.1	0.3	1.0	—	—	—	—
Return, Tax-Adjusted (%)	1.1	2.1	1.0	7.4	4.8	8.4	—	—	—	—
Dividends, Net Income ($)	0.52	0.59	0.59	0.62	0.64	0.69	—	—	—	—
Expense Ratio (%)	0.50	0.50	0.50	0.35	0.35	0.35	—	—	—	—
Yield (%)	5.28	5.87	5.78	5.86	6.12	6.65	—	—	—	—
Total Assets (Millions $)	114	113	147	169	152	126	—	—	—	—

SHAREHOLDER INFORMATION

Minimum Investment
Initial: $5,000   IRA: $2,000
Subsequent: $1,000   IRA: $1,000

Maximum Fees
Load: none   12b-1: none
Other: none

T Rowe Price GNMA
(PRGMX)

Mortgage-Backed Bond

800-638-5660
www.troweprice.com

PERFORMANCE AND PER SHARE DATA   fund inception date: 11/26/85

	3yr Annual	5yr Annual	10yr Annual	Category Risk Index	
Return (%)	2.9	5.0	5.5	1.14—abv av	
Differ From Category (+/-)	0.2 abv av	0.4 abv av	0.2 abv av	**Avg Mat**	5.0 yrs

	2005	2004	2003	2002	2001	2000	1999	1998	1997	1996
Return (%)	2.7	3.8	2.3	9.0	7.6	10.9	0.2	6.5	9.4	3.1
Differ From Category (+/-)	0.2	0.5	0.0	1.2	0.2	0.7	-1.0	0.2	0.9	-1.4
Return, Tax-Adjusted (%)	1.1	2.2	0.9	7.2	5.3	8.3	-2.2	3.9	6.7	0.4
Dividends, Net Income ($)	0.44	0.43	0.39	0.43	0.56	0.60	0.60	0.62	0.65	0.65
Expense Ratio (%)	0.67	0.69	0.70	0.69	0.70	0.71	0.71	0.70	0.74	0.74
Yield (%)	4.62	4.46	3.99	4.33	5.94	6.37	6.65	6.49	6.74	6.97
Total Assets (Millions $)	1,262	1,353	1,319	1,408	1,139	1,091	1,089	1,146	1,063	928

SHAREHOLDER INFORMATION

Minimum Investment
Initial: $2,500   IRA: $1,000
Subsequent: $100   IRA: $50

Maximum Fees
Load: none   12b-1: none
Other: none

USAA GNMA Tr
(USGNX)

Mortgage-Backed Bond

800-531-8181
www.usaa.com

PERFORMANCE AND PER SHARE DATA — fund inception date: 2/1/91

	3yr Annual	5yr Annual	10yr Annual	Category Risk Index
Return (%)	2.7	4.8	5.2	1.09—av
Differ From Category (+/-)	0.0 av	0.2 av	-0.1 av	**Avg Mat** 4.2 yrs

	2005	2004	2003	2002	2001	2000	1999	1998	1997	1996
Return (%)	2.7	3.4	2.0	9.2	7.1	12.1	-3.6	8.2	9.5	2.9
Differ From Category (+/-) ..	0.2	0.1	-0.3	1.4	-0.3	1.9	-4.9	1.9	1.0	-1.6
Return, Tax-Adjusted (%)....	1.0	1.7	0.3	7.0	4.7	9.3	-6.0	5.7	6.8	0.3
Dividends, Net Income ($)..	0.48	0.47	0.49	0.57	0.61	0.66	0.63	0.65	0.68	0.69
Expense Ratio (%).........	0.48	0.47	0.46	0.41	0.32	0.32	0.31	0.30	0.30	0.32
Yield (%)	4.99	4.82	4.92	5.61	6.14	6.69	6.73	6.28	6.61	6.91
Total Assets (Millions $).....	563	610	649	727	533	439	449	453	347	307

SHAREHOLDER INFORMATION

Minimum Investment
Initial: $3,000   IRA: $250
Subsequent: $50   IRA: $50

Maximum Fees
Load: none   12b-1: none
Other: none

Vanguard GNMA
(VFIIX)

Mortgage-Backed Bond

800-662-7447
www.vanguard.com

PERFORMANCE AND PER SHARE DATA — fund inception date: 6/27/80

	3yr Annual	5yr Annual	10yr Annual	Category Risk Index
Return (%)	3.3	5.4	6.0	1.41—high
Differ From Category (+/-)	0.6 high	0.8 high	0.7 high	**Avg Mat** 5.6 yrs

	2005	2004	2003	2002	2001	2000	1999	1998	1997	1996
Return (%)	3.3	4.1	2.4	9.6	7.9	11.2	0.7	7.1	9.4	5.2
Differ From Category (+/-) ...	0.8	0.8	0.1	1.8	0.5	1.0	-0.5	0.8	0.9	0.7
Return, Tax-Adjusted (%).....	1.7	2.5	0.8	7.4	5.4	8.4	-1.7	4.4	6.6	2.4
Dividends, Net Income ($) .	0.48	0.48	0.51	0.59	0.66	0.68	0.67	0.69	0.72	0.73
Expense Ratio (%)	0.20	0.20	0.22	0.27	0.27	0.27	0.30	0.31	0.27	0.29
Yield (%)	4.66	4.62	4.86	5.46	6.31	6.67	6.77	6.60	6.89	7.11
Total Assets (Millions $) ...	13,890	18,858	19,408	21,792	15,531	13,911	12,548	10,993	8,725	7,441

SHAREHOLDER INFORMATION

Minimum Investment
Initial: $3,000   IRA: $3,000
Subsequent: $100   IRA: $100

Maximum Fees
Load: none   12b-1: none
Other: none

Government: Short-Term Bond Funds
Category Performance Ranked by 2005 Returns

Fund (Ticker)	Annual Return (%)				Category Risk	Total Risk
	2005	3Yr	5Yr	10Yr		
Sit US Government Securities (SNGVX)	2.4	2.3	4.2	5.1	high	low
AMF Short US Government (ASITX)	2.2	1.8	3.4	4.3	blw av	low
Vanguard Short Term Federal (VSGBX)	1.8	1.7	4.2	5.0	abv av	low
Vanguard Short Term Treasury (VFISX)	1.7	1.7	4.1	4.9	abv av	low
Excelsior Short Term Govt Sec (UMGVX)	1.7	1.5	3.7	4.4	av	low
Payden US Government R (PYUSX)	1.0	1.2	4.0	4.7	high	low
Gov't: Short-Term Bond Category Average	**1.6**	**1.4**	**3.4**	**4.3**	**av**	**low**

AMF Short US Government (ASITX)

800-527-3713
www.amffunds.com

Government: Short-Term Bond

PERFORMANCE AND PER SHARE DATA — fund inception date: 11/26/82

	3yr Annual	5yr Annual	10yr Annual	Category Risk Index	
Return (%)	1.8	3.4	4.3	0.76—blw av	
Differ From Category (+/-)	0.4 high	0.0 av	0.0 av	Avg Mat	7.0 yrs

	2005	2004	2003	2002	2001	2000	1999	1998	1997	1996
Return (%)	2.2	1.4	1.8	4.6	7.3	7.7	2.3	6.6	6.2	3.6
Differ From Category (+/-)	0.6	0.3	0.4	-1.2	0.1	-0.2	0.1	0.4	0.1	-0.5
Return, Tax-Adjusted (%)	0.9	0.4	0.9	3.2	5.3	5.3	0.3	4.3	3.8	1.2
Dividends, Net Income ($)	0.39	0.30	0.29	0.39	0.52	0.61	0.56	0.61	0.63	0.63
Expense Ratio (%)	na	0.48	0.47	0.49	0.51	0.51	0.49	0.50	0.49	0.48
Yield (%)	3.80	2.87	2.70	3.57	4.88	5.84	5.39	5.72	5.96	6.01
Total Assets (Millions $)	154	151	231	167	190	98	113	118	106	176

SHAREHOLDER INFORMATION

Minimum Investment
Initial: $10,000   IRA: $10,000
Subsequent: $1   IRA: $1

Maximum Fees
Load: none
Other: none
12b-1: 0.15%

Excelsior Short Term Govt Sec (UMGVX)

800-446-1012
www.excelsiorfunds.com

Government: Short-Term Bond

PERFORMANCE AND PER SHARE DATA — fund inception date: 12/31/92

	3yr Annual	5yr Annual	10yr Annual	Category Risk Index	
Return (%)	1.5	3.7	4.4	0.88—av	
Differ From Category (+/-)	0.1 abv av	0.3 abv av	0.1 abv av	Avg Mat	1.9 yrs

	2005	2004	2003	2002	2001	2000	1999	1998	1997	1996
Return (%)	1.7	1.4	1.4	6.7	7.6	7.6	2.4	6.3	5.8	3.9
Differ From Category (+/-)	0.1	0.3	0.0	0.9	0.4	-0.3	0.2	0.1	-0.3	-0.2
Return, Tax-Adjusted (%)	0.5	0.3	0.3	5.1	5.6	5.3	0.4	4.3	3.7	1.8
Dividends, Net Income ($)	0.24	0.21	0.21	0.27	0.36	0.39	0.34	0.35	0.37	0.38
Expense Ratio (%)	0.75	0.53	0.49	0.51	0.57	0.54	0.58	0.62	0.61	0.61
Yield (%)	3.46	2.96	2.91	3.70	5.04	5.53	4.93	4.95	5.28	5.47
Total Assets (Millions $)	355	417	458	387	148	58	69	51	32	30

SHAREHOLDER INFORMATION

Minimum Investment
Initial: $500   IRA: $250
Subsequent: $50   IRA: $50

Maximum Fees
Load: none
Other: none
12b-1: none

Payden US Government R
(PYUSX)

800-572-9336
www.payden.com

Government: Short-Term Bond

PERFORMANCE AND PER SHARE DATA · fund inception date: 1/2/95

	3yr Annual	5yr Annual	10yr Annual	Category Risk Index	
Return (%)	1.2	4.0	4.7	1.41—high	
Differ From Category (+/-)	-0.2 av	0.6 abv av	0.4 abv av	**Avg Mat**	2.7 yrs

	2005	2004	2003	2002	2001	2000	1999	1998	1997	1996
Return (%)	1.0	1.4	1.1	8.1	8.5	8.8	1.7	7.7	6.6	2.9
Differ From Category (+/-)	-0.6	0.3	-0.3	2.3	1.3	0.9	-0.5	1.5	0.5	-1.2
Return, Tax-Adjusted (%)	-0.1	0.5	0.0	6.2	6.5	6.6	-0.3	5.5	4.4	0.8
Dividends, Net Income ($)	0.35	0.27	0.29	0.45	0.54	0.59	0.58	0.58	0.57	0.58
Expense Ratio (%)	0.45	0.45	0.45	0.45	0.40	0.40	0.40	0.34	0.45	0.45
Yield (%)	3.32	2.55	2.58	3.90	4.89	5.51	5.54	5.35	5.38	5.54
Total Assets (Millions $)	43	52	70	68	50	57	69	71	24	26

SHAREHOLDER INFORMATION

Minimum Investment
Initial: $5,000   IRA: $2,000
Subsequent: $1,000   IRA: $1,000

Maximum Fees
Load: none   12b-1: none
Other: none

Sit US Government Securities
(SNGVX)

800-332-5580
www.sitfunds.com

Government: Short-Term Bond

PERFORMANCE AND PER SHARE DATA · fund inception date: 6/2/87

	3yr Annual	5yr Annual	10yr Annual	Category Risk Index	
Return (%)	2.3	4.2	5.1	1.12—high	
Differ From Category (+/-)	0.9 high	0.8 high	0.8 high	**Avg Mat**	20.8 yrs

	2005	2004	2003	2002	2001	2000	1999	1998	1997	1996
Return (%)	2.4	3.3	1.1	5.7	8.5	9.1	1.3	6.5	8.1	5.0
Differ From Category (+/-)	0.8	2.2	-0.3	-0.1	1.3	1.2	-0.9	0.3	2.0	0.9
Return, Tax-Adjusted (%)	1.1	2.1	0.3	3.9	6.2	6.6	-0.7	4.2	5.7	2.5
Dividends, Net Income ($)	0.41	0.36	0.26	0.50	0.62	0.64	0.56	0.57	0.64	0.66
Expense Ratio (%)	0.80	0.80	0.80	0.80	0.80	0.80	0.80	0.80	0.80	0.80
Yield (%)	3.90	3.40	2.40	4.60	5.73	6.12	5.48	5.28	5.99	6.31
Total Assets (Millions $)	245	263	301	391	208	140	151	142	93	65

SHAREHOLDER INFORMATION

Minimum Investment
Initial: $5,000   IRA: $2,000
Subsequent: $100   IRA: $100

Maximum Fees
Load: none   12b-1: none
Other: none

Vanguard Short Term Federal (VSGBX)

800-662-7447
www.vanguard.com

Government: Short-Term Bond

PERFORMANCE AND PER SHARE DATA   fund inception date: 12/28/87

	3yr Annual	5yr Annual	10yr Annual	Category Risk Index	
Return (%)	1.7	4.2	5.0	1.06—abv av	
Differ From Category (+/-)	0.3 abv av	0.8 high	0.7 high	**Avg Mat**	2.1 yrs

	2005	2004	2003	2002	2001	2000	1999	1998	1997	1996
Return (%)	1.8	1.3	1.9	7.6	8.6	9.1	2.0	7.2	6.4	4.7
Differ From Category (+/-)	0.2	0.2	0.5	1.8	1.4	1.2	-0.2	1.0	0.3	0.6
Return, Tax-Adjusted (%)	0.6	0.3	0.9	5.7	6.5	6.7	-0.1	4.9	4.0	2.4
Dividends, Net Income ($)	0.33	0.29	0.31	0.43	0.55	0.61	0.57	0.58	0.61	0.61
Expense Ratio (%)	0.20	0.22	0.26	0.31	0.28	0.27	0.27	0.27	0.25	0.27
Yield (%)	3.25	2.78	2.95	3.97	5.22	5.96	5.71	5.68	6.06	6.05
Total Assets (Millions $)	1,698	2,432	2,673	2,851	1,783	1,502	1,521	1,635	1,429	1,338

SHAREHOLDER INFORMATION

Minimum Investment
Initial: $3,000   IRA: $3,000
Subsequent: $100   IRA: $100

Maximum Fees
Load: none   12b-1: none
Other: none

Vanguard Short Term Treasury (VFISX)

800-662-7447
www.vanguard.com

Government: Short-Term Bond

PERFORMANCE AND PER SHARE DATA   fund inception date: 10/28/91

	3yr Annual	5yr Annual	10yr Annual	Category Risk Index	
Return (%)	1.7	4.1	4.9	1.00—abv av	
Differ From Category (+/-)	0.3 high	0.7 high	0.6 high	**Avg Mat**	1.9 yrs

	2005	2004	2003	2002	2001	2000	1999	1998	1997	1996
Return (%)	1.7	1.0	2.3	8.0	7.8	8.8	1.8	7.3	6.3	4.3
Differ From Category (+/-)	0.1	-0.1	0.9	2.2	0.6	0.9	-0.4	1.1	0.2	0.2
Return, Tax-Adjusted (%)	0.6	0.1	1.2	6.2	5.8	6.4	-0.2	5.1	4.0	2.1
Dividends, Net Income ($)	0.32	0.28	0.27	0.42	0.52	0.59	0.53	0.55	0.59	0.59
Expense Ratio (%)	0.24	0.26	0.28	0.29	0.27	0.27	0.27	0.27	0.25	0.27
Yield (%)	3.11	2.65	2.53	3.79	4.94	5.78	5.27	5.30	5.78	5.76
Total Assets (Millions $)	1,383	1,886	2,086	2,211	1,394	1,200	1,235	1,184	998	960

SHAREHOLDER INFORMATION

Minimum Investment
Initial: $3,000   IRA: $3,000
Subsequent: $100   IRA: $100

Maximum Fees
Load: none   12b-1: none
Other: none

Government: Intermediate-Term Bond Funds
Category Performance Ranked by 2005 Returns

Fund (Ticker)	Annual Return (%)				Category Risk	Total Risk
	2005	3Yr	5Yr	10Yr		
Amer Century Target Maturity 2015 Inv (BTFTX)	4.8	5.9	7.7	7.5	high	abv av
Fidelity Spartan Govt Income (SPGVX)	2.7	3.0	5.4	5.8	av	blw av
Fidelity Government Income (FGOVX)	2.6	2.8	5.1	5.5	av	blw av
Vanguard Inflation Protected Securities (VIPSX)	2.5	6.2	8.5	na	high	blw av
Amer Century Government Bond Inv (CPTNX)	2.4	2.2	4.8	5.5	low	low
Wells Fargo Advtg Govt Securities Inv (STVSX)	2.1	2.7	5.4	5.6	av	low
Fidelity Inflation & Protected Bonds (FINPX)	2.1	6.0	na	na	high	blw av
Amer Century Target Maturity 2010 Inv (BTTNX)	1.3	2.8	6.0	6.5	high	blw av
Gov't: Intermediate-Term Bond Category Average	2.1	3.2	5.3	5.5	av	blw av

Amer Century Government Bond Inv (CPTNX)

800-345-2021
www.americancentury.com

Government: Intermediate-Term Bond

	3yr Annual	5yr Annual	10yr Annual	Category Risk Index	
Return (%)	2.2	4.8	5.5	0.66—low	
Differ From Category (+/-)	-1.0 blw av	-0.5 av	0.0 abv av	**Avg Mat**	5.0 yrs

	2005	2004	2003	2002	2001	2000	1999	1998	1997	1996
Return (%)	2.4	2.4	1.9	10.9	6.7	12.6	-2.0	8.9	8.3	4.0
Differ From Category (+/-) ..	0.3	-1.7	-1.5	-0.8	0.0	-0.7	1.2	-0.4	-1.6	2.2
Return, Tax-Adjusted (%)....	1.1	1.3	0.5	8.8	4.9	10.4	-4.0	6.4	6.0	1.8
Dividends, Net Income ($)..	0.39	0.28	0.30	0.40	0.51	0.55	0.50	0.56	0.59	0.58
Expense Ratio (%).........	0.50	0.51	0.51	0.51	0.51	0.51	0.51	0.51	0.51	0.53
Yield (%)	3.74	2.57	2.74	3.51	4.70	5.20	5.05	5.14	5.63	5.61
Total Assets (Millions $).....	521	436	486	588	440	352	352	444	361	337

SHAREHOLDER INFORMATION

Minimum Investment		Maximum Fees	
Initial: $2,500	IRA: $2,500	Load: none	12b-1: none
Subsequent: $50	IRA: $50	Other: none	

Amer Century Target Maturity 2010 Inv (BTTNX)

800-345-2021
www.americancentury.com

Government: Intermediate-Term Bond

	3yr Annual	5yr Annual	10yr Annual	Category Risk Index	
Return (%)	2.8	6.0	6.5	1.53—high	
Differ From Category (+/-)	-0.4 abv av	0.7 high	1.0 high	**Avg Mat**	5.0 yrs

	2005	2004	2003	2002	2001	2000	1999	1998	1997	1996
Return (%)	1.3	4.0	3.2	18.2	4.2	22.5	-11.8	15.0	16.7	-3.5
Differ From Category (+/-) ..	-0.8	-0.1	-0.2	6.5	-2.5	9.2	-8.5	5.7	6.8	-5.4
Return, Tax-Adjusted (%)....	-0.2	2.1	0.6	15.6	1.8	20.1	-13.8	12.4	14.4	-6.6
Dividends, Net Income ($) .	3.85	3.86	3.94	3.46	3.69	3.27	3.21	2.78	2.46	2.82
Expense Ratio (%)	0.58	0.59	0.59	0.59	0.59	0.59	0.59	0.59	0.62	0.67
Yield (%)	4.34	4.35	4.47	4.16	5.34	4.98	5.98	4.47	4.64	6.08
Total Assets (Millions $).....	218	212	236	305	252	270	219	246	158	109

SHAREHOLDER INFORMATION

Minimum Investment		Maximum Fees	
Initial: $2,500	IRA: $2,500	Load: none	12b-1: none
Subsequent: $50	IRA: $50	Other: none	

Amer Century Target Maturity 2015 Inv (BTFTX)

800-345-2021
www.americancentury.com

Government: Intermediate-Term Bond

PERFORMANCE AND PER SHARE DATA   fund inception date: 9/1/86

	3yr Annual	5yr Annual	10yr Annual	Category Risk Index	
Return (%)	5.9	7.7	7.5	2.36—high	
Differ From Category (+/-)	2.7 high	2.4 high	2.0 high	**Avg Mat**	10.0 yrs

	2005	2004	2003	2002	2001	2000	1999	1998	1997	1996
Return (%)	4.8	9.1	3.9	21.2	0.6	26.6	-14.5	14.6	22.9	-6.0
Differ From Category (+/-) . . .	2.7	5.0	0.5	9.5	-6.1	13.3	-11.3	5.3	13.0	-7.8
Return, Tax-Adjusted (%). . . .	3.1	7.1	1.4	19.1	-1.6	23.9	-16.5	12.6	19.6	-8.4
Dividends, Net Income ($) .	3.29	3.21	3.64	2.84	3.04	2.81	2.46	2.10	2.11	2.05
Expense Ratio (%)	0.58	0.59	0.59	0.59	0.59	0.59	0.59	0.59	0.61	0.65
Yield (%)	4.26	4.31	5.27	4.40	5.71	5.32	5.89	4.29	4.79	5.85
Total Assets (Millions $)	204	162	144	164	130	159	200	178	134	118

SHAREHOLDER INFORMATION

Minimum Investment		Maximum Fees	
Initial: $2,500	IRA: $2,500	Load: none	12b-1: none
Subsequent: $50	IRA: $50	Other: none	

Fidelity Government Income (FGOVX)

800-544-8544
www.fidelity.com

Government: Intermediate-Term Bond

PERFORMANCE AND PER SHARE DATA   fund inception date: 4/4/79

	3yr Annual	5yr Annual	10yr Annual	Category Risk Index	
Return (%)	2.8	5.1	5.5	1.00—av	
Differ From Category (+/-)	-0.4 av	-0.2 abv av	0.0 av	**Avg Mat**	6.1 yrs

	2005	2004	2003	2002	2001	2000	1999	1998	1997	1996
Return (%)	2.6	3.6	2.2	10.9	6.7	12.6	-2.2	8.5	8.9	2.0
Differ From Category (+/-) . . .	0.5	-0.5	-1.2	-0.8	0.0	-0.7	1.0	-0.8	-1.0	0.2
Return, Tax-Adjusted (%) . . .	1.3	2.4	0.9	9.0	4.5	10.0	-4.4	6.1	6.4	-0.5
Dividends, Net Income ($) . .	0.39	0.31	0.33	0.43	0.55	0.62	0.56	0.60	0.61	0.67
Expense Ratio (%)	0.45	0.63	0.65	0.68	0.60	0.66	0.67	0.68	0.73	0.72
Yield (%)	3.86	2.99	3.14	4.00	5.51	6.27	6.03	5.92	6.18	6.94
Total Assets (Millions $)	5,590	4,478	3,886	3,381	2,402	1,699	1,589	1,583	1,165	973

SHAREHOLDER INFORMATION

Minimum Investment		Maximum Fees	
Initial: $2,500	IRA: $500	Load: none	12b-1: none
Subsequent: $100	IRA: $100	Other: maint fee for low bal	

Fidelity Inflation & Protected Bonds (FINPX)

800-544-8544
www.fidelity.com

Government: Intermediate-Term Bond

PERFORMANCE AND PER SHARE DATA   fund inception date: 6/26/02

	3yr Annual	5yr Annual	10yr Annual	Category Risk Index
Return (%)	6.0	na	na	1.43—high
Differ From Category (+/-)	2.8 high	na	na	**Avg Mat** 9.7 yrs

	2005	2004	2003	2002	2001	2000	1999	1998	1997	1996
Return (%)	2.1	8.2	7.7	—	—	—	—	—	—	—
Differ From Category (+/-)	0.0	4.1	4.3	—	—	—	—	—	—	—
Return, Tax-Adjusted (%)	1.0	7.2	6.8	—	—	—	—	—	—	—
Dividends, Net Income ($)	0.15	0.16	0.18	—	—	—	—	—	—	—
Expense Ratio (%)	0.45	0.50	0.50	—	—	—	—	—	—	—
Yield (%)	1.30	1.32	1.57	—	—	—	—	—	—	—
Total Assets (Millions $)	1,619	1,317	724	—	—	—	—	—	—	—

SHAREHOLDER INFORMATION

Minimum Investment
Initial: $2,500   IRA: $500
Subsequent: $250   IRA: $100

Maximum Fees
Load: none   12b-1: none
Other: maint fee for low bal

Fidelity Spartan Govt Income (SPGVX)

800-544-8544
www.fidelity.com

Government: Intermediate-Term Bond

PERFORMANCE AND PER SHARE DATA   fund inception date: 12/20/88

	3yr Annual	5yr Annual	10yr Annual	Category Risk Index
Return (%)	3.0	5.4	5.8	1.02—av
Differ From Category (+/-)	-0.2 abv av	0.1 abv av	0.3 high	**Avg Mat** 6.3 yrs

	2005	2004	2003	2002	2001	2000	1999	1998	1997	1996
Return (%)	2.7	4.0	2.3	11.5	6.9	12.7	-2.0	9.0	9.2	2.6
Differ From Category (+/-)	0.6	-0.1	-1.1	-0.2	0.2	-0.6	1.2	-0.3	-0.7	0.8
Return, Tax-Adjusted (%)	1.2	2.7	0.9	9.6	4.7	10.1	-4.3	6.6	6.7	0.0
Dividends, Net Income ($)	0.46	0.39	0.40	0.49	0.58	0.65	0.63	0.62	0.64	0.68
Expense Ratio (%)	0.45	0.50	0.50	0.50	0.49	0.50	0.51	0.60	0.60	0.65
Yield (%)	4.20	3.55	3.56	4.36	5.48	6.22	6.33	5.77	6.16	6.62
Total Assets (Millions $)	831	860	890	1,212	875	720	468	643	280	277

SHAREHOLDER INFORMATION

Minimum Investment
Initial: $25,000   IRA: $25,000
Subsequent: $1,000   IRA: $1,000

Maximum Fees
Load: none   12b-1: none
Other: maint fee for low bal

Vanguard Inflation Protected Securities (VIPSX)

800-662-7447
www.vanguard.com

Government: Intermediate-Term Bond

fund inception date: 6/29/00

	3yr Annual	5yr Annual	10yr Annual	Category Risk Index
Return (%)	6.2	8.5	na	1.38—high
Differ From Category (+/-)	3.0 high	3.2 high	na	**Avg Mat** 10.8 yrs

	2005	2004	2003	2002	2001	2000	1999	1998	1997	1996
Return (%) 2.5	2.5	8.2	8.0	16.6	7.6	—	—	—	—	—
Differ From Category (+/-) . . .0.4	0.4	4.1	4.6	4.9	0.9	—	—	—	—	—
Return, Tax-Adjusted (%). 0.6	0.6	6.5	6.5	14.8	5.7	—	—	—	—	—
Dividends, Net Income ($) . 0.68	0.68	0.57	0.45	0.46	0.45	—	—	—	—	—
Expense Ratio (%) 0.20	0.20	0.18	0.22	0.25	0.25	—	—	—	—	—
Yield (%) 5.57	5.57	4.47	3.64	3.86	4.16	—	—	—	—	—
Total Assets (Millions $) . . . 6,332	6,332	7,182	4,746	2,988	772	—	—	—	—	—

SHAREHOLDER INFORMATION

Minimum Investment		Maximum Fees	
Initial: $3,000	IRA: $3,000	Load: none	12b-1: none
Subsequent: $100	IRA: $100	Other: none	

Wells Fargo Advtg Govt Securities Inv (STVSX)

800-368-3863
www.wellsfargofunds.com

Government: Intermediate-Term Bond

fund inception date: 10/29/86

	3yr Annual	5yr Annual	10yr Annual	Category Risk Index
Return (%)	2.7	5.4	5.6	0.85—av
Differ From Category (+/-)	-0.5 av	0.1 abv av	0.1 abv av	**Avg Mat** 5.3 yrs

	2005	2004	2003	2002	2001	2000	1999	1998	1997	1996
Return (%) 2.1	2.1	3.2	2.8	10.4	8.7	11.3	-1.0	8.1	9.0	2.8
Differ From Category (+/-) . . .0.0	0.0	-0.9	-0.6	-1.3	2.0	-2.0	2.2	-1.2	-0.9	1.0
Return, Tax-Adjusted (%) 0.6	0.6	1.8	1.4	8.2	6.4	8.9	-3.1	5.4	6.6	0.5
Dividends, Net Income ($) . .0.45	0.45	0.37	0.34	0.46	0.55	0.59	0.56	0.61	0.65	0.63
Expense Ratio (%) . . . . na	na	1.05	0.90	0.90	0.90	0.90	0.80	0.80	0.80	0.90
Yield (%) 4.26	4.26	3.43	3.08	4.04	5.03	5.59	5.59	5.59	6.00	6.02
Total Assets (Millions $) 982	982	1,170	1,731	2,317	1,630	1,336	1,288	1,327	907	660

SHAREHOLDER INFORMATION

Minimum Investment		Maximum Fees	
Initial: $2,500	IRA: $1,000	Load: none	12b-1: none
Subsequent: $100	IRA: $100	Other: none	

Government: Long-Term Bond Funds
Category Performance Ranked by 2005 Returns

Fund (Ticker)	Annual Return (%)				Category Risk	Total Risk
	2005	3Yr	5Yr	10Yr		
Amer Century Target Maturity 2025 Inv (BTTRX)	14.4	10.7	9.7	na	high	high
Wasatch Hoisington US Treasury (WHOSX)	10.4	7.2	8.2	8.5	abv av	abv av
Amer Century Target Maturity 2020 Inv (BTTTX)	10.2	8.6	8.9	8.4	high	high
Rydex US Government Bond Inv (RYGBX)	8.3	5.2	6.8	5.6	abv av	high
Vanguard Long Term Treasury Inv (VUSTX)	6.6	5.4	7.3	7.1	av	av
Dreyfus US Tsy Long Term (DRGBX)	5.6	4.6	5.5	5.8	blw av	blw av
Gov't: Long-Term Bond Category Average	6.5	5.2	6.0	5.5	av	abv av

Amer Century Target Maturity 2020 Inv (BTTX)

800-345-2021
www.americancentury.com

Government: Long-Term Bond

PERFORMANCE AND PER SHARE DATA   fund inception date: 12/29/89

	3yr Annual	5yr Annual	10yr Annual	Category Risk Index
Return (%)	8.6	8.9	8.4	1.22—high
Differ From Category (+/-)	3.4 high	2.9 high	2.9 high	**Avg Mat** 15.0 yrs

	2005	2004	2003	2002	2001	2000	1999	1998	1997	1996
Return (%)	10.2	12.4	3.4	21.4	-1.5	30.6	-18.3	16.5	28.6	-8.4
Differ From Category (+/-) . . .	3.7	5.2	1.3	8.2	-3.5	12.7	-10.1	5.0	12.8	-8.0
Return, Tax-Adjusted (%)	8.5	10.3	0.7	17.4	-6.3	26.0	-22.2	10.4	22.9	-10.6
Dividends, Net Income ($) .	2.49	2.38	2.47	2.13	2.43	1.79	1.85	2.06	2.35	1.45
Expense Ratio (%)	0.58	0.59	0.59	0.59	0.59	0.59	0.59	0.59	0.53	0.61
Yield (%)	4.18	4.36	4.91	4.32	5.72	4.30	5.65	5.00	7.09	6.04
Total Assets (Millions $)	185	173	169	204	193	304	271	424	599	890

SHAREHOLDER INFORMATION

Minimum Investment
Initial: $2,500   IRA: $2,500
Subsequent: $50   IRA: $50

Maximum Fees
Load: none   12b-1: none
Other: none

Amer Century Target Maturity 2025 Inv (BTTRX)

800-345-2021
www.americancentury.com

Government: Long-Term Bond

PERFORMANCE AND PER SHARE DATA   fund inception date: 2/15/96

	3yr Annual	5yr Annual	10yr Annual	Category Risk Index
Return (%)	10.7	9.7	na	1.44—high
Differ From Category (+/-)	5.5 high	3.7 high	na	**Avg Mat** 20.0 yrs

	2005	2004	2003	2002	2001	2000	1999	1998	1997	1996
Return (%)	14.4	16.4	2.0	20.4	-2.6	32.6	-20.6	21.8	30.1	—
Differ From Category (+/-) . . .	7.9	9.2	-0.1	7.2	-4.7	14.7	-12.4	10.3	14.3	—
Return, Tax-Adjusted (%) . . .	13.3	11.8	-0.7	16.5	-5.8	29.1	-22.1	19.5	28.6	—
Dividends, Net Income ($) . .	1.34	2.54	2.08	2.06	2.26	2.00	1.11	1.28	0.70	—
Expense Ratio (%)	0.58	0.59	0.59	0.59	0.59	0.59	0.59	0.59	0.62	—
Yield (%)	2.54	4.92	5.03	5.05	6.92	6.02	4.50	4.06	2.74	—
Total Assets (Millions $)	239	86	125	187	244	593	696	303	193	—

SHAREHOLDER INFORMATION

Minimum Investment
Initial: $2,500   IRA: $2,500
Subsequent: $50   IRA: $50

Maximum Fees
Load: none   12b-1: none
Other: none

Dreyfus US Tsy Long Term
(DRGBX)

Government: Long-Term Bond

800-645-6561
www.dreyfus.com

PERFORMANCE AND PER SHARE DATA   fund inception date: 3/27/87

	3yr Annual	5yr Annual	10yr Annual	Category Risk Index
Return (%)	4.6	5.5	5.8	0.65—blw av
Differ From Category (+/-)	-0.6 blw av	-0.5 blw av	0.3 av	**Avg Mat** 29.7 yrs

	2005	2004	2003	2002	2001	2000	1999	1998	1997	1996
Return (%)	5.6	3.8	4.4	11.4	2.5	17.7	-8.2	10.8	11.7	0.8
Differ From Category (+/-) . .	-0.9	-3.4	2.3	-1.8	0.5	-0.2	0.1	-0.7	-4.1	1.3
Return, Tax-Adjusted (%). . . .	4.0	2.3	3.0	9.6	0.5	15.4	-10.2	8.7	9.1	-1.6
Dividends, Net Income ($). .	0.71	0.71	0.66	0.72	0.79	0.82	0.82	0.80	0.93	0.99
Expense Ratio (%).	na	0.97	0.80	0.80	0.80	0.80	0.80	0.80	0.80	0.80
Yield (%)	4.32	4.43	4.05	4.43	5.17	5.23	5.83	4.95	6.10	6.77
Total Assets (Millions $)	83	82	100	101	109	116	121	142	134	136

SHAREHOLDER INFORMATION

Minimum Investment
Initial: $2,500   IRA: $0
Subsequent: $100   IRA: $0

Maximum Fees
Load: none   12b-1: none
Other: none

Rydex US Government Bond Inv (RYGBX)

Government: Long-Term Bond

800-820-0888
www.rydexfunds.com

PERFORMANCE AND PER SHARE DATA   fund inception date: 1/3/94

	3yr Annual	5yr Annual	10yr Annual	Category Risk Index
Return (%)	5.2	6.8	5.6	1.19—abv av
Differ From Category (+/-)	0.0 av	0.8 av	0.1 blw av	**Avg Mat** 24.7 yrs

	2005	2004	2003	2002	2001	2000	1999	1998	1997	1996
Return (%)	8.3	9.4	-1.7	19.0	0.3	21.5	-19.0	15.5	17.4	-7.1
Differ From Category (+/-) . . .	1.8	2.2	-3.9	5.8	-1.7	3.6	-10.8	4.0	1.6	-6.7
Return, Tax-Adjusted (%).	7.0	8.1	-3.0	17.3	-1.1	19.5	-20.6	13.9	14.6	-9.1
Dividends, Net Income ($) .	0.42	0.41	0.41	0.41	0.39	0.44	0.46	0.39	0.67	0.54
Expense Ratio (%)	0.93	0.95	0.97	0.88	0.96	0.92	0.96	1.11	1.49	1.26
Yield (%)	3.68	3.69	3.92	3.75	4.04	4.38	5.30	3.47	6.65	5.88
Total Assets (Millions $)	42	21	41	30	11	58	22	45	58	4

SHAREHOLDER INFORMATION

Minimum Investment
Initial: $25,000   IRA: $25,000
Subsequent: $1   IRA: $1

Maximum Fees
Load: none   12b-1: none
Other: none

Vanguard Long Term Treasury Inv (VUSTX)

800-662-7447
www.vanguard.com

Government: Long-Term Bond

PERFORMANCE AND PER SHARE DATA   fund inception date: 5/19/86

	3yr Annual	5yr Annual	10yr Annual	Category Risk Index	
Return (%)	5.4	7.3	7.1	0.77—av	
Differ From Category (+/-)	0.2 av	1.3 av	1.6 abv av	**Avg Mat**	17.1 yrs

	2005	2004	2003	2002	2001	2000	1999	1998	1997	1996
Return (%)	6.6	7.1	2.6	16.6	4.3	19.7	-8.6	13.0	13.9	-1.2
Differ From Category (+/-) . . .	0.1	-0.1	0.5	3.4	2.3	1.8	-0.4	1.5	-1.9	-0.8
Return, Tax-Adjusted (%).	4.7	5.2	0.8	14.2	2.1	17.2	-11.0	10.6	11.3	-3.6
Dividends, Net Income ($) .	0.57	0.58	0.56	0.59	0.60	0.63	0.61	0.63	0.64	0.65
Expense Ratio (%)	0.24	0.26	0.28	0.29	0.29	0.28	0.27	0.27	0.25	0.27
Yield (%)	4.83	4.96	4.87	4.93	5.60	5.74	6.24	5.55	6.05	6.55
Total Assets (Millions $). . .	1,422	1,444	1,489	1,682	1,373	1,358	1,224	1,416	1,035	918

SHAREHOLDER INFORMATION

Minimum Investment
Initial: $3,000   IRA: $3,000
Subsequent: $100   IRA: $100

Maximum Fees
Load: none   12b-1: none
Other: none

Wasatch Hoisington US Treasury (WHOSX)

800-551-1700
www.wasatchfunds.com

Government: Long-Term Bond

PERFORMANCE AND PER SHARE DATA   fund inception date: 12/19/86

	3yr Annual	5yr Annual	10yr Annual	Category Risk Index	
Return (%)	7.2	8.2	8.5	1.07—abv av	
Differ From Category (+/-)	2.0 abv av	2.2 abv av	3.0 high	**Avg Mat**	20.8 yrs

	2005	2004	2003	2002	2001	2000	1999	1998	1997	1996
Return (%)	10.4	10.2	1.2	16.8	2.8	21.9	-12.3	14.6	15.7	7.8
Differ From Category (+/-) . . .	3.9	3.0	-0.9	3.6	0.8	4.0	-4.1	3.1	-0.1	8.3
Return, Tax-Adjusted (%)	9.7	8.5	-0.6	14.8	0.4	19.9	-14.5	13.5	13.6	5.8
Dividends, Net Income ($) . .	0.29	0.60	0.73	0.63	0.77	0.56	0.73	0.28	0.56	0.51
Expense Ratio (%)	0.75	0.75	0.75	0.75	0.75	0.75	0.75	0.75	0.75	0.93
Yield (%)	2.00	4.48	5.67	4.73	6.46	4.48	6.86	2.18	4.85	4.88
Total Assets (Millions $).	159	47	57	77	59	63	65	89	14	9

SHAREHOLDER INFORMATION

Minimum Investment
Initial: $2,000   IRA: $1,000
Subsequent: $50   IRA: $50

Maximum Fees
Load: 2.00% redemption   12b-1: none
Other: redemption fee applies for 2 months

General Bond Funds
Category Performance Ranked by 2005 Returns

Fund (Ticker)	Annual Return (%)				Category Risk	Total Risk
	2005	3Yr	5Yr	10Yr		
Vanguard Long Term Bond Index (VBLTX)	5.3	6.4	8.2	7.3	high	av
Metropolitan West Total Return Bond M (MWTRX)	3.1	7.2	5.9	na	abv av	low
USAA Income (USAIX)	2.9	4.1	5.7	5.8	high	low
Fidelity Invmnt Grade Bond (FBNDX)	2.8	4.0	5.9	5.9	av	low
Preferred Fixed Income (PFXIX)	2.8	5.1	6.4	6.0	high	low
T Rowe Price New Income (PRCIX)	2.8	4.3	5.7	5.4	av	low
Managers Fremont Bond (MBDFX)	2.7	4.4	6.5	6.8	high	low
Fidelity Spartan Invmt Gr Bd (FSIBX)	2.6	4.2	6.1	6.1	abv av	low
Fidelity Total Bond (FTBFX)	2.5	4.6	na	na	high	low
TIAA-CREF Bond Plus (TIPBX)	2.4	3.6	5.9	na	abv av	low
Vanguard Total Bond Market Index (VBMFX)	2.4	3.5	5.4	5.8	abv av	low
Managers Bond (MGFIX)	2.2	6.0	7.7	7.0	high	blw av
Fidelity US Bond Index (FBIDX)	2.2	3.8	5.9	6.1	abv av	low
Dodge & Cox Income (DODIX)	1.9	3.8	6.4	6.3	blw av	low
Janus Flexible Bond (JAFIX)	1.7	3.9	5.7	6.1	high	low
Vanguard Intermediate Term Bd Idx (VBIIX)	1.7	4.1	6.5	6.3	high	blw av
General Bond Category Average	**2.0**	**3.1**	**5.0**	**5.3**	**av**	**low**

Dodge & Cox Income
(DODIX)

General Bond

800-621-3979
www.dodgeandcox.com

	3yr Annual	5yr Annual	10yr Annual	Category Risk Index	
Return (%)	3.8	6.4	6.3	0.91—blw av	
Differ From Category (+/-)	0.7 abv av	1.4 high	1.0 high	**Avg Mat**	5.0 yrs

	2005	2004	2003	2002	2001	2000	1999	1998	1997	1996
Return (%)	1.9	3.6	5.9	10.7	10.3	10.7	-0.8	8.0	10.0	3.6
Differ From Category (+/-) . .	-0.1	0.3	1.7	3.1	2.6	0.9	-1.0	0.7	1.7	0.1
Return, Tax-Adjusted (%)	0.4	2.1	4.3	8.5	7.7	7.9	-3.1	5.6	7.5	1.1
Dividends, Net Income ($) .	0.55	0.54	0.60	0.66	0.74	0.78	0.71	0.72	0.73	0.74
Expense Ratio (%)	na	0.44	0.45	0.45	0.45	0.46	0.46	0.47	0.49	0.50
Yield (%)	4.38	4.20	4.64	5.14	6.03	6.61	6.20	5.84	6.04	6.33
Total Assets (Millions $) . . .	9,393	7,870	5,697	3,405	1,512	1,021	974	952	706	533

SHAREHOLDER INFORMATION

Minimum Investment		Maximum Fees	
Initial: $2,500	IRA: $1,000	Load: none	12b-1: none
Subsequent: $100	IRA: $100	Other: none	

Fidelity Invmnt Grade Bond
(FBNDX)

General Bond

800-544-8544
www.fidelity.com

	3yr Annual	5yr Annual	10yr Annual	Category Risk Index	
Return (%)	4.0	5.9	5.9	1.21—av	
Differ From Category (+/-)	0.9 high	0.9 high	0.6 abv av	**Avg Mat**	6.3 yrs

	2005	2004	2003	2002	2001	2000	1999	1998	1997	1996
Return (%)	2.8	4.5	4.6	9.3	8.5	10.8	-1.0	7.9	8.9	3.0
Differ From Category (+/-) . . .	0.8	1.2	0.4	1.7	0.8	1.0	-1.2	0.6	0.6	-0.5
Return, Tax-Adjusted (%)	1.3	3.1	3.3	7.3	6.2	8.2	-3.2	5.5	6.3	0.5
Dividends, Net Income ($) .	0.30	0.25	0.24	0.32	0.41	0.45	0.43	0.42	0.45	0.47
Expense Ratio (%)	0.45	0.63	0.66	0.66	0.64	0.69	0.70	0.72	0.76	0.76
Yield (%)	4.05	3.32	3.11	4.13	5.55	6.27	6.18	5.70	6.20	6.56
Total Assets (Millions $)	7,539	6,283	5,523	4,767	3,702	2,497	2,079	2,191	1,650	1,455

SHAREHOLDER INFORMATION

Minimum Investment		Maximum Fees	
Initial: $2,500	IRA: $500	Load: none	12b-1: none
Subsequent: $100	IRA: $100	Other: maint fee for low bal	

Fidelity Spartan Invmt Gr Bd
(FSIBX)

800-544-8544
www.fidelity.com

General Bond

	3yr Annual	5yr Annual	10yr Annual	Category Risk Index	
Return (%)	4.2	6.1	6.1	1.24—abv av	
Differ From Category (+/-)	1.1 high	1.1 high	0.8 high	**Avg Mat**	6.1 yrs

	2005	2004	2003	2002	2001	2000	1999	1998	1997	1996
Return (%)	2.6	4.9	5.0	9.5	8.8	11.0	-0.7	8.7	9.2	3.1
Differ From Category (+/-)	0.6	1.6	0.8	1.9	1.1	1.2	-0.9	1.4	0.9	-0.4
Return, Tax-Adjusted (%)	1.0	3.4	3.5	7.3	6.3	8.3	-3.0	6.1	6.7	0.7
Dividends, Net Income ($)	0.42	0.40	0.39	0.49	0.60	0.65	0.62	0.63	0.65	0.63
Expense Ratio (%)	0.45	0.50	0.50	0.50	0.50	0.50	0.47	0.38	0.48	0.65
Yield (%)	3.95	3.65	3.54	4.48	5.69	6.36	6.33	5.96	6.22	6.27
Total Assets (Millions $)	3,174	2,523	2,542	2,653	2,681	1,892	1,554	1,261	658	360

SHAREHOLDER INFORMATION

Minimum Investment		Maximum Fees	
Initial: $25,000	IRA: $25,000	Load: none	12b-1: none
Subsequent: $1,000	IRA: $1	Other: maint fee for low bal	

Fidelity Total Bond
(FTBFX)

800-544-8544
www.fidelity.com

General Bond

	3yr Annual	5yr Annual	10yr Annual	Category Risk Index	
Return (%)	4.6	na	na	1.27—high	
Differ From Category (+/-)	1.5 high	na	na	**Avg Mat**	6.1 yrs

	2005	2004	2003	2002	2001	2000	1999	1998	1997	1996
Return (%)	2.5	5.4	5.8	—	—	—	—	—	—	—
Differ From Category (+/-)	0.5	2.1	1.6	—	—	—	—	—	—	—
Return, Tax-Adjusted (%)	1.0	4.1	4.7	—	—	—	—	—	—	—
Dividends, Net Income ($)	0.44	0.36	0.31	—	—	—	—	—	—	—
Expense Ratio (%)	0.45	0.65	0.65	—	—	—	—	—	—	—
Yield (%)	4.17	3.39	2.89	—	—	—	—	—	—	—
Total Assets (Millions $)	497	366	300	—	—	—	—	—	—	—

SHAREHOLDER INFORMATION

Minimum Investment		Maximum Fees	
Initial: $2,500	IRA: $500	Load: none	12b-1: none
Subsequent: $100	IRA: $100	Other: maint fee for low bal	

Fidelity US Bond Index
(FBIDX)

General Bond

800-544-8544
www.fidelity.com

fund inception date: 3/8/90

	3yr Annual	5yr Annual	10yr Annual	Category Risk Index	
Return (%)	3.8	5.9	6.1	1.24—abv av	
Differ From Category (+/-)	0.7 abv av	0.9 abv av	0.8 high	**Avg Mat**	6.5 yrs

	2005	2004	2003	2002	2001	2000	1999	1998	1997	1996
Return (%)	2.2	4.3	4.9	10.2	8.0	11.4	-0.9	8.8	9.5	3.3
Differ From Category (+/-) . . .	0.2	1.0	0.7	2.6	0.3	1.6	-1.1	1.5	1.2	-0.2
Return, Tax-Adjusted (%)	0.8	2.8	3.3	8.1	5.7	8.6	-3.4	6.3	6.7	0.7
Dividends, Net Income ($) .	0.45	0.43	0.41	0.51	0.63	0.72	0.67	0.70	0.74	0.74
Expense Ratio (%)	0.53	0.32	0.32	0.31	0.31	0.31	0.31	0.31	0.31	0.31
Yield (%)	4.07	3.79	3.62	4.52	5.81	6.78	6.50	6.33	6.84	6.96
Total Assets (Millions $) . . .	5,842	5,263	4,765	4,405	2,954	1,785	1,533	1,225	665	552

SHAREHOLDER INFORMATION

Minimum Investment
Initial: $10,000   IRA: $10,000
Subsequent: $1   IRA: $1,000

Maximum Fees
Load: none   12b-1: none
Other: none

Janus Flexible Bond
(JAFIX)

General Bond

800-525-3713
www.janus.com

PERFORMANCE AND PER SHARE DATA   **fund inception date: 7/7/87**

	3yr Annual	5yr Annual	10yr Annual	Category Risk Index	
Return (%)	3.9	5.7	6.1	1.24—high	
Differ From Category (+/-)	0.8 high	0.7 abv av	0.8 high	**Avg Mat**	7.0 yrs

	2005	2004	2003	2002	2001	2000	1999	1998	1997	1996
Return (%)	1.7	3.8	6.3	9.9	7.2	4.8	0.4	8.8	11.4	6.8
Differ From Category (+/-) . .	-0.3	0.5	2.1	2.3	-0.5	-5.0	0.3	1.5	3.1	3.3
Return, Tax-Adjusted (%)	0.3	2.1	4.7	7.9	4.8	2.1	-2.0	5.9	8.2	3.8
Dividends, Net Income ($) . .	0.40	0.46	0.43	0.48	0.57	0.64	0.64	0.66	0.68	0.74
Expense Ratio (%)	0.78	0.85	0.83	0.81	0.77	0.79	0.81	0.82	0.86	0.87
Yield (%)	4.22	4.78	4.41	4.97	6.15	7.03	6.86	6.60	6.73	7.60
Total Assets (Millions $)	912	1,105	1,425	1,645	1,273	1,080	1,204	1,169	766	625

SHAREHOLDER INFORMATION

Minimum Investment
Initial: $2,500   IRA: $500
Subsequent: $100   IRA: $100

Maximum Fees
Load: none   12b-1: none
Other: none

Managers Bond
(MGFIX)

General Bond

800-835-3879
www.managersfunds.com

PERFORMANCE AND PER SHARE DATA   fund in   date: 6/1/84

	3yr Annual	5yr Annual	10yr Annual		ory Risk Index
Return (%)	6.0	7.7	7.0		high
Differ From Category (+/-)	2.9 high	2.7 high	1.7 high		at 5.1 yrs

	2005	2004	2003	2002	2001	2000		998	1997	1996
Return (%)	2.2	5.1	10.7	10.9	9.6	9.4		.2	10.4	4.9
Differ From Category (+/-) . .	0.2	1.8	6.5	3.3	1.9	-0.4		4.1	2.1	1.4
Return, Tax-Adjusted (%). . . .	0.9	3.5	8.9	8.8	7.0	6.5			7.9	2.6
Dividends, Net Income ($). .	0.88	1.03	1.11	1.24	1.45	1.50		5	1.40	1.36
Expense Ratio (%).	na	1.06	0.99	0.99	1.18	1.19			1.27	1.36
Yield (%)	3.62	4.17	4.47	5.28	6.48	6.84			5.89	5.95
Total Assets (Millions $).	406	259	179	129	67	5.			41	32

SHAREHOLDER INFORMATION

Minimum Investment		Maximum Fees	
Initial: $2,000	IRA: $1,000	Load: none	· none
Subsequent: $100	IRA: $100	Other: none	

Managers Fremont Bond
(MBDFX)

General Bond

.funds.com

PERFORMANCE AND PER SHARE DATA   fund   date: 4/30/93

	3yr Annual	5yr Annual	10yr Ann		ory Risk Index
Return (%)	4.4	6.5	6.8		–high
Differ From Category (+/-)	1.3 high	1.5 high	1.5 high	Avg Mat	6.5 yrs

	2005	2004	2003	2002	2001	2000	1999	1998	1997	1996
Return (%)	2.7	5.3	5.3	9.7	9.7	12.7	-1.2	10.0	9.7	5.2
Differ From Category (+/-) . .	0.7	2.0	1.1	2.1	2.0	2.9	-1.4	2.7	1.4	1.7
Return, Tax-Adjusted (%). . . .	1.5	4.0	3.9	7.7	7.0	9.8	-3.5	7.0	6.9	2.5
Dividends, Net Income ($) .	0.35	0.26	0.35	0.39	0.57	0.71	0.58	0.62	0.64	0.69
Expense Ratio (%)	na	0.71	0.61	0.59	0.57	1.83	0.60	0.60	0.61	0.68
Yield (%)	3.37	2.37	3.29	3.61	5.54	7.11	6.13	5.89	6.25	6.90
Total Assets (Millions $).	994	879	851	1,228	783	298	175	216	109	73

SHAREHOLDER INFORMATION

Minimum Investment		Maximum Fees	
Initial: $2,000	IRA: $1,000	Load: none	12b-1: none
Subsequent: $100	IRA: $100	Other: none	

Metropolitan West Total Return Bond M (MWTRX)

800-241-4671
www.mwamllc.com

General Bond

	3yr Annual	5yr Annual	10yr Annual	Category Risk Index	
Return (%)	7.2	5.9	na	1.21—abv av	
Differ From Category (+/-)	4.1 high	0.9 high	na	**Avg Mat**	6.9 yrs

	2005	2004	2003	2002	2001	2000	1999	1998	1997	1996
Return (%)	3.1	5.1	13.8	-0.9	9.1	10.2	1.7	9.9	—	—
Differ From Category (+/-)	1.1	1.8	9.6	-8.6	1.4	0.4	1.6	2.6	—	—
Return, Tax-Adjusted (%)	1.1	3.0	11.5	-3.6	6.0	6.5	-1.1	6.9	—	—
Dividends, Net Income ($)	0.55	0.59	0.63	0.71	0.76	0.92	0.76	0.72	—	—
Expense Ratio (%)	0.65	0.65	0.65	0.65	0.65	0.65	0.65	0.65	—	—
Yield (%)	5.72	6.03	6.32	7.55	7.45	9.05	7.59	6.66	—	—
Total Assets (Millions $)	492	453	499	568	621	278	187	83	—	—

SHAREHOLDER INFORMATION

Minimum Investment

Initial: $5,000   IRA: $1,000

Subsequent: $1   IRA: $1

Maximum Fees

Load: none   12b-1: 0.21%

Other: none

Preferred Fixed Income (PFXIX)

800-662-4769
www.preferredgroup.com

General Bond

	3yr Annual	5yr Annual	10yr Annual	Category Risk Index	
Return (%)	5.1	6.4	6.0	1.33—high	
Differ From Category (+/-)	2.0 high	1.4 high	0.7 high	**Avg Mat**	6.5 yrs

	2005	2004	2003	2002	2001	2000	1999	1998	1997	1996
Return (%)	2.8	5.9	6.8	9.4	7.2	10.5	-0.7	6.9	8.4	2.9
Differ From Category (+/-)	0.8	2.6	2.6	1.8	-0.5	0.7	-0.9	-0.4	0.1	-0.6
Return, Tax-Adjusted (%)	1.2	4.5	5.5	7.9	4.9	8.0	-3.0	4.2	5.7	0.6
Dividends, Net Income ($)	0.44	0.34	0.32	0.37	0.57	0.60	0.58	0.61	0.65	0.60
Expense Ratio (%)	0.68	0.71	0.74	0.69	0.69	0.68	0.65	0.67	0.74	0.93
Yield (%)	4.08	3.07	2.95	3.45	5.66	6.03	6.08	5.88	6.22	5.82
Total Assets (Millions $)	396	365	308	236	187	183	173	162	148	131

SHAREHOLDER INFORMATION

Minimum Investment

Initial: $1,000   IRA: $250

Subsequent: $50   IRA: $50

Maximum Fees

Load: none   12b-1: none

Other: none

T Rowe Price New Income
(PRCIX)

General Bond

800-638-5660
www.troweprice.com

PERFORMANCE AND PER SHARE DATA   fund inception date: 10/15/73

	3yr Annual	5yr Annual	10yr Annual	Category Risk Index	
Return (%)	4.3	5.7	5.4	1.18—av	
Differ From Category (+/-)	1.2 high	0.7 abv av	0.1 av	**Avg Mat**	7.2 yrs

	2005	2004	2003	2002	2001	2000	1999	1998	1997	1996
Return (%)	2.8	4.6	5.5	7.4	8.1	11.1	-1.5	5.0	8.9	2.3
Differ From Category (+/-) . .	0.8	1.3	1.3	-0.2	0.4	1.3	-1.7	-2.3	0.6	-1.2
Return, Tax-Adjusted (%)	1.3	3.2	4.2	5.6	5.8	8.5	-3.8	1.9	6.3	-0.1
Dividends, Net Income ($) . .	0.38	0.34	0.33	0.42	0.50	0.53	0.51	0.71	0.58	0.59
Expense Ratio (%).	0.69	0.71	0.74	0.72	0.73	0.73	0.72	0.71	0.74	0.75
Yield (%)	4.17	3.69	3.64	4.74	5.74	6.27	6.28	8.00	6.42	6.65
Total Assets (Millions $) . . .	3,387	2,883	2,290	2,018	1,803	1,715	1,795	2,103	1,945	1,688

SHAREHOLDER INFORMATION

Minimum Investment
Initial: $2,500   IRA: $100
Subsequent: $100   IRA: $50

Maximum Fees
Load: none   12b-1: none
Other: none

TIAA-CREF Bond Plus
(TIPBX)

General Bond

800-223-1200
www.tiaa-cref.org

PERFORMANCE AND PER SHARE DATA   fund inception date: 9/2/97

	3yr Annual	5yr Annual	10yr Annual	Category Risk Index	
Return (%)	3.6	5.9	na	1.24—abv av	
Differ From Category (+/-)	0.5 abv av	0.9 abv av	na	**Avg Mat**	6.9 yrs

	2005	2004	2003	2002	2001	2000	1999	1998	1997	1996
Return (%)	2.4	4.2	4.3	10.5	8.1	11.6	-1.0	8.9	—	—
Differ From Category (+/-) . . .	0.4	0.9	0.1	2.9	0.4	1.8	-1.2	1.6	—	—
Return, Tax-Adjusted (%)	0.9	2.9	2.6	8.1	5.6	9.1	-3.1	6.5	—	—
Dividends, Net Income ($) .	0.44	0.40	0.40	0.52	0.59	0.62	0.57	0.56	—	—
Expense Ratio (%)	na	0.30	0.30	0.30	0.30	0.30	0.30	0.30	—	—
Yield (%)	4.29	3.83	3.80	4.89	5.70	6.18	5.87	5.41	—	—
Total Assets (Millions $)	483	469	426	371	285	232	205	—	—	—

SHAREHOLDER INFORMATION

Minimum Investment
Initial: $2,500   IRA: $2,000
Subsequent: $50   IRA: $50

Maximum Fees
Load: none   12b-1: none
Other: none

USAA Income
(USAIX)

General Bond

800-531-8181
www.usaa.com

	3yr Annual	5yr Annual	10yr Annual	Category Risk Index	
Return (%)	4.1	5.7	5.8	1.24—high	
Differ From Category (+/-)	1.0 high	0.7 abv av	0.5 abv av	**Avg Mat**	6.3 yrs

	2005	2004	2003	2002	2001	2000	1999	1998	1997	1996
Return (%)	2.9	4.5	4.9	8.6	7.5	13.3	-3.8	8.7	11.0	1.3
Differ From Category (+/-)	0.9	1.2	0.7	1.0	-0.2	3.5	-4.0	1.4	2.7	-2.2
Return, Tax-Adjusted (%)	1.3	2.9	3.2	6.4	4.9	10.5	-6.3	5.4	8.3	-1.1
Dividends, Net Income ($)	0.58	0.55	0.58	0.67	0.79	0.79	0.76	0.84	0.83	0.83
Expense Ratio (%)	na	0.52	0.50	0.55	0.41	0.42	0.38	0.38	0.39	0.40
Yield (%)	4.76	4.40	4.63	5.38	6.56	6.64	6.74	6.45	6.51	6.74
Total Assets (Millions $)	1,807	1,753	1,757	1,736	1,547	1,339	1,319	1,769	1,722	1,738

Minimum Investment		Maximum Fees	
Initial: $3,000	IRA: $250	Load: none	12b-1: none
Subsequent: $50	IRA: $50	Other: none	

Vanguard Intermediate Term Bd Idx (VBIIX)

General Bond

800-662-7447
www.vanguard.com

	3yr Annual	5yr Annual	10yr Annual	Category Risk Index	
Return (%)	4.1	6.5	6.3	1.85—high	
Differ From Category (+/-)	1.0 high	1.5 high	1.0 high	**Avg Mat**	7.4 yrs

	2005	2004	2003	2002	2001	2000	1999	1998	1997	1996
Return (%)	1.7	5.2	5.6	10.8	9.2	12.7	-3.0	10.0	9.4	2.5
Differ From Category (+/-)	-0.3	1.9	1.4	3.2	1.5	2.9	-3.1	2.7	1.1	-1.0
Return, Tax-Adjusted (%)	0.1	3.4	3.7	8.5	6.7	10.0	-5.4	7.4	6.7	0.0
Dividends, Net Income ($)	0.49	0.51	0.53	0.60	0.65	0.65	0.63	0.65	0.66	0.65
Expense Ratio (%)	na	0.18	0.20	0.21	0.21	0.21	0.20	0.20	0.20	0.20
Yield (%)	4.74	4.72	4.91	5.55	6.33	6.52	6.57	6.13	6.48	6.50
Total Assets (Millions $)	3,009	3,501	2,749	2,415	2,096	1,642	1,449	1,102	687	460

Minimum Investment		Maximum Fees	
Initial: $3,000	IRA: $3,000	Load: none	12b-1: none
Subsequent: $100	IRA: $100	Other: none	

Vanguard Long Term Bond Index (VBLTX)

800-662-7447
www.vanguard.com

General Bond

PERFORMANCE AND PER SHARE DATA — fund inception date: 3/1/94

	3yr Annual	5yr Annual	10yr Annual	Category Risk Index
Return (%)	6.4	8.2	7.3	2.94—high
Differ From Category (+/-)	3.3 high	3.2 high	2.0 high	**Avg Mat** 19.6 yrs

	2005	2004	2003	2002	2001	2000	1999	1998	1997	1996
Return (%)	5.3	8.4	5.5	14.3	8.0	16.4	-7.8	11.9	14.3	-0.2
Differ From Category (+/-)	3.3	5.1	1.3	6.7	0.3	6.6	-8.0	4.6	6.0	-3.8
Return, Tax-Adjusted (%)	3.5	6.5	3.3	12.0	5.5	13.7	-10.1	9.4	11.6	-2.7
Dividends, Net Income ($)	0.60	0.62	0.63	0.66	0.67	0.66	0.66	0.67	0.68	0.67
Expense Ratio (%)	na	0.18	0.20	0.21	0.21	0.21	0.20	0.20	0.20	0.20
Yield (%)	5.07	5.21	5.36	5.64	6.21	6.22	6.76	5.85	6.28	6.68
Total Assets (Millions $)	1,893	1,310	951	794	542	417	313	210	88	44

SHAREHOLDER INFORMATION

Minimum Investment
Initial: $3,000   IRA: $3,000
Subsequent: $100   IRA: $100

Maximum Fees
Load: none   12b-1: none
Other: none

Vanguard Total Bond Market Index (VBMFX)

800-662-7447
www.vanguard.com

General Bond

PERFORMANCE AND PER SHARE DATA — fund inception date: 12/11/86

	3yr Annual	5yr Annual	10yr Annual	Category Risk Index
Return (%)	3.5	5.4	5.8	1.24—abv av
Differ From Category (+/-)	0.4 abv av	0.4 av	0.5 abv av	**Avg Mat** 7.0 yrs

	2005	2004	2003	2002	2001	2000	1999	1998	1997	1996
Return (%)	2.4	4.2	3.9	8.2	8.4	11.3	-0.7	8.5	9.4	3.5
Differ From Category (+/-)	0.4	0.9	-0.3	0.6	0.7	1.5	-0.9	1.2	1.1	0.0
Return, Tax-Adjusted (%)	0.8	2.6	2.3	6.0	5.9	8.7	-3.1	6.0	6.8	1.0
Dividends, Net Income ($)	0.45	0.45	0.47	0.57	0.63	0.65	0.62	0.62	0.65	0.64
Expense Ratio (%)	na	0.20	0.22	0.22	0.22	0.22	0.20	0.20	0.20	0.20
Yield (%)	4.46	4.33	4.60	5.50	6.22	6.50	6.44	6.06	6.39	6.50
Total Assets (Millions $)	21,643	19,479	17,032	16,676	14,116	11,180	9,477	7,765	5,129	2,962

SHAREHOLDER INFORMATION

Minimum Investment
Initial: $3,000   IRA: $3,000
Subsequent: $100   IRA: $100

Maximum Fees
Load: none   12b-1: none
Other: none

MUNICIPAL BOND FUNDS

National Muni: Short-Term Bond Funds
Category Performance Ranked by 2005 Returns

Fund (Ticker)	Annual Return (%) 2005	3Yr	5Yr	10Yr	Category Risk	Total Risk
Wells Fargo Advtg Short Term Muni Bd Inv (STSMX)	2.6	3.3	4.0	4.3	abv av	low
USAA Tx Ex Short Term (USSTX)	1.7	2.0	3.2	3.8	high	low
Vanguard Short Term TE (VWSTX)	1.6	1.4	2.5	3.2	blw av	low
Vanguard Limited Term TE (VMLTX)	1.1	1.8	3.4	3.9	high	low
Nat'l Muni: Short-Term Bond Category Average	1.7	1.8	2.8	3.4	av	low

USAA Tx Ex Short Term
(USSTX)

800-531-8181
www.usaa.com

National Muni: Short-Term Bond

PERFORMANCE AND PER SHARE DATA   **fund inception date: 3/19/82**

	3yr Annual	5yr Annual	10yr Annual	Category Risk Index	
Return (%)	2.0	3.2	3.8	1.30—high	
Differ From Category (+/-)	0.2 high	0.4 abv av	0.4 abv av	**Avg Mat**	1.7 yrs

	2005	2004	2003	2002	2001	2000	1999	1998	1997	1996
Return (%)	1.7	1.5	2.9	5.0	5.1	6.0	1.6	4.9	5.8	4.0
Differ From Category (+/-) . .	0.0	0.1	0.6	1.1	0.4	0.9	-0.3	0.3	0.9	-0.1
Return, Tax-Adjusted (%)	1.7	1.5	2.9	5.0	5.1	6.0	1.6	4.9	5.8	4.0
Dividends, Net Income ($) . .	0.33	0.27	0.30	0.37	0.44	0.49	0.47	0.49	0.49	0.45
Expense Ratio (%)	0.55	0.56	0.54	0.48	0.38	0.38	0.38	0.39	0.41	0.42
Yield (%)	3.08	2.53	2.74	3.37	4.13	4.63	4.52	4.55	4.53	4.23
Total Assets (Millions $) . . .	1,177	1,319	1,367	1,226	1,122	1,003	988	1,006	937	786

SHAREHOLDER INFORMATION

Minimum Investment
Initial: $3,000   IRA: $0
Subsequent: $50   IRA: $0

Maximum Fees
Load: none   12b-1: none
Other: none

Vanguard Limited Term TE
(VMLTX)

800-662-7447
www.vanguard.com

National Muni: Short-Term Bond

PERFORMANCE AND PER SHARE DATA   **fund inception date: 8/31/87**

	3yr Annual	5yr Annual	10yr Annual	Category Risk Index	
Return (%)	1.8	3.4	3.9	1.70—high	
Differ From Category (+/-)	0.0 abv av	0.6 high	0.5 high	**Avg Mat**	2.6 yrs

	2005	2004	2003	2002	2001	2000	1999	1998	1997	1996
Return (%)	1.1	1.5	2.7	6.3	5.5	6.3	1.4	5.1	5.1	4.0
Differ From Category (+/-) . .	-0.6	0.1	0.4	2.4	0.8	1.2	-0.5	0.5	0.2	-0.1
Return, Tax-Adjusted (%)	1.1	1.5	2.7	6.3	5.5	6.3	1.4	5.1	5.1	4.0
Dividends, Net Income ($)	0.33	0.32	0.35	0.41	0.47	0.47	0.46	0.46	0.47	0.48
Expense Ratio (%)	na	0.14	0.17	0.17	0.19	0.18	0.18	0.21	0.19	0.21
Yield (%)	3.06	2.89	3.12	3.71	4.34	4.40	4.33	4.23	4.39	4.45
Total Assets (Millions $) . . .	2,169	3,494	3,256	2,773	2,104	2,932	2,569	2,391	2,023	1,792

SHAREHOLDER INFORMATION

Minimum Investment
Initial: $3,000   IRA: $0
Subsequent: $100   IRA: $0

Maximum Fees
Load: none   12b-1: none
Other: none

Vanguard Short Term TE
(VWSTX)

800-662-7447
www.vanguard.com

National Muni: Short-Term Bond

PERFORMANCE AND PER SHARE DATA   fund inception date: 9/1/77

	3yr Annual	5yr Annual	10yr Annual	Category Risk Index	
Return (%)	1.4	2.5	3.2	0.60—blw av	
Differ From Category (+/-)	-0.4 blw av	-0.3 av	-0.2 av	**Avg Mat**	1.1 yrs

	2005	2004	2003	2002	2001	2000	1999	1998	1997	1996
Return (%)	1.6	1.1	1.6	3.4	4.7	4.9	2.5	4.3	4.0	3.6
Differ From Category (+/-) . .	-0.1	-0.3	-0.7	-0.5	0.0	-0.2	0.6	-0.3	-0.9	-0.5
Return, Tax-Adjusted (%)	1.6	1.1	1.6	3.4	4.7	4.9	2.5	4.3	4.0	3.6
Dividends, Net Income ($) .	0.35	0.29	0.31	0.42	0.61	0.63	0.58	0.60	0.62	0.60
Expense Ratio (%)	na	0.14	0.17	0.17	0.19	0.18	0.18	0.20	0.19	0.20
Yield (%)	2.28	1.88	1.94	2.65	3.87	4.06	3.73	3.86	3.95	3.85
Total Assets (Millions $) . . .	1,305	2,164	2,153	2,022	1,359	2,117	1,917	1,657	1,492	1,456

SHAREHOLDER INFORMATION

Minimum Investment

Initial: $3,000   IRA: $0

Subsequent: $100   IRA: $0

Maximum Fees

Load: none   12b-1: none

Other: none

Wells Fargo Advtg Short Term Muni Bd Inv (STSMX)

800-368-3863
www.wellsfargofunds.com

National Muni: Short-Term Bond

PERFORMANCE AND PER SHARE DATA   fund inception date: 12/31/91

	3yr Annual	5yr Annual	10yr Annual	Category Risk Index	
Return (%)	3.3	4.0	4.3	1.10—abv av	
Differ From Category (+/-)	1.5 high	1.2 high	0.9 high	**Avg Mat**	4.1 yrs

	2005	2004	2003	2002	2001	2000	1999	1998	1997	1996
Return (%)	2.6	3.2	4.0	5.0	5.1	5.0	1.1	5.5	6.9	4.8
Differ From Category (+/-) . . .	0.9	1.8	1.7	1.1	0.4	-0.1	-0.8	0.9	2.0	0.7
Return, Tax-Adjusted (%)	2.6	3.2	4.0	5.0	5.1	5.0	1.1	5.5	6.9	4.8
Dividends, Net Income ($) . .	0.31	0.31	0.34	0.39	0.43	0.46	0.46	0.49	0.48	0.49
Expense Ratio (%)	na	0.66	0.60	0.60	0.60	0.60	0.60	0.60	0.70	0.70
Yield (%)	3.15	3.11	3.43	4.03	4.43	4.81	4.73	4.89	4.82	5.05
Total Assets (Millions $)	655	499	528	597	511	312	282	264	181	145

SHAREHOLDER INFORMATION

Minimum Investment

Initial: $2,500   IRA: $0

Subsequent: $100   IRA: $0

Maximum Fees

Load: none   12b-1: none

Other: none

National Muni: Intermediate-Term Bond Funds
Category Performance Ranked by 2005 Returns

Fund (Ticker)	Annual Return (%)				Category Risk	Total Risk
	2005	3Yr	5Yr	10Yr		
USAA Tx Ex Intermediate Term (USATX)	3.0	4.1	5.1	5.2	blw av	low
Fidelity Intermediate Muni Inc (FLTMX)	2.5	3.8	5.2	5.2	av	low
Amer Century Tax Free Bond Inv (TWTIX)	2.4	3.0	4.6	4.9	blw av	low
T Rowe Price Summit Muni Intm (PRSMX)	2.2	3.2	4.7	5.0	blw av	low
Vanguard Intermediate Term TE (VWITX)	2.2	3.3	4.5	4.8	av	low
TIAA-CREF Tax Exempt Bond (TCTEX)	2.1	4.1	5.6	na	high	blw av
Northern Intermediate Tax Exempt (NOITX)	2.0	3.2	4.7	4.7	av	low
Dreyfus Intm Muni Bd (DITEX)	2.0	3.0	4.0	4.3	abv av	low
Nat'l Muni: Interm-Term Bond Category Average	1.8	2.9	4.3	4.5	av	low

Amer Century Tax Free Bond Inv (TWTIX)

800-345-2021
www.americancentury.com

National Muni: Intermediate-Term Bond

PERFORMANCE AND PER SHARE DATA   fund inception date: 3/2/87

	3yr Annual	5yr Annual	10yr Annual	Category Risk Index	
Return (%)	3.0	4.6	4.9	0.97—blw av	
Differ From Category (+/-)	0.1 abv av	0.3 abv av	0.4 high	**Avg Mat**	9.0 yrs

	2005	2004	2003	2002	2001	2000	1999	1998	1997	1996
Return (%)	2.4	2.6	4.0	9.1	5.2	9.8	-0.9	5.8	7.4	3.9
Differ From Category (+/-) ...	0.6	-0.2	-0.2	0.5	0.5	0.9	0.4	0.2	0.1	0.1
Return, Tax-Adjusted (%).....	2.4	2.6	4.0	9.0	5.1	9.8	-0.9	5.6	7.2	3.8
Dividends, Net Income ($) .	0.39	0.37	0.38	0.41	0.47	0.49	0.47	0.48	0.49	0.49
Expense Ratio (%)	0.50	0.51	0.51	0.51	0.51	0.91	0.51	0.51	0.58	0.60
Yield (%)................	3.63	3.35	3.42	3.73	4.42	4.68	4.70	4.51	4.57	4.68
Total Assets (Millions $).....	639	590	605	556	316	163	161	147	133	79

SHAREHOLDER INFORMATION

Minimum Investment
Initial: $5,000   IRA: $0
Subsequent: $50   IRA: $0

Maximum Fees
Load: none   12b-1: none
Other: none

Dreyfus Intm Muni Bd (DITEX)

800-645-6561
www.dreyfus.com

National Muni: Intermediate-Term Bond

PERFORMANCE AND PER SHARE DATA   fund inception date: 8/11/83

	3yr Annual	5yr Annual	10yr Annual	Category Risk Index	
Return (%)	3.0	4.0	4.3	1.03—abv av	
Differ From Category (+/-)	0.1 abv av	-0.3 blw av	-0.2 blw av	**Avg Mat**	8.2 yrs

	2005	2004	2003	2002	2001	2000	1999	1998	1997	1996
Return (%)	2.0	3.3	3.8	6.9	3.9	7.7	-1.5	5.5	7.6	3.8
Differ From Category (+/-) ...	0.2	0.5	-0.4	-1.7	-0.8	-1.2	-0.2	-0.1	0.3	0.0
Return, Tax-Adjusted (%)	2.0	3.3	3.8	6.9	3.9	7.7	-1.6	5.3	7.4	3.6
Dividends, Net Income ($) ..	0.50	0.50	0.54	0.61	0.65	0.65	0.66	0.68	0.70	0.72
Expense Ratio (%)	0.73	0.74	0.74	0.74	1.01	0.75	0.75	0.74	0.73	0.71
Yield (%)................	3.72	3.69	3.93	4.45	4.88	4.80	5.01	4.76	4.90	5.14
Total Assets (Millions $).....	828	895	967	1,059	1,057	1,066	1,133	1,321	1,372	1,430

SHAREHOLDER INFORMATION

Minimum Investment
Initial: $2,500   IRA: $0
Subsequent: $100   IRA: $0

Maximum Fees
Load: 0.10% redemption   12b-1: none
Other: redemption fee applies for 1 month

Fidelity Intermediate Muni Inc (FLTMX)

800-544-8544
www.fidelity.com

National Muni: Intermediate-Term Bond

PERFORMANCE AND PER SHARE DATA   fund inception date: 4/15/77

	3yr Annual	5yr Annual	10yr Annual	Category Risk Index	
Return (%)	3.8	5.2	5.2	0.97—av	
Differ From Category (+/-)	0.9 high	0.9 high	0.7 high	**Avg Mat**	8.5 yrs

	2005	2004	2003	2002	2001	2000	1999	1998	1997	1996
Return (%)	2.5	3.7	5.3	9.0	5.4	9.2	-1.0	5.4	8.2	4.4
Differ From Category (+/-) . .	0.7	0.9	1.1	0.4	0.7	0.3	0.3	-0.2	0.9	0.6
Return, Tax-Adjusted (%). . . .	2.4	3.6	5.0	8.8	5.4	9.2	-1.0	5.3	8.1	4.3
Dividends, Net Income ($). .	0.38	0.39	0.41	0.43	0.46	0.48	0.47	0.43	0.49	0.49
Expense Ratio (%).	na	0.43	0.43	0.42	0.39	0.49	0.48	0.50	0.55	0.56
Yield (%)	3.83	3.87	3.96	4.18	4.65	4.87	4.95	4.33	4.85	5.01
Total Assets (Millions $) . . .	1,936	1,809	1,797	1,752	1,487	1,210	1,061	1,146	912	901

SHAREHOLDER INFORMATION

Minimum Investment		Maximum Fees	
Initial: $10,000	IRA: $0	Load: 0.50% redemption	12b-1: none
Subsequent: $1,000	IRA: $0	Other: redemp fee applies for 1 mo; maint fee for low bal	

Northern Intermediate Tax Exempt (NOITX)

800-595-9111
www.northernfunds.com

National Muni: Intermediate-Term Bond

PERFORMANCE AND PER SHARE DATA   fund inception date: 4/1/94

	3yr Annual	5yr Annual	10yr Annual	Category Risk Index	
Return (%)	3.2	4.7	4.7	1.00—av	
Differ From Category (+/-)	0.3 abv av	0.4 high	0.2 abv av	**Avg Mat**	9.5 yrs

	2005	2004	2003	2002	2001	2000	1999	1998	1997	1996
Return (%)	2.0	3.1	4.6	9.1	4.9	8.0	-1.0	8.2	5.8	3.3
Differ From Category (+/-) . . .	0.2	0.3	0.4	0.5	0.2	-0.9	0.3	2.6	-1.5	-0.5
Return, Tax-Adjusted (%).	1.9	3.0	4.3	8.6	4.7	8.0	-1.0	8.0	5.8	3.1
Dividends, Net Income ($) .	0.34	0.34	0.33	0.37	0.40	0.42	0.39	0.69	0.40	0.41
Expense Ratio (%)	0.85	0.85	0.85	0.85	0.85	0.85	0.85	0.85	0.85	0.85
Yield (%)	3.27	3.21	3.08	3.38	3.90	4.04	3.89	6.59	3.85	3.97
Total Assets (Millions $)	572	587	629	677	690	664	682	330	291	254

SHAREHOLDER INFORMATION

Minimum Investment		Maximum Fees	
Initial: $2,500	IRA: $0	Load: none	12b-1: none
Subsequent: $50	IRA: $0	Other: none	

T Rowe Price Summit Muni Intm (PRSMX)

800-638-5660
www.troweprice.com

National Muni: Intermediate-Term Bond

fund inception date: 10/29/93

	3yr Annual	5yr Annual	10yr Annual	Category Risk Index
Return (%)	3.2	4.7	5.0	0.97—blw av
Differ From Category (+/-)	0.3 abv av	0.4 high	0.5 high	**Avg Mat** 8.1 yrs

	2005	2004	2003	2002	2001	2000	1999	1998	1997	1996
Return (%)	2.2	3.0	4.4	8.6	5.6	8.7	-1.2	5.7	8.4	4.6
Differ From Category (+/-)	0.4	0.2	0.2	0.0	0.9	-0.2	0.1	0.1	1.1	0.8
Return, Tax-Adjusted (%)	2.2	3.0	4.4	8.6	5.6	8.7	-1.2	5.7	8.3	4.6
Dividends, Net Income ($)	0.38	0.38	0.43	0.46	0.47	0.48	0.46	0.48	0.48	0.49
Expense Ratio (%)	0.50	0.50	0.50	0.50	0.50	0.50	0.50	0.50	0.50	0.50
Yield (%)	3.53	3.41	3.90	4.15	4.48	4.58	4.60	4.48	4.53	4.74
Total Assets (Millions $)	222	169	119	110	94	82	79	81	53	31

SHAREHOLDER INFORMATION

Minimum Investment		Maximum Fees	
Initial: $25,000	IRA: $0	Load: none	12b-1: none
Subsequent: $1,000	IRA: $0	Other: none	

TIAA-CREF Tax Exempt Bond (TCTEX)

800-223-1200
www.tiaa-cref.org

National Muni: Intermediate-Term Bond

fund inception date: 4/3/00

	3yr Annual	5yr Annual	10yr Annual	Category Risk Index
Return (%)	4.1	5.6	na	1.28—high
Differ From Category (+/-)	1.2 high	1.3 high	na	**Avg Mat** 8.4 yrs

	2005	2004	2003	2002	2001	2000	1999	1998	1997	1996
Return (%)	2.1	4.5	5.8	10.6	5.0	—	—	—	—	—
Differ From Category (+/-)	0.3	1.7	1.6	2.0	0.3	—	—	—	—	—
Return, Tax-Adjusted (%)	2.0	4.4	5.5	10.4	4.7	—	—	—	—	—
Dividends, Net Income ($)	0.38	0.38	0.42	0.43	0.47	—	—	—	—	—
Expense Ratio (%)	na	0.30	0.30	0.30	0.30	—	—	—	—	—
Yield (%)	3.53	3.46	3.72	3.90	4.51	—	—	—	—	—
Total Assets (Millions $)	484	194	168	146	74	—	—	—	—	—

SHAREHOLDER INFORMATION

Minimum Investment		Maximum Fees	
Initial: $2,500	IRA: $0	Load: none	12b-1: none
Subsequent: $50	IRA: $0	Other: none	

USAA Tx Ex Intermediate Term (USATX)

800-531-8181
www.usaa.com

National Muni: Intermediate-Term Bond

	3yr Annual	5yr Annual	10yr Annual	Category Risk Index	
Return (%)	4.1	5.1	5.2	0.92—blw av	
Differ From Category (+/-)	1.2 high	0.8 high	0.7 high	**Avg Mat**	9.5 yrs

	2005	2004	2003	2002	2001	2000	1999	1998	1997	1996
Return (%)	3.0	4.2	5.1	7.6	5.5	9.8	-2.6	6.3	9.3	4.4
Differ From Category (+/-)	1.2	1.4	0.9	-1.0	0.8	0.9	-1.3	0.7	2.0	0.6
Return, Tax-Adjusted (%)	3.0	4.2	5.1	7.6	5.5	9.8	-2.6	6.3	9.3	4.4
Dividends, Net Income ($)	0.55	0.58	0.62	0.65	0.68	0.69	0.69	0.71	0.72	0.72
Expense Ratio (%)	0.55	0.51	0.49	0.46	0.36	0.36	0.36	0.37	0.37	0.38
Yield (%)	4.18	4.31	4.65	4.85	5.21	5.30	5.53	5.22	5.36	5.59
Total Assets (Millions $)	2,783	2,676	2,601	2,564	2,397	2,230	2,147	2,252	1,936	1,711

SHAREHOLDER INFORMATION

Minimum Investment
Initial: $3,000   IRA: $0
Subsequent: $50   IRA: $0

Maximum Fees
Load: none   12b-1: none
Other: none

Vanguard Intermediate Term TE (VWITX)

800-662-7447
www.vanguard.com

National Muni: Intermediate-Term Bond

	3yr Annual	5yr Annual	10yr Annual	Category Risk Index	
Return (%)	3.3	4.5	4.8	0.97—av	
Differ From Category (+/-)	0.4 high	0.2 abv av	0.3 abv av	**Avg Mat**	6.0 yrs

	2005	2004	2003	2002	2001	2000	1999	1998	1997	1996
Return (%)	2.2	3.2	4.4	7.9	5.0	9.2	-0.5	5.7	7.0	4.2
Differ From Category (+/-)	0.4	0.4	0.2	-0.7	0.3	0.3	0.9	0.1	-0.3	0.4
Return, Tax-Adjusted (%)	2.2	3.2	4.4	7.8	5.0	9.2	-0.5	5.7	7.0	4.1
Dividends, Net Income ($)	0.55	0.55	0.56	0.60	0.63	0.65	0.65	0.66	0.67	0.67
Expense Ratio (%)	na	0.14	0.17	0.17	0.19	0.18	0.18	0.21	0.19	0.20
Yield (%)	4.11	4.05	4.05	4.38	4.75	4.87	5.05	4.87	4.96	5.04
Total Assets (Millions $)	4,682	6,897	6,970	7,338	6,653	8,925	7,920	7,896	6,891	6,139

SHAREHOLDER INFORMATION

Minimum Investment
Initial: $3,000   IRA: $0
Subsequent: $100   IRA: $0

Maximum Fees
Load: none   12b-1: none
Other: none

National Muni: Long-Term Bond Funds
Category Performance Ranked by 2005 Returns

nd (Ticker)	Annual Return (%)				Category Risk	Total Risk
	2005	3Yr	5Yr	10Yr		
lls Fargo Advtg Municipal Bond Inv (SXFIX)	5.0	7.3	6.6	5.0	blw av	low
eyfus Muni Bond (DRTAX)	3.9	4.2	4.5	4.5	abv av	blw av
AA Tx Ex Long Term (USTEX)	3.8	5.4	6.0	5.7	av	low
elity Tax Free Bond (FTABX)	3.7	4.9	na	na	high	blw av
Rowe Price Tx Fr Inc Tr Income (PRTAX)	3.7	4.3	5.3	5.2	blw av	low
elity Municipal Income (FHIGX)	3.6	4.7	5.9	5.9	abv av	blw av
nguard Insrd Long Term TE (VILPX)	3.3	4.3	5.4	5.6	high	blw av
nguard Long Term TE (VWLTX)	3.0	4.1	5.4	5.5	high	blw av
at'l Muni: Long-Term Bond Category Average	3.5	4.4	5.3	5.2	av	low

Dreyfus Muni Bond
(DRTAX)

800-645-6561
www.dreyfus.com

National Muni: Long-Term Bond

PERFORMANCE AND PER SHARE DATA			fund inception date: 10/4/?

	3yr Annual	5yr Annual	10yr Annual	Category Risk Index
Return (%)	4.2	4.5	4.5	1.05—abv av
Differ From Category (+/-)	-0.2 av	-0.8 blw av	-0.7 low	Avg Mat 16.9 yrs

	2005	2004	2003	2002	2001	2000	1999	1998	1997	19
Return (%)	3.9	4.2	4.6	7.1	2.7	11.9	-5.9	5.6	7.9	3
Differ From Category (+/-)	0.4	-0.4	-0.5	-1.9	-1.6	-0.3	-1.1	-0.5	-1.7	-0
Return, Tax-Adjusted (%)	3.9	4.2	4.6	7.1	2.7	11.9	-5.9	5.3	7.8	3
Dividends, Net Income ($)	0.52	0.49	0.50	0.60	0.62	0.60	0.61	0.63	0.66	0.6
Expense Ratio (%)	0.72	0.72	0.72	0.71	0.72	0.76	0.73	0.73	0.71	0.7
Yield (%)	4.38	4.15	4.23	5.02	5.31	5.01	5.47	4.94	5.18	5.4
Total Assets (Millions $)	2,024	2,109	2,280	2,467	2,489	2,611	2,606	3,249	3,415	3,60

SHAREHOLDER INFORMATION

Minimum Investment
Initial: $2,500   IRA: $0
Subsequent: $100   IRA: $0

Maximum Fees
Load: 0.10% redemption   12b-1: none
Other: redemption fee applies for 1 month

Fidelity Municipal Income
(FHIGX)

800-544-8544
www.fidelity.com

National Muni: Long-Term Bond

PERFORMANCE AND PER SHARE DATA			fund inception date: 11/30/?

	3yr Annual	5yr Annual	10yr Annual	Category Risk Index
Return (%)	4.7	5.9	5.9	1.09—abv av
Differ From Category (+/-)	0.3 abv av	0.6 abv av	0.7 high	Avg Mat 15.6 yrs

	2005	2004	2003	2002	2001	2000	1999	1998	1997	199
Return (%)	3.6	4.7	5.8	10.4	5.0	12.3	-2.4	6.0	9.2	4
Differ From Category (+/-)	0.1	0.1	0.7	1.4	0.7	0.1	2.4	-0.1	-0.4	1
Return, Tax-Adjusted (%)	3.4	4.5	5.5	10.2	4.9	12.2	-2.4	6.0	9.0	4
Dividends, Net Income ($)	0.55	0.57	0.54	0.60	0.61	0.63	0.60	0.60	0.61	0.6
Expense Ratio (%)	na	0.47	0.47	0.46	0.43	0.48	0.49	0.53	0.55	0.5
Yield (%)	4.20	4.31	4.02	4.48	4.82	4.95	5.00	4.69	4.78	5.2
Total Assets (Millions $)	4,670	4,619	4,775	4,801	4,514	4,452	4,063	4,639	2,347	1,79

SHAREHOLDER INFORMATION

Minimum Investment
Initial: $10,000   IRA: $0
Subsequent: $1,000   IRA: $0

Maximum Fees
Load: 0.50% redemption   12b-1: none
Other: redemp fee applies for 1 mo; maint fee for low

idelity Tax Free Bond
TABX)

ational Muni: Long-Term Bond

800-544-8544
www.fidelity.com

ERFORMANCE AND PER SHARE DATA   fund inception date: 4/10/01

	3yr Annual	5yr Annual	10yr Annual	Category Risk Index
Return (%)	4.9	na	na	1.18—high
Differ From Category (+/-)	0.5 abv av	na	na	**Avg Mat** 13.4 yrs

	2005	2004	2003	2002	2001	2000	1999	1998	1997	1996
turn (%)	3.7	4.8	6.1	10.6	—	—	—	—	—	—
ffer From Category (+/-)	0.2	0.2	1.0	1.6	—	—	—	—	—	—
turn, Tax-Adjusted (%)	3.7	4.7	6.0	10.6	—	—	—	—	—	—
vidends, Net Income ($)	0.42	0.44	0.44	0.43	—	—	—	—	—	—
pense Ratio (%)	0.51	0.23	0.14	0.06	—	—	—	—	—	—
eld (%)	3.94	4.03	4.07	4.05	—	—	—	—	—	—
tal Assets (Millions $)	365	253	220	257	—	—	—	—	—	—

HAREHOLDER INFORMATION

inimum Investment
tial: $25,000   IRA: $0
bsequent: $1,000   IRA: $0

Maximum Fees
Load: 0.50% redemption   12b-1: none
Other: redemp fee applies for 1 mo; maint fee for low bal

Rowe Price Tx Fr Inc Tr
ncome (PRTAX)

ational Muni: Long-Term Bond

800-638-5660
www.troweprice.com

ERFORMANCE AND PER SHARE DATA   fund inception date: 10/26/76

	3yr Annual	5yr Annual	10yr Annual	Category Risk Index
Return (%)	4.3	5.3	5.2	0.95—blw av
Differ From Category (+/-)	-0.1 abv av	0.0 av	0.0 av	**Avg Mat** 14.1 yrs

	2005	2004	2003	2002	2001	2000	1999	1998	1997	1996
eturn (%)	3.7	4.3	5.1	9.2	4.3	12.2	-3.9	5.9	9.3	3.2
iffer From Category (+/-)	0.2	-0.3	0.0	0.2	0.0	0.0	0.9	-0.2	-0.3	-0.7
eturn, Tax-Adjusted (%)	3.7	4.3	5.1	9.2	4.3	12.2	-3.9	5.9	9.3	3.2
vidends, Net Income ($)	0.44	0.43	0.45	0.47	0.48	0.49	0.49	0.51	0.52	0.51
pense Ratio (%)	0.54	0.54	0.55	0.54	0.54	0.55	0.55	0.55	0.57	0.58
eld (%)	4.35	4.30	4.46	4.67	4.98	5.10	5.41	5.10	5.20	5.34
tal Assets (Millions $)	1,465	1,454	1,492	1,503	1,416	1,396	1,328	1,481	1,385	1,345

HAREHOLDER INFORMATION

inimum Investment
tial: $2,500   IRA: $0
bsequent: $100   IRA: $0

Maximum Fees
Load: none   12b-1: none
Other: none

USAA Tx Ex Long Term
(USTEX)

800-531-8181
www.usaa.com

National Muni: Long-Term Bond

PERFORMANCE AND PER SHARE DATA   **fund inception date: 3/19/8**

	3yr Annual	5yr Annual	10yr Annual	Category Risk Index	
Return (%)	5.4	6.0	5.7	1.02—av	
Differ From Category (+/-)	1.0 high	0.7 high	0.5 high	**Avg Mat**	14.2 yrs

	2005	2004	2003	2002	2001	2000	1999	1998	1997	199
Return (%)	3.8	5.6	7.0	9.7	4.3	12.1	-5.0	5.9	10.3	4.4
Differ From Category (+/-) . .	0.3	1.0	1.9	0.7	0.0	-0.1	-0.2	-0.2	0.7	0.5
Return, Tax-Adjusted (%)	3.7	5.6	7.0	9.7	4.3	12.1	-5.0	5.9	10.3	4.4
Dividends, Net Income ($) . .	0.62	0.63	0.65	0.67	0.72	0.74	0.76	0.77	0.78	0.79
Expense Ratio (%)	0.56	0.56	0.54	0.46	0.36	0.36	0.36	0.36	0.37	0.37
Yield (%)	4.39	4.47	4.64	4.86	5.45	5.57	6.01	5.45	5.56	5.87
Total Assets (Millions $) . . .	2,376	2,282	2,238	2,229	2,075	2,071	1,910	2,173	2,002	1,873

SHAREHOLDER INFORMATION

Minimum Investment
Initial: $3,000   IRA: $0
Subsequent: $50   IRA: $0

Maximum Fees
Load: none   12b-1: none
Other: none

Vanguard Insrd Long Term TE
(VILPX)

800-662-7447
www.vanguard.com

National Muni: Long-Term Bond

PERFORMANCE AND PER SHARE DATA   **fund inception date: 10/1/8**

	3yr Annual	5yr Annual	10yr Annual	Category Risk Index	
Return (%)	4.3	5.4	5.6	1.11—high	
Differ From Category (+/-)	-0.1 av	0.1 abv av	0.4 abv av	**Avg Mat**	8.4 yrs

	2005	2004	2003	2002	2001	2000	1999	1998	1997	199
Return (%)	3.3	3.9	5.7	10.0	4.3	13.6	-2.9	6.1	8.6	4.0
Differ From Category (+/-) . .	-0.2	-0.7	0.6	1.0	0.0	1.4	1.9	0.0	-1.0	0.1
Return, Tax-Adjusted (%)	3.3	3.9	5.6	9.8	4.1	13.6	-2.9	6.0	8.5	3.8
Dividends, Net Income ($) .	0.58	0.58	0.58	0.59	0.62	0.64	0.64	0.66	0.67	0.67
Expense Ratio (%)	na	0.15	0.17	0.18	0.19	0.19	0.19	0.21	0.19	0.20
Yield (%)	4.55	4.54	4.46	4.55	5.00	5.10	5.52	5.15	5.28	5.40
Total Assets (Millions $) . . .	1,027	1,875	1,944	1,962	1,847	2,439	2,153	2,268	2,091	1,965

SHAREHOLDER INFORMATION

Minimum Investment
Initial: $3,000   IRA: $0
Subsequent: $100   IRA: $0

Maximum Fees
Load: none   12b-1: none
Other: none

'anguard Long Term TE
/WLTX)

800-662-7447
www.vanguard.com

ational Muni: Long-Term Bond

	3yr Annual	5yr Annual	10yr Annual	Category Risk Index	
Return (%)	4.1	5.4	5.5	1.18—high	
Differ From Category (+/-)	-0.3 blw av	0.1 abv av	0.3 abv av	Avg Mat	8.4 yrs

	2005	2004	2003	2002	2001	2000	1999	1998	1997	1996
turn (%)	3.0	4.1	5.2	10.1	4.6	13.4	-3.5	6.0	9.2	4.4
ffer From Category (+/-)	-0.5	-0.5	0.1	1.1	0.3	1.2	1.3	-0.1	-0.4	0.5
turn, Tax-Adjusted (%)	3.0	4.1	5.2	10.0	4.5	13.4	-3.5	5.8	9.1	4.3
vidends, Net Income ($)	0.51	0.52	0.52	0.54	0.57	0.58	0.57	0.58	0.59	0.59
pense Ratio (%)	na	0.15	0.17	0.17	0.19	0.19	0.18	0.21	0.19	0.20
eld (%)	4.52	4.53	4.53	4.64	5.15	5.24	5.48	5.07	5.18	5.33
tal Assets (Millions $)	641	1,127	1,146	1,248	1,187	1,746	1,487	1,537	1,291	1,147

HAREHOLDER INFORMATION

inimum Investment
tial: $3,000   IRA: $0
bsequent: $100   IRA: $0

Maximum Fees
Load: none   12b-1: none
Other: none

Wells Fargo Advtg Municipal
3ond Inv (SXFIX)

800-368-3863
www.wellsfargofunds.com

ational Muni: Long-Term Bond

	3yr Annual	5yr Annual	10yr Annual	Category Risk Index	
Return (%)	7.3	6.6	5.0	0.91—blw av	
Differ From Category (+/-)	2.9 high	1.3 high	-0.2 blw av	Avg Mat	12.7 yrs

	2005	2004	2003	2002	2001	2000	1999	1998	1997	1996
eturn (%)	5.0	10.3	6.7	6.4	4.7	3.3	-6.4	6.6	12.1	2.4
iffer From Category (+/-)	1.5	5.7	1.6	-2.6	0.4	-8.9	-1.6	0.5	2.5	-1.5
eturn, Tax-Adjusted (%)	5.0	10.3	6.7	6.4	4.7	3.3	-6.4	6.6	12.1	2.4
vidends, Net Income ($)	0.41	0.42	0.40	0.37	0.40	0.48	0.50	0.51	0.51	0.49
xpense Ratio (%)	na	0.80	0.80	1.10	0.80	0.80	0.70	0.70	0.80	0.80
eld (%)	4.26	4.44	4.42	4.18	4.66	5.59	5.65	5.14	5.14	5.35
tal Assets (Millions $)	205	186	196	243	249	243	313	349	241	234

HAREHOLDER INFORMATION

inimum Investment
itial: $2,500   IRA: $0
bsequent: $100   IRA: $0

Maximum Fees
Load: none   12b-1: none
Other: none

National Muni: High-Yield Bond Funds
Category Performance Ranked by 2005 Returns

Fund (Ticker)	Annual Return (%)				Category Risk	Total Risk
	2005	3Yr	5Yr	10Yr		
T Rowe Price Tx Fr Inc Tr High Yield (PRFHX)	6.2	6.6	6.2	5.4	blw av	low
Northern High Yield Muni (NHYMX)	4.8	5.9	6.3	na	high	low
Vanguard High Yield TE (VWAHX)	4.3	5.2	5.6	5.5	high	low
Nat'l Muni: High-Yield Bond Category Average	**5.5**	**5.9**	**6.2**	**5.5**	**av**	**low**

Northern High Yield Muni
(NHYMX)

800-595-9111
www.northernfunds.com

National Muni: High-Yield Bond

PERFORMANCE AND PER SHARE DATA   fund inception date: 12/31/98

	3yr Annual	5yr Annual	10yr Annual	Category Risk Index	
Return (%)	5.9	6.3	na	1.06—high	
Differ From Category (+/-)	0.0 abv av	0.1 high	na	Avg Mat	17.4 yrs

	2005	2004	2003	2002	2001	2000	1999	1998	1997	1996
Return (%)	4.8	6.5	6.4	7.3	6.3	6.3	-6.2	—	—	—
Differ From Category (+/-)	-0.7	0.8	-0.1	-0.5	0.8	-1.8	-2.6	—	—	—
Return, Tax-Adjusted (%)	4.8	6.5	6.4	7.3	6.3	6.3	-6.2	—	—	—
Dividends, Net Income ($)	0.42	0.43	0.45	0.46	0.49	0.48	0.39	—	—	—
Expense Ratio (%)	0.85	0.85	0.85	0.85	0.85	0.85	0.85	—	—	—
Yield (%)	4.31	4.43	4.68	4.93	5.29	5.25	4.28	—	—	—
Total Assets (Millions $)	185	122	84	47	34	28	19	—	—	—

SHAREHOLDER INFORMATION

Minimum Investment
Initial: $2,500   IRA: $0
Subsequent: $50   IRA: $0

Maximum Fees
Load: none   12b-1: none
Other: none

T Rowe Price Tx Fr Inc Tr High Yield (PRFHX)

800-638-5660
www.troweprice.com

National Muni: High-Yield Bond

PERFORMANCE AND PER SHARE DATA   fund inception date: 3/1/85

	3yr Annual	5yr Annual	10yr Annual	Category Risk Index	
Return (%)	6.6	6.2	5.4	0.94—blw av	
Differ From Category (+/-)	0.7 high	0.0 av	-0.1 av	Avg Mat	17.3 yrs

	2005	2004	2003	2002	2001	2000	1999	1998	1997	1996
Return (%)	6.2	6.6	7.1	6.3	4.6	8.1	-5.1	5.5	10.1	4.9
Differ From Category (+/-)	0.7	0.9	0.6	-1.5	-0.9	0.0	-1.5	-0.4	-0.1	0.4
Return, Tax-Adjusted (%)	6.2	6.6	7.1	6.3	4.6	8.1	-5.1	5.4	10.1	4.9
Dividends, Net Income ($)	0.58	0.60	0.61	0.64	0.66	0.67	0.65	0.67	0.69	0.70
Expense Ratio (%)	0.70	0.71	0.71	0.71	0.72	0.71	0.71	0.72	0.74	0.75
Yield (%)	4.89	5.10	5.24	5.58	5.80	5.81	5.77	5.34	5.49	5.78
Total Assets (Millions $)	1,370	1,220	1,139	1,119	1,089	1,084	1,132	1,345	1,200	1,033

SHAREHOLDER INFORMATION

Minimum Investment
Initial: $2,500   IRA: $0
Subsequent: $100   IRA: $0

Maximum Fees
Load: none   12b-1: none
Other: none

Vanguard High Yield TE
(VWAHX)

800-662-7447
www.vanguard.com

National Muni: High-Yield Bond

PERFORMANCE AND PER SHARE DATA   fund inception date: 12/27/78

	3yr Annual	5yr Annual	10yr Annual	Category Risk Index	
Return (%)	5.2	5.6	5.5	1.22—high	
Differ From Category (+/-)	-0.7 low	-0.6 low	0.0 abv av	**Avg Mat**	7.3 yrs

	2005	2004	2003	2002	2001	2000	1999	1998	1997	1996
Return (%)	4.3	4.9	6.3	7.3	5.3	10.7	-3.3	6.4	9.2	4.4
Differ From Category (+/-) ..	-1.2	-0.8	-0.2	-0.5	-0.2	2.6	0.2	0.5	-1.0	-0.1
Return, Tax-Adjusted (%)....	4.3	4.9	6.3	7.3	5.3	10.7	-3.3	6.3	9.1	4.4
Dividends, Net Income ($)..	0.49	0.50	0.52	0.56	0.58	0.58	0.57	0.58	0.60	0.59
Expense Ratio (%)...........	na	0.15	0.17	0.17	0.19	0.19	0.18	0.20	0.19	0.20
Yield (%)	4.54	4.64	4.81	5.23	5.48	5.54	5.70	5.21	5.45	5.52
Total Assets (Millions $)...	1,745	2,764	2,668	2,669	2,650	3,143	2,753	2,767	2,320	2,042

SHAREHOLDER INFORMATION

Minimum Investment
Initial: $3,000   IRA: $0
Subsequent: $100   IRA: $0

Maximum Fees
Load: none   12b-1: none
Other: none

STATE-SPECIFIC BOND FUNDS
Category Performance Ranked by 2005 Returns

Category	Fund (Ticker)	Annual Return (%)				Category Risk	Total Risk
		2005	3Yr	5Yr	10Yr		
MS-MN	Sit MN Tax Free Income (SMTFX)	4.4	4.1	5.0	4.9	av	low
MS-CA	USAA Tx Ex California Bond (USCBX)	3.7	4.6	5.0	5.6	abv av	blw av
MS-CA	Vanguard CA Long Term TE Inv (VCITX)	3.7	4.3	5.1	5.7	abv av	blw av
MS-NY	USAA Tx Ex New York Bond (USNYX)	3.7	4.6	5.5	5.7	high	blw av
MS-CA	Fidelity CA Muni Inc (FCTFX)	3.6	4.4	5.3	5.6	abv av	low
MS-MA	Fidelity MA Muni Inc (FDMMX)	3.6	4.4	5.4	5.5	high	low
MS-CA	T Rowe Price CA Tax Free Bond (PRXCX)	3.5	4.1	4.9	5.3	av	low
MS-FL	USAA Florida Tx Fr Income (UFLTX)	3.4	4.8	5.6	5.5	av	blw av
MS-NY	T Rowe Price Tx Fr Inc Tr NY Tx Fr Bond (PRNYX)	3.4	4.0	5.1	5.2	av	low
MS-WI	Wells Fargo Advtg WI Tax Free Inv (SWFRX)	3.3	4.4	na	na	high	low
MS-NJ	Fidelity NJ Muni Inc (FNJHX)	3.3	4.2	5.3	5.4	high	blw av
MS-CA	Amer Century CA Long Term Tax Free Inv (BCLTX)	3.3	3.9	4.9	5.2	high	blw av
MS-CA	Schwab Inv CA Long Term Tax Free Bond (SWCAX)	3.3	4.3	5.2	5.4	av	low
MS-MD	T Rowe Price Tx Fr Inc Tr MD Tx Fr Bond (MDXBX)	3.3	3.8	5.2	5.2	high	low
MS-VA	T Rowe Price Tx Fr Inc Tr VA Tx Fr Bond (PRVAX)	3.2	4.0	5.3	5.3	av	low
MS-MA	Vanguard MA Tax Exempt (VMATX)	3.2	4.1	5.1	na	abv av	low
MS-GA	T Rowe Price Tx Fr Inc Tr GA Tx Fr Bond (GTFBX)	3.2	4.1	5.1	5.2	high	low
MS-NY	Fidelity NY Muni Inc (FTFMX)	3.0	4.3	5.6	5.6	abv av	blw av
MS-VA	USAA Tx Ex Virginia Bond (USVAX)	2.9	4.3	5.3	5.4	high	blw av
MS-NY	Dreyfus NY Tax Exempt Bond (DRNYX)	2.9	3.3	4.6	4.8	abv av	blw av
MS-OH	Fidelity OH Muni Inc (FOHFX)	2.9	4.3	5.4	5.4	av	blw av
MS-NJ	Vanguard NJ Long Term TE Inv (VNJTX)	2.8	3.9	5.2	5.4	abv av	blw av
MS-NY	Vanguard NY Long Term TE Inv (VNYTX)	2.8	4.0	5.3	5.5	high	blw av
MS-FL	Fidelity FL Muni Inc (FFLIX)	2.7	4.0	5.3	5.3	high	blw av
MS-PA	Vanguard PA Long Term TE Inv (VPAIX)	2.7	4.0	5.3	5.5	abv av	blw av
MS-AZ	Fidelity AZ Muni Inc (FSAZX)	2.7	3.8	5.2	5.1	high	blw av
MS-PA	Fidelity PA Muni Inc (FPXTX)	2.7	4.0	5.2	5.2	av	low
MS-MI	Fidelity MI Muni Inc (FMHTX)	2.6	4.1	5.3	5.2	high	low
MS-KY	Dupree KY Tax Free Income (KYTFX)	2.6	4.1	4.9	4.8	high	low
MS-OH	Vanguard OH Long Term Tax Exempt (VOHIX)	2.6	4.0	5.4	5.5	high	blw av
MS-MN	Fidelity MN Muni Inc (FIMIX)	2.6	3.9	4.9	5.0	high	low
MS-FL	Vanguard FL Long Term Tx Ex (VFLTX)	2.5	4.1	5.5	5.7	high	blw av
MS-MD	Fidelity MD Muni Inc (SMDMX)	2.5	3.8	4.9	5.1	high	low
MS-TN	Dupree TN Tax Free Income (TNTIX)	2.5	3.8	4.8	5.2	high	low
MS-HI	Hawaii Municipal Inv (SURFX)	2.3	3.8	4.7	4.6	high	low
MS-CA	Amer Century CA Intermediate Tax Free Inv (BCITX)	2.2	2.7	4.2	4.7	blw av	low
MS-CT	Fidelity CT Muni Inc (FICNX)	2.2	3.5	5.0	5.3	high	blw av
MS-AZ	Northern AZ Tax Exempt (NOAZX)	2.0	3.1	4.7	na	abv av	low
MS-CA	Vanguard CA Intm Term TE Inv (VCAIX)	1.8	2.9	4.4	5.1	blw av	low
MS-CT	Dreyfus CT Intm Muni Bd (DCTIX)	1.7	2.6	4.1	4.3	blw av	low
MS-WV	WesMark West Virginia Muni (WMKMX)	1.6	2.6	4.0	na	high	low
MS-NY	Bernstein NY Municipal (SNNYX)	1.6	2.7	3.9	4.3	low	low
MS-CO	Westcore CO Tax Exempt (WTCOX)	1.5	2.8	4.1	4.4	high	low
MS-FL	T Rowe Price Tx Fr Inc Tr FL Int Tx Fr (FLTFX)	1.5	2.5	4.1	4.4	blw av	low
MS-CA	Bernstein CA Municipal (SNCAX)	1.4	2.5	3.6	4.1	blw av	low
MS-CA	Schwab Inv CA Short Intm Tax Free Bond (SWCSX)	0.7	1.9	3.3	3.8	low	low
MS-KY	Dupree KY Tax Free Short to Med (KYSMX)	0.4	1.9	3.5	3.7	av	low

Fidelity AZ Muni Inc
(FSAZX)

800-544-8544
www.fidelity.com

Muni: Arizona Bond

fund inception date: 10/11/9

	3yr Annual	5yr Annual	10yr Annual	Category Risk Index	
Return (%)	3.8	5.2	5.1	1.09—high	
Differ From Category (+/-)	0.5 high	0.4 high	0.1 high	**Avg Mat** 13.2 yrs	

	2005	2004	2003	2002	2001	2000	1999	1998	1997	199
Return (%)	2.7	3.7	5.2	9.9	4.8	10.9	-1.8	5.3	7.9	3.5
Differ From Category (+/-)	0.4	0.4	0.9	0.3	-0.1	0.3	-0.5	-0.2	0.5	-0.
Return, Tax-Adjusted (%)	2.6	3.6	5.1	9.7	4.8	10.9	-1.8	5.2	7.8	3.
Dividends, Net Income ($)	0.42	0.43	0.43	0.44	0.46	0.49	0.46	0.47	0.48	0.49
Expense Ratio (%)	0.55	0.53	0.52	0.48	0.41	0.48	0.55	0.55	0.53	0.30
Yield (%)	3.63	3.67	3.70	3.79	4.18	4.49	4.47	4.23	4.42	4.6
Total Assets (Millions $)	99	86	76	73	54	40	27	26	20	22

Minimum Investment
Initial: $10,000   IRA: $0
Subsequent: $1,000   IRA: $0

Maximum Fees
Load: 0.50% redemption   12b-1: none
Other: redemp fee applies for 1 mo; maint fee for low b

Northern AZ Tax Exempt
(NOAZX)

800-595-9111
www.northernfunds.com

Muni: Arizona Bond

fund inception date: 10/1/9

	3yr Annual	5yr Annual	10yr Annual	Category Risk Index	
Return (%)	3.1	4.7	na	1.05—abv av	
Differ From Category (+/-)	-0.2 abv av	-0.1 abv av	na	**Avg Mat** 11.2 yrs	

	2005	2004	2003	2002	2001	2000	1999	1998	1997	199
Return (%)	2.0	3.5	3.9	9.9	4.6	11.2	—	—	—	—
Differ From Category (+/-)	-0.3	0.2	-0.4	0.3	-0.3	0.6	—	—	—	—
Return, Tax-Adjusted (%)	1.9	3.3	3.8	9.6	4.3	11.2	—	—	—	—
Dividends, Net Income ($)	0.41	0.41	0.44	0.41	0.43	0.44	—	—	—	—
Expense Ratio (%)	0.85	0.85	0.85	0.85	0.85	0.85	—	—	—	—
Yield (%)	3.93	3.82	4.08	3.72	4.10	4.17	—	—	—	—
Total Assets (Millions $)	55	69	80	81	80	73	—	—	—	—

Minimum Investment
Initial: $2,500   IRA: $0
Subsequent: $50   IRA: $0

Maximum Fees
Load: none   12b-1: none
Other: none

Amer Century CA Intermediate Tax Free Inv (BCITX)

800-345-2021
www.americancentury.com

Muni: California Bond

PERFORMANCE AND PER SHARE DATA   fund inception date: 11/9/83

	3yr Annual	5yr Annual	10yr Annual	Category Risk Index	
Return (%)	2.7	4.2	4.7	0.98—blw av	
Differ From Category (+/-)	-0.8 blw av	-0.3 blw av	-0.2 av	Avg Mat	9.0 yrs

	2005	2004	2003	2002	2001	2000	1999	1998	1997	1996
Return (%)	2.2	2.7	3.2	8.7	4.3	10.1	-1.0	5.5	7.4	4.2
Differ From Category (+/-)	-0.6	-0.9	-0.8	0.9	0.1	-1.4	1.5	-0.3	-0.7	0.1
Return, Tax-Adjusted (%)	2.2	2.7	3.2	8.7	4.2	10.1	-1.0	5.3	7.1	4.1
Dividends, Net Income ($)	0.46	0.44	0.44	0.46	0.49	0.50	0.49	0.51	0.53	0.54
Expense Ratio (%)	0.50	0.50	0.51	0.51	0.51	0.51	0.51	0.51	0.48	0.48
Yield (%)	4.09	3.88	3.85	3.93	4.38	4.47	4.60	4.49	4.64	4.84
Total Assets (Millions $)	439	418	450	479	440	445	439	480	437	439

SHAREHOLDER INFORMATION

Minimum Investment
Initial: $5,000   IRA: $0
Subsequent: $1   IRA: $0

Maximum Fees
Load: none   12b-1: none
Other: none

Amer Century CA Long Term Tax Free Inv (BCLTX)

800-345-2021
www.americancentury.com

Muni: California Bond

PERFORMANCE AND PER SHARE DATA   fund inception date: 11/9/83

	3yr Annual	5yr Annual	10yr Annual	Category Risk Index	
Return (%)	3.9	4.9	5.2	1.24—high	
Differ From Category (+/-)	0.4 av	0.4 abv av	0.3 abv av	Avg Mat	18.0 yrs

	2005	2004	2003	2002	2001	2000	1999	1998	1997	1996
Return (%)	3.3	4.0	4.4	8.6	4.2	14.8	-5.2	6.3	9.7	3.5
Differ From Category (+/-)	0.5	0.4	0.4	0.8	0.0	3.3	-2.7	0.5	1.6	-0.6
Return, Tax-Adjusted (%)	3.0	4.0	4.4	8.6	4.2	14.8	-5.2	6.1	9.3	3.5
Dividends, Net Income ($)	0.52	0.51	0.53	0.53	0.55	0.56	0.56	0.58	0.61	0.61
Expense Ratio (%)	0.50	0.50	0.51	0.51	0.51	0.51	0.51	0.51	0.48	0.48
Yield (%)	4.47	4.31	4.50	4.44	4.83	4.85	5.37	4.93	5.13	5.41
Total Assets (Millions $)	461	468	498	544	310	320	300	340	312	297

SHAREHOLDER INFORMATION

Minimum Investment
Initial: $5,000   IRA: $0
Subsequent: $1   IRA: $0

Maximum Fees
Load: none   12b-1: none
Other: none

Individual Fund Listings   421

Bernstein CA Municipal
(SNCAX)

Muni: California Bond

212-486-5800
www.bernstein.com

	3yr Annual	5yr Annual	10yr Annual	Category Risk Index
Return (%)	2.5	3.6	4.1	0.76—blw av
Differ From Category (+/-)	-1.0 blw av	-0.9 blw av	-0.8 blw av	**Avg Mat** 5.4 yrs

	2005	2004	2003	2002	2001	2000	1999	1998	1997	199
Return (%)	1.4	2.5	3.6	5.8	4.5	8.5	0.0	5.1	6.3	3.
Differ From Category (+/-)	-1.4	-1.1	-0.4	-2.0	0.3	-3.0	2.5	-0.7	-1.8	-0.
Return, Tax-Adjusted (%)	1.4	2.5	3.6	5.8	4.5	8.5	-0.1	5.0	6.3	3.
Dividends, Net Income ($)	0.43	0.42	0.46	0.50	0.56	0.57	0.55	0.56	0.59	0.6
Expense Ratio (%)	0.65	0.64	0.65	0.66	0.65	0.64	0.64	0.65	0.67	0.6
Yield (%)	3.06	2.95	3.19	3.44	3.98	4.09	4.04	3.96	4.19	4.4
Total Assets (Millions $)	983	878	711	605	513	447	561	576	430	31

SHAREHOLDER INFORMATION

Minimum Investment
Initial: $25,000   IRA: $0
Subsequent: $5,000   IRA: $0

Maximum Fees
Load: none   12b-1: none
Other: none

Fidelity CA Muni Inc
(FCTFX)

Muni: California Bond

800-544-8544
www.fidelity.com

	3yr Annual	5yr Annual	10yr Annual	Category Risk Index
Return (%)	4.4	5.3	5.6	1.10—abv av
Differ From Category (+/-)	0.9 high	0.8 high	0.7 high	**Avg Mat** 12.9 yrs

	2005	2004	2003	2002	2001	2000	1999	1998	1997	199
Return (%)	3.6	4.8	4.9	8.4	4.7	12.5	-2.8	6.5	9.8	4.
Differ From Category (+/-)	0.8	1.2	0.9	0.6	0.5	1.0	-0.2	0.7	1.7	0.
Return, Tax-Adjusted (%)	3.5	4.6	4.7	8.3	4.6	12.5	-2.8	6.3	9.8	4.
Dividends, Net Income ($)	0.51	0.53	0.54	0.54	0.56	0.57	0.55	0.57	0.59	0.6
Expense Ratio (%)	0.48	0.48	0.47	0.43	0.42	0.49	0.52	0.53	0.59	0.5
Yield (%)	4.10	4.16	4.21	4.23	4.50	4.64	4.78	4.58	4.81	5.1
Total Assets (Millions $)	1,566	1,470	1,520	1,686	1,603	1,430	1,224	1,319	1,210	48

SHAREHOLDER INFORMATION

Minimum Investment
Initial: $10,000   IRA: $0
Subsequent: $1,000   IRA: $0

Maximum Fees
Load: 0.50% redemption   12b-1: none
Other: redemp fee applies for 1 mo; maint fee for low

Schwab Inv CA Long Term Tax Free Bond (SWCAX)

800-435-4000
www.schwab.com/
schwabfunds

Muni: California Bond

PERFORMANCE AND PER SHARE DATA — fund inception date: 2/24/92

	3yr Annual	5yr Annual	10yr Annual	Category Risk Index	
Return (%)	4.3	5.2	5.4	1.07—av	
Differ From Category (+/-)	0.8 abv av	0.7 high	0.5 abv av	**Avg Mat**	15.7 yrs

	2005	2004	2003	2002	2001	2000	1999	1998	1997	1996
Return (%)	3.3	5.0	4.6	8.2	4.9	15.2	-6.1	6.4	10.0	4.3
Differ From Category (+/-)	0.5	1.4	0.6	0.4	0.7	3.7	-3.6	0.6	1.9	0.2
Return, Tax-Adjusted (%)	3.2	4.9	4.6	8.2	4.9	15.2	-6.1	6.4	10.0	4.3
Dividends, Net Income ($)	0.49	0.50	0.49	0.52	0.54	0.55	0.54	0.54	0.56	0.56
Expense Ratio (%)	0.61	0.61	0.58	0.49	0.49	0.49	0.49	0.49	0.49	0.49
Yield (%)	4.21	4.23	4.18	4.43	4.73	4.85	5.24	4.63	4.92	5.18
Total Assets (Millions $)	197	185	190	233	216	190	166	198	138	108

SHAREHOLDER INFORMATION

Minimum Investment
Initial: $2,500   IRA: $0
Subsequent: $500   IRA: $0

Maximum Fees
Load: none   12b-1: none
Other: none

Schwab Inv CA Short Intm Tax Free Bond (SWCSX)

800-435-4000
www.schwab.com/
schwabfunds

Muni: California Bond

PERFORMANCE AND PER SHARE DATA — fund inception date: 4/20/93

	3yr Annual	5yr Annual	10yr Annual	Category Risk Index	
Return (%)	1.9	3.3	3.8	0.59—low	
Differ From Category (+/-)	-1.6 low	-1.2 low	-1.1 low	**Avg Mat**	4.3 yrs

	2005	2004	2003	2002	2001	2000	1999	1998	1997	1996
Return (%)	0.7	1.9	3.0	6.1	4.9	7.2	0.6	4.8	5.1	3.9
Differ From Category (+/-)	-2.1	-1.7	-1.0	-1.7	0.7	-4.3	3.2	-1.0	-3.0	-0.2
Return, Tax-Adjusted (%)	0.7	1.9	3.0	6.1	4.9	7.2	0.6	4.8	5.1	3.9
Dividends, Net Income ($)	0.33	0.32	0.32	0.34	0.38	0.40	0.39	0.40	0.42	0.43
Expense Ratio (%)	0.61	0.61	0.58	0.49	0.49	0.49	0.49	0.49	0.49	0.49
Yield (%)	3.20	2.98	2.96	3.17	3.62	3.86	3.90	3.91	4.14	4.21
Total Assets (Millions $)	128	153	170	184	146	139	118	107	61	49

SHAREHOLDER INFORMATION

Minimum Investment
Initial: $2,500   IRA: $0
Subsequent: $500   IRA: $0

Maximum Fees
Load: none   12b-1: none
Other: none

T Rowe Price CA Tax Free Bond (PRXCX)

800-638-5660
www.troweprice.com

Muni: California Bond

PERFORMANCE AND PER SHARE DATA   fund inception date: 9/15/86

	3yr Annual	5yr Annual	10yr Annual	Category Risk Index	
Return (%)	4.1	4.9	5.3	1.07—av	
Differ From Category (+/-)	0.6 abv av	0.4 av	0.4 abv av	**Avg Mat**	13.4 yrs

	2005	2004	2003	2002	2001	2000	1999	1998	1997	1996
Return (%)	3.5	4.2	4.5	8.5	3.8	12.8	-3.3	6.0	9.0	4.5
Differ From Category (+/-) . .	0.7	0.6	0.5	0.7	-0.4	1.3	-0.7	0.2	0.9	0.4
Return, Tax-Adjusted (%). . . .	3.4	4.2	4.5	8.5	3.8	12.8	-3.3	5.9	9.0	4.5
Dividends, Net Income ($). .	0.47	0.48	0.49	0.50	0.51	0.53	0.52	0.49	0.54	0.55
Expense Ratio (%).	0.53	0.53	0.53	0.54	0.54	0.56	0.58	0.58	0.62	0.63
Yield (%)	4.28	4.32	4.35	4.45	4.78	4.87	5.13	4.44	5.00	5.21
Total Assets (Millions $)	283	265	267	273	249	236	214	220	188	156

SHAREHOLDER INFORMATION

Minimum Investment
Initial: $2,500   IRA: $0
Subsequent: $100   IRA: $0

Maximum Fees
Load: none
Other: none

12b-1: none

USAA Tx Ex California Bond (USCBX)

800-531-8181
www.usaa.com

Muni: California Bond

PERFORMANCE AND PER SHARE DATA   fund inception date: 8/1/89

	3yr Annual	5yr Annual	10yr Annual	Category Risk Index	
Return (%)	4.6	5.0	5.6	1.17—abv av	
Differ From Category (+/-)	1.1 high	0.5 abv av	0.7 abv av	**Avg Mat**	15.3 yrs

	2005	2004	2003	2002	2001	2000	1999	1998	1997	1996
Return (%)	3.7	4.8	5.3	8.3	3.2	14.3	-5.2	6.8	10.3	5.3
Differ From Category (+/-) . . .	0.9	1.2	1.3	0.5	-1.0	2.8	-2.7	1.0	2.2	1.2
Return, Tax-Adjusted (%).	3.7	4.7	5.2	8.3	3.2	14.3	-5.2	6.8	10.3	5.3
Dividends, Net Income ($) .	0.48	0.49	0.49	0.51	0.55	0.57	0.58	0.59	0.60	0.60
Expense Ratio (%)	0.57	0.58	0.54	0.49	0.39	0.39	0.39	0.40	0.41	0.42
Yield (%)	4.30	4.33	4.36	4.54	5.03	5.13	5.66	5.21	5.37	5.64
Total Assets (Millions $)	692	669	670	701	666	647	575	608	511	439

SHAREHOLDER INFORMATION

Minimum Investment
Initial: $3,000   IRA: $0
Subsequent: $50   IRA: $0

Maximum Fees
Load: none
Other: none

12b-1: none

Vanguard CA Intm Term TE Inv (VCAIX)

800-662-7447
www.vanguard.com

Muni: California Bond

PERFORMANCE AND PER SHARE DATA   fund inception date: 3/4/94

	3yr Annual	5yr Annual	10yr Annual	Category Risk Index	
Return (%)	2.9	4.4	5.1	0.95—blw av	
Differ From Category (+/-)	-0.6 av	-0.1 av	0.2 av	**Avg Mat**	5.9 yrs

	2005	2004	2003	2002	2001	2000	1999	1998	1997	1996
Return (%)	1.8	2.8	4.1	9.1	4.4	10.9	-0.5	6.0	7.6	5.4
Differ From Category (+/-)	-1.0	-0.8	0.1	1.3	0.2	-0.6	2.0	0.2	-0.5	1.3
Return, Tax-Adjusted (%)	1.8	2.8	3.9	9.0	4.4	10.9	-0.5	6.0	7.6	5.3
Dividends, Net Income ($)	0.43	0.44	0.45	0.47	0.49	0.50	0.48	0.49	0.50	0.51
Expense Ratio (%)	na	0.15	0.17	0.17	0.17	0.17	0.17	0.19	0.18	0.19
Yield (%)	3.94	3.90	3.95	4.08	4.47	4.53	4.63	4.46	4.66	4.83
Total Assets (Millions $)	1,003	1,523	1,494	1,655	1,499	1,783	1,262	1,034	627	353

SHAREHOLDER INFORMATION

Minimum Investment
Initial: $3,000   IRA: $0
Subsequent: $100   IRA: $0

Maximum Fees
Load: none   12b-1: none
Other: none

Vanguard CA Long Term TE Inv (VCITX)

800-662-7447
www.vanguard.com

Muni: California Bond

PERFORMANCE AND PER SHARE DATA   fund inception date: 4/7/86

	3yr Annual	5yr Annual	10yr Annual	Category Risk Index	
Return (%)	4.3	5.1	5.7	1.20—abv av	
Differ From Category (+/-)	0.8 abv av	0.6 abv av	0.8 high	**Avg Mat**	7.2 yrs

	2005	2004	2003	2002	2001	2000	1999	1998	1997	1996
Return (%)	3.7	4.1	4.9	9.4	3.3	15.1	-3.1	6.2	9.1	4.9
Differ From Category (+/-)	0.9	0.5	0.9	1.6	-0.9	3.6	-0.5	0.4	1.0	0.8
Return, Tax-Adjusted (%)	3.7	4.1	4.7	9.4	3.3	15.1	-3.1	6.1	8.9	4.7
Dividends, Net Income ($)	0.53	0.54	0.54	0.55	0.57	0.58	0.56	0.58	0.59	0.60
Expense Ratio (%)	na	0.15	0.17	0.18	0.18	0.18	0.18	0.19	0.16	0.19
Yield (%)	4.48	4.56	4.52	4.59	4.93	4.93	5.26	4.93	5.08	5.28
Total Assets (Millions $)	651	1,286	1,284	1,464	1,479	1,808	1,493	1,503	1,235	1,061

SHAREHOLDER INFORMATION

Minimum Investment
Initial: $3,000   IRA: $0
Subsequent: $100   IRA: $0

Maximum Fees
Load: none   12b-1: none
Other: none

Westcore CO Tax Exempt
(WTCOX)

800-392-2673
www.westcore.com

Muni: Colorado Bond

PERFORMANCE AND PER SHARE DATA   fund inception date: 6/3/91

	3yr Annual	5yr Annual	10yr Annual	Category Risk Index	
Return (%)	2.8	4.1	4.4	1.00—high	
Differ From Category (+/-)	0.0 high	0.0 high	0.0 high	**Avg Mat**	10.0 yrs

	2005	2004	2003	2002	2001	2000	1999	1998	1997	1996
Return (%)	1.5	2.5	4.4	7.9	4.3	9.0	-2.2	5.5	7.3	4.3
Differ From Category (+/-)	0.0	0.0	0.0	0.0	0.0	0.0	0.0	0.0	0.0	0.0
Return, Tax-Adjusted (%)	1.5	2.5	4.4	7.9	4.3	9.0	-2.2	5.5	7.3	4.3
Dividends, Net Income ($)	0.42	0.42	0.41	0.43	0.45	0.45	0.46	0.48	0.50	0.50
Expense Ratio (%)	0.65	0.65	0.65	0.65	0.65	0.63	0.53	0.50	0.50	0.44
Yield (%)	3.77	3.65	3.59	3.76	4.06	4.13	4.34	4.24	4.54	4.66
Total Assets (Millions $)	58	62	52	50	47	43	37	40	27	19

SHAREHOLDER INFORMATION

Minimum Investment		Maximum Fees	
Initial: $2,500	IRA: $0	Load: 2.00% redemption	12b-1: none
Subsequent: $100	IRA: $0	Other: redemption fee applies for 3 months	

Dreyfus CT Intm Muni Bd
(DCTIX)

800-645-6561
www.dreyfus.com

Muni: Connecticut Bond

PERFORMANCE AND PER SHARE DATA   fund inception date: 6/26/92

	3yr Annual	5yr Annual	10yr Annual	Category Risk Index	
Return (%)	2.6	4.1	4.3	0.93—blw av	
Differ From Category (+/-)	-0.3 abv av	-0.3 abv av	-0.4 blw av	**Avg Mat**	7.2 yrs

	2005	2004	2003	2002	2001	2000	1999	1998	1997	1996
Return (%)	1.7	2.7	3.4	8.1	4.9	7.5	-1.1	5.4	7.5	3.7
Differ From Category (+/-)	-0.1	-0.2	-0.5	-0.8	0.2	-2.0	0.9	-0.5	-0.9	-0.1
Return, Tax-Adjusted (%)	1.6	2.7	3.4	8.1	4.9	7.5	-1.1	5.4	7.5	3.7
Dividends, Net Income ($)	0.52	0.53	0.55	0.58	0.61	0.59	0.58	0.58	0.60	0.59
Expense Ratio (%)	0.78	0.78	0.78	0.77	0.79	0.79	0.80	0.78	0.78	0.72
Yield (%)	3.79	3.74	3.84	4.05	4.44	4.33	4.32	4.14	4.29	4.37
Total Assets (Millions $)	137	139	153	157	140	131	132	139	130	130

SHAREHOLDER INFORMATION

Minimum Investment		Maximum Fees	
Initial: $2,500	IRA: $0	Load: 1.00% redemption	12b-1: none
Subsequent: $100	IRA: $0	Other: redemption fee applies for 1 month	

Fidelity CT Muni Inc
(FICNX)

800-544-8544
www.fidelity.com

Muni: Connecticut Bond

	3yr Annual	5yr Annual	10yr Annual	Category Risk Index	
Return (%)	3.5	5.0	5.3	1.10—high	
Differ From Category (+/-)	0.6 high	0.6 high	0.6 high	**Avg Mat**	12.4 yrs

	2005	2004	2003	2002	2001	2000	1999	1998	1997	1996
Return (%)	2.2	3.4	5.0	10.0	4.9	10.9	-2.1	5.8	9.1	4.2
Differ From Category (+/-)	0.4	0.5	1.1	1.1	0.2	1.4	0.0	-0.1	0.7	0.4
Return, Tax-Adjusted (%)	2.0	3.3	4.8	9.9	4.8	10.9	-2.1	5.7	8.9	4.2
Dividends, Net Income ($)	0.46	0.48	0.49	0.49	0.52	0.55	0.53	0.54	0.56	0.57
Expense Ratio (%)	na	0.49	0.49	0.46	0.41	0.42	0.49	0.54	0.55	0.52
Yield (%)	3.98	4.03	4.06	4.14	4.61	4.88	4.89	4.66	4.81	5.10
Total Assets (Millions $)	434	430	439	468	411	356	330	373	344	330

SHAREHOLDER INFORMATION

Minimum Investment
Initial: $10,000   IRA: $0
Subsequent: $1,000   IRA: $0

Maximum Fees
Load: 0.50% redemption   12b-1: none
Other: redemp fee applies for 1 mo; maint fee for low bal

Fidelity FL Muni Inc
(FFLIX)

800-544-8544
www.fidelity.com

Muni: Florida Bond

	3yr Annual	5yr Annual	10yr Annual	Category Risk Index	
Return (%)	4.0	5.3	5.3	1.07—high	
Differ From Category (+/-)	0.6 abv av	0.5 abv av	0.3 abv av	**Avg Mat**	12.9 yrs

	2005	2004	2003	2002	2001	2000	1999	1998	1997	1996
Return (%)	2.7	4.4	4.9	9.2	5.2	10.8	-2.7	6.2	8.7	3.9
Differ From Category (+/-)	0.5	1.1	0.2	0.0	0.5	0.7	-0.5	0.2	0.5	0.1
Return, Tax-Adjusted (%)	2.5	4.4	4.6	9.0	5.2	10.8	-2.7	6.1	8.6	3.9
Dividends, Net Income ($)	0.45	0.47	0.48	0.51	0.53	0.54	0.52	0.53	0.54	0.55
Expense Ratio (%)	na	0.49	0.48	0.47	0.40	0.49	0.55	0.55	0.55	0.55
Yield (%)	3.90	3.98	4.04	4.27	4.62	4.74	4.79	4.50	4.65	4.91
Total Assets (Millions $)	519	521	573	614	520	438	413	455	419	393

SHAREHOLDER INFORMATION

Minimum Investment
Initial: $10,000   IRA: $0
Subsequent: $1,000   IRA: $0

Maximum Fees
Load: 0.50% redemption   12b-1: none
Other: redemp fee applies for 1 mo; maint fee for low bal

T Rowe Price Tx Fr Inc Tr FL Int Tx Fr (FLTFX)

800-638-5660
www.troweprice.com

Muni: Florida Bond

PERFORMANCE AND PER SHARE DATA   fund inception date: 3/31/93

	3yr Annual	5yr Annual	10yr Annual	Category Risk Index	
Return (%)	2.5	4.1	4.4	0.89—blw av	
Differ From Category (+/-)	-0.9 low	-0.7 blw av	-0.6 blw av	**Avg Mat**	7.5 yrs

	2005	2004	2003	2002	2001	2000	1999	1998	1997	1996
Return (%)	1.5	2.1	3.9	8.7	4.7	8.6	-1.1	5.6	6.7	3.6
Differ From Category (+/-) ..	-0.7	-1.2	-0.8	-0.5	0.0	-1.5	1.1	-0.4	-1.5	-0.2
Return, Tax-Adjusted (%)....	1.5	2.1	3.9	8.7	4.7	8.6	-1.1	5.6	6.7	3.6
Dividends, Net Income ($)..	0.41	0.41	0.43	0.44	0.46	0.46	0.45	0.46	0.46	0.46
Expense Ratio (%).........	0.55	0.55	0.54	0.56	0.59	0.60	0.60	0.60	1.65	0.60
Yield (%)	3.76	3.74	3.86	3.95	4.27	4.35	4.38	4.24	4.28	4.32
Total Assets (Millions $).....	108	120	126	126	106	101	99	116	96	90

SHAREHOLDER INFORMATION

Minimum Investment
Initial: $2,500   IRA: $0
Subsequent: $100   IRA: $0

Maximum Fees
Load: none   12b-1: none
Other: none

USAA Florida Tx Fr Income (UFLTX)

800-531-8181
www.usaa.com

Muni: Florida Bond

PERFORMANCE AND PER SHARE DATA   fund inception date: 10/1/93

	3yr Annual	5yr Annual	10yr Annual	Category Risk Index	
Return (%)	4.8	5.6	5.5	1.05—av	
Differ From Category (+/-)	1.4 high	0.8 high	0.5 high	**Avg Mat**	14.2 yrs

	2005	2004	2003	2002	2001	2000	1999	1998	1997	1996
Return (%)	3.4	4.7	6.5	8.7	4.9	12.8	-6.3	6.3	11.1	4.3
Differ From Category (+/-) ...	1.2	1.4	1.8	-0.5	0.2	2.7	-4.1	0.3	2.9	0.5
Return, Tax-Adjusted (%).....	3.4	4.7	6.5	8.7	4.9	12.8	-6.3	6.3	11.1	4.3
Dividends, Net Income ($) .	0.42	0.43	0.45	0.45	0.48	0.49	0.49	0.50	0.51	0.52
Expense Ratio (%)	0.63	0.64	0.63	0.56	0.49	0.48	0.47	0.50	0.50	0.50
Yield (%)	4.20	4.19	4.38	4.53	5.02	5.09	5.48	4.95	5.15	5.49
Total Assets (Millions $).....	285	267	240	228	202	187	170	181	137	95

SHAREHOLDER INFORMATION

Minimum Investment
Initial: $3,000   IRA: $0
Subsequent: $50   IRA: $0

Maximum Fees
Load: none   12b-1: none
Other: none

Vanguard FL Long Term Tx Ex (VFLTX)

800-662-7447
www.vanguard.com

Muni: Florida Bond

	3yr Annual	5yr Annual	10yr Annual	Category	Risk Index
Return (%)	4.1	5.5	5.7	1.16—high	
Differ From Category (+/-)	0.7 high	0.7 high	0.7 high	**Avg Mat**	7.0 yrs

	2005	2004	2003	2002	2001	2000	1999	1998	1997	1996
Return (%)	.2.5	4.0	5.6	10.8	4.5	13.2	-2.7	6.6	8.9	4.1
Differ From Category (+/-) . . .	.0.3	0.7	0.9	1.6	-0.2	3.1	-0.5	0.6	0.7	0.3
Return, Tax-Adjusted (%).	.2.5	4.0	5.4	10.6	4.4	13.2	-2.7	6.5	8.9	4.1
Dividends, Net Income ($) .	0.51	0.51	0.51	0.53	0.55	0.56	0.54	0.55	0.56	0.55
Expense Ratio (%)	na	0.14	0.17	0.18	0.15	0.15	0.18	0.20	0.19	0.19
Yield (%)	4.36	4.25	4.18	4.39	4.83	4.90	5.13	4.76	4.94	5.02
Total Assets (Millions $)	326	694	735	793	805	994	885	893	695	550

SHAREHOLDER INFORMATION

Minimum Investment
Initial: $3,000   IRA: $0
Subsequent: $100   IRA: $0

Maximum Fees
Load: none   12b-1: none
Other: none

T Rowe Price Tx Fr Inc Tr GA Tx Fr Bond (GTFBX)

800-638-5660
www.troweprice.com

Muni: Georgia Bond

	3yr Annual	5yr Annual	10yr Annual	Category	Risk Index
Return (%)	4.1	5.1	5.2	1.00—high	
Differ From Category (+/-)	0.0 high	0.0 high	0.0 high	**Avg Mat**	12.9 yrs

	2005	2004	2003	2002	2001	2000	1999	1998	1997	1996
Return (%)	.3.2	4.0	5.0	8.8	4.7	11.6	-3.6	6.1	9.6	3.9
Differ From Category (+/-) . . .	.0.0	0.0	0.0	0.0	0.0	0.0	0.0	0.0	0.0	0.0
Return, Tax-Adjusted (%) . . .	.3.2	4.0	5.0	8.8	4.7	11.6	-3.6	6.1	9.6	3.9
Dividends, Net Income ($) .	.0.46	0.46	0.47	0.49	0.51	0.52	0.50	0.51	0.51	0.51
Expense Ratio (%)	.0.64	0.65	0.65	0.65	0.65	0.65	0.65	0.65	0.65	0.65
Yield (%)	.4.07	4.08	4.14	4.33	4.70	4.78	4.90	4.59	4.69	4.93
Total Assets (Millions $)	106	95	86	87	75	67	58	59	47	38

SHAREHOLDER INFORMATION

Minimum Investment
Initial: $2,500   IRA: $0
Subsequent: $100   IRA: $0

Maximum Fees
Load: none   12b-1: none
Other: none

Hawaii Municipal Inv
(SURFX)

Muni: Hawaii Bond

808-988-8088
www.fpchawaii.com

PERFORMANCE AND PER SHARE DATA   fund inception date: 11/30/88

	3yr Annual	5yr Annual	10yr Annual	Category Risk Index	
Return (%)	3.8	4.7	4.6	1.00—high	
Differ From Category (+/-)	0.0 high	0.0 high	0.0 high	**Avg Mat**	4.6 yrs

	2005	2004	2003	2002	2001	2000	1999	1998	1997	1996
Return (%)	2.3	3.8	5.3	8.2	4.3	8.5	-1.9	4.8	7.1	4.1
Differ From Category (+/-)	0.0	0.0	0.0	0.0	0.0	0.0	0.0	0.0	0.0	0.0
Return, Tax-Adjusted (%)	2.2	3.7	5.3	8.2	4.3	8.5	-1.9	4.8	7.1	4.1
Dividends, Net Income ($)	0.41	0.44	0.46	0.48	0.50	0.52	0.53	0.54	0.55	0.55
Expense Ratio (%)	1.00	1.01	1.01	1.02	1.03	0.98	0.94	0.89	0.98	0.98
Yield (%)	3.68	3.93	4.06	4.29	4.62	4.77	5.09	4.85	4.89	4.96
Total Assets (Millions $)	151	145	144	134	123	115	113	115	109	55

SHAREHOLDER INFORMATION

Minimum Investment
Initial: $1,000   IRA: $0
Subsequent: $100   IRA: $0

Maximum Fees
Load: none   12b-1: 0.15%
Other: none

Dupree KY Tax Free Income
(KYTFX)

Muni: Kentucky Bond

800-866-0614
www.dupree-funds.com

PERFORMANCE AND PER SHARE DATA   fund inception date: 7/2/79

	3yr Annual	5yr Annual	10yr Annual	Category Risk Index	
Return (%)	4.1	4.9	4.8	1.09—high	
Differ From Category (+/-)	1.1 high	0.7 high	0.6 high	**Avg Mat**	7.0 yrs

	2005	2004	2003	2002	2001	2000	1999	1998	1997	1996
Return (%)	2.6	4.1	5.5	7.2	5.0	8.0	-1.4	5.6	8.0	3.6
Differ From Category (+/-)	1.1	1.2	1.0	0.4	-0.2	1.3	-0.9	0.5	1.4	-0.2
Return, Tax-Adjusted (%)	2.6	4.1	5.5	7.2	5.0	8.0	-1.4	5.6	8.0	3.6
Dividends, Net Income ($)	0.31	0.33	0.34	0.35	0.37	0.37	0.37	0.38	0.40	0.40
Expense Ratio (%)	0.58	0.58	0.58	0.59	0.60	0.61	0.61	0.62	0.63	0.62
Yield (%)	4.10	4.27	4.37	4.64	4.96	5.04	5.14	4.96	5.15	5.32
Total Assets (Millions $)	696	654	617	576	498	443	414	413	349	312

SHAREHOLDER INFORMATION

Minimum Investment
Initial: $100   IRA: $0
Subsequent: $100   IRA: $0

Maximum Fees
Load: none   12b-1: none
Other: none

Dupree KY Tax Free Short to Med (KYSMX)

800-866-0614
www.dupree-funds.com

Muni: Kentucky Bond

PERFORMANCE AND PER SHARE DATA   fund inception date: 9/15/87

	3yr Annual	5yr Annual	10yr Annual	Category Risk Index	
Return (%)	1.9	3.5	3.7	0.94—av	
Differ From Category (+/-)	-1.1 av	-0.7 av	-0.5 av	**Avg Mat**	3.3 yrs

	2005	2004	2003	2002	2001	2000	1999	1998	1997	1996
Return (%)	0.4	1.8	3.5	6.5	5.3	5.4	0.2	4.6	5.1	3.9
Differ From Category (+/-)	-1.1	-1.1	-1.0	-0.3	0.1	-1.3	0.8	-0.5	-1.5	0.1
Return, Tax-Adjusted (%)	0.4	1.8	3.5	6.5	5.3	5.4	0.2	4.6	5.1	3.9
Dividends, Net Income ($)	0.15	0.16	0.17	0.20	0.21	0.22	0.21	0.21	0.22	0.21
Expense Ratio (%)	0.69	0.68	0.69	0.69	0.70	0.69	0.72	0.74	0.72	0.75
Yield (%)	2.90	2.91	3.15	3.62	4.07	4.33	3.99	3.95	4.07	4.05
Total Assets (Millions $)	90	101	104	93	78	50	58	61	53	57

SHAREHOLDER INFORMATION

Minimum Investment		Maximum Fees	
Initial: $100	IRA: $0	Load: none	12b-1: none
Subsequent: $100	IRA: $0	Other: none	

Fidelity MD Muni Inc (SMDMX)

800-544-8544
www.fidelity.com

Muni: Maryland Bond

PERFORMANCE AND PER SHARE DATA   fund inception date: 4/22/93

	3yr Annual	5yr Annual	10yr Annual	Category Risk Index	
Return (%)	3.8	4.9	5.1	1.26—high	
Differ From Category (+/-)	0.6 abv av	0.5 high	0.5 high	**Avg Mat**	14.4 yrs

	2005	2004	2003	2002	2001	2000	1999	1998	1997	1996
Return (%)	2.5	4.0	5.0	8.6	4.7	11.0	-2.1	5.9	8.8	3.8
Differ From Category (+/-)	0.2	0.9	0.9	0.9	-0.1	1.4	-0.4	0.3	1.4	0.3
Return, Tax-Adjusted (%)	2.4	4.0	5.0	8.6	4.7	11.0	-2.1	5.9	8.8	3.8
Dividends, Net Income ($)	0.41	0.43	0.43	0.44	0.46	0.48	0.46	0.46	0.46	0.48
Expense Ratio (%)	0.55	0.53	0.52	0.47	0.40	0.55	0.55	0.55	0.55	0.39
Yield (%)	3.72	3.83	3.87	4.02	4.39	4.58	4.60	4.32	4.44	4.73
Total Assets (Millions $)	109	101	95	101	81	60	46	47	39	45

SHAREHOLDER INFORMATION

Minimum Investment		Maximum Fees	
Initial: $10,000	IRA: $0	Load: 0.50% redemption	12b-1: none
Subsequent: $1,000	IRA: $0	Other: redemp fee applies for 1 mo; maint fee for low bal	

T Rowe Price Tx Fr Inc Tr MD Tx Fr Bond (MDXBX)

800-638-5660
www.troweprice.com

Muni: Maryland Bond

PERFORMANCE AND PER SHARE DATA   fund inception date: 3/31/87

	3yr Annual	5yr Annual	10yr Annual	Category Risk Index
Return (%)	3.8	5.2	5.2	1.21—high
Differ From Category (+/-)	0.6 high	0.8 high	0.6 high	**Avg Mat** 13.3 yrs

	2005	2004	2003	2002	2001	2000	1999	1998	1997	1996
Return (%)	3.3	3.5	4.8	9.4	4.9	11.4	-3.1	6.1	8.6	3.7
Differ From Category (+/-) ..	1.0	0.4	0.7	1.7	0.1	1.8	-1.4	0.5	1.2	0.2
Return, Tax-Adjusted (%)....	3.3	3.4	4.8	9.4	4.9	11.4	-3.1	6.1	8.6	3.7
Dividends, Net Income ($)..	0.47	0.47	0.48	0.50	0.51	0.53	0.54	0.55	0.56	0.56
Expense Ratio (%).........	0.48	0.48	0.49	0.49	0.49	0.51	0.51	0.51	0.54	0.54
Yield (%)	4.40	4.35	4.36	4.56	4.92	5.10	5.41	5.12	5.23	5.40
Total Assets (Millions $)...	1,356	1,288	1,318	1,334	1,186	1,083	990	1,039	908	808

SHAREHOLDER INFORMATION

Minimum Investment		Maximum Fees	
Initial: $2,500	IRA: $0	Load: none	12b-1: none
Subsequent: $100	IRA: $0	Other: none	

Fidelity MA Muni Inc (FDMMX)

800-544-8544
www.fidelity.com

Muni: Massachusetts Bond

PERFORMANCE AND PER SHARE DATA   fund inception date: 11/10/83

	3yr Annual	5yr Annual	10yr Annual	Category Risk Index
Return (%)	4.4	5.4	5.5	1.02—high
Differ From Category (+/-)	0.9 high	0.6 high	0.6 high	**Avg Mat** 15.3 yrs

	2005	2004	2003	2002	2001	2000	1999	1998	1997	1996
Return (%)	3.6	4.5	5.3	9.7	4.4	11.8	-2.1	5.6	9.3	3.6
Differ From Category (+/-) ...	1.0	1.2	0.7	0.4	0.0	0.8	0.3	-0.2	0.8	0.0
Return, Tax-Adjusted (%).....	3.4	4.3	5.1	9.5	4.3	11.8	-2.1	5.5	9.3	3.5
Dividends, Net Income ($) .	0.50	0.52	0.53	0.53	0.55	0.57	0.56	0.57	0.60	0.61
Expense Ratio (%)	0.47	1.15	0.46	0.42	0.42	0.49	0.49	0.53	0.56	0.54
Yield (%)	4.14	4.25	4.23	4.30	4.66	4.80	5.02	4.77	5.00	5.28
Total Assets (Millions $)...	1,843	1,754	1,841	1,999	1,885	1,614	1,278	1,367	1,210	1,138

SHAREHOLDER INFORMATION

Minimum Investment		Maximum Fees	
Initial: $10,000	IRA: $0	Load: 0.50% redemption	12b-1: none
Subsequent: $1,000	IRA: $0	Other: redemption fee applies for 1 month	

Vanguard MA Tax Exempt
(VMATX)

800-662-7447
www.vanguard.com

Muni: Massachusetts Bond

PERFORMANCE AND PER SHARE DATA   fund inception date: 12/9/98

	3yr Annual	5yr Annual	10yr Annual	Category Risk Index
Return (%)	4.1	5.1	na	1.00—abv av
Differ From Category (+/-)	0.6 high	0.3 abv av	na	**Avg Mat** 8.0 yrs

	2005	2004	2003	2002	2001	2000	1999	1998	1997	1996
Return (%)	3.2	4.0	5.1	9.0	4.3	13.7	-4.1	—	—	—
Differ From Category (+/-)	0.6	0.7	0.5	-0.3	-0.1	2.7	-1.7	—	—	—
Return, Tax-Adjusted (%)	3.2	4.0	5.1	9.0	4.3	13.7	-4.1	—	—	—
Dividends, Net Income ($)	0.42	0.42	0.44	0.46	0.47	0.48	0.44	—	—	—
Expense Ratio (%)	na	0.14	0.16	0.14	0.16	0.19	0.20	—	—	—
Yield (%)	4.10	4.04	4.27	4.53	4.82	4.87	4.77	—	—	—
Total Assets (Millions $)	505	456	409	386	290	196	117	—	—	—

SHAREHOLDER INFORMATION

Minimum Investment   **Maximum Fees**
Initial: $3,000   IRA: $0   Load: none   12b-1: none
Subsequent: $100   IRA: $0   Other: none

Fidelity MI Muni Inc
(FMHTX)

800-544-8544
www.fidelity.com

Muni: Michigan Bond

PERFORMANCE AND PER SHARE DATA   fund inception date: 11/12/85

	3yr Annual	5yr Annual	10yr Annual	Category Risk Index
Return (%)	4.1	5.3	5.2	1.00—high
Differ From Category (+/-)	0.0 high	0.0 high	0.0 high	**Avg Mat** 11.3 yrs

	2005	2004	2003	2002	2001	2000	1999	1998	1997	1996
Return (%)	2.6	3.9	5.8	9.7	4.7	11.1	-2.6	5.2	9.0	3.3
Differ From Category (+/-)	0.0	0.0	0.0	0.0	0.0	0.0	0.0	0.0	0.0	0.0
Return, Tax-Adjusted (%)	2.5	3.7	5.8	9.7	4.7	11.1	-2.6	5.2	8.8	3.3
Dividends, Net Income ($)	0.47	0.49	0.51	0.53	0.55	0.57	0.55	0.51	0.57	0.63
Expense Ratio (%)	0.50	0.49	0.55	0.48	0.44	0.45	0.52	0.55	0.56	0.59
Yield (%)	3.94	4.01	4.19	4.40	4.80	4.96	5.07	4.35	4.86	5.57
Total Assets (Millions $)	563	559	559	571	505	458	424	478	456	453

SHAREHOLDER INFORMATION

Minimum Investment   **Maximum Fees**
Initial: $10,000   IRA: $0   Load: 0.50% redemption   12b-1: none
Subsequent: $1,000   IRA: $0   Other: redemp fee applies for 1 mo; maint fee for low bal

Fidelity MN Muni Inc
(FIMIX)

800-544-8544
www.fidelity.com

Muni: Minnesota Bond

PERFORMANCE AND PER SHARE DATA   fund inception date: 11/21/85

	3yr Annual	5yr Annual	10yr Annual	Category Risk Index
Return (%)	3.9	4.9	5.0	1.31—high
Differ From Category (+/-)	-0.1 av	-0.1 av	0.0 high	**Avg Mat** 12.2 yrs

	2005	2004	2003	2002	2001	2000	1999	1998	1997	1996
Return (%)	2.6	3.9	5.2	8.5	4.6	10.6	-2.4	5.5	8.8	3.7
Differ From Category (+/-) . .	-0.9	0.1	0.4	0.7	-0.6	1.3	0.7	-0.3	0.3	-1.1
Return, Tax-Adjusted (%). . . .	2.5	3.8	5.1	8.5	4.6	10.6	-2.4	5.5	8.8	3.7
Dividends, Net Income ($). .	0.46	0.46	0.46	0.51	0.52	0.53	0.51	0.53	0.55	0.56
Expense Ratio (%).	na	0.51	0.49	0.49	0.46	0.46	0.51	0.55	0.56	0.60
Yield (%)	4.01	3.93	3.94	4.38	4.67	4.70	4.80	4.65	4.86	5.13
Total Assets (Millions $).	343	355	343	344	315	293	284	311	296	294

SHAREHOLDER INFORMATION

Minimum Investment
Initial: $10,000   IRA: $0
Subsequent: $1,000   IRA: $0

Maximum Fees
Load: 0.50% redemption   12b-1: none
Other: redemp fee applies for 1 mo; maint fee for low bal

Sit MN Tax Free Income
(SMTFX)

800-332-5580
www.sitfunds.com

Muni: Minnesota Bond

PERFORMANCE AND PER SHARE DATA   fund inception date: 12/1/93

	3yr Annual	5yr Annual	10yr Annual	Category Risk Index
Return (%)	4.1	5.0	4.9	0.69—av
Differ From Category (+/-)	0.1 high	0.0 high	-0.1 av	**Avg Mat** 12.6 yrs

	2005	2004	2003	2002	2001	2000	1999	1998	1997	1996
Return (%)	4.4	3.6	4.4	7.0	5.8	8.1	-3.8	6.1	8.1	5.8
Differ From Category (+/-) . . .	0.9	-0.2	-0.4	-0.8	0.6	-1.2	-0.7	0.3	-0.4	1.0
Return, Tax-Adjusted (%).	4.4	3.6	4.4	7.0	5.8	8.1	-3.8	6.1	8.1	5.8
Dividends, Net Income ($) .	0.42	0.44	0.46	0.47	0.50	0.52	0.51	0.53	0.55	0.57
Expense Ratio (%)	0.80	0.80	0.80	0.80	0.80	0.80	0.80	0.80	0.80	0.80
Yield (%)	4.15	4.30	4.51	4.61	4.99	5.24	5.25	4.99	5.27	5.59
Total Assets (Millions $).	251	223	213	211	185	173	180	230	128	83

SHAREHOLDER INFORMATION

Minimum Investment
Initial: $5,000   IRA: $0
Subsequent: $100   IRA: $0

Maximum Fees
Load: none   12b-1: none
Other: none

Fidelity NJ Muni Inc
(FNJHX)

800-544-8544
www.fidelity.com

Muni: New Jersey Bond

PERFORMANCE AND PER SHARE DATA   fund inception date: 12/31/87

	3yr Annual	5yr Annual	10yr Annual	Category Risk Index
Return (%)	4.2	5.3	5.4	1.04—high
Differ From Category (+/-)	0.4 high	0.3 abv av	0.3 high	**Avg Mat** 13.4 yrs

	2005	2004	2003	2002	2001	2000	1999	1998	1997	1996
Return (%)	3.3	3.9	5.4	9.7	4.2	11.4	-1.4	6.1	8.3	4.1
Differ From Category (+/-)	0.5	0.2	0.5	0.3	-0.3	0.8	0.7	0.1	0.1	0.7
Return, Tax-Adjusted (%)	3.1	3.7	5.2	9.6	4.1	11.3	-1.4	6.0	8.2	3.7
Dividends, Net Income ($)	0.46	0.47	0.49	0.49	0.53	0.56	0.53	0.59	0.56	0.59
Expense Ratio (%)	na	0.49	0.49	0.47	0.41	0.45	0.55	0.55	0.55	0.52
Yield (%)	3.92	3.98	4.06	4.14	4.66	4.91	4.89	5.11	4.90	5.22
Total Assets (Millions $)	555	535	549	580	495	400	366	391	364	351

SHAREHOLDER INFORMATION

Minimum Investment
Initial: $10,000   IRA: $0
Subsequent: $1,000   IRA: $0

Maximum Fees
Load: 0.50% redemption   12b-1: none
Other: redemp fee applies for 1 mo; maint fee for low bal

Vanguard NJ Long Term TE Inv (VNJTX)

800-662-7447
www.vanguard.com

Muni: New Jersey Bond

PERFORMANCE AND PER SHARE DATA   fund inception date: 2/3/88

	3yr Annual	5yr Annual	10yr Annual	Category Risk Index
Return (%)	3.9	5.2	5.4	1.04—abv av
Differ From Category (+/-)	0.1 av	0.2 av	0.3 abv av	**Avg Mat** 9.0 yrs

	2005	2004	2003	2002	2001	2000	1999	1998	1997	1996
Return (%)	2.8	3.9	5.1	9.9	4.5	12.4	-2.3	6.3	8.5	3.1
Differ From Category (+/-)	0.0	0.2	0.2	0.5	0.0	1.8	-0.2	0.3	0.3	-0.3
Return, Tax-Adjusted (%)	2.7	3.8	5.0	9.8	4.5	12.4	-2.3	6.2	8.5	3.1
Dividends, Net Income ($)	0.53	0.55	0.55	0.57	0.58	0.60	0.59	0.60	0.61	0.61
Expense Ratio (%)	na	0.14	0.17	0.18	0.20	0.19	0.19	0.20	0.18	0.20
Yield (%)	4.41	4.49	4.44	4.66	4.93	5.07	5.32	4.99	5.11	5.32
Total Assets (Millions $)	438	907	918	978	931	1,284	1,118	1,124	972	844

SHAREHOLDER INFORMATION

Minimum Investment
Initial: $3,000   IRA: $0
Subsequent: $100   IRA: $0

Maximum Fees
Load: none   12b-1: none
Other: none

Bernstein NY Municipal
(SNNYX)

212-486-5800
www.bernstein.com

Muni: New York Bond

fund inception date: 1/9/89

PERFORMANCE AND PER SHARE DATA

	3yr Annual	5yr Annual	10yr Annual	Category Risk Index	
Return (%)	2.7	3.9	4.3	0.78—low	
Differ From Category (+/-)	-0.4 blw av	-0.5 blw av	-0.4 low	**Avg Mat**	4.9 yrs

	2005	2004	2003	2002	2001	2000	1999	1998	1997	1996
Return (%)	1.6	2.5	3.9	7.2	4.5	8.2	0.0	5.2	6.5	3.5
Differ From Category (+/-)	-0.6	-0.6	-0.1	-1.6	0.5	-3.2	3.1	-0.6	-1.8	0.1
Return, Tax-Adjusted (%)	1.6	2.5	3.9	7.2	4.5	8.2	-0.1	5.1	6.5	3.5
Dividends, Net Income ($)	0.46	0.46	0.49	0.53	0.57	0.57	0.56	0.58	0.61	0.63
Expense Ratio (%)	0.63	0.63	0.65	0.66	0.64	0.64	0.64	0.64	0.65	0.66
Yield (%)	3.29	3.27	3.44	3.74	4.18	4.20	4.25	4.17	4.41	4.68
Total Assets (Millions $)	1,285	1,145	1,018	935	782	683	791	836	705	570

SHAREHOLDER INFORMATION

Minimum Investment
Initial: $25,000   IRA: $0
Subsequent: $5,000   IRA: $0

Maximum Fees
Load: none   12b-1: none
Other: none

Dreyfus NY Tax Exempt Bond
(DRNYX)

800-645-6561
www.dreyfus.com

Muni: New York Bond

fund inception date: 7/26/83

PERFORMANCE AND PER SHARE DATA

	3yr Annual	5yr Annual	10yr Annual	Category Risk Index	
Return (%)	3.3	4.6	4.8	1.10—abv av	
Differ From Category (+/-)	0.2 abv av	0.2 abv av	0.1 abv av	**Avg Mat**	16.7 yrs

	2005	2004	2003	2002	2001	2000	1999	1998	1997	1996
Return (%)	2.9	3.4	3.6	9.0	4.5	11.1	-3.8	6.7	9.1	2.4
Differ From Category (+/-)	0.7	0.3	-0.4	0.2	0.5	-0.3	-0.7	0.9	0.8	-1.0
Return, Tax-Adjusted (%)	2.9	3.4	3.5	8.8	4.5	11.0	-3.9	6.5	8.9	2.3
Dividends, Net Income ($)	0.60	0.63	0.65	0.71	0.74	0.71	0.73	0.74	0.75	0.77
Expense Ratio (%)	0.72	0.71	0.71	0.70	0.73	0.75	0.75	0.73	0.74	0.71
Yield (%)	4.04	4.20	4.29	4.61	4.94	4.77	5.13	4.73	4.81	5.12
Total Assets (Millions $)	1,257	1,290	1,381	1,459	1,431	1,456	1,441	1,660	1,682	1,761

SHAREHOLDER INFORMATION

Minimum Investment
Initial: $2,500   IRA: $0
Subsequent: $100   IRA: $0

Maximum Fees
Load: 0.10% redemption   12b-1: none
Other: redemption fee applies for 1 month

Fidelity NY Muni Inc
(FTFMX)

800-544-8544
www.fidelity.com

Muni: New York Bond

PERFORMANCE AND PER SHARE DATA — fund inception date: 7/10/84

	3yr Annual	5yr Annual	10yr Annual	Category Risk Index	
Return (%)	4.3	5.6	5.6	1.15—abv av	
Differ From Category (+/-)	1.2 high	1.2 high	0.9 high	AvgMat 14.2yrs	

	2005	2004	2003	2002	2001	2000	1999	1998	1997	1996
Return (%)	3.0	4.4	5.5	10.9	4.3	12.8	-3.2	6.3	9.7	3.8
Differ From Category (+/-)	0.8	1.3	1.5	2.1	0.3	1.4	-0.1	0.5	1.4	0.4
Return, Tax-Adjusted (%)	2.9	4.2	5.1	10.6	4.3	12.8	-3.3	6.0	9.6	3.7
Dividends, Net Income ($)	0.51	0.53	0.55	0.57	0.58	0.60	0.59	0.60	0.62	0.63
Expense Ratio (%)	0.48	0.48	0.47	0.44	0.42	0.49	0.53	0.55	0.59	0.58
Yield (%)	3.92	4.02	4.07	4.23	4.58	4.73	4.94	4.64	4.85	5.11
Total Assets (Millions $)	1,402	1,375	1,421	1,494	1,316	1,151	1,042	1,171	445	411

SHAREHOLDER INFORMATION

Minimum Investment
Initial: $10,000   IRA: $0
Subsequent: $1,000   IRA: $0

Maximum Fees
Load: 0.50% redemption   12b-1: none
Other: redemp fee applies for 1 mo; maint fee for low bal

T Rowe Price Tx Fr Inc Tr NY
Tx Fr Bond (PRNYX)

800-638-5660
www.troweprice.com

Muni: New York Bond

PERFORMANCE AND PER SHARE DATA — fund inception date: 8/28/86

	3yr Annual	5yr Annual	10yr Annual	Category Risk Index	
Return (%)	4.0	5.1	5.2	1.05—av	
Differ From Category (+/-)	0.9 high	0.7 abv av	0.5 abv av	AvgMat 15.0yrs	

	2005	2004	2003	2002	2001	2000	1999	1998	1997	1996
Return (%)	3.4	3.8	4.9	9.6	4.1	12.8	-4.7	6.4	9.5	3.7
Differ From Category (+/-)	1.2	0.7	0.9	0.8	0.1	1.4	-1.6	0.6	1.2	0.3
Return, Tax-Adjusted (%)	3.4	3.8	4.9	9.6	4.1	12.8	-4.7	6.1	9.5	3.7
Dividends, Net Income ($)	0.47	0.47	0.48	0.50	0.51	0.53	0.52	0.55	0.57	0.57
Expense Ratio (%)	0.55	0.55	0.55	0.56	0.56	0.58	0.59	0.61	0.65	0.65
Yield (%)	4.16	4.11	4.19	4.38	4.73	4.86	5.11	4.78	5.06	5.29
Total Assets (Millions $)	246	239	241	229	208	201	188	210	171	142

SHAREHOLDER INFORMATION

Minimum Investment
Initial: $2,500   IRA: $0
Subsequent: $100   IRA: $0

Maximum Fees
Load: none   12b-1: none
Other: none

USAA Tx Ex New York Bond
(USNYX)

Muni: New York Bond

800-531-8181
www.usaa.com

	3yr Annual	5yr Annual	10yr Annual	Category Risk Index
Return (%)	4.6	5.5	5.7	1.17—high
Differ From Category (+/-)	1.5 high	1.1 high	1.0 high	**Avg Mat** 15.6 yrs

	2005	2004	2003	2002	2001	2000	1999	1998	1997	1996
Return (%)	3.7	4.7	5.5	9.5	4.3	14.8	-5.0	6.6	10.6	3.7
Differ From Category (+/-) . .	1.5	1.6	1.5	0.7	0.3	3.4	-1.9	0.8	2.3	0.3
Return, Tax-Adjusted (%). . . .	3.7	4.7	5.5	9.5	4.3	14.8	-5.0	6.6	10.6	3.7
Dividends, Net Income ($). .	0.50	0.53	0.54	0.54	0.58	0.60	0.60	0.62	0.63	0.64
Expense Ratio (%).	0.70	0.69	0.68	0.61	0.50	0.50	0.50	0.50	0.50	0.50
Yield (%)	4.21	4.41	4.47	4.56	5.06	5.21	5.72	5.25	5.45	5.76
Total Assets (Millions $).	140	130	127	127	113	96	84	81	66	56

SHAREHOLDER INFORMATION

Minimum Investment
Initial: $3,000   IRA: $0
Subsequent: $50   IRA: $0

Maximum Fees
Load: none   12b-1: none
Other: none

Vanguard NY Long Term
TE Inv (VNYTX)

Muni: New York Bond

800-662-7447
www.vanguard.com

	3yr Annual	5yr Annual	10yr Annual	Category Risk Index
Return (%)	4.0	5.3	5.5	1.27—high
Differ From Category (+/-)	0.9 abv av	0.9 high	0.8 high	**Avg Mat** 8.8 yrs

	2005	2004	2003	2002	2001	2000	1999	1998	1997	1996
Return (%)	2.8	3.9	5.3	10.7	4.1	13.7	-3.3	6.2	8.7	4.0
Differ From Category (+/-) . . .	0.6	0.8	1.3	1.9	0.1	2.3	-0.2	0.4	0.4	0.6
Return, Tax-Adjusted (%).	2.7	3.9	5.3	10.5	4.0	13.7	-3.3	6.1	8.7	3.9
Dividends, Net Income ($) .	0.49	0.49	0.48	0.50	0.52	0.55	0.55	0.56	0.57	0.57
Expense Ratio (%)	na	0.14	0.17	0.18	0.20	0.20	0.20	0.21	0.20	0.20
Yield (%)	4.27	4.22	4.16	4.31	4.72	4.99	5.31	4.98	5.11	5.23
Total Assets (Millions $).	689	1,317	1,325	1,367	1,296	1,725	1,426	1,421	1,166	950

SHAREHOLDER INFORMATION

Minimum Investment
Initial: $3,000   IRA: $0
Subsequent: $100   IRA: $0

Maximum Fees
Load: none   12b-1: none
Other: none

Fidelity OH Muni Inc
(FOHFX)

Muni: Ohio Bond

800-544-8544
www.fidelity.com

800-544-8544
www.fidelity.com

PERFORMANCE AND PER SHARE DATA   fund inception date: 11/15/85

	3yr Annual	5yr Annual	10yr Annual	Category Risk Index	
Return (%)	4.3	5.4	5.4	1.00—av	
Differ From Category (+/-)	0.2 high	0.0 high	0.0 av	**Avg Mat**	13.1 yrs

	2005	2004	2003	2002	2001	2000	1999	1998	1997	1996
Return (%)	2.9	4.4	5.7	9.6	4.7	11.6	-2.8	5.3	8.7	4.2
Differ From Category (+/-) . . .	0.2	0.2	0.2	-0.5	0.1	-0.6	0.1	-0.5	0.1	0.0
Return, Tax-Adjusted (%)	2.6	4.2	5.6	9.5	4.7	11.6	-2.8	5.2	8.5	4.0
Dividends, Net Income ($) .	0.48	0.50	0.51	0.52	0.54	0.55	0.54	0.49	0.55	0.56
Expense Ratio (%)	na	0.50	0.50	0.49	0.46	0.46	0.51	0.55	0.56	0.59
Yield (%)	4.01	4.09	4.16	4.33	4.67	4.79	4.92	4.15	4.68	4.87
Total Assets (Millions $)	424	423	430	434	398	379	352	392	388	381

SHAREHOLDER INFORMATION

Minimum Investment
Initial: $10,000   IRA: $0
Subsequent: $1,000   IRA: $0

Maximum Fees
Load: 0.50% redemption   12b-1: none
Other: redemp fee applies for 1 mo; maint fee for low bal

Vanguard OH Long Term Tax Exempt (VOHIX)

Muni: Ohio Bond

800-662-7447
www.vanguard.com

800-662-7447
www.vanguard.com

PERFORMANCE AND PER SHARE DATA   fund inception date: 6/18/90

	3yr Annual	5yr Annual	10yr Annual	Category Risk Index	
Return (%)	4.0	5.4	5.5	1.00—high	
Differ From Category (+/-)	-0.1 av	0.0 av	0.1 high	**Avg Mat**	7.2 yrs

	2005	2004	2003	2002	2001	2000	1999	1998	1997	1996
Return (%)	2.6	4.1	5.3	10.7	4.6	12.9	-3.0	6.2	8.4	4.2
Differ From Category (+/-) . .	-0.1	-0.1	-0.2	0.6	0.0	0.7	0.0	0.4	-0.2	0.0
Return, Tax-Adjusted (%)	2.5	3.9	5.2	10.6	4.5	12.9	-3.0	6.2	8.4	4.0
Dividends, Net Income ($) .	0.53	0.55	0.54	0.56	0.58	0.59	0.58	0.59	0.60	0.60
Expense Ratio (%)	na	0.14	0.15	0.14	0.17	0.19	0.19	0.20	0.17	0.20
Yield (%)	4.35	4.40	4.35	4.51	4.87	5.00	5.26	4.93	5.03	5.20
Total Assets (Millions $)	529	506	497	536	478	419	366	327	260	216

SHAREHOLDER INFORMATION

Minimum Investment
Initial: $3,000   IRA: $0
Subsequent: $100   IRA: $0

Maximum Fees
Load: none   12b-1: none
Other: none

Fidelity PA Muni Inc
(FPXTX)

800-544-8544
www.fidelity.com

Muni: Pennsylvania Bond

PERFORMANCE AND PER SHARE DATA   fund inception date: 8/6/86

	3yr Annual	5yr Annual	10yr Annual	Category Risk Index	
Return (%)	4.0	5.2	5.2	1.00—av	
Differ From Category (+/-)	0.4 abv av	0.3 abv av	0.1 abv av	**Avg Mat**	11.9 yrs

	2005	2004	2003	2002	2001	2000	1999	1998	1997	1996
Return (%)	2.7	4.2	5.1	9.1	5.0	10.9	-1.8	5.4	8.3	4.0
Differ From Category (+/-)	0.4	0.5	0.2	0.1	0.3	-0.8	0.6	-0.3	0.1	0.1
Return, Tax-Adjusted (%)	2.6	4.2	4.9	9.0	4.9	10.9	-1.9	5.2	8.2	3.8
Dividends, Net Income ($)	0.44	0.45	0.43	0.48	0.50	0.50	0.52	0.45	0.50	0.52
Expense Ratio (%)	na	0.50	0.50	0.49	0.45	0.44	0.50	0.55	0.55	0.53
Yield (%)	4.03	4.08	3.80	4.33	4.64	4.65	5.11	4.11	4.62	4.95
Total Assets (Millions $)	306	298	291	299	268	243	241	267	264	271

SHAREHOLDER INFORMATION

Minimum Investment

Initial: $10,000   IRA: $0
Subsequent: $1,000   IRA: $0

Maximum Fees

Load: 0.50% redemption   12b-1: none
Other: redemp fee applies for 1 mo; maint fee for low bal

Vanguard PA Long Term TE Inv (VPAIX)

800-662-7447
www.vanguard.com

Muni: Pennsylvania Bond

PERFORMANCE AND PER SHARE DATA   fund inception date: 4/7/86

	3yr Annual	5yr Annual	10yr Annual	Category Risk Index	
Return (%)	4.0	5.3	5.5	1.07—abv av	
Differ From Category (+/-)	0.4 high	0.4 high	0.4 high	**Avg Mat**	7.8 yrs

	2005	2004	2003	2002	2001	2000	1999	1998	1997	1996
Return (%)	2.7	3.8	5.6	10.0	4.7	12.7	-2.6	6.1	8.2	4.3
Differ From Category (+/-)	0.4	0.1	0.7	1.0	0.0	1.0	-0.2	0.4	0.0	0.4
Return, Tax-Adjusted (%)	2.6	3.8	5.5	9.9	4.6	12.7	-2.6	6.0	8.2	4.1
Dividends, Net Income ($)	0.52	0.53	0.52	0.54	0.57	0.58	0.58	0.60	0.60	0.60
Expense Ratio (%)	na	0.14	0.17	0.18	0.20	0.19	0.19	0.20	0.18	0.19
Yield (%)	4.55	4.53	4.38	4.64	5.07	5.19	5.47	5.18	5.24	5.41
Total Assets (Millions $)	704	1,457	1,525	1,627	1,514	2,007	1,793	1,940	1,778	1,640

SHAREHOLDER INFORMATION

Minimum Investment

Initial: $3,000   IRA: $0
Subsequent: $100   IRA: $0

Maximum Fees

Load: none   12b-1: none
Other: none

Dupree TN Tax Free Income (TNTIX)

800-866-0614
www.dupree-funds.com

Muni: Tennessee

PERFORMANCE AND PER SHARE DATA   fund inception date: 12/15/93

	3yr Annual	5yr Annual	10yr Annual	Category Risk Index
Return (%)	3.8	4.8	5.2	1.00—high
Differ From Category (+/-)	0.0 high	0.0 high	0.0 high	**Avg Mat** 6.1 yrs

	2005	2004	2003	2002	2001	2000	1999	1998	1997	1996
Return (%)	2.5	3.9	5.1	8.4	4.4	9.7	-2.7	7.6	9.0	5.1
Differ From Category (+/-)	0.0	0.0	0.0	0.0	0.0	0.0	0.0	0.0	0.0	0.0
Return, Tax-Adjusted (%)	2.5	3.9	5.1	8.4	4.4	9.7	-2.7	7.5	8.9	5.1
Dividends, Net Income ($)	0.43	0.44	0.46	0.50	0.52	0.53	0.53	0.53	0.54	0.54
Expense Ratio (%)	0.67	0.67	0.65	0.54	0.54	0.54	0.48	0.44	0.55	0.54
Yield (%)	3.87	3.94	4.14	4.53	4.85	4.88	5.09	4.76	4.96	5.16
Total Assets (Millions $)	85	78	66	55	48	42	40	43	17	10

SHAREHOLDER INFORMATION

Minimum Investment
Initial: $100   IRA: $0
Subsequent: $100   IRA: $0

Maximum Fees
Load: none   12b-1: none
Other: none

T Rowe Price Tx Fr Inc Tr VA Tx Fr Bond (PRVAX)

800-638-5660
www.troweprice.com

Muni: Virginia Bond

PERFORMANCE AND PER SHARE DATA   fund inception date: 4/30/91

	3yr Annual	5yr Annual	10yr Annual	Category Risk Index
Return (%)	4.0	5.3	5.3	0.98—av
Differ From Category (+/-)	0.4 abv av	0.5 high	0.4 abv av	**Avg Mat** 13.3 yrs

	2005	2004	2003	2002	2001	2000	1999	1998	1997	1996
Return (%)	3.2	4.0	5.0	9.7	4.8	11.9	-3.4	6.2	9.0	4.1
Differ From Category (+/-)	0.8	0.4	0.0	0.6	0.7	0.0	0.6	0.5	0.2	0.3
Return, Tax-Adjusted (%)	3.2	4.0	4.9	9.7	4.8	11.9	-3.4	5.9	9.0	4.1
Dividends, Net Income ($)	0.49	0.49	0.49	0.52	0.54	0.55	0.54	0.56	0.58	0.57
Expense Ratio (%)	0.51	0.52	0.52	0.53	0.54	0.55	0.57	0.58	0.65	0.65
Yield (%)	4.16	4.19	4.17	4.38	4.79	4.94	5.11	4.83	5.03	5.15
Total Assets (Millions $)	471	432	417	402	352	307	265	270	227	190

SHAREHOLDER INFORMATION

Minimum Investment
Initial: $2,500   IRA: $0
Subsequent: $100   IRA: $0

Maximum Fees
Load: none   12b-1: none
Other: none

USAA Tx Ex Virginia Bond
(USVAX)

800-531-8181
www.usaa.com

Muni: Virginia Bond

fund inception date: 10/10/90

	3yr Annual	5yr Annual	10yr Annual	Category Risk Index
Return (%)	4.3	5.3	5.4	1.09—high
Differ From Category (+/-)	0.7 high	0.5 abv av	0.5 high	**Avg Mat** 11.6 yrs

	2005	2004	2003	2002	2001	2000	1999	1998	1997	1996
Return (%)	2.9	4.4	5.5	9.2	4.3	13.1	-4.6	6.0	9.5	5.0
Differ From Category (+/-)	0.5	0.8	0.5	0.1	0.1	1.2	-0.6	0.3	0.7	1.2
Return, Tax-Adjusted (%)	2.9	4.4	5.5	9.2	4.3	13.1	-4.6	6.0	9.5	5.0
Dividends, Net Income ($)	0.49	0.50	0.49	0.52	0.57	0.59	0.59	0.61	0.62	0.63
Expense Ratio (%)	0.60	0.61	0.59	0.52	0.43	0.43	0.43	0.44	0.46	0.48
Yield (%)	4.25	4.26	4.19	4.47	5.07	5.24	5.67	5.25	5.41	5.70
Total Assets (Millions $)	531	511	502	504	461	418	371	385	331	285

SHAREHOLDER INFORMATION

Minimum Investment
Initial: $3,000   IRA: $0
Subsequent: $50   IRA: $0

Maximum Fees
Load: none   12b-1: none
Other: none

WesMark West Virginia Muni Bond (WMKMX)

800-864-1013
www.wesbanco.com

Muni: West Virginia

fund inception date: 4/14/97

	3yr Annual	5yr Annual	10yr Annual	Category Risk Index
Return (%)	2.6	4.0	na	1.00—high
Differ From Category (+/-)	0.0 high	0.0 high	na	**Avg Mat** 5.4 yrs

	2005	2004	2003	2002	2001	2000	1999	1998	1997	1996
Return (%)	1.6	2.7	3.5	8.0	4.3	9.9	-1.7	5.3	—	—
Differ From Category (+/-)	0.0	0.0	0.0	0.0	0.0	0.0	0.0	0.0	—	—
Return, Tax-Adjusted (%)	1.6	2.7	3.5	8.0	4.3	9.9	-1.7	5.3	—	—
Dividends, Net Income ($)	0.32	0.35	0.33	0.40	0.45	0.45	0.44	0.43	—	—
Expense Ratio (%)	1.03	0.97	0.74	0.30	0.65	0.65	—	—	—	—
Yield (%)	3.05	3.35	3.07	3.75	4.38	4.38	4.48	4.16	—	—
Total Assets (Millions $)	73	74	75	71	64	63	64	67	—	—

SHAREHOLDER INFORMATION

Minimum Investment
Initial: $1,000   IRA: $0
Subsequent: $100   IRA: $0

Maximum Fees
Load: none   12b-1: 0.25%
Other: none

Wells Fargo Advtg WI
Tax Free Inv (SWFRX)

Muni: Wisconsin

800-368-3863
www.wellsfargofunds.com

fund inception date: 4/6/01

	3yr Annual	5yr Annual	10yr Annual	Category Risk Index
Return (%)	4.4	na	na	1.00—high
Differ From Category (+/-)	0.0 high	na	na	**AvgMat** 11.6yrs

	2005	2004	2003	2002	2001	2000	1999	1998	1997	1996
Return (%)	3.3	4.3	5.5	9.9	—	—	—	—	—	—
Differ From Category (+/-) . . .	0.0	0.0	0.0	0.0	—	—	—	—	—	—
Return, Tax-Adjusted (%)	3.3	4.0	5.4	9.9	—	—	—	—	—	—
Dividends, Net Income ($) .	0.40	0.44	0.42	0.47	—	—	—	—	—	—
Expense Ratio (%)	0.51	0.40	0.10	0.10	—	—	—	—	—	—
Yield (%)	3.73	4.08	3.88	4.42	—	—	—	—	—	—
Total Assets (Millions $)	56	49	59	69	—	—	—	—	—	—

SHAREHOLDER INFORMATION

Minimum Investment

Initial: $2,500   IRA: $0
Subsequent: $100   IRA: $0

Maximum Fees

Load: none   12b-1: none
Other: none

INTERNATIONAL BOND FUNDS

Category Performance Ranked by 2005 Returns

Fund (Ticker)	Annual Return (%)				Category Risk	Total Risk
	2005	3Yr	5Yr	10Yr		
T Rowe Price Emerging Markets Bond (PREMX)	17.2	19.2	15.2	13.4	abv av	blw av
Fidelity New Markets Income (FNMIX)	11.5	18.0	14.5	14.8	high	blw av
Loomis Sayles Bond Retail (LSBRX)	4.0	14.1	11.4	na	av	blw av
Fidelity Strategic Income (FSICX)	3.4	10.3	9.3	na	blw av	blw av
T Rowe Price Intl Bond (RPIBX)	-8.1	6.7	7.4	4.2	high	blw av
Amer Century Intl Bond Inv (BEGBX)	-8.2	7.5	8.6	4.7	high	av
International Bond Category Average	**3.2**	**9.7**	**9.3**	**7.4**	**av**	**blw av**

Amer Century Intl Bond Inv (BEGBX)

800-345-2021
www.americancentury.com

International Bond

PERFORMANCE AND PER SHARE DATA

fund inception date: 1/7/92

	3yr Annual	5yr Annual	10yr Annual	Category Risk Index
Return (%)	7.5	8.6	4.7	1.48—high
Differ From Category (+/-)	-2.2 av	-0.7 av	-2.7 av	**Avg Mat** 6.0 yrs

	2005	2004	2003	2002	2001	2000	1999	1998	1997	1996
Return (%)	-8.2	13.1	19.9	23.5	-1.6	-1.2	-10.3	17.8	-5.7	6.3
Differ From Category (+/-) .	-11.5	3.7	2.6	11.0	-6.8	-6.5	-16.5	15.3	-11.9	-9.6
Return, Tax-Adjusted (%). . . .	-9.3	11.5	17.3	22.5	-1.6	-1.7	-12.0	16.7	-6.1	3.6
Dividends, Net Income ($) .	0.41	0.59	0.85	0.26	0.00	0.11	0.43	0.17	0.06	0.73
Expense Ratio (%)	na	0.83	0.84	0.85	0.86	0.87	0.85	0.84	0.84	0.83
Yield (%)	3.08	3.98	6.18	2.09	0.00	1.06	3.98	1.34	0.50	6.10
Total Assets (Millions $) . . .	1,040	973	593	301	116	111	113	158	170	253

SHAREHOLDER INFORMATION

Minimum Investment
Initial: $2,500   IRA: $2,500
Subsequent: $100   IRA: $100

Maximum Fees
Load: none   12b-1: none
Other: none

Fidelity New Markets Income (FNMIX)

800-544-8544
www.fidelity.com

International Bond

PERFORMANCE AND PER SHARE DATA

fund inception date: 5/4/93

	3yr Annual	5yr Annual	10yr Annual	Category Risk Index
Return (%)	18.0	14.5	14.8	1.33—high
Differ From Category (+/-)	8.3 high	5.2 high	7.4 high	**Avg Mat** 13.6 yrs

	2005	2004	2003	2002	2001	2000	1999	1998	1997	1996
Return (%)	11.5	12.5	31.1	12.6	6.6	14.3	36.6	-22.3	17.5	41.3
Differ From Category (+/-) . .	8.3	3.1	13.8	0.1	1.5	9.0	30.5	-24.9	11.4	25.4
Return, Tax-Adjusted (%)	8.7	9.9	28.5	9.4	2.5	9.7	32.2	-26.0	12.1	37.6
Dividends, Net Income ($) . .	0.91	0.88	0.79	0.91	1.21	1.30	1.01	1.22	1.32	0.93
Expense Ratio (%)	na	0.94	0.97	1.00	0.99	0.99	1.07	1.13	1.08	1.09
Yield (%)	6.04	6.00	5.69	8.02	11.06	11.37	9.07	13.53	9.52	7.19
Total Assets (Millions $)	1,720	1,089	866	425	293	258	214	207	371	306

SHAREHOLDER INFORMATION

Minimum Investment
Initial: $2,500   IRA: $500
Subsequent: $250   IRA: $1

Maximum Fees
Load: 1.00% redemption   12b-1: none
Other: redemp fee applies for 6 mos; maint fee for low bal

Fidelity Strategic Income
(FSICX)

800-544-8544
www.fidelity.com

International Bond

PERFORMANCE AND PER SHARE DATA   fund inception date: 5/1/98

	3yr Annual	5yr Annual	10yr Annual	Category Risk Index
Return (%)	10.3	9.3	na	0.77—blw av
Differ From Category (+/-)	0.6 abv av	0.0 abv av	na	**Avg Mat** 9.1 yrs

	2005	2004	2003	2002	2001	2000	1999	1998	1997	1996
Return (%)	3.4	9.4	18.6	9.3	6.5	4.0	6.3	—	—	—
Differ From Category (+/-)	0.2	0.0	1.3	-3.2	1.4	-1.3	0.2	—	—	—
Return, Tax-Adjusted (%)	1.4	7.4	16.4	6.9	4.1	1.2	3.5	—	—	—
Dividends, Net Income ($)	0.58	0.55	0.58	0.57	0.56	0.68	0.66	—	—	—
Expense Ratio (%)	na	0.76	0.80	0.84	0.94	0.99	1.10	—	—	—
Yield (%)	5.46	5.07	5.48	6.11	6.16	7.40	7.03	—	—	—
Total Assets (Millions $)	3,444	3,166	2,320	771	163	63	41	—	—	—

SHAREHOLDER INFORMATION

Minimum Investment
Initial: $2,500   IRA: $500
Subsequent: $250   IRA: $100

Maximum Fees
Load: none   12b-1: none
Other: maint fee for low bal

Loomis Sayles Bond Retail
(LSBRX)

800-633-3330
www.loomissayles.com

International Bond

PERFORMANCE AND PER SHARE DATA   fund inception date: 1/2/97

	3yr Annual	5yr Annual	10yr Annual	Category Risk Index
Return (%)	14.1	11.4	na	1.08—av
Differ From Category (+/-)	4.4 abv av	2.1 abv av	na	**Avg Mat** 7.2 yrs

	2005	2004	2003	2002	2001	2000	1999	1998	1997	1996
Return (%)	4.0	11.0	28.8	13.1	2.2	4.0	4.2	4.5	—	—
Differ From Category (+/-)	0.8	1.6	11.5	0.6	-2.9	-1.3	-1.9	2.0	—	—
Return, Tax-Adjusted (%)	1.9	8.5	26.3	10.3	-0.7	0.9	1.1	0.8	—	—
Dividends, Net Income ($)	0.81	0.92	0.77	0.76	0.87	0.92	0.93	0.92	—	—
Expense Ratio (%)	1.04	1.00	1.00	1.00	1.00	1.00	1.00	1.00	—	—
Yield (%)	5.97	6.69	5.79	6.93	8.34	8.30	8.04	7.36	—	—
Total Assets (Millions $)	900	344	180	71	63	79	61	56	—	—

SHAREHOLDER INFORMATION

Minimum Investment
Initial: $2,500   IRA: $2,500
Subsequent: $50   IRA: $50

Maximum Fees
Load: none   12b-1: 0.25%
Other: none

T Rowe Price Emerging Markets Bond (PREMX)

800-638-5660
www.troweprice.com

International Bond

PERFORMANCE AND PER SHARE DATA   fund inception date: 12/30/94

	3yr Annual	5yr Annual	10yr Annual	Category Risk Index	
Return (%)	19.2	15.2	13.4	1.28—abv av	
Differ From Category (+/-)	9.5 high	5.9 high	6.0 high	**Avg Mat** 13.4 yrs	

	2005	2004	2003	2002	2001	2000	1999	1998	1997	1996
Return (%)	17.2	14.8	26.0	9.5	9.3	15.2	22.9	-23.0	16.8	36.5
Differ From Category (+/-)	14.0	5.4	8.7	-3.0	4.2	9.9	16.8	-25.6	10.7	20.6
Return, Tax-Adjusted (%)	13.7	12.5	23.5	6.3	5.0	11.1	18.3	-27.1	12.9	31.7
Dividends, Net Income ($)	0.97	0.79	0.75	0.85	1.16	1.05	1.08	1.31	1.15	1.01
Expense Ratio (%)	na	1.08	1.10	1.14	1.16	1.21	1.25	1.25	1.25	1.25
Yield (%)	6.68	5.92	6.12	8.13	11.22	9.92	10.71	13.95	8.23	7.59
Total Assets (Millions $)	454	278	252	211	156	164	173	148	113	40

SHAREHOLDER INFORMATION

Minimum Investment
Initial: $2,500   IRA: $1,000
Subsequent: $100   IRA: $50

Maximum Fees
Load: 2.00% redemption   12b-1: none
Other: redemption fee applies for 1 year

T Rowe Price Intl Bond (RPIBX)

800-638-5660
www.troweprice.com

International Bond

PERFORMANCE AND PER SHARE DATA   fund inception date: 9/10/86

	3yr Annual	5yr Annual	10yr Annual	Category Risk Index	
Return (%)	6.7	7.4	4.2	1.36—high	
Differ From Category (+/-)	-3.0 av	-1.9 av	-3.2 blw av	**Avg Mat** 7.9 yrs	

	2005	2004	2003	2002	2001	2000	1999	1998	1997	1996
Return (%)	-8.1	11.4	18.7	21.8	-3.4	-3.1	-7.9	15.0	-3.1	7.1
Differ From Category (+/-)	-11.4	2.0	1.4	9.3	-8.6	-8.5	-14.1	12.5	-9.3	-8.8
Return, Tax-Adjusted (%)	-9.2	9.9	17.0	20.5	-4.9	-4.8	-9.7	12.9	-5.2	4.4
Dividends, Net Income ($)	0.26	0.25	0.25	0.25	0.32	0.39	0.48	0.51	0.55	0.71
Expense Ratio (%)	na	0.88	0.91	0.93	0.95	1.15	0.90	0.88	0.86	0.87
Yield (%)	2.76	2.25	2.36	2.71	4.12	4.65	5.26	4.89	5.69	6.80
Total Assets (Millions $)	1,575	1,663	1,306	1,058	762	753	779	926	826	969

SHAREHOLDER INFORMATION

Minimum Investment
Initial: $2,500   IRA: $1,000
Subsequent: $100   IRA: $50

Maximum Fees
Load: 2.00% redemption   12b-1: none
Other: redemption fee applies for 3 months

Appendix:
Index Funds

DOMESTIC STOCK INDEXES

S&P 500
Vanguard 500 Index Inv (Stk-LC: VFINX)

Wilshire 4500
Vanguard Extended Market Index Inv (Stk-MC: VEXMX)

Wilshire 5000
Vanguard Total Stock Market Index Inv (Stk-LC: VTSMX)

S&P MidCap 400
Dreyfus Index Midcap Index (Stk-MC: PESPX)

MSCI US Prime Market Growth
Vanguard Growth Index Inv (Stk-LC: VIGRX)

MSCI US Prime Market Value
Vanguard Value Index Inv (Stk-LC: VIVAX)

MSCI US Midcap 450
Vanguard Mid Cap Index Inv (Stk-MC: VIMSX)

CRSP 9-10 Decile
Bridgeway Ultra Small Company Market (Stk-SC: BRSIX)

MSCI US SmallCap 1750
Vanguard Small Cap Index Inv (Stk-SC: NAESX)

MSCI US SmallCap Growth
Vanguard Small Cap Growth Inv (Stk-SC: VISGX)

MSCI US SmallCap Value
Vanguard Small Cap Value Inv (Stk-SC: VISVX)

Schwab 1000
Schwab Inv 1000 Index I (Stk-LC: SNXFX)

NASDAQ 100
Rydex OTC Inv (Stk-LC: RYOCX)
USAA NASDAQ 100 Index (Stk-LC: USNQX)

American Gas Association
FBR Gas Utility Index (Sec-U: GASFX)

FOREIGN INDEXES

MSCI EAFA
Vanguard Developing Markets Index (IntS-F: VDMIX)

MSCI Europe
Vanguard European Stock Index (IntS-R/C: VEURX)

MSCI Pacific
Vanguard Pacific Stock Index (IntS-R/C: VPACX)

MSCI Emerging Markets Free
Vanguard Emerging Mkts Stock Index (IntS-E: VEIEX)

MSCI EAFA / MSCI Emerging Markets Free
Vanguard Total Intl Stock Index (IntS-F: VGTSX)

BOND INDEXES

Lehman Brothers Aggregate Bond
Fidelity US Bond Index (B-Gen: FBIDX)
Vanguard Total Bond Market Index (B-Gen: VBMFX)

Lehman Brothers Intermediate (5-10) Government/Corporate
Vanguard Intermediate Term Bd Idx (B-Gen: VBIIX)

Lehman Brothers Long (10+) Government/Corporate
Vanguard Long Term Bond Index (B-Gen: VBLTX)

BALANCED INDEXES

S&P 500 (55%)/Wilshire 4500 (15%)/MSCI EAFA (15%)/LB Bond (15%)
Fidelity Four-In-One Index (Bal: FFNOX)

Wilshire 5000 (60%)/Lehman Aggregate Bond (40%)
Vanguard Balanced Index Inv (Bal: VBINX)

Index

D

E

F